Long Waves of Growth, Hegemonic Power, and Climate Change in the World Economy

Phillip Anthony O'Hara

Long Waves of Growth, Hegemonic Power, and Climate Change in the World Economy

Dutch, British, US and Chinese Capitalism and Structural Polycrises

Springer

Phillip Anthony O'Hara
Global Political Economy Research Unit (GPERU)
Perth, WA, Australia

ISBN 978-981-96-4131-4 ISBN 978-981-96-4132-1 (eBook)
https://doi.org/10.1007/978-981-96-4132-1

This Springer imprint is published by the registered company Springer Nature Singapore Pte Ltd.
The registered company address is: 152 Beach Road, #21-01/04 Gateway East, Singapore 189721, Singapore

This book is dedicated to a major piece of art, one that has stimulated and engrossed many long wave, hegemony, and climate change scholars and analysts through the ages:

Under the Wave off Kanagawa *(1830-1832)*
(Kanagawa oki nami ura)
By Katsushika Hokusai (1760-1849)
[Also known as The Great Wave, *by Japanese artist Katsushika Hokusai (1760-1849), is a digital copy made by 'The Met' of a work held by the Metropolitan Museum of Art (*'The Met'*), 1000 Fifth Avenue, New York, NY 10028, Phone*

Preface

Much of what I know about long waves, hegemony, and climate change was inspired by colleagues I met and got to know over several decades. I started working on long waves in 1982 when I wrote, in a loft overlooking the Sydney Harbor Bridge, a very long analysis of the different theories, empirics, and schools of long waves. Around this time my correspondence with Ernest Mandel inspired me to go further into the subject. Mandel's emphases on the rate of profit and endogenous–exogenous factors have kept with me ever since. When I moved to Canberra in 1983, I had several discussions with Walt Whitman Rostow, and his emphases on the irreducible complexity of history, prices, and sectoral analysis enhanced my understanding of the world. Also in Canberra, Noel Butlin gave me much needed advice on how to go about studying long waves through economic history, and Ernst Boehm also helped in this regard.

In New Orleans my first meetings with and further communications with David Gordon impressed on me the importance of institutions, accumulation, and growth. Numerous meetings with Victor Lippit, in Riverside and elsewhere, and Martin Wolfson, in various places in the USA, helped me understand the dynamics of capitalism, institutions, and crises. In Fremantle, Galway, and New York City I had numerous discussions with Terry McDonough (who also provided many comments), which assisted my understanding of long-term motion.

My good friend and confidant, Thea Biescheuvel, novelist, poet, artist, and linguist, translated several papers on long waves for me into English from Russian, German, and Dutch and gave me comments on papers over the years. Many thanks Thea! Barry Gordon enabled me to meet Jules Ginswick who took me though his library in Lindfield and suggested numerous useful hypotheses to investigate. Allen Oakley was kind enough to provide comments on a multitude of chapters and papers for a decade! The provision of a three-year Scholarship from the Australian Government was of enormous help in getting my ideas together in print and at conferences.

Asimina Christoforou offered me comments on several versions of my paper on SSAs, long waves, and history. Svetlana Chandler-Kirdina, in Moscow and Nice, provided comments and advice regarding my theoretical-empirical work on waves vis-a-vis Kondratieff, Trotsky, Braudel, Polanyi, and Gordon. Solomos Solomou was good enough to send me his PhD thesis, hot off the press, and comments on my work, which gave me much food for thought, while Hironori Tohyama whether in Tokya or Riverside was a good source of ideas. In France and Atlanta, Pascal Pettit gave me good comments on my empirical methods and analysis.

Ron Stanfield and Bill Dugger offered advice and organizational support for the development of my ideas over several decades, especially through discussions in Portugal, Chicago, San Diego, Philadelphia, New Orleans, the Rocky Mountains, Albuquerque, Atlanta, and Boston. Also in Boston, Fariba Alipour provided much support to my research in numerous ways at Harvard University, while my discussions there with Hyman Minsky on long waves of finance were extremely helpful. Andrew Tylecote was proactive in our meetings regarding the critical things to highlight in long wave studies. At several venues Jim Devine was always forthcoming with comments on my work, while Gordon Tullock was inspiring with his comments on my papers on potential financial social structures of accumulation and neoliberalism, in Georgia and Washington DC.

Over two decades Immanuel Wallerstein guided my work on long waves and hegemony and inspired me with several of his theses on capitalist development. Meetings with Gunder Frank at South Beach, Miami, and surroundings instilled in me the importance of an historical analysis of waves. It was a great pleasure to be on the Veblen-Commons (VC) Committee and discuss with the recipient of the VC Prize, Paul Sweezy, issues associated with capitalism, Schumpeter, the socioeconomic circuit, surplus, and conditions generating long-term upswing and downswing.

Several editors and colleagues helped a great deal through providing comments and anonymous referee reports, especially Kosta Josifidis, John Davis, Hazel Gunn, Alpar Lošonc, Anne Mayhew, Mario Seccareccia, Hassan Bougrine, Steve Pressman, Patrick Welsch, John Lodewijks, John King, Richard V. Adkisson, Francisco Louca, Geoffrey Hodgson, Wolfram Elsner, William Waller, Frank Stilwell, and Glen Atkinson. Numerous publishers were *personally* encouraging, including Edward Elgar and Alan Jarvis. Geoff Harcourt always demonstrated an interest, as did Ian Kerr and Thomas Lambert.

My desire to integrate into long wave and hegemony studies issues of climate change was due to my longstanding interest in environmental issues, which link to work published in *Ecological Economics*, my assistance to *Pacific Peacemaker*, and my previous studies of biology and evolution. I was also helped by comments and materials prepared by John Bellamy Foster, Andrew Brennan, Nicola Scafetta, Eric Schutz, and IPCC members over several years.

My interest in long waves was part of a longer process of studying crises of capitalism, business cycles, great depressions, and other unstable dynamics, which started with my Honours dissertation, supervised by Herb Thompson and Frank Harman, and examined by Geoffrey Harcourt. Lewis Havercamp, Patricia Harney, and Garth Hartley helped me get through that year with a first for that thesis. Also, the work I did on economic power (for a previous thesis) helped a great deal, and it was thanks in part to Roslyn Jones, Ted Wheelwright, and Robert Greig that I got a first for this thesis.

Much of what I know about business cycles I learnt from Howard Sherman, my dear friend and mentor, who inspired me with many meetings over lunch or dinner over the years, usually in Los Angeles, San Diego or Riverside, and numerous outstanding books on the subject. He also helped me a great deal when it comes to developing principles of political economy.

The process of meeting long wave, hegemony, and climate change scholars and others in several places around the world was the most exciting thing about analysing the long-term motion of capitalism through several long waves and phases of evolution.

Note that this book is the second volume in the series on political economy principles, the first one being *Principles of Institutional and Evolutionary Political Economy: Applied to Current World Problems,* which I published with Springer Nature in 2022 (revised edition 2023), and which won the 2025 Joan Robinson Prize for book of the Year from EAEPE. There is also a third volume to publish in this series.

This is also the third volume I have written on long waves. The first won the Myrdal Prize for Book of the Year from EAEPE (I have used some extracts from Part C for parts of chap. 7 in this current book). The second won Book of the Year Award from CBS (some of the ideas from this I have used for chap. 9). A section of chap. 9 emanates from a paper that won Journal Article of the Year from CBS. And my climate change paper that won Journal Article of the Year Awards from EAEPE and CBS informed some ideas that are used in several parts of this book.

Many thanks also go to Kala Palanisamy who did a lot of work proofing, formatting, and editing the manuscript, as well as to Joseph Daniel, Emily Wong, Mamun Mishra, and Cynthia Kroonen from Springer who were a source of important information and flexible deadlines.

Readers of this book should feel free to contact me with questions or queries on any aspect of this book, areas covered within it, or the other two books of mine on the trilogy of political economy volumes.

Perth, WA, Australia Phillip Anthony O'Hara

Acknowledgements

'Long Waves of Growth, Hegemonic Power, and Climate Change in the World Economy ...'

Artwork For Cover-Dedication
The artwork for the cover-dedication of this book, *Under the Wave off Kanagawa* (1830-1832) (Kanagawa oki nami ura), also known as *The Great Wave*, by Japanese artist Katsushika Hokusai (1760-1849), is a digital copy made by 'The Met' of a work held by the Metropolitan Museum of Art (*'The Met'*), 1000 Fifth Avenue, New York, NY 10028, Phone 1-212-535-7710. 'This artwork is identified as *Open Access*. By waiving any rights to Materials identified as Open Access, the Museum makes those Materials available for any purpose, including commercial and non-commercial use, free of charge and without requiring permission from the Museum. Open Access works are made available under a Creative Commons Zero (CC0) license'. https://www.metmuseum.org/art/collection/search/45434

Chapters of This Book
Earlier versions of some parts of this book were published in journals and authored books. The following is a list of publications and copyright acknowledgements I have been asked to provide. I wish to thank the various parties for allowing me to use some previous writings of mine in this current book.

A Paper entitled "Economic Growth, Hegemonic Power, and Climate Change in the Netherlands, Britain, United States and China", which is currently under consideration at a journal, was an inspiration for the content, style and direction of especially Chaps. 1 and 5–9. An earlier version of parts of Chap. 7 was originally published in sections of Part C of Phillip Anthony O'Hara, *Marx, Veblen, and Contemporary Institutional Political Economy: Principles and Unstable Dynamics of Capitalism.* Cheltenham: Edward Elgar. Licensor: EDWARD ELGAR PUBLISHING. Reproduced with permission of the Licensor through PLSclear. (Won *Gunnar Myrdal Prize* for *Book of the Year Award* from EAEPE.) https://www.e-elgar.com/shop/gbp/marx-veblen-and-contemporary-institutional-political-economy-9781858980676.html

Parts of an earlier version of 'Section 7.3.6' of Chap. 7 were originally published as Phillip Anthony O'Hara. 1995. Household Labor, the Family, and Macroeconomic Instability in the United States: 1940s-1990s, *Review of Social Economy,* 52(1), 89-120. London & New York: Routledge (Taylor & Francis Group). Licensor: INFORMA UK LIMITED. Reproduced with permission of the Licensor through PLSclear. (Won *Journal Article of the Year Award from CBS.)* https://www.tandfonline.com/doi/abs/10.1080/00346769500000004

An earlier version of Section 9.5 from Chap. 9 was originally published as Phillip Anthony O'Hara, The Securitized Subprime Market Crisis. *Review of Radical Political Economics* 41(3): 318–334. Licensor: SAGE JOURNALS. Reproduced with permission of the Licensor through CCC. https://journals.sagepub.com/doi/abs/10.1177/0486613409336179

An earlier version of Sect. 9.7 of Ch. 9 was published as Sect. '6' of Phillip O'Hara, 'Global Coronavirus Pandemic Crisis and Future Crisis Prevention', *Panoeconomicus,* 2021, Vol. 68, Issue 5, pp. 587-623. Permission is granted to publish this (in full or part, updated, etc.) in this book without charge, covering all future editions, formats, platforms, and printings of the publication. Thanks go to copyright holder, Association of Economists of Vojvodina and Serbian Association of Economists—Kosta Josifidis and Public Knowledge Project. https://panoeconomicus.org/index.php/jorunal/article/view/1550

An earlier version of chap. 11 was originally published as Phillip Anthony O'Hara, 'Short-, Long-, and Secular-Wave Growth in the World Political Economy Periodicity, Amplitude, and Phases for 8 Regions, 108 Countries, 1940–2010', *International Journal of Political Economy,* 41(1): 3–46. Licensor: INFORMA UK LIMITED. Reproduced with permission of the Licensor through PLSclear. https://www.tandfonline.com/doi/abs/10.2753/IJP0891-1916410101

About the Book

Long Waves of Growth, Hegemony, and Climate Change in the World Economy: Dutch, British, US and Chinese Capitalism and Structural Polycrises investigates eras of major geopolitical and socioeconomic power, development, relative demise and potential renewal, for four major political economies. It concentrates on the Dutch Golden Age of the late 1500s and 1600s, British hegemony of the 1800s, Pax Americana of the 1900s, and Chinese potential hegemony of the 2000s, as well as long wave patterns of change over successive centuries to the present (and to some degree into the future).

These economies are situated within patterns of long-term successive rise and fall (and fall and rise) of economic growth, hegemony, and climate change in the world political economy, including linkages between core, periphery, and semi-periphery. Patterns of multiple crises tend to appear between hegemonic periods, and climate change often undergoes complex dynamics through time, while currently climate anomalies are emerging during mostly long wave downswings and polycrises in the world economy.

Contemporary themes of the book include the ongoing competition for world domination between the USA and China, the conflict over Ukraine-Taiwan that some think may generate World War III, the climate change crisis that continues to plague the world, and whether the world and its major economies are likely to undergo a Golden Age into the future. Chapter 7 of this book on US hegemony and long waves includes extracts of material that won the Myrdal Prize for Book of the Year Prize from EAEPE as well as Journal Article of the Year from Curtin Business School. Ideas from parts of Chap. 9 emanate from a volume that won Book of the Year Award from CBS. A climate change paper that won Journal Article of the Year Awards from EAEPE and CBS informed ideas that are used in several parts of this book.

The book outlines key stylized facts from the analysis and presents hypotheses for further investigation on the relationship between long-term growth, hegemony, and climate change. The book uses the work of Kondratiev, Schumpeter, and company, themes in economic history, modern political economy schools, and the principles of political economy contingency paradigm to reformulate long wave, hegemony, and climate change hypotheses and empirics.

Contents

About the Author

Phillip Anthony O'Hara Phillip Anthony O'Hara has a PhD in political economy, held a personal chair at Curtin University, and is currently Director of the Global Political Economy Research Unit (GPERU) in Perth, Australia. He specializes in studying concepts and principles, major problems of the world, institutional change and adjustment, global political economy, history of the world, and scholarly biography. He has published over 100 articles in refereed journals and edited books, 16 volumes of books and special issues of journals, was President of the Association for Evolutionary Economics (AFEE), and currently is on the editorial or international advisory boards of the *Review of Evolutionary Political Economy, Panoeconomicus, the International Journal of Pluralism and Economics Education,* and *Terra Economicus.* His major books include (among others) *Principles of Institutional and Evolutionary Political Economy: Applied to Current World Problems,* the two-volume *Encyclopedia of Political Economy,* the four-volume *International Encyclopedia of Public Policy,* plus *Growth and Development in the Global Political Economy,* as well as *Global Political Economy and the Wealth of Nations.* He has won many awards for his research, including Journal Article of the Year, two prizes for 'Book of the Year, from the European Association for Evolutionary Political Economy (EAEPE) ('Gunnar Myrdal Prize' and 'Joan Robinson Prize') and from Curtin Business School, plus Researcher of the Year from CBS, as well as the Clarence Ayres Award from AFEE.

Abbreviations

AAGR	Annual average growth rates
AFEE	Association for Evolutionary Economics
AFRICA	West African Monsoonal System
AI	Artificial intelligence
AIDS	Acquired immunodeficiency syndrome
AMAZ	Amazon rainforest
AMOC	Atlantic meridional overturning circulation
ANZUS	Australia, NZ and USA military alliance
AUKUS	Australia, UK and USA military alliances
AP	Autocratic Powers
APG	Alpine glaciers
ARCTIC	Summer Arctic Sea Ice
ASSI	Arctic summer sea ice
ATHC	Atlantic Thermohaline Circulation
AWIS	Arctic winter ice sheet
BARENT	Barents Sea Ice loss
BBC	British Broadcasting Commission
BRI	Belt-and-Road-Initiative
BGW	Samuel Bowles, David Gordon, and Thomas Weisskopf
BP	Before the present
BOE	Bank of England
BP or B	Borderline performance
BWS	Bretton Woods System (or Agreement)
CC	Climate change
CCC	Circular and cumulative causation
CE	Circular economy
CEE	Central and Eastern Europe
CGTP	Cascading global tipping point(s)
CH_4	Methane
CIA	Central Intelligence Agency
Co_2	Carbon dioxide

CO_2-eq	Carbon dioxide equivalent
COP28	28th UN Climate Change Conference of the Parties 2023
COVAX	COVID-19 Vaccines Global Access
CPSP	Core, Periphery, Semi-Periphery
CSM	Cyclical Sine Model
CSD	Circuit of Socioeconomic Dynamics
CTP	Cascading Tipping Point(s)
CW	Cold War
CWE	Capitalist world-economy
d	Destabilizing
EAEPE	European Association for Evolutionary Political Economy
EAIS	Eastern Antarctic ice sheet
EFI	Economic Freedom Index
EIC	English East India Company
EIU	*Economist* Intelligence Unit
EMF	Electromagnetic field
ENR	El-Nino regime
ERF	Effective radiative forcing
ENSO	El Niño–Southern Oscillation
EU	European Union
FAO	Food and Agricultural Organization
FIH	Financial Instability Hypothesis
F&L	Christopher Freeman and Francisco Louçã
FLP	Freeman, Louçã, Perez, et al
FDI	Foreign direct investment
FPE	Feminist political economy
GA	1 billion years
GATT	General Agreement on Tariffs and Trade
GCTP	Global cascading tipping points
GD	Great Depression
GDP	Gross Domestic Product
GER	David Gordon, Richard Edwards, and Michael Reich
GF	Gravitational field
GFC	Global financial crisis
GGI	Global Governance Index
GHG	Greenhouse gas(ses)
GHGE	Greenhouse gas emissions
GHSI	Global Health Security Index
GII	Global Innovation Index
GIS	Greenland ice sheet
GLAC	Mountain Glacier
GMT	Global Methane Tracker
GPERU	Global Political Economy Research Unit
GPI	Global Power Index
GPR	Geopolitical Risk

GPU	Geopolitical Uncertainty
GREEN	Greenland Ice Sheet
H	Hydrogen
He	Helium
HRU	High risk uncertainty
HIV	Human immunodeficiency virus
H_2O	Water (vapour)
HSH	Hegemonic stability hypothesis
ICT	Information and communications technology
I-E	Institutional and evolutionary
IEPE	Institutional and evolutionary political economy
IMF	International Monetary Fund
IMS	Indian monsoonal system
INDIA	Indian Summer Monsoon
IPCC	Intergovernmental Panel on Climate Change
JHU	Johns Hopkins University
KWS	Keynesian Welfare State
Kyr	1,000 years
LAC	Latin America & the Caribbean
LACA	Latin America and the Caribbean
LDA	Liberal-Democratic Allies
LGBTQIA	Lesbian, gay, bisexual, transsexual, queer, intersexual, asexual
LIA	Little Ice Age
LTP	Lower turning point (in the wave or cycle)
LWD	Long wave downswing
LWHegCC	Long waves, hegemony, and climate change
LWU	Long wave upswing
MA	1 million years
MEI	Multilateral embedded institutions
MENA	Middle East and North Africa
M&A	Mergers and acquisitions
MIC	Military industrial complex
MIT	Massachusetts Institute of Technology
MMT	Modern Monetary Theory
₼	Moderate
MOR	Mode of Regulation
MPSW	Millennial plus scale waves
MSW	Millennial scale waves
N	Nitrogen
NA	North America
NATO	North Atlantic Treaty Organization
NBF	Northern boreal forests
NEP	Northeast permafrost
NH	Northern hemisphere
NINO	*El Nino*

NLWM	New Long Wave Method
NOE	Neighbourhoods of equilibrium
NOx	Nitrogen oxides
NPF	Northern permafrost
NTI	Nuclear Threat Initiative
PCS	Postwar corporate system
PBID	Performance-based institutional dynamics
PE	Political economy
PERM	Permafrost
PKI	Post-Keynesian institutionalism
PoPE	Principles of political economy
RCP	Representative Concentration Pathways
RH	Research Hypothesis
ROA	Regime of Accumulation
R&D	Research and development
s	Stabilizing
š	Strong
SCC	Socialism with Chinese characteristics
SCE	Small cool era (1940-1970)
SECWU	Secular wave upswing
SEG	Social, Environmental and Governance ethic
SF	Structure forms (institutions)
SH	Southern hemisphere
SO_2	Sulphide Dioxide
SPI	Social and political institutions
SPRC	Science Policy Research Centre
SSA	Social structure(s) of accumulation
SSA	Sub-Saharan Africa
SSP	Shared Socioeconomic Pathway(s)
SWD	Short wave downswing
SWU	Short wave upswing
TCR	Tropical coral reefs
TEP	Techno-economic-paradigm
TFP	Total Factor Productivity
TQM	Total quality management
TP	Tipping Point(s)
TSR	Total solar radiation
U	Uncertainty
ű	Unclear
UK	United Kingdom
UN	United Nations
UNUI	United Nations University
UNDP	United Nations Development Program
USDOA	US Department of the Army
USSR	Union of Soviet Socialist Republics

UTP	Upper turning point
v or vs.	versus
VOC	Dutch East India Company
ώ	Weak
WAIS	Western Antarctica Ice Sheet
WAMS	West African Monsoonal System
WANT	Western Antarctic Ice Sheet
WE	Western Europe
WB	World Bank
WDI	World Development Indicators
WE	Western Europe
WHO	World Health Organization
WIC	Dutch West India Company
WMO	World Meteorological Organization
WSA	World Systems Analysis
WSS	World-Systems School
WUI	World Uncertainty Index
WW1	World War 1
WW2	World War 2
WW3	World War 3

Chapter 1
Long Waves of Growth, Hegemonic Power, and Climate Change

Abstract This chapter outlines the main theory and empirics of this book and summarizes the contents of the chapters. I commence with an overview of the *Standard Model of Long Waves*, as developed by Kondratieff, Schumpeter, and most schools of long wave analysis. I also mention areas where some protagonists and schools differ from the standard model and from each other. I then *introduce* an alternative to the standard model, including (a) the *principles of political economy (PoPE) contingency paradigm* for analyzing long waves (and other world problems and issues) and (b) the *new long wave method* (NLWM), which enables the analysis to deviate significantly from the standard model. Then I *outline* how the PoPE contingency paradigm and NLWM, respectively, interpret long waves from the past to the present and potentially into the future, including the Dutch, British, US, and Chinese cases. Then I summarize each of the chapters and provide a conclusion.

Keywords Long waves · Innovation · Standard model · PoPE contingency paradigm · New long wave method · Economic growth · Hegemonic power · Climate change · Netherlands · Britain · USA and China · Structural polycrises · Principles

1.1 Introduction

The purpose of this book is to provide an integrated analysis of long-term growth, global power, and climate change for the Netherlands, Britain, the United States, and China, plus to some degree core, periphery, and semi-periphery (CPSP) linkages. To this end, I use long wave, hegemony, and climate change (LWHegCC) theory and empirics to inform the analysis. I go back to the start of long wave and hegemony historical inquiry, scrutinize the literature, and re-fashion it on different foundations. Then I examine climate change theory and evidence and inculcate this with Dutch, British, US, and Chinese history. The chapter's case studies

P. A. O'Hara, *Long Waves of Growth, Hegemonic Power, and Climate Change in the World Economy*, https://doi.org/10.1007/978-981-96-4132-1_1

start with *Pax Netherlandia,* which provides an outline of the Dutch situation during the 1500s–1600s and summarizes the results up to the 2020s. The second case study is for *Pax Brittanica*, starting with a summary of the British situation during the 1500s–1700s, then concentrating on the 1800s, and concluding with an outline of the situation during the 1900s–2000s. The third case study is that of *Pax Americana*, where I start the analysis of the USA during the 1800s, provide details of the 1900s, and conclude with the 2000s. The fourth case study is the potential *Pax Chinesia*, starting with a broad outline of China during the late 1700s and 1800s, and providing some details of Chinese growth, global power, and climate dynamics into the 1900s–2040s. After this, I analyze the structural polycrises of the (1970s-)1980s–2020s, the current situation vis-à-vis international conflict relating to Ukraine and Taiwan, and more details of national, regional, and global long waves during the 1940s–2020s. I conclude with a summary of the main results of the analysis, hypotheses for further research, and a glossary of major terms.

In the first volume of this series on political economy principles and applications (O'Hara 2023), I presented eight core principles and a whole subseries of subprinciples for analysis and applied some of them to nine core world problems. In *this* current book, I add one principle to make it nine core principles, which are introduced in this chapter (outlined in Table 1.1). One of these core principles is the *principle of innovation and novelty*, namely, that it is necessary to consistently and repeatedly develop innovations and novel solutions to help solve world problems and issues. Consistent with this innovation principle, in this book I make four novel modifications or additions to long wave analysis.

The first innovation develops and applies the first new principles of political economy (PoPE) paradigm and method of analysis for long waves of growth and metamorphosis in a generation. The PoPE paradigm applies the major principles of (institutional and evolutionary) political economy to economic growth, hegemony, and climate change, showing that these applications are contingent upon integrating forces merging to potentially constitute long waves of upswing and downswing. Long waves of growth, hegemony, and climate change (LWHegCC) are thereby hypothesized to be contingent upon and interrelated with several factors, which are linked to the principles that allude to several processes generating these contingencies. These principles (and contingencies) include (1) history and evolution, (2) uneven development and hegemony, (3) the new principle of *the circuits and pathways of socioeconomic dynamics* (CSD) (also called the circuits of socioeconomic reproduction [CSR], and for short the 'socioeconomic circuits'), (4) heterogeneous agents and groups, (5) the amplified and magnified multifactor circular and cumulative causation (CCC) forces at work, (6) the contradictory processes in motion, (7) the degree of uncertainty in the socioeconomic environment, (8) the nature of and uneven impact of innovation and novelty, and (9) the role of policies and governance. These principles are detailed later in this chapter, and applied sequentially to the Dutch (Chap. 5), British (Chap. 6), US (Chap. 7), Chinese (Chap. 8), and structural polycrises (1980s–2020s) situations.

I also develop a *new long wave method* (NLWM) of inquiry. The NLWM relates to (a) investigating the Dutch, British, US, and Chinese cases (Chaps. 5–8), (b) studying LWs through decadal average annual real GDP growth rates (AAGR) per

Table 1.1 100 concepts and principles. 9 core general plus 91 specific concepts/principles of political economy (PoPE) contingencies

1. Historical Specificity & Evolution	2. Hegemony & Uneven Development	3. Circuits of Socioeconomic Dynamics [CSD]	4. Innovation & Novelty	5. HeteroGeneous Groups & Agents	6. Circular & Cumulative Causation [CCC]	7. Contradiction & Destructive Creation	8. Uncertainty & Risk	9. Policy & Governance
Historical Time	Capitalist World-System	Ecological & Geo-spatial Environment	Community's Joint Stock of Knowledge	Social Circles, Trust and Cooperation	Multifactor Method and Multicausality	Power & Authority	Circuit of Money Capital	Social Provisioning, Standard of living & Quality of Life
Phases & Stages of Evolution	Absolute & Relative Hegemony	Technology Styles	Creative Destruction	Gender and Class	Interdependence	Disembedded Economy	Prevailing Business Climate	Participatory Democracy
Scientific Realism	Hegemonic Stability Theory	Institutional Spheres	Technology Styles	Ethnicity and Nationality	Emergence and Complexity	Vested Interests vs. Common Good	Cycles, Waves, Crises and Polycrises	Climate Change Mitigation and Adaptation
Culture, Institutions, Habits & Instincts	Core/ Periphery/ Semi-Periphery (CPSP)	Production-Distribution Systems	Social Structures of Accumulation & Modes of Regulation	Species and Age	Multiplication & Amplification	Instrumental vs. Ceremonial Functions	Recovery, Boom, Recession, and Depression	Ideologies, Parties, Monarchs & Parliaments
Long Duree, Conjunctures & Events	Production, Commercial & Financial (PCF) Dominance	Familial & Community Relations	Clusters & Systems of Innovation	AI, Robotics, Intelligent Machines	Effective Demand	Monopoly vs. Competition	Endogenous Money & Credit	Principles of Community Health
Path Dependence & Hysteresis	International Regimes	State & Governance Systems	Embodied Cognition and Neurobiology	Emulation & Conspicuous Consumption	Economic Surplus	Capital vs. Labor	Financial Instability Hypothesis	Functional Finance, Monetary & Fiscal Policies

(continued)

Table 1.1 (continued)

1. Historical Specificity & Evolution	2. Hegemony & Uneven Development	3. Circuits of Socioeconomic Dynamics [CSD]	4. Innovation & Novelty	5. HeteroGeneous Groups & Agents	6. Circular & Cumulative Causation [CCC]	7. Contradiction & Destructive Creation	8. Uncertainty & Risk	9. Policy & Governance
Blind Drift and Irreducible Complexity of History	Varieties of Capitalism (and other Systems)	Corporate Institutional Systems	Labor Power and Human Capital	Inequality of Income, Wealth and Power	Economies of Scale & Scope	Industry vs. Finance	Modern Monetary Theory	Social, Ecological, & Governance (SEG) Ethic
Stylized Facts	Hard & Soft Power & Authority	Financial Systems	Intellectual Property	Enabling Myths & Interactive Agency	Positive & Negative Feedback	Capital vs. Ecology	Cascading Tipping Points	Agreements, Accords & Contracts
Evolution, Metamorphosis, & Transformation	Wars, Conflicts, Disputes, & Treaties; Imperialism	Commodity Markets, Storage, and Transportation Systems	Mutation, Variation, & Selection	Bounded Rationality	Agglomeration and Networks	Men vs. Women	Debt Deflation	Legal-Economics Nexus
Routines, Mores, and Norms	Bilateral and Multilateral Agreements	Circular Economy	Knowledge and Creativity	Multiple Capital Paradigm	Growth and Development	Conflict and Cooperation	Structural Crises of Adjustment	Neoliberalism, Keynesian Welfare State, et al.

Source: Adapted from O'Hara (2023, 48). It would be a useful exercise to compare these principles with the concepts espoused by Dugger (1988, 1995, 2022)

capita, (c) introducing linear trend lines (using least squares), (d) transforming the linear lines into bars of borderline performance (BP) (Schumpeter's "neighborhoods of equilibrium?") (more on this later); (e) ascertaining long wave dynamics by differentiating between the AAGR growth per capita pattern and the trend bars (wave versus trend), (f) from this delineating long- and short-wave upswings (U), downswings (D), and borderline (B, in between U and D) positions, and (g) linking to the long wave apparatus hegemony and climate change dynamics. NLWM is explained and demonstrated further below.

The second innovation advanced in this book is that, to my knowledge, this is the first time, in a full book manuscript, that a long wave approach has been structurally and historically applied to *long waves of climate change*. To understand climate change, we scrutinize its history in the distant past, up to the present, and into the future. The Intergovernmental Panel on Climate Change (IPCC 2021, 2022a, b, 2023) has tended, in their four volume reports (including the synthesis report) every 6 years (circa), to examine climate change leading up to the present and the future, but they have not recently explicitly included a *detailed* analysis of the distant past (before 1800 AD), so we can link the past to the present and future. The last time they *attempted* to do this (that I am aware of) was in IPCC (2007, ch 6), but this was inadequate for our purposes. Hence, Chap. 4 below surveys the cycles and waves of climate change from the past to the future. Long wave scholars, on the other hand, have tended to ignore climate change, or at least not include it as a core, structural, and processual part of their analysis, *in a book-length project.* We seek to rectify these anomalies by scrutinizing long waves of climate change in the distant past, and certainly long before the 1800s, and after the 2020s (Chap. 4 provides details). This climate change analysis is especially crucial for the case studies on the Netherlands, Britain, US, China (Chaps. 5–8), and on polycrises (Chap. 9).

In this context, the third innovation is that this is the first book to incorporate (a) real economic growth per capita, (b) hegemony, and (c) climate change in an integrative theory and empirics of long waves. To do this, the history of these phenomena has been pushed back to the origins of climate change dynamics, the first possible hegemonic nation or area of proto-capitalism (the Netherlands or United Provinces), and the economic growth process going back to the mid-1500s. We thus investigate the background history of growth, phases, hegemony, and climate change, and situate the four (actual and potential) hegemonic capitalist nations (Netherlands, Britain, US, and China) within the framework of growth, phases, CSD, global power, and climate change dynamics.

We investigate, first, the Dutch case in light of growth, early capitalism, hegemonic power, and the "Little Ice Age"[1] (LIA, the Sporer and Maunder solar cycle minima during the 1400s–1700s) affecting Europe and much of the world (eventually). Second, we examine the British case in light of the outcome of the Napoleonic

[1] The "Little Ice Age" (LIA) is a phenomenon that especially affected the Northern Hemisphere (and other places perhaps later) during the 1400s–1800s, often seen as encompassing the whole world or variously mostly the northern hemisphere. The dating differs depending upon author, some extending it to 1300–1850 (e.g., Sam White 2014), whereas others variously discuss the LIA solar cycle declines, which include (1) the "Wolf Minimum" (1270–1350), (2) Sporer Minimum (1430–1570), (3) Maunder Minimum (1650–1750), and the 4) Dalton Minimum (1800–1855) (Wikipedia 2024).

Wars, the Dalton solar cycle minimum of the LIA (especially during 1800–1855), and the so-called industrial revolution and its impact on climate. Third, we study the US case for the 1800s–2020s, including the heatwaves of the 1930s and "small colder period" of 1940–1970, increasing temperatures (climate crises) thereafter, plus US hegemony rise and fall, and postwar boom and crisis. Fourth, we study the Chinese situation (actual and potential) through the 1800s–2040s, paying special attention to the 1950s–2040s, and notably during the 1980s–2020s (onto 2100), during the era of rising global GHGs and temperatures and the Chinese phases and hegemony-push.

The fourth innovation of this volume is that this is the first time a scholar has established a long wave paradigm and model that *explicitly* accepts core elements of the Garvy (1943), Kuznets (1940), Sweezy (1943), and other criticisms of the Kondratieff and Schumpeter et al.'s *Standard Model of Long Waves*. In relation to Garvy (who analyzed Kondratiev et al.), we recognize that long waves are conditioned by and contingent upon several complex processes of capitalism's evolutionary dynamics, while still being a potentially useful frame of critically analyzing the evolution and transformation of capitalism (and potentially other economies). Kuznets critiqued Schumpeter for, among other things, providing an anomalous view of cycles, which I agree with. Long waves, in my view, are not cycles but long movements, although they have a strong association with shorter business fluctuations (which tend to be deeper during long wave downswings and shallower during long wave upswings). Sweezy critiqued Schumpeter for paying insufficient attention to capitalists as a class, who tend to periodically innovate, accumulate, and seek profits even in the circular flow scenario.

We thus accept the caveats that ensure that long waves are often discontinuous, asymmetric, complex, and problematic, but nevertheless, despite, or rather *because* of these potential anomalies, still a potentially useful tool of socioeconomic, political, evolutionary, and climate change analysis in certain contexts. The outcome of this book are certain hypotheses that can be subject to further analysis in the future (outlined later in this chapter and especially in the conclusion).

1.2 Standard Model of Long Waves

Let me, first, set the stage for long wave analysis and how this book accepts certain long wave theoretical and empirical concepts/hypotheses while recognizing they are subject to a myriad of contingencies. The literature review provides more detail on this (Chaps. 2–3 below), but briefly, long waves started as a serious subject for scientific analysis as several scholars, particularly Jacob van Gelderen (1913, a.k.a. J. Fedder), Nikolai Kondratiev, and D.I. Oparin (1928), Salomon de Wolff (1929) and later Joseph Schumpeter (1939) and others established the basic parameters of the theory and empirics. This was the *first long wave upswing (boom) of long wave scholarship* (1900s-to-mid-1940s), because the major innovations of theory and empirics occurred through the works of these and other scholars, plus the major critiques developed by numerous Russian authors, including Leon Trotsky (1923) and D.I. Oparin, plus several "non-Soviet" scholars such as Kuznets (1940), Sweezy (1943), and Garvy (1943) already mentioned (see Chap. 2 for details).

By the end of the Second World War, as long wave growth upswings emerged through especially in the core Western nations and many others, long wave *scholarship* underwent the first major downswing, partly initiated by the critiques provided by Kuznets, Sweezy, Garvy, and others, even though numerous scholars kept the long wave hypothesis (and cycles analysis) ongoing in one form or another during the 1940s–1960s including, for instance, by Leon H. Dupriez (1947), Paolo Sylos-Labini (1950), and W.W. Rostow (1952), plus critical and sympathetic commentary by others including Burns and Mitchell (1946), Clemence and Doody (1950), and Alvin Hansen (1951). Perhaps, more importantly, the postwar boom (1945–early-1970) in the wave gave many scholars and policymakers the idea, especially by the mid-1960s, that long-term *growth* upswing (subject to some minor cyclical downswings) may be ongoing, at least for certain core nations. (See Barr 1979.)

It was not until the fourth Kondratieff long wave (postwar) boom (1945–1973) started to come undone during the late 1960s and early 1970s that long wave scholarship upswing really came of age, especially during the 1970s, 1980s, and 1990s. This *second long wave scholarship upswing* (boom) emerged and became more sophisticated through several schools of thought, as the *long wave downswing of postwar economic growth* (for the postwar corporate system) was apparently set in motion during the 1970s/1980s–2020s. (For some scholars, downswing was during the 1970s–1980s, with a new long wave upswing from the 1990s, perhaps with a downswing from the GFC in 2008 onwards.) But whereas much of the first major expansion of long wave scholarship (1900s–mid-1940s) centered on prices, and *where possible* output and other variables (partly due to inadequate data for real output), this second expansion of long wave scholarship was focused mainly on growth, accumulation, innovation, and the rate of profit; with some exceptions (e.g., Rostow 1978; Mager 1987; Goldstein 1988).

This is a crucial point, concerning growth rather than simply prices. Long wave scholars who were active during the second long wave upswing (boom) of long wave scholarship (1970s–1990s) were *predominantly* interested in real variables such as growth, accumulation (net investment), real wages, technology, plus global, regional, national, and sub-national processes (CPSP). During this time, growth became subdued as several successive short-cycle recessions led to a cessation of major long wave booms in the core. Productivity and investment also took a major hit during the downswing. Stagflation also became a major problem throughout the world as higher rates of unemployment, subdued growth, and rising prices became ubiquitous throughout much of the world during the 1970s–early-1990s. Inflation became a core part of the long wave analysis, but not so much as before when prices tended to take on a long wave character (rising in the upswing and declining in the downswing). Rather this was a case of prices rising during the downswing, at least for a time (see Grinin and Korotayev 2018 for a CPSP view of inflation).

Also, most long wave scholars analyzed long waves during the 1940s–1990s–2020s circa, or for some back to the early 1900s, and others certain segments of the institutions going back to the 1780s, while a few very thorough long wave scholars did go back to a macro or global view of long waves from the 1500s. Going back to the 1500s–1800s naturally raises the issue of prices and how they fluctuate during the long wave, especially since data used to be (and still is to some degree) quite scarce for many variables going that far back. Price data was much easier to come by, which is why Kondratieff used that often, even though he also used output data where possible, and his research in the Gulag in Siberia during the 1930s reveals his special interest in national income accounting (and growth). As for Schumpeter, some argue (Bloch 2018) that the vertical axis of his cycle curves from *Business Cycles* was prices, especially since during recessions he thought real output could increase (perhaps due to declining prices). In light of the second boom in long wave scholarship, which I was part of, one can understand why real output and related variables become the focus. Nevertheless, when one engages in a much fuller historical analysis of long waves, as we do in this book, some engagement in prices is inevitable and probably desirable. I do this where practicable in this book, even though I still think real variables are the core. Some recent empirical papers have come back to prices and situated them impressively in a long wave (often standard model) framework (e.g., Fischer 1996; Gallegati et al. 2017).[2]

Regarding the second boom in long wave scholarship, Ernest Mandel (1964) was very cognizant of structural forces emerging from upswing to maturity, being probably the first to note the fragile state of the postwar long wave upswing. Mandel (1995) generated an important school of long waves, which emphasized changes in the rate of profit, accumulation, innovation, and the organic composition of capital. Second, Walt Rostow (1978), the main one who emphasized prices, attracted renewed attention during the 1970s–1990s as he researched waves of (primary/manufacturing relative) prices, sectoral analysis, and the irreducible complexity of history. Third, neo-Schumpeterians came alive during this time with their theories–empirics of the bunching of innovation, the life cycle of inventions/products, systems of innovation, and phases of capitalist development (e.g., Mensch 1979; Perez 1983, 2015; Kleinknecht 1987; Freeman 1996). Fourth, David Gordon (1978, 1980) instigated the social structure of accumulation (SSA) school of long cycles, through the analysis of institutions, accumulation, profit, growth, and phases of evolution of capitalism. Fifth, Jay Forrester (1977) and others used system dynamics analysis to investigate investment, technological change, and capital and consumer goods sectors over the long wave. Sixth, numerous others adopting a more eclectic approach, scrutinized long waves through some innovative tools, including, among several others, J.J. van Duijn (1983), Andrew Tylecote (1992), Brian Berry (1991), and Manfred Neumann (1997) to mention a few notable ones. And seventh, many world-system analysts (WSA) studied long waves in association with hegemonic power

[2] To my mind, however, while one should include prices in the analysis to some degree (when relevant), too often scholars of long waves of prices get confused between (or don't sufficiently compare) (a) changes in the general price level, (b) the rate of change of prices, (c) relative prices between different sectors (e.g., primary vs. manufacturing), and (d) micro, meso, macro, regional, and global prices.

and core–periphery trends, including Immanuel Wallerstein, Chris Chase-Dunn, and numerous others.

By the late 1990s, the theoretical and empirical edifice of long wave analysis and policy had developed to the point where papers and chapters could be edited into substantial collections of reference books (e.g., Louçã and Reijnders 1999). By the 1990s, it could be well-established that the postwar wave had been on the upswing during the 1940s/1950s through to the 1970s/1980s and that downswing had developed into the 1970s/1980s onwards, in most nations of the core and many others in the semi-periphery. It was also during this time, including into the 2000s, that complicating factors started to especially impinge on the analysis, as the second major long wave upswing *of long wave scholarship* (boom) evolved onto a *period of crisis and instability* after which it went into long wave *scholarship downswing* (slump). The second long wave *scholarship* crisis and downswing thus emerged during the 2000s to the 2020s.

At this stage, it is appropriate to introduce the hypothesized modular patterns of long waves, whether of prices, growth, innovation, and/or structural changes in the techno-institutions: the *Long Wave Standard Model* (LWSM). There are two main modules to the standard model, the first module being the pattern (of prices, and/or growth, productivity, accumulation, profit, and techno-institutional) and the second module including hegemony and war. This *standard model* (in stylized form) is shown below in Fig. 1.1.

The basic parameters of the standard model of long waves include analyzing capitalism as a dynamic system characterized by cycles, waves, and phases of evolution. The major cycles are Juglar cycles of 7–11 years in periodicity (along with perhaps "Kitchin cycles" of 2–3 years), which have been moderately regular right up until the present in many areas of the world (especially the US) (see Sherman 1990; Sherman and Kolk 1996; Spinola 2023). There are also potential Kuznets cycles of about 20 years long, which correspond to the population-housing cycle; some think they ceased operating by the early 1900s (see Abramovitz 1968), but others doubt this (e.g., EU/UN 2017). Then there are the long waves (or Kondratiev "cycles") of perhaps 35–80 years in periodicity, in which long wave scholars initially hypothesized the existence of four such waves up until the 2020s since global growth per capita has not rebounded (e.g., Louçã 2021; O'Hara, 2023). But for many others, as noted, it was five (or even six) long waves, an extra one during the 1990s to the 2020s, either to showcase the rise of neoliberalism and its crises and relative demise, or the rise of aspects of information and communications technology (ICT) and/or biotechnology (e.g., Tsoulfidis and Papageorgiou 2019); while others see it as being based on rising nations in the semi-periphery (Grinin et al. 2016).

At this point, it should be noted briefly that some scholars only study long *cycles*, being entirely endogenous up and down movements in the core variables or processes. For instance, Solomous (1987, 1998) is one such scholar. His analysis is usually critical, for he specializes in critiquing the literature mainly from the view of statistical techniques and he ignores writers who argue long waves are partly endogenous and partly exogenous. (See Chap. 3 for more on this.) This current

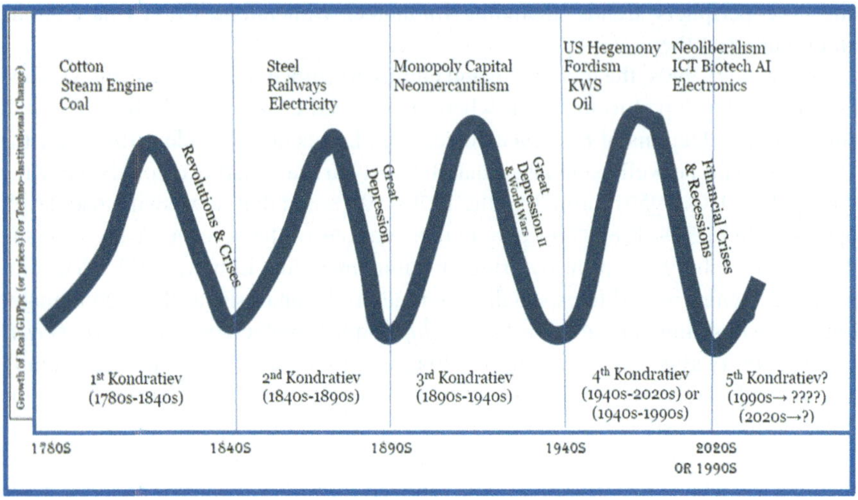

Fig. 1.1 Standard model of long waves, 1780s–2020s (stylized), variously for prices, real growth, techno-institutional change, etc.

book, on the other hand, includes writers who deal with both long cycles (in the endogenous sense) and long waves (being partly exogenous). I use the generic term "long waves" often to refer to authors using both meanings of the process (endogenous and exogenous), unless otherwise noted, but I also try and differentiate between authors who do distinguish between the two types of long dynamic in their own analysis, where useful.

The First Long "Wave" (or "First Kondratiev," following Schumpeter) in the standard model was thought to have begun during the late 1700s through to the mid-1800s (e.g., 1780s–1840s), usually divided into upswing (1780s–1810s) and downswing (1810s/1820s–1840s) (some authors start it in the 1790s). The long wave upswing is seen usually as beginning in Britain and having as its basis numerous core innovations. These include a set of political and social changes corresponding to a combined monarchy and an active parliamentary system along with common law, and the development of a useful system of class alliances. It also includes the extensive canal system of transportation, the putting out system (domestic arrangement of workshops for producing clothes, ironmongery, and even firearms); the spinning jenny, water frame, and spinning mule for textiles; the steam blast for smelting coke and iron; the steam engine for all sectors, and the rotation of crops for agriculture. Other "innovations" such as the scientific revolution, primary accumulation, enclosures, laissez-faire, and the very early stages of the factory system are said to have generated high rates of growth and employment (and/or prices and/or techno-institutional transformation) through what is often called the first industrial revolution, which was the organizing principle underlying efficiency, productivity, and exports. There was a price revolution in the late 1700s and early 1800s, in light of the Napoleonic Wars, which went into downswing during the 1820s–1840s.[3]

Some authors argue that these innovations led to the growth in demand for British goods and services, but that the downswing phase of the long wave started by the 1820s and especially into the 1830s and 1840s, as social revolt, deep recession, higher unemployment along with declining prices which led to lower profits and accumulation. Some authors say that the first industrial revolution was a qualitative change in the organization of production, distribution, and exchange which led to a substantial decline in demand and innovation through the long structural crises of the 1820s–1840s, which also included considerable pauperism, workhouses, and poor laws. The British developed an extensive system of colonial and settler systems (plus involvement in several wars) during this period which assisted the process of developing imperial preferences and exploitations. Other "core" nations are said to have undergone the industrial revolution much later in the nineteenth century, as they could learn from the premier capitalist economy and save themselves much of the original cost of renewal (e.g., France, USA, and Germany).

The Second Long Wave (or Kondratiev) upswing of growth (and/or prices/ techno-institutions) is thought to have emerged in the 1840s–1870s, on the back of the (second) industrial revolution in Britain, and the gold discoveries of California and Australia, manifesting in the railway and steam engine expansions, especially in the core. Railway expansion started in the 1830s–1840s and continued into the 1860s–1870s, with major benefits accruing through heightened turnover of capital, reduced transportation costs, and major passenger services. It also enabled reduced costs for coal and iron production, and, eventually, steel that benefited all industrial areas of Britain (the British "second industrial revolution") and later elsewhere. The contribution of mass production, especially of the factories and related dynamic structures, was a great boon for productivity, domestic sales, and exports during this time.

British hegemony is said to have emerged by 1815 and declined during the 1870s and 1880s (or for some authors, the 1890s) in areas of production, commerce, finance, and overall leadership (but commercial and especially financial hegemony continued for a time after absolute hegemonic decline). The British were said to have lost interest in innovation as they could rest on their laurels, established business institutions, imperial linkages, human capital, and social relationships. The US especially (and Germany) began to overtake Britain, once the civil war was over and a large market-landmass of business and consumers propelled economies of scale, agglomeration, and turnover of capital. Structural crises of overproduction are said to have developed during the first so-called Great Depression (1870s–1890s), as prices and profits declined, and the free-market philosophy began to dissipate in favor of beggar-thy-neighbor policies, higher tariffs, and imperial pursuits in Africa

[3] For this and many other so-called price waves, see David Hackett Fischer (1996). In this book, Fischer provides empirical evidence and theory associated with various price waves, especially (for our purposes) those of 1550–1660 (p.82), late 1700s–early 1800s (p. 137), and the 1970s–1980s (p. 209).

and elsewhere. With the crises and Great Depression(s), overproduction is said to have existed in the main sectors of steel, manufacturing, and transportation, especially in the core nations, while profits and prices declined (with real wages tending to rise).

The Third Long Wave ("Kondratiev") upswing is said to have started in the late 1890s through to the First World War (or the 1920s), based on changes to capitalism in the core (especially the US). These included changes to policy and institutions designed to reverse the low profitability and prices of the previous downswing, including advances in accounting techniques to better assess costs, revenues, and hence profit; as well as the European "scramble for Africa" to expand surplus expropriation and distribution from minerals, labor, and markets; increases in corporate concentration through mergers and acquisitions; plus other financial innovations via investment banks and central banking ("financial capital"). Several innovations were made in chemicals, rubber, turbines, pharmacology, and metallurgy that enabled the growth of the automobile industry, hydroelectricity, and electro-chemicals.

For some, the First World War upset the motion of the so-called Third Kondratieff (van Duijn 1983), while the 1920s deep recessions in many places and speculative bubble rises and crashes culminated in the (second) Great Depression of the 1930s. J.M. Keynes saw the 1930s crisis as a consequence of deficient aggregate effective demand, the power of the Treasury view which predisposed economies to austerity, and the dominance of finance at the expense of productive capital. Charles Kindleberger (1973) viewed this great contraction from the perspective of there being no effective hegemonic power willing to provide the public goods of lender of last resort, global accord, and overall leadership.

Meanwhile, Germany was situating itself through the First and Second World Wars as a dictatorial and oppressive (potential) hegemon. The excesses of the reparations and (second) "Great Depression" of the 1930s led Germany to initiate another world war, and a defeated Germany, big government, and US hegemony led eventually to the Fourth Kondratiev long wave upswing (1940s–1970s). This upswing was the consequence of a series of techno-institutional changes, in light of the Depression and world war, which benefited especially the core capitalist economies, but also many in the semi-periphery. The core economies mostly developed the Keynesian-welfare (-warfare) state (KWS), Fordism (including automobile and oil sectors), regulated finance, the two-tier system of corporate arrangements (oligopolies and smaller businesses), and the familial-household system of consumption and reproduction, plus the arrangements associated with the United Nations, Marshall Plan, NATO, and the Bretton Woods System (BWS). Most core and some semi-peripheral nations experienced the biggest boom of capitalism ever during the postwar corporate system of the 1940s to the 1970s.[4] Many in the periphery did not benefit so much from this upswing, and indeed a number had to suffer from the

[4] Part of the postwar long wave upswing was, of course, the hegemony of the West (led by the US) versus the so-called communist powers. Some Marxists deny that, e.g., the USSR was socialist or communist, calling it either a new socioeconomic and political system, or simply calling it "state

imperialist endeavors of wars, takeovers, and massacres (e.g., in Vietnam, Cambodia, Indonesia, and so on).

Cracks started to appear in the upswing during the late-1960s and early-1970s which initiated long wave "maturity" followed by the so-called fourth Kondratieff downswing. Workers gained relative power vis-à-vis capital for a time, OPEC gained at the expense of consumers/non-oil nations, the US (and their allies) lost the Vietnam War, while Europe and Japan started to emerge as potential new powers as US hegemony declined. As a result, structural crises of adjustment emerged during the 1970s and 1980s, while the Internet bubble and bust of the late 1990s–early 2000s, 9/11, the GFC of 2008–2010, and the Eurocrisis of 2010–2014-ff (especially in Greece; to a lesser extent in Italy, Portugal, and Spain) gave many the idea of long wave downswing being longer than usual. This idea was extended through polycrises of the ongoing climate crisis, the coronacrisis emerging into the 2020s, and the current "pre-war" situation (alluding to the possibility of World War 3).

More extensive research emerged that revealed severe cracks in the standard model of long wave scholarship during the long downswing. Most schools had gone through the long wave scholarship highs of dozens of research articles, books, conferences, and promotions during the 1970s, 1980s, and 1990s. The postwar corporate system (1940s–1970s) was the first long wave upswing and the start of the subsequent downswing (1980s–1990s) that fit (many thought) *perfectly* the standard model of long waves being of a certain dynamic of rise and fall, a certain amplitude, and as of the 1990s or 2000s a certain periodicity (of rise and fall of growth, accumulation, profit, and innovation). But the new structure of institutions (especially during the 1980s through to the 2010s), which in most places was influenced by neoliberalism (and perhaps the associated fusion with the flexible system of production/Taylorism), did not provide the usual high growth and investment necessary for a long wave upswing in the core or most of the semi-periphery or periphery. Some scholars interpret the short boom of the 1990s (in some areas), anomalously I think, as a long wave upswing. The age of neoliberalism, 1980s–2010s as Kindleberger recognized in his classic study of financial crises (Aliber and Kindleberger 2015), was the greatest period of recurring financial crises and their consequences in the history of capitalism, classic signs of a long wave downswing.

During this time (1980s–2020s), most nations of the world (and the world itself, excepting China and much of Asia) experienced decadal rates of GDP growth per capita about half that of the upswing during the postwar corporate system of the 1940s–1960s and possibly 1970s. As mentioned, some saw the 1980s and/or 1990s not only as a new set of institutions but also as a (new) long wave upswing for much of capitalism, while they saw the GFC as the onset of systemic crises of neoliberalism. Others saw the rise of ICT and biotechnology since the 1990s as the (new) long wave upswing, still underway. But the evidence shows, in the core and much elsewhere especially in the Americas, Europe, and Africa, that growth of GDP per

capitalist." Some research also viewed especially the USSR (and other "Soviet-style" economies) as undergoing long waves, often similar ones to the West.

capita, investment, productivity, and world income has been getting lower and lower since the 1970s and/or 1980s (broadly speaking, with varying amplitudes and cyclicality) (see Chaps. 9 and 11 below for details).

Meanwhile, as indicated, China and much of Asia underwent a long wave upswing during the 1990s through to the 2010s (except the "Asian crisis" during 1997–1998, which adversely affected notably Thailand, Malaysia, the Philippines, Indonesia, South Korea, and Hong Kong) with growth declining in half during the early 2020s in many nations (especially China), while still being much higher than the core. China itself has been developing state capitalism (see Schweinberger 2014; Chap. 8, below) very successfully, through the state direction of sociopolitical forces and state-market direction of economic activities. More recently (during the 2020s), as China has been explicitly seeking a degree of hegemonic power, it also has been changing governance by seeking more financial stability (and lower debt especially for construction and infrastructure), more equality, more inward development, and to some degree the development of second, third, and fourth-tier rural towns and cities to challenge big city eastern and south/east dominance.

Fractures thus emerged in long wave scholarship. Also, the new schools and re-emerging scholarship of the 1970s–1990s were bound to dissipate, especially as no new set of techno-institutions has produced a major rebound of durable (long-term) growth and accumulation in the core during recent decades; indeed, quite the reverse. The overall confusion in the field is compounded by some long wave scholars having stopped discussing the subject as long waves, while including chapters on long waves in their books (e.g., McDonough et al. 2021).

These fracture, uncertainty, and discontinuity in the field (though not emphasized elsewhere, to my knowledge) are happening while many scholars and schools of long waves have started (or continued) discussing the importance of linking together different traditions of long waves. In some respects, almost all schools have done this from the start; it is a question of emphasis. Neo-Schumpeterians have long emphasized not only technology but also institutions (e.g., Freeman and Louçã 2001). SSA scholars have sometimes (not often) linked institutions with technology and the regulation approach (e.g., O'Hara 2000, 2009). Several other long wave schools have encouraged shared research visions for the future (e.g., Wallerstein 1992; Kleinknecht et al. 1992). All schools have somewhat influenced others, and where this has not happened this school or trend may have dissipated from the field of long wave analysis. But still, a lot of scholars and schools in the broad field of long waves ignore other schools or concentrate on some scholars rather than others. Like much of academia, scholars tend to keep to their respective areas, fields, groups, and clans, despite some trends against this.

We have thus outlined the standard model of long waves, some who deviate from the model somewhat, and the general confusion in the literature in recent decades. Now it is time to argue the case for a new model of long waves, which must necessarily emerge out of the long wave scholarship downswing if we are to propel scholarly innovation to stimulate socioeconomic and politico-institutional innovation in the social formation. I hope this contributes to a third long wave of long wave scholarship (broadly defined).

But first I must emphasize that, regardless of the criticisms made of the standard model throughout this book, as I make especially clear in Chaps. 2 and 3, and more specifically in Chaps. 5–9 and 11, below, many scholars building on the standard model, or modifying it slightly or even significantly, have done some remarkable work to comprehend the long-term dynamics of capitalism (and sometimes other formations). Perhaps the best of these, which emphasizes the qualitative-historical elements of long waves, are the studies by Tylecote (1992) and Freeman and Louçã (2001). Even though, for instance, they point out the quite reasonable criticisms of the standard model, especially regarding Britain before 1850 vis-à-vis data unavailability or the data not fitting the periodicity of the model (on this see, e.g., Solomou 1987, 1998), not to mention other criticisms, they do an outstanding job of arguing for developing the theory-empirics and a qualitative-historical approach to the standard model that is persuasive. (This current book is quite different from these trends in linking waves with hegemony and climate change.)

Charles Kindleberger (especially in relation to hegemonic waves) and Eric Hobsbawm (long waves of growth), who also consistently used a qualitative-historical method, would have been impressed especially with the work of Freeman and Louçã. Others have also taken to the qualitative-historical approach, sometimes with statistical-diagrammatical information. One notable one, which for some reason virtually everyone ignores, is the work of Nathan Mager (1987), who applied long wave analysis to the whole history of US capitalism, not just for, e.g., capital–labor relations, from the 1780s to the 1990s (as done by Gordon et al. 1982); but including details of every one of the first four Kondratieffs, and a prospective fifth. I am perplexed that no one has, to my knowledge, critically analyzed the work by Mager or used it as a foundation for a more complete study of long waves in the US (perhaps the reason is that he emphasizes long waves of prices, but with extensive linkages to other processes).

We must now discuss briefly some (other) authors who deviate substantially from the standard model. Immanuel Wallerstein (1979), Christopher Chase-Dunn, and the world-systems school (WSS) (RWG 1979) extended the inquiry from long waves of growth and innovation to (also) hegemonic power, uneven development, and wars, especially in the *Review* (Fernand Braudel Centre) and later the *Journal of World-Systems Research*. Likewise, political scientists such as George Modelski, David Wilkinson, and others examined long cycles of global leadership, war, and conflict (see, e.g., Modelski 1987), while Joshua Goldstein (1988) followed a broadly similar mode of analysis (as well as doing a survey of much of the whole long wave literature up to then). Some others investigated the long movements of capitalism, including the Regulation School*s* (e.g., Aglietta 1976; Boyer and Saillard 2002), especially relating to the movement from Taylorism to Fordism and the flexible system of production. There is also the work of Angus Maddison (1982, 1991), who is not a long wave scholar per se, but who studied the empirical record of phases of capitalist development with the emphasis on growth *per capita* (and the associated Maddison Project which has done excellent work on, e.g., historical statistics and broad trends). The work of Wallerstein et al., Goldstein[5] et al., and Maddison Project et al., as well as the critiques mentioned earlier, and numerous other scholars, has been highly influential in the development of this current book.

Outstanding work of a statistical-historical nature on waves regarding the standard model, including many modifications and additions, has also been done by numerous scholars (see Chaps. 2 and 3, below). Some of the best is done by a collection of numerous authors, which I group together as the "East, Central and South European Long Wave Group" (see Chap. 3, Glossary), including Leonid Grinin, Anton Grinin, Andrey Korotayev, Arno Tausch, cowriters, and many others. See their work on long waves, such as Grinin et al. (2016) and Grinin et al. (2017), and on the decline of US hegemony by Grinin and Korotayev (2020). With works such as Grinin et al. (2016), Grinin et al. (2017), and Grinin and Korotayev (2020), to mention only a few, they have transformed long waves with a new vitality and enthusiasm. Several dimensions have been explored, such as linkages between long cycles and Juglar cycles, technological cycles, big history waves, aging populations, revolutions, and the decline in US hegemony. These innovations have played a key role in generating new energy into long *cycle* analysis, providing several hypotheses for further research.

These works are very pathbreaking, but some of the symptoms of the (a) crisis of long wave scholarship have been ongoing for several decades now, as have (b) the polycrises of modern capitalism; these two crises being interrelated. A major reason for the crisis of long wave scholarship is the incessantly unstable, nonlinear, and complex transformation of the world system of capitalism, *especially over recent decades*, which makes it hard for scholars and policymakers to understand global and regional dynamics. Nonetheless, as indicated above, long wave scholarship continues to make headway, and new works emerge, especially in the journals, every year or so (e.g., see Tsoulfidis and Papageorgiou 2019; Tomás Gutiérrez-Barbarrusa 2019; Kılıç 2021; Espinosa-Gracia and Sanchez-Choliz 2023).[6]

Works mentioned in the above two paragraphs are different in some respects from this current book, which seeks to examine long waves rather than long cycles, to basically accept the major criticisms of long cycles by Garvy, Kuznets, Sweezy, and some others, and to integrate broadly long wave motion with phases of evolution, changes in hegemony, and climate change ("LWHegCC"). No other major manuscripts or books have emerged since the 1970s or 1980s which have sought this reorienting of long waves vis-à-vis LWHegCC. These changes in long wave styles require modifications and reconstructions to make the analysis more consistent with the evidence, while also changing the concept of long waves toward an

[5] Joshua Goldstein (1988) especially tries to analyze the long wave relationships between real output, prices, wars, and other variables, noting especially certain lags and other anomalies between the processes involved. See especially page 275 (Fig. 12.7) and the surrounding explanation (re. output and prices).

[6] The *Kondratieff Medal*, for major contributions on long waves, has been won by Leonid Grinin and Andrey Korotayev, Christopher Freeman, Carlotta Perez, George Modelski, and Immanuel Wallerstein (among others).

evolutionary and transformative process of *complexity*. In this context, we turn to an alternative to the standard model, to comprehend the structural-historical integrated long wave motion of growth, hegemony, and climate change since the 1500s. It is hoped that this alternative will stimulate more work of a critical and reconstructive nature that makes further innovations in long wave analysis (a third long wave upswing in long wave scholarship), or more generally presents a constructive critique and reconstruction.

It was shown above that the standard model of long waves primarily revolves around the pattern of growth, productivity, innovation, and profit, with some additions involving wars, revolutions, and price waves, during the 1780s–2020s. Much of the actual long wave analysis before 1970 centers on price waves, but we regard these as secondary because the core apparatus must center on socioeconomic output and performance rather than prices per se, although I try where possible to show the relationship between price waves and real output growth per capita, hegemony, and climate change waves where desirable or feasible. If we are to add/replace modules vis-à-vis the standard model, we move into new terrain.

There are three main methods I use to study LWHegCC. The first and most important is the PoPE contingency paradigm of principles. This is closely linked to historical specificity (economic history of the periods). The second is the new long wave method of statistical method. The third mode is the primary and secondary literature on waves, history, and empirics. This three-pronged approach ensures multiple layers of argument relating to the details of LWHegCC. I try to make my argument throughout this book consistent with all three tiers where possible, so that I have three areas of scrutiny on LWHegCC. *All three supporting the same argument are a strong test of the three areas collectively.* Section 1.3 outlines the PoPE contingency paradigm (and the associated economic history). Section 1.4 outlines the new LW method, and how we specify periodicity, amplitude, and regularity of waves (vis-à-vis hegemony and climate change). The chapters that follow also detail the primary or secondary literature on the subject.

1.3 PoPE Contingency Paradigm of Long Waves

The first and most important part of my argument throughout this book is associated with the PoPE contingency paradigm (CP). PoPE CP postulates that long waves, hegemony, and climate change mitigation and adaptation are subject to an array of factors that may or may not generate a standard model result depending upon their net influences on global, regional, national, and sub-national events, conjunctures, and long movements. In this context, the *core* PoPE concepts/principles include (1) historical specificity and evolution; (2) hegemony and uneven development; (3) pathways and circuits of socioeconomic dynamics (CSD); (4) innovation and novelty; (5) circular and cumulative causation (CCC); (6) heterogeneous groups and agents; (7) contradiction and creative destruction; (8) risk and uncertainty; and (9) policy and governance (see Table 1.1). We refer to these principles continually throughout this book (directly and indirectly). There are other such concepts and potential principles listed under the umbrella of these nine core principles, and some others are not mentioned in Table 1.1 (see O'Hara 2023 for details). In round figures, this is our "100 principles." Three of the nine "core general principles" (Nos 1, 2, and 4) have already been very briefly discussed relative to the general environment associated with this book. Below we outline how all the principles apply to the concerns of this book.

The *first concept/principle is historical specificity and evolution.* This states in the current context that long waves, hegemonies, and climate change mitigation and adaptation are contingent on the specific array of historical processes at work. In general terms, they involve "*long duree*" (long duration), conjunctures, and events (Braudel 1979, 71–88), i.e. processes and events that variously impinge on the long, intermediate, and near-term; an array of processes impinging on LWHegCC dynamics. Processes of the long duration involve hegemony and climate change, as well as an array of other elements. Conjunctures include long waves and short cycles, but long waves also involve long-term processes and so are affected by hegemony and climate change dynamics. Historical events such as the Dutch revolution of the late 1500s, the Treaty of Westphalia of 1648, the various Anglo-Dutch wars, the Congress of Vienna (1815), the assassination of the heir to the Austrian throne in 1914, Hitler becoming Chancellor in 1933, the Bretton Woods Agreement of 1944 are all affected by long-term and conjunctural processes. All elements of historical time are affected by all the other elements of history. Processes are thus interdependent, yet also relatively autonomous.

This interdependency and relative autonomy make historical analysis more complex than otherwise, but it also makes the analysis more qualitative since strict determinacy does not exist. People live and die in an ecological and geo-spatial environment, as well as in an economic, social, and political context. Students of political economy are thus required to recognize this historical and contextual embeddedness of their inquiry.

This leads to the *second principle of hegemonic power and uneven development.* Historically power has tended to have varying degrees of centripetal and centrifugal distribution within and between nations, regions, and the world. The exact configuration between these various forces must be ascertained by historical, ecological, geospatial, economic, and social-political inquiry. Uneven developments between various cores, peripheries, and semi-peripheries (CPSP) are forever changing through time, and these CPSP uneven developments exist at all levels of reality, including towns, cities, states, nations, regions, and the globe. This current study delimits the inquiry to questions of power differentials within capitalism, starting with the Dutch Republic and continuing through to *Pax Britannica*, US hegemony, and potential Chinese hegemony. The main thesis is that the building of eco-spatial and techno-institutional dynamic structures impacts especially on the nature of long wave upswings, hegemonies, and the manner of dealing with the dynamics of climate change. In other words, LWHegCC relationships tend to coalesce or agglomerate through historical time, but the centripetal forces also move toward centrifugal dynamics at other times, and so on and so forth in a circular and cumulative process.

This raises the issue of the *third principle,* namely, the *circuit of socioeconomic dynamics* (CSD). The CSD, see Fig. 1.2, provides a stylized summary of the architecture associated with the structures, interactions, and flows within and between the (6–8) primary dynamic interrelated techno-institutional-ecological spheres of the CSD that impact on the contingencies of long-term performance and phases of evolution. The concept of the CSD[7] states that the building of sustainable technologies, institutions, and geo-spatial-ecological modules of a durable nature can provide a basis for long-term productivity, GDP per capita growth, investment and profit underlying hegemonic power, climatic, and durable long wave upswings.

The *principle of CSD* states that one should utilize this concept to understand the process of building dynamic structures that generate the long-term turnover of economic activities and cultures of production, distribution, exchange, ecology-spatial, and overall reproduction. Each potential hegemon attracts agents and groups to

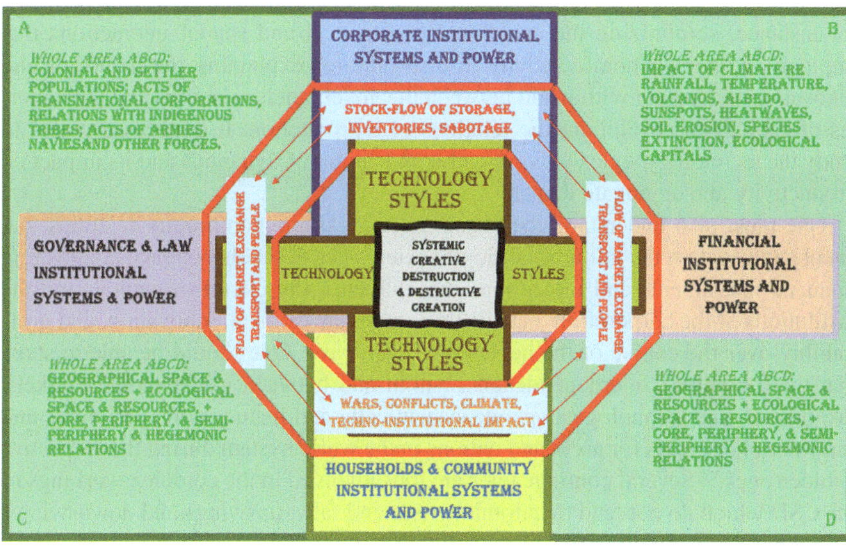

Fig. 1.2 Principle 3, the pathways and circuits of socioeconomic dynamics (CSD), stylized

[7]The concept of the CSD was first developed in O'Hara (1992). In my published work after this I reconstructed the CSD as a social structure of accumulation notion, without the terminology of CSD. But in reviewing my analysis of long waves, I have come to believe that the CSD is a superior form of analysis to the SSA framework, for three reasons. First, because it links institutions, technologies, and climate change/geo-spatial processes together (which SSA does not usually do). Second, because it emphasizes that the CSD is linked to pathways and circuits, flows, stocks, relationships, and organizations. Third, that the CSD can be modified according to changes in history and different hegemons. Fourth, it links structures, relationships, and historical metamorphoses. It is a modern-day re-growth from the original *Economic Tableau* of the Physiocrats, the circuit of social capital of Marx, and the circular and cumulative models of Kaldor and Myrdal (and other models of macrodynamic transformation).

build networks of business, marketing, research and development, distribution-households, and ecological-spatial fields that contribute to higher (and lower) growth per capita, accumulation, and profitability. One should construct a modular CSD appropriate to each potential hegemon to comprehend the interactions and relative autonomies and human/resource flows within and between spheres (dynamic structures). We do this in Chaps. 5–8 below for the Dutch, British, US, and Chinese cases (and briefly in Chap. 9 for neoliberalism).

One must also necessarily explain the workings of the CSD as-a-whole, especially the technologies, institutions, and geo-ecological-spatial structures, in some detail (at least in outline), since their precise nature comprise core contingencies affecting long waves, hegemonies, and climate change.

The *fourth principle of innovation and novelty* is especially relevant here, as core changes in technology, institutions, ecologies, resources, markets, and relationships provide the durable base from which the central focus of this study depends: the emergence of hegemony, long waves of growth, and climate change. This involves, for instance, scrutinizing the ecological-geophysical and spatial interactions that impinge on socioeconomic activity. It also requires explaining the nature of and innovations occurring within and between the governance structures and the varieties of capitalism enveloping the relations of reproduction. It is necessary also to study the technology style evolving within the circuit of dynamics and its impact on productivity and aggregate demand.

One must also understand the changing familial and community relations that enable and sustain the cultural fabric of society. The CSD also engages innovating financial instruments and institutions that influence the circuit of capital, and the institutions of the corporation that enable ongoing investment, innovation, and profitability over the course of the hegemonic long wave. One should be able to show that these complex interdependencies within and between geo-dynamic markets, institutions, and technologies operate systemically and include core, periphery, and semi-periphery roles for areas and nations in the world system during the respective "golden ages."[8] Several contingencies are thus involved in the complex workings of the CSD which do not lead to automatic rises and falls, upswings and downswings, and climate change ups-and-downs. But certain dynamics can certainly be established supporting/inhibiting hegemonic processes, growth waves, and climate changes, given certain relationships and metamorphoses.

The CSD is important to recognize and outline the process whereby hegemons engage in innovation, investment, and expanded demand through institutions, technologies, and ecologies, to produce high-value commodities for domestic markets and export, thereby trading with nations that variously provide numerous other facilitators, including both cheap mainly primary products for import (especially

[8] While the term *Golden Age* usually refers to the *Dutch Golden Age* of cultural, economic and political age of transformation, which I tend to date during the period 1570–1650 (or more restrictedly during the 1570s–1610s); it may also refer generally to the British age of 1820–1880 and to the US (and other western) age of rising expectations during 1945–1975. For the Chinese maybe the period 1980–2020 could be a similar era (or maybe their best is yet to come?).

from the periphery) and high-technology products (especially from the core), to produce a surplus, and by extension often a trade surplus (including re-exports), and regularly a budget surplus to provide the hegemonic goods and services required by their domestic consumers, capitalists, state-workers, and others.

The resulting profit, usually extended by credit (including trade credit, accommodative and structural endogenous funds), can assist with the expanded reproduction required for durable investment and accumulation of capital, and the reproduction of class, gender, ethnic, and species structures of relationships (including alliances and modes of control) that underpin hegemony and long wave upswings. Through time, these structures and relationships become majorly affected by contradictions, which evolve and lead to declining rates of realized surplus, accumulation, consumption, and profitability, and often to trade and budget deficits (including fiscal crises of the state) that interdependently often lead/lag declining hegemony and long wave downswings.

The *fifth principle of heterogeneous groups and agents* is instructive in this context, as these institutions, technologies, and ecologies become activated through the agencies of certain roles associated with various classes, genders, ethnic groups, species, other technical groupings, individuals, and prominent machines. This involves the emergence of workforces of managers, skilled technicians, laborers, farmers, houseworkers, and transporters. It also involves a variety of merchants, industrial capitalists, money capitalists, entrepreneurs, and related officers. It is necessary to explain the role of professional administrators, state agents, politicians, teachers, sales workers, and scientists. Various forms of durable machines, structures, and infrastructures (including potentially robots and AI) become part of this CSD. The reproduction of human and non-human populations is involved, requiring a combination of natural reproduction and migration, replacement investment, and innovation, in relation to GDP per capita and productivity per capita/worker/agent during periods of hegemony and beyond. This requires describing the roles of agents/classes in the core, periphery, and semi-periphery, including the manner of extraction of surplus from slavery, sharecropping, and wage-labor, plus the manner of "handling" of "original inhabitants" and migrants of colonial sites and settler colonies. Substantial contingencies emanate from these complex processes for long wave, hegemonic, and climate change dynamics.

The *sixth principle of circular and cumulative causation* (CCC) is crucial, as the historical circumstances, hegemonic processes, agencies of the classes, and a host of other factors must be capable of providing multiplier and accelerator forces to the upswing in economic power, performance, and profitability upon which the various golden ages depend. The key periods when Dutch, British, US, and, potentially, Chinese capitalisms undergo rapid expansion comprise nonlinear changes, new relationships, upheavals of expectations, a buoyancy of cultural arrangements, and success or suitable "management" of conflicts-wars. These new phases of upward development thus typically involve economies of scale and scope, agglomeration, multiplier effects of aggregate demand expansions, accelerator impacts of investment upgrades, exuberance of financial innovation, non-equilibrium forces of path dependence and forward motion, plus the (cyclical) motion of creative destruction and profit expansions. Again, the contingencies involved here are considerable for our three main areas of investigation (LWHegCC). But as with the other principles/ processes, the facilitation of LWHegCC processes can be expansive when set in motion.

As the *eighth principle of risk and uncertainty* implies, the calculable risks of insurance and financial assessments, and environmental proclivities of uncertainties underlying business and consumer confidence, can be moderated to enable durable confidence and relative stability to prevail during the golden ages of hegemonies. The contingencies of ensuring adequate certainty, trust, and embeddedness become potentially dubious in most environments, but the forces underlying the emergence of a sustainable circuit of capital (and the wider CSD) are capable of moderating uncertainty as the accelerated turnover of transactions through the institutions, technologies, and geo-eco-structures become established on a (sub-)national, regional, and global scale. Sufficient embeddedness of socioeconomic processes must be capable of generating effective coordination of transactions involving markets, distributional arrangements, reciprocities, householdings, and ecologies. This may be possible by moderating the destructive impact of wars, financial crises, depressions, rebellions, revolutions, and severe bankruptcies, which impose numerous further contingencies, but also facilitation, on/of the processes. Often this happens through various types of accords, agreements, treaties, congresses, and other styles of dissolution of conflicts and instabilities.

As the *ninth principle of policy and governance* implies, structures of cooperation, community involvement, participatory institutions, social safety nets, democratic liberalism, and other public goods such as lender of last resort facilities and international treaties and arrangements, including various regimes, are typically needed for a sustainable long wave upswing during times of hegemonic dominance in the respective golden ages through specific forms of climate change. A semblance of such relative and dynamic stability was achieved in periods of Dutch, British, and US ascendency. Domestic liberalism and free trade (imperialism), along with often settler capitalism and/or colonial exploitation, plunder, and war, also pervaded such hegemonic periods, so conflicts were not entirely emasculated, but usually contained at some stage during the hegemonic era (especially domestically). Domestically states and governance structures usually intervened in the interests of competing but partially reconcilable interests, and citizens usually felt themselves part of a national or international movement of buoyancy, while the poorest of the poor were usually disenfranchised from these gains while often being part of the national euphoria. Polity and governance thus involve several contingencies for our three main processes, while agencies can propel such forces through certain historical eras.

Through the *(seventh) principle of contradiction*, these contingencies extend to the conflicting arrangements that potentially inflicted political economies. A moderation of contradictions is necessary for absolute hegemony (and high/durable long wave upswings) to prevail, as the dominant nation arranges for the moderation of conflicts within and between nation-states, classes, and ethnic (including religious) groups, as well as minimizing the impact of climatic and other crises. The pathways and circuits of socioeconomic dynamics need to be effective enough to reduce risk and uncertainty to a minimum while enabling interest rates to fall to moderate-low levels. Technology and property rights need to be structured for rents to be moderated but not excluded. The rights of property ownership need to be balanced by the rights of citizenship, at least for certain classes, such as capitalists/landowners, merchants, skilled workers, and specific migrants. International organizations, treaties, and regimes are always necessary to moderate conflict between nations areas and ensure supply of resources and energy. The vested interests need moderation in the interests of the common good (to the extent desirable), at least domestically. Contingencies abound where contradictions are endemic or widespread. In the colonies, usually, the hegemon and others in the core have carte blanche to inflict whatever crimes against humanity they want on the darker ethnic groups who they see as inferior, and after hegemony, they often inflict worse massacres on the darker colonial groups partly to enhance their own surplus expropriation and exert power and authority to illustrate their superior might (especially against ideological threats).

These public goods, coordination mechanisms, embedded processes, international treaties, and temporary balancing mechanisms are fraught with contingencies, especially when set in a core, periphery, or semi-periphery context. The golden ages, hegemons, long wave upswings, and climate change resolutions also have within their organizational structure the seeds of their own demise. Structural crises are close to inevitable eventually as the institutions, technologies, and geo-ecological structures exhaust their potential. Liberalism draws other powers into the production, commercial, and trade systems to compete against the hegemon and benefit from the lessons of the powerful nation. Existing jealousies and hatred (usually with adoration) bring competitors to engage in mercantilism and (trade) wars against the main power (and eventually by the previous hegemon [where relevant]), and/or otherwise to learn from the hegemon's experience. Multiple product cycles generate maturation and declining profits for previously established monopolies and oligopolies. Financial instability and rising debt ratios generate more extreme financial crises and deep recessions (and eventually debt crises in the periphery), along with rising interest rates and inflationary forces, or otherwise deflation in an environment of deficient demand. The habits and institutions underlying CSD buoyancy eventually evolve toward complacency and stagnant innovation through insufficient renewal and reinvigoration. Declining (relative) hegemony leads to rising tension and ineffective public goods between nations, and therefore to more extreme wars, conflicts, and instabilities. Polycrises of adjustment become more common as the contradictions magnify. Contingencies abound and certainties of polycrises get stronger through time.

These potentially powerful contingencies are so vast that one wonders how the CSD components can periodically become synchronized sufficiently to propel major long wave upswings, hegemonies, golden ages, and climate change resolutions. Agglomerations, multipliers, accelerators, cumulations, buoyancies, and confidences tend to feed off each other precipitating upward propelling motion through multiple tipping points that cumulate through cascading processes. Psychologies of mass euphoria, technological ascendency, institutional optimism, and geospatial expansion aggregate through cycles of upward motion. Phases of evolution of capitalism undergo stages of metamorphosis through the establishment of new systems, followed by ascendency, maturation, and decline. However, counter to the usual stylistic presentation of long waves, institutional transformation, technological change, and climatic adjustment, these phases of evolution are not easily patterned and neatly phased due to the magnitude of the contingencies and the complexity of the processes involved.

The new phases of evolution undergo continual and periodic stresses and strains that pose threats to upward motion. Juglar cycles, for instance, periodically go from highs to lows. Long-term processes (the *long duree)* such as climate change and the rise and fall of cultures impinge upon the medium-term waves of motion. Current events that partially have their own momentum and dynamic affect waves, hegemonies, golden ages, and ecologies. Forces of the universe associated with sunspots, eccentric movement of planets, changing revolutions around the sun, comets, earthquakes, volcanoes, and GHG emissions are forever impacting Earthly dynamics. Charismatic personalities, powerful groups of people, and other nations and areas also influence the course of history. For these and other reasons, hegemonies, long wave upswings, golden ages, and climate regularities may never materialize or may themselves be subject to the irregular distortions of the real world. Contingencies always prove the rule that dynamics will always be complex, disruptive, and often hard to explain or understand. Nonetheless, some patterns do emerge, despite the limitations of human intelligence and the difficulties of resolving conflict. The results will be complex, multi-variant, irregular, uncertain, and subject to certain forces that hinge together and clump into degrees of confluence, regularity, and periodicity.

1.4 New Long Wave Method and LWHegCC

Here the *new long wave method* (NLWM) of long wave structure, periodicity, amplitude, and regularity is outlined. The statistical method linked to NLWM to analyze core waves (long, short, and borderline) of growth is as follows. I want to use a relatively simple method of statistical analysis, since this is a book with a wide audience in mind. I will show how my statistical method can be applied to the standard model which readers are already familiar with; see Fig. 1.3. Then I show how it relates in summary to Dutch, British, US, and Chinese cases to date (see details in Chaps. 5–8).

Figure 1.3 applies the NLWM statistical method to a stylized view of the standard model, using *hypothesized* decadal AAGRs for GDP per capita, over history from the 1770s to the 2020s. This is so that readers get an introduction to the method using an already known standard model, although the main reason for the NLWM is to apply it to the new situation under scrutiny (below also Chaps. 5–8).

First, starting with *stylized* time series data of real GDP *levels*, I, second, calculate hypothetical growth *rates* for every year, and then, third, estimate average

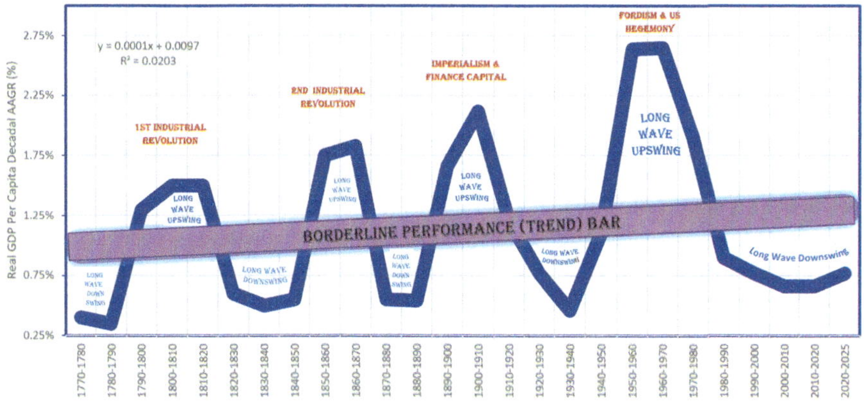

Fig. 1.3 Standard model of long waves (stylized) 1770–2025 (blue line); borderline performance (BP, trend linear purple bar), LWU and LWD, real GDP per capita decadal AAGR (percent) (using New LW model stats. Method)

annual growth rates (AAGR) for each *decade*. Fourth, I compute a trend line for the hypothetical data (using ordinary least squares), and then transform the trend line into a trend bar (20 points wide), to approximate Schumpeter's "neighborhoods of equilibrium" (see Chap. 2; for partly different reasons). Fifth, I compare the decadal AAGR of real GDP per capita with the trend bar (i.e., compare the growth curve with the trend bar). Sixth, this enables me to differentiate between areas of the wave: (a) the upswing, above the trend bar; (b) the "borderline performance" within the trend bar; and (c) the downswing below the trend bar. For the 1780–2022 period, I am thus able to ascertain the standard model results for long waves, including upswings, downswings, and areas of performance in between these two for the four waves. There is no ambiguity about the results. The standard model performs perfectly with the hypothetical data utilized (in this stylized example).[9]

Let me now briefly emphasize a critical point about this book, its use of statistics, and the conceptual foundations of growth. It is this: I make no apology for emphasizing real GDP *per capita* levels and real GDP *per capita* decadal average annual growth rates (AAGR) in the long wave analyses. Specifically, I am interested in changes in levels and rate of growth of *per capita* real goods and services output for

[9] Some scholars may think it strange that wave upswings include areas above "borderline" performance but in part of the *declining* wave; while wave downswings include areas below "borderline" but in the *upward* sloping line. These scholars may think that wave upswings should include the upwardly increasing blue bar, while downswings should include the downwardly decreasing blue bar. This would be a mistake with the method of analysis used here. Upswings include all areas where growth is higher than the borderline bar; while downswings include all areas where growth is lower than the borderline bar. Even Schumpeter argued that during the first half of the downgrade (in the four-phase model) production may increase, and that long waves should (or could) be defined from borderline up to the next borderline up (see Chap. 2 below). Also, if we are using downswings with very negative rates of growth, we need this method of calculating ups and downs, because the upward bar would often include very negative figures (e.g., see Chaps. 5–9).

an economy (and comparative analysis thereof). The general level of the real standard of living (per capita), and its rate of change with decadal averages, is my point of departure for long waves. Of course, I am also interested in other variables, such as hegemonic power, climate change, inequality levels, population growth changes, total GDP, and so on. The point to make is that I am not going to use simply "real GDP growth rates (period)" as I do not believe they reflect the processes we should be concentrating on. However, occasionally I do point out some differences between my conclusions on waves and those who use real GDP growth rates (period), where they are important (e.g., Chap. 5). Put simply: I am interested in per capita rates of growth averaged ten-yearly and not the growth rates per se (not per capita), because I do not believe the latter are very meaningful. (And if I were to estimate the onset of recessions associated with business cycles, I would use GDP per capita AAGR.)

Now I want to provide a brief review of my four case studies of Dutch, British, US, and Chinese long waves, (potential) hegemony, and climate change. The longer explanation of Chaps. 5–8 studies in addition some details of the PoPE applications using the CSD for each case, and the primary-secondary literature. Here I will just use the NLWM statistical analysis for brevity. Readers should not confuse this brevity with the more detailed analysis in Chaps. 5–8. The NLWM here is used simply to introduce the subject.

Hence, using NLWM analysis, I show the results of applying it to three actual empirical cases during 1780–2022 (where possible) for the British, US, and Chinese cases. After this, I utilize the NLWM statistical method to illustrate how it operates before the standard model's periodicity, during Dutch history circa 1550–2022 (broken into three periods to reduce the length of each case). (Chaps. 5–8 study the Dutch, British, US, and Chinese cases for growth, hegemony, and climate change in some detail.) In this context, Fig. 1.4 presents the actual empirical British long wave decadal AAGRs and long-run linear trend bar (wave v trend) for the 1780s–2020s to highlight/clarify times when long wave upswings and British and US hegemonies were at their height (and how they differ from the standard model).

This NLWM summary of British waves illustrates three things, which are detailed in Chap. 6 (using PoPE, NLWM and other literature). First, long wave upswings only occurred during periods of hegemony. During eras of British (1820s–1860s) and US hegemony (1950s–1980s), Britain underwent very long wave upswings. Second, in between hegemonies, the highest growth rates experienced for Britain were short-wave upswings (1790s, 1880s): they were periods of uncertainty and polycrises. Third, there were no full long waves as per the periodicity of the standard model, except (mostly) for the fourth Kondratiev (1940s–2020s); although it is not quite a full long wave due to no recovery to borderline performance (yet, if at all). (See Chap. 6 for the British experience during the period 1570–2022.)

Now we compare Fig. 1.4 with the standard model in more detail. During the periodicity of the standard model's so-called First Kondratiev (1780s–1840s), this NLWM empirical analysis shows "in reality" in Fig. 1.4 there was no LWU during the 1780s–1810s (there was a SWU in the 1790s), and no LWD during the 1820s–1840s. During the standard model's "second Kondratieff," in our NLWM

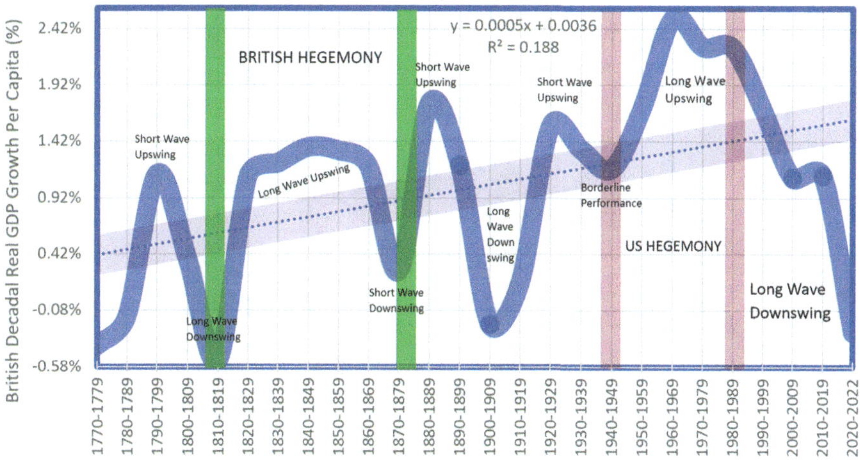

Fig. 1.4 British decadal growth of real GDP per capita (AAGR) 1770–2022 (blue line). Linear trend bar (purple) [Source: Adapted from raw figures of Maddison Project (2024, 1770–2022)]. Conroy and Emerson (2007) use a similar method. ($y=0.0005x+0.0036$; $R^2=0.188$ is for the trend *line*)

"real world," there was a LWU but it lasted from the 1820s to the 1860s (rather than for the 1850s–early-1870s); and there was no LWD during the mid-1870s to the early-1890s, although 1873–1893 was a period of major uncertainty; borderline performance and short waves (see Chap. 6). There also was no "empirical" long wave upswing during the so-called Third Kondratieff (1890s–1930s), and there was borderline performance during the 1930s–1940s. The Fourth Kondratieff (1940s–2022) includes a very dynamic and durable LWU during the 1950s–1980s, borderline performance during the 1990s, and a very durable LWD during the 1990s–2020s. The only thing that prevents a perfect long wave during the postwar long wave is a lack of a return to borderline (if we define LWs as: borderline to borderline). (The evidence does not support multiple long waves between the 1940s and the 2020s.)

We can say overall that the British experience of waves is much more complicated than the standard model, and mostly centers around strong LWU during times of hegemonic dominance (British, US), with periods lacking hegemony being more erratic with more short waves and long wave downswings (and borderlines-downswings). However, the full story must include many more pieces of the puzzle, including the qualitative-historical survey of the rise and fall of the circuits of socio-economic dynamics, including the eco-techno-institutional details, hegemony and climate change (see Chap. 6, below, and further below in this chapter).

Figure 1.5 shows the NLWM statistical approach for the USA during the standard model's 1800–2022 timeline (yearly US Maddison Project data starts in 1800).

Meaningful US growth patterns start during the mid-1800s with a few decades of erratic growth, including short upswing (1830s), short downswing (1840s), short

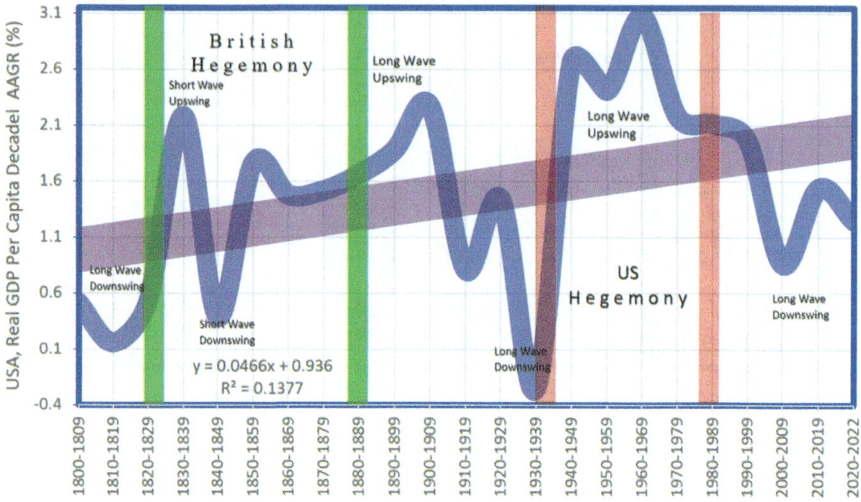

Fig. 1.5 USA real GDP per capita decadal AAGR, 1800–2022 (blue line). Linear trend bar (purple). (Source: Adapted from raw figures of the Maddison Project 2024) ($y=0.0466x+0.936$; $R^2=0.1377$ is for the trend *line*)

upswing (1850s), and a cross between borderline (B) and upswing (U) performance during the civil war (1860s) and the 1870 crises. Clear long wave upswing emerges in the 1880s–1900s. Thereafter, the 1910s represents a short-wave downswing, followed *possibly* by downswing (or B) during the 1920s, and LWD during the [1920–]1930s (given the slight favor to downswing in the 1920s). Thereafter, we have the postwar Golden Age *very high* long wave upswing during the 1940s–1960s, and a *much lower* long wave upswing during the 1970s–1980s (close to B). Thereafter, we have neoliberal (a) borderline in the 1990s and (b) long wave downswing during the 2000s–2020s. (Overall much more subdued growth during the 1970s–2020s.)

The differences between the USA NLWM and the USA standard model of waves are (1) no evidence for *long* wave upswing during the First Kondratiev of the 1780s–1840s (although yearly data only starts in 1800), (b) no evidence for long wave upswing during the Second Kondratieff of the 1850s–1870s (1860s–1870s is close to both B and U) (LWU emerged during the 1880s–1900s, the tail-end of the second long wave and the beginnings of the Third Kondratiev). The best periods when this PoPE wave model corresponds to the standard model are (1) during the Third Kondratiev LWU of 1890s–1900s, the *possible* LWD of the 1910s–1930s (if we interpret LWDs loosely); and (2) during the Fourth Kondratieff (1940s–2020s), with very high LWU during the 1940s–1960s, weak upswing during the 1970s–1980s, borderline performance for the 1990s, and LWD performance in 2000–2022. (Again, not quite long wave material due to no borderline yet to end it off [from B to B].)

The US data reveals two eras of long wave upswing, one just after British hegemony (some would say during the latter part of British hegemony), and during US hegemony in the 1940s–1970s, which accords with a core hypothesis of this current

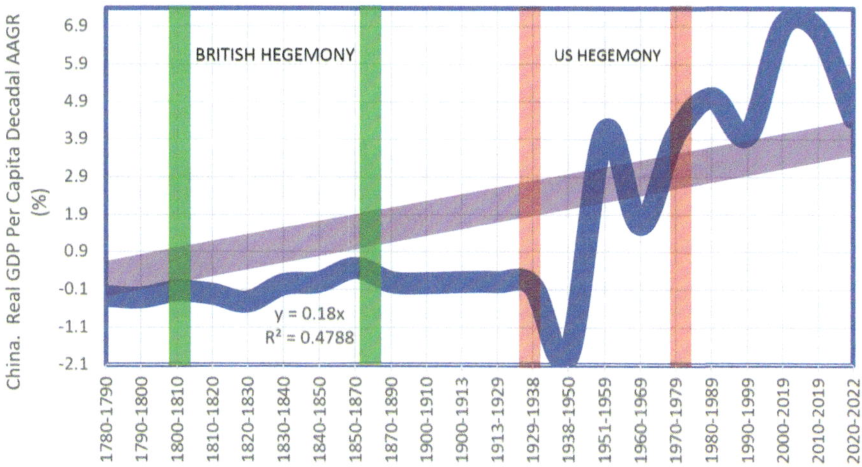

Fig. 1.6 China, decadal AAGR real GDP per capita, 1780–2022 (blue line), showing borderline linear trend bar (purple), upswing, and downswing performances. (Source: Adapted from Maddison Project 2024 database 1780–2022) (y=0.18x; R^2=0.6258; is for the trend *line*)

study. However, as with the British experience, we need much more historical analysis, especially of the rise and fall of the circuits of socioeconomic dynamics, hegemony rise and fall, and climate change fall and rise, which is provided in Chap. 7, below (also briefly below and in Chap. 4, especially vis-à-vis climate change). Note also an important point about the US experience, if we take a looser interpretation of the data. Namely: we could *possibly* hypothesize that the US underwent a major era of techno-institutional development which gradually ushered in a very long period of structural performance and eventually LWU followed by LWD during the 1850s–1930s (90 years). Further research may assist with this hypothesis (see brief comments in Chap. 7, below).

Figure 1.6 illustrates the Chinese record of GDP per capita AAGR for the 1780–2022 period, to compare the empirics with the standard model.

Comparing this figure with the standard model shows little similarity except declining performance during the 1930s–1940s, and rising performance during the 1950s–1970s. In terms of performance during eras of hegemonic dominance, this shows very slightly higher growth in China during some decades of British hegemony, higher ones during US hegemony, and much higher growth during US *relative* hegemony (as hypothesized).

Moving away again from the standard model, we apply a NLWM statistical method to the period before, during, and after 1780, specifically 1530–2022, for the Dutch. Figure 1.7 illustrates Dutch performance, which introduces much more complexity due to the longer periodicity: 220 years longer than the standard model. To make it more manageable/explicit, we differentiate three periods, in Fig. 1.7. The first, (a) is for the period 1530–1779, including during the early phases of the Dutch Revolution (1570–1590) to immediately before the so-called first industrial revolution (1780–1848 circa). The second, (b) is for the years 1780–1939, from the

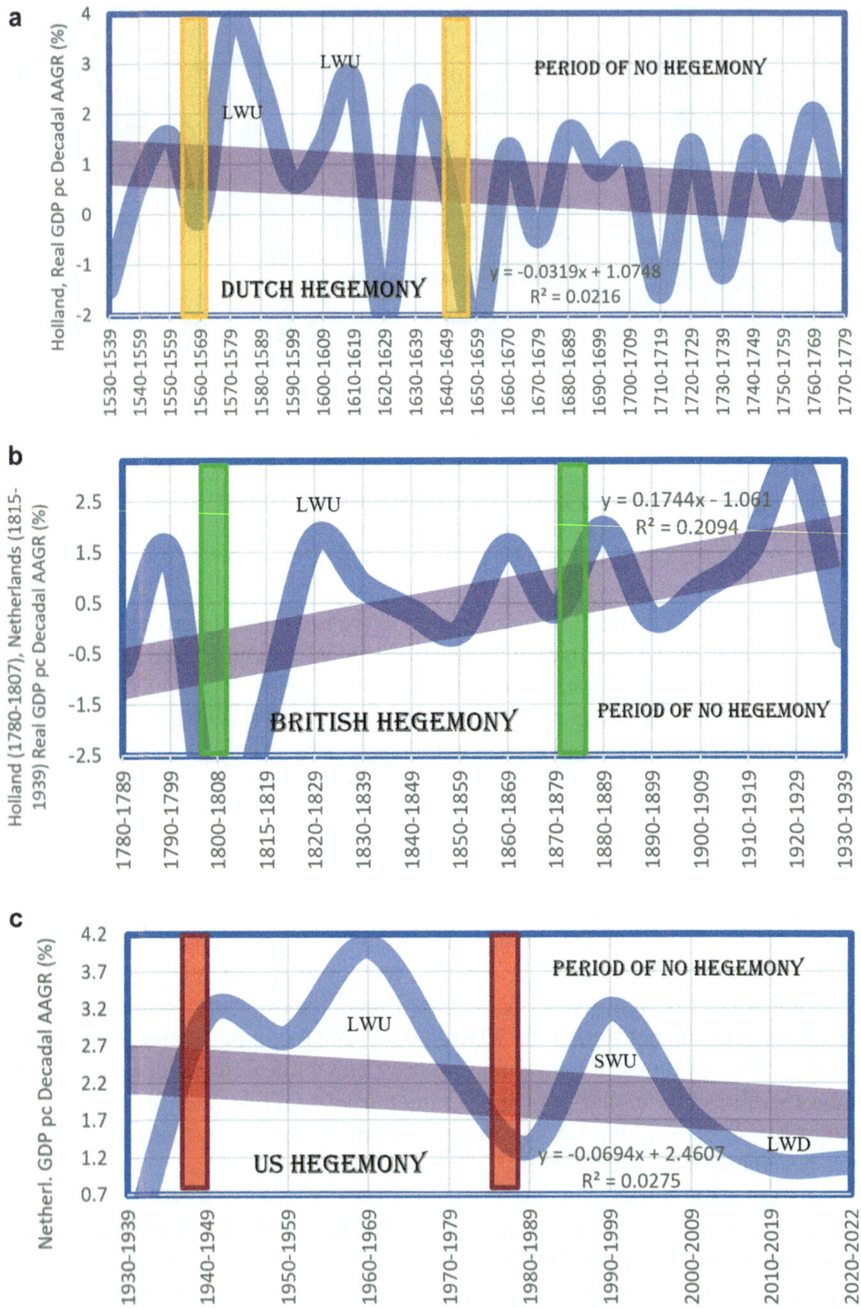

Fig. 1.7 (**a–c**) Decadal annual average GDP per capita growth rates (AAGR) (%), Holland/Netherlands, 1530–2022 (blue line); Linear trend bar (purple). (Source: Adapted from the raw data from the Maddison Project 2024). (See Footnote 11). (**a**) Holland, 1530–1779. Real GDP per capita decadal AAGR (blue line); Linear trend bar (purple). (**b**) Holland (1780–1808)/Netherlands (1815–1939), 1780–1939, real GDP per capita decadal AAGR (blue line), and linear trend bar (purple). (**c**) Netherlands, 1930–2022. Real GDP per capita decadal AAGR (blue line); Linear trend bar (purple). LWU=long wave upswing; LWD=long wave downswing

so-called first industrial revolution to the end of the Great Depression. And the third, (c) is for the period 1930–2022, from the Great Depression to the 2020s.

Figure 1.7a–c illustrates that the most conspicuous eras of LWU are during/around periods of hegemony. There are two LWUs during the broad era (circa) of Dutch hegemony: 1570–1590 and 1600–1620, and there is a very extensive and durable long wave upswing during US hegemony: 1940s–1970s. Introducing Fig. 1.7 does introduce more detail, especially for the 1780–1939 period. Notably, it shows that, when this segment is analyzed in detail, there is a weak long wave upswing during the 1820s–1830s, during the beginning of British hegemony. Overall, areas when there was no hegemony were characterized by periods of uncertainty, poor performance, and polycrises: 1660s–1810s, 1890s–1930s, and 1990s–2020s. See Chap. 5 for details of Dutch performance, Chap. 6 for the British (for the 1500s–2020s), Chaps. 7 and 8 for the US and China; and Chap. 9 for much more detail on polycrises during periods of no hegemon, especially during the 1980s–2020s (in between US hegemony and potential Chinese hegemony).[10]

The NLWM is applied to the empirics of the three dominant hegemonic nations of the capitalist-world economy: the Dutch (1600s, Chap. 5), British (1800s, Chap. 6), and US (late 1990s, Chap. 7); and to some degree the potential hegemon China (2000s, Chap. 8). Our analysis of LWHegCC, based on the *principle of historical specificity and evolution*, illustrates core stylized facts over 200–500 years (circa), that specifically relate to our four countries. The *first stylized fact* is that the model *is complex, irregular, asymmetrical, uneven*, and subject to changes based on further analysis. We present no simple-minded representation of reality nor try to oversimplify the dynamics of the nations examined. This presentation of the model is a summary since more detail is necessary based on eco-geo-spatial, technological, and institutional world-system complexities of specific cores, peripheries, and semi-peripheries (PoPE) and other literature. The NLWM is a representation of a reality impinging on many areas of the world, since the four countries in their respective golden ages exerted powerful forces on other areas of the globe.

The *second stylized fact*, based on the *principle of hegemony and uneven development*, is that during periods of hegemony, the power of the core does exert influences on other regions; during hegemony, impressive long wave upswings tend to be generated by the hegemonic power in their respective nation-state, and often at least reasonable performance by related neighbors (*or* allies, and even enemies). And while long wave upswings generate growth and related socioeconomic performance, once the growth waves undergo long wave downswing (and depressions of performance), GDP per capita *levels* are always high for a considerable time into the future. Hence, during the 1600s and into the 1700s, Dutch GDP per capita *levels* were the highest in the world by a long way; similarly (though not as strong) for the British after their hegemonic dominance faded, but much weaker for the US after

[10] For sources of data from the Maddison Project, see Jutta Bolt and Jan Luiten van Zanden (2024) and the Maddison Project dataset notes. Data for 1500–1808 is for Holland (Van Zanden and van Leeuwen 2012), while 1815–1913 (Smits et al. 2000) and 1913–2022 (Maddison Project) are for the Netherlands. There is no data for 1809–1814 due to war/conflict.

their absolute hegemony faded (vis-à-vis *major* economies of the core). Hence, declining hegemony reduces the power of the hegemon, but per capita living standards are always high for a (long) time.

The *third stylized fact* is that in between periods of hegemony, there is usually dislocation in the world political economy (or much of it), leading to (usually) poor performance, major financial crises, world wars, systemic uncertainties, revolutions, and the like ("polycrises"). This was especially true during the 1700s, between 1885 and 1945, and between the 1980s and the 2020s (it was also true, for many nations, during the 1600s due to the little ice age; more on that below). As Charles Kindleberger (1973, 1996) long argued, hegemonic periods are when the hegemon provides public goods such as leadership, lender of last resort, and facilitating institutions that benefit at least one side of the powerful groupings in the world, and often others. Typically, however, the hegemonic power and their allies exploit especially certain areas of the periphery by way of wars, massacres, surplus expropriation, cultural destruction, ecological devastation, and the like (which often continue when the hegemon is only *relatively* powerful, rather than absolutely).

The *fourth stylized fact* of the NLWM of LWHegCC concerns wars, and especially world wars. Some long wave scholars have indicated that world wars tend to be generated just before the hegemonic power achieves its absolute dominance ("wars of ascendency"). Hence, the revolutionary and Napoleonic Wars of the 1790s–1810s the ending of which ensured British hegemony (1815–1870); and the two world wars of 1914–1918 and 1939–1845, the ending of which ensured US hegemony (1945–1970s). These two cases resulted in a long wave upswing for Britain and the US, respectively, but also for other nations and areas (especially during the period of the 1940s–1970s).

The Dutch case is more difficult to specify vis-à-vis this stylized fact. In this context, authors have variously cited the 30-year war (1618–1648), fought mainly in central Europe, in which 40–60 million people died, which involved the Dutch. But the 30-year war was part of the 80-year war (1568–1648), including, early on, the Dutch War of Independence (also called the Dutch revolution or revolt) after which 11 of the Dutch counties, lordships, dutchies, and cities merged to provide the underlying structure for the Dutch Republic in the aftermath of the *Treaty of Utrecht* (1579). This Dutch revolt is likely a good war of ascendency for the Dutch case (though nothing like a world war). The most impressive long wave upswings for Holland during this time were 1570–1589 (the biggest until the postwar period of the 1940s–1980s) and 1600–1619; and as Kindleberger (1996, 89) points out, "[t]he spurt of growth that ran from 1590 to 1620 has been called an economic miracle" (quoting Slicher van Bath 1982, 23); and "by the early seventeenth century the Dutch Republic had established a *Pax Neerlandica* [sic] over the waters of the Baltic and North Sea" (Israel 1989, 38). Dutch hegemony (see Chap. 5) is thus more complicated than British (Chap. 6) and US (Chap. 7) hegemony.

The *fifth stylized fact,* which is also a hypothesis for further analysis, is that the 1700s was a depressed period for the Netherlands and Britain, mainly because of two factors, first, the socioeconomic structures of the Dutch circuit of capital had deteriorated, and second, due to several wars that the Netherlands and Britain were involved in, especially against (and with) France and against each other. The British were unable to establish strong long wave upswings on the back of their innovations involving the first industrial revolution's so-called upswing (1780–1820), due to the dislocation imposed by the revolutionary and Napoleonic Wars. It certainly did not undergo a "take-off" ("when growth becomes a normal condition," Rostow 1990, 38) during 1783–1802, but that may be a reasonable description for British growth when it commenced the long wave upswing after 1815, when it defeated France in the Napoleonic Wars (and due to the *Congress of Vienna*, which many hypothesize established "100-years of peace").

The *sixth stylized fact* is that after each absolute hegemon has achieved its major long wave upswing(s) during its "Golden Age" and is in the process of undergoing the *relative* (rather than absolute) hegemony phase, when growth is much lower, but GDP per capita levels are high, the country that will eventually (or most likely) become the next hegemon undergoes a period of somewhat impressive performance for a time. For instance, in the case when Dutch performance and hegemony started to decline in relative terms (mid-1600s), Britain underwent a couple of good *short*-wave upswings (interspersed with downswings) (see Chap. 6). When Britain had begun to deteriorate, relatively speaking (after 1870), the US underwent a 30-year long wave upswing during the late 1800s and early 1900s. And when *Pax Americana* and its Golden Age faded in the 1980s–2000s, China (and some other Asian nations) experienced what was to be a major long wave upswing of several decades during 1980–2010, until it declined majorly (but still at around 4–5% growth per capita) during the 2020s. What does this indicate? We hypothesize that historical processes do provide processual indicators as to what may be forthcoming in the future. The Chinese example certainly does indicate that China is a serious contender for replacing the US as the hegemonic nation of the world in the future. We also have good reasons for thinking it may *not* become the next hegemon (see Chap. 8 on China).

The *seventh stylized fact* relates to the so-called *First Great Depression* (supposedly during the 1870s–early-mid-1890s) discussed earlier in the context of the Standard Model. Much has been written about this supposed downswing in the long wave, discussed in some detail in Chap. 6, below. The NLWM indicates it did not eventuate. Examining the 1870s–1890s in more detail, as we do in Chap. 6, reveals that there was a major "price downswing," a profit downswing, and several deep depressions of GDP during 1873–1893 in Britain. While many other nations did (and did not) undergo this decline, the evidence supports this period as a *borderline* performance for the British (neither depression nor long wave upswing). It is a complicated area of analysis in need of much more research.

We can now understand better how climate change fits into the equation of long waves and hegemonic periods, especially in light of the Little Ice Age (circa 1500s–1855), including the Dutch Golden Age of the 1570s–1650s (or 1570–1620), the British industrial revolution, growth, and hegemonic dominance of the 1800s, and the postwar corporate system of the 1950s–1970s and its aftermath into the 2000s (2020s and beyond). These periods of climate change do not easily fit the usual hypothesis of GHGs and global/regional temperatures rising during periods of expanding GDP per capita growth and declining during low growth per capita periods (such as the GFC, Euro debt crisis, and corona crisis).

Here we summarize the *eighth (set of) stylized fact(s)*, relating to climate change, growth, and hegemony. The first fact is that during 300 years, there was a "Little Ice Age" (LIA), as noted, especially in the northern hemisphere (NH), but also elsewhere to a lesser extent, when temperatures were on average about 1 °C (or more) colder than average in the NH (it was preceded by a medieval warm era). There have been different assessments of exactly when the LIA occurred, some dating it during 1400–1855 and others during the 1500s–1600s. We can perhaps safely say that it occurred at least during 1500–1850, including three cyclical cold periods, the Spörer Minimum (1500s), Maunder Minimum (1600s), and Dalton Minimum (1800–1855). Several factors caused the LIA. A significant one was the intrusion of Atlantic waters into the Nordic Seas, so that the "warmer water led to a breakup of sea ice and calving of tidewater glaciers [which] … allowed the volume of ice that had accumulated to be exported into the North Atlantic. This led to a weakening of the subpolar gyre ['a giant circular oceanic surface current,' Merriam-Webster 2024], setting the stage for the subsequent LIA" (Lapointe and Bradley 2021). Other/related factors also played a role, including, for instance, the core one of cycles of solar radiation with a lower floor (Sporer and Maunder Minima for the Dutch and Dalton minimum for the British), heightened volcanic activity, orbital forcing, and changes in Earth's orbit (Mann 2002).

In this context, Geoffrey Parker (2018) has argued that the LIA helped to precipitate a series of crises throughout the world, especially during the 1600s (which was the colder of the three cold periods), and he documents cases in, for instance, the Americas, Africa, Europe, Asia, and Australia. Special reference in Parker's analysis is given to the impact of this climate crisis on the nature and severity of crop failures, trade crises, wars, uprisings, diseases, revolutions, and invasions. This notion of major crises during the 1600s is a theme with a long history, having been debated by several scholars in numerous journals and books, notably in light of the work of Eric Hobsbawm (1954a, b), Hugh Trevor-Roper (1967), and others (e.g., Mousnier et al. 1960), especially vis-à-vis Europe. Parker's innovation was to center on the role of the LIA in these crises (although White 2014 argues he should have concentrated on economic history rather than purely climate crises).

What is the significance of this for the Dutch Golden Age, the *Pax Netherlandea*, and the great Dutch long waves of the late 1500s and early 1600s? It is generally agreed among authors that for the Dutch to lead the capitalist system through the crises of especially the late 1500s and 1600s was a great achievement. In an environment wrought with fear, perpetual war, pandemics, extreme weather events, and socioeconomic rebellions, the Dutch managed to innovate profusely, adapt, change their arrangements, and indeed improve their livelihood and economic position (de Groot 2018). This was seen as a major development at the time, and indeed other states (e.g., British, French) perpetually looked to the Dutch to emulate their successes, while also, as many mentioned, eschewing the fact (because of jealousies) that the Dutch were prime movers of change and at the center of financial, commercial, and productive systems of proto-capitalism. Dutch hegemony and their major long waves of the late 1500s–early 1600s, however, as we see in Chap. 5, gradually dissolved as the British fought them through trade and military wars after mid-century while the French sought to also negate their momentum through wars and trade disputes (and the Spanish fought them off and on for 80 years until 1648).

If the great Dutch Golden Age of, broadly 1570–1650, operated in an Ice Age environment, and European (and international) crises, what was the experience of British and US hegemony in terms of climate and associated responses? We find that the greatest era of capitalist expansion, during the postwar corporate system of Fordism, the Keynesian-welfare state, and *Pax Americana* (1940s–1970s) was in an environment of a *Small Cool Era* (SCE), while the growth waves experienced by Britain (plus the Dutch) during *Pax Britannica* (1815–1870) seem to be mixed. First, we deal with the easiest period to scrutinize, that of the period of US absolute hegemony.

Again, counter-intuitively, as with the period of Dutch hegemony and climate change, the 1940s–1970s era of huge growth and accumulation was a time of climate *cooling* around the world. Data specifically shows the cooling being greatest counter-intuitively during the Second World War (1939–1945) and the 5 years thereafter (1945–1950), followed by a cyclical pattern of low-level cooling and heating (1950–1975) (IPCC 2007, ch 1, 101; IPCC, 2022a, ch 2, 322). Thus, during the largest and greatest worldwide battles and long wave upswings ever recorded there was a substantial period of climate cooling. Why?

Most analysts now believe that this global cooling was due to a rise in anthropogenic aerosols from pollution which dimmed the sun's rays through smog and cloud-type cover preventing a proportion of the solar energy from reaching the oceans and lands. It is also recognized that to some degree volcanic ash played a role; for instance, the eruption of Mount Agung in 1963 cooled the lower atmosphere by perhaps half a degree (Brahic 2007). Regarding the aerosols, there are two processes at play. As Flynn et al. (2023, 15122) states, "Aerosols may affect the radiation balance through aerosol-radiation interactions (ARIs), or the scattering and absorption of radiation directly by aerosols, and through indirect aerosol-cloud interactions (ACIs). The ARIs include the aerosol-cloud albedo effect, also known as the first indirect or Twomey effect …, and the aerosol-cloud lifetime effect, or the second indirect effect …; these interactions exist for all cloud phases." However, these aerosol impacts do not seem to totally explain the cooling period circa 1940–1970, and there is a high degree of uncertainty and complexity associated with them, which may in time lead to a better explanation of the total effect, especially relating to aerosol interactions with other aspects of the climate system (Flynn et al. 2023, 15130). (See Chap. 7 for details.)

Regarding the dynamic long wave and hegemonic dominance of *Pax Britannica* during the 1820s–1880s (and the associated long wave upswing of the 1820s–1860s), there is difficulty ascertaining the record of climate change. *Prima facie*, as noted, one expects industrialization to heighten greenhouse gasses and raise global temperatures on land, sea, and upper atmospheres (depending on aerosol, etc., patterns). Most contemporaneous climate records extend back to 1850 (IPCC 2021) or 1840 (IPCC 2007), and what they show is a recurring cyclical pattern of global temperature changes resembling those of the 10-year sunspot ("Schwabe") cycle, with perhaps a slowly declining trend from 1840 to 1880. Regarding the earlier period of 1815–1840, there are competing trends and cycles that show no obvious and consistent pattern, except the contradictory one of the "Dalton minimum" (a declining part of a 120-year solar cycle) and the rising temperatures of a 1000-year cycle (see Chap. 4 below for details). In Chap. 6, we clarify this conundrum and basically conclude that there was likely cooling during 1800–1855 during the third solar cycle minima of the LIA, and rising temperatures from 1855 to the 1880s.

In relation to China, its 1980s–2000s long wave upswing and the lower growth trajectory of the 2010s–2020s (see Chap. 8, below) coincided with the emergence of the most recent long wave escalation in climate change, between 1975 and the present, when global temperatures rose more than at any other time in "recent" climatological-history. While the West and several other nations have been mostly undergoing long wave (growth) downswing since the 1980s, China and much of Asia have been engaging in an escalation of productive, financial, commercial, and military power in the global political economy. Currently, China produces 30% of global GHG emissions (and rising, with a rising trend), followed by a previous hegemon (US) at 11% (rising, with a falling trend), the EU27 at 7% (rising, with a falling trend), and 18% for "rest of the world" (UNEP 2023, XXVIII). Per capita emissions for 2021 are the highest for the old hegemon (USA) at around 15.3 tCO_2-e/capita) (rising with a declining trend), followed by Russia at 14.5 tCO2-e/capita (rising, with an increasing trend), and China at 10.2 tCO2-e/capita (rising with an increasing trend).

We can thus see that climate change fits relatively well into the long wave and hegemony discourse but certainly not as would be expected vis-à-vis rising temperatures during upswings and declining temperatures during downswings. The historical setting is always much more complex than expected. (For more details applying the principles to the nations see Chaps. 5–9.)

1.5 Chapters of This Book

Chapter 2, below, is a critical literature review of long wave theories and empirics, summarily presented, within the context of the *PoPE contingency paradigm,* with special reference to the *first wave of long wave scholarship*. These include scholars such as Jacob van Gelderen, Salamon de Wolff, and especially the work of the Russian economist, Nikolai Kondratiev, who contributed to earlier versions of the standard model of long waves. Kondratieff posited critical hypotheses concerning (a) upswing and downswing, (b) discoveries and inventions, (c) wars and revolutions, (d) agriculture, (e) gold, and (f) a theory of long waves based on the life of durable fixed capital, which still to this day are inspiring authors toward theory and empirics on the subject. We accept the main criticisms of Kondratieff's work as being subject to a degree of rigidity, determinism, and speculation regarding questions of long wave periodicity, amplitude, and endogeneity. Instead, we agree with D.I. Oparin, Leon Trotsky, and George Garvy that we should aim to study the long-term evolution of capitalism in its various waves and phases subject to more correspondence with the empirical, institutional, and technological (and I would add climatological) tendencies of historical transformation. If long waves were mere price phenomena, our job would be much easier, especially up to the 1950s. But since we are primarily interested in long waves of growth (per capita), hegemony, and climate change, the job becomes more complicated and contingent.[11]

Joseph Schumpeter especially continued the tradition of the standard model of waves through the second part of the first wave of long wave scholars during the 1900s–1940s. Significant was Schumpeter's circular flow process where there is no innovation, with the subsequent introduction of credit, innovation, and the three-cycle schema in his method of successive approximations. A core contribution was in emphasizing the importance of inventions and swarms of innovation as the main dynamic pushing long waves forward. He also hypothesized the process of interaction between Kondratiev waves, Juglar and Kitchin cycles through a long historical time. Keeping more-or-less to the periodicities and amplitudes of the standard model, he also infused it with core hypotheses concerning the role of credit, especially distinguishing between productive credit that underlay innovation and unproductive credit that lay the foundations for speculative bubble crashes and depressions.

Undergoing innovation in theory and empirics, he nevertheless was subject to the valid criticisms especially of Kuznets and Sweezy. We endorse many of these criticisms, especially regarding the inadequacies of the business cycle aspects of waves and shorter fluctuations, as well as, more fundamentally, regarding the importance of capitalists (and surplus) in the circular flow of socioeconomic activity (Sweezy). Our own circuits of socioeconomic dynamics (CSD) is more pragmatic by including core elements of reality in the model, while also identifying the core process of innovation not only by capitalists, but also members of the state apparatus, as well as financiers, members of households-communities, and ecologies, where relevant.[12]

[11] Had Kondratiev (1892–1938) lived a normal life cycle he may have lived to the 1970s and could have been part also of the second long wave of long wave scholarship (late-1960s to the 1990s), as well as contributing to the debate into the 1940s–1960s. Note that while in prison in Siberia in the 1930s, he did quite a bit of research and even prepared models of national income. Hence, he would likely have done much more work not only on price waves, but especially on real GDP growth (per capita) waves and other indicators of performance had he not been executed.

[12] A potential criticism of Kondratiev and Schumpeter is that they may sometimes have engaged in anomalous statistical methods. Eugene Slutsky developed the thesis that the summation of random factors is capable under certain conditions of producing a wave-like motion in the data. A second thesis is that the data's wave-like motion may exhibit periodic regularity over time. Together Slutsky posits that recurring long waves of economic motion may result from data that has no real causal basis. This may occur when random data is analyzed using moving averages. Cycles and waves of a random nature may thus become confused with cycles and waves with specific causal

Chapter 3 extends this analysis, criticism, and reconstruction to the schools of thought constituting the second long wave of long wave scholarship, in the late 1960s to the 1990s (and beyond). This was the most vibrant, innovative, and extensive period of long wave analysis, mainly because the postwar corporate system and its demise was the most obvious example of the standard model in practice (relating to growth) ever seen in the history of capitalism. Up to the 1980s and 1990s, especially it seemed to accord with virtually all the requirements of the standard model of long wave theory in practice, plus its so-called long wave upswing (1940s/1950s–1970s) was arguably the most revolutionary period of all history for the resurgence of progressive scholarship, especially through the boom in university education, the Keynesian-welfare state, and including members of the radical, intelligent, and innovative bourgeoisie and the New Left. But it did not generally include a sustainable long wave recovery or upswing through the 1990s to the 2020s (although some may disagree).

Numerous schools of long wave thought developed during this time, the first one being the Mandelian school concerning accumulation, innovation, the rate of profit, the organic composition of capital, and the role of class conflict, wars, and revolutionary periods in history. Neo-Schumpeterians emerged under the wings of Schumpeter's main hypotheses of circular flow, swarms of innovation, and later the role of credit and bubbles, institutions, and the role of government. The best of these neo-or-post-Schumpeterians reduced majorly the degree of determinateness of the long wave model. A smaller grouping of Rostovians emerged from Rostow's theory of primary goods relative prices, sectoral change, and the irreducible complexity of history. David Gordon started the social structure of accumulation (SSA) school with its emphasis on institutional spheres, class, and ethnic groupings in the (segmented) labor markets, plus US hegemony, state-citizen accord, and the two tiers of the corporate SSA (in the postwar era). Numerous other schools and authors contributed to long wave analysis during this period, including the regulation approach, Andrew Tylecote, Jay Forrester and his coworkers, plus numerous other scholars who are discussed especially in Chap. 3.

By-and-large these schools adhered to the standard model of long waves, but they did contribute much to innovation through the work of several dozen scholars who worked on issues associated with the rate of profit, innovation, institutions, capital and consumer goods sectors, relative prices, and political long waves. World system and international relations scholars to a degree went beyond the standard model by linking long waves with hegemony, wars, and world history since at least the 1500s. Others also went beyond the standard model by scrutinizing phases of the evolution of capitalism and previous historical epochs; Angus Maddison and colleagues being a supreme example of this trend. Others still have started with long waves and then branched out into numerous fields associated with world (big)

processes. One must be the lookout for these anomalies. It helps to use data methods not subject to these problems. It helps to use other methods (e.g., historical analysis, other studies' results) for alternative "tests" of the data. This does not mean that moving averages will certainly result in this problem. (See Glossary, "Slutsky-Yule Effect"; Chaps. 2 and 3; below.)

history, such as hegemony, wars, and cycles (e.g., Andre Korotayev and Leonid Grinin). (See also the work of David Christian.)

This current work (this volume) has some similarities with the Mandelian, post-Schumpeterian, Regulation, and SSA approaches, and with the final trend in long-term history just discussed, including world-systems theory, Maddisonian dynamics, and Korotayev–Grinin–Christian big historical inquiry. It differs in some respects, however, from these trends, mainly because we start with long wave analysis, present critical points, and reconstruct the inquiry based on contingencies, principles, CSD, hegemony, and climate change. It is in this context that we introduce Chap. 4, the analysis of climate change waves and cycles.

Chapter 4 takes the recent IPCC (2021, 2022a, b, 2023) four volumes of climate change empirics, mitigation, and adaptation analysis as the point of departure, plus their earlier chapter on paleoclimatology (IPCC 2007). In this section, we show that the IPCC does acknowledge climate change waves and cycles from ancient history on planet Earth, but then goes on to mostly ignore them in recent volumes. We build on the earlier analysis by the IPCC (2007) that goes through the past 4.5 billion years of Earth's climate history. We start with especially the research of Harris (2023) and Waters et al. (2023) by showing the emergence of the Hedeon Long Wave (4.5b–4.0b years BP) involving the evolution of planet Earth. Following this is the Archean Long Wave (4b–2.5b years BP) which saw the emergence of simple life on Earth, followed by the Proterozoic Long Wave (2.5b–540m years BP) through alternating global glacial and hotter periods. Finally, we introduce the Anthropocene long wave since 1975 when climate change began to generate several climate crises on a global scale (thus far, we have only seen an upswing of this wave).

Waves and cycles associated with the Proterozoic Long Wave were well formulated with regular periodicities, amplitudes, and endogenous mechanisms. Liu et al. (2011) illustrate the linkages between weather cycles and broader waves between 1400 BC and 2100 AD, including two long climate waves between 230 BC–1000 AD and 1000 AD–2200 AD, indicating we are currently in an upwave of this aspect of climate change. Other scholars have advanced our knowledge of these cycles and waves, including Scafetta and Bianchini (2023) who developed a Planetary Model of Solar Activity and Climate Waves. This model is based, first, on planetary movements within the solar system generating systemic oscillations, which in turn change crucial solar dynamics (through luminosity, wind, electromagnetic field, and gravitational field), and which further impact the solar system. Second, these further impacts affect dust, cloud cover/albedo, total solar irradiance, and cosmic rays in Earth's atmosphere, which in turn impact Earth's climate systems.

A combination of these processes is thought to create 10- to 11-year sunspot (Schwabt) cycles, 120-year waves, and 1000-year waves/cycles on planet Earth. These cycles are encapsulated within the Little Ice Age (1500s–1850s), including the cyclical (down-up) period (1800–1875); the Small Cooler Period (1940–1970); and subsequent climate crises of the 2000s–2020s. These variously impacted Dutch, British, US, and potential Chinese hegemony. Several cycles and waves operate concurrently, and authors debate how the current and immediate future trend of climate change will evolve, and how this links to the IPCC. Chapter 4 examines

IPCC studies, and the long waves of climate change generated into the present and the future, especially in light of the currently emerging and future trend of cascading tipping points of climate change on planet Earth as China seeks to establish hegemonic patterns in the global political economy.

The next five chapters (Chaps. 5–9) study the four past and potentially emerging hegemonic trends involving the Dutch, British, US, and Chinese experiences and the associated long waves of expansion and decline, including the systemic polycrises that typically emerge in between hegemony periods during waves of deteriorating performance especially in the core (e.g., during the 1980s–2020s).

Chapter 5 centers on the Dutch experience of hegemony, long waves, and climate change. The Dutch circuits of socioeconomic dynamics emerged out of the successful Dutch Republic from the late 1500s through to the early-middle 1600s. The geo-eco-spatial structures of Dutch proto-capitalism were potentially anomalous for growth and development due to the Little Ice Age, when rain and snowfall were heavier than usual, temperatures more challenging for human, animal, and plant life, and lowlands potentially being lost in the waterways which were gaining ground. But, much more than others, the Dutch were resilient, in that they found effective ways of not only reducing these barriers but surmounting them through new innovations of windmills, dykes, habitual institutions of land reclamation, floodgates, dams, and a whole series of other novelties. Their techno-institutional innovations included the Fluyt design of shipping which reduced costs and improved productivity; the expansion of knowledge, including arithmetic, language, legality, and trade; and the establishment of industrial districts, textiles manufacturing, the fishing industry, the peat fertilizer industry, and a world-class publishing industry. Under the influence of the Reformation and the Renaissance, the Dutch sought to instill an element of liberalism into policymaking and strengthen elements of religious freedom in the Republic. State institutions contributed majorly to a combination of central and local interests, through the provision of first-class legal institutions, property rights, defense technologies and strategies, education and human capital, infrastructure, and (some degree of) poor relief. They established core–peripheral relations involving, most notably, monopoly control of the Baltic trade and the spice trade in the Indies, as well as some shifting power in the Caribbean latifundia using slave labor, along with shipping supremacy, financial hegemony, and the most sophisticated warehousing and storage businesses in the world.

The (Dutch) United Provinces became the first successful capitalist economy wherein the productive, commercial, and financial relationships enabled high levels of growth and accumulation, especially during the late 1500s and early 1600s. The bourgeoisie matured as captains of industry, lieutenants of finance, and masters of trade. Wage labor expanded as towns and cities evolved while farms and market gardens thrived. Double-entry book-keeping reduced the calculative risk of investment, while prudential and central banking functions reduced uncertainty in markets. Sound monetary measures and limitations on overextended credit reduced financial instability while 3–5% interest rates during the Golden Age enabled credible real rates of return on business. Stability was also enabled by the functions performed in households and communities, such as child development, intra-class relations among the aristocracy and skilled labor, and pension and other benefits of citizenship and guild membership.

However, there were major contradictions within the Dutch Golden Age, long wave upswings, and hegemony which began to moderate and later negate these high-performance metrics. These included other powers, particularly the British and the French, who copied Dutch successes, escalated mercantile measures such as embargos, tariffs, and wars against them, and developed innovative technologies, institutions, and climate change responses. It also included declining innovation and rates of investment in the Dutch Republic, even as Westphalia (and Munster) agreements (1648) established conciliation regarding the geopolitical balance of power. Eventually, the Dutch edge in production evaporated, much later also the edge in trade, and finally in finance, whereupon many scholars argued it was the eventual dominance of finance over production that led to demise.

Chapter 6 discusses the establishment of the institutions and technologies within the CSD circuit via *Pax Britannica* and the waves of growth and climate change experienced during the 1600s–2020s. Some argue that Britain (or England) underwent hegemony in the early to mid-1700s, and that industrialization led to long waves of the late 1700s to early 1800s. We can find no convincing evidence of this. By the time Britain defeated Napoleon in 1815 which saw the so-called 100-year peace established at the *Congress of Vienna,* as recovery emerged after some recovery period, hegemony thrived and continued through to the 1870s–1880s. Defeating Napoleon also activated Britain's durable long wave upswing which continued until 1870. Britain and much of the world underwent down-and-up cycles of climate change during the sunspot cycle Dalton minimum (1800–1855) and the subsequent rising temperatures of the second half of the 1800s.

The British circuits of socioeconomic dynamics that provided the foundation for hegemony and long wave upswing was established from eco-techno-institutional changes made through the late 1700s onto the late 1800s. Geo-ecological factors were very important, especially their extended coastlines, shipping, and naval structures, which enabled geospatial processes crucial for the Empire. During the mercantile period, the British imposed effective Navigation Acts and import/export controls to destroy especially Dutch power in trade and shipping, as well as four wars against the Dutch which eventually led to the defeat of this former hegemonic power. Coal in its various forms was crucial, being the main fuel input into iron and later steel production, as well as heating, and later railways, which majorly assisted the workshop of the world in its quest for global supremacy. Innovations such as the spinning jenny, the Bessemer converter, and the steam engine were crucial for productivity improvements, the factory system, and exports.

As with the Dutch experience, households and immigration provided a basis for labor supply, consumption demand, and intra-class relations. The state assisted through monarchy being balanced with (and eventually dominated by) parliamentary representation, the gold standard upon which the balance of payments was based, and the merchant navy which played a key role in colonial and trade growth. Political economists and ideologues became hired prize fighters for free trade (imperialism), which enabled the most productive and powerful nation to sell its products overseas while cheaper imports of especially primary products flowed inwards, and onward exports flourished. The City of London played a key role in organizing finance and promoting the circuit of money capital. Industrial cities such as Birmingham, Leeds, Manchester, Newcastle, and Glasgow generated agglomeration benefits through economies of scale and scope, with circuitous linkages to railways, docklands, colonies, and further industrialization via energy, internal combustion, and chemicals sectors. *Pax Britannica* was well and truly in place in the 1800s and Britain used their colonial and settler peripheries and semi-peripheries along with internal markets to expand its networks of power.

However, the contradictions of British hegemony manifested themselves through declining productivity as innovation diminished while other countries such as Germany and especially the US started to converge with Britain. Domestic institutions failed to reinvent themselves as capitalists satisficed, landlords rested on their laurels, and even the great universities of Oxford and Cambridge fell into mediocrity. British innovators often helped competitors, foreign powers learned the lessons of British success, while the limitless domestic market in the US and increasing German militarism led to major changes in the global political economy. Britain fell into relative decline in the 1880s–1920s, and the US recovered from its civil war and economic crises into 30 years of long wave upswing circa 1880s–1900s. In between periods of British and US hegemony (i.e., during the 1880s–1940s), polycrises plagued much of the world via the mediocre years of 1873–1893, the scramble for Africa, two world wars, and the Great Depression.

Chapter 7 outlines the rise and fall of US hegemony, long wave upswings, and climate change dynamics. The US had been unable or unwilling to act as a hegemon during the late 1800s–early-1900s wars and depressions. But they were drawn into the second world war by Japan's attack on Pearl Harbor and efforts to defeat European fascism, thereby enhancing their leadership substantially. Near the end of the second world war, they helped to organize the Bretton Woods Agreement (BWS), and then instituted the Marshall Plan, and in association with others set up the United Nations and NATO. As the 1940s evolved into the 1950s, much of the Western world (and beyond) instituted the system of Fordism, the Keynesian-welfare state, the dominance of US transnationals, the regulated financial system, and the set of familial household arrangements typical under US hegemony. These eco-spatial, technological, and institutional innovations provided the basis of both US hegemony and long wave upswings during the 1940s–1970s.

The 1940s/1950s through to the 1970s was the biggest boom capitalism has ever experienced, while it affected much of the core and many semi-peripheral areas. It also affected nations in the periphery, notably through the Korean and Vietnam Wars, the bombing of Cambodia (and Laos), the Monroe Doctrine, and several other instances. Alongside the postwar corporate system in the West and elsewhere, the *so-called* socialist countries ("state capitalism" to many Western Marxists) also underwent a boom, especially in the Soviet Union and other areas in the Eastern Bloc. As pollution surged the spread of aerosols (and other factors) led to declining world temperatures in the oceans, atmospheres, and land surfaces, during this period. As the 1960s passed into the 1970s, 1980s, and 1990s, the contradictions of the KWS, Fordism, and the postwar corporate system began to manifest themselves as the CSD evolved and fell into disarray. Borderline conditions and long wave downswings set in during this time, characterized typically by decadal/Juglar speculative bubble rises leading to successive crashes, recessions, debt anomalies, as well as other crises decade after decade, including notably the GFC, Euro crisis, corona crisis, and the climate crises.

The contradictions initially involved stagflation which implicated the KWS, declining productivity which involved Fordism, rising divorce rates and social instability associated with the family breakdowns, greater competition which threatened US hegemony, declining profit rates for corporations, and rising bubbles and crashes of the financial system. Systemically the postwar boom was over by the 1970s and 1980s and long wave downswing emerged in much of the world during the 1990s–2020s. This led to a structural policy shift around the world, involving the rise of neoliberalism and the Washington consensus. New governance arrangements during the late 1970s, 1980s, and beyond included reducing the power of labor while expanding that of capital, deregulating of the financial system, free-market parties being instituted, the rise of individualism and instability within households and elsewhere, the priority of shareholder value within corporations, and more globalization internationally.

(Former) Eastern Bloc countries also started to undergo long wave downswings, followed by demise, as privatization, declining state activities, and "mafia capitalism" fundamentally transformed these areas. While this was happening in the West and elsewhere, China and other nations of Asia (especially in the semi-periphery) started undergoing long wave upswing into the 1990s, 2000s, and 2010s as a counterforce to the downswing happening elsewhere. Climate change crises have intensified through numerous heatwaves, droughts, floods, wildfires, coastal erosion, and more intense hurricanes/typhoons/cyclones, which have also engendered greater social conflict within and between various classes, ethnic groups, and regions.

Chapter 8 examines the Chinese system of state capitalism, including its circuits of socioeconomic dynamics, hegemony potential, long wave patterns, and climate crises. From the 1980s to the 2010s, China developed a successful CSD system based on its institutions, technologies, and spatial-eco dynamics. Its agents and processes were situated in the global political economy as a major power and contributed to heightened prestige and authority in areas of diplomacy, military, production, commerce, and finance. It built a system of state capitalism inculcating market relations, strategic alliances, and agglomeration benefits, accepting the logic of capitalism despite the supposed ideology of its leaders. Its technological expertise especially developed in areas of science and research, and it successfully moved from mass production of consumer items increasingly to higher value-added technology. The financial system became more sophisticated through advances in economic freedom as often state money capitalists became part of the ruling class of powerful entrepreneurs. And crucially its system of rural-to-urban dynamics enabled many households to move into town's and city's manufacturing, trade, and finance sectors while often elders and children were left behind. Its military rose to new heights as it expanded geospatial power in the region and beyond, while its belt-and-road initiative enabled it to gain soft power in certain areas (despite anomalies).

Several contradictions, and internal limits to growth and development, have led to a near-halving of growth in China and in some cases declining hegemonic potential. Rising oligarchy and militarism have reduced the potential for China to become a liberal-democratic nation as all previous hegemonies have been. Declining rural-urban dynamics has exhausted a core force underlying long-term growth. Restrictions on research freedom and socio-political innovation will continue to hamper creative direction. Increasing controls on business and a change in business philosophy to quality, national self-sufficiency, and self-censorship are likely to inhibit creative destruction. A declining rate of profit is inhibiting corporate dynamics, especially due to excess debt, the collapse of infrastructure projects, and high levels of competition, as other powers such as India and Indonesia likely inhabit some of the space previously held by China, and core nations attempt to emasculate Chinese power. In short, current developments may foresee no major long wave upswing in view nor absolute hegemonic power (except in the military and high-technology realms), and no solutions to climate crises, into the foreseeable future.

Chapter 9 scrutinizes the polycrises affecting the world in light of the failure of neoliberalism, the absence of hegemony, and long wave downswings. Neoliberalism did not resolve problems such as low growth, financial crises, climate crises, anomalous industrial profits, and periodic high unemployment in the core or elsewhere. Recessions started getting deeper, culminating in the GFC during 2007–2009 and the Eurocrisis during 2009–2014 (and onto 2018, especially, in Greece). Partly due to neoliberal underinvestment in medical systems, the coronavirus crisis affected the whole world (which the GFC did not) during 2020–2022/2023, while many are (still) suffering from long Covid. Meanwhile, environmental crises have been getting worse through declining biodiversity, global warming, rising sea-levels, major heatwaves, droughts, and floods which are contributing to several conflicts, wars, and civilian unrest in numerous areas. Recently, with the war in Ukraine and conflict over Taiwan, we have moved into what some call a "pre-war era" alluding to the threat of World War 3.

Chapter 10 continues the theme of polycrises by analyzing the nature, causes, and trajectory of the ongoing conflicts and periodic crises between several *Liberal-Democratic Allies* [LDA] (especially NATO) and numerous *Autocratic Powers* [AP] (especially Russia and China) using core general principles of war and political economy. We situate this chapter within the context of the ongoing wars and conflicts involving the situation in southern Europe (e.g., Ukraine) and the Asia-Pacific (e.g., Taiwan), especially involving agreements, military bases, competitive struggles, hegemonic battles, and geopolitical rivalry. The ten dialectical (contradictory) principles of war in the information age are interrelated with the core principles of political economy such as historical specificity, contradiction, uncertainty, circular & cumulative causation, plus uneven development & hegemony, heterogeneous groups and agents, innovation and novelty, policy and governance, and the circuits of socioeconomic dynamics. We make preliminary conclusions about the likely trajectory and possible outcomes of this ongoing conflict into the future using these principles and concurrent developments.

Chapter 11 compares the stylized model with the world pattern of long waves for the period 1940s–2020s, including the wave pattern for various regions and continents, such as Asia (south and east), the Middle East and North Africa (MENA), Latin America and the Caribbean (LACA), sub-Saharan Africa (*SSA*), Western Europe (WE), Central and Eastern Europe (CEE), and North America (NA). The pattern of decadal change is analyzed vis-à-vis amplitude, periodicity, and phases of evolution of short, long, and secular waves. The objective is to evaluate the evolutionary changes of the world and its continents/regions for the period examined, in the era of US hegemony rise and decline, China's rise, and climate change escalation. We conclude that, at least in terms of periodicity and amplitude, several nations and areas underwent well-formed long waves, while others (especially in the periphery) underwent recurring short cycles of up and down activity, while some went through no long wave dynamics. Further research, especially for those with long wave dynamics, should be forthcoming with PoPE and other literature analyzing the eco-spatial, institutional, and technological bases of this dynamic.

Chapter 12 summarizes the whole book by presenting a saliant outline of the new approach to long waves, hegemony, and climate change through the PoPE paradigm and the technical analysis. The chapter then outlines 23 stylized facts and hypotheses for further research, ranging from, for instance, those concerning wars of ascendency, hegemonic stability hypothesis, tendencies toward liberal democracy, the circuits of socioeconomic dynamics, structural polycrises, class alliances, structural contradictions, heatwaves and greenhouse gasses, climate mitigation and adaptation, future wars, and the prognosis of the capitalist-world system into the future. This is followed by a glossary of major terms and scholars.

1.6 Conclusion

This chapter has outlined the innovations of this book, the standard model of long waves, the alternative PoPE contingency paradigm, the new long wave method, and the chapters of this book. Now, in successive chapters, we deal with a literature review of long waves theories, including first, the first wave of long wave scholarship associated with Kondratieff, Schumpeter, and company (Chap. 2), and second, the schools associated with the second wave of long wave scholarship (Chap. 3). Thereafter, we have chapters on waves and cycles of climate change (Chap. 4), how waves, hegemony, and climate change apply to Dutch, British, US, and Chinese capitalism (Chaps. 5–8), polycrises (Chap. 9), the pre-war era and possible World War 3 (Chap. 10), long waves in the postwar era (Chap. 11), followed by a conclusion (Chap. 12) and a Glossary.

References

Abramovitz, Moses. 1968. The Passing of the Kuznets Cycle. *Economica* 35 (140): 349–367.

Aglietta, Michel. 1976. *A Theory of Capitalist Regulation: The US Experience*. London: New Left Books, 1979. Translated from the French edition by David Fernbach.

Aliber, Robert Z., and Charles P. Kindleberger. 2015. *Manias, Panics and Crashes: A History of Financial Crises*. 7th ed. New York: Palgrave Macmillan.

Barr, Kenneth. 1979. Long Waves: A Selected Annotated Bibliography. *Review (Fernand Braudel Centre)* 2 (4): 675–718.

Berry, Brian J. L. 1991. *Long-Wave Rhythms in Economic Development and Political Behavior*. Baltimore: John Hopkins.

Bloch, Harry. 2018. *Schumpeter's Price Theory*. New York: Routledge.

Bolt, Jutta, and Jan Luiten van Zanden. 2024. Maddison-Style Estimates of the Evolution of the World Economy: A New 2023 Update. *Journal of Economic Surveys*1–41. https://onlinelibrary.wiley.com/doi/10.1111/joes.12618.

Boyer, Robert, and Yves Saillard, eds. 2002. *Regulation Theory: The State of the Art*. London & New York: Routledge.

Brahic, Catherine. 2007. Climate Myths: The Cooling after 1940 Shows CO_2 Does Not Cause Warming. *New Scientist*, 16 May.

Braudel, Fernand. 1979. *The Perspective of the World: Civilization & Capitalism 15th-18th Century*. Vol. 3. New York: Harper & Row.

Burns, Arthur F., and Wesley C. Mitchell. 1946. *Measuring Business Cycles*. New York: NBER.

Clement, Richard V., and Francis S. Doody. 1950. *The Schumpeterian System*. Cambridge, MA: Addison-Wesley.

Conroy, Stephen J., and Tisha L. N. Emerson. 2007. Ethical Cycles and Trends: Evidence and Implications. *Journal of Business Ethics* 8 (4): 905–911.

De Groot, Dagomar. 2018. *The Frigid Golden Age: Climate Change, The Little Ice Age, and the Dutch Republic, 1560-1720*. Cambridge: Cambridge University Press.

De Wolff, Salomon. 1929. *Het Economisch Getij: Bijdrage Tot de Verklaring van Het Conjunctuurverschijnsel*. Amsterdam: J. Emmering.

Dugger, William M. 1988. Radical Institutionalism: Basic Concepts. *Review of Radical Political Economics* 20 (1): 1–20.

Dugger, William M. 1995. Veblenian Institutionalism: The Changing Concepts of Inquiry. *Journal of Economic Issues* 29 (4): 1013–1028.

Dugger, William M. 2022. The Doleful Dynamics of Competition: Inequality and Fakery in Modernity. *Forum for Social Economics* 51 (1): 43–64.

Dupriez, Leon H. 1947. *Des Mouvements Economiques Generaux: Tome II*. Louvain: Institut de Recherches Economiques et Sociales, de L'Universite de Louvaine.

Espinosa-Gracia, Adrian, and Julio Sanchez-Choliz. 2023. Long waves, Paradigm Shifts, and Income Distribution, 1929–2010 and Afterwards. *Journal of Evolutionary Economics* 33:1365–1396. https://doi.org/10.1007/s00191-023-00843-5.

EU and UN (European Union and United Nations). 2017. *Handbook on Cyclical Composite Indicators for Business Cycle Analysis*. Luxembourg: Eurostat. Publications Office of the EU.

Fischer, David Hacket. 1996. *The Great Wave: Price Revolutions and the Rhythm of History*. Oxford: Oxford University Press.

Flynn, Claire Marie, Linnea Huusko, Angshuman Modak, and Thorsten Mauritsen. 2023. Strong Aerosol Cooling Alone Does Not Explain Cold-Based Mid-Century Temperatures in CMIP6 Models. *Atmospheric Chemistry Physics* 23:15121–15133.

Forrester, Jay W. 1977. Growth Cycles. *De Economist* 125 (4): 525–543.

Freeman, Chris, ed. 1996. *Long Wave Theory*. Cheltenham: Edward Elgar Publishing.

Freeman, Chris, and Francisco Louçã. 2001. *As Time Goes By: From the Industrial Revolution to the Information Revolution*. Oxford: OUP.

Gallegati, Marco, Mauro Gallegati, James B. Ramsey, and Willi Semmler. 2017. Long Waves in Prices: New Evidence from Wavelet Analysis. *Cliometrica* 11 (2): 127–151. Long waves in prices: new evidence from wavelet analysis | Cliometrica (springer.com).

Garvy, George. 1943. Kondratieff's Theory of Long Cycles. *The Review of Economic Statistics* 25 (4): 203–220.

Goldstein, Joshua S. 1988. *Long Cycles: Prosperity and War in the Modern Age*. New Haven: Yale University Press.

Gordon, David M. 1978. Up and Down the Long Roller Coaster. In *U.S. Capitalism in Crisis*, ed. by Crisis Reader Editorial Collective, Union for Radical Political Economists. New York: URPE.

Gordon, David M. 1980. Stages of Accumulation and Long Economic Cycles. In *Processes of the World System*, ed. Terence Hopkins and Immanuel Wallerstein, 9–45. Beverly Hills, CA: Sage Publications. Reprinted in David M. Gordon. 1998. *Economics and Social Justice: Essays on Power, Labor and Institutional Change.* Cheltenham: Edward Elgar.

Gordon, David M., Richard Edwards, and Michael Reich. 1982. *Segmented Work, Divided Workers: The Historical Transformation of Labor in the United States*. Cambridge: Cambridge University Press.

Grinin, Leonid, Andrey Korotayev, and Arno Tausch. 2016. *Economic Cycles, Crises, and the Global Periphery*. Switzerland: Springer.

Grinin, Leonid, Anton Grinin, and Andrey Korotayev. 2017. Forthcoming Kondratieff Wave, Cybernetic Revolution, and Global Ageing. *Technological Forecasting and Social Change* 115 (February): 52–68.

Grinin, Leonid, and Andrey Korotayev. 2018. The Future of the Global Economy in the Light of Inflationary and Deflationary Trends and Long Cycles Theory. *World Futures: The Journal of New Paradigm Research* 74 (2): 84–103.

Grinin, Leonid, and Andrey Korotayev. 2020. Seven Weaknesses of the U.S., Donald Trump and the Future of American Hegemony. *World Futures: The Journal of New Paradigm Research* 77 (1): 23–54.

Gutiérrez-Barbarrusa, Tomás. 2019. The Interpretation of the Cyclical History of Capitalism. A Comparison between the Neo-Schumpeterian and Social Structure of Accumulation (SSA) Approaches in Light of the Long Wave Theory. *Journal of Evolutionary Economics* 29 (4): 1285–1314.

Hansen, Alvin H. 1951. *Business Cycles and National Income*. New York: Norton & Co.

Harris, Stuart A. 2023. Evolution of the Climate of the Earth. *Journal of Civil Engineering Research and Technology* 5 (2): 1–15.

Hobsbawm, Eric J. 1954a. The General Crisis of the European Economy in the 17th Century. *Past and Present* 5 (1): 33–53.

Hobsbawm, Eric J. 1954b. The Crisis of the 17th Century-II. *Past and Present* 6 (1): 44–65.

IPCC (Intergovernmental Panel on Climate Change). 2007. Paleoclimate. Chapter 6 of *Climate Change 2007: The Physical Science Basis. Contribution to Working Group I to the Fourth Assessment Report of the IPCC*, 433–497. Cambridge: Cambridge University Press.

IPCC (Intergovernmental Panel on Climate Change). 2021. *Climate Change 2021: The Physical Science Basis. Contribution of Working Group I to the Sixth Assessment Report of the Intergovernmental Panel on Climate Change* [Masson-Delmotte, V., P. Zhai, A. Pirani, S.L. Connors, C. Péan, S. Berger, N. Caud, Y. Chen, L. Goldfarb, M.I. Gomis, M. Huang, K. Leitzell, E. Lonnoy, J.B.R. Matthews, T.K. Maycock, T. Waterfield, O. Yelekçi, R. Yu, and B. Zhou (eds.)]. Cambridge: Cambridge University Press, 2391 pp. https://doi.org/10.1017/9781009157896.

IPCC. 2022a. *Climate Change 2022: Impacts, Adaptation, and Vulnerability.* Contribution of Working Group II to the Sixth Assessment Report of the Intergovernmental Panel on Climate Change [H.-O. Pörtner, D.C. Roberts, M. Tignor, E.S. Poloczanska, K. Mintenbeck, A. Alegría, M. Craig, S. Langsdorf, S. Löschke, V. Möller, A. Okem, B. Rama (eds.)]. Cambridge: Cambridge University Press, 3056 pp. https://doi.org/10.1017/9781009325844.

IPCC. 2022b. *Climate Change 2022: Mitigation of Climate Change. Contribution of Working Group III to the Sixth Assessment Report of the Intergovernmental Panel on Climate Change* [P.R. Shukla, J. Skea, R. Slade, A. Al Khourdajie, R. van Diemen, D. McCollum, M. Pathak, S. Some, P. Vyas, R. Fradera, M. Belkacemi, A. Hasija, G. Lisboa, S. Luz, J. Malley, (eds.)]. Cambridge: Cambridge University Press. https://doi.org/10.1017/9781009157926.

IPCC. 2023. *Climate Change 2023: Synthesis Report. Contribution of Working Groups I, II and III to the Sixth Assessment Report of the Intergovernmental Panel on Climate Change* [Core Writing Team, H. Lee and J. Romero (eds.)]. Geneva: IPCC, 184 pp. https://doi.org/10.59327/IPCC/AR6-9789291691647.

Israel, Jonathan. 1989. *Dutch Primacy in World Trade, 1585-1740*. Oxford: Clarendon Press.

Kilic, Sadik. 2021. Does COVID-19 as a Long Wave Turning Point Mean the End of Neoliberalism? *Critical Sociology* 47 (4-5): 609–623.

Kindleberger, Charles M. 1973. *The World in Depression, 1929-1939*. Berkeley: University of California Press.

Kindleberger, Charles M. 1996. *World Economic Primacy: 1500-1990*. Oxford: Oxford University Press.

Kleinknecht, Alfred. 1987. *Innovation Patterns in Crisis and Prosperity: Schumpeter's Long Cycle Reconsidered*. London: Macmillan.

Kleinknecht, Alfred, Ernest Mandel, and Immanuel Wallerstein, eds. 1992. *New Findings in Long-Wave Research*. London: Macmillan.

Kondratiev, Nikolai, and D. I. Oparin. 1928. *Bovshie tsikly kon'iunktury (Major Economic Cycles)*. Moscow: Krasnaya Presnya.

Kuznets, Simon. 1940. Schumpeter's Business Cycles. *American Economic Review* 30 (2): 257–271.

Lapointe, Francois, and Raymond S. Bradley. 2021. Little Ice Age Abruptly Triggered by Intrusion of Atlantic Waters into the Nordic Sea. *Science Advances* 7:1–12.

Liu, Y., Cai, Q., Song, H. et al. 2011. Amplitudes, Rates, Periodicities and causes of Temperature Variations in the Past 2485 Years and Future trends over the Central-Eastern Tibetan Plateau. *Chinese Science Bulletin* 56, 2986. https://doi.org/10.1007/s11434-011-4713-7

Louçã, Francisco. 2021. As Time Went By – Why is the Long Wave So Long? *Journal of Evolutionary Economics* 31 (3): 749–771.

Louçã, Francisco, and Jan Reijnders, eds. 1999. *The Foundations of Long Wave Theory. 2 vols*. Cheltenham: Edward Elgar.

Maddison, Angus. 1982. *Phases of Capitalist Development*. Oxford: Oxford University Press.

Maddison, Angus. 1991. *Dynamic Forces of Capitalist Development: A Long-Run Comparative View*. Oxford: Oxford University Press.

Maddison Project. 2024. *Maddison Historical Statistics Database: Real GDP Per Capita*. Groningen, Netherlands: Groningen Growth & Development Centre, Faculty of Economics & Business, University of Groningen. https://www.rug.nl/ggdc/historicaldevelopment/maddison/releases/maddison-project-database-2023.

McDonough, Terrence; Cian McMahon and David M. Kotz. Eds. 2021. *Handbook on Social Structures of Accumulation Theory*.

Mager, Nathan H. 1987. *The Kondratieff Waves*. New York: Praeger.

Mandel, Ernest. 1964. The Economics of Neo-Capitalism. *Socialist Register* 1 (1): 56–67.

Mandel, Ernest. 1995. *Long Waves of Capitalist Development: A Marxist Interpretation*. London: Verso. Revised Edition.

Mann, Michael E. 2002. Little Ice Age. In *The Earth System: Physical and Chemical Dimensions of Global Environmental Change*, ed. Michael C. MacCracken and John S. Perry, 504–509. New York: Wiley.

Mensch, Gerhard. 1979. *Stalemate in Technology*. Cambridge, MA: Balinger. (Original German Edition, 1975).

Merriam-Webster. 2024. Gyre. *Merriam-Webster Dictionary*.

Modelski, George, ed. 1987. *Exploring Long Cycles*. London: Pinter Publishers.

Mousnier, Roland, J. H. Elliott, Lawrence Stone, E. H. Kossmann, E. J. Hobsbawm, and J. H. Hexter. 1960. Discussion of H. R. Trevor-Roper, The General Crisis of the Seventeenth Century. *Past and Present* 18 (Nov): 8–42.
Neumann, Manfred. 1997. *The Rise and Fall of the Wealth of Nations: Long Waves in Economics and International Politics*. Cheltenham: Edward Elgar.
O'Hara, Phillip Anthony. 1992. *A Critical Analysis of the Reproduction of Institutions Within Capitalism: Integrating Macroinstitutional Themes from Marxist and Institutionalist Political Economy*. PhD Thesis. Supervised by Allen Oakley. University of Newcastle, Australia, Department of Economics.
O'Hara, Phillip Anthony. 2000. *Marx, Veblen and Contemporary Institutional Political Economy: Principles and Unstable Dynamics of Capitalism*. Cheltenham: Edward Elgar.
O'Hara, Phillip Anthony. 2009. *Growth and Development in the Global Political Economy: Social Structures of Accumulation and Modes of Regulation*. London & New York: Routledge. Paper edition.
O'Hara, Phillip Anthony. 2023. *Principles of Institutional and Evolutionary Political Economy: Applied to Current World Problems*. Revised Edition. Singapore: Springer Nature.
Parker, Geoffrey. 2018. *Global Crisis: War, Climate Change and Catastrophe in the Seventeenth Century*. Abridged & Revised Edition. New Haven: Yale University Press.
Perez, Carlotta. 1983. Structural change and assimilation of new technologies in the economic and social systems. *Futures* 15 (5): 357–375. https://doi.org/10.1016/0016-3287(83)90050-2.
Perez, Carlotta. 2015. From Long Waves to Great Surges: Continuing in the Direction of Chris Freeman's 1997 Lecture on Schumpeter's *Business Cycles*. *European Journal of Economic and Social Systems* 27 (1–2): 69–80.
Rostow, Walt Whitman. 1952. *The Process of Economic Growth*. New York: Norton.
Rostow, Walt Whitman. 1978. *The World Economy: History and Prospect*. London: Macmillan.
Rostow, Walt Whitman. 1990. *The Stages of Economic Growth*. 3rd ed. Cambridge: Cambridge University Press.
RWG (Research Working Group on Cyclical Rhythms and Secular Trends). 1979. Cyclical Rhythms and Secular Trends of the Capitalist World-Economy: Some Premises, Hypotheses, and Questions. *Review* 2 (4): 483–500.
Scafetta, Nicola, and Antonio Bianchini. 2023. Overview of the Spectral Coherence between Planetary Resonances and Solar and Climate Oscillations. *Climate* 11 (44): 77. https://doi.org/10.3390/cli11040077.
Schumpeter, Joseph Alios. 1939. *Business Cycles*. 2 Vols. Philadelphia, PA: Porcupine Press.
Schweinberger, Albert. 2014. State Capitalism, Entrepreneurship, and Networks: China's Rise to a Superpower. *Journal of Economic Issues* 48 (1): 169–180.
Sherman, Howard Jay. 1990. *The Business Cycle: Growth and Crisis Under Capitalism*. New Haven: Yale University Press.
Sherman, Howard Jay, and David X. Kolk. 1996. *Business Cycles and Forecasting*. New York: Harper Collins.
Slicher van Bath, Bernard Hendrik. 1982. The Economic Situation in the Dutch Republic during the Seventeenth Century. In *Dutch Capitalism and World Capitalism*, ed. Maurice Aymard, 23–35. Cambridge: Cambridge University Press.
Smits, J.P., E. Horlings, and J.L. van Zanden. 2000. *The Measurement of Gross National Product and its Components 1800–1913*. Groningen Growth and Development Centre Monograph series no 5.
Solomou, Solomos. 1987. *Phases of Economic Growth 1950-1973: Kondratieff Waves and Kuznets' Swings*. Cambridge: Cambridge University Press.
Solomou, Solomos. 1998. *Economic Cycles: Long Cycles and Business Cycles Since 1870*. Manchester: Manchester University Press.
Spinola, Danilo Sartorello. 2023. Instability Constraints and Development Traps: An Empirical Analysis of Growth Cycles and Economic Volatility in Latin America. *CEPAL Review* 139 (April): 7–28.

Sylos-Labini, Paolo. 1950. Le problème des cycles économiques de longue durée. *Economie appliquée: Archive de l'Institut de Science Economique Appliquée* 3 (3–4): 481–495.

Sweezy, Paul. 1943. Professor Schumpeter's Theory of Innovation. *Review of Economic Statistics* 25 (1): 93–96.

Trevor-Roper, Hugh. 1967. *The Crisis of the Seventeenth Century: Religion, the Reformation and Social Change*. Indianapolis: The Liberty Fund.

Trotsky, Leon. 1923. The Curve of Capitalist Development. In *Problems of Everyday Life, New York 1973*, ed. Leon Trotsky, 273–280. (Original 2023 publication in Russian).

Tsoulfidis, Lefteris, and Aris Papageorgiou. 2019. The Recurrence of Long Cycles: Theories, Stylized Facts and Figures. *World Review of Political Economy* 10 (4): 415–448.

Tylecote, Andrew. 1992. *The Long Wave in the World Economy: The Present Crisis in Historical Perspective*. London and New York: Routledge.

UNEP (United Nations Environmental Program). 2023. *Emissions Gap Report 2023: Broken Records*. Nairobi: UNEP.

Van Duijn, J. J. 1983. *The Long Wave in Economic life*. London: Allen & Unwin.

Van Gelderen, Jacob. 1913. Springtide: Reflections on Industrial Development and Price Movements. In *Long Wave Theory*, ed. C. Freeman, 1–56. Cheltenham: Edward Elgar.

Wallerstein, Immanuel. 1979. Review Essay: Kondratieff Up or Kondratieff Down? *Review* 2 (4): 663–673.

van Zanden, Jan Luiten & van Leeuwen, Bas, 2012. Persistent but not consistent: The Growth of National Income in Holland 1347–1807, *Explorations in Economic History*, Elsevier, vol. 49 (2): 119–130.

Wallerstein, Immanuel. 1992. A Brief Agenda for the Future of Long-Wave Research. In *New Findings in Long-Wave Research*, ed. Alfred Kleinknecht, Ernest Mandel, and Immanuel Wallerstein, 339–342. London: Macmillan.

Waters, Colin N. et al. Response to Merritts et al. 2023. The Anthropocene is Complex. Defining it is Not. *Earth-Science Reviews* 238 (March): 1–4.

White, Sam. 2014. The Real Little Ice Age. *Journal of Interdisciplinary History* 44 (3): 327–352.

Wikipedia. 2024. Solar Cycle. *Wikipedia Encyclopedia,* 15 May. file:///C:/Users/Phillip%20 O'Hara/Downloads/Solar_cycle.pdf

Chapter 2
Capitalism's Long Waves: Kondratiev, Schumpeter, *et al.*

Abstract This chapter utilizes the principles of political economy (PoPE) contingency paradigm of long waves to provide a sympathetically critical literature review of long wave theories and empirics, and to extend the inquiry to hegemony and climate change. We review the early history of long wave studies, paying special attention to Kondratiev's contributions in association with his critics including Trotsky. From this, we agree with Garvy's survey and critique that scholars should concentrate on establishing the pattern of long-term evolution and performance of capitalism devoid of preconceptions such as strict periodicities, amplitudes, and regularities. Then we scrutinize the work of Schumpeter and reject his assumptions of rigid links between waves and cycles, while being open-minded about periodicities of long wave upswings and downswings. We agree with the criticisms of Schumpeter's long wave inquiry especially by Simon Kuznets and Paul Sweezy. Nonetheless, some core insights of Kondratiev and Schumpeter et al. are still useful for long wave analysis as we reconstruct the framework. A conclusion follows.

Keywords PoPE paradigm · First long wave theory upswing · Long wave history · Nikolai Kondratiev · Joseph Schumpeter · Criticisms · Hegemony · Climate change

2.1 Introduction

The purpose of this chapter is to outline the main research of relevance in the history of long waves, to assess its importance and anomalies, and to provide a summary of the reconstruction of long waves provided in this book (see O'Hara 2001). Throughout we analyze and critique long wave approaches from the point of view of various principles of political economy (PoPE) (see O'Hara 2023 for details), based on capitalism's institutional, technological, and eco-geo-spatial evolution and transformation; plus the new long wave method (NLWM).

P. A. O'Hara, *Long Waves of Growth, Hegemonic Power, and Climate Change in the World Economy*, https://doi.org/10.1007/978-981-96-4132-1_2

The *principle of historical specificity and evolution* states that to understand any world problem requires that it be situated historically, with its evolutionary metamorphosis followed through various changes, innovations, phases, and mutations. In this context, we start by examining the early works on long waves including the approach taken by Nikolai Kondratiev. The theory, empirics, and stylized facts of Kondratiev's work on long waves are outlined, as well as a brief assessment of the criticisms of his work, plus the lessons this provides for long wave research. Briefly, following Garvy, we conclude that long waves should be viewed in terms of the *complex* long-term *evolution, transformation,* and *performance* of *capitalism* in its various *phases* and *forms* through *historical time*. We delimit the scope of the analysis to long waves, hegemony, and climate change.

Then we turn our attention to Joseph Schumpeter's work on long waves, including his method of successive approximation, where he starts with the circular flow, introduces innovation, as well as credit, the two- and four-phase cycles models, and the multiple cycle phases of the model. We outline major criticisms of his theory and empirics of long waves, especially noting that, from the point of view of our PoPE Contingency Paradigm, Schumpeter places insufficient attention to the complex nexus between technology, institutions, and geo-spatial-ecology, and the process of hegemony in the evolution of capitalism. On the other hand, his model of the circular flow can be updated based on our (a) "circuits of socioeconomic dynamics" (CSD), while his four-phase model that includes the "bar of neighborhoods of equilibrium" can also be updated as our (b) "trend bar of borderline performance" in between waves of upswing and downswing, while being subject to circular and cumulative causation (CCC) rather than equilibrium per se. Thereafter, in Chap. 3, below, we scrutinize various contributions to the renascence of long wave theory and empirics from the 1960s through to the 2020s.

2.2 Early Long Wave Works: Kondratiev et al.—Isolating Essential Problems

Hyde Clarke's (1847) article was the first to emerge which hypothesized the generation of long waves (of 54 years duration), divided between years of above-average growth (the first 27 years) and later years of below-average growth (second 27 years). This was based on what later long wave scholars would call (in the standard model) the "first long wave" of capitalism, during 1793–1847; and he suggested this period was broken up into five 10–11 years what we now call Juglar cycles (1793–1804, 1804–1815, 1815–1826, 1826–1837, and 1837–1847). Clark emphasized the role of astrological and meteorological factors, though he did not cite a specific cause, which was to be the object of a new science of "physical economy."

Near the end of the second (1850–1895) and into the third (1890s–1940s) long wave, major investigations into waves re-emerged on a grander scale. This included the work of Stanley Jevons (1884), Mikhail Tugan-Baranovski (1894) on fixed capital, and Kurt Wicksell (1898) on real production and wars. An avalanche of research on waves appeared early in the twentieth century, by, for instance, "Alexander Parvus" (Israel Lazarevich Gelfand 1901), Karl Kautsky (1901–1902), Jean Lescure (1907), T.T. Williams (1912), R.A. MacDonald (1912), J. van Gelderen (1913), Vilfredo Pareto (1913), Marcel Lenoir (1913), Albert Aftalion (1913), C. Bresciani-Turroni (1917), Gustav Cassell (1918), and Arthur Spiethoff (1923). Many of these were concerned merely with the price level and its relationship to gold and money over the wave, rather than an analysis of real production, and very few sought to investigate the causal processes involved in these long movements of the economy.

The first major theoretical statement of the long wave hypothesis was made in 1901 by a Marxist economist by the name of Israel Lazarevich Gelfand (who often wrote under the pseudonym of "Parvus") (born in present-day Belarus), into a Lithuanian Jewish family.[1] He used a holistic approach and emphasized the idea that (Ekland 1980, 384) "the secular wave movement ... was determined by the expansion of the world market[,] on the basis of changes occurring in all spheres of capitalist commercial and industrial life—technical changes, changes in the money market, in trade, in the colonies—and putting the whole of world production on a new and wider basis" (Parvus 1901). This statement is reasonably typical of the general and all-embracing nature of many of the long wave theories, even to the present day, including the one enunciated in this current book, as many authors did and still do argue that waves appear as the manifestation of the total operation of the capitalist system in its concrete functioning (or at least nation-states and their colonial linkages). According to this approach, neither a simplified analysis of a component part of the economy (e.g., the monetary sector), nor an investigation that emphasizes the "general laws of capitalist accumulation" with special reference to "capital in general," is sufficient for understanding the highly "real" phenomena of long waves.

The first technical theory of the wave was by a Dutch Marxist known as "Fedder" (J. van Gelderen), who argued in 1913 that the relationship between the consumer and capital goods sectors is the central factor explaining waves. The consumer goods sector periodically grows rapidly, due to either colonization or domestic expansion of consumer items, which he thought provided the basis for recovery and subsequent expansion of economic activity. The contractionary phase sets in when market saturation occurs, which takes an extended amount of time. The consumer and capital goods sectors re-emerge much later in several other theories of the wave (e.g., Jay Forrester), and indirectly in most of them. Other notable theories include that of Wicksell (1898) and more especially that of Francois Simiand (1932), who studied waves of the nineteenth century, concluding that contractions were dominated by capital deepening (qualitative improvements or major innovations) associated with competitive forces, with long expansions being associated with capital widening (quantitative growth of the capital stock).

The most significant theory and empirics of long *cycles* in the early twentieth century, however, was that of Nikolai Dmitrievich Kondratiev (1892–1938) (also translated as "Kondratieff"), hence the justification for what has been called

[1] Gelfand ("Parvus") was also known as Alexander Helphand.

"Kondratiev cycles" (or "Kondratievs"). Kondratiev was a minister in the Kerensky Russian Government prior to the 1917–1919 revolution, and, after the revolution, he was head of the Moscow Conjuncture Institute until 1928. Two years later, he was sent to Siberia (and in 1938, he was shot dead), during the Stalin Great Purge, mostly for supporting the economic role of the agricultural sector and market socialism in the face of collectivization and/or supporting the idea that capitalism could rebound from depression through the long cycle dynamic.

Most of his research and that of his associates, on long cycles/waves, was carried out at the Institute, where he first mentioned long waves in 1922, in a book titled *The World Economy and its Conjunctures* (in Russian) (Kondratiev 1922). He discussed concepts such as "crisis" and "disequilibrium," in response to the "Bolshevik argument" that the capitalist crisis of 1920–1921 heralded the decline of capitalism. Kondratiev preferred an explanation focusing on "the crisis" as being necessary for the periodic (and temporary) reinstatement of the equilibrium of economic activity. His long cycle theory was used as a means of situating the crisis of that time within the wider context of the long-period development of capitalism. 1920 was thought to mark the end of the *transition* between the long wave expansion of 1896–1913 and the beginning of a contractionary phase. Stagnation was, therefore, a method by which the moving equilibrium could be temporarily re-established.

Some of Kondratiev's critics in Russia, especially Leon Trotsky, had much in common with Kondratiev. Firstly, they both thought "long-period dynamics" were plausible phenomena. Secondly, they agreed on the timing of these "long-periods." And thirdly, they agreed that the crisis heralded not a decline of capitalism, but the commencement of a long period of declining economic activity. They disagreed, however, on the substance of such "long-periods." Trotsky argued that such periods had no cyclical component; it was not a cycle-type motion. He thought they were caused by largely exogenous factors, such as wars, revolutions, class struggle, imperialism, and the like. Such periods, Trotsky thought, were not consistently patterned, and the trend of capitalist evolution was too complicated and uneven to constitute a wave phenomenon. Trotsky denied the operation of an *endogenous mechanism* (or process) that would produce long fluctuations of a cyclical variety. The disagreement was over whether long periods were determined endogenously by the inner dynamic of capitalism, plus several "empirical" factors (Kondratiev's position, see below); or whether such waves were not fully determined or proved due to the dominance of exogenous factors such as wars, revolutions, class struggle, etc. (Trotsky's position; more on this later).

Kondratiev incorporated both fundamental mechanisms and core empirical conditions and was well on the way to developing a complex *cycle* system. Initially, Kondratiev had not isolated one or a series of mechanisms that would endogenously determine cycle-type economic behavior. But his exchanges with Trotsky and other critics pressed him to formalize his schema, perhaps prematurely. Out of this exchange emerged his primary mechanism concerning the "life of fixed capital." As Kondratiev stated (see also Day 1976, 76):

> [I]f Marx affirmed that the material basis for these crises that periodically recurred in each decade … was the material wear and tear, replacement, and increase in the mass of instruments of production in the form of machines with a service life lasting ten years, one may assume that the material basis for the long cycles is the wear and tear, replacement, and increase in those basic capital goods requiring a long period of time and tremendous investment for their production. *The replacement and expansion of the fund of these goods does not take place smoothly but in spurts, and the long waves in economic conditions are another expression of that.* (Kondratiev 1928, 93.)

Long cycles for Kondratiev are thus considered to be pure reinvestment cycles in durable fixed capital, including transport facilities, factories, warehouses and to some degree the associated innovatory process of capital deepening, which all help promote the expansion, and the subsequent spreading of net investment as capital is (re)installed. The expansions of the producer and consumer sectors tend to decline, however, as investment and consumption spending adjust to the initial burst of activity, as capital is replaced during expansion. Associated with this, according to Kondratiev, is an accumulation of free loanable funds and *significant process and product inventions* of the basic type during the contraction, to provide a sound base for recovery.

Another Dutch Marxist, Sam de Wolff, made substantial contributions to long wave analysis, initially concentrating on empirical matters (de Wolff 1924), but eventually citing a cause identical to Kondratiev's: the periodic replacement of durable capital goods through reinvestment cycles (de Wolff 1929). These cycles were said to have been set in motion by the industrial revolution in Britain, and through time they would likely become more frequent in periodicity as the life of capital goods shortened.

Kondratiev had to rely on the rather limited data available at the time, and thus used prices and production data on various commodities to develop his theory and empirics. Statistically, he often calculated the trend of the data, and then assessed the deviation from the trend, which was smoothed through the medium of moving averages to establish a possible wave[2] (see Barnett 1998, ch 5). Kondratiev's empirical analysis of long waves, including three "long cycles" (specifically just more than two and a half) from 1793 to 1920 (onwards), along with some general features of upswings and downswings associated with these waves, are outlined in Table 2.1:

Associated with this chronology, Kondratiev provided "five supporting empirical conditions" of long waves, as illustrated below (Kondratiev 1925, 1926).

Kondratiev's Five Supporting Empirical Stylized Facts

1. Prosperity and Downturn: During long waves of upturn and expansion, periods of prosperity are significantly more numerous than during downturn and contraction; and during long wave downturns, contraction years of recession are significantly more numerous than during upturn and recovery.

[2] I discuss this method in more detail further below and in the section on Schumpeter (as well as the Glossary).

Table 2.1 Kondratiev's long cycle periodicity and empirics, 1793–1920

Wave & features	Upswings: Dates & features	Downswings: Dates & features
First long wave→	1793–1810/17	1810/17–1844/51
Second long wave→	1844/51–1870/75	1870/75–1890/96
Third long wave→	1890/96–1914/20	1914/20–19??/??
Empirical conditions→	Innovations *spread*	Bunching of discoveries & inventions
	Extensive wars & revolutions	Sharp agricultural recessions
	New countries enter world market	Stimulates gold production

Source: Adapted from Kondratiev (1925, 111; O'Hara 2001)

2. Discoveries and Inventions: During the downturn and contraction of the long cycle a significantly larger number of important discoveries and inventions in production techniques and communications are made than during other phases of the long cycle (innovations *spread* during upturns and expansions).
3. Wars and Revolutions: During the upturn and expansion of the cycle, the most disastrous and extensive wars and revolutions occur.
4. Agriculture: During the downturn and contraction of the cycle, agriculture experiences an especially pronounced and long depression, e.g., especially of (agricultural) prices.
5. Gold production increases during the beginning of the long expansion, while during that same period, the market for goods is promoted by new and especially colonial countries.

Based on these chronologies and empirics, for both price and production variables of numerous especially "Western"' nations (e.g., England, Germany, USA, and France), he concluded that "The available data are sufficient to declare the cyclical character [of waves] to be very probable" (Kondratiev 1925, 112). It is difficult to specify where in his overall theoretical structure these supporting empirical conditions belong, mainly because they were developed prior to his endogenous theory. In general, they are reasonably common hypotheses in the empirical analysis of waves, even to this present day. They are what many analysts have called "exogenous" or "necessary empirical conditions," for the wave-like economic patterns.

The first of these conditions, concerning the length of recessions and prosperities during long wave upswings and downswings, is common to many long cycle theorists and empiricists. This should be called *the most important empirical stylized fact of long wave analysis*, so crucial it has been for long wave scholars, especially (but not only) for the second long wave boom and slump of long wave scholarship during the 1970s–2000s. The second condition concerning inventions and discoveries during downswings has a particularly Schumpeterian and hence Menschian flavor to it and has been subject to much empirical work (often rejecting it). The third condition, concerning wars and revolutions, is very generally related to Mandel's model, and Trotsky's framework; often being examined by other long wave scholars (such as Goldstein and Modelski et al. in the case of war). The last two factors concerning agriculture and gold have an especially Rostovian flavor and are often the subject of long wave scrutiny.

As with much early speculation on complicated matters of science, Kondratiev's theory left much to be desired, as did his statistical testing of the waves.[3] Garvy (1943) has provided the most comprehensive survey of criticisms of Kondratiev's theory, mostly from Russian scholars during the 1920s, and below we deal with some of them to gain further insights into Kondratiev's analysis. Garvy's encyclopedic treatment of these criticisms likely had a numbing impact on global long cycle research, as no one sympathetically critical of long waves, to my knowledge, made a detailed and systematic rebuttal to Garvy's arguments, nor explained how they could support a modified wave analysis.

The first major criticism relates to the nature of long waves vis-à-vis short cycles. While Kondratiev was head of the Business Research Institute in Moscow, the debate on long waves was energetic. Motyleff (1923), for instance, supported Kondratiev's empirical findings, a position described by Kenneth Barr (1979, 689) as "a rarity among … Soviet economists." Several writers, such as Trotsky (1921, 1923), Sukhanov (1926), Pervushin (1926), and Studensky (1930) did not doubt the existence of long periods of expansion and contraction but questioned the assertion that these movements were strictly cyclical and related to one major economic mechanism (a position I agree with). Many critiques centered on a rejection of Kondratiev's view that long waves existed in both prices and general economic activity. For instance, Guberman (1927) and Granowsky (1928) agreed that waves operate only in the price sphere, while Gerzstein (1928) went further to indicate that prices and production, in some instances, were inversely related over the long wave. Others, such as Bagdanov (1928), Anderson (1929), and Eventov (1929) argued that Kondratiev's statistical methodology was flawed (see the Reijnders 1990 rebuttal to some of these arguments).

The most important of these specific theoretico-empirical criticisms was Trotsky's notion of the "double periodicity" of capitalism, where the shorter 7–11-year Juglar cycle was due to the "specific inner laws of capitalist accumulation"—the laws of reproduction, competition, falling rate of profit, as Marx explained in the three volumes of capital—but that the longer "curve of capitalist evolution" (long movements) was caused by the interplay of largely exogenous factors. As Trotsky noted about these "long periods":

[3] Those interested in Kondratiev's original works (especially on long waves but also related topics) as well as secondary commentaries and criticism/support for his works (and of long waves in general) by the editors plus Andrew Tylecote and Solomos Solomou, should consult the four-volume work edited by Natalia Makasheva, Warren J. Samuels, and Vincent Barnett (translated by Stephen S. Wilson) (2024). It was originally published in hardcover by Pickering and Chatto (1998), then by Routledge (2016), with 2024 seeing the publication of the ebook edition. It is, however, very hard to obtain any edition in libraries, and the hardcover edition costs around US$550 (when I checked, the ebook was not available).

> [T]heir character and duration are determined not by the internal interplay of capitalist forces but by those external conditions through whose channel capitalist development flows. The acquisition by capitalism of new centers and continents, the discovery of new natural resources and, in the wake of these, such major facets of "superstructural" order as wars and revolutions, determine the character and the replacement of ascending, stagnating or declining epochs of capitalist development. (Trotsky 1923, 277)

Trotsky's theory of "exogenous" factors was thus somewhat different to Kondratiev's endogenous theory of the long wave/cycle. The "separate historical periods" that Trotsky theorized postulated a form of capitalist development that was uneven over time and subject to marked "external conditions and ... the relative autonomy of superstructural phenomena" (quoted by Day 1976, 71). Trotsky thought there was no essential "internal regulator" that determined long-run patterns of capitalist accumulation, and he therefore thought no proof adequately explained the periodicity, regularity, and amplitude of these historical epochs in a consistent manner. Thus Kondratiev's "attempt to invest epochs labelled ... as major cycles with the same 'rigidly lawful rhythm' that is observable in minor [Juglar] cycles ... is [a] false generalization from a formal analogy" (Trotsky 1923, 276). I agree with Trotsky on this point.

The second criticism of Kondratiev relates to the endogenous mechanism of durable fixed capital. Put simply, Kondratiev failed to provide theoretical or empirical "proofs" of the existence of long waves according to this so-called endogenous factor. To rely on Marx's very tentative theory of short cycles was no substitute for specifically delineating the nature of periodicity, regularity, cyclicality/variable oscillations, and amplitude. Kondratiev did not provide evidence that economic agents reinvest in durable fixed capital every 40–60 years, or that they synchronize their actions with respect to either inventions or innovations. Given these prerequisites, cyclicality may have been assumed but, as the theory stands, neither periodicity, regularity, nor amplitude is justified within the model. There is a basis for qualitative improvements in technology, but there is little in the theory to differentiate between capital widening and capital deepening upon which this condition depends.

Thirdly, in relation to durable fixed capital, moreover, Kondratiev further ignored problems such as the possibility that changes in the obsolescence rate, the cost of maintenance, interest rates, wages, technological progress, and the rate of capacity utilization may negate the "normal life of capital" theory of reinvestment, thus making reinvestment periods more continuous and less cyclical. If there was little synchronization of new and replacement investment, then the "sudden or shock effect" of massive clusters of reinvestment activity could not be supported. Also, the use of loanable funds is a doubtful main source of funds for innovation or investment (or consumption) especially as credit became more generally available.

Kondratiev may have thought assuming total endogeneity was the only way of arguing for "systematic long periods," since he was pushed into a theoretical corner by Trotsky and his other critics, many of who believed in long waves of general economic life, but not purely endogenous roots. This is important as the work of Mandel and Rostow must be taken seriously since Mandel argues for an endogenous-exogenous theory of waves, while Rostow believes in the "irreducible complexity of history" (see Chap. 3 below).[4]

A fourth criticism, from a modern perspective, is that long waves may be associated with different qualitative stages of capitalism: mercantilism, competitive capitalism, largescale production, finance capitalism, Fordism, and the KWS, followed by neoliberal globalization and electronics-biotechnology, and possibly the recent trend to anti-globalization (e.g., industry policy, subsides/tariffs, and domestic reinvention). Linked to this could be the hypothesis that there are several *varieties of capitalism* even in the same phases or historical epochs of development. This method of analysis is not mechanistic, but rather postulates that qualitative changes occur within the structure of long-period mechanisms which, when linked to the concrete workings of the system, ensure that long waves can be substantiated in general evolutionary terms but not as wholly endogenous mechanisms. This is a viable theory of general long wave phases of capitalist evolution.

On the fifth criticism, as Garvy noted, Kondratiev's analysis has been criticized for providing insufficient evidence for the existence of international long waves (see [van] Duijn 1983). In this context, different countries may be in neither the same wave nor the same phase of the wave simultaneously. It has been noted that shorter business cycles do not necessarily affect different countries, sectors, or firms uniformly. In this context, Trotsky's *principle of combined and uneven development* would certainly be a better framework from which to view the global dimensions and differentiations of long waves. In a contemporary view, modern scholars of world systems analysis, such as Immanuel Wallerstein, Christopher Chase-Dunn, and many others have been continuing versions of this theme of uneven development in the global system, and we utilize this principle in this book by situating non-deterministic long waves in the world system, including its regions and nations.

A fifth criticism is that Kondratiev used potentially anomalous statistical methods, as shown indirectly by Eugen Slutzky (1937) (who worked at the Moscow Conjuncture Institute with Kondratiev). Many writers have since applied Slutzky's papers (and those of G.U. Yule and Ragnar Frisch) on the generation of cycles from random factors as potentially applying to Kondratiev (and Schumpeter and potentially others). Exactly how Slutzky's work may apply to that of Kondratiev is subject to debate. I discuss this in more detail in the section on Schumpeter (and in the Glossary).[5]

---

[4]Andrew Tylecote (1998) believes that a further analysis of Kondratiev's papers, especially Kondratiev's (1926) paper on "Long Waves on Economic Conjuncture" (and Oparin's (1926) "Critical Analysis of Professor Kondratiev's Long Cycles of Conjuncture and an Explanation for the Long Fluctuations of Certain Economic Elements: Counter Paper"), demonstrates a much more concerted attempt by Kondratiev to develop a complex endogenous analysis of long cycles or waves (plus many crucial criticisms by Oparin).

[5]In this context, a recent published paper by Jason Hecht (2023) examined the data, chronologies, and amplitudes established by Kondratiev (and Schumpeter) and undertook a series of statistical tests, concluding with respect to numerous core economies variously during 1750/1800 to 2018, for wholesale prices and GDP growth per capita, that endogenous cycles of capitalism of approximately 50 years (circa) do operate in numerous countries.

My main critique of Kondratiev's work is that he did not incorporate a thoroughgoing institutional and evolutionary approach to long waves. An explicit investigation of the dominant techno-institutional and eco-geo-spatial processes influencing his core variables was missing from his analysis. Kondratiev did not explore linkages between long waves, hegemony, and climate change, probably because these topics were not well-developed in the literature at the time, although certainly at the time there was adequate material on sunspots (e.g., Jevons 1884) and international hegemony (e.g., Veblen 1915, 1917) to provide some foundations along these lines. In any case, he was soon isolated from his colleagues in a *Gulag* in Siberia, and while he continued to research this was not subject to the same national and global scrutiny as was his earlier work, and, by the late 1930s, he was deceased.

Garvy wrote a beautifully crafted paragraph, in the context of a critical analysis of Kondratiev's long cycle, regarding future work on long waves, that guides our own work in this current volume:

> Although the hypothesis of *cyclical* swings of long duration upon which shorter cyclical movements are superimposed, should be discarded, the view that the capitalist economy has passed through successive stages of development characterized by different rates of growth and geographic expansion deserves attention. Economic analysis of the present day would probably gain in precision and significance if it were based on a more closely articulated distinction among the different phases of capitalist economy. The "curve of ... capitalist evolution" would then yield a picture more complicated than a curve, and certainly more irregular than Kondratiev's long cycles. We should substitute for the hypothesis of periodic swings the study of the successive stages of our present economic system, of its increasing geographic scope and its changing relations to the non-capitalist spheres. This would divert us from the construction of abstract models of time sequences toward the study of the actual dynamics of our economic system. (Garvy 1943, 219–220; emphasis added.)

This conclusion is one the current writer fully accepts. However, it should be noted that, at times, Garvy exaggerated problems with Kondratiev's analysis of long waves. As Barnett (2024, xlix) said: "If one wanted to criticise Garvy, it would be possible to point out that … Garvy treated the criticisms of long cycles published in the USSR at the end of the 1920s at face value, when in fact they were part of a programme designed to vilify Kondratiev politically. For example, Garvy used a paper published by L. Eventov in *Problemy ekonomiki* in 1929, which can hardly be taken as a balanced treatment of Kondratiev's work."

Phases of capitalist development need to be infused with theoretical and empirical insights into various performance measures, so that it can be considered successive long waves of upswing and downswing of both phases and performance. The current book seeks neither to impose rigid periodicities and amplitudes nor purely endogenous mechanisms, on the long wave and phases of evolution analysis of capitalism. Rather we link waves and phases to the empirical as well as historical techno-institutional and geo-spatial-climatic patterns of evolution through long historical time especially among and between the dominant (hegemonic) powers and their peripheral and semi-peripheral dominions.

In this way, our PoPE contingency paradigm seeks to analyze capitalism's institutional, technological, and climate change evolutionary transformation, performance, and hegemonic trends through historical time. In this light, we scrutinize in some depth numerous other theories, perspectives, and empirics of long waves, including those provided by Schumpeter (and then further work of successive generations of scholars and schools in the next chapter).

2.3 The Schumpeterian Entrepreneur and Long Waves

Many of Kondratiev's hypotheses concerning inventions and innovations were carried forward by others, especially Joseph Alios Schumpeter (1883–1950) and his followers. We investigate the work of Schumpeter, and in Chap. 3 neo-Schumpeterians (and many others), to ascertain whether their studies into long waves sufficiently analyzed the institutional and evolutionary context in which they operated (or otherwise). Even those who posited long *cycles*, such as Schumpeter, provided useful tools for those interested in long-period *waves* rather than cycles. And when the postwar boom came to an end in the 1970s this generated massive new works on long waves, which provided many more fruitful hypotheses and empirical stylized facts to help with this current long wave book.

Schumpeter introduced his general business cycle theory in 1911 with *The Theory of Economic Development*, and his theory of the long cycle formally in 1939 with the publication of the two-volume work, *Business Cycles: A Theoretical, Historical and Statistical Analysis of the Capitalist Process,* in which he suggested in the Preface that "The younger generation of economists should look at this book merely as something to shoot at and to start from—as a motivation program for further research. Nothing, at any rate, could please me more" (1939, v).

We investigate Schumpeter's work to provide greater insights into the problems and hypotheses relevant to this present research on long waves. An excellent starting point is provided by the sub-title of *Business Cycles: A Theoretical, Historical and Statistical Analysis of the Capitalist Process*. As he suggested, "Cycles are not, like tonsils, separate things that might be treated by themselves, but are, like the beat of the heart, the essence of the organism that displays them" (1939, v). The meaning of Schumpeter is clear: To understand capitalism one must investigate, as a high priority, the associated cyclical relations; to understand business cycles, one must investigate the phenomena as they relate to the endogenous functioning of the capitalist system (see Oakley 1990).

The question of the endogenous versus exogenous determination of waves thus arises again as a major problem. Schumpeter generally agrees with Kondratiev that waves are determined from within the system of the model. However, in Schumpeter's research program, an analysis of long cycles was less important than an overall analysis of capitalist dynamics. To inspect his theory of waves within this framework we shall look briefly, first, at his method of successive approximation and, secondly, at the mechanisms that he proposes are fundamental to an overall understanding of cycles for capitalism.

2.3.1 Successive Approximation

Successive approximation is a method by which complicated phenomena may be closely investigated via a series of more concrete models: a method of approximating the real world gradually to understand the many interrelated factors upon which, for instance, economic structure and evolution depend. It requires a set of variable models, assumptions, and conditions whereby the ceteris paribus assumption enables many processes and forces to be studied without being "upset" by the introduction of variables that the analysis precludes from study at a specific moment in scientific development. Stable theoretical conditions must be constructed so that extraneous conditions do not prevent a detailed investigation into the stage(s) of development included in the model; but then certain conditions must be relaxed, and others extended to make the model more complex and realistic through time.

2.3.2 The Circular Flow and Steady State

Before Schumpeter introduced his three successive approximations, he started with an economic system in equilibrium, with no propensity to change, in the *circular flow model* of the stationary state. Here there are certain conditions, such as, firstly, perfect competition, where no firm has any influence over price, there is perfect knowledge, and production functions are constant. Secondly, in the circular flow, there is perfect adjustment with prices, wages, and rents, and households and firms are in equilibrium (including general equilibrium). Thirdly demand for means of production and consumer goods are for present use only, as there are no future markets, stocks, or expectation of future changes (no uncertainty). Fourthly there are *two classes* of economic agents, *workers* (doing ordinary work and receiving wages) and *landlords* (who receive rent). No changes are expected in population size, age distribution, or consumer tastes, and land is not bought or sold.

In this circular flow, there are only landlords and workers, and hence no (money) capitalists (no interest) and no entrepreneurs ("surplus value," as he called it). There is no growth; and money is a veil and constant; with no transaction costs. This circular flow was important for Schumpeter in a similar sense that for Marx simple reproduction was important (although different from Schumpeter's model): it provided a starting point of no change, equilibrium, and a setting for introducing more realistic phenomena which are crucial for cycles and waves.

2.3.3 First Approximation: Innovation and the Entrepreneur

The first approximation to the real world includes many simplifying assumptions to examine the endogenous mechanism: he introduced innovation through the activities of the entrepreneur. The entrepreneur was not considered to be a class in the sense of "workers" and "capitalists" since entrepreneurial actions are relatively unpredictable and hence not stable enough for these agents to constitute a class with its own system of reproductions and ongoing activities through historical time.

Schumpeter laid great stress on the importance of equilibrium in the economic environment and in economic theory. Generally, he defined the "normal business environment" as an approximation to the Walrasian general equilibrium position. As noted in *Business Cycles*, he initially assumes conditions of simple reproduction, a constant population, a given institutional framework, constant tastes, plus conditions of perfect competition. His theoretical economic system was in equilibrium when there was no tendency toward change. He then changed his assumptions slightly by introducing the functions of the entrepreneur plus the more concrete conditions of general rigidity, friction, and lags in the economic system, all of which promoted disequilibrium, and eventually a movement back toward the "theoretical norm" of equilibrium or the normal business environment.

He asks the question: what explains the movement from equilibrium? He then postulates that: "Factors of change [endogenous] to the economic system, are changes in tastes, changes in quantity (or quality) of factors of production, and changes in methods of supplying commodities" (Schumpeter 1939, 73). Included in the category "exogenous factors" (some with qualifications) are wars, the danger of wars, evolution and general social unrest, gold discoveries, government fiscal and monetary policies, migration, crop variations due to natural causes (e.g., weather), earthquakes, and the like.

His theory was used to explain deviations from successive general equilibrium situations, by endogenous (and sometimes exogenous) factors, and is based on several propositions. He starts off with "a theory of business fluctuations to the effect that they are caused by exogenous factors [which] would not lack verifying evidence" (1939, 12). However, for Schumpeter, the most fundamental and most determinate, consistent, and fruitful explanation of the periodicity, amplitude, regularity, cyclicality, observability, and synchronization of the evolution of the capitalist disequilibrium growth path corresponds to one endogenous factor. This associated factor is innovation, technological change, and the role played by the entrepreneur.

For Schumpeter "development" is defined as the action of successive swarms of innovation that occur discontinuously in industrial and commercial life. These endogenous factors tend to recurringly disrupt socioeconomic processes by introducing changes in the ways of doing things that produce novelty. As he said about this development process of swarms of innovation, in his magnum opus, *The Theory of Economic Development*:

> Development in our sense is then defined as the [discontinuous] carrying out of new combinations. This concept covers the following five cases:

(1) The introduction of a new good—that is one with which consumers are not yet familiar—or of a new quality of a good[,]...
(2) The introduction of a new method of production, that is one not yet tested by experience in the branch of manufacturing[,] ...
(3) The opening of a new market, ... into which the particular branch of manufacturing ... has not yet entered[,] ...
(4) The conquest of a new source of supply of raw materials or half-manufactured goods[,] ...[and:]
(5) The carrying out of a new organization of any industry, like the creation of a monopoly position (for example through trustification) or the breaking up of a monopoly position. (Schumpeter 1911, 66)

The introduction of discontinuous swarms of innovation thus involves *entrepreneurs* who innovate and receive *surplus value*, as well as *money capitalists* who lend innovators money (credit) to generate novelty and receive *interest*. To Schumpeter capitalism is an economic society in which credit is the fulcrum by which activities are generated. Innovation, financed by credit,[6] operates *sui generis*, is forceful in its operation on existing economic processes, generates surplus value, and compels pre-existing firms to adopt the new processes or go bankrupt. Innovation thus changes the course of industrial evolution, generating metamorphosis throughout the economy. Surplus value accrues to innovating firms until enough new entrants enter the industry and reduce temporary surplus values to zero.

With the introduction of systemic swarms of innovation financed by credit, the economy moves from the circular flow to the two-phase business cycle, where there are the phases of prosperity and recession. The "Primary Wave" introduces innovation along with the entrepreneur which generates moderate periods of instability between prosperity and recession, starting from neighborhoods of equilibrium (NOE). NOE are broad areas (bars) rather than points, "ranges within which the system[,] as a whole[,] is more nearly in equilibrium than it is outside of them. These ranges … we call *neighborhoods of equilibrium* (the terms must not be used in the mathematical sense)" (Schumpeter 1939, 71). Schumpeter was of the view that moving through successive business cycles led to changes in the economic life of the community. See Fig. 2.1:

By moving from area "A" through a single business cycle to another area "B," many changes have occurred, including:

This new neighborhood of equilibrium ["B"] is characterized [compared with "A"] by a "greater" social product of a different pattern, new production functions, equal sum total of money incomes, a minimum (strictly zero) rate of interest, zero profits, a different system of prices, and a lower level of prices … in the shape of increased real incomes. (Schumpeter 1939, 137)

[6] Schumpeter (1939, 113) goes on to say that "By confining the manufacture of credit to banks, we are roughly conforming to fact. But this restriction is not necessary. … Manufacturers and traders dr[a]w bills on each other which, after acceptance, [are] used for the settlement of debts due to other manufacturers and traders, much as bank notes would be."

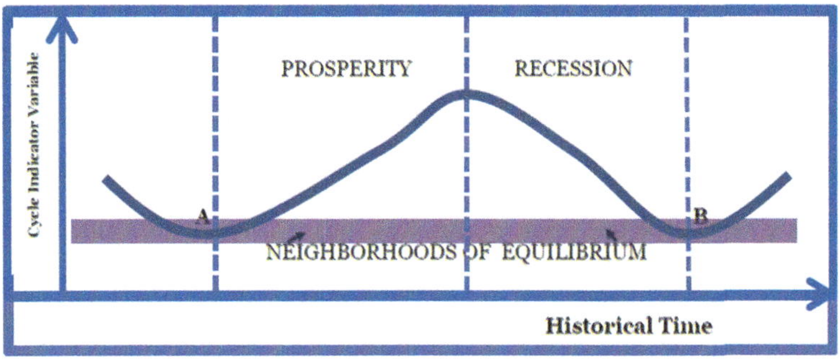

Fig. 2.1 Schumpeter's two-phase model of cycles (first approximation). Source: Adapted from Schumpeter (1939, 138) and Oakley (1990, 171)

In this light, what does the "cycle indicator variable" (Oakley 1990, 171) refer to? For Harry Bloch (2018) it is prices. Oakley is not sure. Examining Schumpeter's (1939) Chaps. 8 and 9 reveals both price and output variables being used for cycle analysis. But the price variables seem to predominate vis-à-vis the vertical axis (see also Schumpeter 1939, 469). Schumpeter clearly notes this above since the move from "A" to "B" results in, among other things, increasing social output and lower prices *vis-à-vis the upper turning point.*

With the two-phase schema, instability and uncertainty are bounded, as several further tiers of uncertainty have not been introduced. When Schumpeter introduces a further layer of successive approximation, we move from the two-phase model of cycles to the four-phase system.

2.3.4 Second Approximation: Four-Phase Model—Speculation, Credit Overextension, and Crisis

This second approximation introduces the "secondary wave," which involves secondary factors such as bootstraps, speculation, credit overextension, financial crises, absorption, and depression, which modify the workings of the system, without negating the fundamental positions that innovation and especially credit hold in the model. Introducing these additional factors in the cyclical motion of capitalism generates credit not simply for innovation but also for general accumulation (introducing saving as a source of funds), over-speculation, and over-indebtedness. It admits of overextensions of optimism and pessimism, larger lags through cycles, greater instability, and amplitude, periodic debt-deflation *à la* (in the style or manner of) Irving Fisher (1932), and hence depression, including deep depression. Other irregularities impact on economic activity, including not simply over- and under-extended credit but also uneven levels of saving that may finance productive and unproductive activities; varying levels of oligopoly power; uncertainty and indeterminateness in calculative analytics; along with banking, financial, and commercial crises.

These aspects of the second approximation led to a more realistic analysis of economic activity, a four-phase model of recovery, boom, recession, and depression; major deviations into disequilibrium or non-equilibrium (greater areas of "neighborhoods of equilibrium"); major errors of forecasting as well as extremes of optimism and pessimism. Instead of "starting" from the lows of depression, when depression becomes a periodic norm, the economy may recover from depression into recovery (or settle into protracted depression). The four-phase model is shown in Fig. 2.2.

In this four-phase model of the second approximation, the more concrete forces such as the unproductive use of credit and savings, speculation, debt-deflation, cycles of optimism and pessimism, oligopoly enterprises, and exogenous-accidental factors increase the amplitude and lags of the cycle. Neighborhoods of equilibrium are not just bars but *larger bars* of relatively indeterminate boundaries, introducing varying degrees of disequilibrium and major deviations from the center of gravity for economic activity.

Readers will notice that my long wave method (NLWM) of construction from Chap. 1 (e.g., Figs. 1.3 and 1.4) is very much influenced by this way of examining waves (not cycles). The only difference is that my long wave statistical illustrations often trend upwards/downwards (and/or vary) through historical time and have (a) a "trend (borderline) bar" as well as (b) a growth wave-curve, providing us with a dialectic of (c) "growth wave v trend bar", from which we ascertain wave upswings, downswings, and borderline areas. My "Figures" have growth on the vertical axis; otherwise, they are very similar to this Fig. 2.2 "map." It is a perfect example of the long wave process in motion (see Chap. 1), where above the bar are generally good periods especially for workers, whereas below the bar are often very bad times for workers (especially in terms of output and employment). But the core thing, for me at least, is not the "equilibrium area," but rather

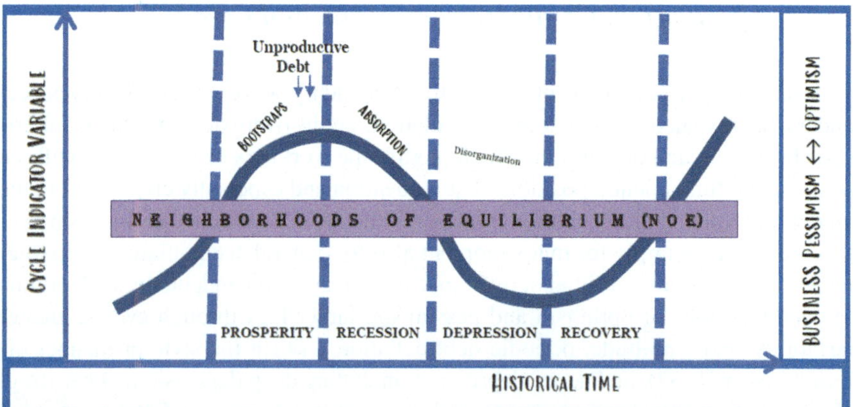

Fig. 2.2 Schumpeter's four-phase cycles model: Second approximation. Source: Adapted from Schumpeter (1939, 145–161); Oakley (1990, 172)

the "borderline area" ("neighborhoods") which represents a large area of output variation, which provides a buffer zone for long wave growth upswings and downswings (both "sides" of them) For me, the vertical axis is growth per capita, the long wave upswing is the area *above* the "borderline bar", and (long) wave downswing is the area *below* borderline (see Chaps. 1 and 5–8 below for details).

Schumpeter tended to treat the large area of neighborhoods of equilibrium in the secondary wave (the second approximation) as one where equilibrium was much less of a fulcrum, and that economic activity could *settle* for long periods at depression rather than "borderline" areas of activity. Much more flexibility was included in the model since potential instability and uncertainty were very much more generally a periodic phenomenon rather than being seldomly generated (or outside the model). Especially important for Schumpeter was the process of "absorption" occurring during a "recession," where real output increases may heighten as the innovations become more general throughout the community. As he said regarding absorption:

> ...besides being a time of harvesting the results of preceding innovation, it is also a time of harvesting its indirect effects. The new methods are being copied and improved; adaptation to them or to the impact of the new commodities consist in part in "induced" inventions; some industries expand into new investment opportunities created by the achievements of entrepreneurs; others respond by rationalization of their technological and commercial processes under pressure; much dead wood disappears. (Schumpeter 1939, 143)[7]

This can easily lead to depression (or deep recession) as these changes lead to heightened uncertainty, instability, chains of bankruptcy and so on as low profits lead to deteriorating investment and overall conditions. Declining expectations are often magnified during this downgrade which "may for a time acquire a causal role:" (Schumpeter 1939, 148), The circular and cumulative causative (CCC) processes becomes self-sustaining as it "has a way of feeding upon itself and of setting into motion a mechanism which ... could in fact run on indefinitely under its own steam" (p. 151). Schumpeter thus believed that the system may require assistance from outside the business system, such as by government (p. 143).

He then completes his analysis of the second approximation by mentioning some critical points about, firstly, the equilibrium neighborhoods becoming more complex due to the impact of previous waves and the next upswing likely not emerging from the equilibrium areas. He notes the need to emphasize the importance of economic growth, and expanded credit likely financing a whole host of activities including general accumulation, financial derivatives, and other purely business activities. He considers sectors such as construction that are likely more volatile to changes in interest rates, and where full employment may result from the process of (upward) disequilibrium rather than equilibrium.

---

[7] One can clearly see the operation of Polanyi's (1944) destructive creation (the disembedded economy) here as change generates destruction, sectoral adaptation, and variation in geographical location and evolution, as well as often declining prices which leads to some lines of business undergoing obsolescence.

2.3.5 Third Approximation: Kitchins, Juglars, Kondratievs

The third and last approximation introduces many simultaneous cycles such as Kitchin cycles (3–4 years) (Kitchin 1923), Juglar cycles (7–11 years) (Juglar 1862), and Kondratievs (40–60 years). The position that Kondratievs have in Schumpeter's system is problematic to say the least. In essence, the existence of Kondratievs per se did not follow strictly from his model, but he used the "long cycle phenomena" as an important descriptive device all throughout the 800-page "historical outline" of *Business Cycles,* because it was thought to be a very useful tool. For instance, in a critical paragraph he said:

> There [is] no particular virtue … in … just three classes of cycles. Five would perhaps be better, though … improvement in the picture would not warrant the increase in cumbersomeness. … *[T]he three-cycle schema does not follow from our model–though multiplicity of cycles does.* … If we discuss the behavior of time series in terms of Kondratieffs, Juglars, and Kitchins, this will be done simply because the writer has found it useful in his own work and in marshalling the facts. … [It is] a convenient descriptive device. (Schumpeter 1939, 169–70.) (Emphases added)

One may conclude from this that long waves are hardly an essential feature of his schema, and therefore do not deserve special discussion. But this would be wrong for three reasons. First, Schumpeter clearly sees the importance of long cycles since he emphasizes the interlinked nature of the three cycles. Second, his theory of the entrepreneur is important for more contemporary theories of the wave (e.g., Gerhard Mensch and Chris Freeman). Third, Schumpeter hypothesized about the relationship between the capitalist system and cycles (including the Kondratiev).

In the third approximation of his cyclical system, he considers the relationship of the main mechanisms associated with Kitchins, Juglars, and Kondratievs. Multiplicity of cycles, which must be posited in the analysis of long cycles or waves, is interrelated insofar as processes, lags, amplitudes, and periodicities are concerned. In this context, see Fig. 2.3, below.

Schumpeter makes the simplifying assumption, indicated in Fig. 2.3, that there are three Kitchins to every Juglar and six Juglars to every Kondratiev. The important point is we must take this pattern of interconnection into account; critically assess the core theoretical and empirical factors of relevance; and note when smaller cycles may be particularly critical in determining the timing of downturns or upturns of the long cycles. The periodicity, amplitude, and regularity of long cycles will be affected by the dynamic interconnections between Kondratievs, Kitchins, and Juglars. Upswings of the two smaller cycles may help determine the regularity of the long cycle, and possibly also the depth of the long downswing.

2.3.6 Schumpeter's Long Waves and Epochs of Transformation

As noted, three cycles did not follow strictly from Schumpeter's analysis, though a multiplicity of cycles did. He concluded that five such cycles would be too complex, and one too simple; three cycles were considered reasonable. One could, for

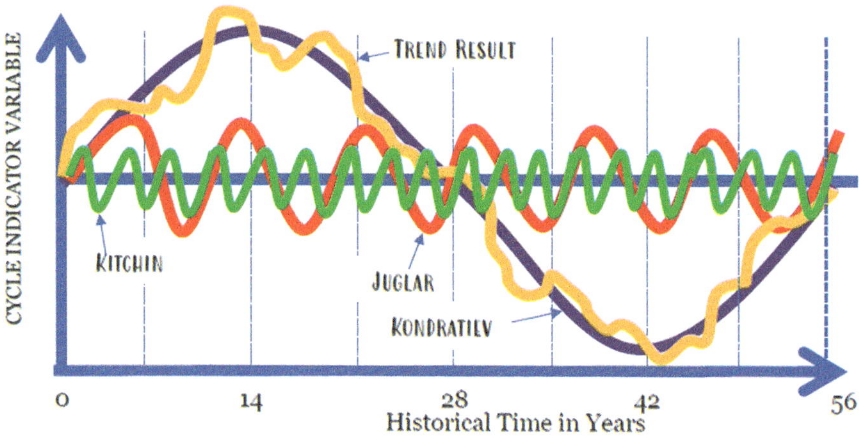

Fig. 2.3 Three-cycle model of third approximation (stylized). Source: Adapted from Schumpeter (1939, 213)

Table 2.2 Schumpeter's three Kondratiev long cycles, circa

Number	Age or epoch	Core innovations	Other novelties
First Kondratiev: 1780s–1840s	Industrial Revolution age (England)	Cotton manufacture, canal construction, water power, flying shuttle, and spinning jenny	Enclosure system, machine tools, paper, watchmaking, fertilizers, and grain improvements
Second Kondratiev: 1840s–1890s	Railway, steam, and steel Age	Sewing machines, Bessemer converter, typewriter, oil & natural gas, firearms, and trams	Clockmaking, rubber, tank furnaces, screw machine, fertilizers, and paper
Third Kondratiev 1890s–[1930s]	Electricity & automobiles age	US Far West conquest, light tractors, rail, firm mergers, steam turbine, cement, and open-hearth	Porphyry ores, high-speed steel cutters, rubber fabrics, oil & gas, cotton looms, and glass

Source: Adapted from general discussion in Schumpeter (1939; also p. 469)

instance, add a Kuznets cycle, and a multitude of others, but three cycles are probably sufficient for our purposes, although some comments on the Kuznets cycle will be made later in this chapter and in others. Schumpeter required a longer cycle, such as a Kondratiev. He thus hypothesized "Three Kondratievs" having likely impacted the capitalist world economy and its major constituents up until the late 1930s when he wrote, as illustrated in Table 2.2 about the various phases of capitalist development through long movements in economic life.

In Schumpeter's system, not all innovations and novelties are necessarily specifically associated with Kondratievs, but major ones do generally play a role in their dynamics. Certain innovations and "ages" also tend to be associated with certain nations and areas rather than others (e.g., Britain during the first Kondratiev). Uneven developments do appear in Schumpeter's cycle historical analysis, as certain nations and areas develop much slower than the core, propelling changes much later in history than for the core economies. Obviously, Kondratievs play a more important role in his cycle schema than Juglars, and Juglars much more than Kitchins.

Two things are juxtaposed in Schumpeter's analysis of Kondratievs, as they are in most other wave theories and empirics. The first is the role of economic activity, including innovation and general performance (e.g. changes in growth of aggregate output). And the second is the role of various historical epochs and ages, whereby certain qualitative changes in the institutions and industries signify broader transformations of the political and social economies. This also links to whether we are discussing cycles or broader waves of socioeconomic change.

Now we deal briefly with issues that link the second and third approximations. One is the issue of unproductive debt when the financial sector expands the financing of general accumulation rather than innovation per se. This leads to higher output but unless economies of scale, scope, and agglomeration enter the picture lower productivity is likely. Unproductive debt also increases the role of the financial system in the economy, as sophisticated assets and liabilities complicate the innovation picture, often generating a financial crisis, leading to a recession (see Schumpeter 2014).

As recession occurs, this introduces the absorption process (noted above), and the crucial role of the "downswing" in enabling the previous bunching of innovations to spread impacts over the whole economy through declining prices and a multiplicity of associated factors. The upper turning point of the *long wave* not only leads to absorption during the recession, but unstable finance leads to greater uncertainty and likely deep depression and disorganization. The secondary cycle of unproductive debt, over-speculation, and uncertainty usually follows from high prosperity to recession and deep depression. When debt is used for general accumulation, not major innovation, it tends to generate a misallocation of resources, and greater power for finance capital and speculative agents. The four-phase model thus endogenizes uncertainty as the highs of the boom influence the depths of the deep depression when financial elements increase volatility, amplitude, dislocation, depression, and high unemployment. In this respect, Schumpeter's analysis is closely linked to that of Minsky, Veblen, Marx, and Keynes (see O'Hara 2023; Bloch 2018), although of course there are differences.

The four-phase model thus led Schumpeter to conclude that the "recuperative forces" of the capitalist economy are often not dominant. Depression, he said: "has a way of feeding upon itself, and of setting into process a mechanism which, considered in isolation, could in fact run on definitively under its own steam" (1939, 151). A series of bankruptcies, market collapses, and breakdowns in credit linkages may thus accelerate the downward spiral into deep depression. The capitalist economy is thus inherently unstable due to the multiplicative primary waves of swarms of innovation and the secondary waves of credit and uncertainty, leading to depressions so critical that "the system may never conquer the breathing space in which it could recover of itself" (Schumpeter 1939, 154). Schumpeter thus stated quite explicitly that there:

> Seems in fact to be [an] element of truth in the popular opinion that there must be help from outside of the business organism, from government action or some favorable chance element for instance, if there is to be recovery at all or, at any rate, recovery without a preceding period of complete disorganization ... of indefinite length. (Schumpeter 1939, 154)

It was for this reason that Schumpeter gave "no support to any general principle of *laisser faire*" [sic] (p. 143), while the state could provide the skills of "statecraft." Innovation is thus not unique to the private sector, and can be instigated, especially through an organization, to promote surplus value and institutional stability required for long-term sustainable development.

2.3.7 Critical Assessment of Schumpeter's Long Cycle Analysis

In *Business Cycles*, Schumpeter suggests that long cycles are inextricably associated with phases in the evolution of capitalist technological development, including the industrial age (1780s–1840s), the age of steam and steel (1840s–1890s), and the age of electricity, chemistry, and motorization (1890s–[1940s]). We could add "the age of plastics, chemistry and internal combustion" (1940s–1990s), and the "age of electronics, biotechnology, AI and renewables" (1990s–2020s). In the overall scheme of things, as noted in *The Theory of Economic Development*, the "entrepreneur is merely the bearer of the mechanism of change" (1911, 61), whereas innovation is the process upon which the mechanism underlying cycles is based. Development is defined as changes in economic life that are not forced upon it from without but arise from its own initiative, from within. "Development in our sense is a distinct phenomenon, *entirely foreign* to what may be observed in the circular flow or in the tendency towards equilibrium" (1911, 61, 64; emphasis added).

Lots of criticisms and updates of Schumpeter's system have been proposed over the decades. Here we deal with some of the core criticisms, and in Chap. 3 introduce updates that link to the resurgence of (neo-or-post-) Schumpeterian themes since the 1970s.

Criticism 1: Creative Destruction Underestimated Destructions

Schumpeter's principle of "creative destruction" underplayed the destructive elements ("dead wood"), including unemployed resources, destruction of ecological capital (including climate change and declining species biodiversity), obliterated cultures, skill obsolescence, and regional uneven development. In the modern era, such destructions need to be integrated through Polanyi's disembedded economy framework (O'Hara 2000, 2023), as we do in this current book.

Criticism 2: Capitalism, Monopoly, and Surplus

In Paul Sweezy's (1943) review of Schumpeter's theory of innovation, he reviews two models of modern business relations. The first examines Schumpeter's circular flow, where there are no surpluses, only the existence of landowners and laborers; and where the introduction of entrepreneurs introduces innovation, competition, and surplus value. The second is the model that Sweezy notes is perhaps more common among large corporations, including "the capitalist," or CEO, who accumulates capital for a surplus and introduces change through innovation usually through commodity improvements or market developments. Under monopoly capitalism, Sweezy implies that the model of capitalism operating through the large corporation and producing surplus via accumulation and change, including the capitalist CEO, is more powerful than the entrepreneurial model. Perhaps this is one reason why Schumpeter wrote and dedicated his book on the large corporation implicitly to Marx, *Capitalism, Socialism and Democracy* (Schumpeter 1942), which has a chapter on "creative destruction" (ch. 7, pp. 81–86), and discusses the "destruction of the institutional framework of capitalist society" (ch. 12).

Criticism 3: Demand

Schumpeter is said to underplay the role of demand and employment theory (Heertje 1977; Lange 1941). To some degree, this is true since Schumpeter saw his theory as an alternative (to some degree) to that of Keynes. Specifically, it has some validity in relation to Schumpeter's analysis of unproductive debt not financing new innovations but promoting established processes, products, markets, and structures. The role of economies of scale and scope is especially relevant here where productivity increases can continue without innovation through increased demand for products and processes that have these characteristics. On the other hand, Schumpeter's analysis of uncertainty has much relevance to Keynesian, Marxian, and Veblenian economics.

Criticism 4: Swarming of Innovations

Schumpeter failed to "prove," theoretically or empirically, the process of swarming of innovations and innovations tending to occur in bunches. Numerous authors have taken issue with this thesis (e.g., Kuznets 1940), while others disagree about whether innovations occur during downswings or upswings ([van] Duijn 1983). What appears to happen is that while some innovations occur during all phases of "cycles," they are important during downswings, especially depressions, but due to demand and positive expectations for profit, they tend to especially expand, swarm, and spread during recovery and the early phases of boom in the cycle or wave. This is discussed more in the next chapter on contemporary schools of long wave thought.

Criticism 5: The Reference Cycle

There is an important question in Schumpeter's works, and that of many of his followers, as to what the reference cycle is on the vertical axis of Figs. 2.1–2.3, above (see Bloch 2018; Oakley 1990). When discussing "economic activity" (see Fellner 1956) vis-a-vis cycles and waves, Schumpeter is sometimes vague as to what he is referring to. Is it GDP growth per capita? GDP growth? Prices? Inflation? Investment? Or something else? Often for Schumpeter, it is prices. On the other hand, Schumpeter does discuss sectoral transformation as being crucial, so perhaps it is sometimes the development of new sectors where economic activity needs to be centered. (See Oakley 1990, chs 8 and 9, for a discussion of the "cycle indicator variable" and Bloch 2018 for an analysis of "prices" in Schumpeter's work.)

Criticism 6: Insufficient Institutional and Long-Duration Context

Schumpeter's technical approach to innovation and development did not adequately examine the role of institutions and the long historical evolution of capitalism in affecting/situating long waves. There is, for instance, very little in *Business Cycles* about policy and governance; the structure and evolution of the financial system; the development and evolution of the corporation; the world economy; the role of households; and most importantly, how these institutions and others interrelate with technological systems, plus macro and global contexts. Also, understandably perhaps, there is little or nothing in Schumpeter's works about the eco-geo-spatial transformation of capitalism, even though he was writing during the decade of the great heatwaves in the USA. Overall, nowhere did Schumpeter provide an adequate eco-geo spatial, techno-institutional evolutionary approach to waves. He also said little or nothing in his cycle investigations about hegemonies and their linkages to peripheries and semi-peripheries. Some neo-Schumpeterians, in response to this criticism, have tried to integrate some institutional and historical factors into the analysis. This is discussed in the next chapter. (Of course, we have already referred to his work on the institution of the large corporation, Schumpeter 1942, in which he made no reference to long cycles or waves.)

Despite these likely anomalies, here are many examples of where Schumpeter was extremely useful for this current book on long waves, hegemony, and climate change. In this context, three things stand out. The first is the linkage between long waves and short cycles. Throughout this study, we often scrutinize long wave performance by indicating that during long wave upswings, there are higher rates of growth of GDP per capita (and hence higher floors and ceilings in the shorter cycles), and during long wave downswings there are lower rates of GDP per capita (lower floors and ceilings in the shorter cycles) (see, e.g., Sherman and Kolk 1996 for Juglar cycle evidence and methods). We often allude to the point that during long wave upswings growth of GDP per capita tends to be significantly higher than during long wave downswings. (Kondratiev was also cognizant of this empirical point.)

Criticism 7: The Slutzky–Yule–Frisch Effect

This raises the issue of trend versus cycle. This relates to having data on prices or GDP (or "output"), calculating a (linear) trend (using ordinary least squares), estimating the deviations from the trend, and subjecting these deviations to a filter using (9-year) *moving averages* of the deviations from trend to establish a [wave] pattern (with phases of the wave being determined in certain ways) (Reijnders 1990, ch 2). Kondratiev and Schumpeter are said to have used this method at various times in their analysis.

Many authors have discussed the work of Kondratiev and Schumpeter vis-à-vis the "Slutzky–Yule effect." As mentioned, Eugen Slutzky (also spelled as 'Slutsky') worked with Kondratiev at the Moscow Conjunctural Institute, and, in the late 1920s, published a paper (Slutzky 1929), also publishing other papers (Slutzky 1925, 1927), one of which was an updated version of the 1929 one (Slutzky 1937), where he examined the method of using data, calculating trend, deleting the trend, and notably using a moving average filter to establish the wave (method of establishing phases). Judy Klein (1999) believes that "Slutsky was searching for a model of business cycles based on moving summations of random disturbances. He was not trying, as Yule [1926] had done, to demonstrate the spurious effects of a colleague's linear combinations of random disturbances, but rather to make a statement of the way capitalism works."

Vincent Barnett (2006) notes, without acknowledging Klein's paper, that there are two related ideas. The first is that the use of *moving averages* (overlapping techniques) might result in a structured cycle even from random data, and that this data may take on a recurring-like dynamic (statistical manipulation) (the process Klein links to Yule). The second idea is that the random element is in the economic process(es) and not in the method per se (real phenomena) (the process Klein links to Slutsky). Barnett emphasizes (a) the *possibility* of *moving averages* contributing to the Yule effect, (b) the differences between spurious and real random waves, and (c) that Slutzky did not define randomness as exogenous. Overall, the moving average technique may not have this anomalous effect (though it might), but the randomness may be real and hence economies may impart waves of a real random nature. The core point is that Slutsky argued the use of a moving average *could* result in a long wave from purely random sources. Moving averages thus may or may not have a negative result, depending on circumstances.

As Solomou (1998, lxiv) says in addition that:

> Fitting a deterministic trend line to the data assumes that there exists a trend-stationary growth path in the relevant time series. This assumption is unlikely to hold over long periods. Assuming a deterministic trend when the assumption is invalid will lead to inappropriate trend-cycle decomposition.

In this context, it may be more appropriate to peruse the use of structural breaks in the data, which recognize the likely existence of stochastic processes that exhibit degrees of uncertainty. The moving average technique could be substituted by use of a method without overlapping contours and with these breaks.

My own method of organizing the data is, in general, not subject to this problem. The NLWM seeks to provide a straightforward method by which readers can follow the GDP per capita growth patterns examined in this book. Our method is to (a) obtain (e.g.,) data on real GDP per capita levels; for shorter periods where they cut at likely structural breakpoints (notably for the Dutch case where several hundreds of years is investigated); (b) calculate decadal AAGR for the GDP per capita data, (c) establish a trend (usually linear, using ordinary least squares), (d) transform this trend into a trend bar (20-point thickness) (a "neighborhood of borderline performance" [BP]), (e) differentiate between the trend bar and the decadal growth fluctuations, and (f) on this basis establish whether there are (long) wave upswings (above BP), borderline performances (within the trend bar, BP), and (long) wave downswings (below BP). We variously define whole waves, usually from the upward borderline trend bar to the next upward trend bar.[8] These results can usually be established from a close visual inspection of the figures; we also detail each hege-

[8] But waves could be measured as operating from upper turning point to next upper turning point, or from lower turning point to next lower turning point, depending upon circumstances.

mon's respective wave periodicities in a table. This is the method used for especially Chaps. 1, 5–8, and 11. Our long wave/hegemony/climate change periodicity is, more importantly, also determined through the use of CSD details and secondary literature.

The third usage of Schumpeter's long wave analysis relates to the linkage between waves and phases of the evolution of capitalism. Schumpeter tended to assume that economic performance was positively related to different epochs or different phases of evolution of capitalism. A new bout of renewed performance, of a sustained nature, he considered to be related to different qualitative epochs in the development of capitalism. Generally, we agree with him, and many other long wave analysts have used this performance-phases link to examine capitalism. When it comes to scrutinizing the details of epochs of capitalism in some detail, which Schumpeter did not do, there tend to be complex issues relating to phases of evolution, which go far beyond that of Schumpeter (and often his followers).

Some scholars have said specifically that they use certain long wave theories (e.g., SSAs) to apply to various phases of evolution of capitalism, *rather than* to performance (growth waves) per se (Kotz et al. 2010). Others fuse "phases" with "performance" (e.g., Freeman and Louçã's Techno-Economic Paradigm [TEP], see next chapter). In this current work, we examine the relationship between performance and epochs of hegemony and climate change, as well as varieties of capitalism, to see what the empirical evidence suggests, since an analysis of phases linked to certain dimensions of performance, varieties, power, and geo-spatial-climate analysis is necessary for the inquiry.

2.4 Conclusion

In this chapter, we have presented an outline of the main contours of the first long wave upswing in long wave scholarship, and the anomalies that laid the foundation for the downswing (during the 1950s and 1960s) in scholarship especially in light of the criticisms made by several authors. But we also made clear that there were innovations made by Kondratiev, Schumpeter, and company, in the sense that they presented some core hypotheses and empirical regularities that could be scrutinized in further works on the evolution of capitalism into the future, even if some of the criticisms were well-founded. We also presented our own clear message about the importance of capitalism's performance, its phases of evolution, varieties, and the linkage of long-term growth with hegemonic and climate change (eco-geo-spatial) dynamics.

In this context, the chapter that follows examines the second long wave upswing (boom) of long wave theory and empirics, from the 1970s to the 1990s, and the subsequent long wave downswing of this second long wave slump of theory and empirics (and related controversies). I start with some of the earlier long wave revivalists, such as W.W. Rostow, Jay Forrester, Ernest Mandel, and Gerhard Mensch. Here we specify what the nature and limitations of these works are. We synthesize more systematically many of these long wave analysts into our PoPE long wave contingency paradigm, including especially neo-Schumpeterians such as Chris Freeman, Francisco Louçã, Carlotta Perez, Andrew Tylecote, and company; infusing their framework with that of Regulation and SSA approaches; as well as the important work of world systems, hegemony, and power cycle analysts such as Immanuel Wallerstein and company, Jushua Goldstein, George Modelski, and several other scholars.

We reconstruct the analysis by integrating climate change dynamics into the long waves and hegemony framework (Chap. 4). It also involves going back to the Dutch golden age and its demise of the late 1500s through the 1600s and beyond (Chap. 5), onto British hegemony and its demise (Chap. 6), then US hegemony and decline (Chap. 7), and finally Chinese potential hegemony of the 1980s–2040s (Chap. 8). This is followed by an investigation of the recent structural polycrises (Chap. 9), one core aspect of the polycrises being the "pre-war" era in light of the Ukraine–Taiwan conflicts (Chap. 10), the empirics of long waves during the 1940s–2020s for many areas and nations (Chap. 11), a conclusion (Chap. 12), and a Glossary of Terms.

References

Aftalion, Albert. 1913. *Les crises generales et periodiques de surproduction*. 2 vols. Paris: Marcel Riviere.

Anderson, O. 1929. *Zur Problematik der empirisch-statistischen Konjunktur-forschung: Kritische betrachtung der Harvard- methoden*, 1929. Bonn: Kurt Schroeder.

Bagdanov, V. 1928. On the Question of the Regularity of the Historical Evolution of Capitalism. *Pod znamenim marksizma* June:80–89.

Barnett, Vincent. 1998. *Kondratiev and the Dynamics of Economic Development: Long Cycles and Industrial Growth in Historical Context*. New York: St Martin's Press.

Barnett, Vincent. 2006. Chancing an Interpretation: Slutzky's Random Cycles Revisited. *European Journal of the History of Economic Thought* 13 (3): 411–432.

Barnett, Vincent. 2024. Dating the Long Cycle Turning Points: Kondratiev and After. In *The Works of Nikolai D Kondratiev Vol 1*, xxxv-1, eds. Natalia Makasheva, Warren J Samuels, and Vincent Barnett. London: Routledge. online edition.

Barr, Kenneth. 1979. Long Waves: A Selected Annotated Bibliography. *Review (Fernand Braudel Centre)* 2 (4): 675–718.

Bloch, Harry. 2018. *Schumpeter's Price Theory*. London: Routledge.

Bresciani-Turroni, C. 1917. Movimento di lunga durato dello sconto e dei prezzi. *Giornale degli economisti*. II:1–11.

Cassell, Gustav. 1918. *Theoretische Sozialokonomie*. Leipzig: C.F. Winter.

Clarke, Hyde. 1847. Physical Economy-A Preliminary Inquiry into the Physical Laws Governing the Periods of Famine and Panics. *British Railway Register* 2–15. Reprinted in Francisco Lou and Jan Reijnders (Eds), *The Foundations of Long Wave Theory: Models and Methodology*, 3–20. Cheltenham: Edward Elgar, 2 vols.

Day, Richard D. 1976. The Theory of the Long Cycle: Kondratiev, Trotsky, Mandel. *New Left Review* 98 (July–August).

De Wolff, Sam. 1924. Prosperitats-und Depressionsperioden. In *Der lebendige Marxismus: Festgabe zum 70 Geburtstage von Karl Kautsky*, ed. Otto Jenssen, 13–43. Jena: Thuringer Verlagsanstalt.

De Wolff, Sam. 1929. *Het economisch getij*. Amsterdam.

Duijn, Jacob J. van. 1981. Fluctuations in Innovations over time. *Futures* 13 (4).

Ekland, Klas. 1980. Long Waves in the Development of Capitalism? *Kyklos* 33:3.

Eventov, L. 1929. On the Nature of Fluctuation of Long Duration in the Capitalist Economy. *Problemy ekonomiki* 1 and 2: 54–73, and 47–68.

Fellner, William. 1956. *Trends and Cycles in Economic Activity*. New York: Henry Holt & Co.

Fisher, Irving. 1932. *Booms and Depressions: Some First Principles*. New York: Adelphi Company.

Garvy, George. 1943. Kondratieff's Theory of Long Cycles, The Review of Economic. *Statistics* 25 (4).

Gelfand, Israel Lazarevich. ('Parvus', 'Helphand'). 1901. *Die Handelskrise und die Gewerkschaften*. Munich: M. Ernst. (Olle & Wolter 1972.)

Gerzstein, A. 1928. Do Major Economic Cycles Exist? *Mirovoe khoziaistvo i mirovaia politika* III (8/9 and 10): 3–42, and 13–35.

Granowsky, E. 1928. On the Business Cycle Theory of the 'Soviet' Bourgeois Economists. *Vestnik kommunisticheskaia akademiia* XXX:6.

Guberman, S. 1927. The Problems of the Short and Long Cycles. *Sotsialisticheskoe khoziaistvo* 1:28–59.

Hecht, Jason. 2023. Are Long Waves 50 Years? Reexamining Economic and Financial Long Wave Periodicities in Kondratieff and Schumpeter. *Review of Political Economy*. Published online 12 December 2023. https://doi.org/10.1080/09538259.2023.2280803

Heertje, Arnold. 1977. *Economics and Technical Change*. New York: Wiley.

Jevons, W. Stanley. 1884. *Investigations in Currency and Finance*. London: Macmillan.

Juglar, Clement. 1862. *Des Crises commerciales et leur retour periodique en France, en Angleterre, et aux Etats-Unis*. Paris: Guillaumin.

Kautsky, Karl. 1901–1902. Krisentheorien. *Die Neue Zeit* XX:37–47 & 133–143. Reproduced in *Die langen Wellen der Konjunktur*, Berlin, Olle & Wolter, 1972.

Kitchin, Joseph. 1923. Cycles and Trends in Economic Factors. *Review of Economic Statistics* 5 (1): 10–16.

Klein, Judy L. 1999. The Rise of "Non-October" Econometrics: Kondratiev and Slutsky at the Moscow Conjuncture Institute. *History of Political Economy* 31 (1): 137–167.

Kondratiev, Nikolai Dmitrievich. 1922. *Mirovoe khoziaistvo i ego kon1 iunktury vo vremia i posle voiny (The World Economy and its Conjunctures During and After the War)*. Oblastnoe Otdelenie Gosudartsvennogo lzdatelstva: Volgada.

Kondratiev, Nicholai Dmitrievich. 1925. Bol'shie tsikly kon"yunktury. *Voprosy kon"yunktury* 1:28–79. Translated into German as Die langen Wallen der Konjunktur, *Archiv fur Sozialwissenschaft and Sozialpolitik* 61(1926)(3): 573-600. An abridged translation of the German appears as The Long Waves in Economic Life, *Review of Economic* Statistics 17(1935) (6): 105-115. The complete English translation of the German appears in *Review* (Fernand Braudel Centre) 2(1979)(4): 519-562.

Kondratiev, Nikolai Dmitrievich. 1926. *Long Waves on Economic Conjuncture*. Paper presented at the Moscow Conjuncture Institute. Reprinted in *The Works of Nikolai D. Kondratiev*. Volume 1, 25–63. Eds. Natalia Makasheva, Warren J. Samuels, and Barnett Vincent. 1998. Translated by Stephen S. Wilson. London: Pickering & Chatto. Reprinted, London: Routledge, 2016. (ebook 2024). https://doi.org/10.4324/9781003552864

Kondratiev, Nikolai Dmitrievich. 1928. Bol'shie tsikly ekonomieskoi kon'iunktury. In *Bol'shie tsikly kon'iunktury*, ed. N. D. Kondratiev and I. Oparin. Moscow: Krasnaya Presnya. Edited version translated published as *The Long Wave Cycle, Foundations of Long Wave Theory: Models and Methodology, Volume 1*, 25-126, eds. Francisco Lou and Jan Reijnders, eds. Cheltenham: Edward Elgar, 1999.

Kotz, David, Terrence McDonough, and Michael Reich. Eds. 2010. *Social Structures of Accumulation: The Political Economy of Growth and Crisis*. Cambridge: Cambridge University Press.

Kuznets, Simon. 1940. Schumpeter's Business Cycles. *American Economic Review* 30 (2): 257–271.
Lange, Oscar. 1941. Book Review of Schumpeter's Business Cycles. *Review of Economic Statistics* XXIII (4): 190–193.
Lenoir, Marcel. 1913. *Etudes sur la formation et la mouvement des prix*. Paris: M. Giard.
Lescure, Jean. 1907. *Des Crises generales et periodiques de surproduction*. Paris.
MacDonald, R. A. 1912. The Rate of Interest Since 1844. *Journal of the Royal Statistical Society* 75 (IV): 361–379.
Makasheva, Natalia, Warren J. Samuels, and Barnett Vincent, ed. 1998. *The Works of Nikolai D. Kondratiev.* 4 volumes. Translated by Stephen S. Wilson. London: Pickering & Chatto. Reprinted, London: Routledge, 2016. (ebook 2024). https://doi.org/10.4324/9781003552864
Motylef, W.E. 1923. The Accumulation Theory of Rosa Luxemburg. *Vestnik sotsialisticheskaia akademiia* IV.
Oakley, Allen. 1990. *Schumpeter's Theory of Capitalist Motion: A Critical Exposition and Reassessment*. Cheltenham: Edward Elgar.
O'Hara, Phillip Anthony. 2000. *Marx, Veblen and Contemporary Institutional Political Economy: Principles and Unstable Dynamics of Capitalism*. Cheltenham: Edward Elgar.
O'Hara, Phillip Anthony. 2001. Long Waves of Growth and Development. In *Encyclopedia of Political Economy*, ed. P. A. O'Hara, 673–677. London and New York: Routledge. Paper Edition.
O'Hara, Phillip Anthony. 2023. *Principles of Institutional and Evolutionary Political Economy: Applied to Current World Problems*. Singapore: Springer Nature. Revised Edition.
Oparin, D. I. 1926. *Critical Analysis of Professor Kondratiev's Long Cycles of Conjuncture and an Explanation for the Long Fluctuations of Certain Economic Elements: Counter Paper*. Reprinted in *The Works of Nikolai D. Kondratiev.* Volume 1, 64-107. Eds. Natalia Makasheva, Warren J. Samuels, and Barnett Vincent. 1998. Translated by Stephen S. Wilson. London: Pickering & Chatto. Reprinted, London: Routledge, 2016. (ebook 2024). https://doi.org/10.4324/9781003552864
Pareto, Villlfredo. 1913. Alcune relazioni fra lo stato sociale e le variazioni del la prosperita economica. *Rivista italiana di sociologia* Sept-Dec.
Pervushin, S. A. 1926. Fundamental Questions of the Theory and the Methodology of Economic Fluctuations. *Planovoe khoziaistvo* 12:120–136.
Polanyi, Karl. 1944. *The Great Transformation*. Harmondsworth, Penguin, 2024.
Reijnders, Jan. 1990. *Long Waves of Economic Development*. Aldershot: Edward Elgar.
Schumpeter, Joseph. 1911. *The Theory of Capitalist Development*. Harvard: Harvard University Press, 1934.
Schumpeter, Joseph. 1939. *Business Cycles: A Theoretical, Historical and Statistical Analysis of the Capitalist Process*. London: McGraw-Hill, 1980.
Schumpeter, Joseph. 1942. *Capitalism, Socialism and Democracy*. 3rd ed. New York: Harper & Row, 1950.
Schumpeter, Joseph A. 2014. *Treatise on Money.* Aalten: Wordbridge Publishing. Translated from the 1970 German Edition by Rubin Alvarado.
Sherman, Howard J. and David Kolk. 1996. *Business Cycles and Forecasting*. New York: Harper Collins.
Simiand, Francois. 1932. *Le salaire l'evolution sociale et la monnaie*. 3 Vols. Paris: Lib. Felix Alcan.
Slutzky, Eugen. 1925. Ueber stochastische Asymptoten und Grenzwete. *Metron* 5:3–89.
Slutzky, Eugen. 1927. Slozhenie sluchainykh prichin, kak istochnik tsiklicheskikh protsessov. *Voprosy kon"yunktury* 3:34–64.
Slutzky, Eugen. 1929. Sur l'erreur quadratique mogenne du coefficient de correlation dans le cas des suites des epreuves non independantes. *Comptes rendus* 189:612–614.
Slutzky, Eugen. 1937. The Summation of Random Causes as the Source of Cyclic Processes. *Econometrica* 5 (2): 105–145.

Solomou, Solomos. 1998. Kondratiev Cycles: An Evaluation. In *The Works of Nikolai D. Kondratiev*, ed. Makasheva, Natalia, Warren J. Samuels, and Barnett Vincent, vol. lxiii–lxx, 4 volumes. Translated by Stephen S. Wilson. London: Pickering & Chatto. Reprinted, London: Routledge, 2016. (ebook 2024). https://doi.org/10.4324/9781003552864

Spiethoff, Arthur. 1923. Krisen. In *Handworterbuch der Staatswissenschaften*, vol. 6. Jena. Translated into English as Business Cycles, *International Economic Papers* 3(1953): 75-171.

Studensky, G. A. 1930. The Agricultural Depression and the Technical Revolution in Farming. *Journal of Farm Economics* 4 (October): 552–572.

Sukharov, G. A. 1926. *Major Economic Cycles. Planovoe khoziaistvo* 4:159–169.

Sweezy, Paul. 1943. Professor Schumpeter's Theory of Innovation. *Review of Economic Statistics* 25 (4): 93–96.

Trotsky, Leon. 1921. Flood-Tide: The Economic Conjuncture and the World Labor Movement. *Pravdaz* 272, Dec. 25. An English translation appears in, Leon Trotsky, *The First Five Years of the Communist International*. Vol. 2. New York: Monad Press, 1972, 74–84.

Trotsky, Leon. 1923. The Curve of Capitalist Development. *Vestnik sotsialisticheskaia akademiia* 4 (April–July): 3–12. An English translation appears in Leon Trotsky, *Problems of Everyday Life*. New York: Monad Press, 1973, 273-80.

Tugan-Banarovski, Mikhail. 1894. *Promyshlennye krizisy v souremennoi Anglii*. Petersburg.

Tylecote, Andrew. 1998. Politics, Technology and Economics: Kondratiev's Endogenous Theory of Long Waves. In *The Works of Nikolai D. Kondratiev*, ed. Natalia Makasheva, Warren J. Samuels, and Barnett Vincent, 4 volumes, LXXi-LXXXiii. London: Pickering & Chatto. Translated by Stephen S. Wilson. Republished, London: Routledge, 2016. ebook 2024.. https://doi.org/10.4324/9781003552864

Van Duijn, J. J. 1983. *Long Waves of Economic Life*. London: Allen & Unwin.

van Gelderen, J. ('J. Fedder'). 1913. Springvloed - Seschouwingen over industrieele ontwikkel ing en prijsbevJeging. *Die Nieiwe Tijd* XVI 11, 4, 5 & 6; April, May & June, 1913 (pp. 254–77, 370–84, 446–64).

Veblen, Thorstein Bunde. 1915. *Imperial Germany and the Industrial Revolution*. New Brunswick: Transaction Books, 1990.

Veblen, Thorstein Bunde. 1917. *An Inquiry into the Nature of Peace and the Terms of its Perpetuation*. Los Angeles: Tutis Digital Publishing, 2008.

Wicksell, Kurt. 1898. *Geldzins und Guterpreise*. Jena: G. Fischer. An English translation appears as *Interest and Prices: A Study of the Causes Regulating the Value of Money*. New York: Augustus Kelley, 1965.

Williams, T.T. 1912. Rate of Discount and the Rate of Consols. *Journal of the Royal Statistical Society* 75 (March).

Yule, G. U. 1926. Why Do we Sometimes get Nonsense Correlations between Time Series? *Journal of the Royal Statistical Society* 89 (1): 1–64.

Chapter 3
Long Wave Schools of Thought: Rostovian, Mandelian, Neo-Schumpeterian, Eastern, SSA, WSA, *et al.*

Abstract In this chapter, I analyze the *second wave of long wave scholarship* (late 1960s–2020s), including the upswing (late 1960s–1990s) and the relative downswing (2000s–2020s), paying special attention to schools of thought. We accept in principle the importance of Rostow's concept of the irreducible complexity of history; Mandel's rate of profit analysis and his notion about long wave upswings being largely exogenously determined, while upswings tend to endogenously decline; Forrester's use of circular and cumulative causation (CCC); and Mensch's sectoral analysis. From there, we analyze several schools of thought, some following scholars just mentioned, and others recognizing the importance of post-Schumpeterian technology styles and institutional clusters; regulation school regimes of accumulation and structural forms; social structures of accumulation (SSAs); world systems analysis and international politics. We then outline the principles of political economy (PoPE) contingency paradigm by reconstructing long wave hypotheses through an integrated principles analysis of eco-geo-spatial, technological, and institutional dynamic spheres through the circuits of socioeconomic dynamics (CSD).

Keywords Long wave schools · Rostovian analysis · Mandelian approaches · Neo-Schumpeterian style · Social structures of accumulation (SSA) · Regulation School · World systems analysis · PoPE contingency paradigm · New long wave method (NLWM)

3.1 Introduction

The second long wave of long wave scholarship emerged into the late-1960s to the 1990s, after the first wave earlier in the century (O'Hara 2001). Several individuals reinvigorated long wave discourse during the 1970s–1990s, in terms of real GDP per capita growth, investment, rate of profit, and related performance measures. Price changes did not enter the long wave debate, except for a minority of scholars, but stagflation, energy prices, real wages and interest rates were important to the growth factors. The debate was mostly about the expansion and decline of

P. A. O'Hara, *Long Waves of Growth, Hegemonic Power, and Climate Change in the World Economy*, https://doi.org/10.1007/978-981-96-4132-1_3

macro-aggregates and related processes, often decomposed into various sectors and institutions. It was the relative decline of growth, hegemony, and profit rates in light of changing oil prices, workers power, corporate performance, and global change that set the whole debate going.

After a while these individual contributions turned into full-fledged schools of thought. For instance, several scholars started taking the Mandelian approach seriously and thus turned to capitalism's contradictory dynamics associated with accumulation, rate of profit, organic composition of capital, and the importance of wars, revolutions, and other socioeconomic forces impinging on long waves. Walt Whitman Rostow's earlier work influenced others to analyze the role of (relative) prices, sectoral analysis, and the irreducible complexity of history. Modern (or post-)Schumpeterians recognized the importance of the earlier work for what had happened during the 1940s–1970s circa and earlier/later and thereby researched the role of clusters of innovation, research and development, systems of innovation, life cycles of products/processes, and policies to stimulate novelty. Regulationists took a cue from the history of capitalism, especially in the twentieth century vis-à-vis the rise and demise of modes of regulation, including the role of regimes of accumulation, institutional forms, and phases of evolution of capitalism. David Gordon started the social structure of accumulation (SSA) school of long waves through the emphasis on several institutional spheres, accumulation, rate of profit, and phases of evolution. Immanuel Wallerstein initiated the Fernand Braudel Centre for the Study of Economies, Historical Systems and Civilizations and the journal simply called *Review* (Fernand Braudel Centre), and inspired further work on long waves, hegemony, and the periodic rise and fall of capitalism, especially since the 1500s (later the *Journal of World-Systems Research* continued this work).

Through the early years of long wave renascence (second boom) several individuals made innovations and developed alternative explanations of long waves, often taking an eclectic approach, and influencing others. George Modelski, David Wilkinson, and others examined cycles of world leadership, linkages between navel supremacy (sea-power, growth, and changing power relations/wars) before and during the Dutch Golden Age, to the British and US cases), and beyond. Jay Forrester developed the system dynamics research group, explaining waves through an analysis of capital and consumer goods sectors, bootstraps mechanism, circular and cumulative causation (CCC), and interactions between investment and innovation. Andrew Tylecote centered on the interplay of technology styles, (mis)matches with socio-political factors, forms of integration, crises, feedbacks (e.g., monetary, population, and inequality), and a historical account of waves. J.J. van Duijn analyzed (especially global) long waves of production, fluctuations in innovation, stagnation in the 1970s, and policy. Brian Berry (1991) investigated long waves of politics and economics, cycles of war and world leadership, and price and growth waves through historical time (including Kuznets cycles). Several others sought to innovate through long wave theory and empirics. Some specialized in a critical (and often sympathetic) analysis of long wave theory and empirics, especially vis-à-vis technical empirics (e.g., Solomos Solomou, Jan Reijnders, etc.).[1]

In this chapter, we use the schools of thought and others that evolved through this second long wave of long wave scholarship, to build an understanding of the innovations that were made, and also the limitations of the various explanations, and why this current work seeks to develop a more inclusive yet also in some respects quite different explanation for the irregular patterns of long waves through various forms of growth, hegemony, and irregular climate change dynamics. We build a theory and empirics of the contingency patterns of long waves, hegemony, and climate change, paying attention to the various limitations of standard long wave models.

3.2 Rostow's Irreducible Complexity of History

Long wave theorists are variously concerned with issues of circular and cumulative long-run growth, and in the case of Rostow (and some others), a sectoral analysis of capitalism, including price dynamics. Walt Whitman Rostow (1916–2003) differs from other long wave theorists by postulating a "fifth Kondratiev upswing" beginning in the late 1970s–early 1980s, but noted that, "Before we've fully squared a way to deal with [this] upswing, we may need an intellectual revolution as profound as the Keynesian revolution itself" (Rostow 1977). Such a revolution would place less emphasis on short-run aggregate investment, gross national product, and a one-commodity economy, and more emphasis on changes in the direction of investment, structural adjustment, and research and development activity. In terms of policy options, Rostow argues that fiscal and monetary policy have both been "oversold," and that the emphasis should be on public and private sector research and development (R&D). Reasons he posits for this are, firstly, because R&D has declined since the 1960s in many advanced nations, and second, since it forms the basis of future growth (and/or changes in relative prices).

Of all long wave theories, Rostow's is the least mono-causal, since he stresses the dynamic interplay of (1) leading sectors, (2) the changing profitability of the primary sector, and (3) the large international process of migration, its relationship to the size of the workforce and demand for housing. These are his core factors in the continual "process of adjustment towards a moving equilibrium, never attained—a process for which we lack an adequate dynamic theory" (1975, 719).

His theory of the long wave has not been elaborated with a high degree of sophistication (but see Rostow 1984 where he does develop some technical analyses),

[1] Mention should also be made to numerous other books on long wave. For instance, several long wave scholars apply their analysis to issues of business and finance, such as Robert Beckman (1983) and I know of some "financial specialists" who utilize long waves for providing financial advice to the public and corporations. Some long wave scholars apply their investigation to regional issues in the global economy, including Michael Marshall (1987). Numerous long wave analysts apply the subject to international politics, such as Manfred Neumann (1997).

mainly because, as an economic historian, Rostow was more concerned with the "complex process of economic growth" rather than a theory that abstracts greatly from complexities. He rejects the position that there are long waves with an endogenous mechanism propelling the cyclical movement of the economy over successive 40–60 years. The Schumpeterian innovator is especially denounced as a major functionary in the Rostovian "trend periods" (rather than cycles). Wars, extensive primary sector expansion, and long gestation periods for investment are more important to Rostow in providing a dynamic framework within which the international economy exhibits periodic, regular, trend (not cyclical) and internationally synchronized movements in prices. Movements in prices constitute the dominant empirical variable upon which he periodizes "long trends" since, as he said (1960, 133):

> Historical evidence does not appear to support the view that the periods of rising trends in general prices were caused primarily by the coming of major new industries. For instance, without the external events of 1793–1800, it is doubtful that the rapid growth of the British cotton industry would have caused a period of sharply rising general prices; or that, without the great extensive investments of the pre-1914 years in many parts of the world, prices would have risen owing to the growth of the automobile, electricity, and chemical industries. Trends are therefore defined primarily in terms of relative price movements, resulting from distortions in the composition of output and capacity (1960, 127).

Within the context of "trend periods," he considers the importance of a sectoral enquiry yet downplays the importance of the growth of some important sectors in the growth process. What Rostow appears to mean is that endogenous sectoral growth does not provide a framework for the expansion of prices (a new long trend), but that this is due largely to war, the primary sector, and international movements of people and capital. Also, while the periodization of long movements of history is said to be based largely on the general price level within the international economy, Rostow postulates a systematic relationship between prices and production: large increases in the relative price of agricultural and raw material products provide the basis for rapid growth and a new long upward trend, while reduced relative prices for these commodities provides an impetus for a downward long trend.

Based on this schema, Rostow provides a periodization of long trends corresponding to the following ranges:

First Long Trend 1790–1848 (Rise, 1790–1815; decline, 1815–1848).

> This period reflected "pressure on the grain supply caused by the rise of the European population" (Eklund 1980, 410), related to the growth of cotton (in England).

Second Long Trend 1849–1896 (Rise, 1849–1873; decline, 1874–1896).

> This was initiated by the opening up of the grain areas of the American Middle West and the Mississippi, which is closely linked to the United States transcontinental railway network. Pig iron and steel were particularly important developments during this time.

Third Long Trend 1897–1936 (Rise, 1897–1920; decline, 1921–1936).

The upswing during this period was largely due to the rising populations of the United States and Europe, and the subsequent increasing demand for infrastructure, plus food supplies from Canada, Australia, Argentina, and Ukraine.

Fourth Long Trend 1937–1972 (Rise 1937–1951; decline 1952–1972).

This trend was promoted by the scarcity of food and energy during the depression and World War Two industrial growth.

Fifth Long Trend 1972-? (Rise 1972-?).

This trend was said to be due to the worldwide grain shortage and oil price rises of the early–mid-1970s.

In very general terms, Rostow's analysis of growth appears to have similarities with Simon Kuznets' analysis of the "Long Swing" (variable oscillations of about 20 years); although the periodicities are different. For instance, in Rostow's system, migration to new areas puts a strain on agricultural and raw materials prices, which promotes their production and through time eventually lowers their price. In the meantime, that same migration promotes infrastructure and housing growth, and leading sectors evolve in these and related consumer sectors. Hence the boosting of investment in important sectors, a process that eventually dampens and finally becomes negative as an overextension of the system becomes evident. Accompanying this is the declining part of the life cycle of leading consumer-goods sectors, which then produce lower prices in these and related areas. Twenty years or so of relative stagnation is eventually negated by exogenous factors such as war, or (what Rostow calls the) "endogenous" opening-up of new territory (promoting migration, new products, etc.) leading to a new, long trend after primary product prices have risen.

While there is no specific *"endogenous" mechanism* generating successive long trends, the complex, dynamic, flexible, and growth-orientated nature of capitalism is said to ensure that the quest for new territory, war, or improvements in productivity in existing or leading sectors from largely domestic changes propel new long trends. He does suggest, however (Rostow 1960, 135), that, due to the exhaustion of the field of territory, the number of precipitating factors promoting primary product prices (and hence the upward portion of the long wave) may have declined "lately," resulting in a weaker tendency toward trend movements of economic factors over the long-period but by no means their obliteration as a general process (hence possibly his anomalous long wave periodicities from 1950).

Rostow gained a great deal of stimulus from Kondratiev, Schumpeter, and Kuznets. However, he did not appreciate Kondratiev's endogenous theory of durable fixed capital, but Kondratiev's analysis of the empirical nature of prices and the role of war, and so on, were very important to Rostow. He rejected Schumpeter's theory of innovation since, "as far as innovation and technological developments are concerned, I remain skeptical that, in the past, these have had a great deal to do, as initiating factors, with the secular pattern of events" (1960, 143); but he did retain the significance of leading sectors which Schumpeter had emphasized. And, while he realized that the population-related basis of the Kuznets cycle has receded somewhat (since 1913?), due to the relative exhaustion of new territory for expansion, a modified version of the theory of population, which emphasized war, "internal economic developments" and other exogenous factors were adequate substitutes, according to Rostow. As he noted:

> In 1972, the world economy experienced a turning point in foodstuff and raw material prices, a break as sharp as those of the [post depressionary] 1790s, 1840s, 1890s and 1930s. As on earlier occasions, one can attribute the turn to ad hoc events: in this case a convergence of bad harvests and a new consciousness of their oligopolistic power among the members of OPEC. But the central fact is that the immediately available American agricultural and energy reserves were running down. These … helped to keep world prices relatively low. ... But the global pace of population increase and industrialization suggest that the pressure of demand on the supply of foodstuffs and raw materials will not prove to be a short-term phenomenon. I am inclined to believe that the fifth Kondratiev upswing is upon us. [Rostow 1975, 49–50]

Rostow's "trend periods" are thus by no means endogenously determined, and since certain important mechanisms (such as the expansion of territory) have become less important, price rises that would normally signal a boom or upswing may necessitate other movements to sectoral investment and innovation. Of critical importance here is the importance of conscious policy: since the market fails due to various externalities (which Rostow hypothesizes increase during periods of low growth) and innovation. The government or state can facilitate the new trend expansion by enabling the internalization of significant pollution costs (which may promote more feasible energy and industrial alternatives) and by guiding and nurturing R&D. Especially important for R&D is a shortening of the invention/innovation lag for basic developments in knowledge, which essentially means the promotion of the "sectoral planning of investment." In this context, he said that:

> The last four Kondratiev upswings were (more or less) transited by the redirection of private investment resources in response to changes in relative prices and evolving technological possibilities... However, energy and agricultural relative price changes are a necessary but not sufficient condition for the appropriate change in investment patterns [Rostow 1978, 632.]

While he does not delve very deeply into this very crucial issue, Rostow suggests that the role of the state is the most important extra condition needed for recovery. Thus, for Rostow, this "exogenous" factor, the state, must promote private-public planning into sectoral innovation before the upswing which he notes, "is upon us" (in 1977) will be sustained. The following represent areas of planning that Rostow (1978) particularly emphasizes:

1. Development of appropriate statistics relating to different sectors of the economy.
2. A careful assessment of multiplier-accelerator rates for specific sectors and different economies (in relation to North-South dialogue).
3. Constraint on further massive investment into automobiles, durable consumer goods, and other oil-intensive forms of private consumption; the freeing of resources for more innovation.
4. Developments in pollution control, housing investment (especially insulation and solar heating), public transport, and basic/applied R & D.
5. Studies into levels of welfare spending by governments and whether they affect (to what degree and in what way(s)) resources available for private investment.

6. Studies into the "plough back rate" of firms (the "own profit-investment rate") and the effect of actual and potential state policy on this.

Clearly, then, Rostow's system relies heavily on "exogenous" factors, and a form of historical inquiry which is not heavily theoretical. Nevertheless, he does provide a useful and important set of core factors from which are derived the following six hypotheses:

Hypothesis One: Long period trends are consistently propelled by (largely) exogenous factors which determine periodicity, regularity, and trend movements in prices and investment; there is a strong qualitative dimension involved.

Hypothesis Two: The Primary Factors for explaining long waves are (1) leading sectors, (2) changing relative prices for energy and grain, and (3) the international flow of capital and people.

Hypothesis Three: Large increases in the relative prices of primary commodities are necessary *but not sufficient* for the expansionary component of sectoral growth.

Hypothesis Four: The long wave is not necessarily realized in gross national product, gross investment, or macro variables in general, but rather in changing investment patterns and structural changes between sectors.

Hypothesis Five: If the long wave is only realized through sectoral change this may be a fruitful line of inquiry relative to an understanding of long period movements of the economy.

Hypothesis Six: 1975 represents the turning point between the contractionary component of the long wave and the new expansionary wave.

A review of Rostow's theory and empirics teaches us several things. First, it teaches us to stress the importance of a dynamic historical approach. Second, Rostow teaches us that much happens at the micro and meso-levels that need attention for the emergent macro and global changes that develop. And third, he teaches us that likely he placed too much emphasis on the agricultural sector (ratio of primary to manufacturing prices), and prices in general, since 1975 is not the start of a long wave upswing, but likely a downswing, although China and parts of the region did likely undergo upswing from the 1980s or 1990s. We thus learn from Rostow about the irreducible complexity of history and the subsystems that gradually interfuse at the macro and global levels. In addition, even though Rostow had been an adviser and speech writer on economic and foreign policy for several US Presidents, he did not integrate into his analysis of long waves core issues of hegemony and global climate change, which are crucial to this current book (although he does discuss pollution, solar energy, and the need for resource innovation along these lines).[2]

---

[2] Although Rostow (1971) did cite the word "hegemony" in six places in *Politics and the Stages of Growth*, in relation to potential or actual Mediterranean, German, Asian, and/or US hegemony, he did not link hegemonic process specifically to long waves. In this book, he briefly discusses issues relating to "cultures [being] shaped by geography and climate," but no link is given to climate change per se, or climate change *and* long waves.

3.3 Forrester's Model of Excess Capital and Bootstraps

Jay Wright Forrester (1918–2016) was a leading figure in the Club of Rome's Limits to Growth computer model, and he invented the random-access magnetic memory for computers (see Eklund 1980, 405–6). His analysis of long waves was undertaken in his capacity as Germeshausen Professor at the Systems Dynamic Group, Alfred P. Sloan School of Management, MIT, and represents a continuation of his research on *Industrial Dynamics* (1961), *Principles of Systems* (1968), *Urban Dynamics* (1969) and *World Dynamics* (1973).

The Systems Dynamic Group National Model was structured as a computer simulation model of economic and social change in the United States for public policy purposes. It includes six main sectors: production, labor, demography, finance, households, and government, with all sectors being aggregated to form an overall macro model, after interconnections with factors such as money, goods, services, orders, expectations, affluence, technology, labor mobility, and associated feedback mechanisms. He noted that "Systems dynamics is a way of combining all available information, including written description and personal experience, with computer simulation to yield a better understanding of social systems" (Forrester 1976, 52).

The National Model analyzes longer-run issues such as "economic growth, resources, energy, population, and capital investment as well as the shorter-term dynamics of the business cycle and economic stabilization policies" (Forrester 1976, 52). The system does not proceed initially with abstract theory, but with numerical information, later augmented by written description, theory, feedback (for selection and filter), and eventually with computer simulation to analyze the complicated data for determining interactions and changing patterns of behavior. The broad "information base," the "fully dynamic disequilibrium" approach, the relations illustrated between short, medium, and long-term phenomena, the emphasis on "policy" rather than "decision making," and the generation of change from endogenous (not exogenous) factors make the model especially relevant to long *cycles*.

The model is built on sectors, including capital goods, consumer durables, energy, agriculture, and building construction, where each sector possesses behavior incorporating "a typical firm" of the respective industry in question. Forrester notes that production processes are being "represented" in detail especially vis-à-vis inputs into industries being determined or simulated from inventories, prices, costs, order backlogs, growth rates, marginal productivities, liquidity, profitability, return on investment, accounting systems, and a market clearing function (that normally does not clear in the short-to-medium run). Labor mobility, banking, monetary authority, government, and households are included in the model to approximate the concrete workings of the economy. The critical thing about the model is that the resulting macroeconomic totality is built from microeconomic interactions, rather than being a purely aggregate model of GNP, prices, and employment. The long- and short-term forces incorporated in the system enable it to deal with the variable behavioral patterns corresponding to dynamics associated with the short economic cycle (3–7 years), intermediate cycles (15–50 years), and the life cycle of systemic economic development (200 years or more): a research task that has some similarities with Schumpeter's model. An important point is that the National Model was not initially concerned with the pattern of long waves, since:

> In fact, I was unaware of the [']scant['] literature on the long wave while we were initially formulating the model. But when we assembled a consumer durable sector ... [and a] capital equipment [sector], ...the model exhibited strong fluctuating growth and collapse in the capital sector with about 50 years between peaks of capital output. ... When such unexpected behavior is encountered in a simulation model, the prudent investigator first questions the structure and plausibility of the model. ... In the early stages, anomalous behavior often points to dubious assumptions in model structure. After we analyzed the reasons for the 50-year [wave] in the National Model, we concluded that the underlying assumptions [were] reasonable. It was only then that the literature on the Kondratiev cycle became a part of the investigation. ... [T]he National Model now provides a theory of how the economic long wave is generated. [Forrester 1981, 325–326]

Such a theory is based on three core factors: capital goods growth, "bootstraps" and related structures, plus uncertainty. In this context, firstly, long cycles are endogenously determined by the nature of expansion of the capital goods sector, and, more especially, due to the interaction between capital and consumer goods sectors. Buildup, overexpansion, and the relative decline of the capital or means of production sector are the essential characteristics (and dynamic) of the long cycle. Technological change is not primary in the determination of these cycles, and long waves have been both theorized and simulated in the model without technological innovation. However, since the expansion of the capital goods sector is embodied in both capital deepening and widening, a changing technological structure is an important form of sectoral growth.

Secondly, if demand for means of production increases suddenly, inventions are said to become moderated, prices begin to rise, and q, the relationship between the prospective yield from investing in capital goods (P) and the supply price of that investment (S), $q = P/S$, increases, resulting eventually in an increased supply of capital. If this increased demand for means of production is derived from the consumer goods sector, then the means of satisfying consumer demand in the long run is to use more capital goods to move closer to the new "optimum" capital stock. The means of production sector is thus being "pulled up by its own bootstraps," and the increasing value of q results initially in less capital being supplied to the consumer sector in response to the demand for more (so that demand for capital goods can be supplied). These "bootstrap structures," mechanisms ignored in the simple supply–demand curves, are destabilizing factors and tend to lengthen considerably from 20 to 50 years the cycle of capital acquisition, and hence provide a central mechanism for producing long cycles. These long cycles are unstable in nature since the oscillation is promoted rather than dampened after a small source of change.

Thirdly, an assumption of the National Model is that change is something economic agents do not usually quickly respond to. Time delays between a change in economy, and adjustment of economic agents to that change, is a core factor influencing dynamics. Especially important is the relationship between the marginal productivities of the "factors of production," (§F), and the marginal productivities perceived by decision-makers (§P), §F/§P, as this strongly impacts on lags by adjusting investment over long time periods.

Expectations of economic growth is a core variable in the National Model, where expectations are based on past rates (with recent rates having more weight than previous rates), and where adjustments of perceptions to the workings of the economy take considerable time. Such delays in the decision process tend to promote *disequilibrium* rather than a strong, speedy movement toward equilibrium at the sectoral and macroeconomic levels.

The most important dynamic and descriptive components of the model are the interactions ("loops," positive and negative feedback) affecting capital and consumer goods sectors, due to, for instance, an initial random fluctuation in consumer demand. Figure 3.1, below, shows the major interrelations between these two sectors, where long cycles are the result of the interwoven workings of the primary factors—bootstrap structures, uncertainty, and related processes. Increasing consumer demand, as noted above, stimulates orders for more capital, which is produced in the capital goods sector by denying the consumer goods sector normal periodic supply, which increases further the demand for capital; the tendency of the capital sector to demand more from itself thus continues. Only after a long, lagged process is the initial demand satisfied, but by this time the capital sector is vastly overextended, which provides the basis for contraction.

Figure 3.2 shows this extended CCC destabilizing process as to why the periodization of long waves occurs in the extended manner suggested.

Six processes, as indicated by the six loops, are important for the promotion of the capital goods sector, given an initial increase in consumer goods demand. Higher demand in the consumer sector promotes demand for more capital so that consumer items can be produced to satisfy demand. This increases both desired production of capital and desired capital stock, with the result that the capital sector pulls itself up by its own bootstraps, which reduces the supply of capital to the consumer goods sector (initially). This process is then repeated (Loop A). In the process inventories of capital are reduced drastically which itself also adds to desired production and the capital stock (Loop B). Meanwhile, there is a backlog of unfilled orders in the capital sector which reinforces these tendencies (Loop C). Since demand for capital

Fig. 3.1 Capital and consumer goods sectors in Forrester's model. (Source: Adapted from Graham and Senge 1980, 285)

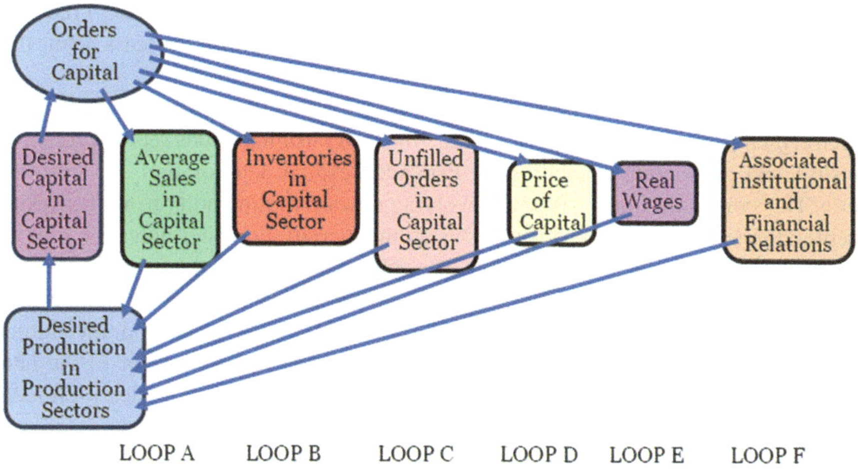

Fig. 3.2 CCC bootstraps and related mechanisms/processes. (Source: Adapted and Extended from Graham and Senge 1980)

exceeds supply by a substantial amount, the price of capital increases, as also does the value of q, the relation between the prospective yield and supply price (or the ratio of market share price/interest), and these changes propel capital investment, capital stock, and capital production (Loop D). As the demand for capital increases substantially, the economy gets closer to full employment, and therefore the real wage of labor (especially in the capital sector) rises, along with rising general prices. This motivates capitalists to increase the capital/labor ratio to reduce costs, and the subsequent increased demand for labor-saving capital reinforces the expansion of production, capital stock, and prices (Loop E). Throughout this entire complex process, financial institutions rely on the institutionally acceptable growth of the capital sector, and thus become "locked into" the dynamics of the process through *path dependency*, thus aiding the process of capital growth further (Loop F). Hence the basis of the long cyclical expansionary long wave through circular and cumulative causation (CCC).

Eventually, the demands of the consumer goods sector are met and the supply of capital to that sector continues. In time, the capital goods sector overexpands beyond the demands of intersectoral equilibrium, due to the "deviation amplifying," CCC nature of its growth, and the lags between actual demand for capital goods and business expectations of demand. The rate of growth of capital demand falls off through the reverse effects of the multifarious CCC processes described above. The lower demand for capital reduces the desired capital stock in both sectors; reduced demand for labor increases unemployment; lower real wages eventually reduce the capital–labor ratio; falling capital demand increases inventories which reduces delivery delays; prices of capital goods decrease which dampens further the desired capital stock and investment in the capital sector, as the value of q declines; and the associated changes in the desirability of financial institutions to lend to the capital sector (plus the reduced ability and effective desire of business to borrow money) reduces the financial interlock in the capital growth process. The extended process forms the basis of the CCC long cyclical downturn.

The "suddenness" or "sharpness" of the reduced investment in the capital goods sector, plus the intersectoral linkages affecting the consumer goods sector, promotes insufficient production capacity after expanded capital deterioration and destruction. This constitutes the basis of the evolving upward turning point from recession/depression to long wave expansion. During this period, Forrester notes the importance of new technological innovation, as a subsidiary factor in the overall analysis. He theorized that different technologies are involved in each successive long cycle, and that they occur in "bunches" during late depression–early expansion. Inventions and improvements in knowledge during the three decades or so prior to the late depression can be utilized, since the endogenous mechanism provides a climate consistent with the replacement of the old capital with many new basic processes and products, while bootstraps and associated psychology enable the transformation of technical production relations and productivity.

For instance, "the period of late depression and early upswing following the Great Depression of the 1930s ... produced nylon, jet airplanes, helicopters, electronic computation, radar, television, catalytic petroleum, refining and many other important innovations" (Graham and Senge 1980, 291). During the middle of the upswing, the 1950s and 1960s, when many technologies became institutionalized, "basic" innovation is said to give way to improvement innovation, as the dynamics of the upswing promote only modest novelty in the technological structure. Innovation rigidity is then said to set in because the new dominant technological base has formed institutional relationships, especially social acceptance, technological associations with dominant energy forms, intersectoral production linkages, plus government financial backing. The time from "rigidity" to the upper turning point, approximately 13 years (one-quarter of a complete cycle), represents years of building upon the production base of the capital, consumer, transport, communications, energy, financial, and technological requirements of the new cycle. Eventually, as noted above, the capital stock is oversupplied, because the dynamics that promoted the long upswing come up against a structural limit. As Forrester said:

> For more than a decade, from 1965 to 1978, physical capital [was] forced into many … economies beyond the point where capital earns an adequate return. But such growing investment in the face of falling incentive[s] cannot continue indefinitely. Eventually, an excess rate of capital construction saturates the need for more capital plant. Such excess capacity on a worldwide basis is now appearing in steel production, shipping, diesel-engine manufacture, synthetical textile fibers, chemicals, electronics, and automobiles. [Forrester 1981, 327]

The theory behind the model, as it explains long waves, has been subject to some criticism. Delbeke (1981) suggests that his model is only quasi-endogenous, because the role of the consumer goods sector is underdetermined; it is too passive vis-à-vis the capital goods sector. He argues that the model is hence too mechanical, "although the results are spectacular." Eklund (1980) reinforces this criticism by arguing that "the model is little more than a formalized version of Kondratiev's thesis concerning the life of durable fixed capital, or a lagged 'echo effect,' where one intense period of investment in capital goods with a long, set, lifetime, is sufficient to produce periodic long swings as these investments are replaced, successively" (1980, 408).

The criticism concerning the underdetermination of the model with respect to the consumer goods sector seems to be true. This suggests that Forrester should have included in the theory factors originating from the consumer-goods side of the economy, such as (1) migration, (2) population growth, (3) new territorial conquests or colonies, (4) radical changes in tastes (whether under conditions of consumer or producer sovereignty), (5) changes in wealth, inflation expectations, normal income and interest rates in the consumption function, (6) the importance of the agricultural sector, and (7) important fluctuations of the luxury goods sector (in an expanded, three sector model).

These factors have not been adequately examined in the published work of the National Model, though many of them were supposedly included in the initial model. This highlights the dichotomy between the theories of Rostow and Forrester. The seven consumer goods variables are critical "exogenous-type determinants" of changes in economic activity, which relate to exogenous and endogenous theories. Furthermore, (8) the complicated bootstraps process of the capital goods sector may well also develop in the consumer goods sector. The Forrester theory has its merits, especially if further justification can be given to the "under-dynamics" of the consumer goods sector.

The second criticism, "that the model only shows what has been called the 'echo-phenomenon'" is also important. An echo effect does form part of the model, but the analysis goes beyond this factor through the introduction of the bootstraps effect, related forces, and uncertainty. Forrester interrelates the multiplier-accelerator model with a complicated capital stock adjustment mechanism in a sophisticated inquiry into the dominant role that capital plays in macroeconomics. It is hardly based exclusively on an echo effect because, firstly, as Forrester himself noted, "discussions [of the echo-phenomena] usually imply that the life of capital equipment is relevant to long cycles only if 'life' is sharply defined and if 'life' is the same as the period of the cycle. Neither is necessary" (1977, 534). He goes on to say that the average life of fixed capital is 15 years, whereas long waves occur in periods of 40–60 years, which means that the overall periodicity of the system deviates greatly from the behavior of individual capitalists and the strict shorter cycles of capital.

A more important, third criticism concerns the role of technology in Forrester's model. Eklund (1980) suggests that technology is his primary factor, but that he has not provided proof concerning the dynamic role it plays in the wave process. Eklund's position is likely anomalous since Forrester has determined cycles of long periodicity without technology being included either in the theory or the simulation model. Nevertheless, even as a secondary factor a specific hypothesis must be analyzed vis-à-vis a qualitative analysis of the wave phenomena. But further, since capital goods development and intersectoral growth is embodied in new technology, during critical phases of the wave, it is hypothesized that, in this context, technology does require a more detailed analysis as a core factor. In Forrester's system, the following represent his supporting empirical conditions on the question of technology:

1. During the late years of the long contraction, capital is worn out, or becomes obsolete, and is subsequently replaced by innovation because the institutional stability of the old methods of production has been negated.
2. Then radical basic innovations become established, promoting for a time sustained and reasonably stable growth of the existing economic structure. Then these basic innovations on a large scale give way to improvement innovations near the 12- to 13-year point of the long expansion.
3. Improvement innovations give way to technological stagnation as symptoms of capital sector overproduction appear.

Few wave theorists would question these three points (although the timing of basic innovations may be variably different). But Forrester's theory, the most mechanistic of them all, must especially provide explanations about these crucial technology issues. The study of various sectors, accumulation, and the rate of profit is generally quite adequate, but, in view of the importance of technology in his theory (noted above) it does appear extreme to suggest that cycles have been simulated with no change in the methods of production or consumer goods, especially without explaining this in detail. We therefore agree with Delbeke (1981, 25) when he says that Forrester has neglected some of the "special dynamics that technological change can generate."

Most importantly, Forrester tends to abstract from some of the dominant institutional spheres affecting long wave motion, as well as hegemony and climate change. More specifically, as we show further below, a comprehensive analysis of long wave motion must be placed in the historical context of the late 1700s through to the 2000s, or further back to the 1500s, with a properly assessed interaction between the technological, institutional, and geo-spatial-climatological elements fully included in the model. Forrester's model is an important but obviously limited view of the total historical, contextual, socioeconomic, and political elements required for a total view of long waves as phases of evolution and performance of varieties of capitalism through historical time. In this context, below, we study the neo-Marxian and neo-Schumpeterian long wave theories, some of which have a much better inclusion of these historical, technological, and institutional elements affecting phases and performance of capitalism. We start with Ernest Mandel, below.

3.4 Mandel's Rate of Profit and Endogenous-Exogenous Variables

Ernest Ezra Mandel (1923–1995) developed a theory of long waves which is a continuation of the Trotsky-Kondratiev debate and Schumpeterian concerns in a more recent setting. Mandel mentions long waves in the context of the postwar boom and its likely aftermath, in the *Socialist Register* (Mandel 1964). His theory of waves was first espoused in *Der Spatkapitalismus* in 1972 (English edition, *Late Capitalism*, Mandel 1975), then in the less theoretical work, *The Second Slump* (1978), and the Marshall lectures given at the University of Cambridge (*Long Waves of Capitalist Development*, Mandel 1980) and much elsewhere, for instance, as a contribution to an issue of *Futures* (1981), where many major long wave theorists (except Rostow) and others exchanged ideas; and in a collective volume (Mandel 1992) committed to providing new findings of long wave empirics and theory.

Central to Mandel's theory is the thesis that long waves need to be understood by an investigation of a relatively concrete analysis of the "many capitals in competition" at the level of the world market. To study long waves properly, we should thus examine the dynamic workings and modification of the dynamics of capitalism as they manifest in the *world market*—the last stage of Marx's method of successive approximation (Oakley 1983; O'Hara 2016). Thus, it must eschew statics, a constant economic structure, and strict determinism, and center on a global analysis of capitalism, the dynamic interplay of exogenous and endogenous factors over time, and the movement between different areas and nations in uneven development.

Mandel rejects the idea shared by Kondratiev, Schumpeter, Forrester, and Mensch (see next section), that waves are activated by strictly deterministic variables, such as the life of durable fixed capital or radical innovation. Rather, he considers that the upper turning point is explained endogenously, while the lower turning point is largely exogenously determined. Mandel's theory has one element in common with Rostow, namely, a degree of exogeneity. But Mandel's theory is more sophisticated than Rostow's, due to an emphasis on the rate of profit, accumulation, and the organic composition of capital.

First, on the question of the commencement of the expansionary phase of the long wave, Mandel (1980, 21–22) notes that the wave needs to incorporate many of the concrete forms, many capitals, and contradictions of capitalist development in a given environment. This implies a whole series of factors such as wars of conquest, extensions and contradictions of the area of capitalist operation, inter-capitalist competition, class struggle, revolution and counter-revolution, etc. These changes in the overall social and geographical environment in which the capitalist mode of production operates in turn detonate, so to speak, upheavals in the basic variables of capitalist growth.

Mandel thus disagrees with Kondratiev, de Wolff, and Forrester (in an extended model) that the life of fixed capital per se will explain the long wave. He also disagrees with Trotsky (without emphasizing this himself) that the curve of capitalist growth is too uneven to be called a wave. For Mandel, an analysis in terms of the capitalist mode of production in its pure form is not sufficient for understanding these waves in their totality; one must investigate thoroughly the complex workings of the capitalist socio-politico-economic formation. A pure study of capitalism will help explain the downturn but, according to Mandel, certainly not an upturn, because that can only be explained by concrete capitalist dynamics as a totality. In other words, capitalist development needs radical "innovations," novelties, reorganizations, interventions, revolutions, and wars, outside its inner motion, to propel it into new waves of transformation. I agree with Mandel on this crucial point, as do some others, but in a slightly different context of the circuits of socioeconomic dynamics (CSD).

The basic economics in his theory include all those factors that make up the average rate of profit: defined as $\pi = \acute{\alpha}(1 - \beta)$, where π=rate of profit; $\acute{\alpha}$=rate of surplus value; and β=organic composition of capital. Mandel follows Marx in postulating that the rate of profit is the dominant determinant of the level of economic activity, as well as being itself influenced by the concrete forces of capitalist growth. Speaking more narrowly, the major determinate forces, according to this approach, propelling growth and development, are the production, circulation, distribution, realization, and utilization of surplus value and, more particularly, the relationship between the rate of surplus value and the organic composition of capital:

> The emphasis [I] place ... on the rate of profit is not the monocausal equivalent of the theory of fixed capital or the entrepreneur, since [I] argue ... that the average rate of profit can precipitate a change in the way in which the system grows or does not grow, and "reflects the system's overall modus operandi" [pp. 181, 335]. The average rate of profit is therefore thought to be a generalized variable which encapsulates the dominant over-all changes in the capitalist world economy. In relation to the rate of surplus value and the organic composition of capital, the main factors which determine [a rising] rate of profit [include:] [Mandel 1975, 115]

1. A sudden fall in the average organic composition of capital, for example, [due to a] massive penetration of capital into spheres (or countries) with a very low organic composition.
2. A sudden increase in the rate of surplus-value, as a result, for example, of a rise in the intensity of labor due to a radical defeat and atomization of the working class which ... forces it to sell [labor power] below its value even in a period of economic prosperity.
3. A sudden fall in the price of elements of constant capital [and hence the organic composition of capital], especially of raw materials [energy; and especially] ... fixed capital ... due to a revolutionary advance in the productivity of the [means of production sector].
4. A sudden [increase in] the turnover-time of circulating capital due to perfection of new systems of transport and communications, improved methods of distribution, accelerated rotation of stock, and so on. [Mandel 1975, 115.]

Mandel argues that, at the trough of the wave, forces at work broadly necessitate a rapid rise in the rate of profit, whereas in the expansion forces endogenous to the system promote a fall in the rate of profit. Given suitable changes in many of these factors, 1–4, investment is initially promoted at the trough via, it is argued, free funds which accumulate within corporations during preceding business cycles, and only after such free funds have been accumulating for five, six, or seven (7–10 year) cycles are there enough funds for radical technological innovation. The initial increase in the rate of profit thus provides the basis for the productive investment of free funds, and therefore Mandel's theoretical proof of the operation of qualitatively different successive waves rests fundamentally on the free funds theory (see further below).

With an increase in the average rate of profit, subsequent technological innovation (capital deepening), and a general accumulation of capital (capital widening), both of which reduce average costs of production, a period of long wave expansion is set in motion at the macroeconomic level. Profit rates may be high for an extended period, partly through migration increasing the supply of labor power and further dampening (along with labor-saving technology) the wage rate. While large-scale international migration of labor power "generally accompany expansionary long waves throughout the history of capitalism" (1981, 337), a factor Rostow also emphasized, Mandel notes that, since capital is more mobile than labor, the movement of labor cannot occur without limit, and hence eventually the rate of surplus value falls.

The dominant reason for the falling rate of profit is the rising organic composition of capital through the massive level of accumulation during the upswing. Hence the drop in the average rate of profit (and the turning point from boom to recession) is due to a decline in the ratio of profits to total invested capital, resulting from a disproportionate rise in that part of capital spent on equipment and raw materials as against that spent on wages (1981, 337), while the rate of surplus value declines or is kept constant (or the rise in the organic composition is greater than the rise in surplus value). The upper turning point (from long wave upswing to downswing) is thus largely endogenous, while the lower turning point (from long wave downswing to upswing) is primarily exogenous, since a whole series of changes are required to provide a new set of potentiality underlying growth and accumulation (1981, 338).

There are significant problems with Mandel's system. One is the view of Delbeke (1981) that it is too supply-orientated, and that his emphasis on the average rate of profit rising suddenly as a prelude to the upswing underemphasizes the possibility of the profit rate rising in a few leading sectors, only gradually increasing the rate in other, related sectors. Rowthorn (1980) takes Mandel to task for his "reserve fund" (loanable funds) theory of investment, discussed earlier, which tends to underrate the growing importance of credit as a means of financing investment during the trough and upswing. This critique is a substantial one and accords with our own view of money and credit as largely endogenously generated via state and corporation (especially through "financial innovation" as well as government/reserve bank action).

A crucial criticism from Rowthorn is that Mandel over-emphasizes the organic composition of capital (proxied by the capital-output ratio) in the movement from one portion of the wave to another. Rowthorn suggests that the post-1970 contractionary phase of the wave was due more to a fall in the proportion of output going to profits than to a higher capital value in the production process. The studies by Nordhaus (1974), Glyn and Sutcliffe (1972) and, more generally, a neo-Ricardian-Marxist perspective, tend to negate Mandel's emphasis on the organic composition, and because the organic composition may rise in some and fall in other sectors, resulting in the falls outweighing the rises during the upward turning point. Kleinknecht (1981a), on the other hand, adds weight to Mandel's argument concerning the tendency for the organic composition to rise over the range of the downturn (see Mandel 1978 for his critique of neo-Ricardians).

The rate of profit is important to long wave analysis, in terms of performance measures, to complement phases of evolution of capitalism. Long wave scholars of various persuasions tend to concur with this, such as, apart from those mentioned, Louçã (2019, 2021), Anwar Shaikh (1992), and Louis Fontvielle (1992), to mention just a few. In this context, whether the organic composition is important is mainly an empirical question, as shown above with different conclusions. My own studies in this current book (e.g., see Chaps. 6–8, below) and other outlets show profit rate and organic compositions to be important for long wave analysis, although such data is often not available before 1870–1930. (Although Rowthorn was likely correct regarding the period and nation(s) he examined.)

Crucial is Mandel's analysis of the average rate of profit, especially in the movement from trough to recovery. Eklund (1980) notes, for instance, that the emphasis he places on the average rate of profit results in the blurring of the difference between endogenous and exogenous factors. He considers the average rate of profit to be a conglomerate variable that includes the net effect of certain variables—primary, secondary, and tertiary—and that it begs the question of the nature of any mechanism. Day (1976) isolates the real problem as a confusion in Mandel's mind between Trotsky and Kondratiev: he suggests that Mandel wants to agree with both, in certain respects, when this is not possible because Trotsky rejected long waves and Kondratiev argued they were completely endogenously determined (cycles). I can appreciate the conundrum Day mentions, but if one is "in-between" Trotsky and Kondratieff one can surely agree with certain aspects of each. For instance, the *current* work is closer to Trotsky given our critique of the standard model, but I heap praise on Kondratieff as an innovator, a great scholar, and one who we take as a critical point of departure.

We noted earlier that Trotsky, who was an important influence on Mandel's thought, rejected the operation of waves or cycles of a long-term nature, because of the uneven nature of the evolution of the capitalist curve of development. Development was neither smooth nor predictable. Kondratiev, on the other hand, as shown above, thought cycles were "most probable." Mandel attempts to resolve the issue by suggesting that "long waves," "long cycles," and "the capitalist curve of development" are purely semantic differences. Hence his conclusion that exogenous factors prevent the waves from exhibiting a "natural necessity" of high order, but that, after all, a basic rhythm still operates (at least until the downswing).

This current book seeks to examine the long wave hypothesis as potentially representing phases of capitalist development and performance measures of capitalism through a long historical time. We agree with Trotsky that the curve of capitalist development is complex and partially indeterminate or difficult to predict. We reject Kondratieff's and Schumpeter's position that these waves are cycles, with well-formed dynamics. This whole question is well represented by what I call *The Long Wave Scholarship Quadrant* (see Fig. 3.3).

This quadrant posits the principle of various wave/cycle/curve/evolution scholars/schools having differing perspectives on the number of systems and subsystems

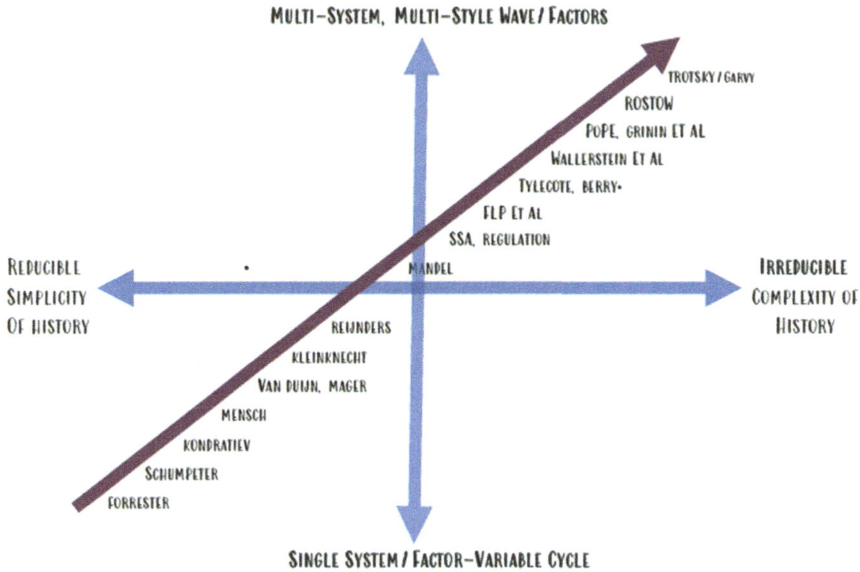

Fig. 3.3 Long cycle-wave-curve-evolution scholarship quadrant. Key: Progressive arrow from long cycle to long wave to evolution-curve analysis. NOTE: *FLP* Freeman, Louçã, Perez (et al.)

plus the degree of simplicity/complexity of history incorporated into their "models" of long-term change of capitalism. This ranges from Trotsky and Garvy's view that history is too complex and subject to so many sub-systems that the long-term motion of capitalism cannot be viewed as a cycle or wave; to Forrester's view of some sub-systems and limited history that easily fits into aspects of the standard model. In between these extremes are numerous wave/cycle scholars who recognize that even though capitalism is subject to numerous systems and sub-systems and varying degrees of historical complexity, it is still open to the perspective of being a wave or a cycle. For some, such as Rostow, a long trend is very broadly defined when subject to a large degree of the irreducible complexity of history. For others, such as Kondratieff and Schumpeter, even given such a modest degree of complexity and sub-system inclusion, the cycle term is very much appropriate. Others such as Freeman, Louçã, and Perez follow in the footsteps of Schumpeter, but add fresh impulses from regulation, Mandelian, and other influences, taking a qualitative-historical view of phases and performance (as "waves").

A priori we accept neither Kondratiev's nor Trotsky's propositions (although the latter is closer to the mark), but tentatively accept conceptually the general framework of exogenous-endogenous factors suggested by Mandel, even if he does "fudge Kondratiev and Trotsky," in terms of the degree of complexity of the analysis. However he does not specifically link his analysis of waves to hegemony, the role of institutions, and geo-spatial-climate change as we do. We do have caveats about Mandel's more technical analysis, however, as mentioned above. Overall, we follow the general prescriptions of Garvy, who hoped the future of this sort of inquiry would have fewer preconceptions about the empirical record and be more flexible about the evolutionary path of capitalism.

Overall, Mandel is a much more important wave scholar than Rostow and Forrester. While his theory may have anomalies, especially concerning his limited specific discussion of institutions and climate (vis-à-vis the theories discussed later in this chapter), he raised crucial questions about a whole range of issues, concerning the nature and source of upswings and downswings, the rate of profit, technological change, and phases of evolution of capitalism. And in his very last major article on long waves (Mandel 1992), he posited the notion that is crucial to this current book, that long waves and hegemonies tend to be structurally aligned, with British wave upswings and hegemonic power being codetermined while their hegemony demise and wave downswings are also coevolutionary. The same applies to the United States. In this context, he was not surprised that long wave downswing has continued for decades and is likely to continue along those lines into the future (i.e., into the 2000s and beyond). Otherwise, however, he kept to the standard model's periodicity despite the evidence against much of it.

In this context, our empirical investigations of the long wave throughout this book (Chaps. 5–8) accept the basic Mandelian proposition that long waves do not undergo an upswing automatically and require quite complex processes to undergo a new phase of evolution of capitalism, to promote certain performance measures to ensure better performance than during the previous downswing. But once in motion a new phase combined with improved performance (upswing; phase A of a long wave) eventually comes to a halt, leading to downswing (phase B of long wave) as the potentiality of the structures exhausts themselves from their own contradictions. Of course, the theory of long waves in this current book is different from that of Mandel, so the endogenous forces ensuring downswing from long wave upswings are also somewhat different from his; but the basis process is very similar.

Hence, long waves I believe do endogenously move from upswing to downswing as the contradictions rise and potentialities fall, but they require quite substantial reconstructions of institutions, technologies, hegemonies, and eco-geo-climatic conditions and responses to generate new long wave upswings. Given that long waves correspond to capitalist dynamics (and possibly other systems), the rate of profit (broadly defined and determined) is an important factor along with investment, consumption, government spending, and net exports (as well as innovations) in determining the degree of long-term performance. In this context, we call our approach the *principles of political economy (PoPE) contingency paradigm*, as mentioned, due to the inclusion of various sub-systems of capitalism's institutional, technological, and climatological evolution and hegemonic transformation through phases of differential performance matrices and the nine core principles.

3.5 Mensch's Metamorphosis Model

Gerhard Mensch's (1937–2021) theory is an obvious extension of Schumpeter's, since he places emphasis on conjunctures providing clusters of technological innovation during depressions for renewed growth and development. He first devised the theory in *Stalemate in Technology* (1975 in German; English 1979), that 1886 and 1935 represent transitional years between the "stalemate" of technology, when existing process and product lines go beyond their capacity to promote institutional revolution (or disequilibrium growth) and the "phase of new clusters" of technology which provides the basis for structural change and further development. The creation of new sectors in these years is said to be promoted by new internal markets, which enable further product and process innovation, and later external markets, while eventually markets mature and become exhausted, resulting in new sectors and products for further growth and evolution of the capitalist economy.

Once in the position of stalemate, again, only suitably abrupt technological innovations are said to negate depression. During the stalemate "pseudo-innovations" ("improvement changes" in product lines), low investment and reorganization (crisis) occur; but during the "clustering," the marginal efficiency of capital rises, with the economy later surging away from depression toward recovery and boom for an extended time. Mensch follows Schumpeter in emphasizing the role of innovation in the evolutionary process, which led him to emphasize the propensity to invest. As Mensch et al. (1981, 276) note:

> We share the view of many economists that, at the heart of … long-term industrial fluctuations, lie some unexpected, yet patterned appreciations and depreciations of certain parts of the capital stock, and subsequent changes in the propensity of capital owners to either invest further in these existing kinds of capital good, or to invest in alternative means of production. [Mensch et al. 1981, 276]

Important here are the marginal efficiencies of capital and, although they suggest the processes of capital widening and deepening are patterned, Mensch and his followers deviate from the Schumpeterian schema in some areas. Schumpeter's theory was based on (dis)equilibrium, the entrepreneurial innovator, and the long period, whereas Mensch proceeds from "nonequilibrium" (an important difference), economic and environmental factors influencing innovation, and a "metamorphosis model" (not waves as such).

Mensch rejects Schumpeter's (dis)equilibrium model in favor of sectoral analysis where different industries may be in *nonequilibrium* simultaneously, with no long-run trend to macro-Walrasian equilibrium. He also suggests (rightly) that Schumpeter provided no real theoretical understanding of the "clusters of innovation" besides the tautological entrepreneur model, and certainly elaborated little on why clusters "appear" in specific periods, regularly and in cyclical form. In working toward an endogenous formulation, Mensch et al. derived their central hypothesis thus:

> That, under certain circumstances (… typical of either expansionist or recessional structural change), entrepreneurs find that their stocks of fixed capital in plant and equipment either

> enjoy or suffer systematic up or down-grading in operative value (appreciation or depreciation). These shifts in value of part of the capital stock induce capital owners to either invest their funds in more of the same types of capital goods or induce them to invest in alternative types of capital goods. … [T]his behavioural theory of the propensity to invest [is called] the contingency theory of capital valuation. [Mensch et al. 1981, 282]

Associated with this are the following five empirical hypotheses:

1. During "prolonged recessional structural change" economies become structurally ready for "basic" innovations, which then evolve.
2. Following the clustering of "basic" innovations, diffusion of product and process innovation drive the economy into growth cycles.
3. Over time, process innovations will substitute for marginal product innovations.
4. These process and product "improvement innovations" give way to "pseudo-innovation," and growth levels decline (after the rate of investment declines in these dominant sectors).
5. Basic innovations increase and the economic regime changes in particular ways, e.g. when producer sovereignty is promoted in older industries.

It has been suggested that Mensch's framework is mono-causal (based on "clusters"); that it underestimates the role of demand; and that the "theory" lacks an adequate set of analyses/categories for identifying (or differentiating) the basic and improvement innovations (Delbeke 1981, 249–50); that he confuses the "depression trigger effect" of innovation during the 1930s with what was really a "pre-war armament process" (van Duijn 1981, 274), that his hypothesis concerning the reduced lag between invention and innovation during the "cluster period" was empirically unfounded (Clark et al. 1981, 312), and that his procedure for selecting innovations to justify the "depression trigger hypothesis" was unsound (Kleinknecht 1981b, 291).

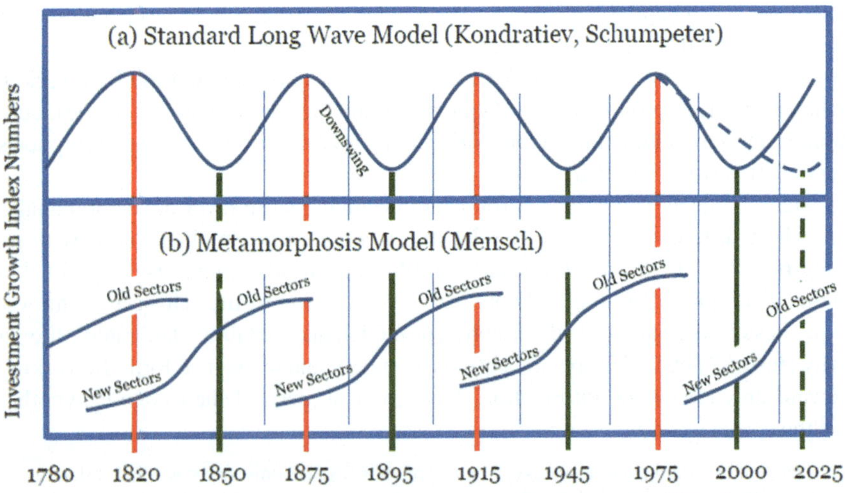

Fig. 3.4 Standard Long wave model vs. Mensch's metamorphosis model. (Source: Adapted from Mensch 1975, 73; Mensch et al. 1981, 277) (stylized)

There is, however, as suggested above, some evidence to suggest that there was a bunching of innovation during the 1930s. Kleinknecht (1981b, 294), for instance, noted that both the risk and the incentive to invest in basic innovation during prosperous times may be low because demand for established lines is strong; hence improvement innovations may dominate during prosperity and radical (process and product) innovations may dominate depressionary times, because in the latter period, there may be (1) decreasing returns to further mere improvements in mature products, (2) overcapacity in existing product lines, and (3) the *chance* for temporary monopoly profits in a new field. (This issue is analyzed further later.)

In this context, see Fig. 3.4 on the relationship between his "metamorphosis model," and the "standard model of long waves" hypothesized by Kondratiev, Schumpeter, and others:

Ideally, the Kondratiev cycle is more cyclical/wave-like and continuous than the metamorphosis model where economic evolution is abrupt and undergoes structural change. Mensch puts special emphasis on the relationship between different sectors of the economy more than most long wave theories, as did Schumpeter, Rostow and Forrester to some degree, although all long wave scholars introduce some subsystems. As Mensch, Coutinho and Kaasch note, "If long waves exist, they are changing trends in structural change, and not mere fluctuations in the level of production prices" (1981, 279), which sounds very similar to Schumpeter and Rostow. In a sense the analysis of different sectors provides a potential significant theoretical breakthrough which may give better insights into economic evolution than the original form of the hypothesis which postulated "trend-cycle" deviations, even if innovations tend to occur later in the wave than Mensch et al. indicated.

Mensch's idea of sectoral changes and the emergence of new inventions being eventually transformed into innovations, through swarms of new product, process, market, raw material, and competition forms of novelty, has become a standard principle of neo-Schumpeterian political economy. Numerous scholars adapt neo-Schumpeterian principles to long waves and establish a post-Schumpeterian lone wave school of thought or paradigm (e.g., Chris Freeman, Fernando Louçã, and Carlotta Perez). They tend to condone some of Mensch's analysis, since Freeman et al. (1982, 63) agree with clustering; but do not think basic innovations cluster systematically during depressions (contra Mensch 1975 and Kleinknecht 1987). For instance, some evidence suggests clustering tends to occur *after* the deep depression phase (e.g., during the late 1930s onwards). Instead (see, e.g., Freeman et al. 1982), there is evidence firms reduce R&D and patenting during severe depressions, while there is a decline in basic innovations during late booms in the wave. In the next section we examine scholarly innovations developed by the post-Schumpeterian school of long wave scholars following on from Mensch.

3.6 Freeman, Louçã, Perez, *et al.*: Techno-Economic Paradigms and Social-Political Institutions

Christopher Freeman and Francisco Louçã (2001) provide a comprehensive history of long waves of capitalism from 1780 to 2000 (from the perspective of the standard model). They include details on all the other major technological and socioeconomic spheres involving every wave during this period. In doing this they argue that successive long waves are phases of evolution of capitalism, that correspond to different techno-economic and socio-political processes and techniques that rise and fall throughout history. These waves are seen as qualitative transformations, with various quantitative elements, but ones that do not necessarily manifest in waves of majorly rising and falling real economic activity. Rather, the long waves tend to represent successive industrial revolutions, associated with socio-political changes during the upswings, followed by downswings characterized by structural crises of adjustment (SCA) to new conditions, techniques, and processes. Upswings and downswings are not deterministic but represent evolutionary processes of nonequilibrium, path-dependent, emergent, and contradictory phases of capitalism.

Freeman and Louçã (2001) situate successive, standard, long waves since the 1780s within six socioeconomic sub-systems, as outlined in Table 3.1:

Central to Freeman and Louçã's ("F&L") long wave analysis is that during the upswing in each wave the "emergence, diffusion, and clustering of innovations" (p. 338) provide the potential for "immense profits" based on the quality of these novelties, with profits being the heart of these upswings during the 1780s–1810s, 1850s–1870s, 1890s–1910s, and 1940s–1970s in the core nations. The upper turning points of the waves tend to occur when the profit potentials decline, and during long wave downswings *crises of structural adjustment* occur as job skills, structural unemployment, and mobility anomalies lead to various mismatches and declining levels of general confidence and investment. Social conflicts are hypothesized to cluster around the peaks of long waves (during high upswings) and during the structural crises of adjustment during downswings (p. 369).

Crucial to the analysis of Freeman and especially Louçã (2021) is the principle that the clustering of techno-economic innovations does not necessarily lead to long wave upswing in performance, because there needs to be a match between the techno-economic and other sub-systems of the political economy. In this context, they include six sub-systems which are seen as being crucial to analyze throughout the so-called Kondratiev waves. These sub-systems include (1) science, (2) technology, (3) economy, (4) politics, (5) culture, and (6) ecology (F&L 2001, 121). Each of these sub-systems are said to have cycles, waves, and tendential trajectories, with the "coordination processes" between them being central to the historical dynamics of the capitalist system. F&L2001 recognize the importance of ecology, and movements in the "periphery" and "semi-periphery," but they usually abstract from ecological ("(6)") movements and center on the "core" (especially the US, Britain, and Europe), as a way of delimiting the scope of inquiry. In the final analysis, then, they seek to isolate five main sub-systems (science, technology, economy, politics, and

Table 3.1 Freeman & Louçã's four/five Kondratiev waves, 1780–2050(?)

	1780s–1840s (K-wave 1)	1840s–1890s (K-wave 2)	1890s–1940s (K-wave 3)	1940s–2020s? (K-wave 4)	1990s–2050s? (K-wave 5?)
Kondratiev Wave Called:	British Industrial Revolution 1	Industrial Revolution 2 in UK; later US, Germany, etc.	Taylorism, Two World Wars, and Depression	Fordism	Electronics Revolution
Age of:	Cotton, Iron & Water Power	Iron Railways, Steam Power, Mechanization, and Machine Tools	Steel, Heavy Engineering, and Electrification	Oil, Automobiles & Mass Production; Golden Growth	Information & Communications Technology (ICT)
Sub-System1: Geopolitics	Primary Accumulation	↓UK Hegemon 1880s–1890s, ↑US & Euro Powers	Scramble for Africa, Hegemonic Rivalry, Protectionism	US & European Hegemony	Global Rivalry: US-Euro vs. China-Russia
Sub-System 2: Sectors	Scientific Revolution	Rail, Steam, Mechanization	Corporate Office & Financial Revolution	Trend to Mass Primary, Secondary, & Tertiary Sectors	Microchips & Semi-Conductors
Sub-System 3: Business	Factory Production (Shopfloor Management)	Rise of Big Business & Managerial Control	Global Cartels, New Factory Organization	Mass Production & Consumption	Strategic Alliances & Networks
Sub-System 4: Policies	Laissez-faire Policy	Nationalism, Socialism	"Beggar-Thy-Neighbor" Policies	Keynesian-Welfare-Warfare State→ Neoliberalism	Neoliberalism→ Post Neoliberal Policy?
Sub-System 5: Classes	Constellation of Classes	Bourgeoisie and Landowners vs. Workers and Poor	Prof. Managers & Finance Capitalists, ↑Admin. Labor, US & Germany	Production Workers & Rising Middle Class	Not yet developed (see SCA below)

(continued)

Table 3.1 (continued)

	1780s–1840s (K-wave 1)	1840s–1890s (K-wave 2)	1890s–1940s (K-wave 3)	1940s–2020s? (K-wave 4)	1990s–2050s? (K-wave 5?)
Sub-System 6: Innovations	Textiles, Iron, Transport, Time, Capital & Consumer Goods	Shipping, Machine Tools, and Steam Engines	Radio, Telephone, Electric Motors, Typewriter, Wireless Telegraph, and Stainless Steel	Reverse Engineering, Aeronautics, Moving Assembly Line, and Consumer Appliances	Computers, Virtual Reality, Internet, Electric Vehicles, Biotechnology Telecommunications, and Internet
Structural Crises of Adjustment (SCA)	High Unemployment of 1830s & 1840s in UK	"Great Depression" of 1880s–1890s	Great Depression of 1930s	Recessions-Crises of 1974–75, 1980–82, 1987, 1991–92, 2000–[02, 2008–2012, 2020–22]	Recovery boom not yet occurred in core: socio-political institutions not yet suitable

Source: Based on O'Hara's interpretation of Freeman and Louçã (2001); Louçã (2019, 2021)

culture), and support the principle that these five sub-systems coevolve, are interdependent, and yet are also relatively autonomous, as part of the system-as-a-whole (p. 121).

Their analysis of the "First Kondratiev Wave" (as they call it), from the 1780s to the 1840s, centered on the industrial revolution in Britain. It was based on the factory production system, through innovations in the leading sectors, including textiles, iron, transportation, capital, and consumer goods, with attention given to specific "times" within the prevailing culture. Britain was a classic case of industrialization due to the ready establishment of a parliamentary-monarchist system, a broadly laissez-faire approach to policy, and the establishment of the British Empire. The invention and then application of the cotton gin, jenny, and water frame set the scene for a revolution in textile production and exports as a leading sector or carrier branch of development. Cheap iron was a core input into most sectors as it was smelted with coke instead of charcoal and became highly malleable for multiple uses. Water-powered machines, canals, turnpike roads, and shipbuilding were said to be crucial for expanding the sphere of circulation of goods, finance, and people. A class of bourgeois landowners, in association with merchants and financiers, skilled craftspeople, and initial proletarians were core classes in the production-distribution processes. A hospitable political, cultural, and scientific climate made industrial coordination more integrated. Foreign wars became an outlet for the production and facilitation of innovation.

Freeman and Louçã (2001) believe that the structural crises of adjustment of the first Kondratiev during the 1820s to the 1840s, did not cause lower growth of output (p. 181), but exhibited social turmoil and heavy unemployment in Britain. The transition to urban life and factory production led to greater rural pauperism, harsh new poor laws and so-called workhouses, heightened cyclicality, and structural unemployment. Greater turbulence and manifest social disruption were said to be the core results of the first Kondratiev downswing.

Freeman and Louçã's "Second Kondratiev Wave" (1850s–1890s) is said to have spread industrialization from Britain gradually to the US, Germany, France, and some other regions, especially during the so-called Victorian prosperity of the 1850s–1860s and the post-civil war US upswing during 1865–1874. The long wave technological style was based on railways, steam engines, shipping, sophisticated machine tools, and the core inputs of iron and steel (with coal). Railways are said to have been the "carrier branch" of the second Kondratiev (p. 212). This wave also saw the transition from British hegemony to increasing US and German power; the trend from laissez-faire policy to nationalism and socialism; the gradual emergence of big business, large-scale production, and economies of scale; and the trend from shopfloor management to centralized managerial control of labor and production.

The structural crises of adjustment that occurred in the leading economies during the late 1870s, 1880s, and 1890s were said to have precipitated greater competition, overproduction, and profit crises in the key sectors, which led to major depressions. These crises eventually initiated greater protectionism, labor unrest, a re-alignment of class interests, social agitation, and discontent (p. 218). There has been much historical research undertaken on the so-called Great Depression of the last quarter of the nineteenth century (see, e.g., Rosenberg 1943; Rostow 1938; Fels 1949), even many who dispute this interpretation of the period. (We discuss this "Great Depression" in more detail in Chap. 6 below.)

The "Third Kondratiev Wave" (1890s–1940s) emerged *out of* business and government strategies to re-establish profitability through key innovations in science and technology (cheap steel, electrification, heavy engineering); African colonization; giant new corporations employing Taylorism in workplaces; and hegemonic rivalry of expanded US and German power. During this time, core–periphery divergence heightened as parts of the core sought to control the world via colonial domination and two world wars. The electro-mechanical revolution is said to have transformed public life, corporate offices, and communication via telephony, typewriters, steel-filing cabinets, and electrification of private and public infrastructure. Radical innovations such as the Bessemer, Siemens, and Gilchrist–Thomas processes enhanced steel productivity as a core input into large-scale manufacturing (p. 233). Mergers and acquisitions; innovation in accounting, sales management, research techniques, and investment banking services helped restore profitability for a time in the leading sectors of especially the US and Germany. Meanwhile, Britain lagged as its educational system failed to advance technical and craft skills adequately for promoting the new regime; finance capital came to dominate the industry to the detriment of productivity; and insufficient domestic investment ensured.

Structural crises of adjustment began to impact not just Britain (much earlier), but also much of continental Europe and America during the 1910s–1940s. Hegemonic rivalry led to a major world war during 1914–1918 (rather than the short one some anticipated), which halted long wave upswing in Europe (and much elsewhere); and re-generated another world war during 1939–1945. The increasing dominance of finance over industry resulted in major speculative excesses, especially during the 1920s, a major crash on Wall Street during late 1929, and several other crises during the 1930s, as the Great Depression affected the whole world. Overcapacity and insufficient demand in core industries (e.g., automobiles and other durable goods sectors) and anomalous fiscal and monetary policies heightened instabilities during the 1920s and the depth of the Depression in the 1930s.

The massive reconstruction after World War Two, the New Deal in the US and the Marshall Plan to prevent communism in western and southern Europe helped to promote confidence during the 1940s and 1950s. The basic accord of the Keynesian welfare and warfare state (KWS) that helped to forge wave upswing during the 1950s–1970s played a key role in generating demand and stability. The Bretton Woods System (BWS) of fixed exchange rates (linked to the US dollar), the World Bank, and the IMF helped to stabilize currency and development markets-sectors. Profitability and investment were ensured through the dominance of Fordist assembly line processes, standardized products, higher wages, and specialized production engineers; as well as a host of product innovations such as televisions, washing machines, and vacuum cleaners. The US led the way through production, financial, commercial, and military dominance for a new wave of capitalist development.

For Freeman and Louçã, as with many others, the "Fourth Kondratiev Wave Upswing" (1950s–1970s) was the greatest golden age of capitalist development.

But several crises of structural adjustment eventually emerged, putting an end to this magnificent set of institutional and technological innovations. The Fordist system of mass production and mass consumption that led the way through demand and accord experienced contradictions that manifested themselves especially into the 1970s and 1980s. The regime of standardized products, assembly line production, and high employment led to declining productivity and greater labor unrest. Japanese systems of production led to a series of innovations involving total quality management, low levels of inventories, and worker participation that challenged the old system. Middle Eastern nations, especially OPEC that supplied much of the cheap oil underpinning Fordist systems, started to rebel several times by controlling production and raising prices. US hegemony was further reduced by losing the war in Vietnam, the rising power of Germany, the European Union, and initially Japan plus the secular rising power of many other Asian economies.

These crises of adjustment manifested themselves, initially, in several recessions and financial crises, including the deep recessions of the mid-1970s and early 1980s, the crash on Wall Street and elsewhere in 1987, and the recession of the early 1990s in many nations/areas The old Fordist system and its giant companies were further challenged by technological and institutional innovations, including the Japanese production style, enhanced electronics and biotechnology, plus the rising power of China and south as well as southeast Asia. The power of oil, internal combustion engines, and coal production was questioned in light of rising greenhouse gasses, global pollution, and climate change. In short, the old systems were declining, crises were getting worse, and the fourth Kondratiev downswing was evident, especially in the West and parts of Latin America and Africa.

Freeman and Louçã (2001, ch 9) posit the start of a new techno-economic revolution, and a *possible* "Fifth Kondratiev Wave," through the development of the electronics, information, and communications technology (ICT) revolution; and we should add biotechnology. This revolution is said to involve four main sub-systems. The first is the ICT industrial base, involving scientific, economic, and educational activities directly and indirectly involved in microelectronics, semi-conductors, computers, and telecommunications. The second is the networked corporation, where firms engage in global, regional, national, and sub-national online and physical linkages between producers, suppliers, distributors, marketers, sellers, and consumers (supply chain business). The third is the culture of virtual reality, access to the Internet, engaging in online social media, shopping, gaming, conferencing, and surfing. And the fourth is the philosophy and practices of neoliberalism, involving the dominance of the corporate society, much self-regulation of business, minimal government, plus deregulated finance, trade, and labor markets.

While Freeman and Louçã do call this ICT revolution, specifically the "Computerization of the entire economy," the core paradigm of the "Fifth Kondratiev Wave" (KW) in Table II.1 (p. 141), there is no date cited for the "upswing (boom)" of the possible Fifth Kondratieff wave ("??" is shown as the date), and the "downswing (crisis of adjustment)" of the Fordist, "fourth Kondratieff wave" only has a starting date: "1973-," with no end date shown. Every chapter of the first four Kondratiev waves cites "Kondratiev wave" in the title, but the "5thKW" chapter's title is, instead, "The Emergence of a New Techno-economic Paradigm: The Age of Information and Communications Technology (ICT)." This demonstrates two things. First, they state many times in the book, vis-à-vis these sub-systems, "our own theory of history is not based on the exclusive dominance of any one sub-system in society, whether economic, technological, scientific, cultural, political, or military-political" (Freeman and Louçã 2001, 365). However, in their book, ICT, as the techno-economic paradigm, is clearly given a privileged position (counter to their principle of "no dominance of sub-systems in theory"). But secondly, it is clear from a more recent work by Francisco Louçã (2021) that he does not think the "crisis of adjustment of Fordism" is over yet, and therefore, the boom of the Fifth Kondratiev wave has not yet emerged. This requires some explanation.

Louçã (2019, 2021) argues that while a new techno-economic regime has been established through the ICT systems, the crisis of Fordism, or the crisis of the new mutant system, is still with us, as the conditions have not been generated to promote renewed profit, productivity, and growth for industrial capital and the macroeconomy (as distinct from finance capital). Hence the Fifth Kondratiev long wave upswing has not yet been established. Sustainable profit, growth, and upswing have not emerged, for the world economy or for its dominant partners (such as the EU and the USA, nor for Russia) because the institutions associated with neoliberalism, financialization (including fictitious capital, see Louçã and Ash 2018), plus current trends in international trade, capital, and military regimes, have not been suitably structured to realize the potential of the techno-economic regime (at least to 2020). As Louçã said:

> If this process of changes in production and distribution leads to a new regime of accumulation, under the form of financialization, which means concentration of power, it also changes the social contract that has been established after the Second World War in most developed countries, replacing it with more authoritarian forms of leadership, based on populism and, in some cases, on militarism. ... [T]wo forms of accumulation were identified as characteristics of the long phase B [downswing] of the fourth Kondratiev; [1] investment in productive capacity, and [2] reproduction as fictitious capital. ... *Th[is] Phase B will give [way] to a new expansionary Phase A of a fifth [Kondratiev] long wave only when the mismatch between the techno-economic paradigm and the socio-institutional conditions is solved and profits and accumulation are reestablished at a high level.* ... A regime of accumulation through financialization or rentism and extractivism, generates inherent instability [e.g., the GFC, Eurodebt crisis]. Economic perturbations and political chaos will endure or even still be aggravated, after forty years of this long Phase B of the long wave. (Louçã 2019, 61–62)

Related to this are the specific causes of the (potential fifth) long wave upswing. We basically accept the view of Freeman and Louçã (2001) that there are two main components of long wave upswing. One concerns the techno-economic paradigm (TEP), for instance, Fordism during the postwar era. And the other relates to the social and political institutions (SPI) required to represent a good fit with the TEP. While Freeman and Louçã state specifically the principle that they privilege neither TEP nor SPI, which we accept, in practice, as mentioned, they do privilege TEP over SPI purely in terms of the priority and relative space and position given to TEP over SPI in their book and elsewhere.

Louçã (2019, 2021) seems to imply that, in the contemporary scene, SPI needs to adjust to TEP, although he is somewhat ambiguous on this since he realizes that the neoliberal SPI (which he perhaps argues is closely linked to the ICT TEP) is insufficient for performance commensurate with long wave upswing (see O'Hara 2023 who has argued this since O'Hara 2000, 2006a). In Mandel's terminology, therefore, long wave upswing may have elements that are endogenous and exogenous, since the TEP and SPI often do depend upon their previous phases of evolution, even if the changes that are happening are somewhat revolutionary. Also, in this context, as we show later, TEP and SPI can be viewed, respectively, as regimes of accumulation and structural forms (regulation approach); or vis-à-vis SSA analysis, various types of institutional systems (some more technological in nature).

Louçã is correct, in my view, that a new long wave upswing has not yet emerged for the world and its core, although I show below in Chap. 8 (and Chap. 11) that long wave upswing did emerge especially for numerous nations of Asia (notably China) in the 1980s–2000s, although anomalies have been growing over the few years even here. Numerous long wave scholars, erroneously in my view, argue for a new long wave emerging during the 1980s (neoliberalism) and declining from the GFC onwards; or alternatively, emerging from the 1990s (ICT) to the present in the core (and generally). But as Chap. 9, below, Louçã and others demonstrate, this was only for a segment of the sub-systems required for a new Kondratiev upswing (for the core or the world).

It is this confusion in the literature between some new and effective sub-systems but not enough for sustainable performance that led a core member of the Sussex SPRC Group, Carlotta Perez, who worked closely especially with Chris Freeman and others, to eschew specific discussions of long waves as such and discuss the substantive issues of the relationship between these techno-economic paradigm(s), or "great surges" as she also calls them, the associated bubble crashes, and the possible ensuring socioeconomic and political changes that may promote a good fit with this current ICT system, but which have not yet been established (see Perez 2002, 2015). Her thesis is that although the ICT great surge has occurred (1980s and 1990s), followed by speculative bubble crashes linked to this surge (e.g., 2000s), sustainable performance has not yet occurred for other reasons. Specifically, we require socioeconomic and political changes, like those she postulates such as the New Deal, a post-Keynesian Welfare State, and the typical social democratic accords and social contracts that we are used to seeing in, for instance, the Scandinavian nations, but more appropriately structured for the twenty-first century, on a global or substantially global, or perhaps regional or "core," basis.

Substantively this is a result similar to Louçã, without the use of the "long waves" tag, although Louçã (2019) *alludes to* neoliberal institutions perhaps being necessary, purely as a good "fit" for the techno-economic institutions. For our purposes, both Perez and Louçã agree that the *techno-economic* "institutions" are in place, but further institutional developments are required for potential major recovery of performance for the core or most nations of the world. The aspect of their analysis that is identical to my own perspective on the evidence is that substantial performance for the world or core has not yet occurred (except for certain regions).

Where we differ is that, as mentioned, I think China and parts of Asia have been undergoing long wave upswing since the 1990s (or based on Perez's terminology, "substantial socioeconomic performance" rather than waves), until about 2018 when it went into *relative* decline. If I interpret Louçã correctly (about "neoliberalism"), my arguments since at least O'Hara (2000), also see O'Hara (2009, 2010, 2012, 2013, 2023), is in line with Louçã that sustainable long wave upswing has not been generated (outside Asia and a few other economies) and in line with Perez that neoliberalism is not an appropriate foundation for substantial socioeconomic performance.

As someone who has done a lot of work on long waves, and especially SSAs and regulation approaches, I can see that the "post-Schumpeterian" work of Freeman, Louçã, and Perez, is very much complementary to my own analysis. Firstly, we both study the system as well as subsystems within the totality of techno-economic, social, and political "institutions." Secondly, these systems and subsystems are substantially similar in both my and Freeman's/Perez's/Louçã's work (at least). And thirdly, we come to much the same conclusions about socioeconomic performance in the core at least (in contrast, as mentioned, to some who think a fifth long wave upswing started in the 1980s or 1990s). And fourthly, our emphasis on non-equilibrium, path dependence, and historical analysis is (almost) on the same level of analysis. Much can be learned by cross-fertilization between the so-called different long wave traditions. Andrew Tylecote's work on long waves seems to be consistent with this as well.

This current book, of course, pushes the boundaries of long wave research further than that of Freeman, Louçã, and Perez (FLP), in several respects. The first is that I scrutinize the interaction between long waves of growth, hegemonic power, and climate change, and more specifically argue that the long wave upswings that were the most impressive were associated with hegemonic power and specific lines of climate change, contra to the standard model. The second is that this current work utilizes the PoPE contingency paradigm, through the principles of historical specificity, hegemony, CSD, heterogeneous groups and agents, CCC, contradiction, uncertainty, innovation, and policy (so it goes beyond FLP somewhat, although much is very similar conceptually). Applying these to the eco-spatial, institutional, and technological dynamic structures of the CSD through growth, hegemony, and climate change dynamics makes my framework somewhat different in emphasis and nature.[3]

Now we turn to some other traditions of long wave inquiry, especially SSA, regulation, world-systems/hegemony/war analysis, and the "Eastern-South-Central European" School, and how these may be important for or impact on the current book.

[3] Also, my CSD, PoPE, LWHegCC framework is somewhat different to the Freeman-Perez-Louçã school in hypothesizing that the technology style may not be the revolutionary system required for long wave upswing, due to its inability to generate substantial long-term productivity and performance (as shown by the research of R.J. Gordon; especially discussed in Chaps. 7, 9, and 12, also the Glossary).

3.7 Regulation and Social Structures of Accumulation Approaches

The regulation approach to political economy does not have an explicit theory of long waves. In a book about its "state of the art," long waves are not mentioned in the contents page or index (Boyer and Saillard 2002). In a five-volume edited work of about 100 articles previously published papers on the approach, there is no substantive analysis of long waves (Jessop 2001), except for some papers linking regulation with SSAs. These five volumes do have four articles on SSAs, and therefore the regulation approach seems to include SSA analysis in its own framework, and SSA analysis is certainly usually about long waves. (But many SSA scholars do not like being encapsulated into the regulation approach, which reduces their originality, and some do not like the idea of SSAs being linked to long waves.)

Most regulation approaches examine Fordism and the flexible mode of regulation; and more recent work on the approach, as shown in the regulation school journal, *Revue de la régulation. Capitalisme, institutions,* pouvoirs (2007–present) (*Regulation journal*, 2007–2023) covers an array of topics, but little or nothing on long waves. However, the approach does provide information to help understand long movements of capitalism during the twentieth and twenty-first centuries, including the long wave of the 1940s–2020s.

There are several sub-schools within the regulation approach, such as "the so-called Parisian School, … the Grenoble School, the German School, the Amsterdam School, British radical geographers, the … [so-called] social structure of accumulation school, and the neo-Gramscian school" (Wikipedia 2023). Several scholars have comparatively analyzed regulation and SSA approaches (e.g., Kotz 1990) or integrated certain aspects of regulation and SSA schools in analyzing the postwar long wave (1940s–2000s) (e.g., O'Hara 2000, 2006a). One type of "basic framework" of regulation theory, according to O'Hara (2003), relates to the mode of regulation (MOR), regime of accumulation (ROA), and certain institutional forms (IF) composite architecture.

I have written two previous books and about 40 articles in journals and edited books linking long waves, regulation, and SSAs. In the first book (O'Hara 2000), which won the *Myrdal Prize for Book of the Year* from EAEPE, I scrutinized the postwar SSA of US, Western and partially global capitalism, including the 1950s–1970s boom and the subsequent 1970s–1990s decline. Special reference was given to the institutional rise and fall of US hegemony, Fordism (using regulation works), the Keynesian welfare state (KWS), the regulated financial system, and household-family systems. A final chapter detailed the factors responsible for the predicted supreme global crisis that was likely to emanate from the new arrangements of the global regime, deregulated finance, neoliberalism, flexible mode of production, and post-familial households during the 2000s (2000). (See Chap. 7 below which draws on some of this material.) This came in the form of the GFC and Eurocrisis, during 2008–2014ff (and the coronacrisis), when disarray deepened especially in the advanced capitalist economies and others majorly dependent upon them.

The second book (O'Hara 2006a; paper edition 2009), which won the *Book of the Year Prize* from CBS, used regulation and SSA frameworks to examine the neoliberal global system that emerged after the breakdown of the postwar accords during the 1970s and 1980s. This book scrutinized the 1990s–2000s neoliberal globalization style with chapters on each of its techno-institutions and the contradictory evolution of the US and global system. In this context, I scrutinized the evolution and problems emerging through neoliberalism, the transnational corporate system, deregulated finance, and the post-familial households, and why this indicated a major crisis arising even greater than the Juglar downswings (and associated bubble crashes) of 1974–1975, 1980–1982, 1990–1991, 1997, and 2000–2003: the GFC, Eurocrisis and coronacrisis. (The pre-publication title for this book was *The Emerging Global Crises of Capitalism*.) (See Chap. 9, below, which draws on some of this material.)

As my research evolved and developed, I recognized that the SSA school was becoming isolated academically, while the regulation school had past its prime, and as I mention especially in Chap. 1 of this current book, long wave theory and empirics had long moved into long wave downswing of scholarship. One problem with wave and phases works is the tendency for many to ignore other schools and tendencies working on this material. Also no one has managed to suitably integrate and fuse long wave frameworks drawing on their innovations and moving away from anomalies. This current volume seeks to rectify this anomaly to some degree.

In this context, one thing that is striking about SSA and regulation works is how innovative were both the seminal book by Michel Aglietta (1976) and the original theoretical essay by David Gordon (1980). Aglietta does nothing less than update Marx's analysis of capitalism to the twenty-first century, including an empirical investigation of how to do this by reference to the previous 70–100 years of capitalist development. He sets the scene with the principle of historical specificity (p. 9). He then posits the *concept of reproduction* (see O'Hara 2001), that the aim of inquiry is to investigate capitalism through the lens of its ongoing transformation through successive qualitative changes to its techno-institutional dynamics (p. 12). He sees this as an alternative to the notion of equilibrium, since while reproduction posits regulation and hence ongoing dynamics, it also includes rupture, due to the *contradictions within the system*. This duality of ongoing reproduction, yet structural and periodic rupture, is set within the framework of US capitalism over the twentieth century (p. 23).

The capitalist mode of production posits certain institutions to generate surplus value, profit, and accumulation. Situating these institutions in a historical phase (postwar) and dominant region (US hegemony) of capitalism requires determining the mode of regulation (MOR) of that socioeconomic formation, including both the regime of accumulation (ROA) and the institutional (structural) forms (SF). During the twentieth century, the ROA evolved into Fordism by mid-century, through the process of mass production reinforced by mass consumption. Crucial to US capitalism during that century was the process of institutionalization, examined through the concept of structural (institutional) forms (p. 27). The five main institutional forms studied include the (1) international regimes, (2) the money-finance regime, (3) the state regime, (4) the wage–labor–employment nexus, and (5) the regime of competition. Together this mode of regulation generated a regime of accumulation with various institutional forms to reproduce in a structured fashion, but subject to structural crisis and rupture, the upswing and downswing characteristic of the 1940s–2000s period (see O'Hara 2010).

Subsequent work on the regulation approach has analyzed all sorts of factors, from the changing forms of regulation through the development of the flexible mode of regulation and the rise of neoliberalism, to further evolution of the mode of regulation, the regime of accumulation, and structural forms. It has also applied and modified this analysis to different areas and problems. But nothing quite like the original work of Aglietta ever (re)emerged to transform the theoretico-historical material into qualitatively different space more recently.

As mentioned, regulation theory and empirics were never a thorough-going analysis of long waves, merely one corresponding to the last century and more of capitalist development. At best it provides critical work to help understand the past two Kondratiev waves, since the 1890s, but unwittingly. If SSA analysis is, as indicated by the multi-volume work edited by Jessop, merely a sub-branch of regulation scholarship, then this SSA framework helps to specify the long wave motion associated with regulation scholarship. And this is where the work of David Gordon and his colleagues (in this context performing a similar function to Aglietta), forms the apex of SSA-long wave analysis.

A few years after the "European/French' regulation school of political economy started their analysis of capitalist development and transformation with Michel Aglietta's (1974) PhD thesis, David Gordon (1944–1996) (1978, 1980) formally commenced his very first investigations into performance-based institutional dynamics. He called his focus social structures of accumulation (SSAs), but they are really institutions (or institutional clusters/spheres), and it is not simply accumulation (investment) that is under investigation, but also profit, growth, and performance more generally considered (as empirical evidence showed). Hence, Gordon-style *performance-based* institutional dynamics (GPID) is a better acronym than SSA. We will use the old SSA acronym merely to avoid confusion, but the reader should highlight this point.

The first of Gordon's (1978) papers was a theoretico-empirical study of the long wave downswing commencing in the US by the late 1960s or mid-1970s. The second was a very long theoretical paper where Gordon (1980) set out his main theses about stages of accumulation and long economic cycles, and where he specified, unwittingly under the umbrella of our notion of "horizontal emergence," the 13 institutions necessary for the establishment of successful SSAs. Gordon saw a strong relationship between industrial profit, investment, and economic growth, recognizing that if capitalists don't have determinate calculations of good profits they will, "leave their money to the financial and commercial spheres." The more uncertain the economic, social, and political institutions that underlie investment, "the less likely it will be that capitalists seek accumulation through production" (real GDP including services) than finance (p. 12).

The institutional clusters, when effective, are seen as impacting on performance by stimulating a climate of relative stability and low levels of uncertainty (emergent phenomena), which promotes industrial investment, plus economies of scale and scope, real GDP per capita, as well as markets and degrees of monopoly. This is the core SSA Research Hypothesis 1 (SSA-RH1), leading to higher productivity and profitability, and, when markets are available (through higher wages, and/or expansions on the world economy, etc.), to greater rates of economic growth per capita (O'Hara 2006a). Another linking mechanism includes higher industrial profits providing a financial source for greater investments and hence growth (Sherman and Kolk 1996). When growth is inclusive to some degree, and not based around finance and commerce per se, this can also enhance levels of relative equality and standards of living for the population (including working and middle classes), at least for a time; even if capitalist industrial enterprises (and the elites) mostly control the central institutional clusters around which improvement is based (while "lumpens" barely survive underneath it all). However, few scholars have raised the issue of what technical conditions or boundaries are required for differentiating between "adequate" and "inadequate" performance, from the point of view of upswing, downswing, and borderline performance measures (see O'Hara 2012; Chaps. 5–9, 11, below; for solutions).

Gordon set out "thirteen specific institutions which comprise the full set of institutions whose stability" is "necessary for rapid and sustained accumulation" (investment) (p. 23); more generally capitalist performance, including profitability and growth (and broader measures): which is SSA-RH2. Four general characteristics for horizontal, meso-emergent SSA include two motors of accumulation of the capitalist mode of production ([1] a moderation of competition and [2] a moderation of class conflict between capital and labor) and two systemic requirements of accumulation (stability in the [3] monetary system and [4] state); along with nine institutions at the level of corporations. These nine institutions include one agent of accumulation internal to the firm ([5] stable internal corporate structure) as well as eight requirements of individual capital accumulation ([6] stable access to raw materials [7] and fixed capital, [8] stable family structure, [9] labor market structure, [10] labor management, [11] final consumer demand, [12] sources of internal and external funds, and [13] administrative management of the firm).

Gordon postulated the operation of numerous contradictions within and between the institutions, but also "the fundamental contradiction in capitalist societies between the social character of accumulation and its dependence upon essentially "private" activities" (p. 25). This postulate of Gordon represented his first self-conscious foray into (vertical) emergent processes, a core part of complexity theory, where "the whole is greater than the sum of the individual parts" (as Gordon stated). In this case the "whole" for Gordon is the complete set of interacting socioeconomic institutions, at the national, regional, and/or global levels; while the "parts" may be the individual institutions, or lower still small groups and individual persons: this is SSA-RH3. But Gordon did not develop this vertically emergent "whole" idea very much at all, nor have SSA scholars since then.

Two years after his 1980 thesis paper was published, Gordon, along with Richard Edwards and Michael Reich ([GER] 1982), produced a remarkable historico-institutional, temporally emergent, investigation of capital–labor relations through the various long waves of capitalism since the 1820s in the United States. Then a host of journal articles appeared, including several by Samuel Bowles, Gordon, and Thomas Weisskopf [BGW], followed by two editions of their more popular and accessible book, initially titled *Beyond the Wasteland* (BGW 1984, 1990); several articles and books by Reich and Edwards; in addition to student-PhD work, and numerous other articles, into the 1990s, 2000s and 2010s. In these papers, Gordon along with his colleagues, and many others, started analyzing SSAs and long waves using (mostly) more empirical and less historico-institutional methods, and their list of horizontally emergent institutions was reduced to 4 (rather than 13).[4]

For instance, Gordon, Edwards, Reich, Bowles, Weisskopf and others established some impressive evidence and theory supporting the emergence of these four successful but ultimately contradictory and eventually declining horizontal institutional clusters that collectively supported high rates of profit, accumulation, and growth in the USA during the 1950s, 1960s, and early 1970s. These institutional clusters of the "postwar corporate system" (PCS) included the [1] capital–labor accord, [2] state–citizen accord, [3] US hegemony, and [4] a system of moderation of competition. They also scrutinized the contradictions within and between the institutions and how they eventually undermined accumulation, leading to the dissolution of the institutions and long wave downswing into the 1970s, 1980s, and 1990s.

In the meantime, other advances were being made, to broaden (yet again) the horizontally emergent scope and size of the institutional dynamic structure, so that it incorporated 8–10 core (or "dominant") institutional processes or spheres (including the four just cited). For instance, additionally these included the role of gender and race by, for instance, Robert Cherry (1991) and Wolfson's (1994) masterly analysis of the rise and demise of the "postwar" financial system in the USA from its roots in the 1930s and 1940s through to the early 1990s. O'Hara (1995, 2000, 2009, 2023) included the "family and community," and the global political economy (O'Hara 2003, 2009), as institutional clusters during the 1950s and 1960s, with the contradictions manifesting themselves into the 1970s to the 2010s (also O'Hara 2023), while Barlow et al. (1993) added the criminal justice system to the SSA framework. Further research along the lines of a broader horizontal emergent array of institutions beyond the core ones has been developed in the literature.

Some SSA scholars believe that potential SSAs only operate at the national level (e.g., Lippit 2005, 2014). The notion of purely national PIDs has been challenged by numerous authors (e.g., O'Hara 2009, 2013; Kotz and McDonough 2010; Wallace and Brady 2010; Nardone and McDonough 2010; Robinson 2012), such that the (potential) (sub)national-regional-global vertically emergent SSA thesis has become institutionalized into the literature; and this broad perspective should be a core part of future research (SSA-RH3). As Gordon et al. (1982, 37) said, vis-à-vis

[4] See McDonough et al. (2014) for an edited selection of *some* of the SSA papers over the decades. Keep in mind this is a skewed *selection* of papers, but nevertheless useful.

a more consistently vertically emergent position, "Since capitalism operates on a world scale, one should analyze its contradictions and [institutions] on a world scale."

Some SSA analysts also believe that neoliberalism was a successful SSA for a time (Lippit 2005), and some also believe that it can be called an SSA even if performance was weak on accumulation and growth. See the counterarguments in Roosevelt (2009), and later evidence by Elsner (2016). O'Hara (2006a, 2013; Chap. 9, below) provided evidence for neoliberalism being an institutional cluster of limited and unstable performance, with below-average rates of industrial profit, accumulation, and growth; and hence not a successful SSA for the system, resulting in major crises (see Chap. 9, below) (SSA-RH4).

In terms of horizontal emergence (e.g., different national economies), Lippit (2005) and O'Hara (2006b; Chap. 5, below) argue that nations such as China (and numerous others in Asia and some elsewhere) have been undergoing SSA development and phase evolution at least since the 1980s (faltering majorly into the 2020s) (SSA-RH5). One underplayed core research hypothesis is that some nations or areas of the world (e.g., many areas of North Africa and the Middle East (and likely Latin America) in the 2010s–2020s) have been experiencing destructively unstable performance-based institutional dynamics of late, as their political economies have been experiencing potentially system-destroying revolutions, wars, terrorist attacks, and associated extreme climate events (SSA-RH6).

Some of the papers by McDonough et al. (2010, 2021) define a new social structure of accumulation as a new phase of evolution of capitalism (i.e., neoliberalism), from the 1980s/1990s, without a major expansion of general accumulation or general performance. Thus, a new phase could emerge, according to this "theory," without sufficient advance in general accumulation (nor profit, growth, overall performance). This is inconsistent with Gordon's theory that a new temporally emergent SSA (performance) phase equates with an expansion of accumulation, profit, and growth; and with O'Hara's (2000, 2009, 2012, 2025) work, where a new temporally emergent phase (neoliberalism) may emerge without a successful new SSA (i.e., unsuccessful accumulation, profit, growth, and general performance) (see also Elsner 2016) (SSA-RH7).

SSA scholars have evaded studying the vertical dimensions of how habits, routines, ways of life, and socialization forces enable people to operate within organizations and institutions, while seemingly not promoting their long-term interests: this is SSA-RH8. Veblen studied these interlinked critical research areas, but most SSA scholars ignore them (see O'Hara 2000). Furthermore, little has been done to extend the vertical micro, meso, macro, regional, and global dimensions of SSA temporally back to the beginnings of industrial capitalism in the 1780s (and none that takes it back to the origins of mercantilism in the 1500s or earlier): this is SSA-RH9. Freeman and Louçã have done a far better job of analyzing this historical dimension of phases of evolution and performance of capitalism through long waves since the 1780s, and as shown above, this framework of techno-economic great surges or revolutions and socio-political institutions is very much complementary to but likely better than SSA and regulation school MOR analyses. The current book seeks to investigate RH9 through a more eclectic and innovative framework.

Similarly, SSA scholars have mostly evaded the equally important research issue of how phases of evolution can be understood in association with capitalism's longer-term functioning, especially regarding processes that are more durable than the core institutions of the SSA (e.g., climate change, hegemonic power, since the 1500s), and the shorter-term events that many think are not explicitly pertinent to the intermediate-institutional analysis of emergent phases and performance of capitalism (wars, coronacrisis): this is SSA-RH10. The current book also seeks to advance RH10 with a more eclectic and innovative approach.

This current book goes beyond the scope of SSA theory and empirics by (1) structurally linking institutions with technology and geo-ecology (including climate change) within the CSD of the long wave of capitalism; (2) emphasizing performance (growth per capita, profit, investment, etc.), phases of evolution and varieties of capitalism; (3) incorporating the PoPE contingency paradigm, and (4) dealing with linkages between long waves of growth per capita, hegemony, wars, and climate change.

3.8 Long Waves, Hegemony, and Wars

In this section, I analyze core long wave literatures associated with integrated themes of (1) long waves, (2) hegemonic trends, and (3) wars (and where relevant climate change). The purpose is to further set this book within an interdisciplinary, complexity, and realistic dynamic. One major scholar, Joshua Goldstein (1988), has reviewed this three-pronged literature (ignoring climate change) and provided guidelines for how they may be linked. He has comparatively scrutinized the work of dozens of scholars, including Immanuel Wallerstein's (1930–2019) world-systems school, Fernand Braudel's (1902–1985) Annales School, and George Modelski's (1926–2014) group. Based on the evidence, he tends to support the analysis of Wallerstein and Braudel. We use the work of these four scholars and followers for furthering the development of our own hypotheses and objectives in this book.

Goldstein's main thesis on the first of these issues, long waves, is that the different schools and scholars working in the area have generally failed to gain sufficient insights from each other. There are exceptions (with caveats), such as the special issues of the journal *Futures* (1981), which merely included papers from different schools and scholars, but did not attempt a synthesis; and the edited book by Kleinknecht, Mandel, and Wallerstein (1992), which attempted less a synthesis and more a joint very general framework of research into the future. For instance, in a concluding proposal by Wallerstein (1992) on long waves, he indicated the need for much more global-world data; more systematic comparisons between core, periphery, and semi-periphery; and more comparisons of long waves over long historical time.

This issue of lack of interaction between and within schools and traditions is a crucial one, and it is partly for this reason that this present book has been written.

Since the passing of the great long wave scholars such as David Gordon, Immanuel Wallerstein, Ernest Mandel, A.G. Frank, Chris Freeman, W.W. Rostow, Jay Forrester, and numerous others, research on long waves has generated fewer new hypotheses and original works. It seems that in many respects the schools and traditions have gone inwards, engaging in navel-gazing within their own traditions, and ignoring the wider issues of interdependency, linkages, and expansion of perspective. This book, in part, seeks to eschew this tendency and stimulate integrative innovation as suggested by Goldstein and others.

Some long wave scholars have not specifically integrated the three issues of waves, hegemony, and wars (nor climate change), but still recognize the three processes being important to their analysis. For instance, Gordon, Bowles, and Weisskopf (in their numerous publications) recognize that US hegemony was an important core institutional sphere of influences affecting performance during the postwar era, and that the world wars, plus the Korean and Vietnam wars, have affected the nature of long waves. In fact, in their empirical work, they typically include four core institutional spheres: capital-labor accord, state-capital accord, US hegemony, and moderation of competition. SSAs are their prime concern; hegemony is one aspect of these (at least during the postwar era); and wars are also important.

Goldstein recognizes that waves, hegemony, and wars are interrelated but also, to some degree, separate processes. The issues of interdependency and relative autonomy are crucial here. The core thing for Goldstein is that we can study the linkages between the three in a systematic fashion. This current book continues this objective and extends it to climate change. Goldstein also posits some hypotheses regarding the relationship between long waves of growth and prices.

In looking at research linking waves, hegemony, and wars, and comparing the efficacy of the various schools and trends working in these areas, Goldstein generally recognizes that Wallerstein, Braudel, and company's research is the most valid, and he uses this work to enhance his own analysis. In the area of long waves, the Freeman *et al.* work on innovation is cited as the best in terms of periodicity and phases. And he accepts the broad periodicity that wave scholars tend to cite in terms of 1780s–1840s (First Kondratiev), 1850s–1890s (Second Kondratiev), 1890s–1930s (Third Kondratiev), and 1940s–1980s->? (Fourth Kondratiev), divided between the generally agreed upswing (A) and downswing (B) phases.

There are two problems with Goldstein's analysis. Firstly, he is mostly concerned with linking performance data (production) and prices, but much less concerned with phases of capitalist development (broadly conceived). And secondly, most of his investigations concentrate on data for specific variables, and little discussion is given to techno-economic and institutional systems and sub-systems. Nothing is provided of substance on ecology or climate change. He also does little to challenge the standard model of long waves.

He summarizes his approach to long waves as follows (Chap. 12), which draws upon all the major schools of thought and scholars on the subject, so that it is a synthesis of what he considers the best of the groups. Firstly, his theory gives production, wars, and prices key roles, with various lags (p. 259). Secondly, there is a

Table 3.2 Long waves and hegemony: Hopkins & Wallerstein et al.'s periodicity

	Netherlands	Britain	USA	Long Wave	Hegemony
A1	1575–1590	1798–1815	1897–1913/20	Upswing	Ascending
B1	1590–1620	1815–1850	1913/20–1945	Downswing	Victory
A2	1620–1650	1850–1873	1945–1967/73	Upswing	Maturity
B2	1650–1672	1873–1897	1967/73–??	Downswing	Decline

Source: Adapted from Research Working Group (1979, 499)

two-way (dialectical) relationship between wars and production. Wars are said to waste economic and other resources and are inflationary (raising prices) but can help the economy move to a new technology style (p. 270).

Wars over successive long waves are closely linked to hegemonic cycles. First, Robert Keohane (1984) is probably right that it is not hegemonic dominance and stability per se that provides the benefits to those who are part of the pact, but the process of establishing regimes of cooperation in the world political economy that generates potential stability, growth, and development. Following the results of Wallerstein and company, if hegemony is defined as the establishment of absolute dominance in the world economy (or a region), then in recent centuries there are likely to have been three major periods of capitalist hegemonic dominance. See Table 3.2 on this:

Firstly, hegemonic periods are said to include the United Provinces (Netherlands) 1625–1672, Britain 1815–1873, and the USA (1945–1967). The hegemon tends to establish dominance in production, followed by commerce and then finance; and loses dominance in the (same) order of production, commerce, and finance (PCF). Military power is derivative of PCF power. This current book debates these stages and dates and tentatively modifies, for instance, especially the Dutch period of hegemony (see Chap. 5).

Secondly, there is some debate about Wallerstein's (1979) hypothesis about there being two Kondratievs to each hegemony cycle. Note that phase A is long wave upswing, and phase B is a long wave downswing. This current book tends to support this for Dutch hegemony (Chap. 5), but not for British (Chap. 6) or US hegemony (Chap. 7).

Thirdly, world-systems theory posits that periods of hegemony tend to be correlated with looser core–periphery relations, multilateral trade, and free trade, while eras with no hegemonic power tend to have close core–periphery relations, bilateral trade, and protectionism. According to Albert Bergeson (1980) (a world-systems analyst), there were two waves of colonial expansion: during 1500–1815 and 1870–1945, the latter being one when no power had hegemonic dominance. Christian Suter (1989) demonstrates that debt crises in the periphery tend to operate during Kondratiev downswings (B-phases), especially notable during the 1870s, 1930s–1940s, and 1980s, primarily caused by recession and protectionist and other policies (e.g., monetary) by the core. By and large, this volume supports these hypotheses (with some modifications).

Fourthly, on the relationship between long waves, hegemony, and wars, there is some agreement that, since the late 1700s, major wars among the great powers have been during long wave upswings, as shown by Kondratiev, Wallerstein; and Raimo Vayrynen (1983). Phases of hegemonic ascendance, followed by victory and maturity, tend to be especially common for crucial wars among the major powers. This is said to fit the pattern of recent periods for the revolutionary and Napoleonic wars (1792–1815), and the two world wars (1914–1918 and 1939–1945). It is likely that these major wars occurred during these times because the ascendant power was more strident, while competitors were more prone to reaction, when a specific hegemonic power is about to or attempting to take up a position of global supremacy. The current book supports the notion of wars of ascendency for Dutch, British, and US hegemony, but not wars of consolidation, nor do we believe these wars (e.g., the revolutionary and Napoleonic wars; and the two world wars) were (necessarily) during upswings (they were generally not).

Britain is said to have established absolute global hegemony around 1815/1820, not long before the first long wave of industrial capitalism is said to have gone into downswing during the 1820s (according to the standard model). Then British hegemony underwent demise around the 1880s (but starting earlier) not long before the third Kondratiev wave upswing is said to have started during the 1890s (standard model). The establishment of US absolute hegemony in the 1940s to the 1960s is said to have been inextricably linked to the postwar long wave boom of the 1950s–1970s, and its relative demise into the 1970s- to 1980s-onwards is said to be closely woven into the fabric of long wave downswing. Partly relying on this evidence, SSA scholars have included US hegemony and its demise as a core institutional cluster affecting long wave dynamics over the 1940s–2000s and beyond. The current book modifies the hypothesized linkages between waves and hegemony by indicating that the most impressive long wave upswings tend to be during periods of hegemony, and that these periods are also eras of specific climate change impact (but usually not adhering to the normal hypothesis of major long wave upswings necessarily generating higher global temperatures).

Currently (2025) no nation or region has absolute hegemony in the world political economy, and US's hegemony has declined majorly from absolute to relative forms. China, on the other hand, is seeking to replace the US as the dominant power in the world. During the 1980s many believed Japan may have begun to fulfill this role, but its spectacular series of bubble crashes and deep recessions since then has long ended such speculation. Whether China does rise to relative or absolute hegemonic power is thus a crucial question for research. For this reason, issues of geopolitics (hegemony), comparative performance, and climate change are linked to long waves in Chap. 4, Chap. 5 (Dutch), Chap. 6 (British), Chap. 7 (US), and Chap. 8 (Chinese) waves and vis-à-vis structural polycrises (Chap. 9) and the ongoing conflict between liberal-democratic allies versus autocratic powers (Chap. 10).

There is also the issue of other players in the hegemonic process apart from the prime ones: such as Europe and Russia. During the immediate postwar era (late 1940s to mid-1970s) US hegemony existed alongside the associated power of Europe, and in contradistinction to that of the Soviet Union. These areas still play core roles in the power stakes of global capitalism. We are currently, for instance, seeing increasing conflict between NATO and Russia (and China, North Korea, etc.)

on the borderlines and Russia's attempt to regain territory lost during the breakup of the 1990s. The success of Russia or Ukraine in their battle plays a key role in the relative power stakes of the US versus China, since if Ukraine won against Russia this would increase the relative power of Europe and the US and be a possible decisive influence on the future of Taiwan. Currently, we are seeing a long wave downswing in the West, as well as Russia, and a long wave upswing (tempered over the past 10 years) in China (see Chap. 8, below). The war in Ukraine is and will continue to have impacts on the state of hegemonic processes, as well as long waves, and indeed climate change. Chapter 10, below, investigates the significance of the war in Ukraine for current and future hegemonic processes, long wave dynamics, and climate change.

3.9 Climate Change in the Long Wave Systems Architecture

A critical area of analysis in long wave discourse is climate change. Here we specifically address how climate change can be structurally integrated into an analysis of waves. The topic is like the question of hegemony and war, in the sense that waves of climate change are interrelated with but relatively autonomous from long wave dynamics. In past, current, and future phases of capitalist development, issues of climate change should be integrated into long wave dynamics. This is because climate change (along with wars and global power politics) impacts on socioeconomic performance and phases of capitalist development. So how can climate change be structurally integrated into long wave dynamics?

Firstly, it is not simply a matter of writing articles and books about climate change in the current scenario, but how to structurally link the subject to our central questions. One possible solution is to include climate change as a sub-system of the political economy, albeit a sub-system that impacts on and is included alongside the other subsystems (as done in O'Hara 2010). In this context we are simply continuing the tradition of the regulation school, SSA scholars, Freeman-Louçã-Perez et al. styles, of utilizing sub-systems as a way of including them in the analysis in a meaningful way. We are also following Mario Bunge, who, as a scientist-philosopher, assumes that everything in the analysis has systems and sub-systems, and by utilizing them core issues can be assembled and scrutinized.

I have surveyed the major literature on major trends and schools of long wave analysis in political economy, including all the schools mentioned above plus in some detail Rostovian, Mandelian, neo-Schumpeterian, regulation, SSA, Freeman-Louçã, world-systems, and "East-Central, European Long Wave Group" (see Glossary). None of them have, from my searches, suitably included climate change as a substantive sub-system or system in their architecture of theory and empirics linked with long waves and hegemony. For instance, no attempt to include climate change structurally as a specific system or sub-system linking to long waves and hegemony is attempted in the *Review of Evolutionary Political Economy*, nor the *Journal of Evolutionary Economics*, nor the most recent *Handbook of Social*

Table 3.3 Climate change system in O'Hara's long wave architecture

	Subsystem 1	Subsystem 2	Subsystem 3	Subsystem 4	Subsystem 5	Subsystem 6	Subsystem 7
A. SSA	Production-Distribution Regime	Competition Regime	Global Economy Institutions	Financial System	Policy & Governance	Family & Community	Climate Change Institutions
B. Regulation	Accumulation Regime A: Technology Style	Accumulation Regime B: Mode of Demand	Institutional Form 1. Global Institutions	Institutional Form 2: Money & Finance	Institutional Form 3: State & Policy	Institutional Form 4: Competition & Monopoly	Institutional Form 5: Climate Change Institutions
C. Pathways and Circuits of Socioeconomic Dynamics (CSD)	Technology Style & Production-Distibution Systems	Demand & Competition Regimes	State-Governance Systems	Business Systems	Finance Systems	Households-Community & Competition-Monopoly Systems	Climate Change Systems (including eco-geospatial systems)

Source: Adapted from O'Hara (2010: 375) (2025)

Structure of Accumulation Theory (McDonough et al. 2021), nor in the *Journal of World Systems Research* or the *Review* (ceased in 2016) (Fernand Braudel Centre, closed in 2020), and nor in *Ecological Economics.*

The only attempt I have seen to *structurally* integrate climate change in the political economy long wave/hegemony architecture as a specific sub-system is the paper by O'Hara (2010) in the *Journal of Economic Issues*. A similar method is used in this current book vis-à-vis the CSD. These examples are shown in Table 3.3:

This method of solving the systems and sub-system problem is by including climate change institutions as a necessary set of arrangements to enable ecology and other sub-systems to function effectively to promote socioeconomic and political performance (long wave upswings and hegemony). In this current book, I include ecological and geospatial structures and relationships, including climate change (and CPSP) dynamics, as part of the circuits of socioeconomic dynamics (CSD). How this is done is illustrated in some depth in Chap. 1 (Table 1.1). Then in Chap. 4, I detail the long waves of climate change over several millennia, thousands, hundreds, and more recent and future years. Chapter 5 situates the climate (eco-geo-spatial relations) as part of the Dutch CSD and provides some details about the Little Ice Age in terms of magnitude and adaptation. Chapters 6–8 also situate climate (re the eco-geo-spatial system) as part of the British, US, and Chinese circuits, providing some details about how these systems impact planet Earth and these nations during such periods and responses to it. Climate change is also included as one of the polycrises in Chap. 9 and in Chap. 10 on the "prewar" (WW3) situation.

3.10 Recent "Empirical" Methods Used to Scrutinize Long Waves

It is also important to survey the empirical material on long waves. Regarding the meaning of "empirical," I put this question to the famous "ChatGPT" (2024), AI platform developed by Microsoft, and, in part, got a response thus (5 August 2024): "Empirical can … be used … broadly to describe something that is practical, factual, or based on real-world examples, as opposed to being abstract, theoretical, or speculative. In various fields, such as science, social sciences, economics, and medicine, empirical methods and evidence are widely used to support the development of theories, models, policies, and decision-making processes."

In this context, there are various types of "empirical" evidence that addresses issues of long waves, and Table 3.4 outlines merely *some* examples of such empirical material (from the second long wave of long wave scholarship).

This shows there are various types of empirical evidence provided by long wave scholars. The first five types all engage in a thoroughly historical (H) analysis of waves, whereas the last two engage in a thoroughly technical (T) analysis of waves that do not engage thoroughly in qualitative-historical detail. The H1 style, provided by Mager (1987), uses mainly history to scrutinize long waves without a sophisticated theory. This book is very good, providing an excellent introduction to the

Table 3.4 Various empirical methods used to scrutinize long waves

Type of empirical work	First exponent	Second exponent	Third exponent
H1. Historical Inquiry	Mager (1987)	Tylecote (1992)	Freeman and Louçã (2001)
H2. Qualitative Phases of Evolution of Capitalism	Freeman and Louçã (2001) (also H3)	McDonough et al. (2010) (Long Waves?)	O'Hara (2025)
H3. Historical Analysis of Specific Long Wave Variables and/or (Sub)Systems	Mandel (1980)	Tylecote (1992)	O'Hara (2000, 2009, 2025)
H4. Sectoral Analysis	Rostow (1978)	Mensch (1975)	Forrester (1977)
H5. C-P-SP, Hegemony Analysis	Wallerstein (1983)	Goldstein (1988)	Chase-Dunn (1998)
S6. Statistical Analysis	Solomou (1990, 1998)	Reijnders (1992)	Kleinknecht (1996)
S7. Spectral Analysis	Reijnders (1990)	Ozouni et al. (2015, 2018)	Korotayev and Tsirel (2010)

subject for a general audience (applied to the USA). The other two examples provide a more rigorous theory to accompany history.

The second type of long wave analysis (H2) is also historically based, providing a "phases of capitalist development" inquiry into waves. The one by Freeman and Louçã (2001), which has already been discussed in general terms, additionally specifies that each long wave is different, and that structural crises of adjustment may impact different variables in a myriad of ways due to qualitative changes. Hence, GDP growth (per capita) may not be the variable most adequate for the analysis of each crisis. Other historical references using qualitative phases, such as McDonough et al. (2010), may have been influenced by Freeman and Louçã (2001), since the editors changed their SSA inquiry from "performance and phases" (in earlier work) to "phases of capitalist development" (often without adequate "performance" and long waves). But this change in theory is not detailed since it is an edited book, and some authors in the volume keep the original theory of "performance and phases" typical of SSA analysis. It is mainly a theoretical history, as distinct from Freeman and Louçã's work which is an exhaustively documented (technological-institutional) history.

H3 wave works use a specific analysis of phases of capitalist development, emphasizing certain variables, processes, and (sub)systems ("performance"). For instance, Mandel places emphasis on the rate of profit as being the dominant empirical variable affecting/influencing upswing and downswing under capitalism. Others agree with Mandel, such as Anwar Shaikh (1992), and Louis Fontvielle (1992), among many others. Tylecote uses various (sub)systems to analyze waves, including successive technology styles (as with Freeman and Louçã), plus monetary, population, inequality, and (to some degree) environmental feedback mechanisms/processes (as well as institutional analysis). In the past, O'Hara has followed a Gordon/Aglietta architecture in viewing SSAs/regulation through the lens of regimes of accumulation, plus various institutional forms such as global, corporate, financial, familial, and environmental subsystems, through phases of evolution (performance) of capitalism. More latterly I have widened the scope of analysis to long wave, hegemony, and eco-geo-spatial relations by, for instance, including sub-systems such as technology styles, institutional spheres (state, business, finance, households), and eco-spatial ecological relations (in this current book).

Another type of historical analysis of long waves includes that of Rostow, who concentrates on the primary versus the manufacturing sectors, set in the framework of the irreducible complexity of history; and that of Mensch, who concentrates on invention and innovation in various sectors as helpful to emasculate depression. Wallerstein also uses a historical framework, as already shown, dealing with core, periphery, and semi-peripheral inquiry, and successive hegemonic states as well as long waves. Goldstein adds to this CPSP framework an emphasis on international relations, and the way in which wars intersect with long waves (of growth and prices).

We also investigate two types of statistical analyses of long waves, which do not include detailed historical inquiry (at least not for LWHegCC), but instead depend almost entirely on statistical and econometric techniques. Solomou, Jan Reijnders, and Kleinknecht are three of the main protagonists of this method.

The second style (but seventh general category; S7) of economic techniques used to examine long waves is that of spectral analysis. Jan Reijnders was an earlier exponent of this method, whereas Ozouni and coauthors plus Korotayev and Tsirel have used aspects of this method more recently. Reijnders (1990) seeks to update Kondratiev's methods of long wave inquiry, since he thinks he was on the right path. He uses spectral analysis, "which is a technique to decompose the total variance of a time series into contributions from various frequencies" (p.218) and different domains of time, with the Kondratiev wave estimated at 40–60 years and the Kuznets wave at a duration of 15–25 years. In between these years is a buffer zone applying to neither Kondratiev nor Kitchin waves.

Using a series of statistics for Great Britain for 1700–1985, which has the fullest data set of all nations, and replacing data for the two world wars with linear interpolations, the series is standardized, and subsequent spectra results are obtained. Reijnders shows that the GDP spectra provide very good results for Kondratiev waves, with employment having a similar wave pattern, and unemployment echoing these wave patterns. He concludes that "Kondratiev's hypothesis [of long waves] survives the spectral analytic test. This accords in a broad sense with the results obtained [from] some other applications of spectral analysis in this field" (p. 236). (See also Chap. 5 on the Dutch Republic for further such work.)

Solomou (1990, 1998) has provided consistent statistical analyses of long "cycles"' (not *waves*), with an emphasis on explanations that have specific, standard, long wave patterns of upswing, downswing, amplitude, periodicity, and endogenous regularity. Summarizing Solomou (1998), he critiques most sympathetic econometric analyses of long cycles, e.g., that of Reijnders, for using data prior to 1870 that is said to be of "doubtful quality," and therefore Solomou concentrates on the period 1870 to the 1990s and finds that while there is fairly good data consistent with the patterns of long waves in numerous areas, these studies do not support long cycles of an endogenous type, since the long upswings, downswings, and turning points are caused by historically specific factors such as certain institutional stabilizing processes that are peculiar to the geographical area and historical eras.

This is a very interesting conclusion since it is almost identical to the *theory of long waves* presented in this current book. Solomou argues, for instance, that there have been three main eras of the world economy since 1870. The first was that of the gold standard era from 1870 to 1913, when fixed exchange rates provided an important foundation for the major industrial economies of Britain, France, Germany, and the USA to engage in core–periphery exchange of primary for manufacturing commodities where factor mobility was relatively high, and the gold standard enabled suitable adjustments in the face of shocks to the system. During this era, he shows Britain and the US displaying two types of cycles, one (Juglar) of about 10 years, and the other (Kuznets) of just less than 25 years in duration.

Solomou (1998, ch 3), in response to van Duijn's thesis of world waves, finds that there were serious depressions in the world economy during the 1870s and early 1880s. But then relatively buoyant upswings during the late 1890s to 1913 in many industrial economies (but not Britain), with some inverse growth tendencies between Europe and the USA, and some less developed nations enhancing their growth tendencies.

This was followed by a new era of global performance during the 1910s to 1940s (which he calls the "interwar era"), including a downswing phase between 1914 and 1938, due to structural factors, such as rising US global power generating global growth instabilities, such as Minsky-style financial fragility and the failure of global leadership (pp. 93–95). This is said to be followed by the postwar era (1945 to 1990s [onwards?]), including strong growth for the world economy from 1945 to 1973, followed by deteriorating performance during the 1970s to the 1990s. Cyclical instability was said to be much lower during the postwar boom, due to, for instance, the rising institutional size and stability of the state and the Bretton Woods System (BWS). This is said to be followed during the 1970s to the 1990s by some deep recessions (including a "depression" in the early 1990s) as instability increased as it did during the 1910s–1940s.

Solomou thus finds statistical evidence for a long wave type motion of downswing (1870s–1980s), followed by upswing (1890s–1910s), then downswing (1910s–1930s), upswing (1940s–1970s), and finally downswing (1970s–1990s); subject to the caveats of uneven development not only between core, periphery (and semi-periphery?) but also within core (and likely periphery, etc.). But he dismisses this as evidence for long cycles, since he argues it is caused by structural changes in the institutional fabric of nations, areas, and the world economy as a whole. As he says:

> Irregular (stochastic) long cycles have been observed in modern economies. Two types of long duration fluctuations have been observed. First, there has been an irregular long cycle

> in the performance of world trade and production since 1870. This is not equivalent to arguing that endogenous Kondratiev [cycles] describe world economic development: however, a series of impulses to world institutions have propagated a cyclical pattern in world economic growth. Secondly, a long duration cycle has been observed at the national level over some historical periods.
>
> The lesson to be learned is that for institutions to endure they need viable adjustment mechanisms. ... The many changes to cyclical features reflect, among other things, changes to economic structures, policy frameworks and behavioral patterns. ... One theme that runs through this survey of economic cycles is that institutional changes have a major effect in determining the nature of economic cycles in different epochs. [Solomou 1998: 117, 104]

This conclusion is remarkably similar, in very general terms, to the current book, but this current book adds some fundamental elements. Solomou argues against long cycles but in favor of cyclical (wave) movements being conditioned by institutional-structural arrangements. This current book also argues against long cycles; but *for* long waves, where the latter are likely irregular and subject to CPSP forces, but nonetheless being conditioned by the interplay of institutional arrangements, technological styles, hegemonies, and forms of eco-geo-spatial change. Solomou and my work on waves could also be considered similar with upswings being exogenous but downswings being endogenous, if he were to accept these types of (long) waves (rather than long cycles). (See also Solomou 2024.)

Numerous, more recent, spectral (and cross-spectral) studies have also been undertaken on long movements of capitalism. For instance, Ozouni et al. (2015) study six European nations (France, England, Sweden, Italy, the Netherlands, and Germany) for the period 1850–2010, using Maddison Project datasets, especially real GDP per capita growth rates, and find clear long waves for these nations. On average, they find upswings from 1850 to 1870, downswings from 1870 to 1890, upswings from the 1890s to 1925, downswings from 1925 to 1945, followed by an upswing from 1945 to 1990. Generally, England's economy tends to be ahead of the others, whereas the other nations lag England in wave dynamics. They also find some evidence for shorter and longer waves. In a follow-up paper, Ozouni et al. (2018) find similar results for the USA, UK, Germany, and France, but regarding causality, they find significant complexity regarding lags and robustness on the link between waves and patents.

Another spectral analysis, Korotayev and Tsirel (2010), finds clear evidence for long waves of slightly more than 50 years duration for World GDP dynamics during the period 1870–2007 (providing backing for van Duijn's (1983) main hypothesis about world waves), and long waves for areas of Europe and North America going back to 1820. They hypothesize that the world system was likely not sufficiently integrated for world long waves to be detected during the 1780–1870 period. They also found evidence for Kitchin and Juglar cycles. In a follow-up paper, Korotayev et al. (2020) provide evidence supporting the notion that recent growth dynamics have shifted from the advanced economies of Europe and North America, etc., to some of the developing nations (especially China, India, etc.).

My own analysis of long waves of growth, hegemony and climate change (LWHegCC) has three main components, in light of the literature review and its main conclusions.

For the first component, I utilize the *PoPE contingency paradigm* for assessing whether there are (long) waves of growth, hegemony, and climate change. This states that whether there are certain phases of a long wave, hegemony or climate change is contingent on numerous factors. It depends upon the historical trajectory in motion, the power dynamics between states, the magnitude of CCC impacts, the array of heterogeneous agents and groups, the contradictory forces, the degree of uncertainty, the extent and nature of innovation, and the efficacy of policy and governance. All these factors influence the manner of reproduction of the circuits of socioeconomic dynamics and its systems and subsystems.

The second component assesses the historical trajectories of LWHegCC dynamics through the use of other references, data, and my own analysis of statistics to complement and integrate with the PoPE paradigm. My empirics include various dimensions. For growth I utilize the Maddison Project (and in places also the WDI World Bank database) to scrutinize growth for the Dutch and British since 1500, the US since 1800 and China since 1800. I use real GDP per capita levels and real GDP per capita decadal AAGRs, plus other statistics. Since this is a book I use materials that can be easily digested by a wide audience, using decadal GDP per capita growth, with a linear trend bar to differentiate from waves. Using trend bar versus wave ("eliminating the trend"), above the trend bar is considered (long or short wave) upswing (U), inside the trend bar is borderline (B) performance, and below the trend bar is (long or short wave) downswing (D). I am specifically looking for long wave upswings (and downswings) that last for several decades, indicating durable structures providing long-term growth potentials (or lack of potentials). I am also linking (long) wave upswings with periods of hegemony and climate change dynamics. In between periods of hegemony, I expect much less buoyant performance as well as polycrises.

Thirdly, I integrate long waves of growth with hegemony and geo-spatial-climate change. In this context, I have chapters on hegemony, growth, and climate change for Dutch (Chap. 5), British (Chap.. 6), US (Chap. 7), and Chinese (Chap. 8) capitalism, including a chapter introducing climate change waves (Chap. 4), polycrises in between hegemonies (Chaps. 9 and 10), and a summary of long waves during the 1940s–2020s for the world and its major nations and regions (Chap. 11).

Using these methods, I find, for the most general conclusions, long wave upswings, hegemonic dominance, and specific forms of climate change to be characteristic of the Dutch Republic of 1580–1640 (or more generally the first half of the 1600s), Britain during 1820–1880/1820–1870, and the United States during the 1950s–1970s/1940s–1980s. I also find long wave upswings during the 1950s–1980s (circa) for these three economies (and many others). These results and many others are documented throughout this book.

3.11 Conclusion: The Way Forward

Chapters 2 and 3 have thus laid the basis for a critical review of the literature on long waves, with supplementary material linking it to hegemony and climate change. We examined the major scholars in the field of long waves and the major issues that need addressing. Our problematic is to examine the waves of growth, hegemony, and climate change and to show how they are interrelated from the time of the Dutch Golden Age to the present and the future. We also seek to illustrate how waves of climate change down the ages provide insights into contemporary issues of growth, hegemony, and climate dynamics.

Broad themes that inform this book involve three core themes. The first is that waves of growth, hegemony, and climate change are generally considered to be indeterminate processes involving multifarious periodicities, amplitudes, and regularities. There are cycles involved in the processes associated with these long movements, but the major dynamics are of less specificity, because they involve very complex issues of time, motion, and variable regularity. Taking Joan Robinson's (1980) distinction between logical and historical time as a point of departure, we try and follow the historical approach, and in doing so "give up the search for grand general laws and [be] content to … inquire [into] how things happen" (p. 95). The waves per se are not cycles but are rather long-term changes impacted by the interface of eco-spatial, institutional, and technological change and actioned by a whole series of heterogeneous groups and agents.

Secondly, three methods or sources of knowledge are utilized to scrutinize this trilogy of waves that are interrelated through long historical time. The main one is the PoPE contingency paradigm, wherein we utilize the main principles of political economy to illustrate how the patterns of long waves (of growth, hegemony, climate change) are conditioned by a whole series of complex processes. In short, they involve dealing with historical processes and its evolution, the forces of hegemony and uneven development, the involvement of heterogeneous groups and agents, the forces of circular and cumulative causation (CCC), the contradictory forces of opposition and conflict, varying levels of risk and uncertainty, innovations and policy interventions that impinge on these processes, and set within the framework of the circuits of socioeconomic dynamics. Ancillary methods to PoPE include the new long wave method (NLWM) of statistical analysis of time series variables (see Glossary), and secondary literature to provide alternative information to supplement PoPE and NLWM.

Thirdly, taking some broad issues from the literature, a core one is that the long waves of growth and hegemony involve exogenous factors to build up resources for upswing, but once they are in motion, they endogenously undergo metamorphosis, maturity, and demise toward downswing. This thesis is so obvious once the literature and the evidence is fully displayed that it becomes a stylized fact involving little doubt or uncertainty. Long waves are thus not cycles in the full endogenous fashion but rather strong forces that tend to agglomerate around the historical forces associated with eco-spatial, institutional, and technological processes wherein groups and agents undertake core roles. The exogenous nature of the upswing does however involve a degree of endogeneity only insofar as core groups and agents do often try and establish a set of conditions to improve their collective performance and more productively cope with environmental conditions.

In this context, the next chapter (Chap. 4) introduces more detail about the climatological aspects of the subject, whereupon Chap. 5 starts the process of examining the first case study involving the Dutch from the mid-1500s to the present but paying special attention to the establishment of the Dutch Golden Age from the late fifteenth through to the mid-to-late sixteenth centuries. Subsequent chapters sequentially investigate the same themes for Britain (Chap. 6), the United States (Chap. 7), and China (Chap. 8). Thereafter, we study the structural polycrises of especially the 1970s–2020s (also alluding to earlier ones) (Chap. 9), the additional crisis of the pre-war era involving the Ukraine–Taiwan conflicts (Chap. 10), stylized empirics of long waves in the world economy during the 1940s–2020 (Chap. 11), the conclusion (Chap. 12), followed by the Glossary. [See O'Hara (Forthcoming) for future developments.]

References

Aglietta, Michel. 1974. *Regulation du mode de production capitaliste dans la longue priode. Exemple des tats-Unis* (1870-1970). Doctoral Thesis. Paris 1: Panth on-Sorbonne.

Aglietta, Michel. 1976. *Regulation et Crises du Capitalism*. Paris: Calmann-Levy. 2nd edition 1982. 3rd edition, Paris: Odille Jacob 1997.

Barlow, D. E., M. H. Barlow, and T. G. Chiricos. 1993. Long Economic Cycles and the Criminal Justice System. *Crime, Law and Social Change* 19 (2): 143–169.

Beckman, Robert. 1983. *The Downwave: Surviving the Second Great Depression*. London: Pan Books.

Bergesen, Albert. 1980. Cycles of formal colonial rule. In *Processes of the World System*, ed. Terence K. Hopkins and Immanuel Wallerstein, 119–126. Beverly Hills: Sage.

Berry, Brian J. L. 1991. *Long-Wave Rhythms in Economic Development and Political Behavior*. Baltimore: John Hopkins University.

BGW. 1984. Bowles, Samuel; David M. Gordon, and Thomas E. Weisskopf. *Beyond the Wasteland: A Democratic Alternative to Economic Decline*. Garden City, NY: Anchor Books.

BGW. 1990. Bowles, Samuel; David M. Gordon and Thomas E. Weisskopf. *After the Waste Land: A Democratic Economics for the Year 2000*. Armonk, NY: M.E. Sharpe.

Boyer, Robert, and Yves Saillard, eds. 2002. *Regulation Theory: The State of the Art*. London and New York: Routledge.

Chase-Dunn, Chris. 1998. *Global Formation: Structures of the World-Economy*. Lanham, MD: Rowman and Littlefield.

Cherry, Robert. 1991. Race and Gender Aspects of Marxian Macro-Models. *Science and Society* 55:60–78.

Clark, John, Christopher Freeman, and Luc Soete. 1981. Long Waves, Inventions and Innovations. *Futures* 13 (4): (Aug).

Day, Richard D. 1976. The Theory of the Long Cycle: Kondratiev, Trotsky, Mandel. *New Left Review* 98 (July–August):

Delbeke, Jos. 1981. Recent Long Wave Theories: A Critical Survey. *Futures* 4 (Aug):

Eklund, Klas. 1980. Long Waves in the Development of Capitalism? *Kyklos* 33 (3):

Elsner, Wolfram. 2016. Speculative Financial Capitalism Wacking Out Over an "Impossible" Profit Rate: The Infeasibility of a "Usual" Real Average Profit Rate, Considering Fictitious Capital, and its Implications. In *Marx, Veblen, and the Foundations of Heterodox Economics: Essays in Honor of John F. Henry*, ed. Tae-Hee Jo and Frederic S. Lee, 199–227. London: Routledge.

Fels, Rendigs. 1949. The Long-Wave Depression, 1873-97. *The Review of Economics and Statistics* 31 (1): 69–73.

Fontvielle, Louis. 1992. Rate of Profit and its Determining Factors from a Regulationist Point of View. In *New Findings in Long-Wave Research*, ed. Alfred Kleinknecht, Ernest Mandel, and Immanuel Wallerstein, 203–244. London: Macmillan.

Forrester, Jay W. 1961. *Industrial Dynamics*. Cambridge, MA: MIT Press.

Forrester, Jay W. 1968. *Principles of Systems*. Cambridge, MA: MIT Press.

Forrester, Jay W. 1969. *Urban Dynamics*. Cambridge, MA: MIT Press.

Forrester, Jay W. 1973. *World Dynamics*. Cambridge, MA: MIT Press.

Forrester, Jay W. 1976. The Systems Dynamic National Model: Understanding SocioEconomic Behavior and Policy Alternatives. *Technological Forecasting and Social Change* 9.

Forrester, Jay W. 1977. Growth Cycles. *De Economist* 125 (4):

Forrester, Jay W. 1981. Innovation and Economic Change. *Futures* 13 (4):

Freeman, Christopher, John Clark, and Luc Soet. 1982. *Unemployment and Technical Innovation: A Study on Long Waves and Economic Development*, 1982. London: Frances Pinter.

Freeman, Chris, and Francisco Louçã. 2001. *As Time Goes By: From the Industrial Revolution to the Information Revolution*. Oxford: OUP.

Futures. 1981. Special issue on long waves. 13 (4): 238–338.

Glyn, Andrew, and Robert Sutcliffe. 1972. *British Capitalism, Workers and the Profits Squeeze*. Harmondsworth: Penguin.

Goldstein, Jushua. 1988. *Long Cycles: Prosperity and War in the Modern Age*. New Haven: Yale University Press.

Gordon, David M. 1978. Up and Down the Long Roller Coaster. In *U.S. Capitalism in Crisis*, ed. Crisis Reader Editorial Collective, 22–35. New York: URPE.

Gordon, David M. 1980. Stages of Accumulation and Long Economic Cycles. In *Processes of the World-System*, ed. Terrence Hopkins and Immanuel Wallerstein, 9–45. London: Sage Publishers.

Gordon, David M., Richard Edwards and Michael Reich. [GER]. (1982). *Segmented Work, Divided Workers: The Historical Transformation of Labor in the United States*. Cambridge: Cambridge University Press.

Graham, A. and Senge, P. 1980. A Long-Wave Hypothesis of Innovation. *Technological Forecasting and Social Change* 17: 283–311.

Jessop, Bob, ed. 2001. *Regulation Theory and the Crises of Capitalism*. 5 Vols. Cheltenham: Edward Elgar.

Keohane, Robert O. 1984. *After Hegemony: Cooperation and Discord in the World Political Economy*. Princeton: Princeton University Press.

Kleinknecht, Alfred. 1981a. Innovation, Accumulation, and Crisis: Waves in Economic Development? *Review* 4 (4):

Kleinknecht, Alfred. 1981b. Observations on the Schumpeterian Swarming of Innovations. *Futures* 13 (4):

Kleinknecht, Alfred. 1987. *Innovation Patterns in Crisis and Prosperity: Schumpeter's Long Cycle Reconsidered*. London: Palgrave Macmillan.

Kleinknecht, A., ed. 1996. *Determinants of Innovation*. London: Palgrave Macmillan. https://doi.org/10.1007/978-1-349-13917-0_4.

Kleinknecht, Alfred, Ernest Mandel, and Immanuel Wallerstein, eds. 1992. *New Findings in Long-Wave Research*. London: Macmillan.

Korotayev, Andrey V., and Sergey V. Tsirel. 2010. A Spectral Analysis of World GDP Dynamics: Kondratieff Waves, Kuznets Swings, Juglar, and Kitchin Cycles in Global Economic Development, and the 2008-2009 Economic Crisis. *Structure and Dynamics* 4 (1): 1–57.

Korotayev, Andrey V., Stanislav E. Bilyuga, and Alisa R. Shishkina. 2020. Which Countries Generate Kondratieff Waves in Global GDP Growth Rate Dynamics in the Contemporary World. *Journal of Globalization Studies* 11 (1): 33–63.

Kotz, David M. 1990. A Comparative Analysis of the Theory of Regulation and the Social Structures of Accumulation Theory. *Science and Society* 54 (1): 5–28.

Kotz, David M. and Terrence McDonough. 2010. Global Neoliberalism and the Contemporary Social Structure of Accumulation. In Terrence McDonough, Michael Reich and David Kotz, 93–120.

Lippit, Victor. 2005. *Capitalism*. London & NY: Routledge.

Lippit, Victor. 2014. The Neoliberal Era and the Financial Crisis in the Light of SSA Theory. *Review of Radical Political Economics* 46:141–161.

Louçã, Francisco. 2019. *As Time Went By - Long Waves in the Light of Evolving Evolutionary Economics*. Science Policy Research Unit (SPRU). University of Sussex, UK. 70pp. www.sussex.ac.uk/spru/swps2019-05

Louçã, Francisco. 2021. As Time Went By - Why is the Long Wave So Long? *Journal of Evolutionary Economics* 31 (3): 749–771. https://link.springer.com/article/10.1007/s00191-021-00724-9\=][PO][P09+.

Louçã, Francisco, and Michael Ash. 2018. *Shadow Networks: Financial Disorder and the System that Caused Crisis*. Oxford: Oxford University Press.

Mager, Nathan H. 1987. *The Kondratieff Waves*. New York: Praeger.

McDonough, Terrence, Michael Reich, and David M. Kotz, eds. 2010. *Contemporary Capitalism and its Crises: Social Structure of Accumulation Theory for the 21st Century*. Cambridge: CUP.

McDonough, Terrence; David Kotz and Michael Reich, ed. 2014. *Social Structure of Accumulation Theory*. 2 Vols. Cheltenham, UK & Northampton, US: Edward Elgar.

McDonough, Terrence, Cian McMahon, and David Kotz, eds. 2021. *Handbook of Social Structure of Accumulation Theory*. Cheltenham: Edward Elgar.

Mandel, Ernest. 1964. The Economics of Neo-Capitalism. *Socialist Register* 1:56–67.

Mandel, Ernest. 1975. *Late Capitalism*. London: New Left Books.

Mandel, Ernest. 1978. *The Second Slump*. London: New Left Books.

Mandel, Ernest. 1980. *Long Waves of Capitalist Development: The Marxist Interpretation*. London: C.U.P.

Mandel, Ernest. 1981. Explaining Long Waves of Capitalist Development. *Futures* 13 (4):

Mandel, Ernest. 1992. The International Debate on Long Waves of Capitalist Development: An Intermediary Balance Sheet. In *New Findings in Long-Wave Research*, ed. Alfred Kleinknecht, Ernest Mandel, and Immanuel Wallerstein, 316–338. London: Macmillan.

Marshall, Michael. 1987. *Long Waves of Regional Development*. New York: St Martin's Press.

Mensch, Gerhard. 1975. *Stalemate in Technology*. Cambridge, MA: Balinger, 1979. Translated from the original German Edition.

Mensch, Gerhard, Charles Coutinho, and Klaus Kaasch. 1981. Changing Capital Value and the Propensity to Innovate. *Futures* 13 (4):

Nardone, E., and T. McDonough. 2010. Global Neoliberalism and the Possibility of Transnational State Structures. In McDonough, Kotz and Reich, eds. 168–194.

Neumann, Manfred. 1997. *The Rise and Fall of the Wealth of Nations: Long Waves in Economics and International Politics*. Cheltenham: Edwards Elgar.

Nordhaus, William. 1974. The Falling Rate of Profits. In *Brookings Papers on Economic Activity*, ed. A. Okun and L. Perry.

Oakley, Allen. 1983. *Schumpeter's Theory of Capitalist Motion*. Aldershot: Edward Elgar.

O'Hara, Phillip Anthony. 1995. Household Labor, the Family and Macroinstitutional Instability in the United States: 1940s-1990s. *Review of Social Economy* 53 (1): 89–120. https://doi.org/10.1080/00346769500000004.

O'Hara, Phillip Anthony. 2000. *Marx, Veblen and Contemporary Institutional Political Economy: Principles and Unstable Dynamics of Capitalism*. Cheltenham: Edward Elgar.

O'Hara, Phillip Anthony. Ed. 2001. *Encyclopedia of Political Economy*. London and New York: Routledge. Paper Edition.

O'Hara, Phillip Anthony. 2003. Recent Changes to the IMF, WTO and SPD: Emerging Global of Regulation or Social Structure of Accumulation for Long Wave Upswing? *Review of International Political Economy* 10 (3): 481–519. https://doi.org/10.1080/09692290308426.

O'Hara, Phillip Anthony. 2006a. A New Neoliberal Social Structure of Accumulation for Sustainable Global Growth and Development? In *Alternative Theories of the State*, ed. Steve Pressman, 91–112. London: Palgrave-Macmillan.

O'Hara, Phillip Anthony. 2006b. A Chinese Social Structure of Accumulation for Capitalist Long Wave Upswing? *Review of Radical Political Economy* 38 (3): 397–404. https://doi.org/10.1177/048661340629090.

O'Hara, Phillip Anthony. 2009. *Growth and Development in the Global Political Economy: Social Structures of Accumulation and Modes of Regulation*. London and New York: Routledge. Paper Edition.

O'Hara, Phillip Anthony. 2010. After Neoliberalism: A Social Structure of Accumulation or Mode of Regulation for Global or Regional Performance? *Journal of Economic Issues* 46 (2): 369–383. https://doi.org/10.2753/JEI0021-3624440209.

O'Hara, Phillip Anthony. 2012. Short-, Long-, and Secular-Wave Growth in the World Political Economy: Periodicity, Amplitude, and Phases for 8 Regions, 108 Countries, 1940-2010. *International Journal of Political Economy* 41 (1): 3–46. https://doi.org/10.2753/IJP0891-1916410101.

O'Hara, Phillip Anthony. 2013. Policies and Institutions for Moderating Deep Recessions, Debt Crises and Financial Instabilities. *Panoeconomicus* 60:19–49. https://doi.org/10.2298/PAN1301019H.

O'Hara, Phillip Anthony. 2016. The Contemporary Relevance of Karl Marx's Heterodox Political Economy. In *Marx, Veblen and the Foundations of Heterodox Economics: Essays in Honor of John F. Henry*, ed. Tae-Hee Jo and Frederic S. Lee, 50–78. London and New York: Routledge.

O'Hara, Phillip Anthony. 2023. *Principles of Institutional and Evolutionary Political Economy: Applied to Current World Problems*. Revised Edition. Singapore: Springer Nature Principles of Institutional and Evolutionary Political Economy: Applied to Current World Problems | SpringerLink

O'Hara, Phillip Anthony. 2025. *Long Waves of Growth, Hegemonic Power, and Climate Change in the World Economy: Dutch, British, US, and Chinese Capitalism and Structural Polycrises*. Singapore: Springer Nature.

O'Hara, Phillip Anthony. Forthcoming. *Advances in Political Economy Principles: Applied to Current World Problems*.

Ozouni, Eirini, Constantinos Katrakylidis, and Grigoris Zarotiadis. 2015. Investigating Long Cycles of Capitalism with Spectral and Cross-Spectral Analysis. *South-Eastern Europe Journal of Economics* 1:7–30.

Ozouni, Eirini, Constantinos Katrakylidis, and Grigoris Zarotiadis. 2018. Technology Evolution and Long Waves: Investigating their Relation with Spectral and Cross-Spectral Analysis. *Journal of Applied Economics* 21 (1): 160–174.

Perez, Carlotta. 2002. *Technological Revolutions and Financial Capital: The Dynamics of Bubbles and Golden Ages*. Cheltenham: Edward Elgar.

Perez, Carlotta. 2015. From Long Waves to Great Surges: Continuing in the Direction of Chris Freeman's 1997 Lecture on Schumpeter's *Business Cycles*. *European Journal of Economic and Social Systems* 27 (1–2): 69–80.

Regulation Journal. 2007–2024. *Revue de la regulation. Capitalisme, institutions, pouvoirs*. https://journals.openedition.org/regulation/

Reijnders, Jan. 1990. *Long Waves of Economic Development*. Aldershot: Edward Elgar.

Reijnders, Jan. 1992. Between Trends and Trade Cycles: Kondratieff Long Waves Revisited. In *New Findings in Long-Wave Research*, ed. Alfred Kleinknecht, Ernest Mandel, and Immanuel Wallerstein, 15–44. London: Macmillan.

Research Working Group. 1979. On Cyclical Rhythms and Secular Trends of the Capitalist World-Economy: Some Premises, Hypotheses, and Questions. *Review (Fernand Braudel Centre)* 2 (4): 483–500. (Wallerstein and Hopkins, Coordinators of RWG.).

Robinson, Joan. 1980. Time in Economic Theory. *Kyklos* 33 (2): 10–22.

Robinson, William I. 2012. Global Capitalism Theory and the Emergence of Transnational Elites. *Critical Sociology* 38 (3): 349–363.

Rosenberg, Hans. 1943. Political and Social Consequences of the Great Depression of 1873-1896 in Central Europe. *Economic History Review* 13 (1–2): 58–73.

Rostow, Walt Whitman. 1938. Investment and the Great Depression. *The Economic History Review* 8 (2): 136–158.

Rostow, Walt Whitman. 1960. *The Process of Economic Growth*. London: Oxford University Press.

Rostow, Walt Whitman. 1971. *Politics and the Stages of Growth*. Cambridge: Cambridge University Press.

Rostow, Walt Whitman. 1975. Kondratieff, Schumpeter and Kuznets: Trend Periods Revisited. *Journal of Economic History* 35 (4): 719–753.

Rostow, Walt Whitman. 1977. Caught by Kondratieff, *Wall Street Journal*, March 8.

Rostow, Walt Whitman. 1978. *The World Economy: History and Prospect*. London: Macmillan.

Rostow, Walt Whitman. 1984. *Why the Poor Get Richer and the Rich Slow Down*. London: Macmillan.

Rowthorn, Bob. 1980. *Capitalism, Conflict and Inflation*. London: Lawrence & Wishart.

Sheikh, Anwar. 1992. The Falling Rate of Profit as the Cause of Long Waves: Theory and Empirical Evidence. In *New Findings in Long Wave Research*, ed. Alfred Kleinknecht, Ernest Mandel, and Immanuel Wallerstein, 174–194. London: Macmillan.

Sherman, Howard Jay, and David X. Kolk. 1996. *Business Cycles and Forecasting*. New York: Harper Collins.

Solomou, Solomos. 1990. *Phases of Economic Growth 1850-1973: Kondratieff Waves and Kuznets Swings*. Cambridge: CUP.

Solomou, Solomos. 1998. *Economic Cycles: Long Cycles and Business Cycles Since 1870*. Manchester: Manchester University Press.

Solomou, Solomos. 2024. Kondratiev Cycles: An Evaluation. In *The Works of Nikolai D. Kondratiev*, ed. Makasheva Natalia, Warren J. Samuels, and Barnett Vincent, vol. 1, 64–70. London: Routledge. ebook. (Original edition published by Pickering & Chatto 1998). https://doi.org/10.4324/9781003552864.

Suter, Christian. 1989. Long Waves in the International Financial System: Debt-Default Cycles of Sovereign Borrowers. *Review (Fernand Braudel Centre)* 12 (1): 1–49.

Tylecote, Andrew. 1992. *The Long Wave in the World Economy: The Current Crisis in Historical Perspective*. London & New York: Routledge.

van Duijn, Jacob J. 1981. Fluctuations in Innovations over Time. *Futures* 13 (4):

van Duijn, J. J. 1983. *The Long Wave in Economic Life*. George Allen and Unwin. London: Boston.

Vayrynen, Raimo. 1983. Economic Cycles, Power Transitions, Political Management and Wars between Major Powers. *International Studies Quarterly* 27 (4): 389–418.

Wallace, Michael and David Brady. 2010. Globalization and Spatialization? The Worldwide Spatial Restructuring of the Labor Process. In ed. McDonough, Kotz and Reich, 121–144.

Wallerstein, Immanuel. 1983. The Three Instances of Hegemony in the History of World-Capitalist Economy. *International Journal of Comparative Sociology* 24 (1–2): 100–108.

Wallerstein, Immanuel. 1979. Kondratieff Up or Kondratieff Down? *Review* 1 (4):

Wallerstein, Immanuel. 1992. A Brief Agenda for the Future of Long-Wave Research. In *New Findings in Long-Wave Research*, ed. Alfred Kleinknecht, Ernest Mandel, and Immanuel Wallerstein, 343–342. London: Macmillan.

Wikipedia. 2023. *Regulation School*. https://en.wikipedia.org/wiki/Regulation_school. Accessed 22 Mar 2023.

Wolfson, Martin H. 1994. *Financial Crises: Understanding the Postwar U.S. Experience*. 2nd ed. Armonk, NY and London: M. E. Sharpe.

Chapter 4
Long Waves of Climate Change on Planet Earth

Abstract This chapter analyzes the long waves of climate change that have occurred over different historical periods on planet Earth, and what the significance of these are for historical and current issues of long waves of growth, hegemony, and climate change (LWHegCC). Special reference is then given to the more recent long waves of climate change and their relevance for the Dutch, British, US, and Chinese experience. In this context, we examine current issues of cascading tipping points, uncertainty, and climate change vis-a-vis long wave growth and hegemony into the future. Throughout the chapter, we utilize some of the principles of political economy (PoPE), explicitly or implicitly, to assist with the investigation. A conclusion follows.

Keywords Long waves of climate change · Principles of political economy · Cascading tipping points · Long waves of growth and hegemony · Dutch · British · US and Chinese experience · Planet Earth

4.1 Introduction

In the first volume of this three-volume series on political economy principles applied to world problems (O'Hara 2023), of which the current book is the second volume, I included a version of a paper from *Ecological Economics* that won the *EAEPE Prize* for journal article of the year (chap. 5) on "Climate Change" (O'Hara 2009). It also won the *Journal Article of the* Year award from CBS. In it I discussed the history of climate change, its contradictions, uneven developments, uncertainties, shared socioeconomic pathways, and cascading tipping points. Another paper examined these anomalies in light of policy issues and actions (O'Hara 2010). *This* current volume that you are now reading seeks to expand on aspects of these themes, written completely anew, especially as they relate to long waves of climate change from the past, the present, and potentially the future. These climate change long

P. A. O'Hara, *Long Waves of Growth, Hegemonic Power, and Climate Change in the World Economy*, https://doi.org/10.1007/978-981-96-4132-1_4

waves are important not only for contextualizing current and future climate trends and stylized facts, but also for situating long waves of growth and hegemonic power historically in these climatological changes, especially regarding the Dutch, British, US, and Chinese experiences, plus the world as a whole.

Scrutinizing the folder on the paper that won the prizes I realized that one of the referees wanted me to summarize and thereby emasculate most of the material I had included on long waves of climate change in the past and how it links to current trajectories. I wondered why they wanted me to very tersely summarize this past wave material, since few or no climate economists and political economists have studied climatological waves (or cycles), and most who do study them (who are usually "natural" scientists) call them cycles. To me cycles are rather deterministic movements with rather precise periodicities and amplitudes and well-delineated endogenous movements (see Huntington 1945; Dewey and Mandino 1973), whereas waves are less regular with greater amplitude and potentially more complex periodicities, determinations, and contingencies (O'Hara 2006, 2022). The waves that I discuss in this current chapter are the longer-term changes in climate that are indeed more irregular, but still with a long-term pattern that is easily comprehensible as being subject to a wave-like trajectory. I will also discuss cycles, especially sunspot cycles, and how they link or otherwise to these longer-term waves of climate change.

The *bible* of climate change theories and evidence that most of us study is usually thought to be the Intergovernmental Panel on Climate Change (IPCC) reports. The latest three volumes of IPCC reports were published as the Sixth Assessment Report, including volume one, *Climate Change 2021: The Physical Science Basis* (IPCC 2021), volume two *Climate Change 2022: Impacts, Adaptation and Vulnerability* (IPCC 2022a), and *Climate Change 2022: Mitigation of Climate Change* (IPCC 2022b). There is also the associated *Climate Change Synthesis 2023: Synthesis Report* (IPCC 2023) which can be considered a summary of the IPCC arguments, models, theories, and evidence. There is good reason to consider these volumes the bible of climate of climate change theory, models, empirics, and policies, given the huge resources, personnel, and organizational tasks committed to them, and the kudos which they rightly deserve.

Of course, there are numerous criticisms of the IPCC reports, ranging from those who challenge the culture of the environment in which their work is undertaken, to those who think they take a relatively conservative approach to the urgency and policies required for dealing with the crises of climate change, to those who think they overlook crucial dimensions of the problem, and even those who think they overstate the problem.[1] I generally accept the science behind the work of the IPCC and the general scientific research underlying it, including even agreeing with some of the criticisms of the reports. Personally, I would argue that the IPCC understates the problem, especially regarding the likely emergence (even now) of the cascading

[1] For some of the criticisms of the IPCC, see, firstly, the very thorough multi-dimensional analysis of the IPCC by over 30 scholars (de Pryck and Hulme 2023), secondly, scholars who think the IPCC understates the importance of solar influences (van Geel and Ziegler 2013), and, thirdly, a scholar who examines the importance of natural cycles on climate change (Jovanovic 2022).

(global) tipping points. It recognizes the likelihood of tipping points but does not specifically link many of them together as *cascading* tipping points in depth. Also, I would take issue with the ad hoc nature of some of the policy measures implied in the reports, rather than, as I would, taking a systemic approach to the required changes needed to engage seriously with mitigation as well as adaptation.

Overall though, as mentioned, I accept the science behind the arguments that the world is warming quickly and that climate change is happening at a fast rate whereby a number of serious climate events are in motion, often at increasingly critical heights of crisis. I am of course referring to the anomalies of much worse floods, rising waterways, heatwaves, droughts, wildfires, typhoons, cyclones, more serious *El Nino* events, and the decimation of numerous species of plants and animals, as well as ecosystems and communities. Research shows that these increasingly extreme events propel conflicts over resources, water, food, housing, migration, finance, and a host of other problems, which contribute to malnutrition, recessions, financial crises, and wars. The generation of polycrises (climate change being a core one, interrelated with some others) has now become institutionalized and is likely to become more extreme through historical time (see chap. 9 below).

In researching the question of long waves and short cycles of climate change, I found some very interesting material, by very serious ("natural") scientists, that in some respects the IPCC does acknowledge. In some of the (shortish) sections of their volumes on the history of climate change, the IPCC presents some data about waves of changing temperatures over successive decades, centuries, millennia, and eons. For instance, Fig. 4.1 is a typical example of this.

This is a stylized figure, from chap. 2 "Changing State of the Climate System," of the first volume of the IPCC's sixth report, where the past 60 million years of climate change is very tersely breezed through without any detail on the dynamics of the cycles and waves. The figure is "cut up" into four time periods, between now

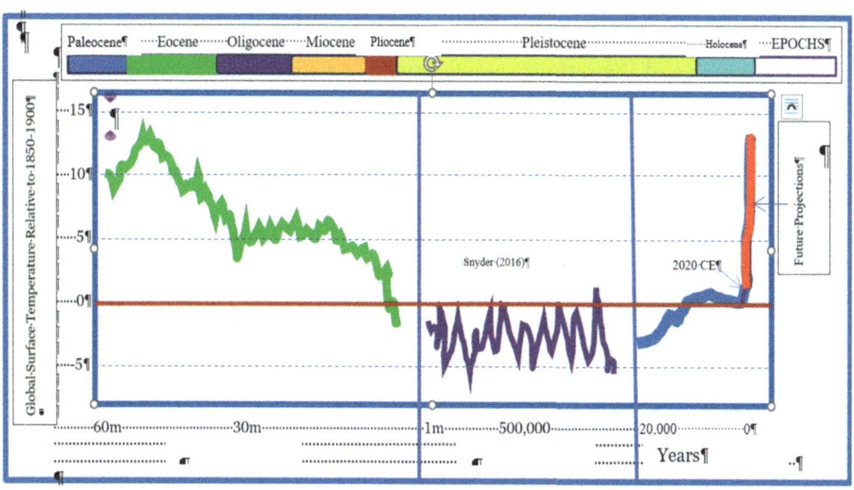

Fig. 4.1 Waves of climate change (°C). Before 2020 and after 2020. Millions, hundreds of thousands, tens of thousands, of years. Planet Earth. (Source: Adapted from IPCC 2021, 296)

and (1) future projections (red bar; "hockey stick") (2) 20 thousand years before the present (BP); (3) one million years BP; (4) 60 million years BP (left-hand side). Recognizable waves of climate change can be seen in (2)–(4) time scales, but the figure has information too condensed for it to be analyzed in detail; this is typical of the 2021/2023 IPCC reports at least for the center and left-hand side sub-figs. (60 million years BP and one million years BP). Generally, the time period between 20,000 years and today is also very summarized and does not enable us to situate various hegemonies adequately into the analysis, but does show some rise and falls. The "hockey stick" major expansion in temperature for planet Earth (continuing into the future) does not show waves or cycles.

All the time periods are too condensed to be analyzed in any clarity. The chapter that it comes from (IPCC 2021, Chap. 2) does recognize that climate change is potentially generated through a number of mechanisms and processes, including especially changes in solar and orbital forcing, volcanic aerosols forcing, and well-mixed greenhouse gasses (GHGs). But no *details* are provided on the degree to which and how especially the solar, orbital, and associated forces such as cosmic dust impact specifically in the past, present, and future. In the last analysis, for instance, on the solar issue, only decadal sunspot cycles seem to have been briefly mentioned in various places by the IPCC, and their contribution to effective radiative forcing (ERF) from 1750 to 2019 is calculated by the IPCC to be −0.02, with uncertainty (U) levels ranging from −0.08 to 0.06. This compares with anthropogenic factors over the same period contributing an ERF of 2.72 (U levels between 1.96 and 3.48), including CO_2 of 2.16 (U = 1.90 to 2.41), CH_4 + N_20 + Halogens of 1.16 (U = 0.94 to 1.38), Ozone of 0.47 (U = 0.24 to 0.71), with stratospheric water vapor being only slightly significant; aerosols having a negative ERF of −1.06 (U = −1.92 to −0.21), and albedo levels being negative but barely significant.

I hope to rectify the problem of information condensation by placing more stress on the *principle of historical specificity*, that current problems and issues in the world need to be situated in a long, medium, and short historical context, before they can be adequately understood and acted upon for policy and structural-actioned governance. None of the serious scientists who contributed to the analysis of these waves and cycles (discussed below) over several historical epochs and stages were included in the IPCC working groups (that I know of), so they understandably may feel under-appreciated. But more seriously, their work should be recognized and an attempt made to fit it into the picture of current and future trajectories (if and when possible), and if not possible be self-conscious of the criticisms made of the work. In the next section, I therefore examine numerous aspects of their theories and empirics on waves and cycles of climate change in order to provide a foundation for doing this. Later we come back to the IPCC approach to these and related matters in order to make some attempt to clarify the issues.

4.2 Historical Specificity of Long Waves of Climate Change

Climatologically inclined geographers, geologists, physicists, and others who study waves and cycles of climate change from the distant past to the present and the future tend to engage in the climate change debate through a discussion of phases of evolution of planet Earth, sunspots, Milanković cycles, interplanetary dynamics, rotation irregularities, volcanic processes, dust particles, aerosols, cloud cover, GHGs, and a host of related factors. I will start this section by summarizing the nature of the various long wave eons that Earth underwent over billions, hundreds of millions, several million and thousands of years as I link the pattern to the present state of climate change and the future.

There have been five major very long waves-eons of change (and four sub-waves within the Phanerozoic eon) for planet Earth, sketched in Table 4.1.

The first, *Hadean Long Wave* (4.6b–4.0b years BP), represents the earliest stage of the formation of planet Earth, with plumes of various substances (such as H [Hydrogen], N [Nitrogen], He [Helium], and H_2O [water vapor]) being ejected from volcanoes to form the atmosphere, with surface molten taking the form of super-hot lava. There are several theories of the origins of the moon, which impacts climate majorly, one being the *giant impact hypothesis*, that the earth was violently assaulted by a large object, perhaps the size of Mars, which sliced a portion off, which became the moon. Eventually, non-gaseous materials formed inside the Earth, with the densest irons and nickels becoming part of the core. The mantle enfolded the core with lighter materials forming igneous (dark) rocks called *sima*. This was encapsulated by lighter-colored granites (feldspar, nickel, and quartz). The atmosphere of early Earth was conditioned by deoxygenated gasses, with the weightier sulfides subsiding on the surface, lighter ones (Ch4 [Methane], He, and H) being distributed into space, nitrogen collecting in the atmosphere, and water vapor rising to form clouds and snow. There was little or no oxygen or carbon in the atmosphere during this wave, but oceans, plate tectonics, and continental crusts were formed.

Table 4.1 Long waves of climate change (CC) and biology on planet Earth

Long waves of evolution	Periodicity	Core processes
1. Hadean long wave	4.6b–4.0b yrs. BP	Evolution of planet earth
2. Archean long wave	4.0b–2.5b yrs. BP	Emergence of simple life
3. Proterozoic long wave	2.5b–540 m yrs. BP	Multicellular organisms
4. Phanerozoic long wave	540 m BP to 1975	Alternating glacial and hot periods
(a) Paleozoic wave	540 m–250 m yrs. BP	Zonal CC mass extinction events
(b) Mesozoic wave	250 m–65 m yrs. BP	Hot uniform CC, reptiles→birds+mammals
(c) Cenozoic wave	65 m–2.6 m yrs. BP	From hot to cold, era of mammals
(d) Quaternary waves	2.6 m BP–11,700 yrs. BP	Several waves of glaciation
(e) Holocene wave	11,700 yrs. BP to 1975	Heating period since 11,700 BP
5. Anthropocene wave	1975–present	Climate extremes deepening

Source: Adapted from Harris (2023), Waters et al. (2023)

During the second, *Archean Long Wave* (4.0–2.5b years), life emerged as oxygen and carbon concentrations developed, and an ozone layer began to protect life from deadly UV rays. As the Earth cooled, rocks, continental plates, and two major continents formed, while high-grade rocks solidified from volcanic flows, which became embryonic continents, and low-grade rocks formed sediments on the sea floors. The Earth's magnetic field began to protect the atmosphere, and the first four glacial movements occurred during the Ice Age, followed by a long warming era. Photosynthesis, oxygenation, and carbonization coevolved with the underlying conditions necessary for the further development of modern climates, and for life itself, especially simple-celled organisms such as cyanobacteria and stromatolites, which formed during this time.

During the third, *Proterozoic Long Wave* (2.5b–540 m years) the so-called Great Oxygen Event, starting 2.4b years ago (circa), enabled the development of more complex life forms and more sophisticated climate systems (Olejarz 2021). During this time there were several global glaciations, surges in oxygen concentration, heightened carbon sequestration, supercontinent cycles, and the first *widespread* evidence of multicellular life on Earth. New fossil records provide "the strongest evidence yet that multicellular eukaryotes (having nucleic cells) with decimetric dimensions and regular developmental programs populated the marine biosphere at least a billion years before the Cambrian Explosion" (Zhu 2016, 1), by 1.5b Years BP. Other multicellular lifeforms of this era include blue-green algae, cnidarians (corals and jellyfish), and earthworms in several areas. There was a major change in the tilting angle of the Earth's magnetic field in the final glacial period of this wave, and a change in both the speed of rotation and the path of the Earth around the sun. Significantly, volcanic land areas merged to resemble current continents, and plates collided to form subduction areas and rift valleys. Tectonic processes, the high level of obliquity of the Earth, and silicate weathering interacted to form five or more major periods of glaciation, during which "land masses as well as marginal marine environments were ice free whereas open oceans were covered with ice" (Sreedhar and Faizal Kahn 2021, 14).

From the fourth, *Phanerozoic Long Wave* (540 m years to the contemporary age, circa), we get clearer data of long waves of ice ages and hot periods, alternating during the era to the present; with more complex evolution of multicellular organisms that diversified into organisms currently on planet Earth; while the supercontinent *Pangaea* separated into the continents we have today. A huge variety of marine organisms and land ecologies emerged, first plants and then animals. Several major periods of extinction occurred alongside four major waves of cold or glacial eras followed by hotter periods. Major extinction events occurred around 500 m BP, 450 m BP, 250 m BP, 190 m BP, 70 m BP, and from the 1970s Anthropocene onwards when temperatures rose 1.45 °C (2023) compared with pre-industrial times. The warm periods of 600–500 m years BP changed to ice ages during the mid-400 m years BP; then again from pre-to-post 400 m years BP (warm) to 350 m–270 years BP (ice age); from 250 m–150 m years BP (warm) to 170 m–130 m years BP (not so cold); and again 130 m–70 m years BP (warm) to 30 m–4 m years BP (ice age). Later we have the transformation through the great warming period of circa 12,000 BP during the Holocene when humans moved around the world with considerable mobility and developed agriculture.

These very long waves of warm and cold ages are shown in Table 4.2, divided into smaller segments of waves, including the Mesozoic wave (250 m–65 m years ago), the Cenozoic wave (62–2.6 m years ago), the Quaternary and Holocene waves (2.6 m–1945 AD), and the Anthropocene (1970s to present and foreseeable future).

There were thus 100 m–140 m year-long waves during the Phanerozoic eon (1 m–500 m years BP), and 70,000–115,000 year-long waves during the Pleistocene era (15,000–500,000 years BP). These two waves/eons were characterized by recurring hot and cold periods, usually culminating in successive glacial or ice ages during cold periods, followed by eras of much warmer weather. Less regular long patterns have been operating during the Holocene period when human beings *settled most of Earth* (12,000BP to the 1970s). For instance, during the Holocene human era, there was a period of rapid change from glacial to warm conditions more suitable for human habitation, between 10,000 and 8000 BC (2–3 C° warmer than "normal"). This was followed by a cooler period from 7000 to 6000 BC (0.5 °C cooler than normal), and then a warmer period from 5500 to 4500 BC (between 0.0 °C and 0.3 °C warmer than normal). The next 2000 years from 4500 to 2250 BC were relatively stable around the norm.

In a long perspective, the whole period from 2250 BC to 1855 AD looks like a transition to colder temperatures until the mid-industrialization period in Britain. Examined more closely, the first 800 years AD shows a stable cold tendency (0.6 to 0.2 °C cooler than the norm), followed by a medieval warm*er* period from 975 to 1425 AD (0 to 0.2 °C *below* norm), a little ice age (especially in Europe) from 1440 to 1855 AD (0.4 to 1.0 °C below norm), during which there were 3–4 cycle minima, within and between Dutch and British hegemony; and then since 1855, a progressively warm*er* era (0.0 to 0.4 °C *below* norm) followed by the era of global warming proper (since 1975) (0.0 to 1.45 °C above norm), during the eras of US relative and potentially Chinese hegemony.

None of these waves or periods before the 1800s (or 1970s) were likely *anthropogenic,* i.e. caused specifically by humans (or other animals). They were caused by factors such as changes in the tilting of the Earth's axis, volcanic forcing, or solar irradiance. The current trends concerning climate are the first to be precipitated by human beings or "non-natural" forces. The current period of expansion of greenhouse gasses commenced at a low base during the industrial revolution from the mid-1850s but did not noticeably increase until the 1970s when it started showing an upward warming trend through to the 2020s and likely beyond.

There are, as mentioned, several dozen studies that seek to comprehend the stylized facts of climate change using various waves and cycles briefly shown by the IPCC but not subject to extensive critical or other examination. Here we summarize some of these studies to gain a more holistic (i.e., comprehensive) understanding of weather and heating/cooling systems on planet Earth.

The first group of scholars who analyze these long and short waves of heating and cooling of planet Earth and its constituents is headed (de facto) by Stuart Harris from the University of Calgary, Canada. He scrutinizes the quite well-established

Table 4.2 Long waves of heating and cooling after multicellular life began: Earth, 1–500 m yrs BP, 20–500,000 yrs BP, 1–12,000 yrs BP, *circa*

1–500 m Yrs BP	Glacial Period	Hot Period	Glacial Period	Hot Period	Glacial Period	Hot Period	Glacial Period	Hot Period
Phanerozoic eon (100–140 m Yr waves)	1 m–35 m	50 m–100 m	140 m–180 m	210 m–260 m	275 m–340 m	360 m–395 m	410 m–460 m	545 m–600 m+
15–500,000 Yrs BP	**Cold period**	**Hot period**	**Cold period**	**Hot period**	**Cold Period**	**Hot period**	**Cold period**	**Hot period**
Pleistocene (70–115,000 Yr waves)	15,000–55,000	100,000–130,000	140,000–190,000	210,000–255,000	270,000–310,000	335,000–360,000	370,000–400,000	440,000–470,000
0–12,000 Yrs BP waves	**Warming trend AD**	**Little ice age AD**	**Medieval warm period AD**	**Stable cold period (NH) AD**	**Normal Temps BC**	**Warming period BC**	**Colder age BC**	**Glacial to warm, BC**
Holocene & Anthropocene waves	1975–present	1440–1850	975–1425	0–800	4500–2250	5500–4500	7000–6000	10,000–8000

Source: Adapted from IPCC-I (2007:477); Moberg et al. (2005:616); Wikipedia (2024)

long waves of climate change that occurred between 600 m years BP and the present, during the whole period of the Phanerozoic, up to the Holocene. These are shown in Fig. 4.2.

Note: "In geochemistry, paleoclimatology and paleoceanography $\delta^{18}O$ or delta-O-18 is a measure of the deviation in the ratio of stable isotopes oxygen-18 (18O) and oxygen-16 (16O). It is commonly used as a measure of the temperature of precipitation, as a measure of groundwater/mineral interactions, and as an indicator of processes that show isotopic fractionation, like methanogenesis. In paleosciences, 18O:16O data from corals, foraminifera and ice cores are used as a proxy for temperature." (Wikipedia 2024).

Two main things stand out from these and related data. The first is the relatively clear long waves of climate change operating from circa 530 m years BP to the Holocene during the Phanerozoic Age. There were four clear *long wave hot periods* of approximately 25–22 °C between, first, 540m (not shown) and 470mBP (70 m years); second, between 400BP and 360mBP (40 m years); third, between 290mBP and 230BP (60 m years); and fourth, between 120mBP and 70mBP (50 m years). In between these periods were glacial/ice ages from 465mBP to 410mBP (55mBP years); 355mBP and 300mBP years (55 m years); 195mBP and 135mBP (60 m years); and 45mBP to more recent times (45 m years). These long waves are not deterministic in the sense of having precise periodicity, amplitude, and endogeneity; but they are quite regular and well-recognized.

Second, the relationship between average global temperatures and atmospheric CO_2 stocks (ppm) is not deterministic (rigid); in fact, not very clearly established at all (not shown here; see Harris 2023, 5). There is a weak correlation between the two indices. Typically, the long waves of average global temperatures are caused by factors associated with solar waves and volcanic activity. The solar waves link to

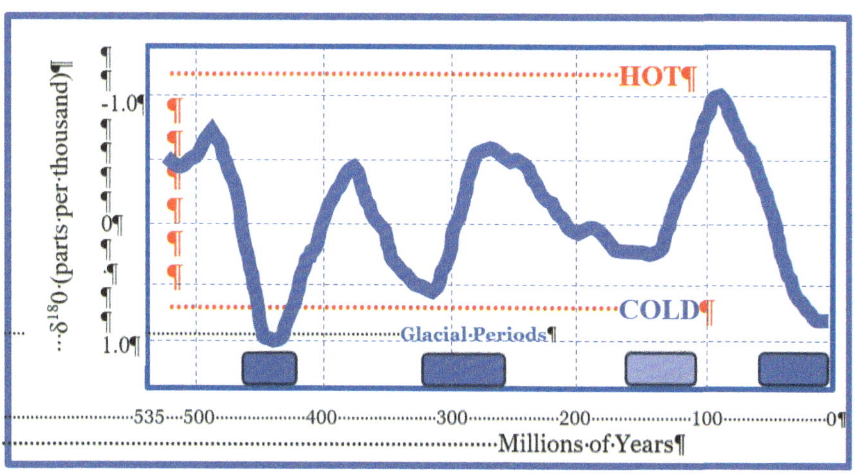

Fig. 4.2 Phanerozoic climate change. 0–530 million years BP. Four hot and glacial/colder waves. Cold and hot periods (Earth surface mean global temperature) and lower atmosphere CO_2. Short-term average. (Source: Adapted from Harris 2023, 10)

sunspots, changes in the tilt of the Earth's axis, changes in the cycle of the Earth around the sun, and changes in the wobbliness of the Earth's rotation. In fact, there are numerous serious and well-regarded scientists who link even the present waves of various warming and cooling to natural forces, because they have studied them in detail and recognize their interconnection with current global and regional climatological trends. The real test here is to recognize how these so-called natural forces can be reconciled with recent trends toward global warming (see later in this chapter).

The *second group of scholars* scrutinizing these long and short waves of heating and cooling of planet Earth, and its constituents seems to be headed by Yu Liu, from the Chinese Academy of Sciences. In this context but dealing with much shorter long waves (in the thousands of years rather than hundreds of millions of years), the most detailed analysis of millennial and 100+ year-long climate waves, broadly from the beginnings of the twenty-first century backward to the time of the Greek Republic, that I have seen, is those by overlapping groups of Chinese and Western scholars. One paper, Liu et al. (2011), scrutinizes temperature changes in *tree rings* within the central-eastern Tibetan Plateau. Their estimates of temperature changes are for a period of almost 2500 years (485 BC to 2000 AD), in addition to future trends to 2134 AD. They also compare their results with numerous other scholars (usually for shorter periods) who studied other areas and nations of the world. It is argued that their results are "*representative*" not only of the central-eastern Tibetan Plateau but also of seven studies of the Northern Hemisphere, with a "teleconnection" to other studies of mid-low latitudes of the Southern Hemisphere (Liu et al. 2011, 2987).

Liu et al.'s (2011) method is as follows. First, half a standard deviation above and below the mean temperature for 2500 years is used to specify warm and cold periods, respectively, for specific years. Second, mean temperature differences between cold and warm successive periods specify the amplitude of the waves. Third, temperature rise and fall rates are the slope of the trend line for a specified period of changing temperatures. Wave periodicities for the 2500-year waves are calculated by using "Reffit35" software, with predictions of future temperature trends using the "Caterpillar-*S.S.A.*" method. Figure 4.3 summarizes the empirical results.

The results are (1) a mean temperature over 2500 years of 2.12 °C, a standard deviation of 0.40 °C, (2) "shortish" waves/cycles of alternating hot and cold weather, and (3) very long waves following the trend line of about 1200 years each.

Specifically, these results for 485 BC to 2000 AD illustrate the existence of, first, two very long waves (from upper turning point to next upper turning point, downswing to upswing) of around 1230 years each during 270 BC and 2200 AD. We may call these *millennial plus scale waves* (MPSWs, or MSW for short). Each of these two MPSWs (MSW) comprises a cooling phase of over 600 years and a heating phase of over 600 years.

The cooling phase of the first long wave (270 BC to 330 AD) of 600 years is a coldish downswing with 7.5 short (full) waves/cycles (between successive upper turning points) of 83 years average length. The heating phase of the first long wave

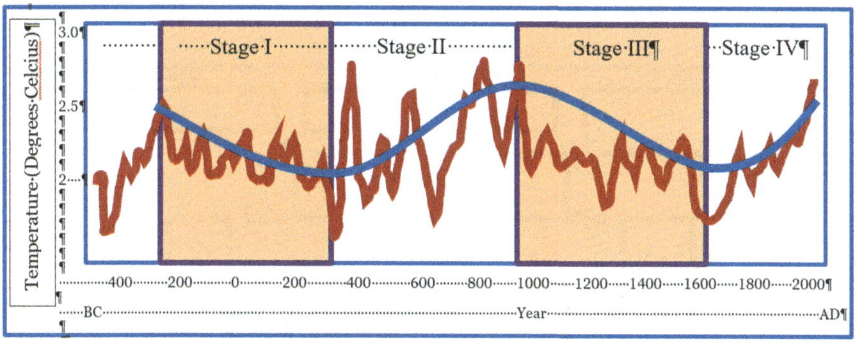

Fig. 4.3 Millennial-scale waves in temperature variation during the previous 2485 years. Tibetan tree rings. (Source: Adapted from Liu et al. 2011, 2990)

(340 AD to 950 AD) of 610 years is a hot upswing, comprising 4.5 shorter (full) waves of around 130 years average length.

The second long wave includes a cooling downswing of 670 years (from 960 AD to 1630 AD), comprising 5.5 shorter waves of around 118 years each, and a hot-rising long wave (likely not yet completed), starting *just after 1600 AD* (1630 AD), likely during Dutch hegemony, and possibly continuing until 2200 AD with shorter waves of perhaps 120 years on average (570 years circa). From our viewpoint, first, this is an impressive series of long waves of climate change of more than one millennium each, circa 1200 years (into the future).

Second, this shows very distinctly the "*Little Ice Age*" (LIA) that Europe, Asia, and much of the rest of the world experienced during 1500–1850 (circa). During this period was the *Dutch Golden Age* (circa 1570–1640) when much of the rest of the world (certainly Europe) was undergoing a major series of crises, including depressions, low growth, numerous wars, famines, floods, and political instabilities. During this LIA, the United Provinces of the Netherlands underwent a period of hegemonic dominance, strong long wave upswings, and high levels of production, commercial, and financial power. *Chap. 5 seeks to explain how this occurred in a regional-global environment of otherwise major dislocation.* (There are also three more cooler periods shown during the 1800s and 1900s, but these are examined with more detail and clarity in Fig. 4.5b much further below, when we raise the issue of British, US, and potential Chinese hegemony.)

Fourth, no mention is made by Liu et al. of climate change being generated by human (anthropogenic) forces since the industrial revolution, and especially since the 1970s. They discuss the role of the so-called natural forces such as changes in solar radiation and atmospheric circulation, but nothing else, including during the heating phase of the second millennial long wave of climate change (1650–2200). For instance, these two studies by Liu et al. indicate, as mentioned, that the current millennial long wave of rising climate temperatures is likely to continue to rise (in an upwardly cyclical fashion) until about 2200, ending the rising phase (1650–2200) of the second MPSW (980–2200).

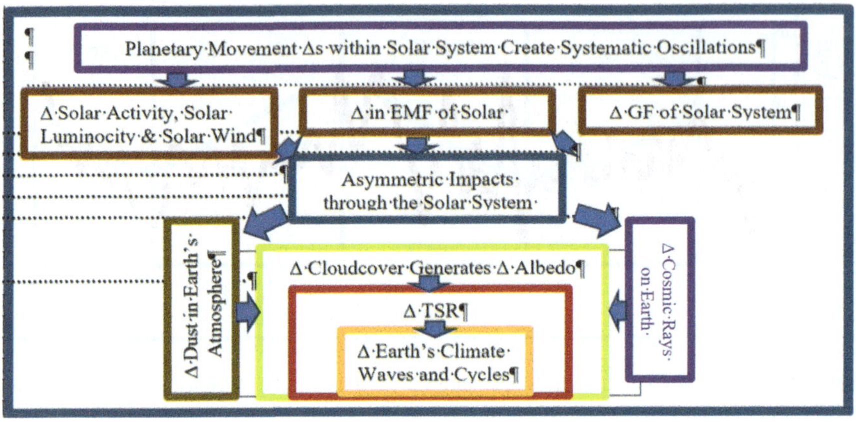

Fig. 4.4 Scafetta and Bianchini's planetary model of solar activity changes and climate waves/cycles. (Source: Adapted from Scafetta and Bianchini 2023, 28)

The third group of scholars examining the long and short waves of climate change cooling and heating of planet Earth, and its constituents headed (de facto) by Nicola Scafetta, from the University of Naples, Federica II. Scafetta attempts to explain many of the crucial long and short waves and cycles of climate change through a model comprising several core variables, summarized in Fig. 4.4. The general point to make about this Scafetta–Bianchini stylized model is the core thesis that the periodic movement of the planets in the solar system that the Earth and the Sun (plus Mercury, Venus, Mars, Jupiter, Saturn, Uranus, Neptune [and Pluto]) generates a series of systematic oscillations. These oscillations create periodic changes in three core processes: first in solar activity, solar luminosity, and solar wind; second, in the electromagnetic field (EMF) of the solar system; and third, in the gravitational field (GF) of the solar system. These three impacts on the solar system in turn affect both the periodic changes in the amount of dust and cosmic radiation entering the Earth's atmosphere, which influence the periodic cloudiness which induces albedo impacts; and the albedo changes that have an important influence on the periodic oscillations in total solar radiation (TSR) reaching Earth's surface; which in turn produce wave and cycle type changes on the Earth's climate.

Scafetta and cowriters demonstrate the existence of several well-correlated cycles and waves of planetary-orbital and global temperature dynamics that signify the importance of these interactions. For instance, they show the relationship between groups of 10-year sunspot ("Schwabe") cycles (Almedeij 2020), 60-year "Milanković waves" (Romano et al. 2021; Scafetta et al. 2020), 1200-year "millennial (plus) waves" (Bond 1997), and global temperatures on planet Earth, including some instances when the IPCC empirics *may* have under-estimated the importance of these planetary-orbit processes for climate change.

The first, sunspots and Earth's climate, are shown in Figure 4.5a, b:

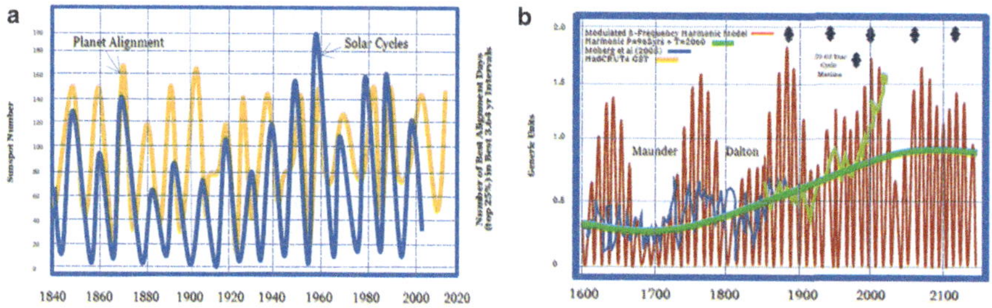

Fig. 4.5 (**a**) The Venus-Earth-Jupiter model plotted against the annual average number of sunspots (using Hung's model). (Source: Adapted from Srafetta 2023, 6.) (**b**) Close linkages between sunspots, planetary alignment, and global temperatures on Earth. (Source: Adapted from Srafetta 2023, 16)

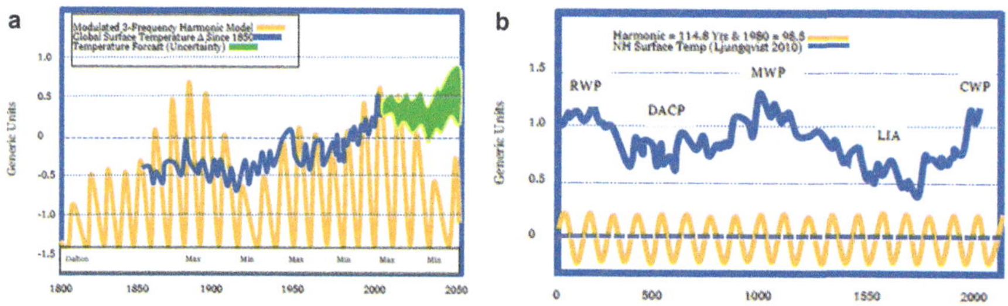

Fig. 4.6 (**a**). Sunspot minima and maxima (1800–2050, actual & forecast), global temperature (1850–2005), and climate forecast for earth (2005–2050). (Source: Scafetta (2012, 305). (**b**) Sunspot and temperature cycles and waves on Earth, 0–2030 AD. Source: Safetta (2012, 306).

In general, there are several dynamics associated with sunspot activity, not simply the observed (well-known) 10–12 year cycle(s), but also the 110-year wave, with the (well-known) sunspot Sporer minima (1450–1570), Maunder minima (1630–1730); around the time of Dutch hegemony; the Dalton minima (1770–1855) including during the first half of British hegemony (which runs from 1820 to 1880, circa) and long wave upswing (1820–1870), the early 1900s (during the mild GDP growth upswing experienced by some nations); plus the next minima during the early 1900s and another during the early 2000s (during Chinese relative downswing). The data indicate a likely sunspot maxima during the mid-late 2000s (e.g., 2060–2080), which could help generate (even) warmer global temperatures on Earth.

To understand the relationship between waves, cycles, and potential conflicts with IPCC predictions, Fig. 4.6 illustrates a wider sphere of data for sunspots, planetary movements, and Earth's climate.

These Figures indicate that, as Scafetta (2012, 310) notes, for much of the late twentieth century, both the 115-year and millennial (plus) waves have been rising, which may have contributed to rising global temperatures. This is consistent with his empirical finding that "up to 70% of the observed post-1850 climate change and warming could be associated [with] multiple solar cycles poorly processed by current general circulation model[s]." He goes on to conclude that:

> The model predicts that the Sun is rapidly entering into a prolonged period of low activity that may last from 2015 to 2050 with a minimum around 2025–2040. This pattern should be due to the forecasted minimum of the quasi-60-year modulation around 2031 that should be further stressed by the forecasted 2030–2040 minimum of the 115-year cycle. Indeed, [our results] show … that there exists an apparent and approximate cyclical repetition between solar cycles 1, 2, 3 and 4, which occurred just before the Dalton Minimum, and the cycles 20, 21, 22 and 23. We observe that the approaching low solar activity may cool the climate slightly more … than … [we calculate], because … the large 115-year cycle was not taken into account. *However, the millennial solar cycle is still slowly increasing and would peak around 2060, while the weaker 130-year cycle would peak in 2035.* [Scafetta 2012, 310; emphasis added.]

The fourth group of scholars examining long and short waves of climate change cooling and heating of planet Earth and its constituents does not seem to be a group (yet), but the current (de facto) leader of this non-group, D.E. Nierode, from the University of Wisconsin, Maddison, may generate a following, or link up with the other three groups (if he has not yet done so). Nierode uses a *Cyclical Sine Model*, nonlinear regression, and three waves/cycles of 11 years (Schwabe), 70 years, and 1000 years to explain climate change temperatures on planet Earth. Taking his most recent data and predictions into account, we examine Fig. 4.7a, b to ascertain a likely trajectory.

Figure 4.7a shows the combined waves/cycles model over the period 1300–2300 AD as well as temperatures on Earth up to 2021. The Little Ice Age is clearly marked, impacting much of the world (especially Europe) notably during the 1500s and 1600s (including the Dutch Golden Age), and the cyclically rising temperatures since then. It illustrates the cyclical upswing predicted to rise until about 2220, when a cyclical downswing starts. It also illustrates that Earth is currently at the top of a 70-year cycle, to be predictably followed by a downswing for a few decades.

Figure 4.7b shows details on the differences between the IPCC5 report findings and the Cyclical Sine Model, providing more micro detail. The IPCC report predicts a rising average temperature into the foreseeable future, with policies as usual, while Nierode predicts that we are at the top of a cycle and likely to have slowly declining average Earth temperatures until 2049, after which they should start to

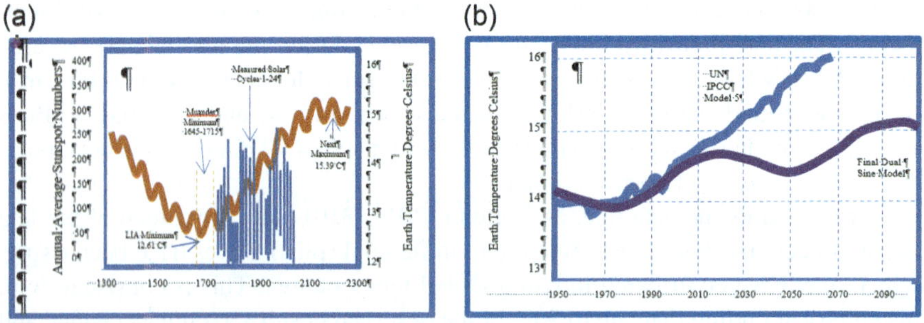

Fig. 4.7 (**a**) Earth's temperature 1300–2300 AD, 3 waves/cycles. (Source: Adapted from Nierode 2022, 181.) (**b**) Earth's temperature 1950–2100, cyclical sine model. (Source: Adapted from Nierode 2022, 183)

rise again, with no changes in the underlying dynamics. Nierode, adds that the proof of the pudding between the IPCC and CSM will be the trend in temperatures for the 2020 decade. (Current results during 2020–2023, with 2023 being a rise of 1.45 °C, compared with pre-industrial times, do not support his thesis. See more on this later in this chapter)

There are other results not yet discussed from wave/cycle results and the empirical evidence of the period. For instance, while we have discussed the evidence for the Little Ice Age (1400–1855), we have not analyzed the evidence *in detail* for climate change during the late-1800s (during British hegemony) and 1900s (during US hegemony), and the significance of possible outcomes for the 2000s (*in detail,* for China and the world). Figure 4.8 enables us to scrutinize these questions in more detail, while the full results are saved for chaps. 5–8, below (summarized in chap. 1 above).

These two sets of data are useful for comparing the details of the IPCC models and empirics (Fig. 4.8b) with those of Nierode (Fig. 4.8a).

It is noteworthy that both the IPCC and the natural wave/cycle scientists tend to underplay or ignore historical processes that should be crucial for climate change dynamics. Specifically, little or no mention is made in these two papers/chapters to an array of greenhouse gas-generating processes that go far beyond issues of solar radiation and atmospheric circulation per se. These include human problems such as the rise of capitalism, changing hegemony, industrial revolutions, world wars, long wave upswings and downswings, innovations such as the internal combustion engine, the gasoline revolution, the rise of China-Asia, declining species diversity, pollution, the rise of large cities, and urbanization. Some mention is made by the IPCC to a few of these historical processes, such as pollution, deforestation, urbanization, but only because they can be easily contextualized as part of the so-called natural science. Overall, both camps are dominated by natural scientists (for the IPCC, at least, in volume one of the main Report). It is unfortunate that economic, social, and historical forces of a broader context are not given major emphasis in a way that could easily provide the necessary conceptualization for explaining climate change, especially since the main theme of the IPCC, for instance, is that climate change is caused mainly by human beings (i.e., within social economies).

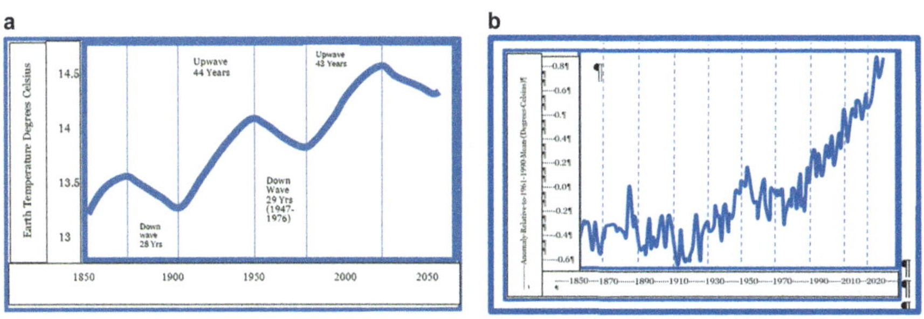

Fig. 4.8 (**a**) Earth temperature changes, 1850–2050, model, and empirical figures. (Source: Adapted from Nierode 2022, 181). (**b**) Historical surface temperature changes, Earth, 1850–2020 (AR6). (Source: Adapted from IPCC 2021, Chap. 2, 322)

Other than that, in general terms, issues that stand out, are, first, that for both studies it is shown that there was no increase in the *trend* of Earth's average temperature between 1850 and 1920. Despite the great advances made through industrialization especially by Britain, Germany, France, and the US during this time, there was if anything a drop in global temperatures. This may be understandable during the 1870s–1890s for those experiencing the so-called Great Depression, and for the associated emerging end of absolute British hegemony, but not for the whole period of the 1800s. Second, during the period 1920 to 1945, there was a substantial increase in global temperatures, and while this may make sense for the pollution emitted during the Second World War, it does not make sense for the 1930s Great Depression, when declining temperatures would be thought possible (as they tend to be during periods of bad economic performance), when there were major heatwaves in the great plains of the US (see chap. 7 on these heatwaves).

Third, there was a drop in global temperatures during 1950 and 1975, which is certainly not what would be expected during the greatest boom in the history of capitalist production, distribution, and exchange, and through the period of absolute US hegemony. This is very strange (though explicable). Fourth, the period of greatest temperature expansion, 1975 to 2024, was the worst synchronized long wave downswing for most of the world (see Chap. 11, below to explain 1940–2024). Granted Asia underwent a very robust upswing, but even so, it is also the period when some very useful anti-pollution legislation was actioned in many core nations. Probably the huge global population increase had a lot to contribute to it, plus the extreme degree of deforestation, pollution, and declining biodiversity of both plants and animals, during the long wave downswing in the core and much elsewhere outside of Asia. (See chaps. 7–9, below, for details.)

These issues do point to a considerable amount of agreement between the IPCC and the natural wave/cycle proponents, in terms of general empirics for the periods discussed. The core of both groups is the so-called natural scientists. It also provides perhaps a prima facie case that maybe the natural wave/cycle scientists' hypotheses should be more extensively analyzed by the IPCC. In this context, we examine in the next section the IPCC climate change results, paying special attention to their explanation of climate change dynamics that are not due to natural forces, and, more especially, we study the IPCC results within the framework of long wave forces and how cascading tipping points, uncertainty, and CCC play core roles in the analysis.

4.3 Long Waves of Climate Change and the IPCC

Here I scrutinize IPCC-style climate change arguments to see if there are wave elements, and if they might in some respects be consistent with the above-mentioned four trends/groups associated with the cycle/wave scientists. The first issue is the recent long waves in temperature dynamics. Figure 4.9 examines the temperature trend during 1850–2023 in light of the 1858–2000 mean for oceans and lands.

First, we deal with anomalous changes in mean temperatures over the period of the 1850s–early 2020s, which are well-delineated by the trend/wave deviations.

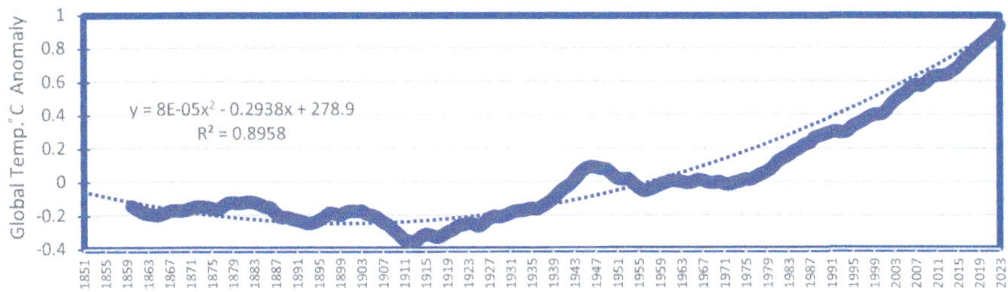

Fig. 4.9 1851–2023, global ocean and land temperature anomalies, compared with 1901–2000 mean (10-year moving average (Tentative apologies to Slutzky, but I don't think the 10-year moving average adversely affected the data results); polynomial trend, second order). (Source: Adapted from figures from NCEI (2024)

Over the long term, one can clearly see (a) two short climate waves, (b) one long climate wave, and (c) half a longer wave of climate upswing. The first short climate wave is between 1865 and 1893, from lower turning point to lower turning point, comprising an upswing from 1865 to 1882 (during the latter period of British absolute hegemony), and a downswing from 1882 to 1893 (during part of British relative hegemony). The second short climate wave is between 1893 and 1912, comprising upswing from 1893 to 1902, and downswing from 1902 to 1912 (all during the standard model's third Kondratiev growth/price upswing).

Then there is a climatic long wave from 1912 to 1973, comprising upswing from 1912 to 1945 and downswing from 1945 to 1972. This long wave is of special interest because the upswing went from virtually the First World War through to the end of the Second World War, including the Great Depression of the 1930s. This makes historical sense in terms of the masses of ammunition and bombs dropped during the two world wars, and the beginnings of Fordism (and war) through the workings of the internal combustion engine. It is not so logical in light of the Great Depression (when GHGs would be expected to have moderated) but made up for by the fact that the major upswing was during the Second World War when GHGs would have heightened.

The strangest result is rapid decline during the late 1940s and 1950s with stabilization through to the 1970s. The last thing one would expect during the greatest golden age in the history of capitalism (mid-to-late 1940s to the 1970s), the period of US hegemony, long wave upswing, the postwar corporate system of Fordism and the Keynesian welfare state is a decline and then stabilization of global temperature anomalies. However, this is becoming more cognizant in the literature, discussed in detail in chap. 7 (and to some degree in ch. 1, above). Briefly, what happened during the period of long wave (growth) upswing and US hegemony is that increasing smog and albedo in the atmosphere acted as a deflector of GHGs back into the outer atmosphere and into space. We do not have all the details yet, but this is the crux of it.

The third cycle or wave is the very long wave climate upswing of temperature anomalies starting in the late 1970s (1977) and continuing to the mid-2020s, with slight declines during Juglar downswings (financial crises and recessions) of the early 1990s, early 2000s, and 2008–2010, and 2020–2022. One would not have expected a surge in global temperature anomalies during the long wave downswing in the West and much elsewhere of the 1980s–2020s (see details in chap. 11 below). But it may be explained by three factors. First, the greatest long wave upswing ever experienced in Asia that data can validate during the 1980s–2020s (especially 1980s–2010s, the major factor). The second factor includes corporations making up for the declining rate of profit and productive investment by shunting environmental protection regulations (especially in the periphery and semi-periphery) and using the periphery as GHG generators through rough and ready regulations and supply of resources and crops to the core. The third factor is the huge increase in human populations especially in the periphery and semi-periphery, and the great masses of populations moving to the (often new) towns and cities thereby engaging in major levels of habitat destruction.

It is instructive that the analysis provided by the wave/cycle scientists in the previous section is consistent with most of this data. This includes the rising wave from the 1850s to the 1880s, the decline from the 1880s through to the early 1910s, then the rise from the 1910s to the 1940s, the decline from the 1950s to the 1970s, and the rise from the 1980s to the present. Could it be that these changes in mean global temperatures are due, in part, to natural forces during these times?

Apart from the global waves and cycles presented at the beginning of this chapter presented by the IPCC, in more recent decades, especially the IPCC has been arguing strongly for the role of anthropogenic forces in promoting global temperatures. Its analysis of the period 1850–2020s is provided by Fig. 4.10.

During the 1910s–1970s, long wave natural and anthropogenic forces seem to be about equal on average (at near zero) in their contribution to temperature changes (comparing H + N with only N forces). But IPCC results confirm, especially during the 1970s–2020s, a much greater impact of anthropogenic forces on temperature changes, and a much lower impact of natural forces (solar and volcanic). The natural forces (planetary movements, solar radiation, etc.) that the IPCC concludes have, overall, especially in recent decades and centuries, little impact on temperature changes, include axial tilt, eccentricity, solar variation, volcanic eruptions,

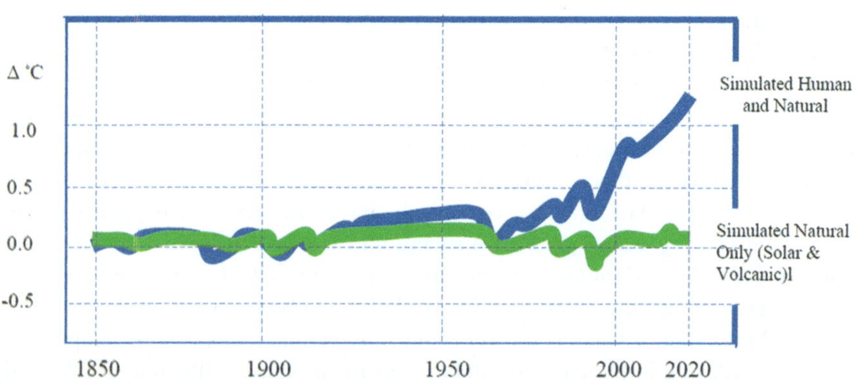

Fig. 4.10 Change in annual surface temperature, 1850–2020, annual average, human (H) + natural (N). (Source: Adapted from the IPCC 2021, 6)

continental drift, ocean currents, natural forest fires, and meteorite impacts. It is unfortunate that the IPCC has not engaged in research and discussions on the specific historical sources of all these impacts on Earth's temperatures, in some detail in recent publications (nor engaging in discussion with the alternative groupings of natural scientists discussed earlier in this chapter).

Thus far for 2023, we know that the Earth has warmed on average by just under 1.5 °C (1.45 °C), but for *details,* we use slightly earlier data. The observed warming (+) in global mean temperatures (GMT) for Planet Earth, up to 2010–2020, relative to 1850–1900, is a net +1.07 °C–1.2 °C, contributed by greenhouse gasses warming of between +1.0 and + 2.0 °C and cooling (−) of between −0.0 and − 0.8 °C (IPCC 2021, TS, 29). Natural sources of GHG over the long-term horizon are generally balanced by sinks such as photosynthesis and the activities of marine plankton. The predominant greenhouse gas contributions to rising (+1.0 to +2.0) temperatures to date include: carbon dioxide (CO_2) (42.80% of total), methane (CH_4) (28.70%) (estimates having nearly doubled in recent years, see GMT 2023), halogenated gasses (CFC + HCFC+HFC) (5.41%), nitrous oxide (4.95%), other gasses (including carbon monoxide) (11.90%), black carbon (4.95%), and aviation contrails (0.83%). The predominant contributions to reductions (−0.0 to −0.8 °C) in temperatures over this period include sulfur dioxide (SO_2) (−61.77%), nitrogen oxides (NOx) (−17.43%), land-use reflectance and irrigation (including albedo) (−10%), organic carbon (−8.84%), and ammonia (−1.82%) (See also IPCC 2021: Table TS14, Tech Sum, pp. TS-129.)

In terms of global sectoral contributors to GHG, during 2016, the major sources were energy use, which constitutes 73.2% of total GHG emissions. These include energy used in industry (24.2%), transport (16.2%), buildings (17.5%), agriculture and fishing (1.7%), fugitive functions (5.8%), and other fuel combustion uses (7.8%). The other major emitter of GHG is "agriculture, forestry and land use" (18.4%), which comprises livestock & manure (5.8%), soils (4.1%), crop burning (3.5%), deforestation (2.2%), crop/grasslands (1.5%), and rice cultivation (1.3%). Further contributors are *direct* industrial activities (5.2%) and waste (3.2%).

In terms of long waves of climate change into the future, as envisaged by the IPCC, generally their reports compare the likely yearly gigatons of $C0_2$-equivalent emissions from, e.g., 2000 to 2100, first according to currently implemented policies, and second compared with various Shared Socioeconomic Pathways (SSPs), corresponding with specific Representative Concentration Pathways (RCPs), relative to pre-industrial times.[2] With current policies into the future, there is likely no real long wave pattern (characteristic steep up and down pattern), and only with

[2] SSPs relate to various styles of socioeconomic scenarios associated with certain climate policies and GHG flows (SSP1 through to SSP6) by (e.g.) 2100; while RCPs (Representative Concentration Pathways) are climate change scenarios indicating future greenhouse stocks (concentrations) (radiative forcing values by (e.g.) 2100) (e.g., RCP 1.9, 2.6, 3.4, 4.5, 6, 7, etc). The IPCC now link SSPs with RCPs. For instance, SSP1–1.19 is SSP1 linked to RCP 1.19, representing the Green Way of mean 1.4 °C by 2100 (U ranges 1–1.8 °C); or SSP5–8.5 (SSP5 and RCP 8.5), representing massive temperature rises to mean 4.5 °C by 2100 (U ranges 3.3–5.7 °C). (See Mohaddes and Raissi 2024).

SSPs consistent with major limits on future GHGs does the typical long wave pattern emerge, where the past rise is patterned with a future crucial decline. IPCC analysis of current policies compared with (below) 1.5 °C (current objective), 2.0 °C (past objective), and current policies impact on the future. 2000–2100 temperatures are shown below in Fig. 4.11, with uncertainty (U) ranges mentioned.

Current policies (red line) are expected to result in a global mean temperature of 3.2 °C by 2100, with uncertainty ranges of between 2.2 °C and 3.5 °C (since pre-industrial times). This result is generally in between SSP2 and SSP3, see below. The previous objective of 2.0 °C by 2100 is a little less climate-friendly than the green line (see below).

The green line, above, has an estimated mean 1.4 °C (U range 1.0 °C–1.8 °C) global mean temperature by 2100, associated with low concentrations. This is close to the SSP1–1.9 scenario of *Taking the Green Road* (Van Vuuren et al. 2017, 2) and includes advancing the state of sustainability to a relatively high degree, promoting environmentally sensitive technology, reducing inequality, lowering carbon footprint, emphasizing quality of life issues rather than growth, and having highly productive land. It could be said that this is the road precisely *not* taken at present by the "global community," and also not taken by the dominant power brokers of the world economy (US and China). Perhaps the EU could be seen as having certain members with an interest in this pathway, but certainly not a general *praxis* working in this direction.

SSP2, at 2.7 °C (2.1–3.5 °C by 2100), RCP of 4.5, with medium concentrations, is a *Middle of the Road* scenario in between SSP1 and SSP3, where historical patterns continue in many areas, including vis-à-vis technological developments; uneven developments; global institutions working slowly toward sustainability; heterogeneous national and regional progress toward mitigation and adaptation; and slowly declining dependency on fossil fuels. This seems to be the most feasible

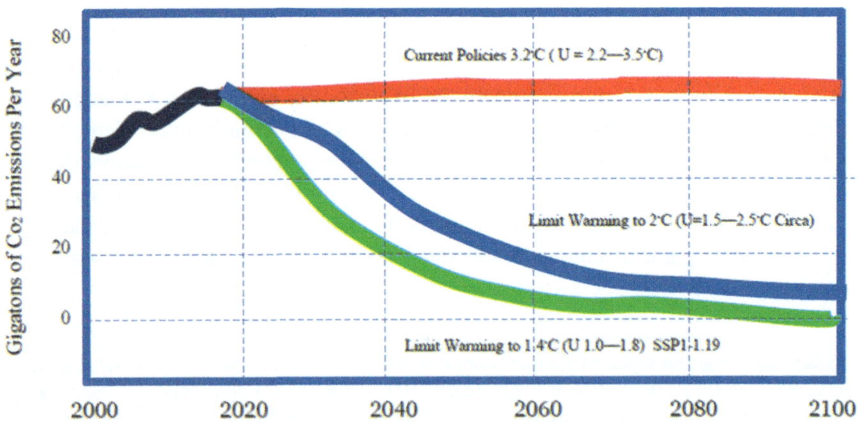

Fig. 4.11 IPCC global emissions pathways, 2000–2100; current policies (red line), green road, current objective (green line), and previous objective of 2 °C (blue line) SSP scenarios. (Source: Adapted from IPCC 2023, 22)

optimistic option for the future in light of recent trends and climate conferences. The result is in between the blue and green lines in Fig. 4.11 with no long wave downswing in temperatures. However, this is a catastrophe for climate and species extinction, but not as bad as the next several scenarios, which are worse than catastrophe.

A worse scenario than even the most feasible/optimistic scenario, but perhaps more realistic on current political trends (not shown above), with an estimated rise (since pre-industrial times) of 3.6 °C (2.8–4.6 °C range) (along with RCP 7.0; high concentrations) is based around *regional rivalry*, high inequality, with rising nationalism, ineffective global institutions, declining investment in education and technology, strong environmental degradation, population decline in core and rise in periphery, fossil fuel dependency, and low levels of sustainability. Some nations especially Russia and North Korea seem to be according to most of these characteristics. But it does not produce an obvious wave (downswing) due to rising expected temperatures. This is best described as annihilation.

Details of SSP4 with rises of about 4.0 °C mean (U range of 3.6–4.4 °C by 2100) are usually ignored in IPCC (and other) analyses.[3] It is conceptually viewed as the divided road of global inequality, where conflict and unrest rise to high levels, and the world is ruled by the high-technology core whereas the low-technology periphery undergoes low standards of living. Internal inequalities also abound, between those with connections and property and others without social capital or capabilities. Pollution expands, species decimate, temperatures rise to very high levels, and the capable engage in adaptation to greater warming and climate crises.

SSP5, with an estimated 4.4 °C in 2100 (3.3–5.7 °C), and RCP 8.5, which is very high, is an interesting case of *High GDP Growth*, competitive economies, a globalizing trend, with rapid technological developments, rising levels of education, but concentration on fossil fuels with little or no sustainable development. There is little mitigation and a strong emphasis on adaptation to severe climate change. This is perhaps outside the pattern of likely contenders given objectives and current trends.

The fact that SSP1–1.19, The Green Road, is considered effectively the only viable pathway to slightly below 1.5 °C by 2100 (compared with pre-industrial times) does not auger well for the future of the planet. This is because at present few of the leading powerful nations and regions are taking the green road seriously, and indeed, from a global perspective, it does not appear to be the leading global operational philosophy of governance at present or in the near future. But this is the path with the most noticeable long wave downswings in temperatures.

Major climate changes have already begun impacting planet Earth, leading to cascading global tipping points (CGTP), with 2023 temperatures being just below 1.5 °C (and early 2024 past 12 months is just over 1.5 °C) increase in global temperatures above 1850–1900 levels. We examine CGTP further below.

---

[3] Scenario SSP4 was underplayed in the report because it was likely considered as not providing sufficient additional information for analysis. For more details about SSP4, see Calvin et al. (2017).

4.4 Uncertainty and CCC of Climate Change

In this section and the next, we analyze how the circular and cumulative causation (CCC) process of climate change is impacting the world and its constituents, drawing on the nonlinear impacts of uncertainty, threshold effects, and cascading global (and regional) tipping points. CCC includes two processes, the first being the interaction between *multiple variables*; and the second being the tendency for the variables to interact in a *cumulative manner* generating instability and dynamic motion through historical time. (See O'Hara 2023.)

We thus need to examine the linkages between three interrelated sub-systems of (1) habitats and species; (2) human activities; and (3) climate change (set within the circuit of capital). Five main factors involved in the circuit of money capital have adversely impacted the ecological environment, especially since the onset of the structural crises of capitalism into the 1970s–2020s (see chap. 9 for details). Land-use clearing and other activities associated with agriculture and forestry (contributing 30.9% of GHGE) left naked whole areas of land, as did human population settlement and housing. Transportation and building (21% GHGE) along with Industry (19.4%) exacerbated the process, as did energy supply (25.9%). Wastes also played a role (2.8%). These commercial and consumption activities reduced the stock of ecological resources, especially flora for photosynthesis and oxygen production, and fauna which provided useful fertilizer and seed-distribution for the reproduction of flora. Atmospheric systems were also changed. These factors coevolved into climate change trends. As this occurred entropy expanded and thus reduced the energy available *for use* by human beings and other animals and plants.

Historical evidence demonstrated that these CCC effects generated anomalous climate events, such as greater unevenness of climate tendencies in different highly populated areas, increased heavy precipitation events, more regular heatwaves, increasing tropospheric water vapor, declining glaciers in the Arctic region and Greenland, more acidic oceans, and rising sea levels (IPCC 2022c). CCC effects have been described well by most of the official reports. In an open system, changes in greenhouse gasses will likely affect climate in nonlinear ways since there are several feedback processes within and between the major processes. Some of the key changes in this regard are as follows:

- *Nonlinear Threshold Effects*. Extreme weather patterns are hypothesized to operate, especially beyond certain temperatures. However, the periods in which the threshold effects come into play are uncertain. While some extremes are already happening, these are thought to be much more pronounced beyond, say, a 1.5 °C increase in global temperatures since pre-industrial times (*above* 450 ppm $C0_2$-e concentrates). These threshold effects include major increases in global temperatures, major variability of temperature (including many more heatwaves and frosts), heavy rainfall events, major droughts and flooding, more tropical cyclones, major bushfires, and extreme winds. Another threshold point is said to possibly emerge at increases of above, say, 2 °C, so that any success in mitigating these higher excesses would be crucial for reducing the even more catastrophic impacts. There is also the possible increase from 3 °C–4 °C (since pre-industrial times) as being "much greater than the consequences of moving from 2 to 3°C" since, for example, "hurricane damage increases as a cube (or more) of wind-speed, which itself scales closely with sea temperatures" (IPCC 2007, 59).

- The Stern Review (2007, 60) demonstrates these CCC effects in terms of heightened costs as climate change accelerates (especially beyond a certain point). For instance, it discussed (a) floods and droughts increasing *exponentially*; a (b) small increase in temperature accelerating the frequency of extreme events (a convex curve); passing into the (c) threshold effects propelling "increasingly negative" impacts on crop growth; an (d) *inverse parabolic "hill function"*; (e) a "sharp increase in mortality once human temperature tolerances are exceeded"; (f) infrastructure damage from storms "increas[ing] as a cube of wind speed"; and (g) "costs of sea-wall construction increas[ing] as a square of defence height."[4]

Uncertainty is critical to the climate change and species extinction problems. The work of Frank Knight (1921), J.M. Keynes (1921, 1936), and G.L.S. Shackle (1970) has laid the ground rules of this analysis, and some environmental experts have taken this further. The informational anomalies associated with greenhouse gas emissions and climate change generate deep uncertainties. Risk and uncertainty can be seen to operate along a continuum, from degrees of risk to high levels of uncertainty: RISK↔UNCERTAINTY. Most elements of climate change relate to the right-hand side of the equation, where there is a combination of risk and uncertainty but more elements of uncertainty. Strictly speaking, according to Keynes (who followed a Bayesian approach to probability), uncertainty concerns the weight with which we place a degree of confidence on a specific probability. The less weight of evidence we have for a specific phenomenon, the greater the uncertainty associated with a specific probability, and the less confidence we have of it occurring.

Climate change poses similar, but more extreme, problems than those posited by Keynes associated with prospective yield and supply price in the *General Theory*, since it concerns events occurring fifty to one hundred years or more into the future. There are many variables, complex processes, nonlinear interactions, and indeed lack of knowledge about many of the climate, carbon cycle, threshold effects, and related matters. Just as important, there are many uncertainties linked to the climate models used to ascertain the nature of the interactions and processes. The major forms of uncertainty are outlined below in Table 4.3.

The major uncertainties (U) associated with the models of climate change are five in number. Initial conditions relate to the basic information about the major factors, such as past knowledge of temperature, rainfall, CO_2 concentration, and the

---

[4] Four of the studies (IPCC 2021, Stern, UNDP, and Garnaut 2008) assume equilibrium analysis in terms of the eventual calming down of impacts, when mitigation is effective. However, this equilibrium terminology is questionable due to "pervasive" uncertainty built into the systems; a medium-term (pragmatic) view shows that no equilibrium of CO_2-e occurs in any of the scenarios; and the assessments make very strict assumptions about the parameters, which are unlikely to prevail. Usage of circular and cumulative causation is a better framework of analysis.

Table 4.3 Deep uncertainties: Modular, ecological, and behavioral

	U_1	U_2	U_3	U_4	U^5
Modular	Initial conditions	Boundary conditions	Parameter	Structural	Subjective
Ecological	Radiative forcing	Ocean heat uptake	Winds & Currents	Climate sensitivity	Feedback, complexity
Behavioral	Investment	Technology	Population	Consumption	Governance

Source: Adapted from Knutti et al. (2008), Knutti (2008), Kandlikar (2005), O'Hara (2023)

like, as well as extrapolations into the future based on these data. Boundary conditions uncertainty relates to the use of technical data for climate change when broader information is necessary about the social and economic behavior of agents and institutions. Parameter uncertainty relates to the use of information about key variables when they are relatively constant but likely to change, often quite radically through time. This especially relates to values of variables that change markedly from stated values (e.g., due to previous lack of knowledge or threshold effects). Structural uncertainty depends upon the "different assumptions, constraints, and choices of models" (Knutti et al. 2008, 2658).

Ecological uncertainties relate to the lack of knowledge about key ecological relationships as they change through historical time. This is mainly due to the complexities, nonlinear relationships, and very long-term prospects that are of concern. Radiative forcing, for instance, is the change in net radiative energy impacting the troposphere, which has a critical input on climate through time. This is a complex process involving many factors such as greenhouse gasses, ozone, water vapor, albedo, aerosols, and solar irradiance. The net *anthropogenic* component is the key that most climate change reports link to global warming. Ocean heat uptake is the degree to which oceans absorb heat, i.e., their sink capacity. Winds and currents relate to, for instance, the transfer of heat pockets through the Gulf Stream and related systems of atmospheric circulation. Climate sensitivity is a general factor relating to how the Earth adjusts to changes in GHGE, in terms of the impact of carbon and related cycles on climate variables. Feedback and complexity are especially problematic with threshold effects associated with West Antarctic ice sheet disintegration, weakening and potential collapse of thermohaline circulation, El Nino changes, coral bleaching, and Greenland ice sheet melting. The extreme weather events and catastrophes linked to these threshold impacts are the primary concerns of climate change studies.

Behavioral uncertainties also play a critical role in the whole matrix of deep uncertainties. How will investment respond to the climate change challenge, and will new technological traverses be successfully introduced? What will be the course of population change in the future, and what choices will consumers make about a negentropic lifestyle? How will the matrix of governance linking states, markets, corporations, individuals and communities coevolve in the future? These questions obviously influence the ecological environment into the future and need to be endogenized into the models and activated.

4.5 Cascading Global Tipping Points

The greatest degree of uncertainty relates to the various "threshold effects," which are also called "tipping points." This means that at certain points of climate change rapid escalations will occur in critical environmental processes that radically upset the climate, producing a whole series of catastrophes (at likely different points). In the literature, there are two major types of tipping points associated with the "climate" or the "environment" broadly conceived. The first are what I call *high-risk-uncertainty interconnected regional environmental tipping points* (HRU TPs), and the second are the *interconnected global cascading tipping points of climate* change (GCTPs).

The HRU TPs are broad environmental uncertainties that represent the proximate cause of major potential anomalies for the planet. They have been documented by several institutions and individuals, with a major report having been recently prepared by the United Unions University, Institute for the Environment and Human Security (UNU EHS 2023).

The first high-risk-uncertainty tipping point is a *chain reaction to ecosystem collapse.* Due to a multitude of human actions, the current rate of species extinction is said to be 10 s–100 s of times faster than usual during the ecological life of human beings. Over 400 vertebrates have become extinct over the past century, 32 million hectares of forest have been decimated over a 5-year period recently, and one million species are threatened with extinction by the mid-twenty-first century or soon after. The HRU1 tipping point is this: "The extinction of a strongly connected species in a given ecosystem can trigger cascading extinctions of dependent species, which can eventually lead to ecosystem collapse" (p. 13). A CCC cascading process of co-extinction is in process due to the interdependent relationships between species on planet Earth.

The second HRU tipping point relates to *groundwater depletion.* Groundwater aquifers have been built up over thousands of years and would take this long to re-establish themselves. Yet the majority of the world's aquifers are becoming degraded faster than they can be replenished. This is leading to an inability to produce enough food for the world's human and non-human populations. The UNU states the tipping point thus: HRU2: "When the water table in a given aquifer drops consistently below the well depth, access to groundwater will become problematic, increasing the risk for farmers to be unable to irrigate their crops" (p. 19).

The third HRU tipping point is linked to mountain glaciers melting. Mountain glaciers hold most of the water required by plants and animals who live in high-altitude communities, and those who are downstream and benefit when it melts. At the current rate of climate change and unsustainable practices, most of these glaciers will melt by 2100 and one-third have melted in the past few decades. By mid-century, it is expected that most of these communities will have insufficient water to survive, and such melting leads to rising sea waterways globally. The UNU states this tipping point thus: HRU3: "When glaciers retreat, long-term ice storage melts and is gradually released as meltwater. Initially, the volume of water released increases until a maximum is reached, known as peak water. After this tipping point, glacier meltwater volume decreases as the glacier continues to shrink with effects on freshwater availability for humans and other species" (p. 25).

The fourth HRU tipping point is associated with the escalating expansion of space debris. Many objects are moving in space, including numerous satellites that enhance communications, space centers that coordinate space travel, and 130 million pieces of debris that are too small to be monitored. Such debris is increasing majorly over time and has already caused significant damage to working capital and its operators. As humanity increases exploration of space the expanding junk poses greater cascading risks-uncertainties through historical time that will impede our trajectory through the solar system and inhibit other functions. The tipping point is stated as: HRU4: "When there is a critical density of objects in orbit around Earth, such that one collision between two objects can set off a chain reaction, it will cause our orbit to become so dense with shrapnel that it becomes unusable. This would threaten our ability to monitor, for example, the weather and environmental changes, and to receive early disaster warnings" (p. 31).

The fifth HRU tipping point relates to unbearable heat associated with climate change. Humans cannot survive more than 6 h above 35 °C, and consequently every year over half a million people (and many other organisms) die from exposure and its affects throughout the world. We are unable to prevent climate change sufficiently to reduce such uncertainties, and many people will be unable to move to evade such threats. This puts the onus more on adaptation through changing behaviors, institutions, and technologies. The tipping point is described thus: HRU5: "Being exposed to above 35°C wet-bulb temperatures for longer than six hours will result in a healthy, young, resting adult in the shade and wind suffering extreme health consequences. This threshold [emerges] far lower as other factors are considered, such as age, medical conditions, or activity level" (p. 37).

These five environmental tipping points led to the issue of *climatological* cascading tipping points, or what some call global (cascading) TPs (GCTPs). These are defined thus:

> [GC] Tipping points occur when change in part of the climate system becomes (i) *self-perpetuating* beyond (ii) a *warming threshold* as a result of *asymmetry* in the relevant *feedbacks,* leading to (iii) substantial and *widespread Earth system impacts* [McKay 2022, 1; emphases added.]

All the threshold effects have some elements of nonlinearity, hysteresis, and irreversibility as feedback processes change parameters, thereby producing cumulative effects. The uncertainty relates to the timing or state when the changes and effects begin to manifest suddenly. The complexities involve a multifarious linking of numerous variables that are difficult to predict. Threshold effects are important because they challenge the idea that climate change will bring linearly related impacts on the system. They also show the problems of equilibrium models such as radiation force/climatic sensitivity analysis. In this context, threshold effects are likely to happen sooner than linear models predict, and Keller et al. (2008, 5) argue that "only subtle warning signs" are likely in many cases "before climate thresholds have been crossed" due to "multiple parameter" interaction (see McInerney and Keller 2008, 29).[5]

GCTPs tend to be irreversible, at least within the framework of human life frames (e.g., 100 years), and while these have global reach, others may be classed as regional but have global teleconnection. It is not just the single TPs that are a concern (although they are a major problem), but more significantly the interconnectedness of some or many of them, that causes the major climate impact. The core likely TPs across the cryosphere (ice), waterways, land, and air that are likely to impact before, at, or just after the 1.5 °C "Paris level" are shown below in Table 4.4.

There are approximately 15–20 actual/potential tipping points of a global, regional, or special character. Table 4.4 shows three global and four regional tipping points that are likely currently in motion or on the cusp of the lower end of the uncertainty areas, plus three regional or special potential TPs that are of major concern. This gives us a total of 10 TPs of special interest *currently* for the future of planet Earth, and if the planet warms more than 2.0 degrees some others will come into play. The average 2023 global warming temperature rise for planet Earth was 1.45 + −0.12 (WMO 2024) (compared with 1850–1900), and 2024 is likely to be higher because *El Nino* and general climate change are still operational in most places. But this is an average, as several areas, especially in the Northern Hemisphere (and parts of Antarctica) have been heating above 2.0 degrees already.

The three global CTPs that are already likely in the process include the (1) Greenland Ice Sheet (GREEN), the (2) Western Antarctic Ice Sheet (WANT), and (3) Atlantic meridional overturning circulation (AMOC). The six regional climatic processes that are in process or on the cusp of TP include (1) coral bleaching (CORAL), (2) West African Monsoonal System (AFRICA), (3) Indian Summer Monsoon (INDIA) (4) Barents Sea Ice loss (BARENT), (5) Mountain Glacier (GLAC) loss, and (6) Boreal Permafrost (PERM) thaw. The other three special areas of concern include the (1) Amazon (AMAZ) Rainforest dieback, (2) *El Nino* (NINO), and (3) Summer Arctic Sea Ice (ARCTIC) loss. The impacts from self-TPs (e.g., AMOC on AMOC) also move into potentially *cascading* TPs with some medium or strong *teleconnections* with other elements of the individual or collective TPs (cross-teleconnections within and between TPs).

For instance, Wunderling et al. (2024) (31 authors) demonstrate some of the core teleconnections within and between TPs as follows. Here I show in Table 4.5 only the destabilizing and stabilizing interactions (not the "unclear"/"competing" impacts that are *linked to neither destabilizing nor stabilizing impacts*):

[5] Lenton et al. (2008) have studied most of the above threshold effects, interviewing experts and assessing the evidence. Their conclusions are as follows. First, they ignored coral bleaching, perhaps because its onset is so close, happening at present. Secondly, summer loss of the Arctic sea-ice and the melting of the Greenland ice sheet were both classed as "high sensitivity" and "low uncertainty." Thirdly, the western Antarctic ice sheet separation, Amazon deforestation, and El Nino amplitude were classed as intermediate sensitivity and highest uncertainty. Lastly, Atlantic thermohaline circulation was classed as low sensitivity with intermediate uncertainty.

Table 4.4 10 Major threshold effects and cascading tipping points

Tipping point/Threshold effect	Tipping problems	^°C Tipping point	Tipping element (nonlinear)	Timing & symptoms	Uncertainty
[1] 1G. Greenland ice sheet (GIS) (global)	(a) Sea ice decline→ (b) Thinning→ (c) Decline over landmass	0.8–3.0 ℃	Positive feedback as ice melts; dark earth reduces reflection to atmosphere	2030 to 2330? Extra warming lately > IPCC assessment. Rising seas	High sensitivity and small uncertainty. Latest data reduces uncertainty.
[2] 2G. Western Antarctic ice sheet (WAIS) (global)	Separation of ice sheet from bedrock	1.0–3.0 ℃	Strong positive feedback: Ocean H2O → ice-bedrock separation	Within 300 years. Sudden rise in sea levels. 5 m rise possible	Intermediate sensitivity and high uncertainty
[3] 3G. Atlantic thermohaline circulation (ATH) (link to gulf stream) AMOC (global)	Insufficient freshwater or heat entering North Atlantic	1.4–8.0 ℃	Hysteresis in all models. Convection collapse. Irreversible (some models reversible)	Sometime in the twenty-first century possible. Cooling in Europe & West North America	AMOC currently on Tipping route (van Westen et al. 2024)
[4] 1R. Coral bleaching (regional)	Rising sea temperature	1.0–2.0 ℃	Multiple cumulative stresses	Threshold near/in process. Food production & tourism	Highly likely already occurring
[5] 2R. Barents Sea ice (abrupt loss) (regional)	Floating ice decline→sea water rise, warmer winters	1.5–1.7 ℃	Fastest warming part of Arctic region	Ice loss during winter →Eurasia winters warmer	BSI vanishes when GW reaches 1.5℃ (since pre-industrial times)
[6] 3R. Mountain glaciers (loss) (regional)	Rise temp. = MG loss: Fracture →cracking→melting→sliding (causes global sea levels to rise)	1.5–3.0 ℃	Positive feedback loops = MG loss from elastic to plastic to fracture as temp. Rises	1.5℃ warming causes 50% melt MG and 85 mm rise in sea levels by 2100	MG loss depends on slope, thickness, snowfall, longitude, basal temp., meltwater, and bed hardness
[7] 4R. Northern permafrost (abrupt thaw) (regional)	Infrastructural damage, rising GHGs, rising sea levels, and habitat destruction	1.0–2.3 ℃	Sudden temp. Increase by thawing of carbon-methane rich soils	Thawing already happening. Irreversible.	Arctic temp. Rising 200% faster than global mean. Uncertainty minimal.

Tipping point/Threshold effect	Tipping problems	^°C Tipping point	Tipping element (nonlinear)	Timing & symptoms	Uncertainty
[8] 0R1. Amazon rainforest (dieback)	Deforestation	2.0–4.0 ℃	20–30% drop in rainfall, dry season longer (↑ El Nino)	Twenty-first century dieback of rainforest	Quite likely in the twenty-first century with *both* land-use changes + ↑ temp
[9] 02-El Nino (ENSO)	Increased ocean heat uptake	2.0–2.5 ℃	Permanent deepening thermocline in east equatorial Pacific	↑El Nino amplitude (not frequency). Transition	"Significant probability" (Lenton differs from IPCC)
[10] 03 Arctic Sea ice	Summer loss (likely September ice-free). Flora & fauna decline	1.5–2.0 ℃	Arctic amplification: Arctic temp. Rise 4–7 times greater than global mean	Already happening	Relatively low

Source: McKay et al. (2022, 3), IPCC (2021, 553–672)

Table 4.5 Teleconnections to TP_1 from $TP_{2,3,4} \rightarrow$ Cascading TPs: Destabilizing (*d*) and stabilizing (*s*); strong (š), moderate (⋔), weak (ώ), unclear (ű)******

To: TP1	From: TP2	From: TP3	From: TP4	Total impact
1. AMOC	*D*GREENš	***d*ARCT⋔ώ**	*D*PERMű	**3*d*-š-⋔ώ-ű**
2. WANT	***d*GREEN⋔**	*d***NINO⋔ώ**	*D*AMOCű	**3*d*-⋔-⋔ώ-ű**
3. AMAZ	*D*NINOš			1*d*-š
4. CORAL	*D*NINOš			1*d*-š
5. NINO	*D*AMOCώ			1*d*-ώ
6. AFRICA	*D*AMOCű			1*d*-ű
7. PERM	*D*ARCTώ			1*d*-ώ
8. GREEN	*D*WANTώ	*S*AMOCš	*D*ARCTώ	2*d*-ώώ,1sš
9. ARCT	***s*AMOC⋔ώ**			**1** *s*-⋔ώ
∑	∑*d* = *3*š **+ 1⋔ + 2⋔ώ + 4ώ + 3ű**		∑*s* = **1š + 1⋔ώ**	∑*d* + *s* = 13*d* + 2 *s*
Net impact = ∑*(d-s)(net)* = 2š **+ 1⋔ + 1⋔ώ + 4ώ + 3ű**				

Source: Adapted from Wunderling et al. (2024, 15)

Based on Table 4.5, we have the following CGTP teleconnection assessments:

[1] AMOC has the greatest number/impact of teleconnections (from other TPs) propelling destructive global cascading tipping points, including a strong destabilizing one from GREEN, a moderate/weak destabilizing one from ARCT, and an uncertain destabilizing one from PERM.

[2] WANT has the second strongest global cascading TPs with at least three, one moderate destabilizing one from GREEN, a moderate/unclear destabilizing one from NINO, and an unclear destabilizing one from AMOC.

[3–4] AMAZ and CORAL have equally strong GCTPs, both having a strong destabilizing impact from NINO.

[5–7] The next three have about equal impacts. NINO has a weak destabilizing effect from AMOC, while AFRICA has an uncertain destabilizing effect from NINO, and PERM has a weak destabilizing effect from ARCT.

[8–9] The last two are the only ones with stabilizing effects, GREEN having a stabilizing impact from AMOC, and two weak destabilizing impacts from AMOC and ARCT, respectively, while ARCT has a stabilizing impact from AMOC.

In aggregate, as shown in the final row of the Table, the results are as follows: first, the total includes 13 destabilizing GTPs and 2 stabilizing TPs: ∑GTPs = 13*d* + 2 *s*. This includes ∑*s* = 1š + 1⋔ώ, one strong and one medium-weak stabilizing TPs. It also includes ∑*d* = *3*š + 1⋔ + 2⋔ώ + 4ώ + 3ű, where the total destabilizing CGTPs include three strong ones, one medium one, two medium-weak ones, four weak ones, and three unclear ones. In net terms, there are ∑*d*Net = 2š + 1⋔ + 1⋔ώ + 4ώ + 3ű, where the total net destabilizing CGTPs include two strong, one medium, one medium-weak, four weak, and three unclear destabilizing impacts on the climate. We have overall 11 known *net* uneven cascading tipping points actually and potentially impacting climate change in the world economy. (See ch. 9 for more details.)

4.6 Conclusion

This chapter has related some core principles of political economy to the problem of climate change. It started with the principle of historical specificity to situate patterns of climate change through the history of planet Earth, paying special attention to waves of warming and cooling during the Phanerozoic, Pleistocene, and Holocene eras. The most recent history of climate change is the only one affected by anthropogenic influences, and it is likely to have major impacts, some of which are already in motion. The principle of circular and cumulative causation centered on the interaction of multiple variables and the feedback loops between them that magnify the atmospheric result.

Natural scientists seem to dominate research for both the IPCC and scientists who scrutinize natural changes in Earth's climate. The natural changes center on 10-year, 70-year, 1200-year, and some other cycles and waves of climate change. Examining the interactions between these cycles and waves produces various scenarios of possible climate change, some of which indicate a declining global temperature for some time (after 2020), but also variously a higher rise until the 2060s circa. Closer scrutiny should ascertain precisely what the outcomes may be when the different cycles and waves are linked to different scenarios and realized temperature rises.

The IPCC, on the other hand, concludes that contemporary changes in GHGEs and global temperatures are closely related and almost entirely caused by anthropogenic (human) agency. They propose various future trends depending upon which socioeconomic patterns of behavior and policies are activated. With no change in structured practices, we are likely to see much greater global warming to under or over 3 degrees, with a middle-of-the-road trajectory it will likely be still over 2 degrees, and with a green road alternative, it will likely be just under or over 1.5 degrees. The green road scenario will require both major mitigation and adaptation, while the other approaches require combinations of mitigation and adaptation, with adaptation being the only option with higher rates of warming. With no changes in structured environmental options, the adaptations cannot reasonably lead to the reproduction of large aggregates of people and other species due to the magnified results, especially in numerous areas and regions.

These magnified results also relate specifically to the principle of uncertainty, since the major uncertainty is how quickly climate change will destroy core elements of ecological capital (including atmospheric patterns and ocean currents). Deep uncertainties associated with the models, ecological factors, and social-behavioral elements generate problems especially as to when tipping points will begin to impact. Likely major threshold effects have to some degree already come into effect, much earlier than expected, which will necessitate more serious efforts at environmental preservation. But if the global tipping points escalate beyond reasonable limits the adaptations will become so severe that much of the world will not be reproducible for a mass of people and other species.

At a broader level, while both schools of thought (IPCC human impact scholars vs. natural temperature change scholars [NTCS]) present scenarios where global mean temperatures likely rise at least through to 2060, they also present contradictory scenarios where temperatures rise to 2100 and beyond (IPCC) while otherwise start declining from 2020 (some NTCS). Hopefully, in the near future, both schools will include the different arguments side by side carefully assessing the respective evidence with fair assessments of both. The IPCC could include the NTCS work in their volumes while the NTCS could include IPCC scenarios in their analyses. Then maybe we will know with hopefully more certainty what the likely future will present for us to likely change (where necessary) through policy and governance measures.

References

Almedeij, Jaber. 2020. Long-term periodic modeling in hydrology: Role of sunspot cycles. *Journal of Hydrological Engineering* 25 (5): 1–11.

Bond, Gerard, William Showers, Maziet Cheseby, Rusty Lotti, Peter Almasi, Peter deMenocal, Paul Priore, Heidi Cullen, Irka Hajdas, and Georges Bonani. 1997. A pervasive millennial-scale cycle in North Atlantic Holocene and glacial climates. *Science* 278 (1257): 1–11. https://doi.org/10.1126/science.278.5341.1257.

Calvin, Katherine, Ben Bond-Lamberty, Leon Clarke, James Edmonds, Jiyong Eom, Corinne Hartin, Sonny Kim, Page Kyle, Robert Link, Richard Moss, Haewon McJeon, Pralit Patel, Steve Smith, Stephanie Waldhoff, and Marshall Wise. 2017. The SSP4: A world of deepening inequality. *Global Environmental Change* 42 (1): 284–296.

de Pryck, Kari, and Mike Hulme. 2023. *A critical assessment of the intergovernmental panel on climate change*. Cambridge: Cambridge University Press.

Dewey, Edward R., and Og Mandino. 1973. *Cycles: The mysterious forces that trigger events*. New York: Manor Books.

Garnaut, Ross. 2008. *The Garnaut climate change review: Final report*. Cambridge, UK: NY: Cambridge University Press.

GMT (Global Methane Tracker). 2023. *Methane and climate change*. Paris: International Energy Association (IEA). https://www.iea.org/reports/https://www.iea.org/reports/global-methane-tracker-2023/understanding-methane-emissions.

Harris, Stuart A. 2023. Evolution of the climate of the earth. *Journal of Civil Enginering Research and Technology* 5 (2): 1–15.

Huntington, Ellsworth. 1945. *Mainsprings of civilization*. New York: Wiley and Sons.

IPCC. 2007. *Climate change 2007: The physical science basis. Contribution of working group 1 to the fourth assessment report*. Cambridge: Cambridge University Press.

IPCC. 2021. *Climate change 2021: The physical science basis. Contribution of working group I to the sixth assessment report of the intergovernmental panel on climate change*. [Masson-Delmotte, V., P. Zhai, A. Pirani, S.L. Connors, C. Péan, S. Berger, N. Caud, Y. Chen, L. Goldfarb, M.I. Gomis, M. Huang, K. Leitzell, E. Lonnoy, J.B.R. Matthews, T.K. Maycock, T. Waterfield, O. Yelekçi, R. Yu, and B. Zhou (eds.)], 2391. Cambridge, United Kingdom and New York, NY, USA: Cambridge University Press. https://doi.org/10.1017/9781009157896.

IPCC. 2022a. *Climate change 2022: Impacts, adaptation, and vulnerability. Contribution of working group II to the sixth assessment report of the intergovernmental panel on climate change*. [H.-O. Pörtner, D.C. Roberts, M. Tignor, E.S. Poloczanska, K. Mintenbeck, A. Alegría, M. Craig,

S. Langsdorf, S. Löschke, V. Möller, A. Okem, B. Rama (eds.)], 3056. Cambridge, UK and New York, NY, USA: Cambridge University Press. https://doi.org/10.1017/9781009325844.

IPCC. 2022b. *Climate change 2022: Mitigation of climate change. Contribution of working group III to the sixth assessment report of the intergovernmental panel on climate change.* [P.R. Shukla, J. Skea, R. Slade, A. Al Khourdajie, R. Van Diemen, D. McCollum, M. Pathak, S. Some, P. Vyas, R. Fradera, M. Belkacemi, A. Hasija, G. Lisboa, S. Luz, J. Malley, (eds.)]. Cambridge, UK and New York, NY, USA: Cambridge University Press. https://doi.org/10.1017/9781009157926.

IPCC. 2022c. Box TS 1, Figure 1. *Climate change 2022: Mitigation of climate change.* "Technical summary".

IPCC. 2023. *Climate change 2023: Synthesis report. Contribution of working groups I, II and III to the sixth assessment report of the intergovernmental panel on climate change.* [Core Writing Team, H. Lee and J. Romero (eds.)], 184. Geneva, Switzerland: IPCC. https://doi.org/10.59327/IPCC/AR6-9789291691647.

Jovanovic, Gordana. 2022. The influence of natural cycles on climate change. *Modern Environmental Science and Engineering* 8 (9): 477–482.

Kandlikar, Miland. 2005. Responding and communicating deep uncertainty in climate change assessments. *C.R. Geoscience* 337:445–455.

Keller, Klaus, Gary Yoke, and Michael Schlesinger. 2008. Managing the risks of climate thresholds: Uncertainties and informational needs. *Climatic Change* 91:5–10.

Keynes, John Maynard. 1921. *A treatise on probability*, 2008. New York: Rough Draft Printing.

Keynes, John Maynard. 1936. *The general theory of employment, interest and money*, 2008. London: BN Publishing.

Knight, Frank H. 1921. *Risk, uncertainty and profit.* New York: Cosimo classics.

Knutti, Reto. 2008. Should we believe model predictions of future climate change? *Philosophical Transactions of the Royal Society* 366:4647–4664.

Knutti, R., M. R. Alen, P. Friedlingstein, J. M. Gregory, G. C. Hegeri, G. A. Meehi, M. Meinshausen, J. M. Murphy, G.-K. Plattner, S. C. B. Raper, T. F. Stocker, P. A. Stott, H. Teng, and T. M. L. Wigley. 2008. A review of uncertainties in global temperature projections over the twenty-first century. *Journal of Climate* 21:2651–2663.

Lenton, Timothy M., Hermann Held, Elmar Kriegler, Wolfgang Lucht, Stephan Rahmstorf, and Hans Joachim Schellnhuber. 2008. Tipping elements in the earth's climate system. *Proceedings of the National Academy of Sciences* 105:1786–1793.

Liu, Yu, Cai Qiu Fang, Song Hui Ming, A. N. Zhi Sheng, and Hans W. Linderholm. 2011. Amplitudes, rates, periodicities and causes of temperature variations in the past 2485 years and future trends over the central-eastern Tibetan plateau. *Chinese Science Bulletin* 56 (28–29): 2986–2994. https://doi.org/10.1007/s11434-011-4713-7.

McInerney, David, and Klaus Keller. 2008. Economically optimal risk reduction strategies in the face of uncertain climate thresholds. *Climatic Change* 91:29–41.

McKay, David I. Armstrong, Arie Staal, Jesse F. Abrams, Ricarda Winkelmann, Boris Sakschewski, Sina Loriani, Ingo Fetzer, Sarah E. Cornell, Johan Rockström, and Timothy M. Lenton. 2022. Exceeding 1.5°C global warming could trigger multiple climate tipping points. *Science* 377 (eabn7950): 1–10.

Moberg, Anders, Dmitry M. Sonechkin, Karen Holmgren, Nina M. Datsenko, and Wibjorn Karlen. 2005. Highly variable northern hemisphere temperatures reconstructed from low-and high-resolution proxy data. *Nature* 433:613–618.

Mohaddes, Kamiar, and Mehdi Raissi. 2024. *Rising temperatures, melting incomes: Country-specific macroeconomic effects of climate scenarios. CAMA working paper 42/2024 (June). Centre for Applied Macroeconomic Analysis.* Crawford Institute of Public Policy. Australian National University. https://crawford.anu.edu.au/sites/default/files/publication/cama_crawford_anu_edu_au/2024-06/42_2024_mohaddes_raissi.pdf.

NCEI (National Centres for Environmental Information). 2024. *Global Land and Ocean December–November Temperature Anomalies. Degrees Celsius. Base Period—1901-2000.* United States of America Government. https://www.climate.gov/news-features/understanding-climate/climate-change-global-temperature.

Nierode, Dale Irwin. 2022. The cyclical sine model for climate change. *International Journal of Plant, Animal and Environmental Sciences* 12 (4): 175–191. https://www.fortunejournals.com/articles/the-cyclical-sine-model-explanation-for-climate.pdf.

O'Hara, Phillip Anthony. 2006. *Growth and development in the global political economy: Social structures of accumulation and modes of regulation*. London & New York: Routledge. Paper Edition 2009.

O'Hara, Phillip Anthony. 2009. Political economy of climate change, ecological destruction, and uneven development. *Ecological Economics* 69:223–234. https://doi.org/10.1016/j.ecolecon.2009.09.015.

O'Hara, Phillip Anthony. 2010. Climate change trends and governance: History, contradictions and prospects. In *International political economy*, ed. Miguel-Angel Galindo Martin, 1–14. New York: Nova Science Publishers.

O'Hara, Phillip Anthony. 2022. Advancing Kondratiev wave complexity through Bunge's emergence, Braudel's history, Veblen's institutions and Polanyi's double movement. *Alter Economics* 19 (1): 51–70. https://doi.org/10.31063/AlterEconomics/2022.19-1.4.

O'Hara, Phillip Anthony. 2023. Principles of institutional and evolutionary political economy: Applied to current world problems. Singapore: Springer Nature.

Olejarz, Jason, Yoh Iwasa, Andrew H. Knoll, and Martin A. Nowak. 2021. The great oxygenation event a consequence of ecological dynamics modulated by planetary change. *Nature Communications* 12 (3985): 1–9.

Romano, Marco, Bruce Rubidge, and Raffaele Sardella. 2021. A century since the recognition of cyclic climatic change by Milanković. *Rendiconti online della Società Geologica Italiana* 52 (23): 1–5.

Scafetta, Nicola. 2012. Multi-scale harmonic model for solar and climate cyclical variation throughout the Holocene based on Jupiter–Saturn tidal Frequencies Plus the 11-Year Solar Dynamo Cycle. *Journal of Atmospheric and Solar-Terrestrial Physics* 80:296–311.

Scafetta, Nicola, and Antonio Bianchini. 2023. Overview of the spectral coherence between planetary resonances and solar and climate oscillations. *Climate* 11 (44): 77. https://doi.org/10.3390/cli11040077.

Scafetta, Nicola, Franco Milani, and Antonio Bianchini. 2020. A 60-year cycle in the meteorite fall frequency suggests a possible interplanetary dust forcing of the earth's climate driven by planetary oscillations. *Geophysical Research Letters* 47:1–11. https://doi.org/10.1029/2020GL089954.

Shackle, George. 1970. *Expectation, enterprise and profit: The theory of the firm*. London: Routledge.

Sreedhar, Arun K., and A. Faizal Kahn. 2021. Proterozoic environment and snowball earth–A review. *Journal of Research in Environmental and Earth Sciences* 7 (3): 13–16.

UNU EHS (United Nations University–Institute for Environment and Human Security). 2023. In *Interconnected disaster risks: Risk tipping points*, ed. Caitlyn Eberle, Jack O'Connor, Liliana Narvaez, Melisa Mena Benavides, and Zita Sebesvari. Bonn: United Nations University—Institute for Environment and Human Security. https://doi.org/10.53324/WTWN2495.

van Geel, Bas, and Peter A. Ziegler. 2013. IPCC underestimates the Sun's role in climate change. *Energy and Environment* 24 (3–4): 431–453.

Van Vuuren, C. P., Elmar Kriegler, Jae Edmonds, Brian C. O'Neill, Shinichiro Fujimori, Katherine Calvin NicoBauer, Rob Dellink, Oliver Fricko, Wolfgang Lutz, Alexander Popp, Jesus Crespo Cuaresma, K. C. Samir, Marian Leimbach, Leiwen Jiang, Tom Kram, Shilpa Rao, Johannes Emmerling, Kristie Ebi, and MassimoTavoni. 2017. The shared socioeconomic pathways and their energy, land use, and greenhouse gas emissions implications: An overview. *Global Environmental Change* 42 (1): 153–168. https://doi.org/10.1016/j.gloenvcha.2016.05.009.

van Westen, René M., Michael Kliphuis, and Henk A. Dijkstra. 2024. Physics-based early warning signal shows that AMOC is on tipping course Science Advances 10(6). https://doi.org/10.1126/sciadv.adk1189

Waters, Colin N., et al. 2023. Response to Merritts et al. the Anthropocene is complex. Defining it is not. *Earth-Science Reviews* 238 (March): 1–4.

Wikipedia. 2024. Alpha 18 0. 13 July 2024. http://en.wikipedia.org/wiki/alpha 18 0

WMO. 2024. World beats previous temperature record. WMO confirms that 2023 smashes global temperature record

Wunderling, Nico, Nico Wunderling, Anna S. von der Heydt, Yevgeny Aksenov, Stephen Barker, Robbin Bastiaansen, Victor Brovkin, Maura Brunetti, Victor Couplet, Thomas Kleinen, Caroline H. Lear, Johannes Lohmann, Rosa Maria Roman-Cuesta, Sacha Sinet, Didier Swingedouw, Ricarda Winkelmann, Pallavi Anand, Jonathan Barichivich, Sebastian Bathiany, Mara Baudena, John T. Bruun, Cristiano M. Chiessi, Helen K. Coxall, David Docquier, Jonathan F. Donges, Swinda K. J. Falkena, Ann Kristin Klose, David Obura, Juan Rocha, Stefanie Rynders, Norman Julius Steinert, and Matteo Willeit. 2024. Climate tipping point interactions and cascades: A review. *Earth Systems Dynamics* 15:41–74.

Zhu, Shixing, Maoyan Zhu, Andrew H. Knoll, Zongjun Yin, Fangchen Zhao, Shufen Sun, Yuangao Qu, Min Shi, and Huan Liu. 2016. Decimetre-scale multicellular eukaryotes from the 1.56-billion-year-old Gaoyuzhuang formation in North China. *Nature. Communications* 7 (11500): 1–7. https://doi.org/10.1038/ncomms11500.

Chapter 5
Dutch Long Waves, Hegemonic Power, and Climate Change

Abstract This chapter examines the Dutch Golden Age of the late 1500s through to the mid-to-late-1600s vis-à-vis institutions, technologies, and geo-spatial-ecological factors (including climate change) that conditioned the Dutch pathways and circuits of socioeconomic dynamics (CSD), set within the context of the world system which they led. We scrutinize the ways the Dutch achieved hegemonic leadership and present data on Dutch GDP per capita growth decadal waves, GDP per capita waves, and other performance measures especially for the 1500s–1700s to ascertain linkages between waves of growth, hegemony, and climate change. We also examine Dutch waves of performance, through to the 2020s, during eras of British, US, and potentially Chinese hegemony. A conclusion follows.

Keywords Dutch hegemony · Long waves · Climate change · Pathways and circuits of socioeconomic dynamics (CSD) · Dutch Golden Age · Institutions · Technologies · Eco-geo-spatial structures · Rise and fall · Principles

5.1 Introduction

In chaps. 2 and 3, I critically examined the literature on long waves to establish problems that need to be resolved so waves may continue to be a potentially useful tool of political economy analysis. The early work of especially Kondratieff and Schumpeter was scrutinized in chap. 2, from which I agreed with Garvy that we should pay attention in future research to the nature of the stylized facts of long-term movements of economic life of the capitalist system and its components. I also agreed with Kuznets' critique that Schumpeter had not adequately scrutinized business cycles, but this current study does not present long waves as cycles, and hence we need to reconstruct long waves as part of the complex long-term transformation of the capitalist economy. I also agreed with Sweezy that in the circular flow, capitalists need to be seen along with other classes as performing various active roles.

P. A. O'Hara, *Long Waves of Growth, Hegemonic Power, and Climate Change in the World Economy*, https://doi.org/10.1007/978-981-96-4132-1_5

This study goes beyond Schumpeter's circular flow model by utilizing the more complex circuits of socioeconomic dynamics (CSD), where the techno-institutional and geo-ecological dynamic structures include many active agents such as classes, genders, and ethnic groups, in the whole process. Rather than using a circuit to establish a system of equilibrium from which change can be introduced as an endogenous factor, I start with a realistic circuit comprising all the major dynamic structures in motion from which we can understand waves of growth, hegemony, and climate change through historical time.

From chap. 3, we learned that the extant schools of thought of long waves have started the process of integrating key lessons from the analysis, especially in relation to technology, institutions, and principles, but that this process needs to be elevated in priority to the core issues of current and future long wave research, hegemony, and climate change. We also learnt that one needs to differentiate between real and price waves, with the emphasis given to real (per capita) performance measures (and the linkage between the two where especially relevant). Other core lessons learnt from chaps. 2 and 3 are that we need to deconstruct the standard model of long waves, not only with respect to the CSD and real variables, but also in relation to empirical anomalies, and to extend the inquiry back to at least the 1500s since statistics and qualitative historical advances make this *more* feasible now.

A core thesis of my first volume on political economy principles and problems (O'Hara 2023) is that it helps to utilize some of the core general principles of (institutional and evolutionary) political economy (PoPE) when analyzing issues such as current anomalies and long-term performance. A myriad of such concepts and principles, including nine core ones, are presented in chap. 1 (Table 1.1) (also see O'Hara 2023, chap. 3 for details). We utilize them in this chapter/book, for two reasons. First, to help generally with the inquiry. And second, to reinforce the hypothesis that the nature of long waves, hegemony, and climate change (LWHegCC) are contingent upon a myriad of factors involving the principles. PoPE teach us that LWHegCC depend upon historical events and processes, uneven developments and power differentials, complexities of circular and cumulative causation (CCC), roles of heterogeneous groups and agents, contradictions, risks and uncertainties, innovation, policies and governance, and the pathways and circuits of socioeconomic dynamics.[1]

In this context, for this chapter, the *first core principle is that of historical specificity and evolution*, which states that political economy should investigate the background history and its movement through time of every core issue it seeks to understand. It also emerged from the above chapters that there are several problems with long wave empirics, with respect to the standard model, that should be brought to the fore and (critically) analyzed. As noted, we should go back to the earlier years

[1] In doing so I utilize "Ian Kerr's (2021) rules" concerning the relationship between concepts and principles, see chap. 1 of O'Hara (2023) for details.

of capitalist development, especially to the 1500s–1700s since modern research shows that industrial, institutional, and climatological/geographical structures did evolve and become transformed within earlier stages of capitalism. Hypothesis One is that scrutinizing the period of the 1500s–2020s, is likely to result in some crucial evidence and ideas about the long-term performance of the capitalist world system.

Hence, long waves, hegemonic power, and climate change are likely to be three core areas associated with current and future analysis of the long-term motion of capitalism. Linking the triadic interdependent processes of LWHegCC is likely to result in substantial knowledge which is important to understanding capitalist development. In this context, we investigate the *second principle of hegemony and uneven development*, namely, that hegemonic power and uneven development are core issues associated with the emergence of long-term socioeconomic performance. We examine the stylized facts associated with key hegemonic regions, starting with (the hypothesis of) Dutch hegemony within the world system of the late 1500s–1600s, then British hegemony of the 1800s, US hegemony of the 1900s, rising Chinese power from the 1980s to the 2020s, and LWHegCC forecasts into the 2030s and 2040s (to 2100 vis-à-vis climate change). The nature of long waves and climate change is partially contingent upon processes linked to uneven power relations in the world economy. Where possible we need to examine the networks of relationships within and between core, periphery, and semi-periphery (CPSP) in this matrix of interdependencies.

The *third principle* of significance is that of *heterogeneous groups and agents*, whereby LWHegCC is contingent upon the different roles played by socioeconomic groups and agents. Central to the forthcoming chapters are the emergence of classes such as wage laborers, household workers, and the middle classes; industrial, financial, and merchant capitalists; landowners, peasants, and rentiers; state workers such as public servants, heads of government, monarchs, nobles, city, and council planners; and so on. Without adequate analysis of the role played by specific groups of human and other agents, long-term motion will be difficult to explain. For instance, the specific dynamics associated with LWHegCC is contingent upon the development of suitable alliances between agents and classes to propel political-economic change.

The *fourth principle,* circular and cumulative causation (CCC), states that analyzing CCC motion is crucial for comprehending the upward and downward motion of socioeconomic activity. Capitalism requires CCC dynamics to ensure a rapid expansion of growth, accumulation, and profit, but expansions incur contradictions that over time lead to deteriorating conditions, conflict, and periodic disarray. In a broader context, CCC is the usual type of continual motion of an 'up-and-down' nature that ensures the rise and fall of economic systems, and the rise and demise of various phases of capitalist development, as well as various hegemonies such as Dutch, British, US and potentially Chinese power. The specific form that LWHegCC takes is contingent in part upon the nature and intensity of these nonlinear CCC forces, rises and falls, (cascading) tipping points, and points of no return (including positive/negative feedback).

The *fifth principle is contradiction*, namely, that the internal dynamics of capitalist development need to be situated within the framework of core anomalies of the system. There is a myriad of such contradictions, including systemic contradictions such as the disembedded economy and creative destruction, where capitalism requires continual global, regional, national, and subnational expansion of markets, changes in production techniques and products, and new ways of arranging corporations and business institutions. These changes in turn lead to destructions and rearrangements of ecological resources, human beings, new skills, technologies, and institutions to push forward accumulation and profit. Capital is also contradictory because it requires extra-institutional resources to provide the public goods of infrastructure, public finance, defense, knowledge, a healthy workforce, and suitable public lands and environments which are not usually provided by profit-oriented business groups (and open markets). There are several other contradictions that are crucial for understanding long-term motion, including the relationships between capital and labor, monopoly and competition, rural versus urban areas, ecology versus capital, state and capital, gender and ethnic (including religious) relations, international relations, and so on. Scrutinizing systemic, group, and agent contradictions is necessary for understanding the contingent nature of LWHegCC and development in promoting (temporary) continuity and durable expansion of the circuits of socioeconomic dynamics, and for comprehending the rise and especially demise of waves, hegemonies, and climate dynamics.

The *sixth principle of risk and uncertainty* (PRU) states that PRU is especially crucial for comprehending these movements from upswing to downswing; from one phase to another; and for the continual reproduction of the institutions-technologies-climate (and CPSP) dynamics underlying capitalist transformation. Risk is linked to factors that are relatively determinate and capable of calculative specificity, such as insurance risk, gambling, taxation and short-term profit, revenue, and cost. Uncertainty concerns the future, especially those factors comprising significant degrees of ambiguity, opacity, and non-transparency.

Uncertainty is the very fabric of capitalism since unstable change and motion are the core of its existence. Uncertainty necessarily arises from a system based on long-term financing of investment and relatively short-term (and intermediate-term) profit and returns to capital. To moderate such uncertainty it is necessary, first, to have continual advances in methods and products; second, for institutional relationships to ensure future investments; and third, for public goods such as education, health, infrastructure, and ecological diversity to provide protection from disarray. Reducing uncertainty associated with anomalous forms of climate change is also required. LWHegCC is contingent upon the form and intensity of risk and uncertainty (including efforts to moderate such intensities).

The *seventh principle of innovation and novelty/creative destruction* is a core one for capitalism, since major new methods, organizations, products, resources, and markets are required for its long-term reproduction. Groups of entrepreneurs and innovative businesses are necessary for continual profit and accumulation to ensure advances in productivity, skills, and knowledge. A dynamic (im)balance between monopoly and competition is required so that rent-seeking is neither too large nor small, and competition is neither too intense nor weak (in a dynamic sense of possibly moving from one extreme to the other). Innovations are also required to moderate the potential conflicts between capital and labor, industrial and finance capital, rural and urban dynamics, men and women, ethnic group vs. ethnic group, state and capital, nature vs. humans, and so on. Innovations are crucial for improving the provision of public goods such as education, health, infrastructure, information, organization, eco-spatial resources, defense, trust, and governance. Non-state and non-corporate agents and organization must also innovate, including families and households, NGOs, communities, and local organizations.

Contradictions, CCC-movements, and uncertainties associated with insufficient coordination between business, state, community, and geo-eco-spatial relations within the circuit tend to periodically generate rises and booms followed by recessions and depressions; typical motions of business cycles in the shorter-time horizon; and the instabilities associated with long-term waves, hegemonic rise and fall and climate change upheavals. LWHegCC are thus contingent upon the nature and intensity of innovations, broadly defined.

This leads logically to the *eighth principle of policy and governance*, and why capitalism in its various styles has historically been closely linked to state, corporate, household, civil society, and global governance. Corporate governance at both the general and specific levels are necessary to provide protection from competitors, be they businesses, states, armies, groups, and individuals. They also provide certain public goods, which often evolve into state forms, such as armies, central banks, technical monopolies, and planners. State forms of governance organize property rights for business, encourage the transition from small landowners (or renters) to wage laborers, organize free trade or protection depending on the degree of hegemony existing at the time, and the expansion (and where relevant protection) of literacy, knowledge, health, infrastructure, and administration. There are more double movements of opposition (or dynamic fusion) to capitalist dynamics in the form of states, civil society groups, households, individuals, even corporate forms themselves, other types of dynamic embeddedness to promote community trust, sociality, and alternative institutions of social provisioning. The nature and intensity of LWHegCC are thereby contingent upon policy and governance.

For this chapter, the *ninth principle* is the *circuits of socioeconomic dynamics* (CSD), which integrates the dominant forms of institutions, technologies, and geo-ecologies to analyze the systemic performance of (for instance) Dutch, British, US, and Chinese varieties of capitalism. CSD is a dynamic circuit for evaluating the major structural forms impacting on the overall performance of capitalist economies in their various forms over a long historical time. CSD involves relative autonomous, interdependencies, and emergent properties of geo-spatial-ecologies, institutions, and technologies, including input-output relations, flows and structural forms within and between the components. It is related to the cultural way of life of the community involving various networks, forms of trust, beliefs, values, and pathways through which people, resources, and capital move and provide structure for the system and its subsystems.

Earlier forms of such circuits, apart from those already discussed, include the *Tableau économique* of the physiocrats (François Quesnay, 1694–1774), Marx's *circuit of social capital* (1885) and extensions thereof, see O'Hara (2001), Keynesian macro-tables, Myrdalian-Kaldorian CCC models, and circular economy frameworks. It also evolved and was adapted from previous techno-institutional models that have the *potential* to be expressed in (modified) matrix or circuit form, such as the Regulation Approach (between, e.g., modes of regulation, regimes of accumulation, and institutional forms), the SSA approach (between 5 and 6 or more institutional spheres, see O'Hara 2000, 2006, 2010), James O'Connor's (1984) extended circuit, Boris Frankel's (1983) potential synchronization between electoral, production, credit and food processes, Freeman and Louçã's (2001) linkage between technologies and institutions, as well as others (see O'Hara 2023).

The CSD shares not only some similarities with these models but also seeks to transcend them in the search for a framework more appropriate to the cases in question. We discussed the general form of the CSD in more detail (see Fig. 1.1 above) and more specific forms for the Dutch (see below), British (chap. 6), US (chap. 7), and Chinese (chap. 8) CSDs (usually in stylized form).

The following chapters will utilize these nine principles and several of their umbrella concepts and principles to examine the interaction between hegemonic power, long waves, and climate change (and CPSP relations) for The Netherlands, Britain, USA, China, and related networks, and circuits. We use the principles of political economy (PoPE) *paradigm of long waves, hegemony, and climate change* (and the NLWM) to analyze the nature of *capitalism* through its institutions, technologies, climatological, core events, conjunctures, and hegemonic (including uneven development) dynamics. The *PoPE paradigm* synthesizes and develops several innovations for analyzing these core processes.[2]

5.2 Dutch Golden Age, Hegemony, and Climate Change

Recent decades have seen major developments in big history, world history, history, economic history, Dutch history, British history, US history, Chinese history, other histories, international statistical analysis of socioeconomic performance, and many other literatures, that enable us to better understand the emergence, evolution, and transformation of the Dutch Golden Age of the late 1500s through the 1600s in the

[2] In the first volume on political economy concepts and principles (O'Hara 2023), the principles were given center stage, so that nine world problems could be scrutinized explicitly through the continual mention/application of each of the (eight) principles (and many of the umbrella concepts) throughout the volume. This was necessary for the first volume to set the scene and ensure that readers knew exactly what principles were being applied and when. In this current volume, I fuse the *principles* more with applications, so they are introduced explicitly in the first chapter and several of the earlier ones, including this one, but after this, they are utilized less explicitly, while highlighting them occasionally to remind readers of what is being done. In this volume, there are nine principles.

context of the capitalist world system emerging at the time (plus other chapters in this volume). Some of these literatures and data will be the subject of this chapter vis-à-vis LWHegCC.

Statistical analysis of real GDP levels, per capita and its growth are data the quality of which has improved immensely both in quantity and quality over recent years. Readers should recognize this for all the data presented in this book. In general, the trend of data quality and goodness can be shown as follows in Fig. 5.1 in a stylized fashion (subject to various caveats and qualifications):

This illustrates that, in general (though there are exceptions and variations based on specific cases) the further back in time we traverse the lower the quality of the data, since the number of errors and uncertainties become greater, especially for GDP, and related types of data. Some data is simply not possible to obtain for certain variables in many nations before say 1950, 1900, or 1850 (e.g., macro profit rates and unemployment). Likely also some data has been getting much better in availability and quality more recently (e.g., possibly for GDP, population, and investment). And as information becomes more available about quality, errors, and uncertainties, one may have to adjust the data accordingly, e.g., perhaps the trade-off gets better or worse; maybe a new and more complex line is necessary (showing error/uncertainty areas). Data for some nations (e.g., China), since they are not core economies, may be questionable even for the 1980s–2000s and maybe further forward, since the data has political influences underlying it (potentially more than some nations of the core), and some nations have few resources to utilize for data improvement (especially in parts of Africa, for instance).

Also, the errors and uncertainties may be quite different, less, or more complicated, or not so historically contingent, for certain variables, e.g., climate change, which is often based on core samples from tree trunks, ice sheets, soil samples, other natural phenomena, especially for data traversing hundreds, thousands, or

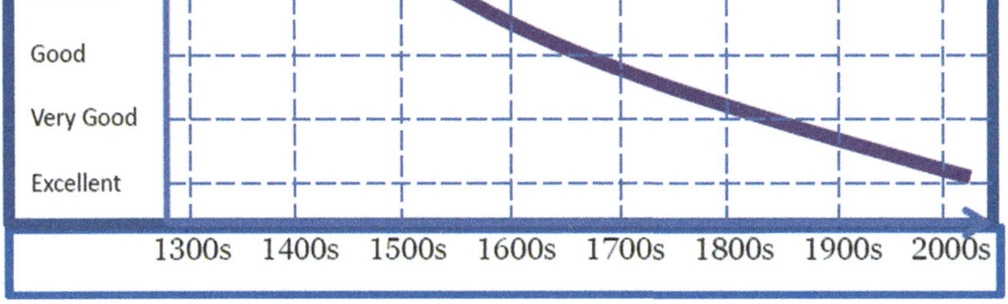

Fig. 5.1 Data quality and errors, stylized, 1300s–2020s (circa)

millions of years or more. Using multiple forms of these estimates from different sources, where possible, will usually improve the analysis.

In terms of my own empirics in these chapters, there are three forms and aspects to consider. First, I use historical analysis of the eco-geo-spatial, institutional, and technological dynamic structures of the CSD to scrutinize Dutch, British, US and Chinese LWHegCC as explained above.

Second, I back the (a) historical analysis up with (b) statistical analysis of core variables to provide a supplementary form of documentation. Here I use several methods, including one which is designed to be understood by a wide range of readers of this book. A core one is stylistically shown (again) in Fig. 5.2.

This new long wave method empirics is the main one utilized in this study. Here we apply the empirical method to the standard model of long waves, a model we seek to critically scrutinize throughout this book. It comprises four main tools or methods or calculations.

First, using the PoPE Model, we first typically utilize the data of, e.g., real GDP per capita growth rates (annually), which we averaged (AAGR) over successive decades to reduce the amplifications of short cycles and fluctuations as well as chance events. These decadal AAGRs are also used to provide the dynamics of the waves. There are typically short (1 decade) and long (2 or more decades) waves of upswing or downswing, or borderline performance.

Second, we differentiate between waves and trends by establishing a trend bar. Trend bars for annual GDP per capita decadal growth are usually linear (using the least squares method), since a linear bar usually provides the best way of illustrating the data and ascertaining the operation of long- and short-wave upswing (LWU, SWU), downswing (LWU, SWU), and borderline (B) performance.

Third, trends are transformed into bars (thick trend "bars" of 20 points) for three reasons. They enable us to effectively delete the trend from the data to see what the result is. In doing this, the trends versus data enable us to differentiate upswings

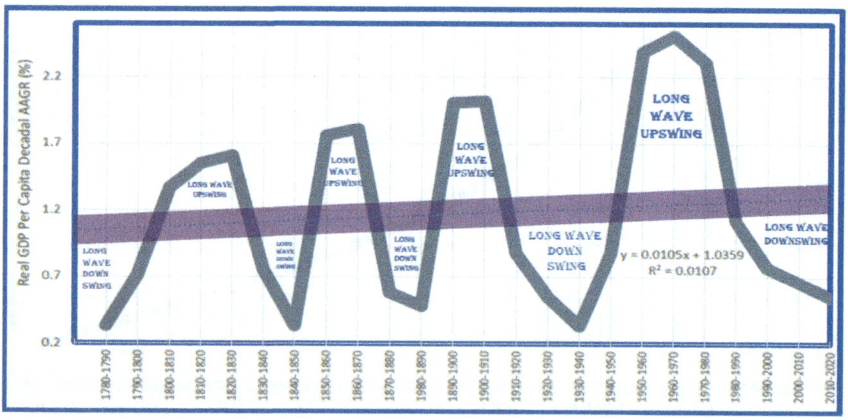

Fig. 5.2 Stylized Standard Model of long wave analysis. Real GDP per capita decadal AAGR (%), LWU, LWD, BP, 1780s–2010s (applied to "standard model") ($y = 0.0105x + 1.0359$; $R^2 = 0.0107$; is the equation for the trend *line*)

from downswings and borderlines. They establish a large area of performance in between up and downswing in the wave; so that we have three main performances, up, down, and borderline. This three-area illustration helps in establishing three areas of performance and thereby assists in establishing upswings and downswings (and their borders).

Schumpeter used a similar method and called these areas "neighborhoods of equilibrium" (NOE). In this study, we do not use equilibrium theory (see Kaldor 1972 as to why), but the technique of NOE helps much in other core ways. Trends are used (with usually a small-medium correlation) since we want some difference between wave and trend.

Fourth, the differences between waves and trends can be easily seen with this method, and these define our waves. Figures 5.4 and 5.5 provide examples of how we shall analyze waves throughout this book (see chap. 1 for details). The empirical results for the Dutch, British, US, and Chinese cases will include categories such as short-wave upswings and downswings, very long wave upswings and downswings, short and long wave borderline performance, and so on.

We used a similar Figure to the above in chap. 1 to critique the standard model (SM), the SM being not the statistical method used to illustrate it but rather the periodicities, amplitudes, and regularities associated with the Figure. In this context, some major authors contributing to the history of The Netherlands, some other nations, and the world have been making the point that positing the "industrial revolution" of the 1800s (1790s–1850s), or the "industrial revolutions" of the late 1780s/1790s–1800s (e.g., 1780s–1820s, 1850s–1870s, also often cited as long waves, especially for Britain/England) as the beginnings of industrial capitalism, is anomalous. It is seen as problematic because capitalism emerged much earlier, for instance, during the 1500s and 1600s, with its skeletal origins going back to the 1300s and 1400s. It is in this context that the general framework of Wallerstein (1974) and world systems analysis (and likely also Braudel 1979) is more valid than earlier criticisms have established (although some authors have numerous reservations, e.g. Israel 1989, 1995, vis-à-vis Braudel). Some discuss the demise of feudalism from the 1300s to the 1500s (Hilton 1978) and the rise of mercantile capitalism typically from the 1600s (Albritton 1991), while others discuss the development of the institutions of capitalism long before these years (Frank and Gills 1990).

Frank's (1990) view that the world system of capitalism is ancient in origin, going back perhaps 5000 years, while an interesting thesis, is unlikely to satisfy those who pay attention to capitalism as a *continual* revolutionary system, with many core elements and historical regularities of periodic abrupt change. Wallerstein's (1990) thesis that the capitalist modern world system evolved from the 1500s to the 2020s and likely beyond certainly pushes the envelope compared with those who seek to commence with the 1780s or 1790s through the emergence of industrial capitalism. This is especially the case when one is hoping to use some statistics and other evidence to sustain aspects of the argument. The 1400s–1500s is about as far back as one can go through an array of sources including statistical and historical. For example, accumulation and profit, which both Frank and Wallerstein use as important *concepts* to guide historiography and history. It is not possible to get good data for macro let alone global profit rate, and for accumulation (net investment) before the 1800s (even for the 1800s is hard for most nations). But one can get modestly reasonable data for GDP, population, migration, and so on, and other fragments, going back to the 1500s and earlier especially for core areas.

Sectoral data at the micro or meso level is more easily obtained for some earlier years. We delimit the commencement of the study to the world system of Dutch capitalism (since the mid-1500s) in a core–periphery setting, first, to limit the scope of inquiry, second to have reasonable data on waves of growth, hegemony, and climate change at our disposal, and third, because we doubt that the core structures and dynamics of *capitalism* can be assessed as going back thousands of years. Hence, we concentrate on (potential) capitalist hegemonies rather than non-capitalist empires.

It has become institutionalized in certain even relatively *avant-garde* establishment history circles now to see European history in the context of world history (e.g., De Zwart 2018). While the East (e.g., Asia) was seen as the center of the world, so to speak, going back to 1000–1500 AD and further (Maddison 2007), as it declined in relative performance, the West rose relatively during the 1500s–mid-1900s, and since then the East has been rising while the West has been in relative decline (1970s–2020s) (Mahbubani 2022 Frank 1998; see Spengler 1923 on the earlier cultural decline). As to why the West rose, many explanations abound, including that it was a matter of culture and institutions (Mokyr 2017). Similarly, explanations abound as to why the East rose again, including that it was a matter of the rise and fall and fall and rise of "culture and institutions" (Mokyr et al. Forthcoming).[3]

It became an established institution to start more recent capitalisms with the phase of *mercantilism* of the 1500s and 1600s. However, while this would help explain British capitalism from the 1600s, I am quite sure it does not adequately encapsulate Dutch capitalism (within the world system). A recent history of The Netherlands, *Pioneers of Capitalism* (Prak et al. 2023), also eschews the description

[3] Mokyr (2017) defines "culture" vis-à-vis growth as: "modern economic growth or 'the Great Enrichment' depended on a set of radical changes in beliefs, values, and preferences—a set I will refer to as 'culture'" (Mokyr 2017, xiii); "*Culture is a set of beliefs, values, and preferences, capable of affecting behavior, that are socially (not genetically) transmitted and that are shared by some subset of society*" (p. 8; emphasis original); "culture involves social learning, so that one's beliefs, values, and knowledge are not built-up from scratch for each individual but are acquired from others" (p. 9). Compare this definition with Anne Mayhew's (1994, 115–117): "Culture [is] the whole of a people's pattern of regular and recurring behaviour. The idea [is] that human behaviour, belief, thought, and artefact [are] all cultural patterns. Emphasis is placed on the interrelatedness of component parts of culture, and upon cultural change as a result of that interrelatedness." The latter view of culture is associated with the *way of life of the community*, in terms of the dominant social habits, views and behavior of its peoples. (Note: Kroeber and Kluckhohn (1952) present 50 definitions of culture.)

of Dutch capitalism as (purely) mercantilist, as do numerous other histories (see sections 5.4 and 5.5 below). This is partly because "the Dutch" examined the practices of other powers, involving trade barriers, conflict, war, and so on, and decided it was not for them. Certainly, they tended to adhere to free trade principles *to some degree domestically* during the Golden Age (p. 187), even while they sometimes used protective measures, and certainly, in their colonial spaces they usually reverted to typical mercantilist or worse activities associated with war, monopolies, slavery, and decimation, especially against local populations (and sometimes others). In my examination of the "Dutch circuit of capital" (CSD) during the late 1500s and 1600s below, the word "mercantile" is not used as a general term to describe the Dutch *domestic* system for these reasons.

Industrial capitalism (of a sort) developed during the time at least as early as the Dutch Golden Age. This was an age when the United Provinces of the Netherlands, especially Holland, was undergoing substantial industrial development as an emerging capitalist economy, leading the charge of the capitalist world system. Different scholars have variable views as to when this Dutch Golden Age occurred. But all of them agree that the 1600–1650 period was within the ballpark of the Golden Age. *Many* scholars start the Golden Age around 1570, and *some* finish the Golden Age in 1750.[4] Probably few would disagree that the years 1575–1650 are within the Golden Age (although some may argue the apogee was during 1575–1620, or others 1630–1650), when the United Provinces established absolute de facto hegemony of the capitalist world economy. Some may agree that they had *relative* hegemony during the 1570s–1620s and 1660s–1710s and absolute hegemony during the 1630s–1650s. I sometimes refer rather loosely to Dutch hegemony, the Golden Age, good long wave upswings, and the Little Ice Age, "during the 1600s," but this should be understood within these other contexts just mentioned. We discuss later in this chapter the details of Dutch long wave upswings, hegemony, climate change elements, and when they may have occurred more precisely (e.g., Sections 5.4, 5.5, and 5.6, below; chap. 4 for climate change). Let us now turn to the "Dutch circuit of social capital" (shorthand description of the CSD).

[4] Some specialists on Dutch history have, from earlier years, argued that Dutch decline did not emerge until the 1700s. For instance, Wilson (1939) castigated those who think (or thought) Dutch decline started from the 1650s, only to argue later in the paper that Dutch decline did start relatively early, but that aspects of it continued into the 1700s. (See also footnote 10 for work by Israel who argues along similar lines.) All Wilson manages to show is that Dutch especially financial dominance continued long after its other edges discontinued. This is exactly what I and many others argue. The core thing is to work out when total Dutch hegemony (production, commercial, and financial edge) started to decline, and how the decline in hegemony coincided with trade dominance for a time and financial dominance for a long time. Writers like Wilson fail to *explicitly* say this even though he does say exactly this, implicitly (but his paper is an early one so he can perhaps be forgiven).

5.3 Dutch-Led World System: Pathways and Circuits of Socioeconomic Dynamics (CSD)

To understand the nature of the Dutch Golden Age, Dutch hegemony, long waves, climate change, and the capitalist world-economy (including CPSP relations) of the time, it helps to establish a realistic structure and flow analysis. In this context, we referred earlier (e.g., Table 1.1 of chap. 1 and Sect. 5.2 above) to the *principle* of the CSD, which structurally links core aspects of the PoPE *Paradigm* to the Dutch case. This CSD is shown in a slightly complex form below in Fig. 5.3, illustrating that the Dutch Golden Age was based around six partially interdependent and relatively autonomous institutional, technological, and geo-spatial-ecological systems. These include (1) geo-spatial-ecological spaces and resources, (2) state and governance systems (3) technology styles, (4) business institutional systems, (5) financial institutions and markets, and (6) household and community relations. These six dynamic structures are part of the circuit of relationships which include the flow of transactions, transportation, and people, urban-rural, and ecological spaces and resources, plus core, periphery, and semi-periphery (CPSP) power relations. These systems are encased in a systemic cultural environment of destructive creation plus double movement (dis)embedded systems generated to potentially counter the destructions and create their own dynamics.

Before we discuss these dynamic interdependent, yet relatively autonomous relational structures, some preliminary comments are required on the situation in the "low countries," particularly in what are *now* termed "The Netherlands," "Belgium",

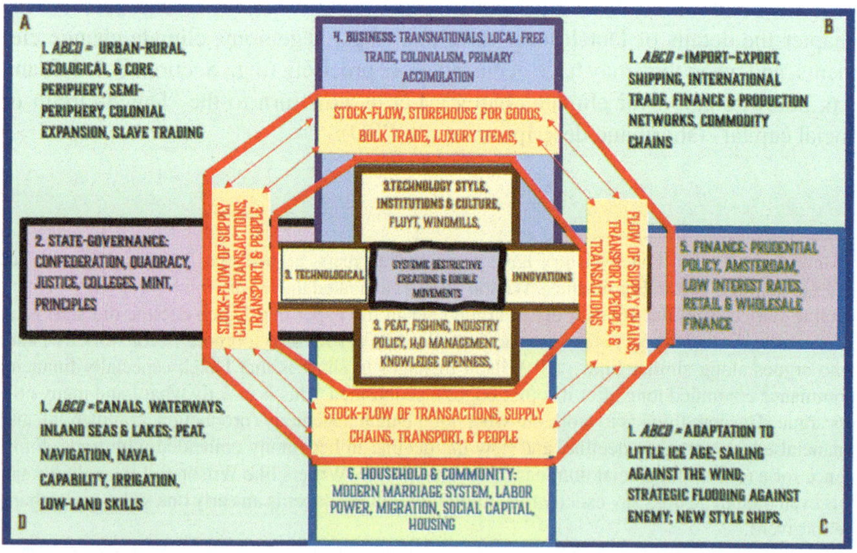

Fig. 5.3 Dutch-led capitalist world economy, 1575–1650, Golden Age, LWHegCC: *Pathways and circuits of Socioeconomic Dynamics* (CSD)

and "Luxembourg" around the time of the (possible) start of the Golden Age in the late 1500s. The Spanish Habsburg monarchy had nominal control over most of this region, although their representatives were resented within most sides of the religious and social spectrum. This elicited a rebellion (revolution) against Habsburg "rule" during the 1560s and 1570s, which resulted in the emergence of the *Union of Utrecht* (1579) against Spanish rule by 10 "Provinces" and 2 "cities" of the low countries, which was followed by the *Act of Abduration* (1581), a formal declaration of independence.[5] By the time of the *Treaty of Antwerp* (1609), which was influenced by Hugo Grotius' (1583–1645) writings on the "freedom of the seas" (see Eric Wilson 2008), the Dutch Republic had achieved de facto independence from Spain (followed by the 12 years truce to 1621), which also enabled "Dutch freedom of trade" within areas that were not Spanish territories or colonies, and trade in Spanish areas under certain conditions.

Much has been made of the fact that for most of the period of the 1570s to the 1710s (especially 1570s to 1648), the period some call the Dutch Golden Age, the "Dutch Provinces" were at war, variously against Spain, France, and Britain. This was not simply a reaction to "oppressive forces," but also constituted a positive act of defense and offense, including in the periphery where the Dutch often aggressively used force, plunder, pillage, decimation of native populations, and enslavement of "colored" colonial peoples, to promote their commercial and political interests. The Dutch Provinces, especially Holland, around the time of the supposed start of the Golden Age (late 1500s or early 1600s), were the most "modern" of all nations of the world, being the most urbanized, with a rapidly rising bourgeoisie, waged workers, scientists, artists, and with an advancing status of women. It was the center of the Reformation and the Renaissance. These stylized facts about Dutch capitalism are detailed especially in the work of Prak et al. (2023).

For much of this period (especially 1570–1648), the Dutch Provinces were formally at war, "war without end," as Prak (2023, chap. 1), calls it. But because they were at the forefront of advances in economics, politics, science, and industry they were able to "hold their own" usually much better than their enemies, and they developed some good specific principles of warfare. Many of the battles or sieges were undertaken at sea, also in or near (present-day) "Belgium" and "Luxembourg," and in the colonies of the New World (the Americas, including the east coast of North America, the West Indies, and north-eastern South America), the East Indies (Asia), and Africa.

One of the core principles of good defense and offense that was well learned by the core hegemons, including the Dutch, was to ensure the majority of major battles are fought outside domestic lands, preferably on other people's areas, hinterlands, at sea, and/or in colonial territories. While this is a very useful principle, another

[5] The Union of Utrecht comprised agreements between 12 areas, including the Counties of Holland, Zeeland, Drenthe, and Flanders; the Lordships of Utrecht, Groningen, Friesland, and Overijssel; the Dutchies of Brabant and Guelders; and the Cities of Valenciennes and Tournai. During the Golden Age, over time, the Cities were lost from the Dutch Republic, as was Flanders, parts of Brabant, and some other segments.

principle is that those defending their territory usually have a decided advantage due to domestic knowledge, skills, and platforms, and the Dutch also used that as an advantage when it was needed. Dutch sea-power (including in the North Sea) saved countless lives in the Dutch Republic while it decimated hundreds of thousands elsewhere. It needs to be mentioned that spending on armaments, wages for the militia, and profits from military innovations were included in GDP and thus were part of the Golden Age "splurge" (paid for by taxes and loans). Mercenaries were often used to fight these wars, and the taxes and loans were well organized to finance such expert fighters. Also, from the 1600s, the Dutch East Indies and Dutch West Indies companies became integrated business-military institutions and engaged in major campaigns, often closely associated with official naval personnel. (See more on this later.)

We present data on socioeconomic performance and long waves later in this chapter, since now we outline the institutional, technological, and geo-spatial-ecological basis of the Dutch system as it evolved before and during the time of the Golden Age. The reason for presenting some details of these dynamic structures is because long waves, hegemonies, and climate processes are generated within the context of these institutional, technological, and geo-eco-spatial relational structures, dynamics, and environments of the regions in question. The rise and fall of the emergent-composite waves, hegemonies, and climate events are "teleconnectedly"[6] associated with these structures. This is one of the core principles of this work (the CSD). We also want to complement numerical and statistical methods with more historico-institutional inquiry, which enables us to have at least two fronts on which to explain the material. (The third front is a summary of the positions of those who have studied all three hegemonies and applied to the Dutch situation. See, e.g., Sect. 5.5 below.)

In each chapter on Dutch, British, US, and potential Chinese LWHegCC, we outline the structure and dynamics of these CSD relationships that underpin specific temporal movements of performance. We hypothesize, therefore, that delimiting the analysis to the techno-institutional-geo-eco structures as they evolve especially during 1575–1700 (Dutch situation), 1780–1900 (British situation), 1800–2024 (US situation [notably 1940s–1970s]), 1978–2040s (Chinese situation), including investigations of the polycrises in between the hegemonies, and extending the analysis of Dutch and British contexts to the present (in summary form), will be the best arrangement for understanding the strongest long waves, (potentially) dominant hegemonic positions, and climate change dynamics during the late 1500s to the present and forward to the 2040s (for China) and 2100 (for climate change).

[6]The notion of teleconnected linkages between the eco-geo-spatial processes, technologies, and institutions across climate, wave, and hegemony relations is one of relational associations and interdependent correlations impacting in a CCC fashion through historical time.

5.3.1 *Ecology, Spatiality, and Geography*

The natural environment plays a large role in reproducing and conditioning the institutions, technologies, and ecologies underlying the socioeconomic performance of every region in all historical epochs. This was especially the case for the Dutch Republic. First, all socioeconomic activity occurs within a certain ecological and geographical area, land, water, and air space. Second, the environment provides certain potential services such as liquid, temperature, humidity, space, animals, fertilizers, resources, defense, and beauty. Third, the environment changes with the seasons, with waves of climate change, alternations in the tilting of the Earth's axis, and movements in the Earth's crust and geochemical pressure pockets within.

The history of The Netherlands is replete with movements that led to the destruction of ecological capital, as most of the forests of Western Europe were destroyed in the Middle Ages and beforehand, which was especially anomalous in the low countries as it led to the creation of many marshlands, bogs, subsided soil, declining biodiversity, and sandy soils that were relatively devoid of nutrients. In addition, the period of Dutch hegemony was right in the middle of the "Little Ice Age" (LIA), a regional (or global) phenomenon that led to greater rainfall, colder temperatures, and the expansion of waterways such as rivers, canals, oceans, and marshes. The incessant wars and conflicts over many centuries between rival powers, clans, and classes led to even greater decimation of wildlife and local ecologies. Using the abundant supply of peat as a fertilizer and energy source, especially in certain regions of the Dutch Republic, became widespread (a core part of the *energy regime*) but also contributed to land subsidence.[7]

These potentialities and destructions variously helped and hindered socioeconomic performance. It helped performance insofar as it was part of the movement of people migrating to north-western Europe (the North Sea region), building houses and businesses, farming rural and even urban areas, and mining the land for resources. It also led to the creation of whole industries the purpose of which was to prevent inundation of the lowlands; reclamation of land from the swamps, lakes, and rivers, and which generated other sectors from these innovations. The building of dikes, weirs, deep-waters, windmills, reclamations, and other forms of fixed capital contributed to GDP, while the windmills came to be modified for use as grain mills, manufacturing motors, iron works, and shipping. People were inculcated into the habit of preparing their lands for flood prevention, using the waterways for commerce and travel, and expanding the fishing and ship-building industries. A major contribution to GDP was the Dutch Republic being part of the North Sea region, also being part of a major continent, close to Mediterranean and Baltic markets and

---

[7] Braudel (see esp. Braudel 1979, chap. 3) and Wallerstein (see esp. 1974, chap. 4; 1980, chap. 2) provide much background history on the economic, political, and environmental foundations of Dutch hegemony. Jonathan Leitner 2007) uses Braudel's analysis in a modern account to explain the Dutch use of ecological resources, and their destruction of ecological resources, including in relation to metabolic rift. This is a very rich and fascinating investigation also in relation to the decline of Dutch hegemony.

produce, and emulating and eventually surpassing Spain and Portugal in shipbuilding while having the most powerful merchant and naval fleet in the world and utilizing these to dominate world trade.

Dagomar DeGroot (2018) has made a special study of the LIA throughout the world, and regionally, for instance, within Europe and especially around the North Sea region of north-west Europe (notably The Netherlands). He calls the Earth's climate, including during the LIA, as a *fantastically complex jigsaw puzzle* (p. 26), which especially during 1560–1720, was influenced by a myriad of factors, including various volcanic eruptions, Earth's orbit including rotational changes, sunspot cycles, positive feedback loops, permafrost impacts, AMOC changes, the strength of the northern polar vortex, arctic oscillation, the Siberian High, and the *El Nino*. Around the time of the Dutch Golden Age, he cites four periods of especially cold temperatures, the 1560s–1570s, 1600–1630, 1645–1670, and the 1690s. For much of the world, especially Europe, the costs of the LIA included *general crisis* (which Parker 2018 documents) as socio-political instability, violence, epidemics, inflation, famines, and numerous wars were regular outcomes of colder temperatures of up to and often greater than 1 °C colder than twentieth-century world averages, that generated regular frosts, extreme rain events, droughts, and storm surges.

While for most areas of the world, including Europe, this was a time of crisis, for some nations it was a time of opportunity. Notably, Japan and the United Provinces (of The Netherlands) undertook very different strategies to overcome the LIA. Japan took the route of closing borders, reinforcing domestic institutions, and reducing risks to a minimum, while the Dutch were more resilient in generating innovations, changing habits, and adapting successfully to crises much of the time. The Dutch were well used to dealing with inundations of water and changing patterns of rainfall, since much of their land was below sea level, and as indicated above, their response was to build huge networks of reinforced riverbanks, reclaimed land, and drainage systems. The Dutch Republic's vitality enabled its agents to use the sea as a vehicle of successful merchant trade and naval innovation, including war power, since while risks rose so too did the advantages of high winds and currents enabling greater speed of voyages, especially with the newly build and agile Fluyt ships.

DeGroot also documents how the more extensive winds from the east during the LIA enabled Dutch ships to easily sail from port while hindering English blocking tactics during the Anglo-Dutch wars.[8] The Dutch also learned effectively to sail against the wind and anticipate changes in weather. They developed the skills of copiously documenting changes in wind conditions and adjusting behavior accordingly. They became masters of effectively harnessing energy from peat, water, and wind during the most extreme climatological events. They developed extensive networks of transportation that were able to often surmount the most challenging circumstances. The periodic colder weather during the LIA also enabled the Dutch to

[8] The four Anglo-Dutch wars were during 1652–1654 (first, won by England), 1665–1667 (second, won by the Dutch), 1672–1674 (third, won by the Dutch, but not before causing major crisis during 1672 in the United Provinces), and 1780–1784 (fourth, won by the British). (Some auhors have more vague assessments of the first three of these wars.)

recognize and act on such changes while their enemies such as the Spanish had more sclerotic cultures and institutions with less adaptability. While some cultures such as again the Spanish used the LIA conflicts to castigate and blame (religious) minorities and the so-called Witches, the Dutch, being under the influence of the Reformation and Renaissance, tended often to act from more scientific and pragmatic mindsets.

5.3.2 State and Governance

State and governance were crucial to the success of the Dutch Republic. It is a complicated topic and needs to be situated within the context of the Dutch history of gradual independence from the rule of the Habsburg Dynasty. Our story rightfully starts with the *Pragmatic Sanction of 1549*, enacted by Charles V, Holy Roman Emperor, which effectively united the 17 Dutch Provinces (north and south "low countries"), with their own decentralized forms of governance, under Charles V's general rule. It was a method of reorganizing the so-called empire (greater Germany) along rational lines. When Charles's son Phillip II took over his father's "Spanish Empire" in 1556, and instituted greater centralization, taxation, and religious intolerance (part of the Spanish inquisition), most of the Dutch population (especially but not only in the Protestant north) were upset and rebelled against this encroachment on their liberty.

The so-called Dutch Revolution, or Revolt, variously also called the Dutch War of Independence, during the 1550s–1570s (which continued into the 1600s), was led especially by the main Dutch *Stadholder* (*de jure* "representative" of the Spanish King): William the Silent, Prince of Orange. The Dutch people had come to enjoy their relative autonomy and decentralized control from the Habsburgs. The early revolts and wars led to the *Union of Utrecht* (1579), which involved initially seven northern Dutch areas (later an extra 5) joining together as the *Republic of the United Provinces of The Netherlands*. This was followed by the *Estates General* in the Hague enacting the *Act of Abjuration* in 1581, which formalized the decision made under the 1579 Union. The Habsburgs did not informally recognize Dutch independence until the *Twelve Years Truce of 1609*, and after war began again in 1621 *formal* independence was again in abeyance until the *Treaty of Westphalia of 1648* (Van Gelderen 1992).

"The Netherlands" therefore achieved varying degrees of independence during 1579–1648. However, into the late 1640s and through the 1650s, as well as over the next 160 years, there were challenges to this power and independence especially from the British and the French, at least until the Congress of Vienna of 1815, soon after which the southern lowlands broke away during the revolutions of 1830 and 1848, to become the independent nations of Belgium, followed by Luxembourg.

Jonathan Israel (1998, 276) makes the bold statement that:

> The institutional framework of the Dutch Republic first took shape between 1572 and 1588 and assumed definitive form in the period from the departure of Leicester [1587-1588][9] down to 1609. From the Twelve Years Truce [1609-1621] onwards, Dutch institutions remained essentially unchanged until the fall of the Republic in 1795. The Republic's institutions, it needs to be stressed, differed markedly from those of the Habsburg Netherlands before 1572, and also from what was *envisaged* in 1579, in the terms of the Union of Utrecht. [Emphasis added.]

By "institutions" Israel infers the system of governance (a narrow definition of institutions), since the relevant chapter deals with the organization of the United Provinces, the system of taxation, "the generality and the generality lands," plus the Stadholderate. But such changes in the system of governance that took place, as the principle of interdependency implies (along with emergence), did impact and were affected by a whole series of changes that enabled a qualitatively new regime of socioeconomic reproduction to be activated in the United Provinces. As it emerged and developed it led to the Dutch Golden Age, some impressive long wave upswings, Dutch hegemony, and resilience in the face of the Little Ice Age.

The governance of the *United Provinces of the Netherlands* during the period of the Dutch Golden Age of the late 1500s to the mid-1600s is complicated and involves several caveats. It can be broadly summarized by saying that, although there were major changes during this period, and some regional variations, there was a *quadratic structure of governance* ("quadracy") for the formal institutions of the state. First was the central government called the *States General* (Federal Assembly); second, the Provincial governments called the *States of the Provinces* (especially the *States of Holland*); third, the *Local Councils*; and fourth there was the *Stadholder* of each Province, which was a type of *Governor-General*. Their functions varied from area to area, time to time, and institution to institution. Some of these institutions met locally as well as centrally.

During the so-called Dutch Golden Age, the various layers of governance contributed majorly to socioeconomic performance. Most elected and appointed members of the four layers of government were members of the "bourgeoisie," including merchants, industrialists, financiers, entrepreneurs, members of the professions, plus clerics, and nobles. There was general support for laissez faire in the *Dutch domestic market*, with substantial state support in the form of a degree of free trade (between *certain* areas), and an efficient system of public finance to provide public goods such as defense, legality, protection of property rights, foreign policy, infrastructure, and poor relief.

There was structurally a *fundamental contradiction* in policy-making that was a source of both revolt and resolution of problems. This was the conflict between local interests and those of the nation. As Prak (2023, 152) points out regarding these

[9] The "departure of Leicester" refers to the return of Robert Dudley (first Earl of Leicester), an English statesman, vis-à-vis his role of Governor General of the United Provinces, to England in 1586, and giving up his post in 1587–1588. In 1584, William of Orange, the head of government in the Dutch Republic, was murdered, and Leicester took over his post as chief, although his duties were vaguely defined, he became unpopular, and lost battles. Hence his return to England.

"two contradictory principles": Article 1 of the *Union of Utrecht of 1579*, which was also important for further articles of constitutional government, proposed two principles that were at odds with each other. One subscribed to the position that the provinces will "join together" to form a united province. But the other principle emphasized the special rights, conditions, customs, and mores of the different areas. This recurringly posed issues and problems of governance, but ones that were constantly resolved to varying degrees, often after considerable resources were used in reaching a workable compromise. Often it was left to Holland to decide, as it was by far the most powerful province, with Amsterdam being its center, emerging as the financial center of the world system during the 1600s (and to some degree thereafter for a time), and often decisions being made after cursory consultation with the other provinces (Israel 1989).[10]

The "Republic" emerged with the *States General*, in which representatives of the provinces met in the Hague, having control of "defence, taxation for defence, and foreign policy," and "after 1590, the federal principle was extended to areas such as regulation of shipping, administration of conquered districts, church affairs, and … colonial expansion" (Israel 1998, 276–277). Increasingly through time the nobles (and the clergy) lost power while the *States of Holland* gained hegemony over the other states, and the *States General* greatly increased its power through time, as it soon began to meet continuously in daily sessions, with all states having representatives, even though not all exerted equal influence. The *Council of State* became the main administrative arm of the *States General*, even though their staff were paid by the provinces, while the *States General* also established a "generality" accounting office dealing with revenue, expenses, and estimates, as well as a military court, a Mint associated with a single currency, and several naval colleges dealing with customs, tariffs, gunboats, borders, shipping, and fisheries. In theory *Stadholders* were appointed by the provinces, but in practice, several states joined together, and there were usually three *Stadholders*, representing an ensemble of states, with powers of administering justice, resolving conflicts, and supervising certain elections. (Israel 1998, chap. 13)

The governance arrangements of the Dutch Golden Age were thus well developed and while contradictory enabled a multifarious apparatus to promote public goods and club goods that assisted various interests and the general welfare of the area for a considerable time.

[10] This "contradiction" is the basis on which Jonathan Israel (1998, Chap. 13) emphasizes that the Republic of the United Provinces of the Netherlands was a cross between a confederacy, where the provinces/states/individual units have dominance over the central authority, and a federation, where the central authority has more power over the individual units; with varying trends from one side of the contradiction to the other through concrete historical time. This is complicated further by the power of the *States of Holland*, and especially the power of Amsterdam, as the hegemonic region/city of the "Republic."

5.3.3 Technology Style

Here we view technological innovations broadly, comprising a *technology style* of scientific knowledge, improvements in industrial processes and products, skill developments, and advances in literacy. During the late 1500s and into the 1600s, the Dutch Provinces had the highest literacy rates in the world, and numerous skills spread throughout the working population. Associated with this was the development of the book industry (and paper manufacturing), initially especially in Deventer, and the rise in schools and universities. The Dutch culture was one of openness to free inquiry in the context of the Reformation, the Renaissance, and the spread of reformist and republican ideas.

Innovations were central to the technology style typically operating in the Dutch Republic. First and foremost, as already mentioned, the "low countries" had to deal with the problem of rising waterways. The Dutch low areas are mostly alluvial plains. Therefore dikes, floodgates, dams, and other tools of water management were developed to save huge areas, including Amsterdam, from being submerged. During the Golden Age, as mentioned, Europe and other areas were seriously affected by the "little ice age," which impinged on provinces especially along the North Atlantic and North Sea belt, with colder temperatures and higher rain and snowfall. The Dutch became specialists in producing innovative windmills, canals, water control boards, and general skills of farmers and landowners to enable the productive use of large areas of potential wastelands (DeGroot 2018a).

Also crucial were the skills and innovations in the fishing industry (especially associated with herring) and ship-building. The *Fluyt Design* for ships was one core innovation advancing the Dutch Golden Age, since it required fewer crew and smaller ships. The introduction of Fluyts halved the cost of constructing merchant ships and doubled cargo capacity, thus providing a durable base for the Dutch merchant and colonial empire. This gave the Dutch a competitive advantage in global shipping for over half a century, since it was not until the second half of the 1600s that effective competition emerged (Tellis and Rosenzweig 2018). Industrial districts developed, providing agglomeration benefits, economies of scale, and scope. Maarten Prak (2023, 89) argues that such districts arose around the River Zaan, partly due to "Cornelis Corneliszoon [who] succeeded in 1592 in using a crankshaft to change the circular motion of a mill into a back-and-forth movement of a saw."

These innovations had a circular and cumulative impact on industry and trade, as a system of vertical integration developed with extensive drainage systems, dykes, windmills, and land reclamations; transportation and processing of timber and other raw materials; building of ships and other vessels and structures; development of harbors and export-import sectors; growth of whaling and fishing industries; a rapidly expanding textiles sector; building of premises for sailors, families, and commodities; emergence of cities and services sectors; in addition to schools, hospitals, state, and scientific institutions (Enthoven 2018). Numerous areas of The Netherlands adopted such complex industrial districts and cities, while the "Dutch Provinces" (especially Holland, where Zann is situated) became the greatest industrial-trade network hub in the world.

Vertically networked systems of mechanization, supply chain management, and export-import activities stimulated growth in numerous other sectors such as tobacco, peat, market gardening (including tulips), the importation of grain from the Baltics, and the spice trade through the monopolies of Dutch traders established especially in the Caribbean and the East Indies. Much of this was made possible by the extensive development of labor power and human capital providing the highest literacy rate in the world, and a sound knowledge of basic mathematics and bookkeeping in many businesses. The Dutch were also able to generate communications within and between merchants, sailors, and others from numerous cultural backgrounds, which enhanced networks of business, through basic multilingual skills and a (usually) moderate degree of religious tolerance (cultural and social capital).

Van Zanden and Van Leeuwen (2012, 127) see a *wave-like pattern* of technological change through the Dutch economy of the 1300s–1700s, summarized thus:

> [W]e can distinguish three phases in the process of economic growth: the first one, between 1347 and 1500, is characterized by rapid structural transformation and (modest) technological change; *the second one, from the middle of the sixteenth century to the middle of the seventeenth century* [1550-1650], *was based on relatively rapid technological development, and is combined with relatively fast growth of population*; during the third phase, which begins in the 1660s, population growth comes to an end, technological change slows down, but changes in relative factor proportions and human capital formation allow for a further increase in per capita incomes during the 18th century. [Emphases added.]

Providing more specificity to these waves, they add that (Van Zanden and Van Leeuwen 2012, 126; emphases added):

> *TFP [total factor productivity] growth was strongest in the final decades of the sixteenth century* [1570s-1590s], *when … the economic basis for the ensuring 'Golden Age' was laid.* It then slowed down during the first half of the 17th century, and even declined from the 1620s onwards. For the 1660s onwards, however, it stabilized and even began to play a … much more *modest* role in economic growth. The *wave-like character* of technological development during the 'long' Golden Age is confirmed by studies of the number of patents granted by Dutch authorities, which peak in the 1620s and 1630s, and slowly declined afterwards …, and by the qualitative information on the rise and decline of Dutch technological leadership collected and analysed by Davids (2008).

Karel Davids' (2008) detailed analysis concludes, *first,* that the northern Netherlands did have considerable technological leadership from 1580 to 1700, and that it was based primarily upon non-market forces of institutions and culture. The leadership pattern is said to be a long wave of rising innovation during the 1500s, *an escalation after 1580, a slight decline from the 1620s*, and from the 1670s a maturation that led to *cessation of leadership during the 1700s.* The pattern of the wave is a life cycle that rises, escalates, slightly declines, matures, and declines majorly. The life cycle is said to be endogenously engrained in the institutions and culture (p. 365).

Second, market rules were not the norm in the United Provinces, since other institutions and cultures usually majorly conditioned the introduction of novelty, new innovations, and changing conditions. These other institutions and cultural conditions enabled innovations to occur, and often encouraged them much more than market relations, through a type of *industry policy* or measures to solve complex problems more quickly. In a similar fashion, inventors usually promoted new products, processes, and coordination mechanisms to enhance the quality of a given technique, solve a complex problem of (re)production, and apply their knowledge and skills to industrial activities. Because of the contradiction of central versus provincial and local governance (mentioned above), a plurality of decision-makers provided a multitude of ways to solve complex problems and introduce/encourage novel arrangements, skills, technologies, and organizations, especially during the Golden Age.

More specifically, market forces were more commonly activated in shipping, foreign trade, new processing, and agrarian sectors; but a plurality of institutional and cultural arrangements were typical in infrastructure, military, land transportation, peat, fishing, ocean navigation, crafts, and some segments of the rural sector. (Davids 2008, 372, 378.) The non-market alternatives were ways of encouraging risk sharing, ensuring safety and quality control, solving specific immediate anomalies, preventing fraud and bribery, providing tests of competence, and defending property rights through patents for a certain minimal period (as briefly as possible for the "common good").

In more general terms, David's analysis of Dutch leadership in technology was based on the Dutch Republic's openness *at the macro level* to the transfer, creation, and application of knowledge, which he describes as "the *de facto* general rule" (p. 390). Foreigners were said to be often surprised at the knowledge available to them in the public arena and the relative absence of industrial secrecy. One reason for this is the slowness with which the corporate form of organization developed in the Republic, although partnerships were widespread. Another reason is that there were few attempts to stem the inflow and outflow of migrants or visitors. Though there was some variation between provinces, there was in general a free flow of information throughout the Republic, including also at the micro level. Windmill technology was especially subject to a seamless transfer of knowledge.

Patents were only one form of reward for invention, which were especially used for improvements of hydraulic equipment and installations, industrial windmills, and heating equipment (notably during 1580–1639) (Davids 2008, 409). The most common patentees during 1580–1719 were merchants, artisans (woodworkers and metalworkers), and the landed gentry (p. 421). The Republic used a variety of other means to stimulate specific inventions, such as rewards, sponsorships, commissions, and contracts. These remunerations were notably useful for navigation (e.g., determining longitude in voyages), shipping and military inventions, especially organized by the *Estates General*, the *Council of State*, and to some degree by the *States of the Provinces* (e.g., Holland), *Local Governments*, cities, and the *Chambers of Commerce,* vis-à-vis especially partnerships. Innovations and knowledge expansion were also encouraged through the private schools of navigation, and university schools of engineering, surveying, and medicine.

Davids (unwittingly) recognizes the importance of the Veblen (1899, 1914) principle of knowledge, termed *"collective social wealth"*, for Dutch leadership during the 1580s–1700s (pp. 456–457, 537). This principle is based on knowledge being in large measure a public good, with its expansion being affected by the stream of knowledge emanating from within the institutions, which is a cumulation of traits from the past. Through the openness of knowledge, the cumulative expansion of innovations and technologies were capable of far greater multiplication (through CCC) than if it were privatized for individual remuneration alone (or via club goods). The Dutch method of knowledge acquisition and generation based on past accumulations generating and being merged with new combinations is thus a recognition of the common good being more important than purely individual initiative. This is seen as the basis of the Dutch system of technology leadership.

So why did Dutch leadership in technology undergo such waves of expansion, escalation, maturity, and relative decline and demise? The expansion, escalation, and maturity are based on the system of institutions underlying the dynamic circuits. But what about the relative decline and demise? We discuss the demise of the Golden Age later in this chapter, but let us say preliminarily how it involved the decline in technological aspects. Davids' assessment of the Dutch decline was complex. He agrees with *Cardwell's Law*, named after Donald Cardwell's (1972) stylized fact about the *rise and decline of technological leadership* from area to area, although Cardwell did not explain the law but treated it as a historical regularity (stylized fact) (Mokyr 1994).

Davids shows that technological change faltered in the Dutch Republic because the life cycle of its development began to decline majorly into the late 1600s. The main reasons cited are changes in the activities of investors from the promotion of invention, innovation, and production to less significant transactions. These include an expansion of relatively unproductive investments into financial instruments, shares, bonds, houses, and land. The economy had moved from a technology and production powerhouse to a *rentier* economy based on the flow of already existing assets, financial returns, rents, and market prices rather than activities that promote productivity and growth in real GDP per capita. The ruling classes, including the bourgeoisie and regents, had become regressive groups rather than continuing to be a progressive alliance promoting the common good and the general interest[11] (p. 515).

[11] Some other scholars have adopted Olson's (1965) thesis about the rise and establishment of vested interests that prevent the flow of resources to new and innovative activities, for the decline of technological leadership. Some scholars working on the Dutch Golden Age also critique the notion of transaction costs in this context as being a disembedded notion abstracted from a set of more complex arrangements.

5.3.4 Business Institutional Systems

As Prak et al. (2023) point out, the Dutch were the first to develop a coherent system of capitalist production, distribution, and exchange, and to acquire commercial, financial, and technological dominance out of this embryonic capitalist dynamic for hegemonic control of the world system into the late-1500s and 1600s. The numerous (sub)classes of *heterogeneous groups and agents* required for this system were well developed, including abundant varieties of workers (including highly skilled artisans), merchants, industrial capitalists, financial capitalists, bookkeepers and accountants, bankers, joint stock companies, and transportation capitals, among others.

By the late 1500s, Medieval institutions had long been transformed in the Dutch Provinces through the movement of people from rural to urban regions and city hubs, and numerous rural areas became more urban-like and developing along capitalist lines. Property rights were protected, *burgeoning* joint stock companies (and partnerships) helped reduce uncertainties associated with market expansion, and profit systems of accountancy ensured financial control over production and distribution systems. Free trade was a dominant philosophy of agents, especially (but not entirely) in the Dutch European sphere of influence (though not in their activities throughout Asia and the Americas), and declining taxes on the movement of goods and services ensured the relatively smooth turnover of capitals through the socio-economic circuits.

The Dutch East India Company (VOC, established 1602) and the Dutch West India Company (WIC, established 1621) were the first effective groups of conglomerate transnational corporations in the world, and VOC itself was the first to be listed on the Dutch stock exchange. They established a separation of ownership from control, with limited liability, and a mandate from the Dutch state for a 21-year (VOC) and 24-year (WIC) state-monopoly global system of (triangular) trade, through the sourcing of labor, and a colonial-type system of exploitation in the periphery. As mentioned, while Dutch business activities and philosophies in the European sphere of interest were mostly conducted in an environment of liberal institutions of trade and policy, their corporate activities in Asia, the Americas, and Africa were conducted in an environment of mercantilism (and worst) through typically cartels, monopoly capital, monocultures, wars, massacres, slavery, and colonial control.

During the early to mid-1600s VOC established colonial-Asian trade and power, especially in the East Indies (Indonesia), India, Formosa, Bengal, Ceylon, and Malacca. VOC also established African trade and colonial settlement in the Cape Colony (South Africa), the Gold Coast (Ghana), and Mauritius (Parthesius 2010). WIC had control, e.g., over parts of the east coast (e.g., New Amsterdam) of what is now the USA, numerous islands in the Caribbean, Guiana (including Surinam), and Brazil (Wallerstein 1982). The activities of VOC and WIC contributed to the primary accumulation of surplus profit, bullion, and labor, providing resources for

Dutch investment, dividends and state finance for growth and rentier income, accruing to the ruling classes, during the early to mid-1600s.

In Part 8 of volume 1 of *Capital*, Marx (1867) has eight chapters on primitive accumulation in the Dutch and British contexts. He discusses the Dutch case of being the *first prototypical domestic capitalist economy*, where during the 1600s, handicrafts were well developed but growth in manufacturing dominated. The colonial exploits of VOC and WIC generated primitive accumulation involving slavery, massacres, wars, plunder, and trade agreements and strategic alliances. In the Dutch domestic economy, the institution of wage labor had been evolving and developing for notably a hundred years or more, as rising productivity in the rural areas led to workers moving to the cities and towns (while many continued "rural" activities), now often without property and dependent upon wages for survival.

Evidence for 1575–1640 shows impressive increases in Dutch total factor productivity, and the most rapidly rising absolute and growth rates of GDP per capita in the world (Raa 2009). Profits were especially high in the leading sectors, middle-class incomes rose majorly, and skilled workers were well off, but the unskilled and lumpen classes were usually impoverished and underwent recurring unstable cycles of bare-subsistence-to-poverty income shares. Inequality thus rose during the Golden Age, due to (initially) regressive taxes and few public goods for the masses. Greater inequality occurred in an environment of high-profit rates and significant primitive accumulation due to the *large luxury goods and services sectors*[12] and the greatest import-export trade system in the world, which generated business-as-usual high rates of turnover of capital. Being the most rapidly growing nation in the world, such modernization attracted masses of migrants, both unskilled and skilled, including numerous Jewish and Protestant workers, innovators and capitalists who were being discriminated against in Catholic Kingdoms, such as France and Spain (Prak 2023, chap. 8.).

The primary accumulation generated from domestic wage labor, whose income shares were declining relative to the middle and upper classes, was added to by the activities of VOC and WIC worldwide. These corporate activities included those of a typical trading company, buying and selling at conventional rates, when the powers of some dynasties were unable to be surmounted, such as when they were dealing with the Japanese. Otherwise, they engaged in whatever practices they could 'get away with' in the environments established in parts of Asia, the Americas, and Africa (e.g., wars, slavery, unequal agreements, markets, and so on).

The application of Dutch *domestic* governance principles led to the outlawing of slavery, but it was allowed in the colonies. VOC, WIC, and other Dutch traders and agents, for instance, transported slaves from Africa to the Americas; used them on the sugar and cotton plantations (latifundia) and in domestic service in the Americas; on the spice plantations and in domestic and industrial service, typically in areas of

---

[12] A robust debate in the literature has developed relating to the significance of luxury goods versus subsistence goods in the trade and development experience of the Dutch Republic during the Golden Age, Hegemonic and Little Ice Age periods. See, for instance, de Vries (1999, 2003) and Israel (1995).

Africa, Asia, and the Americas. Often local Dutch traders and colonists used females (and males) as sex slaves, and inter-marriage was common. Typically, a slave was less productive of total output than a wage-laborer, but they were often relatively more productive of *surplus product* due to the difference between the value of output minus wages of wage labor often being lower than the value of slave output minus slave bare subsistence (Foster et al. 2020).

The surplus from slave latifundia production and slave trading was especially fruitful for sustaining capitalist investment, luxury goods consumption, and the standard of living of merchants and elites. Prak (2023, 187) estimates that Dutch traders transported 250,000 slaves from Africa to the Americas during the 1600s, and 350,000 slaves during the 1700s. He estimates (p. 188) also that in the year 1780, slavery contributed 10% of Holland's GDP and 5% for the Dutch Republic as a whole, while during 1675 the estimates were 5% for Holland and 2.5% for the Dutch Republic. These estimates are said to be far less than that established for slave trade contribution to English, French and Portuguese national income.

These figures are dwarfed by the *social costs* incurred by VOC and WIC in many of the economies, which were not internalized into market prices. These included seafarers and military personnel engaging in forced trade and employment, and war in the colonies. The concern of the Dutch in their forceful dealings with colonial islands and states was purely monetary. Most seamen used for overseas business and wars died before they returned to their ancestral lands. Despite being the greatest trading nation in the world during the late-1500s–1650, the great stain of colonial exploitation and primary accumulation is a contradiction that forever marked the Golden Age, as a Dark Age in some respects. As Prak and van Zanden (2023, 127) state, to reinforce the point:

> The negative consequences of the economic system surfaced mainly in the way the VOC and later the Dutch West India Company (… WIC) dealt with non-European peoples and trade contacts. In general, during this period the Dutch behaved as aggressive overseas colonizers who did not hesitate to oppress other peoples for their own gain. Their conquests in Indonesia-the nadir being the Banda genocide of 1621-are the most striking examples of this. But their treatment of native Americans in New Amsterdam and Surinam, and the Khoikhoi and San peoples in the Cape Colony, could also be pointed to in this respect, not to mention slavery, no doubt the most shameful stain on the Dutch Golden Age.

This also manifested itself in other contradictions as the core "mother country" followed the road to modernization, development, long wave upswings, and hegemonic dominance, while its *long-term periphery* was set on the path to further exploitation, colonization, underdevelopment, and eventually post-colonial antagonisms. Eventually, the contradictions came home to roost as the Dutch Republic underwent disarray, military defeat, hegemonic decline and lower floors and ceilings of the long wave with VOC itself going bankrupt. As Patrick O'Brien (2000) recognized, the Dutch style of colonial and imperial practices had core limits since their activities in the Americas led to failure, and while their pursuits in Asia were more "successful" (for profits), they too were limited as they never developed proper settler colonies and hardly went far beyond the seaboards. By the mid-to-late 1600s, the British (and French) effectively started to negate Dutch export-import trade, shipping, commercial networks and colonies through trade and military wars and very strategic actions seeking to destroy Dutch supremacy in the world system. And the Dutch never were able to develop effective countermeasures through ongoing *innovation* within the CSD on a global scale or nationally.

5.3.5 Financial Institutions

Despite the depression experienced by the United Provinces (and much of Europe) during the 1620s at the end of the *Twelve Years Truce* (caused by war and financial crisis), and the *Tulip Mania* and crash of 1634–1637, the financial system was treated with considerable prudential care by the Dutch authorities during the Golden Age. The relatively frugal financial system contributed majorly to the stability of the Dutch economy, even if other factors periodically promoted balance uncertainty and crises.

An orthodox explanation of private Dutch finance sees it as one of the accumulated savings of spendthrift capitalists financing investment through loans. The institutional and evolutionary (IE) approach explains the situation more realistically by postulating that the relatively stable system of governance, in an environment of wars and revolts, enabled capitalists to use their primitive accumulations of capital to invest in productive capital as well as being able to lend to those who prospectively anticipated good returns on projects. The *financial instability hypothesis* approach additionally postulates the principle that capitalist economies endogenously move from hedge (positive profits and net worth) to speculative (positive net worth but negative profits) and onto Ponzi (negative profits and net worth) financial positions if left purely to their own devices (see Glossary). The implication is that market systems of finance pose systemic risks that need moderating to reduce risk and uncertainty (as argued by also Kindleberger and Aliber 2015).

The banking and financial authorities in the United Provinces evidently thought along similar lines as Hyman Minsky, since they repeatedly sought to regulate the unstable tendencies of market finance to generate trust in the system and promote stability through prudential regulation. Some examples of prudential policies of Dutch governments include, first, their response to the supposedly innovative *bill of exchange* that private financial houses provided for clients from the late 1500s. A bill of exchange is an IOU giving the holder an unconditional right to demand payment upon presenting the bill to the originator by a certain date. In Holland this would have allowed successive chains of endorsement, and thereby successive rounds of buying and selling of goods and services, enabling the generation of endogenous money and credit (see Glossary). Amsterdam's city council banned this endogenous credit mechanism for many decades, which otherwise may have overextended the system of production and generated overexuberant conditions leading to major instability, recession, and depression.

Similarly, as Prak and van Zanden (2023, 120) show, the authorities were cognizant of the need to separate institutions promoting normal retail demand and supply of money from risk-taking institutions generating risk-bearing credit and financial derivatives. Consequently, the monetary authorities established the *Wisselbank* (Bank of Amsterdam), a type of central bank that performed public goods functions such as enhancing the stability of monetary exchange, enabling domestic payments, ensuring proper gold and silver valuation, and protecting the quality of foreign exchange reserves.

There was also the usual array of private sector financial institutions wherein agents could operate in a market-based risk environment. These included stock exchanges, credit banks, insurance companies, and financial advisory institutions. Amsterdam became the financial hub of the world, with traders and capitalists from especially European markets regularly visiting the capital to engage in financial trading (or operating through local agents) (Kindleberger 1978, chap. 4). Government bonds became a universal commodity in the capital and elsewhere in the provinces to promote the turnover of capital. The merging of production dominance with commercial supremacy and financial proficiency contributed not only to systemic macroeconomic buoyancy for the Dutch but also effective reproduction of the world system of which the United Provinces represented for a time the center (despite the climate crisis).

It is argued by many scholars that the stability and efficiency of Dutch finance contributed to higher levels of trust in Dutch business institutions and reduced the systemic risk of engaging in financial instruments, commerce, and industry. This led to comparatively modest interest rates on government bonds, 5% often and regularly as low as 3% (Israel 1995). This reflected the trust and relatively risk-free environment in which the Dutch provinces experienced the Golden Age. Low interest rates enhanced levels of investment for an extended period as it buoyed confidence and stimulated prospective yield from projects. Rates were generally much lower in the maritime west compared with those of the inland provinces (Dehing and Hart 1997; Hart 1997).

These institutional innovations in finance helped the Dutch Republic pay for its military budget, without incurring systemic problems of debt insolvency and periodic major financial crises. It also enabled Amsterdam city to continue to hold the mantle of financial hegemony for the world system, further into the late 1600s and 1700s, even when the Republic's production and commercial hegemony had declined. Indeed, when the technological decline and production hegemony along with commercial and trading hegemony faded after 1650, it was the financial domain that continued to contribute majorly to economic activity and employment in the face of general demise. This is consistent with the principles of hegemonic demise for former hegemonies to hold onto financial power while the other areas have long past their prime and was also used by those explaining the contradictions that led to hegemonic demise as a source of institutional anomaly.[13]

5.3.6 *Households and Community Institutions*

Households and community networks also made a substantial contribution to public, private, and club goods in The Netherlands. This was done by providing a continual supply of quality labor power, establishing guilds that embedded economy within society, instituting levels of trust that placed a floor under business cycles and long waves, developing a system of marital arrangements that ensured a minimal degree of gender empowerment, and providing migrants with established systems of familial and community life. Without these benefits, Dutch social capitalism could not have been reproduced with the level of confidence and stability that prevailed (despite perpetual wars, colonialism, and much poverty) from the late 1500s to the mid-1600s and to some degree onto the 1660s and 1670s.

Four main things stand out as basic stylized facts relevant to household provisioning during the Golden Age. The first is the marriage system common in Dutch states, especially on the west coast, which Prak et al. (2023) calls the "modern style," in which both genders had a basic level of access to the wider community and where roles were significantly egalitarian. The age at which people tended to marry was relatively late in global terms, with the early to mid-20 s being a common age for men and women establishing their own households, as the extended family was becoming less common. This was made possible by the large demand for labor power characteristic of the Golden Age. It was also increasingly recognized that women were just as capable of contributing to the social economy as men, even though the prevailing centers of power were dominated by men. In the household, there was a degree of modernity, where women were generally literate and capable of being part of the wider conversation. They tended to undertake most of the domestic duties, and many were quite knowledgeable of household finances and effective budgetary measures. They also contributed substantially to domestically produced textile and other commodities for sale in markets as well as to the capabilities of other family members. This contributed to household consumption and investment patterns in the long term.

---

[13] This point about the contradictory dual-legacy of finance during later years is highly interesting from a systemic, business, and scholarly point of view. During the late 1600s and through the 1700s, Dutch finance continued to excel and provide income for agents and groups. At the same time, it can be identified as propelling much of the demise of Dutch hegemony, Golden Age, and long wave upswings by crowding out production (especially) and commercial (trading) activities. This leads one to cite this issue as a major one to elucidate in explaining the nature and origins of the paradox, antinomy, and contradiction.

Second, the household, as well as schools and the community, was crucial for the development of labor power, being the skills, knowledge, manners, communication modes, and characters of children and others who contribute to the economy; as well as labor, being the exertion of effort in the (re)production process. Parents and especially women contributed to the economy of the household, but so too did many children who often were expected to undertake tasks such as helping in the kitchen, cleaning, washing, and disposing of garbage. Parents, schools, and the community also contributed to the skills and knowledge of children who were expected in adolescence to contribute to the household economy by bringing in a wage, at least until they likely married and established their own families.

The third is that migration into the United Provinces and especially into Holland from other lands and the interior was very prominent during the Golden Age. As mentioned, many migrants were of Jewish and Protestant faiths suffering persecution in "Catholic lands." They set up heterogeneous forms of households and contributed as household workers, wage laborers, entrepreneurs, farmers, capitalists, and so on. Jewish households with notable members being entrepreneurs were especially prominent in contributing to financial and technological innovations. Overall, as Foldvari et al. (2013, 15, 17) conclude, "the positive effect of migrants on factor accumulation is a strong indication of their significant role in the success of commercial capitalism in Holland during the Golden Age." Migration had a coevolutionary impact along with a high birthrate during especially the late 1500s and early 1600s with the building industry playing a key role in establishing household structures wherein economic roles evolved and developed.

The fourth role is that, especially among the elites, the institutions of marriage and family were a core part of social and political patronage, establishing or moving up the social pyramid, and reproducing children who could transpose the family name into the future and carry on such rights and duties. These ceremonial functions contributed to the relatively high level of inequality characteristic, especially of the early mid-years of the Golden Age. It also contributed to weak *inter-class* interaction while it deepened intra-class relations. The ruling class of protestant nobles, capitalists, and merchants with access to money, wealth, land, knowledge, and connections became better established during the Golden Age, and there was a modest degree of tolerance of especially Catholic and Jewish faiths to the extent that they contributed to economic development in the Dutch Republic.

Households were thus an important institution during the Golden Age, while community institutions contributed to well-being, even if they were partly ceremonial in reproducing privileges and monopoly powers. Guilds, for instance, were important in providing services to their members. They were institutions associated with trades such as carpenters, textile manufacturers, nurses, doctors, medics, chemists, and so on, which charged membership fees, established entry requirements, and ensured the quality of service or product. In return, members received benefits in the form of cartel-type returns, unemployment benefits, pensions, and cheap inputs appropriate to their trade.

There was thus a considerable degree of trust throughout the broad social environment, by all classes, despite several (especially intra-)religious and class antagonisms that rose periodically to great heights. Dutch citizens were thus able to be identified as both citizens of a healthy province and of a well-functioning republic during the Golden Age. As with all hegemonic powers, there was a large degree of integrative social capital associated with being a citizen of a powerful and successful province and nation. Citizenship was well-prized as it bestowed considerable benefits. It enabled one to join a guild if certain requirements were met, such as providing a useful identity; enabling certain citizens to vote in local, state, and national elections; and the privileges of schooling, medical care, poor relief, and inculcating in migrants the desire to become part of the Dutch social economy. (Compare this with the work by Van Zanden (2009, ch 4) on the European Marriage System during this period.)

5.4 Dutch Hegemony Rise and Fall and Long Waves

This chapter has thus far summarized the nature of the six interdependent and relative autonomous techno-institutional and geo-spatial-ecological dynamic structures comprising the basic edifice of the socioeconomic circuits underlying the Dutch Golden Age. Now we place these dynamic structures in aggregate motion through real historical time. It is not simply a circuit but also an interrelated set of processes operating through various dynamic structures in motion. CSD comprises an amalgam of state, technological, business, financial, household, community, ecological-geographical institutions, relationships, and processes in complex motion through time. The subsystems operate through both relative autonomies and interdependencies within and between CSD linkages enabling circular and cumulative upward and as the contradictions and uncertainties mount downward motion through time.

One of the core things about the CSD is the speed with which the durable and dynamic circuit turns over through historical time, but the quality of the transactional motion is also crucial. Care needs to be taken because expanding the speed can generate instability at certain thresholds. This can be seen, for instance, through (a) the financial instability hypothesis (refinance, debt and crises); (b) major changes in migration levels when instability may rise substantially (households); (c) declining trust in business and government when speed takes precedence over quality (e.g., in colonial exploitation, monopolization, and financial flows); (d) when greater market turnover and profit lead to the decimation of original cultures, their islands and spices (e.g., re the Banda Islands population during 1621); and (e) when more speed leads to a decimation of ecological capitals and climate change. Some trade-offs, social safety nets, agreements, institutions, and other resources are thus required to ensure proper reproduction of the CSD, and for the generation of the Dutch Golden Age, hegemony, long wave upswings, and suitable forms of climate change.

The purpose of this section is to continue the analysis of the Dutch Republic vis-à-vis hegemonic dominance, long waves, and climate change, moving from the more qualitative and historical details to the statistical and numerical dimensions of the investigation.

The question of hegemonic dominance is potentially complex since there are various types of hegemony and different ways of delineating the nature of power. There are at least three types of hegemony, or three different ways of understanding it. The first is to determine whether there was absolute dominance by the Dutch Republic in the world system in which they operated. Absolute dominance requires that they establish an enormous amount of power in production, commercial, and financial sectors, which usually leads to a derivative form of military power. This is Wallerstein's definition. Using this type of hegemony, Wallerstein (1983, 103) dated Dutch absolute hegemony as 1620–1672, British hegemony as 1815–1873, and US hegemony as 1945–1967. In an earlier, more detailed research paper, as part of a research team, Wallerstein, and company (Research Working Group 1979, 499) differentiated between four stages of hegemony: (a) ascending hegemony, (b) hegemonic victory, (c) hegemonic maturity, and (d) declining hegemony. Relating these four stages to the three capitalist nations that underwent all stages, generates the following dates and stages, in Table 5.1 (as hypotheses or perhaps stylized facts):

Ascending hegemony is where hegemony is not yet established but is rising majorly; victory is when the state business has hegemonic power in production, commerce, and finance simultaneously; maturity is when the hegemony has absolute power in all three main areas and has the most power in the world system; and declining hegemony is when hegemony is diminishing, absolute dominance is disappearing, but relative hegemony may be in operation, perhaps with power still ahead commercially and financially but not in production (with derivative military power majorly diminishing). The Research Working Group added that the boundaries between these stages are necessarily thick with qualitative (non-deterministic) processes determining the outcome.

In general, the phases outlined in Table 5.1 accord with my own understanding of Dutch history. But it needs emphasizing that Dutch, British, and US hegemony were qualitatively different, even though we can compare several dimensions of their historical processes. Anticipating results here and in further chapters (below), all three hegemons ruled the world system in which they operated; all three had extensive networks of control through several continents as well as where they were geopolitically situated; and all three dominated in the three (or four) "sectors" discussed. Dutch hegemony was the first powerful national force in the world system of capitalism, and its power was less concentrated than either British or US

Table 5.1 Phases of Dutch, British, and US Hegemony, 1575–2000s

	Dutch	British	USA
Ascending	1575–1590	1798–1815	1897–1913/20
Victory	1590–1620	1815–1850	1913/20–1945
Maturity	1620–1650	1850–1873	1945–1967
Decline	1650–1672	1873–1893	1967–

Source: Adapted from Research Working Group (1979, 499)

hegemony. It was a small nation that through luck and prowess managed to hold off competitors economically and militarily for up to half a century or more (or less).

In this context, Dutch hegemony was more impressive than British and US hegemony, especially given that the British managed to organize several large capitalist settler economies as well as submissive colonies (especially into the 1700s and 1800s), while the US did not need control of specific de jure colonies since it ruled through naked power, diplomacy, and business networks and relationships with a huge domestic market (during the 1900s).

The question arises about the relationship between Dutch hegemony, socioeconomic performance, and waves of GDP per capita growth (as well as GDP per capita *levels*, GDP *not* per capita, and several other variables). Data for Holland and some other economies has improved significantly recently, thanks to those, for instance, working on the Maddison Project. As a result, we have data on GDP per capita and GDP per capita growth going back to the 1300s (especially for Holland) and forward to the present (The Netherlands), with few gaps. Some scholars have studied this data, and the Dutch experience, in particular. Prominent ones include Jan Luiten van Zanden and Maarten Prak (who often work together), in addition to Jack Goldstone, Bas van Bavel, Jan de Vries, and van der Wonde. Van Zanden and Prak et al. (2023) argue from their analysis of the data that the Dutch experienced a growth "take-off" between 1350 and 1500 that "set in motion an irreversible process of economic development" (p. 18), and that econometrically there is evidence of a long process of growth with no major structural breaks through to the 1700s at least. By the 1600s "the Dutch Republic [became] the richest and most productive economy in the world" (p. 18): the first specifically capitalist economy with capitalist institutions and dynamics of creative destruction, but numerous social safety nets and other protections to moderate the instabilities somewhat.

More generally, though van Zanden and Prak argue that scholars should see the process of growth in the context of the North Sea area, with the center of growth during the "Middle Ages [e.g., 1400s] [occurring] in Flanders (Bruges, Ghent), [which] shifted in the [1500s] to Brabant (Antwerp) ['Belgium'], before moving north after 1585 to Holland (Amsterdam), and finally, around 1700, to England (London)" (p. 20). Significantly, they add that, "The region as a whole … experienced continuous growth for the *best part* of a millennium, owing to the emergence of a capitalist market economy there in the late medieval period" (p. 20; emphasis added). They conclude by saying that "The Dutch Golden Age was thus part of this much wider process of growth in the North Sea area, and what appears to be a growth cycle is just the century of Holland being the "core" of this region on the long road from 1350 to 1800" (p. 21).

Van Bavel and Goldstone take a more cyclical approach to the general question of growth, particularly for the Dutch Republic. The debates in the literature between, e.g., Goldstone (2021) and Zanden et al. (2021) are especially illuminating, but also conflicting. Goldstone takes note of the much better statistics of growth recently developed. He then goes on to critically examine the results of Van Zanden and others, who argue that modern economic growth started in the North Sea region from the 1400s to the 1700s with an impressive array of modest but consistent increases in GDP per capita (varying between what is now called Belgium, Holland, and England) during the period. Goldstone indicates that such expansions of GDP per capita were concentrated in short periods of time, such as the late 1500s in Holland, with gentle declines after 1600, and after the 1650s, but no major *increases* in GDP per capita between 1600 and 1800. (My results below concur with these.) Similarly for Britain, Goldstone shows evidence for relatively high growth spurts, for a few decades each, during the late 1300s and the late 1600s; with no evidence of a long period of (even modestly) sustained growth during 1350–1800.

In reply to Goldstone, van Zanden and Bolt argue that it is not ideal to concentrate on changes in GDP per capita over short periods because, even though recent data-measuring has improved, the earlier years especially have a larger margin of error than recent estimates, and the econometric evidence indicates no major structural changes. They argue instead we should use the long-term trend data, which shows that *older data under-estimated increases in GDP* per capita, and that therefore the take-off in economic activity can be seen to have occurred in the North Sea region ("Belgium," around the 1400s), Holland (late 1500s to early mid-1600s) and England (late 1600s) and that this modest growth continued into the early-middle 1800s (when another bout of long-term growth occurred, at higher levels, for a time).

Yet Prak and van Zanden do specify medium-term "waves" and "swings" which deviate from the long-term trends (of 0.18% yearly real growth per capita over 1350–1800 for Holland), such as the "temporarily higher levels of GDP per capita in the … 1630s, and other low-level 'outliers' between 1650 and 1680" (p. 17); and the "take-off" they mention "that set in motion an irreversible process of economic development … between 1350 and 1500 (and perhaps already by 1400)" (p. 18). Similar examples of such waves and swings are discussed further in articles and books. It appears that van Zanden and co-authors believe both in decadal-to-multiple decadal swings and waves, but also that "the results do not show the cyclical pattern of growth that Goldstone is finding; on the contrary, after 1348 growth was persistent in Holland" (and England) (Zanden et al. 2021). This is rather confusing, but perhaps it is just that they do not condone empirical statements about "cycles" in Holland during this time but are quite happy to recognize the existence of swings or "waves" which are much longer in temporal space. In this context, my own results (see below) concur with these.

As to whether long waves operated before the 1780s or 1790s, the date(s) at which the standard long wave model commences, many have argued for and against the proposition. Dassbach et al. (1995) surveys the issue and emphasizes some core issues (but not dealing with issues of causality). The first core issue is that some scholars believe long waves did not commence before the advent of industrial capitalism in the late 1700s. Second, price waves have been shown to exist, but without any necessary direct linkage to real output. Goldstein shows a lag of around 15 years between production (first) and price (second) waves prior to the late 1700s. Third, numerous scholars such as Wallerstein and Braudel believe that long waves operated before the late 1700s. Fourth, numerous authors are dubious of waves before the late 1700s or mid-1800s due to data inadequacies (though they may not still argue that if they are still alive). Fifth, some scholars believe long waves existed before the late 1700s, especially if one integrates the analysis with questions of hegemonic power and transformation. Sixth, several authors date various waves during the 1500s–1700s: e.g., Boswell et al. (1991) cites "peaks" or "upper turning points" in long waves for certain regions during this period, including during the 1530s, 1550s/60s, 1580s/90s, 1640s, 1680s, 1710s, and 1750s.

It is time to summarize my analysis of the data for Holland/Netherlands during the "Golden Age" and for longer periods, and to examine how Dutch hegemony fits into the equation, including to British and US hegemony. In chap. 1, I surveyed the whole period 1530–2022 for Holland/Netherlands. I divide the period into two segments for clearer scrutiny. Figure 5.4 looks at the period from the Dutch Revolt of the early mid-1500s through to 1800, while Fig. 5.5 examines the 1780s to the 2020s. From these figures, we outline the record of long and short waves for 1550–2022 in Table 5.2.

Rule Number One applies that long wave decadal growth (AAGR) needs to be greater than the trend bar, for at least two decades, to be defined as a long wave upswing. Without this rule holding the result is short-wave upswing, borderline, or short/long wave downswing. Two factors are crucial for long wave upswings. The first is the strong durability of growth per capita (long periodicity). And the second is a good amplitude of growth per capita. When durability through historical time (periodicity) and high growth (amplitude) both are present then long wave upswings are in process.

Table 5.2, based on Figs. 5.4 and 5.5, reveals some crucial stylized facts about waves, hegemony, and climate change. The first is that the Dutch experienced long wave upswings only during (or closely related to) periods of hegemony. During

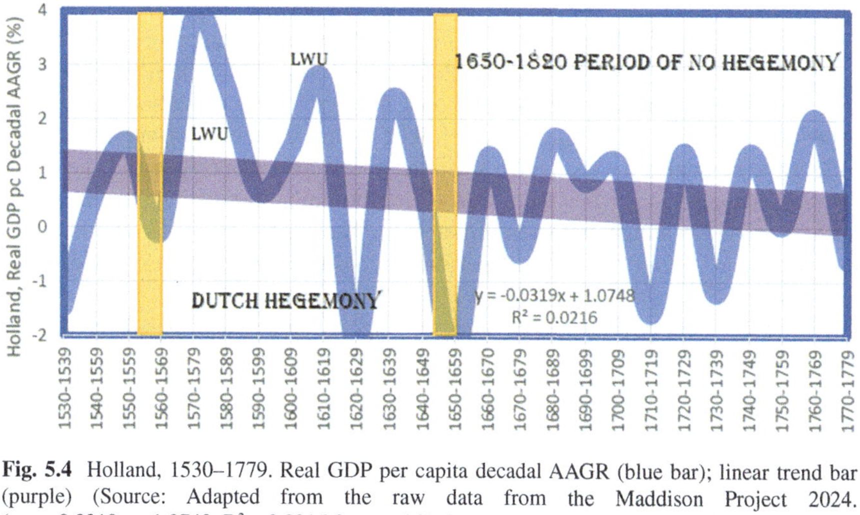

Fig. 5.4 Holland, 1530–1779. Real GDP per capita decadal AAGR (blue bar); linear trend bar (purple) (Source: Adapted from the raw data from the Maddison Project 2024. (y = −0.0319x + 1.0748; R^2 = 0.0216 for trend *line*)

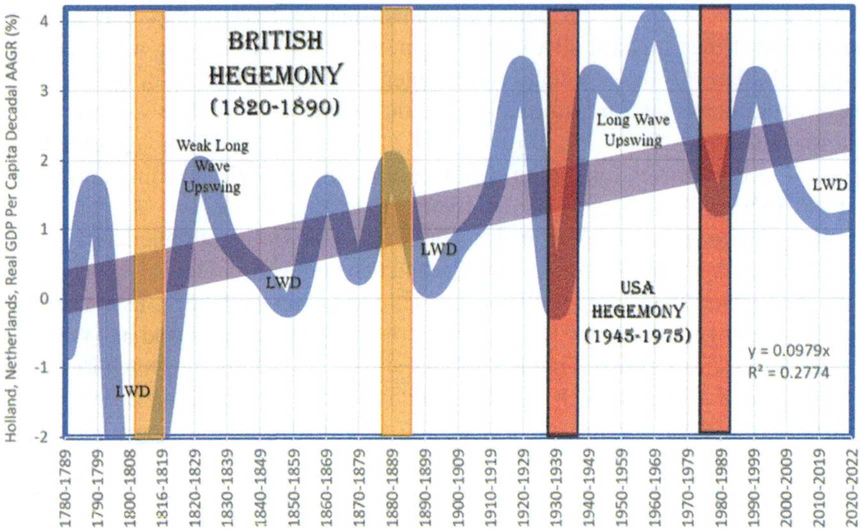

Fig. 5.5 Decadal annual average GDP per capita growth rates (AAGR) (blue line), Holland/The Netherlands, 1780–2022. Linear trend bar (purple) (Source: Adapted from the raw data of the Maddison Project 2024.) (For sources of data from the Maddison Project, see Bolt and van Zanden (2020) and the Maddison Project dataset notes. Data for 1350–1808 is for Holland (Zanden et al. 2012; Maddison Project 2024), while 1816–1913 (Smits et al. 2000) and 1913–2022 data are for the Netherlands (Maddison Project 2024). There is no data for 1809–1815 due to the wars. The Maddison Project date their data as "2023" but since it was published online during (May) 2024, I cite it as "2024.") ($y = 0.0979x$; $R^2 = 0.2774$ for trend *line*)

Dutch hegemony, they had two such long wave upswings, one very major (1570–1589) and one relatively minor (1600–1619). During British hegemony, the Dutch experienced one relatively weak long wave upswing (1820–1839). And during the era of US (and Euro) hegemony, the Dutch experienced one very major long wave upswing of 40 years (1940–1979). This confirms our major hypothesis, that long wave upswings tend to occur only during/close to periods of hegemony, especially for those economies closely linked to the hegemonic power. In general, long wave upswings for the Dutch are phenomena linked purely with hegemonic power. During periods when there was no hegemonic power, the Dutch underwent no long wave upswings, not even minor ones. These periods characterized by no hegemony are periods of poorer performance and often polycrises (see chap. 9 below).

The second stylized fact is that climate change dynamics have usually close connections with hegemonies and long waves. For instance, before and during the era of Dutch hegemony, and indeed through the whole period from Dutch hegemony (1570) through to British hegemony (1855), Europe and to some degree the world underwent a Little Ice Age. Within the wider LIA (1450–1855), there were three 100-year (circa) sunspot cycles, including the Sporer minima (1450–1570) and the Maunder minima (1630–1730) around the time of Dutch hegemony and beyond;

Table 5.2 Long waves "map," borderline, and short-wave performance, Dutch Republic, 1570–2022 (452 Years)

1570–1649 (80 yrs)	1650–1689 (40 yrs)	1690–1819 (130 yrs)	1820–1889 (70 yrs)	1890–1939 (50 yrs)	1940–1979 (40 yrs)	1980–2022 (42 yrs)
During Dutch absolute hegemony	Relative hegemony	No hegemony	British absolute hegemony	No absolute hegemony	US hegemony: Absolute	US relative hegemony
LWU 40 yrs. (1570–89) (1600–19)			LWU 20 yrs. (1820–1839)		LWU 40 yrs. (1940–1979)	
SWU 10 yrs. (1630–1639)	SWU 10 yrs. (1680–89)	SWU 50 yrs. (1700–1709) (1720–1729) (1740–1749) (1760–69) (1790–99)	SWU 20 yrs. (1860–1869) (1880–1889)	SWU (1920–1929)		SWU 10 yrs. (1990–1999)
		SWB 20 yrs. (1690–1699) (1750–1759)		SWB (1910–1919)		
SWB 20 Yrs (1590–1599) (1640–1649)	SWB 10 yrs. (1660–1669)	SWD 20 yrs. (1710–1719) (1730–1739)	SWD (1870–1879)	SWD 10 yrs. (1930–1939)		SWD 10 yrs (1980–1989)
SWD 10 yrs. (1620–1629)	SWD 20 yrs. (1650–1659) (1670–79)	LWD 40 yrs. (1770–1789) (1800–1819)	LWD 20 yrs. (1840–1859)	LWD 20 yrs. (1890–09)		LWD 23 yrs (2000–2022)
50 U/30DB = 1.66	**10 U/30BD = 0.33**	**50 U/80DB 0.625**	**40 U/30D = 1.33**	**10 U/40BD = 0.25**	**40 U/0D = ∞**	**10 U/32D = 0.313**

Note: *U* upswing, *D* downswing, *B* borderline, *LWU* long wave upswing, *LWD* long wave downswing, *SWU* short-wave upswing, *SWD* short-wave downswing, *DB* on border of D and B; ∞ infinity

and the Dalton minima (1770–1855) including during the first half of British hegemony. These cold periods were perfect for groups that specialize in dealing with waterways and navigation such as the Dutch and to some degree the British. And during the era of US hegemony when the Dutch and the British gained from their cultural linkages to the US, there was a small colder age (1940s–1970s) which was followed by increasing climate crises during the era of global warming (circa 1980s to the present and future).

The Dutch have a long history of studying long waves, as we discussed in chaps. 2 and 3, with, for instance, the work by van Duijn (1983) being one of the first on long waves during the second long wave of long wave scholarship. But I could find no papers or books detailing (specifically) Dutch long waves of *growth* before the 1800s (many discuss price waves), although some scholars do discuss "theoretical logic waves" for that period and later[14]; and only one specifically analyzing Dutch long waves of growth for the 1800s.[15]

Now we introduce the record of Dutch real GDP per capita *levels* for 1500–1900, compared with US, France, Spain, and Germany, as shown in Fig. 5.6.[16]

This shows that Dutch real GDP levels tend to move in waves from upswing to downswing, especially from 1500 to 1530s (up) and 1530s to the early 1540s (down); subsequent rise during the mid-late 1540s to the late-1560s, and down in

[14] Discussions of "logistic waves" for the Netherlands during the 1500s–1700s, by Boswell and Misra (1995) and Goldstein (1988, 64–81), are based on arguments concerning "general agreement among historians," otherwise "prices," or "general hypotheses" to be investigated, rather than statistics and analysis, usually by referring to Braudel, Wallerstein, and others as sources. For instance, Boswell and Misra discuss the logistic of Phase A (expansion) for 1500–1600/1650, and Phase B (contraction) for 1600/1650–1700 (with overlap for 1600–1650). These seem to be referring to cycles of the European economy (rather than the Dutch specifically). Similarly, for the period mentioned by Goldstein, he refers to Braudel for "European peaks" of 1529, 1559, 1595, 1650, etc., and "troughs" of 1509, 1539, 1575, 1621, 1689, and so on. This may be useful for hypothesis forming but hardly for the sort of work involved in this chapter. The best that can be gained from this work seems to be the proposition, based on data, that "Dutch *trade* hegemony" was in "ascent from 1578 to 1620, peak from 1620 to 1650, and decline from 1620 to 1671" (Boswell et al. 1991, emphasis added). A similar style is shown in Boswell and Sweat (1991) regarding long waves and wars.

[15] Reijnders' (2009) paper is very complicated but seems to show two long waves for the Netherlands in the 1800s, one centered on the 1820s–1830s (as was ours), and the other centered on the strong performance of the 1880s (see Fig 5, page 96 of his book). But given the very low growth of the 1870s and the 1890s, the high growth of the 1880s cannot be the fulcrum of a longer wave. It may be possible to discover sectoral long waves for the late 1800s (rather than for growth of real GDP), and Reijnders does seem to argue for this disaggregated approach. The second conclusion Reijnders makes is that "long waves in Dutch volume series appear to run contrary to the corresponding long waves in price series," and that "the Keynes effect is responsible for the reversion of the basic price-volume relation" (p. 107). How this works is said to be that a rising "world [output] cycle" leads to an increasing demand for agricultural goods, which leads to rising prices, which then follows through to rising interest rates and hence a declining growth of Dutch output (p. 106).

[16] Note also that Italian and Swedish real GDP per capita levels cut the Dutch lead majorly during the late 1500s to the mid-1600s, but we are especially interested in the English/UK, etc., comparative performance, as Swedish and Dutch performance slid down majorly from the 1700s. (See Fouquet and Broadberry 2015, 230.)

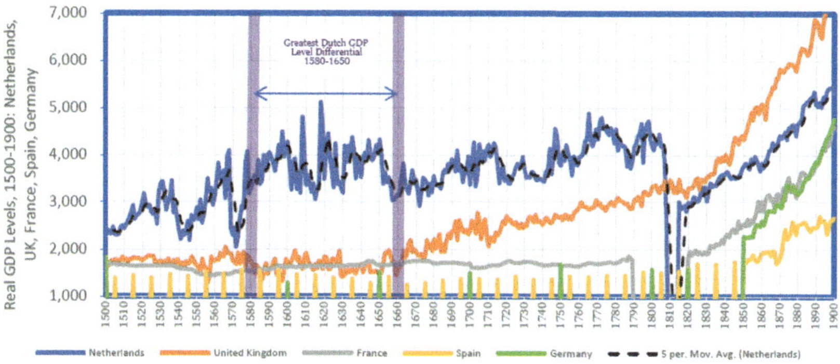

Fig. 5.6 Real GDP per capita *levels*, 1500–1900: Dutch, British, French, Spanish, and German. (Source: Adapted from the raw data provided by the Maddison Project 2024) Note: The yellow and green vertical lines illustrate occasional data for Spain and Germany, respectively (hence vertical lines rather than horizontal-style lines)

the late 1560s-to-early-1570s. This is followed by a very major rise during the 1570s–1600s, and modest downswing during the 1600s–1610s. Then there was a rise during the late 1610s and a decline in the 1620s; followed by a rise in the 1630s–1640s and a drop during the 1650s. This downswing lasted through the entire period of the 1650s-to-mid-1680s, after which the waves tended to become more subdued during the 1700s as the Dutch/British GDP differential declined majorly. When the Dutch emerged from the revolutionary and Napoleonic wars (during which they were temporarily part of the French Empire) an entirely new trajectory commenced as British/Dutch GDP differentials reversed, the British economy expanded majorly, and the Dutch trailed along after them but at an increasingly lower level (but still much higher than the French and Germans).

The core thing here is that for much of the period of the 1580s to the 1650s, with cyclical swings, Dutch real GDP per capita levels were about double that of the UK's. It was not until the 1650s that UK levels of GDP per capita started to catch up with the Dutch, until it finally elevated beyond the Dutch level during the latter years of the Napoleonic wars. After 1815, Dutch GDP per capita levels recovered somewhat but were never again higher than the British (at least not until late into the 1900s). Thus, the two key periods for Dutch GDP levels were, first,1570–1600 when Dutch levels rose majorly (while UK levels declined and/or were low), and the 1650s when Dutch GDP levels began to decline (while UK levels rose substantially). It was essentially the start (1570s) and the end (1650s) of the Dutch Golden Age.

Several conclusions emerge from an analysis of this pattern of long waves and hegemony for The Netherlands. The first, mentioned above, is that the most robust periods of growth and upswings for the Dutch Republic were during eras of hegemony—Dutch (especially), British, and US (most especially). This provides more than prima facie evidence for the notion that hegemonies tend to provide enough stability, trust in institutions, and productivity to enhance long wave upswings (and increasing the floors and ceilings of long waves), at least for the area(s) undergoing hegemonic dominance, but in the case of at least British and US hegemony for a much wider array of nations and areas (especially their "allies" during the later periods). Two periods of hegemonic dominance provided the highest rates of growth for any period, for the Dutch, under Dutch hegemony and US hegemony. But the period of British hegemony also gave the Dutch benefits in the form of one very mild long wave upswing.

The periods of lowest growth (1650–1679 and 1710–1818) were characterized by no-hegemons, especially when the Dutch were involved in the French revolution (and the Napoleonic wars). There was however one modestly healthy period in between these lowest growth decades; namely, the short upswings of 1680–1689 and 1700–1709, plus the borderline performance of 1690–1699. But the modest robustness did not continue while the UK gained ground on the Dutch. The *1815 Congress of Vienna* united south and north Netherlands but during the 1830 revolutions Belgium broke away to become a separate nation, as did Luxembourg in 1848 (as noted earlier).

The second conclusion is that the Dutch circuit of techno-institutional-geo-spatial-ecological reproduction was robust enough by the late 1500s and early 1600s to generate a large era of growth and socioeconomic performance that lasted for two long wave upswings, 1570–1590 (a strong one) and 1600–1620 (a weaker one). After these two long waves was a major war against Spain (and European et al. financial crisis) during the 1620s which caused a depression in the United Provinces, and for 40 years thereafter there was a succession of lower ceilings/floors and short-wave ups and downs (1630–1670). From the 1670s to 1816, growth was subject to a series of relatively short waves of up and down.

A major factor preventing the emergence of more impressive long wave upswings after these two during 1570–1590 and 1600–1620 (circa), apart from the major war/crisis during the 1620s was, as Goldstone (2021) recognizes, that just before the 1600s and early in the 1600s, real GDP growth (Gg, *not* per capita) was robust, but population growth (Pg) was so strong that this did not translate into per capita *growth* (Ggpc) performance, as indicated below in (approximate) eqs. 5.1 and 5.2 and Table 5.3. The same trajectory occurred during especially the 1800s (notably 1850–1900) as mentioned above.

$$Ggpc = Gg - Pg \tag{5.1}$$

$$Gg = Ggpc + Pg \tag{5.2}$$

This illustrates that the most buoyant period of per capita growth was during the 1550–1600 era, especially the very late 1500s, when all three of the factors, g, pg, and gpc were growing at a fast pace. The rate of population growth was the highest of all half-centuries but also was concurrent with very high rates of GDP growth per capita. No other period illustrated this double phenomenon. By the 1600–1650, both population growth and real GDP growth were growing strongly, but without (significant) per capita growth. In other words, the population surge especially in

Table 5.3 Growth of Dutch population and real GDP, GDP per capita, 1400–1850

	GDP growth, 50 Yrs [Gg]	Pop. growth, 50 Years [Pg]	GDPpc growth 50 yrs. [Ggpc]
1400–1450	28%	13%	15%
1450–1500	12%	6%	6%
1500–1550	44%	20%	24%
1550–1600	71% (esp. 1570s, 1580s)	23% (esp. 1580–1600)	48%
1600–1650	29% (esp. 1610s, 1630s)	28%	1%
1650–1700	−17%	5%	−22%
1700–1750	12%	0%	12%
1750–1800	19%	8%	11%
1800–1850	37%	47%	−10%
1850–1900	107%	67%	40%

Source: Based on raw data in Paping (2014) and Maddison Project (2024)

Holland in the very late 1500s had settled down to rates equal to GDP growth by the first half of the 1600s, leaving no significant *increase* in per capita GDP. By the second half of the 1600s the surge, Golden Age, and hegemony had matured and indeed ended with negative population and GDP growth rates. Hence, the *whole period* of the Golden Age and hegemony accorded with one aspect of Kuznets' (1966) style GDP analysis: "a sustained increase in population attained without any lowering of per capita product" (Birdsall 1989, 23); but not the second aspect: "robust growth plus robust population growth" (although the 1580–1620 period did). Nonetheless, the Golden Age and hegemony provided good periods of sound per capita performance which did not return until the era of US hegemony, although during British hegemony Dutch performance became more buoyant (as noted).

Regarding the experience of the 1800s, aggregate data for 1800–1850 compared with 1850-1900 mystifies the results somewhat. Firstly, 1800–1820 was a major long wave downswing due to war, colonisation and recovery; while, in contrast,1820-1840 was a relatively weak long wave upswing as the Dutch became independent from the French and reestablished some reasonable socioeconomic performance. This was followed during 1840–1860 by a long wave downswing, followed by two short wave upswings (1860s, 1880s) and a short wave downswing (1870s). The 1800s was concluded by a long wave downswing which extended into the 1900s (1890–1910). Table 5.3 thus hides this detailed reality by positing an impressive expansion of GDP growth per capita during 1850–1900 and ignoring the best period during the 1820s–1830s. Third, the results of Dutch hegemony and long waves reinforce the conclusion made by Goldstein (1988, 287), that waves and hegemonic dynamics interact and condition each other, but also have their own relative autonomies. However, this current study of the Dutch experience, and knowledge about the British and US ones, does generate a conclusion not, to my knowledge, noticed elsewhere. This is because the Dutch Golden Age can be defined, in the context of our hypotheses, as the simultaneous generation of two successive long waves and (just before [or during]), hegemonic dominance throughout the world system. The Golden Age started with a long wave upswing and hegemonic ascendancy and ended after another (weak) long wave upswing and maturing-declining hegemony. Thereafter, during the mid-late 1600s, 1700s (in general), and very early 1800s, long waves became generally subdued as Dutch absolute hegemony evaporated while relative hegemony likely continued until the mid-1700s.

The fourth conclusion relates, again, to the period of downswing at the end of the 1570–1590 and 1600–1620 long waves (1620s) and a short-wave upswing of the 1630s. During the years of 1570–1620, growth per capita was moderately robust (also growth *not* per capita was strong but so was population growth), and downswing started during the 1620s when a depression emerged in the Dutch Republic, due to a European financial crisis and war against the Spanish. It should be mentioned that the 1620s was said to be the start of what some called the European crisis of the 1600s (during 1620–1720) (see Hobsbawm 1954a, b; Trevor-Roper 1967; Parker and Smith 1978; Parker 2018).[17] Some have even called the whole of the 1600s the global crisis of the seventeenth century, precipitated by the Little Ice Age (as discussed above, Section 5.3.1). The more delimited depression of the 1620s involved numerous factors, but essentially it represented a manifestation of systemic contradictions at the heart of the Dutch circuit of socioeconomic relations. As Israel said of this:

> The malaise gripping the Republic in the … 1620s arose partly from external factors. It was a *malaise* of commerce, navigation, industry, finance, taxation, and other war related burdens and a decidedly grim strategic situation. But it was more than this. For it was a crisis also of the body politic, society and religion. For the time being the State of Holland had indeed lost their soul and ceased to lead. [Israel 1995, 480]

The Dutch economic miracle depended upon trade with European countries, and later world trade via VOC, WIC, and other agents. The major European currency crisis of 1619–1623 hindered the circuit of market relations (Kindleberger 1991), while the ending of the *Twelve Years Truce* in 1621 generated ongoing battles with Spain which contributed to the depression of trade. It also generated domestic upheaval through higher taxes and public disorder. In the middle of the worst decade of the Golden Age, during 1624, plague ravaged Amsterdam, Delft, and numerous other major cities, with tens of thousands of mortalities and major stresses on an already overstretched health system from the war. Spanish embargoes against Dutch traders and their encirclement of the Republic further hindered trade and industry. During the whole of the 1620s, the Republic was engaged in ongoing battles against the Spanish, as the depression got worse. The Republic gradually generated a strong

[17] Hobsbawm places emphasis on the social and economic nature of the crises. Trevor-Roper emphasizes instead state-society crises. Niels Steensgaard (1978) is skeptical and notes the Dutch Golden Age in motion during the alleged crisis. The debate about European crisis in the "1600s" (1620s–1720s) evolved into an analysis of global crisis; see, for instance, the book by Geoffrey Parker (2018). Some authors argue concepts such as "general crisis" and "industrial revolution" are over-generalizations better substituted by the different problems that arise rather than lumping them all together.

arsenal against the invaders and successfully instituted tax reform, e.g., stamp duty paid by the rich on legal documents, which helped finance the war. A major victory by the Republic in 1629 severely dampened the prestige of the Spanish state and enhanced that of the Dutch.

Dutch military successes in the 1620s were difficult in garnishing united support for policies to end the war, even though the Spanish King was willing to agree to an unconditional truce when his army was finally defeated. This was due to two other conflicts. One was between Dutch traders in Europe who benefited from peace involved in the truce, and WIC agents in the Americas and West Africa who would lose markets and colonies if a truce was instituted. The other war was also vicious, involving opposing sides of the Dutch Reform Church (protestants), which raged especially during 1620–1632. Essentially it was a theological war between those who supported the establishment Church and others who were more liberal and advocated tolerance of heterodox interpretations within the Church. It raged for years and adversely affected the ability of especially City Councils to perform effectively and efficiently.

The 1620s depression was a major downswing during the Golden Age but soon after an impressive short-wave upswing emerged during the 1630s during which there was a brief era of moderate peace while trade was relatively buoyant. The techno-institutions and ecologies associated with the Dutch circuit (CSD) continued to generate a semblance of robust economic activity, for a time, even though some of the vibrancy deteriorated and migration to the Dutch Provinces diminished. Many authors thus argue (questionably I think) that the Dutch Golden Age continued until the 1670s, when downswing re-emerged; absolute hegemony disappeared entirely or gradually wilted.[18]

What were the systemic causes of the decline of the Dutch Golden Age, which is the same question concerning the causes of hegemonic demise and the move to subdued long waves (in general terms). Essentially the performance potential imbued in the Dutch socioeconomic circuit became relatively exhausted, during the mid-1600s and especially during the late 1600s, and even more so during the 1700s. It started early on when the growth of real GDP (not per capita) grew at about or less than the rate of population growth. People were fleeing the inquisition and religious intolerance against Protestants and heterodoxies, especially in Spain and France, and moving to where the Golden Age was well known to (have) be(en) in motion. But the Golden Age failed to keep pace with the growth of households. Dutch technologies failed to keep ahead of competitors throughout Europe and elsewhere as productivity faltered.

Furthermore, the circuit of business and colonial relations, including VOC and WIC, was challenged by competitors, especially as numerous nations, especially the British, instituted mercantilist policies against the Dutch, and

[18] Many authors cite 1672 as a terribly critical and depressing year for the Dutch, being part of the third Anglo-Dutch War of 1672–1674, which they eventually did win (as with the second), but with grave crises affecting the Republic especially during 1672.

competitors learned some of the lessons of the Dutch experience to beat them at their own game. Several Navigation Acts were instituted by the British to dislocate Dutch supremacy, which was compounded by the Franco-Dutch War and four Anglo-Dutch wars, the third (with France leading the charge with the English, 1672–1674) being a "disaster" for the Dutch (Israel 1989, 297), which also led to major colonial and trade losses. The objective of this war was specifically to end Dutch trade hegemony, even though it did not achieve its objective. Nonetheless, this and other wars and trade embargoes against the Dutch resulted in major dislocations to its pattern of trade, production and finance, exhausted public finances, and majorly reduced immigration as growth potential-actual declined. It also led through time, along with other factors, to a robust British short wave upswings and robust growth during the 1660s and the 1680s. As Chase-Dunn (1998) stated:

> The Dutch decline exhibited the tendencies … of hegemonic stages: the shift toward financial services, the export of capital and the transformation of the capitalists from entrepreneurs to rentiers[.] … [But] Amsterdam remained an important centre of international commerce and finance 300 years after it lost first position. World cities decline relatively, not absolutely.

5.5 Other Authors on Dutch Hegemony

Now we compare our own conclusions on Dutch hegemony (and to some degree waves) with those of others. But we only consider those who have analyzed all three of the major hegemonies: the Dutch, British, and US, as a way of delimiting the scope of the analysis and comparing similar stories (which we also do in the chapters on British and US hegemony). I investigate five authors who have done a comparative analysis of the three dominant hegemonies of the 1580–2020s period, with special reference to their views of Dutch hegemony. The five analyzed include Roy Kwon, Angus Maddison, Christopher Chase-Dunn, Peter Taylor, and Giovanni Arrighi, who are influenced variously by Wallerstein, Modelski, and Antonio Gramsci, but have their own theoretico-empirical assessments of Dutch (and British-US) hegemony.

I start with Roy Kwon (2011) who calculated the hegemony index for 1550–1830 in relation to the Dutch, British, Spanish, and French positions (see Fig. 5.7).

Kwon seeks to integrate conceptual insights of both world-systems analysis (e.g., Immanuel Wallerstein and Christopher Chase-Dunn) with world politics scholars (e.g., George Modelski and William R Thompson), who both deal with issues of hegemony and world leadership. In this regard, he uses three variables to measure hegemony: real GDP per capita, real GDP, and sea-power. The results show that Dutch hegemonic power was ahead of the Spanish during the 1580s, and again after 1600. The large lead that the Dutch had between 1610 and 1643 provided Kwon with a good argument for concluding that the Dutch experienced

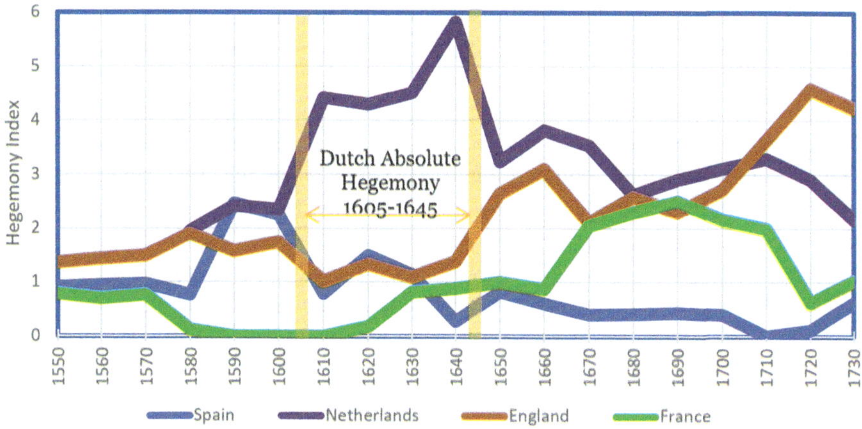

Fig. 5.7 Hegemony index, 1550–1730. Netherlands, Spain, England, and France. (Source: Adapted from raw data, Appendix A, Kwon 2011, 612)

hegemony during this period. By the 1650s, their large lead had deteriorated majorly and by 1680 the English hegemony index was equal to the Dutch.[19]

Maddison's (1991, 31–35) analysis of Dutch hegemony is broader than that of Wallerstein or Kwon, since although he is not very specific about hegemony dates, he stretched it out from 1600 to 1700 or even later. But he calls it "leadership" (like Modelski and company) and does not differentiate between absolute and relative levels. He puts the Dutch success down to three main factors. The first is said to be the "'modernity' of Dutch institutions, which were highly favourable to capitalist enterprise, and the absence of feudalism in most of the country". He argues that the bourgeoisie largely had political power, enterprise was assisted by [relative] religious tolerance, and the Dutch were imbued with the ethos of having "mastery over man and nature". The second factor is geography, especially the major rivers of Europe which gave them access to major markets, as well as ocean ports, low-cost freight, passenger travel, and innovative wind power for drainage and manufacturing. The third factor was said to be mercantile policies in Asia and Latin America, and the blockade against "Antwerp's access to the sea between 1585-1795."

Regarding declining leadership during the 1700s, he cites the destruction of monopolistic trading privileges especially vis-à-vis France and the UK, the stagnation of population, and the decline of production-trade for ship-building, fisheries, and textiles, as being the major factors. The economy is said to have "sank into

[19] The analysis of this chapter indicates that some authors, such as Jonathan Israel (1989, 1995), seem to mistake trade dominance of the Dutch for (total) Hegemony. Israel cites "The Republic at its Zenith I: The 1650s" and "Zenith II: 1659–1672," and "The Age of Decline, 1702–1806" (contents pages). Taking hegemony as a totality (production, commercial, and financial dominance), this current chapter indicates that hegemony started to decline likely at the latest during the 1650s, even though the Republic continued to have commercial (including trade) and financial edge, especially the latter, for some considerable time after the 1650s, into the 1700s.

complacent stagnation" due to French and British mercantilism and the dominance of finance "which kept the currency overvalued and further weakened export potential."

Third, Chase-Dunn's (1998, chap. 9) account of Dutch hegemony like that of Maddison's started with the crucial importance of capitalism to the Dutch success and he is also rather vague on periodicity. He believes that the "seafaring capitalists of Amsterdam held considerable power," and that the free trade ideology and practices led to capitalists underselling their competitors. He agrees with Maddison and Wallerstein that "Dutch hegemony was based on production capital in lead[ing] industries [such as herring, shipbuilding, and windmills], contrary to those who have seen the Dutch as primarily merchant capitalists." He also recognizes the importance of the imperial forces of armed trade and destruction typical of the Dutch activities especially in Asia, and to some degree in their less successful sites in Latin America and New Amsterdam. The decline of Dutch hegemony, as noted above, was said to be due to the dominance of finance, the export of capital, and capitalists becoming rentiers rather than innovators in the late 1600s and 1700s.

Peter Taylor (1996, chap. 2) follows Maddison and Chase-Dunn in recognizing the United Provinces as the "first bourgeois society," which is viewed as "a functioning social collectivity based upon economic linkages." Key aspects of this bourgeois society are said to be, first, the transportation system, especially the role of canals linking "goods, information and people between 30 cities throughout the country to produce a single, large integrated economic space" (p. 48). The second core part of the Dutch system was its federal or confederate system oriented around strong local institutions and a central system of governance specializing in defense. As he said: "This specialized activity was 'subcontracted' out to the House of Orange [which] recruited a mercenary army to do the business. This proved very efficient and effective: for rival states war was a burden creating perennial fiscal crises; for the United Provinces it was an unfortunate but necessary part of the budget" (p. 52). Defense was thus a core industry, where the Dutch were able to often fight at sea, or in the southern part of the low countries, or otherwise "the dikes would be opened, and the core of the United Provinces was converted into 'a fortified island'" (p. 52). This strategic defensive amalgam was said to work all through the era of Dutch hegemony.

While being a pacifist state domestically, the third part of the Dutch success was said to be its foreign and trade policy, where it supposedly employed the balance of power theory. While being hegemonic economically, the Dutch along with some other powers established a series of rolling alliances to ensure they were not dominated by any one power militarily. This enhanced Dutch power ever while it could pursue global trade while not antagonizing other European powers excessively. Taylor, however, goes too far in abstracting from the role of the Dutch East India Company in systematically engaging in genocide in the Banda Islands (East Indies) during 1921, destroying much of the cultural heritage of many areas in especially south-(east) Asia through their monopolization and monoculture policies, and many other practices, such as the massacre in Ambon Island (East Indies) where the VOC executed ten English, numerous

Japanese and Portuguese agents and thereby negated Anglo-Dutch accord in the area while enhancing Dutch power.

Arrighi (1993, chap. 6) is the only one of these five "hegemony" authors to mention the Little Ice Age. But since this article was written before the pathbreaking work of Parker (2017), Arrighi denigrates its importance in amplifying the socioeconomic crises of the 1600s, and thereby its importance for Dutch hegemony in reducing their impact on the United Provinces. Like all the above authors, first, Arrighi emphasizes the importance of the capitalist class in leading and engendering Dutch hegemony. He gives priority to the "liquidation" of the medieval system of rule and its replacement by a "modern inter-state system" and capitalism as a world system, under the leadership of the "Dutch capitalist oligarchy," which was based on "commercial and financial networks that [were] … carved out of the seaborne and colonial empires" (p. 162–163). Arrighi argues that financial networks were more important to Dutch hegemony than merely commercial networks, and thereby rather than being limited by trade competition they could rearrange their portfolio to ensure continuity of financial flows through speculation (e.g., buying at low prices and selling at high prices), thus enhancing the margin and turnover of profit.

Arrighi also argues that the capitalist oligarchy specialized in promoting a system of governance where commercial and financial arrangements were protected from wars and other conflicts. Their general interest was said to be in promoting peace, at least domestically, and moderating wars through alliances, accords, and truces wherever possible. The Dutch were leaders not only in the accumulation of capital and profitability but also in rationalizing military techniques, a theme also covered by Taylor. Governance activated especially by or through the Prince of Orange incorporated some old ideas adopted by the Romans. Especially notable were the practices of scientific management of wars through siege techniques to enhance efficiency, cut costs, and maintain discipline. The standardization of marching, loading, and firing, as well as incorporating drills into daily practices, and divisions into smaller tactical units, along with enhancing the role of normal and non-commissioned officers, improved their effectiveness in war. These are crucial insights to make given the intensity of wars during the Dutch Golden Age, long waves, hegemony, and climate change eras.

These writings variously reinforce my thesis about capitalism in Holland (all the writings), hegemony between 1620 and 1650 (Kwon), and Dutch innovation in warfare (Arrighi). We are thus able to isolate the best Dutch long wave upswings during the 1570s–1610s and hegemony 1620–1650, indicating that long wave upswings can help propel the forces of hegemony, but need not coincide perfectly with eras of hegemony. But can hegemonic power operate during a decade of crisis, warfare, and depression (1620s), or should we date absolute hegemony during the 1630s–1660s (and/or 1570–1610s)? All this while the world, especially the Northern Hemisphere and notably Europe, underwent major crises associated with the Little Ice Age, when especially extremely wetter and windier as well as colder temperatures helped to generate social crises, uprisings, wars, famines, floods, and pandemics. The Dutch were, as argued, the most reliant of all in managing these instabilities and crises while being experts in climate control and management.

5.6 Conclusion

The purpose of this chapter has been to outline the key features of the dynamic Dutch socioeconomic circuit, to explain the nature of the Dutch Golden Age, and to illustrate the dynamics of Dutch hegemony, long wave growth patterns and climate change during the late 1500s, 1600s, and to some degree through to 2022. We found that the Golden Age, long wave upswings, hegemony, and climate change patterns were dependent upon the effective organization of the CSD but that contradictions eventually led to the relative dissolution of the Golden Age, hegemony, and overall performance.

Throughout the 1500s and 1600s, much of the world experienced the Little Ice Age, which the Dutch managed very well through a series of innovations and adjustments which most others were unable to do. It is perhaps in this context that we can understand the Dutch Golden Age as primarily a phenomenon of Dutch resilience in the face of crises other nations were mostly unable to tolerate well. This resilience and effective innovations were also apparent during the persistent wars that the Dutch were battling, where they managed to succeed in moderating Spanish, English, and other incursions into their territory for about 50 years or more. Globally they managed to effectively gain powerful monopolies and trade restrictions, especially in Asia, and to some degree in the Americas, and elsewhere, through various agreements, wars, and massacres, but their efforts to gain a permanent foothold in important areas of the Americas failed.

During the early years, the most pronounced long wave upswing was in the late-1500s, with a much weaker one during the early-1600s when hegemony started to impact. There was a major depression during the 1620s and from the 1630s onwards growth wave upswings were more subdued, but still modestly good into the 1660s, when absolute hegemony was in decline.

The contradictions within these dynamic structures of the circuit came to the fore as the potential for growth and accumulation declined, the Golden Age disappeared, hegemony matured and faltered, and long (and short) waves became much more subdued into the late 1600s and beyond through to the 1810s (with no long wave upswings during this period). The first great capitalist experiment ushered in a period of remarkable optimism and potential, which dissipated and led to a period devoid of hegemonic power and faltering long waves.

This led to a further period of rivalry among the great powers, especially Britain and France, when no hegemony emerged, until finally Waterloo and the Congress of Vienna led to British hegemony into the early to middle 1800s (1820s–1860s). During the period of British hegemony, the Dutch experienced one relatively weak long wave upswing, an experience that was not to be bettered until the onset of US hegemony into the 1940s–1970s when a very long wave upswing emerged for The Netherlands (plus Britain, the US, and many other nations), after which downswing emerged especially in the core and other areas (except Asia) while climate crises were gathering momentum and intensity.

In the next chapter, we scrutinize the period before, during, and after British hegemony, and provide evidence to support a specific pattern of long waves and climate change during these periods for the British, along with their relationships with the periphery and semi-periphery.

In terms of further research, three areas especially stand out. The first relates to the 1620s. More research is required on this decade in terms of how much the Dutch faltered during the depression, which was affected by financial crisis and warfare. Could the Dutch have undergone hegemonic dominance during this period, as a continuation of earlier periods, or did it only emerge afterward (and/or before)? When did and did not the Dutch achieve and lose hegemonic power, specifically? Second, the Dutch were said to have had a large measure of resilience and innovation in the face of the Little Ice Age and continual warfare during the so-called Golden Age. More details concerning this dual resilience would help in understanding their situation. And third, if the Dutch were so successful in terms of their political economy, where were their political economists? Much has been said about lawyers and legal scholars, capitalists, workers, innovators, and governance experts. Did they have people who may be said to have been political economists and who contributed to the understanding of the Dutch Golden Age, hegemony, long wave upswings, and climate change adaptation? Or as seems to be the case from this chapter, did the political economy emanate from some combination of the practical and scientific contributions of the skilled workers, household workers, entrepreneurs, business personnel, merchants, academics, lawyers, public officials, and clerics? Or was there no specific Dutch political economy discourse during the 1500s and 1600s of whatever sort, as seems to be the case, but merely practical policy-making and various forms of governance?

References

Albritton, Robert. 1991. *A Japanese approach to stages of capitalist development*. New York: St Martin's Press.

Arrighi, Giovanni. 1993. The three hegemonies of historical capitalism. In *Gramsci, historical materialism and international relations*, ed. Stephen Gill, 148–185. Cambridge: Cambridge University Press.

Birdsall, Nancy. 1989. Economic analysis of rapid population growth. *Research Observer* 4 (1): 23–50.

Bolt, Jutta and Jan Luiten van Zanden. 2020. *The Maddison project: Maddison style estimates of the evolution of the world economy: A new 2020 update*. Maddison Project Working Paper WP-15.

Boswell, Terry, Joya Misra, and John Brueggemann. 1991. The rise and fall of Amsterdam and Dutch hegemony: Evidence from the Baltic sound tolls. In *Cities in the world system, 55–80*, ed. R. Kasaba. New York: Greenwood.

Boswell, Terry, and Joya Misra. 1995. Cycles and trends in the early capitalist world-economy: An analysis of leading sector commodity trades, 1500-1600/1650-1750. *Review (Fernand Braudel Centre)* 18 (3): 459–485.

Boswell, Terry, and Mike Sweat. 1991. Hegemony, long waves, and major wars: A time series analysis of systemic dynamics, 1496-1967. *International Studies Quarterly* 35:123–149.

Braudel, Fernand. 1979. *The perspective of the world: Civilization and capitalism 15th–18th century, Volume 3*. New York: Harper and Row.
Chase-Dunn, Christopher. 1998. *Global formation: Structures of the world-economy*. 2nd ed. Boulder & New York: Rowman & Littlefield Publishers.
Cardwell, Donald S. L. 1972. *Turning points in Western technology: A study of technology, science and history*. New York: Science History Publications.
Dassbach, Carl H. A., Nurhan Davutyan, Jianking Dong, and Barry Fay. 1995. Long waves prior to 1790s: A modest contribution. *Review (Fernand Braudel Center)* 18 (2): 305–328.
Davids, Karel. 2008. *The rise and decline of Dutch technological leadership: Technology, economy and culture in The Netherlands, 1350–1800*. Vol. 2. Leiden, Netherlands: Brill.
DeGroot, Dagomar. 2018. *The frigid Golden age: Climate change, the little ice age, and the Dutch Republic, 1560–1720*. Cambridge: Cambridge University Press.
DeGroot, Dagomar. 2018a. Climate change, water, and the Golden age of the Dutch Republic. *Europe Now Journal* 12 (10): 1–7.
Dehing, Pit, and Marjolein't Hart. 1997. Linking the fortunes: Currency and banking, 1550-1800. In *A financial history of The Netherlands, 37-63*, ed. Joost Jonker Marjolein 't Hart and Jan Luiten van Zanden. Cambridge: Cambridge University Press.
De Zwart, Pim, and Jan Luiten Van Zanden. 2018. *The origins of globalization: World trade in the making of the global economy, 1500–1800*. Cambridge: Cambridge University Press.
de Vries, Jan. 1999. Luxury and Calvinism/ luxury and capitalism: Supply and demand for luxury goods in the seventeenth-century Dutch Republic. *Journal of the Walters Art Gallery* 57:73–85.
de Vries, Jan. 2003. Luxury in the Dutch Golden age in theory and practice. In *Luxury in the eighteenth century*, ed. M. Berg and E. Eger. London: Palgrave Macmillan. https://doi.org/10.1057/9780230508279_4.
Enthoven, Victor. 2018. Zaanse Jonas: Zaan whaling and shipbuilding in the seventeenth century. In *Navigating history: Economy, society, knowledge, and nature: Essays in honor of prof. Dr C.A. Davids, 123-145*, ed. Pepijn Brandon, Sabine Go, and Wybren Verstegen. Leiden: Brill Publishing.
Foldvari, Peter, Bas van Leeuwen, Jan Luiten, and van Zanden. 2013. The contribution of migration to economic development in Holland 1570-1800. *De Economist* 161:1–18.
Foster, John Bellamy, Hannah Hollman, and Brett Clark. 2020. Marx and Slavery. *Monthly Review* 72 (3): 250–265.
Fouquet, Roger, and Stephen Broadberry. 2015. Seven centuries of European economic growth and decline. *Journal of Economic Perspectives* 29 (4): 227–244.
Frank, Andre Gunder. 1990. A theoretical introduction to 5,000 years of world system history. *Review (Fernand Braudel Centre)* 13 (2): 155–250.
Frank, Andre Gunder, and Barry K. Gills. 1990. *The world system: Five thousand or five hundred?* London & NY: Routledge.
Frank, Andre Gunder. 1998. *ReOrient: Global economy in the Asian age*. Los Angeles: University of California Press.
Frankel, Boris. 1983. *Beyond the state? Dominant theories and socialist strategies*. London: Macmillan.
Freeman, Christopher, and Francisco Louçã. 2001. *As time goes by: From the industrial revolution to the information revolution*. Oxford: OUP.
Goldstein, Joshua. 1988. *Long cycles: Prosperity and war in the modern age*. New Haven: Yale University Press.
Goldstone, Jack A. 2021. Dating the great divergence. *Journal of Global History* 16 (2): 266–285.
Hart, Marjolein't. 1997. The merits of a financial revolution: Public finance, 1550-1700. In *A financial history of The Netherlands, 11-36*, ed. Joost Jonker Marjolein't Hart and Jan Luiten van Zanden. Cambridge: Cambridge University Press.
Hilton, Rodney. 1978. Introduction. In *The transition from feudalism to capitalism*. London: Verso.
Hobsbawm, Eric J. 1954a. The general crisis of the European economy in the 17th century. *Past and Present* 5 (1): 33–53.

Hobsbawm, Eric J. 1954b. The crisis of the 17th century-II. *Past and Present* 6 (1): 44–65.

Israel, Jonathan I. 1989. *Dutch primacy in world trade, 1585–1740*. Oxford: Clarendon Press.

Israel, Jonathan I. 1995. *The Dutch Republic: Its Rise, greatness and fall 1477–1806*. Oxford: Clarendon Press.

Israel, Jonathon. 1998. *The Dutch Republic: Its rise, greatness and fall, 1477–1806*. Oxford: Clarendon Press.

Kaldor, Nicholas. 1972. The irrelevance of equilibrium economics. *Economic Journal* 82 (328): 1237–1255. Reprinted in *the essential* Kaldor, eds. Ferdinando Targetti and Anthony P. Thirlwall. New York: Holmes and Meier, 1989, 373–398.

Kerr, Ian Alexander. 2021. *The relationship between concepts and principles in political economy*. Technical Note.

Kindleberger, Charles P. 1978. *Economic response: Comparative studies in trade, finance, and growth*. Boston: Harvard University Press.

Kindleberger, Charles P. 1991. The economic crisis of 1619-1623. *Journal of Economic History* 51 (1): 149–175.

Kindleberger, Charles, and Robert Z. Aliber. 2015. *Manias, panics and crashes: A history of financial crises*. Hoboken: Wiley.

Kroeber, Alfred L., and Clyde Kluckhohn. 1952. *Culture: A critical review of concepts and definitions*, 47. Cambridge, MA: Harvard University Peabody Museum of American Archeology and Ethnology Papers No.

Kuznets, Simon. 1966. *Modern economic growth: Rate, structure and spread*. New Haven, Connecticut: Yale University Press.

Kwon, Roy. 2011. Hegemonies in the world-system: An empirical assessment of hegemonic sequences from the 16th to 20th century. *Sociological Perspectives* 54 (4): 593–617.

Leitner, Jonathan. 2007. An incorporated comparison: Fernand Braudel's account of Dutch hegemony in a world-ecological perspective. *Review (Fernand Braudel Centre)* 30 (2): 97–135.

Maddison, Angus. 1991. *Dynamic forces in capitalist development: A long-run comparative view*. Oxford: Oxford University3 Press.

Maddison, Angus. 2007. *Contours of the world economy 1-2030 AD: Essays in macro-economic history*. Oxford: Oxford University Press.

Maddison Project. 2024. *GDP per capita data*. Maddison historical statistics project. Groningen Growth and Development Centre | University of Groningen (rug.nl).

Mahbubani, Kistore. 2022. *The Asian 21st century*. Singapore: Springer.

Marx, Karl. 1867. Capital: The process of production of capital. Harmondsworth: Penguin, 1976. Introduction by Ernest Mandel.

Mayhew, Anne. 1994. Culture. In *The Elgar companion to institutional and evolutionary economics*, ed. Geoffrey M. Hodgson, Warren J. Samuels, and Marc R. Tool, 115–119. Cheltenham: Edward Elgar.

Mokyr, Joel. 1994. Cardwell's law and the political economy of technological Progress. *Research Policy* 23:561–574.

Mokyr, Joel. 2017. *Culture and institutions: The origins of the modern economy*. Princeton, NJ: Princeton University Press.

Mokyr, Joel, Avner Greif, and Guido Tabellini. Forthcoming. *Two paths to prosperity: Culture and institutions in Europe and China, 1200–2000*. Princeton, NJ: Princeton University Press.

O'Brien, Patrick Karl. 2000. Mercantilism and imperialism in the rise and decline of the Dutch and British economies 1585-1815. *De Economist* 148 (4): 469–501.

O'Connor, James. 1984. *Accumulation crisis*. New York: Blackwell.

O'Hara, Phillip Anthony. 2000. *Marx, Veblen, and contemporary institutional political economy principles and unstable dynamics of capitalism*. Edward Elgar: Cheltenham, UK.

O'Hara, Phillip Anthony. 2001. Circuit of social capital. In *Encyclopedia of political economy, 84–87*, ed. P. A. O'Hara. London and New York: Routledge.

O'Hara, Phillip Anthony. 2006. *Growth and development in the global political economy: Modes of regulation and social structures of accumulation*. London: Routlege. Paper Edition 2009.

O'Hara, Phillip Anthony. 2023. *Principles of institutional and evolutionary political economy: Applied to current world problems*. Singapore: Springer Nature. Revised Edition.

O'Hara, Phillip Anthony. 2010. After neoliberalism: A social structure of accumulation or mode of regulation for global or regional performance? *Journal of Economic Issues*, 44(2): 369-384. https://doi.org/10.2753/JEI0021-3624440209

Olson, Mancur. 1965. *The logic of collective action: Public goods and the theory of groups*. Boston: Harvard University Press, 1971. Revised Edition.

Paping, Richard. (2014). *General Dutch population development 1400–1850: Cities and countryside*. Conference paper. General Dutch population development 1400–1850: Cities and countryside (rug.nl).

Parker, Geoffrey, and Lesley M. Smith, eds. 1978. *The general crisis of the seventeenth century*. 2nd ed. London & New York: Routledge.

Parker, Geoffrey. 2018. *Global crisis: War, climate change and catastrophe in the seventeenth century*. Abridged & Revised Edition. New Haven: Yale University Press.

Parthesius, Robert. 2010. *Dutch ships in tropical waters: The development of the Dutch East India company (VOC) shipping network in Asia*. Amsterdam: Amsterdam University Press.

Prak, Maarten. 2023. *The Dutch Republic in the seventeenth century*. 3rd ed. Cambridge: Cambridge University Press.

Prak, Maarten, Jan Luiten, and van Zanden. 2023. *Pioneers of capitalism: The Netherlands 1000–1800*. Princeton: Princeton University Press.

Raa, Thijs ten, Pierre Mohnen, Jan Luiten van Zanden, and Bas van Leeuwen. 2009. Invention, entrepreneurship and prosperity: The Dutch Golden age. *SSRN Electronic Journal* 2009.

Reijnders, Jan P. G. 2009. Trend movements and inverted Kondratieff waves in the Dutch economy, 1800-1913. *Structural Change and Economic Dynamics* 20 (1): 90–113.

Research Working Group [on Cyclical Rhythms and Secular Trends]. 1979. (Coordinated by Terrence K. Hopkins and Immanuel Wallerstein.). Cyclical Rhythms and Secular Trends of the Capitalist World-Economy: Some Premises, Hypotheses, and Questions. *Review (Fernand Braudel Centre)* 2 (4): 483–500.

Smits, J.P., E. Horlings and J.L. van Zanden (2000). *The Measurement of Gross National Product and its Components 1800–1913*. Groningen Growth and Development Centre Monograph series no 5.

Spengler, Oswald. 1923. *Decline of the West*. 2 vols. Petoskey, Michigan: Random Shack, 2016. Translated from the German by David G. Payne.

Steensgaard, Niels. 1978. The seventeenth-century crisis. In *The general crisis of the seventeenth century*, ed. Geoffrey Parker and Lesley Smith, 32–56. London & New York: Routledge.

Taylor, Peter J. 1996. *The way the modern world works: World hegemony to world impasse*. New York: Wiley.

Tellis, Gerard, and Stav Rosenzweig. 2018. The Fluyt and the Building of the Dutch Empire. In Gerard and Rosenzweig. In *How transformative innovations shaped the rise of nations: From ancient Rome to Modern America, 157–176*. Cambridge: Cambridge University Press.

Trevor-Roper, Hugh. 1967. *The crisis of the seventeenth century: Religion, the reformation and social change*. Indianapolis: The Liberty Fund.

Van Gelderen, Martin. 1992. *The political thought of the Dutch Revolt 1555–1590*. Cambridge: Cambridge University Press.

Van Zanden, Jan Luiten. 2009. *The long road to the industrial revolution: The European economy in a global perspective, 1000–1800*. Leiden & Boston: Brill Publishing. (Ch. 4 is written with Tine de Moor)

Van Zanden, Jan Luiten, and Bas Van Leeuwen. 2012. Persistent but not consistent: The growth of national income in Holland 1347–1807. *Explorations in Economic History* 49:119–130.

Van Zanden, Jan Luiten, and Jutta Bolt. 2021. Two concerns about the interpretation of the estimates of historical national accounts before 1850. *Journal of Global History* 16 (2): 294–300.

Veblen, Thorstein Bunde. 1899. *The theory of the leisure class: An economic study of institutions*. London: Macmillan.

Veblen, Thorstein Bunde. 1914. The instinct of workmanship and the state of the industrial arts. London: Macmillan.

Wallerstein, Immanuel. 1974. *The modern world-system I: Capitalist agriculture and the origins of the European-world economy in the sixteenth century*. New York: Academic Press.

Wallerstein, Immanuel. 1980. *The modern world-system II: Mercantilism and the consolidation of the European world-economy, 1600–1750*. New York: Academic Press.

Wallerstein, Immanuel. 1982. Dutch hegemony in the seventeenth-century world economy. In *Dutch Capitalism and World Capitalism: Capitalisme Hollandais and Capitalisme Mondial, 93-146*, ed. Maurice Aymard. London: Cambridge University Press.

Wallerstein, Immanuel. 1983. The three instances of hegemony in the history of the capitalist world-economy. *International Journal of Comparative Sociology* 24 (1-2): 100–108. https://doi.org/10.1163/156854283X00071.

Wallerstein, Immanuel. 1990. World-system analysis: The second phase. *Review (Fernand Braudel Centre)* 13 (2): 287–293.

Wilson, C. H. 1939. The economic decline of the Netherlands. *Economic History Review* 9 (2): Reprinted in E.M. Carus-Wilson, ed., *Essays in Economic History: Volume One*. London: Edward Arnold, 1954:254–269.

Wilson, Eric. 2008. *The savage Republic: 'De Indis' of Hugo Grotius, republicanism, and dutch hegemony within the early modern world-system (c. 1600-1619)*. Leiden and Boston: Martinus Nijhoff Publishers.

Chapter 6
British Long Waves, Hegemonic Power, and Climate Change

Abstract This chapter examines the record of long-term growth per capita, and other variables, for the British economy from the late 1500s through to the 2020s, with a view to scrutinizing those periods when long-wave upswings were in line with hegemonic forces, and the way in which climate change linked to these processes. We find two periods when *long-term growth* per capita was above average and associated with *very long-wave upswings*. One of these spurts of long-wave upswing overlapped with British hegemony during the 1820s–1860s. The climate change pattern is complex, with the first half of the 1800s experiencing cooling or constant temperatures, and the second half heating. A more upbeat long-wave upswing occurred during US hegemony (1950s–1980s), and afterward, when long-wave downswing emerged during US relative hegemony, climate change crises operated along with other polycrises.

We seek to understand why these good wave upswings occurred during periods of hegemony. Special attention is then given to the late 1700s through to the late 1800s when the British Pathways and Circuits of Socioeconomic Dynamics (CSD) were forming and developing sufficiently to promote long upswings and hegemony. Much of the chapter outlines the nature of this CSD, comprising global, state, geo-ecological, technological, financial, and household relationships. We then seek to comprehend why CSD declined and how it impacted growth and hegemony. The chapter ends with a discussion of the decline of British hegemony into the late 1800s and early 1900s, through to the later episode of US hegemony and its demise, plus the start of the Asian (especially Chinese) rise.

Keywords British hegemony · Long waves · Pathways and Circuits of Socioeconomic Dynamics (CSD) · Industrial Revolution · Institutions and technologies · Climate change · Rise and fall · Structural polycrises · Principles

P. A. O'Hara, *Long Waves of Growth, Hegemonic Power, and Climate Change in the World Economy*, https://doi.org/10.1007/978-981-96-4132-1_6

6.1 Introduction

The purpose of this chapter is to outline the relationship between British long waves, hegemony, and climate change during the 1500s–2020s. We are also interested in how the British experience affected and was affected by the performance of other nations and areas in the core–periphery dynamics.

6.2 British Growth and Hegemony Pattern 1570–2022

British decadal annual average annual growth per capita (AAGR) patterns for 1570–2022 are shown in Figs. 6.1 and 6.2. I first explain, briefly, my schematic configuration of long waves, hegemony, and climate change. The method is the same as with the Dutch data analytics from Chap. 5. Embedded in these figures is the following method (see Glossary for "New Long-Wave Method"). First, I calculate the patterns of real Gross Domestic Product (GDP) per capita (growth rates [AAGR]) averaged over the decades (1570–2022) and plot the results. Second, I encapsulate a trend line (using the least squares regression method), and convert it to a bar (20 units wide), moving through the time series data. The purpose of the trend bar is to use it as a filter to differentiate between trend and wave so that the

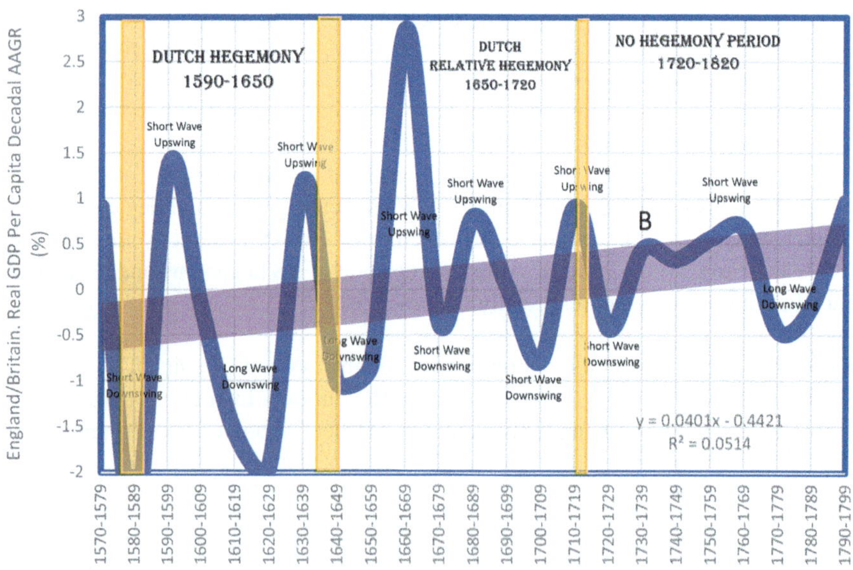

Fig. 6.1 British decadal growth of real GDP per capita (AAGR), percent. 1570–1799 (blue bar). Borderline linear trend bar (purple). No Absolute Hegemony (circa 1650–1820). (Source: Adapted from raw figures of Maddison Project (2024). A similar method of wave and trend analysis is used by Conroy and Emerson (2007). ($y = 0.0401x-0.4421$; $R^2 = 0.0514$ is for the trend *line*)

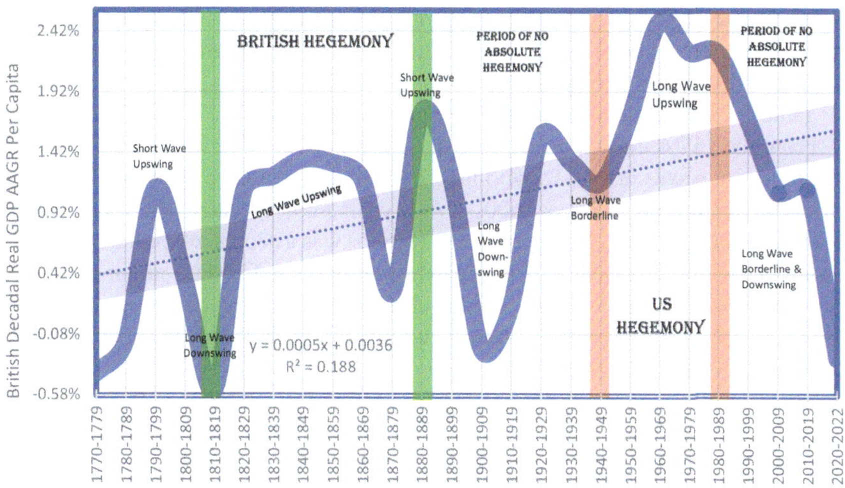

Fig. 6.2 British decadal growth of real GDP per capita (AAGR) 1770–2022 (blue bar). (Purple bar includes the linear trend.) (Source: Adapted from raw figures of the Maddison Project (2024))

trend bar can be used to ascertain the periods of (long-wave) upswing and downswing (which deviate from the trend bar) plus borderline conditions (within the trend bar area). This method enables us to filter the trend out of the picture and concentrate on the deviations from the trend when growth was above, below, or equal to the trend bar.[1]

In this context, I am especially interested in four things. First, a longish (durable) period of upswing in real annual GDP growth per capita averaged over successive decades. Second, certain buoyant amplitude of upswing. Third, a longish period of downswing. Fourth, certain amplitude of downswing. In the traverse of these ups and downs, the data will move through borderline performance. Since capabilities build up over time, long waves are required to be temporally contingent to some degree. The further one moves from the 1500s to the 2020s, the *more* growth is required to be considered a long-wave upswing, for two reasons. First, because, as the rising trend especially toward more recent hegemonic times illustrates, there is a buildup of higher capabilities in the long term; and second, as has been suggested by van Zanden et al. (2012, 2021), earlier years likely underestimate growth figures somewhat.[2]

The durable and buoyant periods of growth per capita indicate that the institutions, technologies, and geospatial ecologies are contributing to sustainable performance at the structural level; they especially put a higher floor on performance,

[1] I am hence less interested in the trend bar correlation; in fact, we usually have a low correlation, so we can ascertain when deviations (amplitudes) may be considered long-wave upswings or downswings (or borderline performance).

[2] Van Zanden was referring to the Dutch statistics, of which he is an expert. But this point is also likely to apply to the British data as well, for similar reasons (insufficient information).

potentially a higher ceiling, and contribute to sustainable growth. For instance, a sudden high (short) upswing and sudden low downswing (volatility) do not indicate a sustainable level of performance.

Table 6.1 summarizes the results of Figs. 6.1 and 6.2.

From the 1570s through to the 1810s, British growth underwent mostly decadal up and down waves or cycles, with the 1660s (one short-wave upswing) being the most buoyant decade of those 1600s–1700s years until the early 1800s. The 1700s through to the end of the Napoleonic Wars (1815) was a depressive period with little notable growth performance (short upswings at best) and several major wars. For the 1500s–1810s, nothing resembled well-formed high and durable long waves (upswings) as they were mostly short-wave changes from decade to decade with no period of long-wave upswing.

These results confirm all the specific "long-wave/hegemony hypotheses" of this study. That is, the ratio of upswings to downswings/borderlines is highest during times of British hegemony (1820–1889), and when Britain benefits from the hegemonic dynamics of closely related allies (e.g., USA during the postwar Golden Age 1950s–1980s). In this context, Britain also benefited *slightly* from Dutch hegemony as both were part of the North Sea performance enhancement impact (during the 1570s–1650). British performance was also modestly reasonable, for merely a decade, when Dutch hegemony began to decline (as an indication that the British were long-term threats to the Dutch).

From the 1720s to the 1810s, there was very subdued growth per capita, at a time when Britain was supposed to be undergoing the "First Industrial Revolution," either from 1760–1820 or 1790–1820 (depending on author(s)), but where especially war debt, notably the Revolutionary and Napoleonic Wars, was crowding out industrial investment and consumer demand. This conclusion that Britain underwent no adequate long waves (especially not sustained upswings), and certainly not yet hegemonic power, during these periods is reinforced by much data and historical sources.

After the Napoleonic Wars, Britain underwent 50 years of long-wave upswing, during the 1820s–1860s, the most sustainable and buoyant of the whole pre-1940s period, and this overlaps with the period during which Britain achieved hegemonic dominance: *Pax Britannica* (1815–1880s). Growth per capita was very durable since periodicity (length of the wave) was impressive, the *durable* structures of the CSD were well organized, even if significantly contradictory. Amplitude (in the upwards direction) was modest because several contradictory limits were ingrained in the eco-spatial, technological, and institutional CSD. (See details further below.)

Overall, as Thomas E. Lambert (2020) showed, during the early 1800s to 1860s, for Britain, the economic surplus[3] per capita rose majorly by around 33% (while it declined slightly from 45% to 38% of NNI, which rose majorly), capital income (as a proportion of NNI) rose just less than half, capital income divided by rental

[3] The economic surplus (S) is defined by Lambert (2024, 1384).

Table 6.1 Long waves "Map," ratio of upswing to borderline and downswing performance, England/Britain, 1570–2022 (452 Years)

1570–1649 (80 yrs)	1650–1719 (70 yrs)	1720–1819 (100 yrs)	1820–1889 (70 yrs)	1890–1939 (50 yrs)	1940–1989 (50 yrs)	1990–2022 (33 yrs)
During/close to Dutch absolute hegemony	Relative Dutch hegemony	No hegemony era	British absolute hegemony	No absolute hegemony	US hegemony: Absolute	US relative hegemony
SWU 30 yrs. (1570s) (1590s) (1630s)	SWU 30 yrs. (1660s) (1680s) (1710s)	SWU 20 yrs. (1760s) (1790s)	LWU 50 yrs. (1820–1869)	SWU 10 yrs (1920s)	LWU 40 yrs. (1950–1989)	
SWB (1600s)	SWB 10 yrs. (1690s)	LWB 30 yrs. (1730s–1750s)	SWU 10 yrs. (1880s)	SWUB 10 yrs (1890s)	½LWB 20 yrs (1930s–1940s) =10 yrs	SWB 10 yrs. (1990s)
SWD 10 yrs. (1580s)	SWD 20 yrs. (1670s) (1700s)	SWD 10 yrs. (1720s)	SWD 10 yrs. (1870s)	½LWB 20 yrs (1930s–1940s) =10 yrs		LWD 23 yrs. (2000–2022)
LWD 30 yrs. (1610–1629) ½(1640–1659)	LWD 10 yrs. ½(1640–1659)	LWD 40 yrs. (1770s–1780s) (1800s–1810s)		LWD 20 yrs. (1900s–1910s)		
30 U/50D = 0.60	**30 U/40BD = 0.75**	**20 U/80BD = 0.25**	**60 U/10D = 6.00**	**10/40 = 0.25**	**40 U/10B = 4.00**	**00 U/33D=**

Note: *U* upswing, *D* downswing, *B* borderline, *LWU* long-wave upswing, *LWD* long-wave downswing, *SWU* short-wave upswing, *SWD* short-wave downswing, *DB* on border of D and B

income rose from 1.5 to about 4.2, wages (divided by the economic surplus) rose about 30%, and the Baran Ratio (investment/economic surplus) also increased from about 2 to 3. In short, capitalism was evolving, the bourgeoisie was productively investing, and some workers were better off[4] (while rentier income was likely not thriving). Some of the increase in investment (the core part of the surplus) occurred between 1780 and1810 (from £70 m to £190 m), but the major investment expansion occurred between 1810 and 1860 (from £190 m to £715 m) (Lambert 2023, 6). However, all was not rosy, see further below, as the recovery from the wars took some time, there were significant, especially decadal downswings (recessions), and some workers were not well off during much of this time.

The first period when long waves operated, from the 1800s (downswing) to the 1870s (downswing) (from lower turning point [LTP] to lower turning point), is within the period of Wallerstein's dating of British hegemony (1815–1885). This is done by dating long waves from floor to floor, with LWU occurring during the 1820s–1860s. This is a period when short- or long-wave downswings are modest on both sides of the LWU, indicating buoyant growth conditions with few negative downswings (but see more on the "first Great Depression" of 1873–1996 below). 1820–1870 is a much more robust and stable period of long-term growth than the earlier British waves of the 1650s–1710s, which (as mentioned) were erratic periods. In a sense, the 1810s–1870s long wave was the very first classically durable very long wave for British capitalism with a high floor and modest ceiling. As mentioned, even this successful long-wave–hegemony–climate change trio had its limitations and contradictions (discussed later), since while it was durable, it was not especially buoyant in terms of amplitude.[5]

Later we examine the hypothesis of the "first Great Depression [GD1] of 1873-1996," but briefly, even though Fig. 6.2 does not indicate GD1 occurred in Britain, other indicators do support a borderline performance (for 1873–1993). If so, this indicates evidence not quite in favor of the standard model during the 1870s–1890s (due to borderline performance; no systemic downswing), but more pertinently indicates lower performance during periods of no hegemon. During the 1870s–1940s, the old pattern of volatility reemerged in successive decadal waves of upswing followed by downswing, with again poor overall performance, two world wars, along with major hegemonic decline (structural polycrises).

---

[4] John L. Brooke (2014, 476) documented his statements that: "By a host of measures the living conditions of British laboring peoples at best stalled during these opening decades of the First Industrial Revolution. Real wages did not rise until 1820, then increased only very slightly, and did not grow consistently until the 1870s. These wages were inadequate to support high-fertility families, leading to serious increases of infant mortality in British cities during the 1830s and 1840s, reflected in higher mortality rates in the cities than in the country as a whole."

[5] Comparing the recessions during 1780–1820 (40 years, 30 years of downswing and 10 years of upswing) and 1820–1860 (40 years, long-wave upswing), according to the research of Broadberry et al. (2023), in terms of how many recessions and how deep they were. During Britain in 1780–1820, there were 12 recessions, with four of them being very deep (over 4% decline in output); whereas in 1820–1860, there were eight recessions, with two of them being deep. Overall, therefore, recessionary periods were 50% worse in 1780–1820 than during 1820–1860.

The British case deviated from the standard model in the following ways. First, Britain did not undergo a long-wave upswing (1780/90–1810s) and did not experience a long downswing (1820s–1840s) during the so-called First Kondratieff downswing. Instead, it underwent a short-wave upswing during the 1790s, long-wave downswing in 1800–1819 plus a long-wave upswing during the 1820s–1860s. Second, it did not undergo long-wave upswing during the late-1890s–1913; instead, while it did have strong growth during the late 1890s, it experienced long-wave downswing during the 1900–1913 period. Third, as distinct from the standard model, good growth occurred during the 1920s, and while the Great Depression did occur during the early 1930s, Britain rebounded strongly from the depression later in the 1930s.

The other period of above-average growth for Britain, the 1950s–1980s (consistent with the standard model), was much more impressive than the 1820s–1860s hegemony era. This was due, as noted, to US hegemony (see chap. 7 below), including the Marshall Plan to assist European nations recover from the Second World War and help prevent "communist" expansion. Also, the postwar Golden Age (circa 1950s–1970s) was an era of "Western dominance," and the greatest era of growth and development for much of the world in the whole history of capitalism. Britain thus benefited from the public goods and network effects of the huge expansion and long-wave upswing for much of the world, as did the Netherlands and many other nations.

During this period, most major economies underwent the transition from downswing and borderline (and short upswing) during the 1910s/1930s–1940s to LWU during the 1950s–1980s, followed by LWD thereafter (1990s–2020s). The British, Dutch, US, and many other nations broadly fit this dynamic, as they moved from the postwar corporate system (LWU) through to neoliberalism and then the neoliberalism experience of the Global Financial Crisis (GFC), Eurocrisis, climate change, pandemic, and pre-(world-)war polycrises.

To some degree following the demise in performance, during the 1990s–2020s, climate change has been accelerating, and more recently has been on the cusp of several cascading tipping points which will likely see average global temperatures of well above 2.0 °C (since pre-industrial times) by 2100. The 2023 annual average global temperature was 1.45 ± 0.12 °C above pre-industrial levels (compared with the 1850–1900 average), according to the World Meteorological Organization (WMO 2024), due to several interacting climate processes (including El Nino, ACAPS 2023) and especially climate change exacerbating several major ecological and political crises and emergencies (see chaps. 4 and 9). Britain, along with many other nations, suffered the excesses of the GFC (especially affecting the core) and the corona crisis (global), along with decadal crises since the 1980s–1990s.

Some stress should also be placed on another major hypothesis of this book, which has been mentioned but not stressed so far in this chapter. Between the period of absolute British hegemony (circa 1820s–1870s) and US hegemony (circa 1940s–1970s), i.e., 1880s–1930s, were periods when growth performance was generally underperforming, and major instabilities, depressions, and world wars occurred (structural polycrises). This fact provides prima facie evidence for the hegemonic stability hypothesis (HSH), namely, that the world economy can be greatly assisted by having (certain types of) hegemonic powers (or hegemonic areas or groups) to provide durable global and international public goods to assist in the building of also impressive domestic institutions, technologies, and ecologies for wave upswings. The hypothetical alternative to hegemony is multilateral embedded institutions (MEI) and regimes of accumulation that are suitable substitutes for hegemonic stability, providing required public goods of lender of last resort, treaties to generate peace and agreement, plus financial, energy, and other regimes to generate stable environments, to build capabilities. (See, e.g., Keohane 1984, Gilpin 2001). Currently, for most continents, this hypothesized option of multilateral embedded institutions is not evident to any major degree (without hegemony) into the 2020s, nor in recent decades, nor in any era of capitalist development since the 1600s. We investigate in Chap. 8 whether Chinese hegemony may develop through a multidimensional view of performance.

During the 1990s, a major decline in GDP per capita growth started, and this decline got worse into the 2000s, 2010s, and 2020s. According to the linear trend, this decline was a combination of borderline and downswing performance, but regardless of the categories, it was a major downswing in activity. This was also the predominant pattern in much of the rest of the western world (and much elsewhere, see Chap. 11), although the long-wave upswing and slump in Britain occurred a decade after many other nations. This performance is contrasted with the buoyant performance of Asia (especially China) and a few other nations, notably during the 1990s, 2000s, and 2010s.

6.3 Other Performance Measures 1760–1901

It needs to be detailed somewhat, first, why there was no classic long-wave dynamic for Britain during what some call the first Industrial *Revolution* of 1760s–1810s, including the hypothetical standard model long-wave upswing (e.g., 1780s/1790s–1810s) followed by downswing (1820s–1840s). Why was the period 1720s–1810s lacking in sustainable long-term socioeconomic performance (long-wave upswings)? And why were the 1820s–1840s devoid of long-wave downswings (or even borderline conditions)? Gallegati et al. (2015) show there to be standard model *price*-long waves for the UK during the late 1700s to the 2000s (see Sect. 6.6 for more information on this), but our analysis above showed this not to be true for real growth per capita for many periods, including the 1780s–1810s.

During the period 1773–1783 (American Revolutionary Wars), 1791–1802 (French Revolutionary Wars), and 1803–1815 (Napoleonic Wars), Britain was engaged in a whole series of conflicts, which stretched their resources and increased especially government debt. During this time, the only reasonable growth in Britain was during the 1790s short-wave upswing, as all other decades were downswing. Yet the 1780s/1790s to the 1810s were seen as a long-wave upswing for Britain in the standard model. Why the discrepancy between the standard model and the evidence?

On the low growth rates, or forces negatively impacting growth, we have much evidence. Take, for instance, the study by Jeffrey G. Williamson, as summarized in Table 6.2, below.

Five conclusions emerge from this data. The first conclusion of Williamson is that the Revolutionary and Napoleonic Wars and related processes severely hampered long-term growth during the 1790s–1815. The second is that these negative impacts were significantly worse during 1790–1815 than during the 1760s–1810s, the former period being the usual long-wave upswing periodicity for Britain during the (so-called first) Industrial Revolution. The third is that the negative impacts of the Wars on British *manufacturing exports* were twice as negative during 1790–1815 than during the 1760s–1810s. Harley (1999, 203) confirms this. Fourth, regarding industrialization, the wars (especially the rising relative prices for agricultural goods) had a much worse impact during 1790–1815 than during the whole period; and thereby majorly inhibited performance especially during an era when supposedly industrialization was higher than average.

According to Williamson, Britain at peace would have enhanced economic growth by 1.51% during each of the years 1790–1815 (0.96% for each year during the 1760s–1810s), while peace would have increased real average wages by 1.21% per year during 1790–1810 (0.84% each year on average during the 1760s–1810s). The counterfactual "Peace Dividend" growth would have comprised greater investment (accumulation) worth 0.94% during each year 1790–1815 (0.68% for each year of 1760s–1810s); and no war-generated price effects are worth annual average growth of 0.59% per year for 1790–1815 (0.30% each year of the 1760s–1810s). The Peace Dividend would have counterfactually promoted major annual average growth of manufacturing, home services, and mining-quarrying, but a major drop in agriculture in both periods, plus expansions in industrialization and manufacturing (notably during 1790–1815). As Williamson states:

> One of the strangest features of the period [1760-1820] is ... the failure of the standard of living of the working classes to rise much[,] until the 1820s. ... [Our results] suggest ... that most of the dismal standard of living performance before the 1820s can be attributed to wars and their financing. Peace would have raised the growth of workers' living standards by 0.84% per year [over 1760-1815]. ... Slow accumulation and thus slow rates of job creation (especially in cities) account for most of the poor performance in living standards up to the 1820s, although war induced price-distortions played a major supporting role. ... [C]rowding-out and forgone accumulation also account for most of the slow aggregate growth, but it does not account for a large share of slow industrialization. Prices and world markets played a far greater role. [Williamson 1984, 711.]

These data and other references cast doubt on the notion that Britain underwent a sudden structural transformation during the late 1700s which ushered in an Industrial Revolution *and high growth*. The conventional view now is that it was a much slower growth during the 1600s, through to the 1700s and the early 1800s. It is thus likely that the institutional and technological changes that generated much higher levels of growth, accumulation, and profit in Britain were also relatively

Table 6.2 British counterfactual peace growth dividends, 1760s–1810s, yearly growth rates (mean, percentage change)

Variable	Period/ Sector counterfactual	No war debt crowd-out. *dK* *Counterfactual* (% increase)	No mobilization effects. *dL* Counterfactual (% increase)	No war distorted price effects. *dP* *Counterfactual* (% increase)	All effects combined. *Counterfactual* (% increase)
Real wages	1790–1815	0.94%	−0.27%	0.59%	1.27%
	1760s–1810s	0.68	−0.13	0.30	0.84
Real income	1790–1815	0.93	0.13	0.46	1.51
	1760s–1810s	0.67	0.06	0.23	0.96
Sectoral outputs: 1790–1815	*dA*	0.40	0.34	−2.76	−2.05
	dM	1.14	0.02	2.93	4.09
	dC	1.13	0.09	0.70	1.93
	dB	1.14	0.02	2.82	3.98
Sectoral outputs: 1760s–1810s	*dA*	0.29	0.15	−1.38	−0.94
	dM	0.82	0.01	1.47	2.30
	dC	0.81	0.05	0.35	1.21
	dB	0.82	0.01	1.31	2.24
Manufactures exports:	1790–1815	1.59	−0.56	11.92	12.95
	1760s–1810s	1.14	−0.28	5.96	6.82
Industrialization index: *dM-dA*	1790–1815	0.74	−0.32	5.69	6.14
	1760s–1810s	0.53	−0.14	2.85	3.24

Source: Adapted from Jeffrey G. Williamson (1984, 709)

medium-paced in development. The hegemony that Britain developed through the period 1820–1880 also overlapped with the first truly sustainable and long-lasting long waves (1820s–1860s).

There has been much debate about wars and their financial crowding out of industrial investment and related matters. Some have questioned the degree of crowding out, such as Heim and Mirowski (1987), who state that there is not good annual data on savings and investment for the period, that the empirical links between real interest rates and accumulation are weak, and that investment is associated with retained earnings and the "web of credit," including trade credit and other payment avenues (see Heim and Mirowski 1991; Black and Gilmore 1990). Temin and Voth (2005) point out that British banks engaged in credit rationing, such that when war was imminent (during the late 1700s), banks anticipated customers transferring funds into government bonds used to finance the war, and banks decreased liquidity and thereby tightened credit. In this circulatory sense, they say government spending on war crowded out liquid funds and thereby reduced investment and growth.

Patrick O'Brien (1992, 2011), using extensive knowledge of history (and lateral thinking), implies that growth may have been slow during the so-called first Industrial Revolution (1760–1820), but that government spending on the war was crucial for the subsequent expansion of accumulation, growth, circulation of funds, and hegemony that Britain acquired and utilized for their global machinery of the empire during the rest of the 1800s. Government financing of war is said to have contributed to the development of a highly sophisticated and globally dominant financial apparatus via the institutional workings of the City of London and its affiliates around the world (Kindleberger 1974). Being able to defeat Napoleon also led, via the *Congress of Vienna* (1815), to what many call the 100 Years Peace (e.g., Polanyi 1944) when major wars on the scale of the Napoleonic Wars were virtually absent for the whole time of British hegemony and soon after (until 1914).[6]

Most economic historians realize the relative lack of growth characteristic of Britain circa 1760–1820 and the negative impact of the Revolutionary and Napoleonic Wars in preventing sustained growth from emerging. Some argue that winning the war was important for establishing British hegemony and enabling long-term growth. Therefore, many of the preconditions for hegemony and sustainable growth were likely present in Britain by the late 1700s, and once the wars were over, this enabled Britain to fully encapsulate these preconditions and thereby enhance its growth and power. However, it took some time for Britain to recover from the wars (Derry 1965, ch 4, discusses "postwar distress"), several short cycle decadal downswings emerged, even during the 1820s–1850s (Flamant and Singer-Kerel 1968), and many unskilled workers (in particular) did not see much

[6] Some long wave scholars have critiqued the outcomes of the Congress of Vienna, e.g., Tylecote (1992, 199), who states that: "The damage done at Vienna was twofold. First, it put almost all the territories which had benefited from French reforms under more or less reactionary regimes. Second, it broke up the large economic units which had been created during the wars in Western Europe. It was the latter effect which was, at least in the short term, the more disastrous."

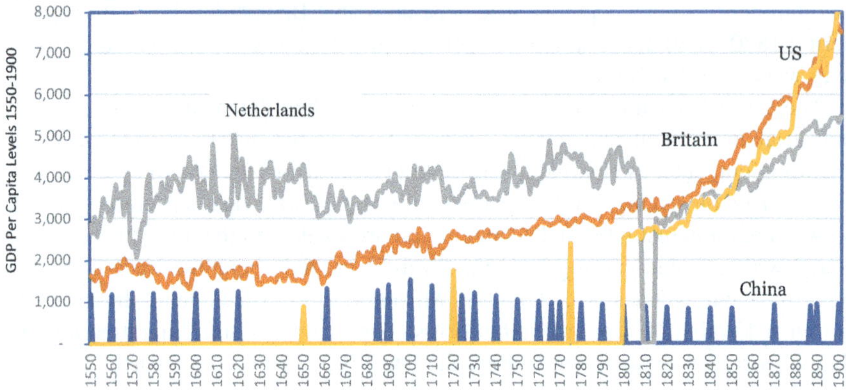

Fig. 6.3 GDP per capita *levels*: Dutch (gray), British (orange), US (yellow), China (blue), 1550–1900. (Source: Adapted from the Maddison Project 2024, Raw Data)

improvement in their wages until the mid-1800s (Broadberry et al. 2015, chs. 6, 8). Overall, though, British long-wave upswings were resurgent during the 1820s–1860s, and like the Dutch, this provided a foundation for the largest GDP per capita *levels* in the world, as shown in Fig. 6.3.

Dutch GDP per capita relative ascendency had been slowly declining since the 1660s, as British levels rose to eventually surmount the Dutch levels by the time of the Napoleonic Wars, when Dutch levels crashed and were never to recover their lead (in the period examined) (during 1810–1913, the Netherlands became part of France and national statistics were poor as a result). British real GDP per capita levels stayed quite high from about 1825 to the 1870s, after which US levels underwent a sudden jump and stayed at about the British level until at least 1900 (when they increased further). Overall, British GDP per capita levels were the highest in the world during the era of their longest and most sustainable long-wave upswing of the 1820s–1860s, and overlapped the period of their absolute hegemonic dominance, which was to last at least until the 1880s (at which point they likely moved into relative hegemony).

6.4 British Pathways and Circuits of Socioeconomic Dynamics: Long Waves, Hegemony, and Climate Change

Below we present an outline of the techno-institutional and geo-ecological conditions that enabled British growth and hegemony to generate fully functioning (but contradictory) pathways and circuits of socioeconomic dynamics (CSD) during the 1800s. I see the core question as: What were the foundations of the British long waves, hegemony, and geo-climatic conditions during the 1800s?

The crucial thing about these conditions within the circuit is that they are multifarious, interactive, and based on circular and cumulative causation (CCC) combined with complex feedback (positive and negative) processes, involving path dependence, evolution, emergence, contradiction, governance, heterogeneous groups and agents, and varying degrees of uncertainty. They all move forward and backward but in an innovative systemic process of multicausal, cybernetic, interactive, and magnified change. Uncertainty involves the future as the conditions are multiplied and forward moving for a while. Contradictory forces operate that both impinge on this forward motion and provide a foundation for relative demise. The total impact is one of long-wave motion with varying degrees of industrial, financial, and commercial dominance since the dynamic structures involve upscale growth and downscale deterioration, but with large temporal movements in both directions depending upon the overall potential momentum of the systems and subsystems.[7]

Before we examine the dynamic circuit, it is important to point out we are especially interested in three things. First, growth performance *durability and amplitude* per capita over the long term. Second, hegemonic power in areas of production, commerce, and finance (where military power is mainly derivative) also involves core, periphery, and semi-periphery relations. And third, the pattern of climate change. If the exhaustive research of Leif van Neuss (2015) is any indication, there is little or no agreement among scholars about the forces that led Britain to dominate the world in political economy performance during the 1800s. Therefore, what follows is a synthetic long-term analysis of the techno/institutional/geo-eco-spatial foundations of British performance; see Fig. 6.4 for an *outline* of the circuits of socioeconomic dynamics (CSD).

In successive subsections of Sect. 6.4, we scrutinize the eco-spatial, institutional, and technological foundations underlying the 1820s–1860s British socioeconomic circuits (CSD), comprising the overall system and its five subsystems, including (a) geo-spatial-ecological dynamic structures, (b) colonialism, trade, and empire, (c) politics and finance, (d) technology and industry, and (e) households and demography.[8]

---

[7] Up to this point of the 1800s, Britain was unique in achieving capitalist hegemony as well as Empire building power. The Dutch achieved capitalist hegemony but not the degree of empire building that Britain experienced. The US achieved capitalist hegemony but not Empire as such, since they ruled through cultural hegemony of their dominant institutions and technologies. The Spanish achieved Empire power but not capitalist hegemony.

[8] Because so much has been written about the processes involved, scholars are likely to have very different ideas about the underlying techno-institutional and geo-eco-political basis of such performance due to their differential ideologies, methodologies, techniques, theories, established preconceptions, and (inter)disciplinary backgrounds. Some are more interested in qualitative phases of evolution of capitalism, others concentrate on cliometrics, while others seek to understand the historical forces operating through time, and still others seek a synthetic account that links different approaches to the subject in a comprehensive manner. The approach undertaken here is to present an outline of the ecological, institutional, technological, historical, statistical, stylized, and synthetic works to develop a relatively general but often quite specific account of the rise of Britain

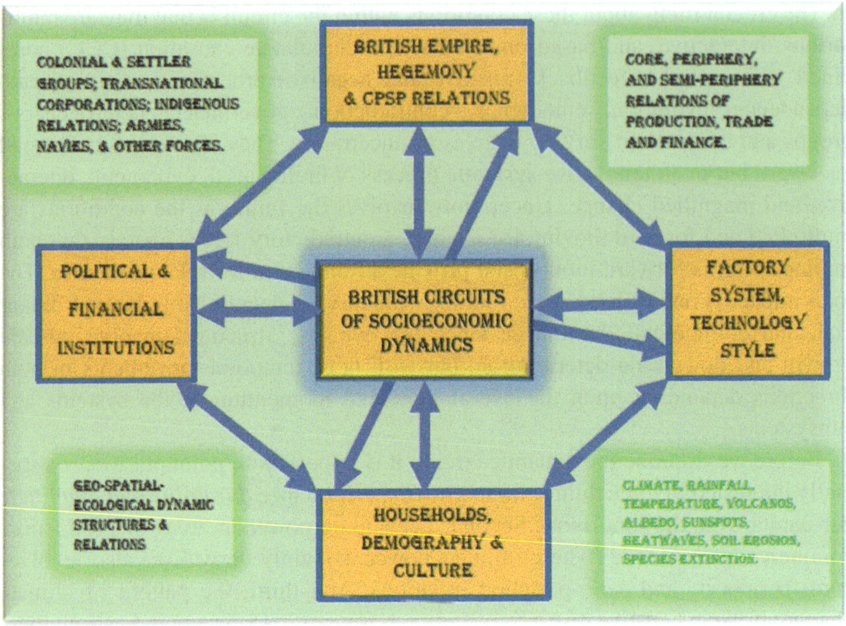

Fig. 6.4 British pathways and circuits of socioeconomic dynamics (CSD, Shortform version)

6.4.1 Geospatial-Ecological Dynamic Structures and Relations

Britain clearly had more access to the seas, rivers, and canals than any other nation in the region in the late 1700s and 1800s. The Dutch utilized this resource for their own Golden Age during 1575–1620 and possibly into the mid-late 1600s and to a lesser degree later. Starting during the 1650s, Britain imposed successive Navigation Acts specifically to destroy Dutch hegemony of the seas and succeed in their own mission to upstage the Dutch in Europe, Asia, and the Americas. Ready access to the North Sea, the Atlantic, and later the Indian Ocean gave Britain an advantage in warfare, trade, and colonization, and they developed innovative shipping, military garrisons, and colonial trading expeditions. Britain had a far greater area of coastline per unit national landscape than any other area of Europe, and elsewhere only Japan had a greater proportion of such access to sea lanes.

Key: ⟷ Inter-sphere interdependencies: flows, stocks, agents, groups.

Internally, Britain lay on a gigantic geological foundation of *coal*, which was crucial for subsequent steam power, steelmaking, weaponry, building materials, and heating. Coal supply was thus a core resource underlying British industrialization.

---

in the growth, hegemony, and climate change dynamics of the world political economy during the period, as well as the contradictory motion that led to its demise.

It also provided a basis for the ongoing climate change that contributed to the global warming crisis (especially later). It assisted industry and provided businesses and households with profitable inputs well below their environmental and social costs, and it was a major pre- and co-condition for industrialization and growth (given the opportunity costs).

Climate change had some well-established stylized facts associated with Dutch and British long-wave upswings and hegemonic processes. The Dutch were able to largely surmount the impacts of the Little Ice Age during the late 1500s and 1600s, which generated major crises throughout the world (especially Europe), in their resilience and techno-institutional innovations that provided counter-movements to the climate norm (see Chap. 4 above). Regarding climate change during the period of British hegemony and the very long-wave upswing of 1820s–1860s, we found an asymmetric flow of factors. A summary of this temperature-long-wave record is shown below in Fig. 6.5.

Abram et al. (2016) illustrate global and regional anomalies for (land) "surface air temperatures" (SAT) and "sea-surface temperatures" (SST), relative to the 1961–1990 mean. Figure 6.5 shows the 25-year moving average of the area-weighted mean terrestrial temperature anomaly (SAT), which is very similar to the European, and hence British, SAT anomaly. It shows two long waves of climate change, during the three-pronged climate cycles of the "Little Ice Age" (the first, not shown, of the Spoerer minimal, 1375–1550), the second during 1550–1770 (Maunder solar cycle), and a third for 1770–1880 (Dalton solar cycle) (from upper turning point (UTP) to UTP). After these 2–3 two cycles/waves, one could argue for two further waves, one during 1880–1945 and the other during 1945–present (UTP to UTP?). These indicate two possible (sub-)LIAs, one during 1570–1715 and the other during 1800–1860 (see above, ch 4, Section 4.2; Nierode 2022, 181).

From the perspective of the 1770–1880 climate long wave, the British likely experienced a long-term cooling during 1810–1855, during about 2/3 of the whole era of combined hegemony and long-wave upswing. During this time the lowest temperatures were during 1820–1850, within the era of hegemony and durable

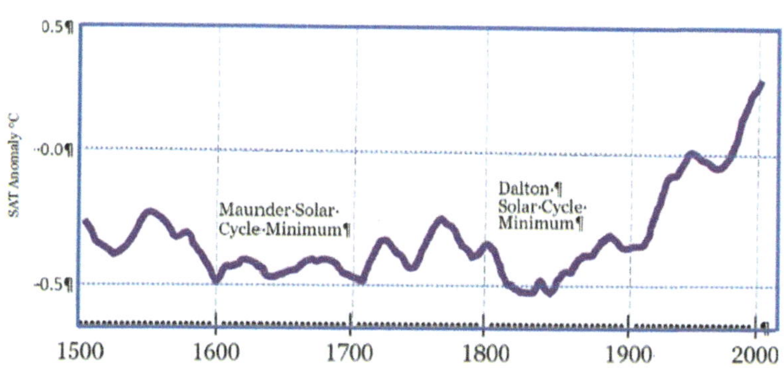

Fig. 6.5 SAT long-wave temperature anomaly (°C), Earth, 1500–2000. (Source: Adapted from Abram et al. 2016, 412)

long-wave upswing. From the 1850s to the present, there was a long-term rise in temperatures (from a low base), but with two periods of slight cooling/leveling off, during 1885–1914 and 1945–1970.

Scientific evidence detailing the nature of and reasons for this asymmetric stock-flow of cooling followed by heating, within British hegemony and long-wave upswing during 1800–1870 (followed by leveling off and then rising again) are scanty. Many popular articles seek to argue simply for rising temperatures during the 1800s in Britain without any evidence. Many excellent book histories (e.g., Brooke 2014) show the basic pattern of declining temperatures followed by rising temperatures over the period 1800–1870, with few details. One journal article details the analysis in general terms over this period, though with no specific reference to Britain or England (Abram et al. 2016).

Brooke mentions the prima facie expectation that the British Industrial Revolution and associated processes globally would have predictably heightened Earth's greenhouse gases, and thereby (depending upon other factors including aerosols) eventually increased global temperatures. This was indeed the case, as total industrial CO_2-equivalent metric tons increased majorly in the UK from 0.5 (1815) to 3.0 (1890) per capita, after which it declined and then leveled off until 1914. The world-long wave of carbon emissions is slightly different, as global emission, *tons per $m of GDP,* increased majorly from 1820 to 1870 (echoing the British rise), followed by an increase in the rate in the light of the US rise from 1870 to the global peak in 1910 (US peak was 1917), and then a continual (cyclical) global rise onto the present (Brooke 2014, 390).

Three factors that were likely responsible for the lowering of temperatures during 1800–1855 in Britain were (a) fewer sunspot cycle upswings, (b) higher aerosols, and (c) lags associated with the growth upswing of the 1820s–1860s. First, the Dalton Minimum areas of the LIA represented two major declining sunspot cycles, during which global temperatures fell. Second, there was also a major spike in volcanic aerosols during the 1820s and 1840s, which would have greatly increased haze and reduced the ability of the sun(spots) to heat the Earth.

The third is the importance of lags. There is always a lag between global and regional carbon emissions and global and regional temperature changes. Abram et al. (2016), including six main coauthors plus a 2 K consortium of other authors, published in *Nature*, argue as follows about the evidence. First, they suggest that the Little Ice Age decline in global temperatures would have abated sometime in the 1850s. Afterward, in some areas, this would have been counteracted by an industrial-era rise in temperatures. Second, they state that the warming of tropical oceans began around 1830 and that (with a lag) the Northern Hemisphere underwent warming by the mid-1800s (Europe specifically by "1852"). Southern Hemispheric temperature increases experience a lag of about half a century, resulting in rises by the early twentieth century (e.g., Australasia and South America), and in *some parts* of Antarctica (West Antarctica and Antarctica Peninsula). Overall, they conclude that "widespread climate warming observed during the twentieth century forms part of a sustained trend that began in the tropical oceans and over *some* Northern Hemisphere *land* areas around the 1830s (about 180 years ago)" (Abram et al. 2016,

413), subject, of course, to several wave declines in temperatures as mentioned, and the rise not really beginning in Europe until 1852.

In other words, the Industrial Revolution that started in Britain with technological changes in the 1700s, and which generated a sustained long-wave upswing and hegemony in Britain during the 1800s after the Napoleonic Wars, did on balance and eventually manifested itself in higher temperatures in regional oceans, the Northern Hemisphere, and the tropics, and much later in the rest of the world. But this process failed to manifest itself immediately in Britain, since it did not eschew the earlier cold temperatures *completely*, until 1915. As Abram et al. (2016) point out, *sea* temperatures around the tropics experienced rising temperatures the earliest, *land areas* surrounding the North Atlantic took some time to start heating, while, as mentioned, many areas in the Southern Hemisphere took half a century or more to begin heating.

6.4.2 British Empire, Hegemony, and Core, Periphery, Semi-Periphery (CPSP) Relations

The complex socioeconomic circuit involved many structural dynamics for the 50-year-long-wave upswing experienced by Britain during the 1820s–1860s. Domestic markets provided a basis for demand in areas of subsistence consumption for all classes as the population expanded. It generated demand from especially capitalists who spent on inputs, machinery, labor, factories, and innovation. Luxury goods had a special place in British culture as upper-class citizens established habits of conspicuous consumption through properties, gardens, garb, food, drink, parties, and weddings. The increasing population from domestic and overseas sources established a relatively free-flowing labor and entrepreneurial supply and real wages especially for skilled workers rose in relative and absolute terms, which gave them access to some non-subsistence goods and services.

Developments in warfare, sea power, shipping, navigation, global production networks, commodity chains, railways, and colonial settlements and outposts enabled the further expansion of the circuit of capital. A core stylized fact is that Britain tended to import raw materials and export final goods and services, which benefited from the periodic trend of high-technology manufacturing products having a price premium over material inputs to manufacturing. Historically, Britain during the 1800s variously imported cotton, wool, spices, silk, grain, minerals, sugar, timber, tea, and wine from the periphery and semi-periphery. They exported notably textiles, steel and iron products, cutlery, machinery, and furniture, along with several re-exports. Initially, after domestic markets, the British relied on trade with European nations, but especially into the 1800s trade with North America grew tremendously while Asia and Oceania contributed significantly.

The British Empire was established and grew as a hegemonic power developed in production, commerce, finance, and sea power. This major modern industrial power had a conspicuous impact on others, especially core nations, as the circuit of capital became more global through the growth of knowledge, capital, and innovation. Europe, America, and parts of Oceania and Latin America especially benefited from the global circuit of relationships and networks. London became the global center of finance while the seaports of the Thames, Liverpool, Glasgow, and Bristol became hubs of trade and fishing. Agglomeration benefits extended into the hinterlands. Eventually, free trade (imperialism) became a dominant ideology and practice of states and agents of British trade and commerce. Export-oriented industrialization benefited British industry through competitive advantages of specialization, more efficient resource allocation, tacit and specific knowledge transfer, and exchange. A long-wave upswing encompassed especially England, Scotland, and to some degree Wales, plus the core trading partners and powerful client states well into the 1800s. During this long-wave upswing Ireland had a series of famines, one especially extended one in the 1840s which led to over two million people either migrating or dying in the process.

The naval supremacy of the British, along with more sophisticated sailing ships and mercantile trading, enabled multiple tiers of colonies, and a dominant British-led world system to develop especially during the 1800s (McMichael 1985). The *first tier* of networks incorporated England, Wales, Scotland, and Ireland in the uneasy union. British naval blockades, extended mercantilist policies, free trade imperialism (Semmel 1970), and cheaper commodities enabled British hegemony to rule in the *second tier* for a time throughout Europe. The British liberal-imperial system of governance helped to weaken the continental class alliances between aristocracy, nobility, and bourgeoisie against the common people who challenged the ruling classes especially during the crises and recessions of the 1830s and 1840s. The rising imperial power enabled a *third tier* of networks to become established through British control of the trading routes to the Americas, Asia, Africa, the Middle East, Oceania, and the Pacific.

Britain was successful in transplanting surplus, especially lumpen and working populations, to settler-pioneer societies where local natives were replaced (decimated) by white ethnic groups, through several wars and rebellions. This enabled the establishment of fledgling capitalist institutions through state control of landholdings, laws, distribution systems, and governing bodies. Empire building also enabled trading partnerships where agricultural and mining imports were exchanged for mostly manufactures, and mid-1800s gold discoveries provided a further source of accumulation, balance of trade surplus, and profitability for the mother country. These colonies eventually provided coherent subsystems for global capitalism, wartime provisions, personnel, and some resolution of the surplus absorption problem. (Denoon 1983.)

As with the Dutch experience of hegemony, the British employed several systemic practices that impinged severely on other cultures. For instance, free trade imperialism engendered two major opium wars against China during 1839–1842 and 1856–1860, which were crucial for reversing the considerable British trade deficit with China and led at one point to around a quarter of Chinese males in the heartland of the opium market being addicted. It also led to a decline in the considerable power of the Chinese empire, a domestic rebellion that extended this decline, and later defeat by Japan, which came to eclipse China (for a time) as the major Asian power (Gelber 2004).

British imperialism in India led to the destruction of indigenous systems of governance and the decimation of many local industries. Karl Marx (1853) wrote on the primary accumulation of surplus from their activities in India. Other writers put forward similar theories, including Dadabhai Naoriji (1901) who postulated the *economic drain theory*, that Britain, on balance, expropriated vast amounts of economic surplus from India, which inhibited their development structurally for more than a century. Nogues-Marco (2021) scrutinizes the literature on the economic drain, including criticisms, and provides statistics as well as profound conclusions about the phenomenon. He summarizes his results thus regarding the East India Company (EIC) and related networks in India:

> [M]y examination of the budgets of the EIC leads me to conclude in favor of the Marxist-nationalist theory of the drain of wealth. ... [Firstly,] the EIC charged extractive land taxes in a society wh[ere] GDP *per capita* fell close to bare-bones subsistence in the early nineteenth century. Because land taxes primarily affected agricultural laborers, they lived below subsistence levels. Taxation based mainly on land revenues intensified poverty and probably made agriculture less productive. ... [Secondly,] [m]ilitary charges, civil charges, and interest on debt consumed [a] vast majority of the fiscal budget. [In] consequence, productive expenses were tiny.... Contrary to Mughal practice, the EIC neither invested in nor repaired irrigation systems, which reduced agricultural productivity and intensified famines during the recurrent episodes of drought. [And thirdly,] [i]n 1858, when the EIC's [East-India Company's] territorial charter was terminated, the ... unrequited exports charged to Indian public debt represented 13% of Indian GDP. [Nogues-Marco 2021, 192]

British imperialism in Ireland is well known and continued over many hundreds of years. It had a major impact on the culture, growth, and standard of living of the Irish. The total costs over the full historical coverage of the dominance would represent decades worth of Irish GDP, millions of deaths (including those not born), and tens of millions of people having stunted growth and malnutrition. Taking one simple example from the period of British hegemony, long waves, and climate change, consider the Irish potato famine of the 1840s (during the middle of the Dalton solar cycle minimum). The English government refused to provide sustenance to the Irish, based on the theory of free trade, and especially the poor suffered over one million deaths, with over one million migrating to other countries (Kinealy 2002).

The British settler colony of Australia experienced the decimation of native populations and an inability to reproduce successive generations of indigenous cultures for sustainable development. There were numerous wars between settlers, armies, police, and aborigines, mainly over extensions to the farming and mining frontier, including more than 400 massacre events and 10,000 indigenous peoples killed, up from a previous estimate of 8400 dead in 302 massacre events. By contrast, it is estimated that 168 non-Aboriginal people were killed in 13 frontier massacre events (Ryan 2024).

6.4.3 Political and Financial Institutions

Several aspects of the state were favorable to capitalism and industrial strength through the 1600s, 1700s, and 1800s in Britain. First, the Glorious Revolution of the 1680s set the scene for a degree of constraint on monarchy and some rule of parliament, along with, critically, eventually relative peace at the national level (especially between England, Wales, and Scotland), which fostered some important domestic institutions. A critical institution was the gradual evolution of tolerance to heterodox ideas, which eventually stimulated establishment institutions, such as science over religion, rational argument over superstition, practical industry over medieval thought, and individual initiative over social control. It also led to the *ongoing alliance between the bourgeoisie and landowners* and evolutionary contests between the Whigs (liberals) and the Tories (conservatives).

Some argue that British patents protected innovations and stimulated technological change, especially from the late 1700s and early 1800s onwards, depending upon the degree of business acumen, legal representation, and access to venture capital (Bottomley 2014). Other specialists on the Industrial Revolution cite patents as providing little protection for innovative property, due to numerous factors, such as the short length of protection, copying, and generic innovation (e.g., Clark 1953). Extending this line of argument, formal institutions such as patents were seen as less important than informal institutions (Mokyr 2008). This view sees innovators concentrating on micro-secrecy, first-mover profits, and public esteem rather than patents per se, which, through lags, enabled them to gain profits while generating social spread through ideas and technologies, which were core to Britain establishing an industrial system. Freedom of the press, assembly, publishing, and literacy led to the spread of the collective social wealth of knowledge and practical applications of technology, which contributed to innovations including the spinning jenny, the Bessemer converter, the steam engine, and the factory system.

The mythical "free trade and liberalism" were principles underlying British policy and its hegemonic role in generating a global system of business and finance during the 1800s. It is said to have manifested itself, especially during the 1820s–1840s, through the dismantling of the Corn and Navigation Laws, reduction in tariffs across the board, the scrapping of export and import controls, and enforcing open trade in the colonies. Freer Trade was said to be supported by a multitude of vested interests, including, especially, Manchester and Nottingham manufacturers who wanted profits on their investments, a multitude of merchants who supported simplified rules to stimulate the circuit of capital, some politicians who reduced the complexity of the tax structure and costs for consumers and workers, and even some landowners who engaged in "High Farming" (improved techniques on the land).

Kindleberger (1975) makes the point that British and to a lesser degree European free trade during the mid-to-late 1800s was primarily a doctrinal force propagated by (British) political economists and officials (and previously the Physiocrats). Some were theorists who believed it would benefit the British and international economies (Smith, Ricardo, Mill), others being trade officials (Jacob, Bowring, MacGregor) who wanted to counter the growing power of German manufacturers, as well as various politicians who had taken a free trade view (Pitt, Gladstone). Kindleberger argued that "Not until the 1830s did economic liberalism burst forth as a crusading passion" (p.49), and politicians henceforth used it to reduce barriers to trade, but before the Tory Robert Peel could act on this, he had to re-introduce income taxes to make up for the (otherwise) public finance deficit.

British capitalism emerged as the most productive system of factory organization and trading empire, the "workshop of the world," whereby free trade became a *form* of imperialism as it enabled their manufacturers to export durable goods throughout the world in exchange for primary products and minerals from especially Europe and the periphery. Britain used free trade arguments to impose such policies on other nations, often through force, such as China in relation to the opium trade/wars (Izumikawa 2001). A general rule has henceforth developed among certain political economists where emerging hegemonies establish free trade to deepen their industrial, commercial, financial, and derivative military power through various production networks and commodity chains and that they tended to negate free trade when it suited them, especially when hegemony waned majorly (e.g., use of mercantilist policies during periods of relative [i.e., declining] hegemony).

A double movement of research has, however, developed, countering this free trade rhetoric to some degree by arguing that, even though it may have been a passion espoused by certain political economists, manufacturers, politicians, and others, in practice it is an oversimplified myth. This counter-movement indicates, for instance, that the French were more oriented to free trade. French tariffs were consistently lower than British ones during 1800–1850, and Napoleon III's reforms opened French markets to foreign goods more than Britain did up to 1870 (Nye 2010), the 1860 Cobden–Chevalier Treaty stimulated further reform on the continent, while British tariffs did not fall lower than France's until 1876 (Nye 1991).

The myth of British free trade, however, was not a complete myth as there was a progressive decline in British tariffs during the 1800s–1870s, but it grossly exaggerated the comparative dynamics of free trade especially between Britain and France. Likely the reasons it was so successful a myth were due to the absolute magnitude of British trade, the trend throughout the 1800s, the movement of certain tariffs, and especially the rhetoric of political economists, officials, and certain business interests. From the 1880s, the protectionist movement began to grow as free trade faltered and inward-looking policies impacted the continent and much elsewhere.

Meanwhile, the Bank of England was important in the generation of public finance for external wars, especially against France in the 1700s and early 1800s, and success in this politico-imperial exercise enabled Britain to establish military hegemony. This, in turn, was crucial for expanding the British merchant navy, foreign trade, and global turnover of capital, which created substantial profitability and accumulation. Following the *Congress of Vienna*, the so-called 100 Years Peace between 1815 and 1914 (Polanyi 1944) enabled British capital to move throughout the world and situate other nations especially Europe, America, and Australia, to accrue benefits through global production chains and commodity networks.

It is sometimes difficult to separate analytically state from finance (as noted earlier in this chapter) because the state played such a key role in transforming financial relationships for the world system that Britain led during especially the 1820s–1860s. London was the financial center of the world and crucial to Britain's hegemonic role, as Amsterdam had lost much of its power due to involvement in wars with France and Britain during the 1700s. London became the center of merchant banking due to its prominence in providing loans and bills for trade finance in Europe and the world. The Bank of England (established in 1694) assisted in the establishment of the gold standard, initially in Britain during the 1810s, more formally in the 1840s, and globally into the 1870s until the 1920s. The gold standard helped to organize finance, exchange, the balance of payments, and protect vested interests, especially those on fixed incomes, businesses, notably Manchester manufacturers, and landed interests to moderate speculation.

As mentioned, political economy, particularly the physiocrats and classical economists, played a key role in the rise of capitalism in Europe and especially Britain, promoting ideas and practices central to British hegemony and long-wave performance. Landed interests especially found the physiocrat idea of productive enterprise originating from agriculture ideally suited to their interests. Adam Smith helped establish the free market philosophy and free trade via the "invisible hand," economies of scale in manufacture, and the circular causation of trade and investment (CCC). Manufacturers were drawn to Ricardian notions of comparative advantage and diminishing returns to justify their global expansion and profitable investment. Thomas Malthus was also attractive, especially to those on fixed incomes and landed interests who indulged in luxury goods, and the role of the state in encouraging spending through the circuit of capital. The export of political economy from Britain and Europe to America and the colonies was a major factor in establishing British, Western, and later US hegemony throughout the world. It also established indigenous versions of political economy in the colonies and later more global visions of the subject.

6.4.4 Technology Style and Factory System

A crucial pre- and co-condition for British industrialization, waves, and hegemony was the development of technology, accumulation, and industry. One avenue for profit involved surplus labor and other resources moving from agriculture to be productively employed in industry, services, and government. The long-term development of enclosures led to the expropriation of many peasants who *often* moved to the cities providing labor for industry (Leonard 1962). Acts of Parliament especially during the late 1700s and early 1800s enabled a major extension of enclosures less through agreement and more from mere legal procedure, resulting from the "1840s [in] several counties [being] on the verge of an *absolute* loss of population, and from 1850 land-flight became general" (Hobsbawm 1962, 188).

The resulting economic surplus from agriculture could be spent on innovations in both agriculture and industry, promoting the development of rural and urban capitalists and the rising working class. The development of new methods of field rotation, fertilizers, breeds of plants and animals, drainage systems, plowing methods, transportation, and knowledge of capitalist farming techniques led to a declining proportion of the population working in agriculture, higher productivity, and lower prices for products. The long-wave *price* upswing in Britain during the 1790s–1810s saw a reversal into a long-wave (price) downswing during the 1810s to the 1840s. The biggest price declines were for cotton, wool, beef, and iron, with timber and coal continuing to decline for decades after the 1840s. Some prices then underwent a long-wave upswing again in Britain, especially during the 1850s–early 1870s during the second half of the *long-wave growth upswing*, including, especially, cotton and beef, and to a very modest extent coal and iron. Many commodities then underwent price declines during the 1870s–1890s, including cotton, iron, beef, coal, and wool (Rostow 1978, 89–90).

Another channel for increasing Britain's industrial surplus was through importing cheaper inputs, agricultural products, handicrafts, and minerals from overseas and exporting manufactured products and re-exports of imports (usually in slightly changed form). This enabled urban capitalists to increase investment in industry, workers to have better diets, including more nutrients and sources of energy, and greater markets to stimulate industry. Industrialization in Britain was to some degree self-generating as industry assisted agricultural productivity while agricultural advances lowered the costs of production and thus advanced industry (once the 1790–1815 wars had ended) (Mykya 1985). This had a profound circular and cumulative impact on socioeconomic development.

There were three main phases of the evolution of British industrialization, growth, and power during the 1700s and 1800s. The first was the building of capabilities through the mid-1600s to the mid-1700s, involving the freedom to develop ideas, engage in wage labor, and experiment with methods and skills of business, technology, and trade. The second was the first stage of technological advances in the late 1700s and early 1800s when especially the textile industry propelled profits and accumulation, but wars reduced the net benefits of this phase. Unskilled labor, skilled craftspeople, and financiers provided a basis for productivity and human labor power. The liberalism of democratic capitalism enabled the promotion of a fledging culture of entrepreneurship, especially through the pragmatic merging of science and industry, significant development of apprenticeships, and learning by doing. The rise of British empiricism and practical learning as well as basic human capital and workmanship enabled the early rise of industrial capitalism in Britain.

The macroeconomic benefits of the first and the truncated second phase of British industrialization were unable to be fulfilled until the circuit of reproduction was given greater freedom after the Napoleonic Wars. This generated the third phase of industrialism, propelling industry and especially finance and investment to utilize technological gains in production, trade, and transportation, which led to several decades of long-wave upswing during the 1820s–1860s. Systemic uncertainty was moderated while buoyant expectations contributed to the most durable period of growth in the history of British capitalism (up to this point). It was during this long-wave upswing that the third stage of industrialization especially embodied the long-term macro-dynamics of the *Age of Railways and Electricity* that led eventually to other nations experiencing industrialization and long-wave upswings (especially the US) in an environment conducive to business evolution.

It was also during this third phase of industrialization of the mid-to-late-1800s onwards that labor power developed through more intensive methods of schooling, literacy, apprenticeships, practical learning, and skill development. Large-scale capital became a dominant factor, creating economies of scale and agglomeration in industrial areas such as Birmingham, Leeds, Manchester, Glasgow, and Newcastle. Circuitous linkages were established via railways, shipping, and more sophisticated docklands, enabling expansion through colonies and other core–periphery modes of development. There were more intimate linkages between industry and science through innovations in electrical and chemical industries, in tandem with the internal combustion engine, oil, and rubber, and with the "systematic extension of the factory system," a technology style characterized by the production of machinery and durable consumer goods via standardization and mechanization (Hobsbawm 1968, 146).

Along with more sophisticated industries came more elaborate financial securities, joint stock companies, and bank holding companies. The merchant bank phase of the early-to-mid-1800s led the way in the mid-to-late 1800s to a new phase of commercial credit to finance longer-term capital formation, durable investment in railways, and social capital business networks (McMichael 1985). More elaborate securities involving extending trade credit, commercial credit, and especially shareholdings in the late 1800s, with the evolution of the telephone, the telegraph, and the stock ticker.[9] These enabled the extended accumulation of investment, economies of scale and scope, and greater potential profitability in core sectors.

Innovation in production was greatly facilitated by rising real wages, especially for skilled labor, and three types of machinofacture, which often merged in performance. The first type was the *workshop*, where textiles, crafts, leather work, tailoring, and brickworks utilized various types of machines, mills, and presses. These were often coordinated by supervisors and managers and could be set close to households or city locales. The second were *larger units of production* variously involving chemicals, iron works, and shipbuilding, with several modules operating in close proximity and often hundreds of workmen in the work yard, usually directed by supervisors. The third was the *factories*, driven by machines, including blast furnaces, rolling mills, and puddling ovens, through standardization and mass

[9] The "stock-ticker," invented in 1867, was a printing telegraph, powered by battery, and covered in glass, whereby stock prices could be communicated, in simple language, throughout the world. It was thus a machine, which used ticker tape to transmit such information (Preda 2006). Similar information now is transmitted through computer terminals, the Internet, and other means. Bliss et al. (forthcoming) examined the use of the stock ticker during the 1900s, and found its widespread use generated financial inefficiencies due to traders undertaking "trend chasing" behavior which created more co-movements rather than efficiency-generating behavior per se.

production. Over time, interchangeable parts were incorporated into the machines to reduce waste and duplication in factories. (Landes 1969, ch 2.)

The crux of British primacy of production lay, at least in principle, in the factory system (Freeman and Louçã 2001), which included three major codetermined processes, requiring simultaneous development. These included, first, factory organization, including the social relations within and between workers, supervisors, and management in the production process. The second was new knowledge embedded in machinery, which enabled productivity to increase through time. The third was quality control which became a core part of the triad generating successful marketing and sales. The *concept of complementarity* (Geraghty 2007) was important to embed in decision-making within the factory system to ensure triangular organizational, mechanical, and quality codetermination for successful profit-making.

Geraghty applied the concept of complementarity to major areas of successful industrialization in Britain, including, for instance, cotton textiles workshops, flax spinning mills, metalworking, and ironmaking. Various integrated advances in machinery with improvements in factory organization and enhanced quality control were shown to generally increase marginal revenue and reduce total costs as well as expand marginal efficiencies of investment. Advances made during "the" Industrial Revolution were relatively slow in manifesting themselves until the 1820s–1860s, not only because of the earlier-mentioned Revolutionary and Napoleonic Wars, but also due to the complexity of the factory process, the learning curve, tacit knowledge, competition, and resistance from vested interests.

There were many inefficiencies endemic in the complexity of the industrialization era in Britain, which inhibited the full development of long-wave upswing during the 1820s–1860s and contributed to delayed performance. Internal financing of investment was the rule during this period since the financial system was often incapable of providing sufficient funds for expanded reproduction. There were also too many agents involved in agriculture compared with manufacturing, as the movement to the cities and factories was less than required. (Williamson 1991.)

Complementary but slowly adjusting triads and inefficient markets help to explain why the long wave of British production hegemony was eventually durable and extensive but not of a particularly high order of magnitude or amplitude in terms of long-wave upswing, although the periodicity was impressive.

6.4.5 Households, Demography, and Culture

Developments in the household are crucial as pre- and co-conditions for long waves and hegemony. On the one hand, much of British development was based on a population of human beings reproduced partly from the household and partly from the community in which they lived. This mode of reproduction was partly domestic and partly due to immigration. The reproduction of British workers, capitalists, landowners, household workers, and others was, in a sense, the foundation of development. In the family and community, these heterogeneous groups and agents were brought up, inculcated in various norms and socialization mores, educated to varying degrees, and taught to perform various functions to sustain the social economy. To some degree a double movement was in play as certain informal rules and norms evolved through time, which were supplemented by a series of more formal institutions, to solve crucial agency, coordination, trust, information, and performative roles.

Demographic factors became more important in Britain during the 1800s as the population doubled every 25 years, rising from circa ten million to 40 million over 1800–1900. This demographic trend was important for supply and demand. Supply provided the potential for labor, capital, and innovation while demand enhanced market turnover, economies of scale, and scope. A greater population also encouraged agglomeration as rural-to-urban movement (though encountering barriers) enabled economies of communication, networks, and production chains to develop. Some urban areas also progressed/expanded into rural towns and cities where agglomerations involved complex interactive processes. (Coleman and Salt 1992.) The circuit of capital required the resolution of many apparently contradictory problems that occurred through time and space within and between the micro, meso, macro, and global realms of the social economy.

During the late-1700s and 1800s, the typical European modern marriage system evolved, involving diminished rates of fertility with the emphasis placed on labor-power (or "human capital") expansion, the potential for human beings to produce goods and services for the community, depending on their specific roles and duties. The "consumer" (Koyama 2009) and "industrious" (de Vries 2008) revolutions enhanced profit and accumulation by spreading the work ethic among workers and the consumption habit among householders. The work ethic expanded productivity while consumption habits enhanced the turnover of capital.

Joel Mokyr (2008) explains many of these informal cultural traits that emanated from interconnected families, classes, agents, and business networks that coalesced to generate, distribute, and reproduce the economic surplus required for capitalist reproduction. He sees a major change happening as the modest innovations and class relations of the 1600s and 1700s transformed and created better conditions for capitalism into the 1800s. The mercantilist tendencies underlying the class coalition between merchants, landowners, and certain politicians were transformed by the early 1800s, as a more liberal approach was taken to incentivize classes contributing to innovation, skills and networks of relationships underlying productive business associations.

The institutions underlying the so-called Second Industrial Revolution (of the 1850s–1870s) included a set of norms and routines ("culture and institutions," Mokyr 2017) underlying interactive business networks, including behavioral traits with a communicative mentality, informal information flows concerning business opportunities, clubs that created friendly interaction, and partnerships of association. This encouraged a productive system of rewards for innovation, including respect, reputation, monetary rewards, patents, and a collegial environment.

Balancing collective interests that generate trust and association with class or individual rewards that advance property rights enhanced the economic surplus underlying innovation during the period of British hegemony. The state became a vehicle for advancing the interests of the bourgeoisie, often redirecting the behavior of landlords to productive pursuits, and inculcating the expertise and tacit knowledge of the skilled technicians through such means as apprenticeships. The system also required business transactions to be expedited based on trust and agreed-upon norms, with formal laws and regulations acting as backup mechanisms, often not required (a social safety net called "redundancy").

As Mokyr concluded about the broader system of informal arrangements underlying the 1800s business environment:

> Observant contemporaries noted that informal institutions, that is customs, institutions, and conventions delineating acceptable behaviour, were at least as important as a formal rule of law. ... What mattered was that within the merchant and artisan classes there existed a level of trust that made it possible to transact with non-kin, and increasingly with people who were, if not strangers, certainly not close acquaintances. ... It is this kind of environment [comprising] ... "social capital," that created the possibility of cooperation even when standard behavior in finite games would suggest that defection and dishonest behavior might have been a dominant strategy. [Mokyr 2008, 75, 76, 78]

Unskilled labor, paupers, and "lumpens" were excluded from this system of informal norms but included in a perfunctory set of institutions such as the Poor Laws, workhouses, and convict settlements. Those found to have committed major crimes were usually put to death, while petty crimes often led to deportation to a convict settlement when jails were full. The flow of convicts to America declined after the Revolutionary Wars, while during 1788–1868, around 162,000 British and Irish petty criminals were sent to the Australian states as convicts. Domestically, workers who depended on home production increasingly joined industrial classes by adopting mechanization in workhouses or working in factories or workhouses. Eventually, a series of regulations were passed providing some protection for children and other workers in relation to hours, conditions of work, wage rates, and eventually holidays.

During the period leading up to and including hegemony and long waves socioeconomic and political "blockages" typical of the 1700s had to be cast aside for the institutions underlying innovation to be advanced. One such blockage was the mercantile mentality that economic activity is a zero-sum game. Monopolies and vested interests need to be broken up for the liberal bourgeoisie to advance a social surplus in their collective factory and workshop systems. Just as important was for the extensive wars of the 1700s and early 1800s to be emasculated, as mostly happened at the *Congress of Vienna,* which reduced the unproductive use of the surplus on weapons and military equipment during the 1800s. The processes enabling the sustainable long-wave upswing of the 1820s–1860s to manifest also generated a series of contradictions that led eventually to declining hegemony and unstable and mediocre performance late in the nineteenth and early twentieth centuries.

6.5 British Hegemonic and Long-Wave Decline and Global Disarray

T.K. Derry (1965) saw the British experiment in modern economic growth during the long nineteenth century (1790s–1890s) as comprising four phases, each lasting a quarter of a century. The first phase was during the Revolutionary and Napoleonic Wars, plus the recovery from these wars, through the 1790s to the mid-1820s, during which growth was slow, prices high, and conditions for working people generally hard and difficult. The second phase during the mid-late 1820s to 1850 was one of the gradually rising expectations, productivity, profit rates, and real wages (for skilled labor), declining prices, but also several crises, recessions, and disruptions as reactions to the establishment of the new order of business and industry (crises of adjustment). The third phase, during the 1850s to the early 1870s, was one of rapid development of industry, some rising prices, rapid expansion of railways, steel, and transportation, expanding real wages and progress and prosperity. The final phase during the mid-late 1870s to the early-mid-1890s involved declining prices, especially for agriculture, in addition to lower growth, profits, and trade.

In this context, the great British industrialization, long-wave upswings, and hegemony that saw the emergence of a major empire, new technologies, and colonization, began to fade after the 1860s. This decline between the 1870s and the 1940s was characterized by a major Depression in the 1870s and shortly afterward, plus a series of short-wave upswings and severe downswings until the postwar boom of the 1950s–1980s. There were two major sources of the decline, the first was endogenous to Britain, and the second was endogenous to the stylized facts of the time.

The first, endogenous source of the decline lay in the British Empire itself, the fact that its potential had become exhausted by the late 1800s, as the contradictions of British hegemony began to magnify. The business culture that provided a basis for upswing, innovation, entrepreneurship, workmanship, and productivity decayed. The maturation and decline of especially small-scale family businesses were no match for the large-scale enterprises that were necessary in the age of mass production and economies of scale and scope. They were unable to adapt to the changing business model, due to inherent and habitual routines, institutions, and ways of life. Hobsbawm (1968, ch 9) puts it down to the decline of enterprise and the conservative nature of British society. Aristocrats associated with the public school system and capitalists who were inculcated into the leisure class failed the test of productive labor, capital, and industry. Mere satisficing with a normal rate of profit in the face of mature industries and productivity decline set the scene for systemic deterioration.

Even the teaching of history, such as the nature and evolution of the Industrial Revolution and British hegemony and its aftermath, was in disarray, as, for instance, "Oxford was locked into a complacent and conservative curriculum that marked it ever after, and while Cambridge debated the intellectual project of history more energetically, its actual teaching and training was little better. The vanguard of change was more to be found in London and Manchester" (Merriment and Winter 2006, 1073). The evolution of liberalism, which had flourished in the age of free trade and freedom for business to operate according to its principles and to stimulate industrialism, began to decay as it appealed to the middle class and aristocrats and was found wanting vis-à-vis the common people who increasingly sought refuge in Labor and socialism (p. 1349).

The decay of British industry led to a shift to finance, commerce, and services, while the monopoly of the Empire enabled foreign direct investment and colonialization to generate and especially absorb the economic surplus. The other endogenous factor responsible for the decline, which occurred through an evolutionary process, led to the rise of Germany, France, other parts of Europe, the USA, and other nations. According to Stearns (2013, Chap. 5) there were three phases of development whereby other nations managed to negate British dominance in the world economy. The first was through the copying, transferring, and modifying of British industrial practices and principles, during the late 1700s and early 1800s, and later during the mid-to-late 1800s. This process expanded via the employment of British workers and entrepreneurs in Europe and America. Competitors were often able to prevent the severe degradation of workers, including especially children, in the factories that were typical of the British experience. The French had more state involvement in industrialization, while the Germans concentrated more on investment banks financing big industry, and Americans surpassed Europe's expertise in science and technology in their efforts to industrialize.

In the US, the copying and adapting of British and European methods evolved to the second stage of developing new military technology during the Civil War of the 1860s, along with intercontinental rail networks that propelled the turnover of the complex capital circuit. Andrew Carnegie took the process developed by Henry Bessemer, extended its scope, and modernized steel production in the US, while investment bankers played a key role in financing capital investment during the new era of business, and sewing machines along with the mechanization of agriculture, enhanced productivity in textiles and primary industry. The ideology of free enterprise spurred Westward expansion and the use of foreign capital to finance industry. Organizational "innovations" such as Taylorism, including time and motion studies, factory police, and workplace hierarchies streamlined workplace-factory management in their efforts to subordinate labor and generate a surplus. (Stearns 2013.)

Stearns and others emphasize the "Great Depression" of the 1870s and 1880s in the US and parts of Europe (certainly Britain), brought on by financial crises and overproduction in large-scale industry. Veblen (2023) also gave heed to this in his analysis of declining prices and profits that led to a major re-evaluation of business practices in the new order of business, especially in the United States. In Veblen's works, businesses reorganized their institutions to emphasize profitability and cash flow, leading to advances in accountancy, finance, mergers and acquisitions, colonial conquests, and the state through protectionism and subsidies. This new order of business involved greater reliance on credit, finance capital, and the sales effort. He saw this as an escalation of relatively unproductive activities which later was said to evolve into speculative bubbles, insufficient demand, and a decline in workmanship characteristic of the period leading up to the Great Depression of the 1930s, which he saw as an outcome of vested interests dominating the common good (Veblen 1919).

We see the evolution of industrial societies from British hegemony in the 1820s–1870s through to rising French and German power and especially US industrial production, commerce, and finance from the late 1800s to the early twentieth century. The failure of German attempts to establish hegemony through two world wars reinforced the movement toward US power. Up to the late 1800s, the US had only partial ascendency, a position it would continue to hold for more than half a century, while it established military dominance and thereby absolute hegemonic power which became characteristic of the US role in the world economy by 1945.

6.6 United Provinces and Great Britain: Long-Wave Upswing, Hegemony, and Climate Change

It is now time to summarize our arguments and analyze some secondary literature on waves, hegemony, and climate change.

First, the Dutch long waves and hegemony of the 1570s–1650s occurred during the Maunder sub-cycle of the Little Ice Age (LIA). The Maunder affected much of Europe and elsewhere (with a lag) during the 1600s "global crisis," which impacted socioeconomic performance, social crises, and epidemics. The Dutch were the best at surmounting these obstacles, due to their habits and institutions associated with adjusting to rising waterways, winds, social impacts, and other innovations. This was a major factor promoting Dutch hegemony and long-wave upswings during this otherwise difficult time.

During British hegemony, there were down-up cycles of climate change (and a classic long wave of climate change) during the last solar cycle (Dalton) LIA minimum. The first half of Britain's hegemony and long waves were characterized by colder temperatures, due to solar cycle declines, volcanic aerosols, and possibly changes to ocean circulation. Lags associated with growth and industrialization waves caught up with the British during the trajectory of the industrialization process when global temperatures rose during the period 1855–1870s.

Second, I examined the "war and hegemony" hypothesis and established some conclusions. The British needed to defeat Napoleon before they could generate hegemony, which was formally done at the *Congress of Vienna*. Dutch hegemony and long-wave upswings were possible after the *Treaty of Utrecht* [1579] (when they expelled the Spanish and established a "(con)federation"), rather than after the *Peace of Westphalia* [1648] which is usually cited as the critical (world) peace treaty (linked to the Treaty/Peace of Munster/Osnabrück).

I have found the notion of "wars of ascendency" very useful, but not "wars of consolidation." For instance, while the Napoleonic Wars could easily be seen as a War of Ascendency, it is questionable to call the Crimean War (1853–1856) a "war of *consolidation*" (as some have proposed), given that the "war underlined the British army's administrative weaknesses" in this "ill-starred campaign" (Holmes 2001, 239). Similarly, it is difficult to consider any of the many wars the Dutch were involved in being a "war of consolidation," while the Dutch Revolution against the Spanish could possibly be seen as a war of ascendency.

During declining hegemony (Dutch, British), some modest growth patterns (slightly better than usual) emerge for the power that will eventually/possibly be the next hegemon (Britain, US, China). This was true of British growth during the 1660s. We scrutinize the case for the US and China in chaps. 7 and 8.

Durable long-wave upswings have a strong tendency to be stronger during hegemonic periods than at other times; British performance was more durable (four decades of upswing) during their hegemonic era compared with the Dutch experience (two bouts of long-wave upswing, two decades each; one strong, one weak). The British case was qualitatively different from the Dutch, also since wars did not disrupt the process after the Napoleonic episodes, compared with, especially, the Dutch depression/war of the 1620s and thereafter.

Technologies are important. The core energy for the Dutch Golden Age/hegemony/long-wave upswings was peat lawn, while the prime mechanical innovation was the Windmill, and the principal governance innovation was the provision of several public goods, such as prudential policy. For British hegemony, the core energy source was coal, the key mechanical innovations were steam power and later railways, and a prime governance policy was free trade and the gold standard (for a time). There were several similarities, such as both the Dutch and British being (a) in the North Sea area, (b) protestant and liberal, (c) promoting free trade at least internally, (d) being master shipbuilders, and (e) having a 'white' heritage.

Now we come to the secondary literature on British hegemony from authors who have studied the first three capitalist hegemonies: the Netherlands, Britain, and the US (as we did for the Dutch in ch 5). First, Roy Kwon (2011) compared the evidence for Dutch, England, the US, France, and Germany "hegemony" from world systems and world politics perspectives, and his calculations of the hegemonic index are shown in Fig. 6.6.

He concluded that "England [sic] is hegemonic only during the 1800s" (p. 606). He believes that "English" hegemony was precipitated in an environment of the war of ascendency which ended in 1815 and is based on the so-called (second) Industrial Revolution, and that the *hegemony index* is adequate for "English" dominance between 1833 and 1918. However, one can see from Fig. 6.6 that the period of greatest hegemonic power for "England" was between 1820 and 1900.

This shows that the "English" developed relative hegemonic power into the 1700s, but their real power thrust forward during and after the Revolutionary and Napoleonic Wars, by the 1820s through to the 1890s, thereafter it declined in absolute terms, and by 1918 the United States was on a par with "England."

Second, Angus Maddison (1991, chap. 2; 1982, chap. 2) also studied these three hegemonies. The main reasons cited for the rise of British hegemony were that they took the advice of Petty, Child, Temple, and Smith in "emulate[ing] the Dutch" through "replication of the Dutch mercantilist capitalist model" (1982, 34) (I doubt this point, as already argued.). British success is said to have depended upon Dutch technology and knowledge, especially in "agriculture, canal building, shipping, banking, and international specialization." The crucial difference between the two is said to have been the rapid technical progress obtained by the British in "cotton

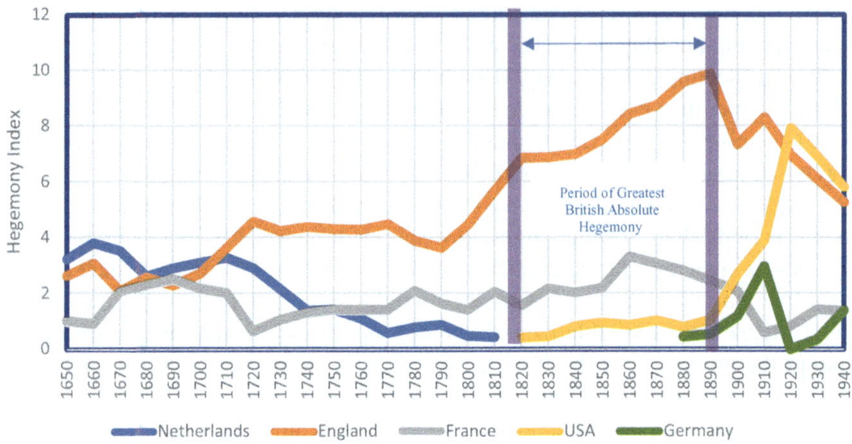

Fig. 6.6 Hegemony Index, 1650–1940, England, Netherlands, USA, Germany, France. (Source: Adapted from raw data in Kwon 2011, 612, Appendix.) NOTE: The hegemony index (HI) was estimated based on three major variables, (1) Total real GDP, (2) real GDP per capita, and (3) sea power. To capture the interactive (CCC) impact of the three variables, after certain quality adjustments, they are multiplied together to ascertain the HI. The exercise is done for eight (some not shown) nations over 446 years (depending upon availability of data for some nations). ("England" is transposed for "Britain")

textiles, iron manufacture, and the use of coal." In general, British dominance in the 1800s is said to have followed the Dutch through, first, the nature of their institutions, second, geography, and third, becoming the new world trade leader. The British are said to have destroyed Dutch trading supremacy through a series of wars and Navigation Acts and their subsequent establishment of monopolies and advantages in Spanish America, India, the West Indies, and Brazil.

Maddison goes on to say that the first phase of British industrialization based on technologies such as Hargreaves' Jenny, Arkwright's spinning frame, Crompton's mule, Cartwright's power loom, and Whitney's cotton gin of the 1760s–1790s textiles industry was not decisive. The real turning point for the British after success in the Napoleonic Wars was the development, especially from the 1820s of the Factory System, mass production, and associated innovations in areas of "steam power, steel, and railways" (p. 38), which depended more on scientific principles and greater investment in capitalist modes of production. However, Britain soon lost its ascendency and matured rapidly during the 1890s. Maddison thus dates hegemony during the 1820s–1880s. This is very similar to my own conclusions (except for his allusion to Dutch mercantilism, and he does not *utilize* waves [he has his own theory of phases of capitalism] nor discuss climate change).

Third, Chase Dunn (1998) dates British hegemony of the world system during the 1820s–1880s. It is said to be based on three stages. The first is a competitive advantage in mass consumption goods, e.g., textiles during the late 1770s and early 1800s. The second stage is expansion of capital goods, e.g. the use of machinery in factories. The third is the export of financial services, and London is the financial center of the world. The main factors promoting hegemony are said to be geographical location, breakthrough technologies, massive investment, access to cheap imports, and especially core production in leading sectors. Politically, it is said to require state support from *a suitable class coalition,* e.g., *bourgeoisie and landlords,* a core issue, willing to invest in profitable production for the world market.

It is also required to have a *relatively* pluralistic and egalitarian political system, compared with its (local) competitors (e.g., Germany and France), to effectively deal with potential threats and solve problems of effective demand. It also had a domestic underclass which could be used as a scapegoat and a source of solidarity through national objectives. Britain is said to have gained all these characteristics by the 1820s. But after sixty years, during the 1880s, it is said to have begun losing hegemonic power *relatively* speaking, to especially the United States, through the spreading of leading core sectors, e.g., steel plants, US success in world trade, a greater domestic market, and greater naval, army and air power. Temporally my dating of British hegemony is identical to that of Chase-Dunn (but he does not *emphasize* waves or climate change).

Fourthly, Immanuel Wallerstein (1993) cites 1815–1883 as the period of British hegemony and defines hegemony as an instance of absolute dominance of production, trade, and finance in the world economy. In his scheme military dominance is derivative from economic hegemony. Hegemonic powers first achieve agro-industrial dominance, followed by trade power and finally financial edge. Hegemony exists when all three forms are dominant in the world system, after which they lose production edge (and hence hegemony), followed by trade dominance, and lastly financial power. Hegemony is procured after a major world war when the rules of international relations are established and military challenges moderate for a time. The British established production dominance when the factory system was generating high rates of accumulation and profitability, when trade power was established in Europe, much of Asia, and the Americas, and when London became the financial center of the world. However, hegemony faltered when especially the US edged Britain from production dominance, and when the British trade system started to mature, while London still held the position of the financial center of the world. (My own analysis has a different assessment of long waves, much more on climate change, and places emphasis on the CSD, while otherwise, it agrees with Wallerstein's periodicity and analysis.)

Fifth, Taylor's (1996) account of the rise and fall of British hegemony is based mainly on politics and imperialism. Britain and France are said to have generated a mercantile system to counter the Dutch, which was successful from the 1650s onward in relegating the Dutch to a minor power during the 1700s. The glorious English revolution of the late-1600s and its aftermath set the scene for a plural democracy, where the *bourgeoisie and landowners developed a class alliance,* which in politics could sway from liberal to conservative with the Crown and Lords providing supplementary institutions during the 1700s and 1800s. The Concert of Europe that developed after the Congress of Vienna (1814–1815), effectively paved the way for relative peace in Europe while Britain had free play to develop its Empire on the global stage. However, the workshop of the world (1820s–1870s) did not last long as especially US and German manufacturing outperformed the British, while the age of imperialism reduced the relative powers of *Pax Britannica* even as British overseas power continued in relative terms.

Regarding the contradictions, domestically Taylor argues that the British upper classes eschewed industry in pursuit of a classical education and statist pursuits, while their partners in business during the late 1800s moved from industry to finance and trade. Meanwhile, the industry had evolved toward overproduction while workers started impinging on the power of the elites through state and union action. As with the Dutch experience, the productive British powerhouse petered out in the face of concerted opposition as the system became a rentier economy, and in both cases, financial power continued long after its base had deteriorated. (My analysis differs from Taylor's view of Britain since I pay more attention to economic and climatological factors; while for the Dutch I periodize hegemony much earlier.)

Arrighi's (1993) analysis of the rise and fall of British hegemony starts with the British systemic need to develop a conceptual and institutional apparatus of governance and political economy to protect Britain from attacks in Europe and beyond. Unlike the Westphalia system of 1648, which did not protect the Dutch as it saw the immediate erosion of Dutch power through the mercantile systems of British and French efforts to destroy their power, the Congress of Vienna left Britain free to deploy its navy and corporations globally while incorporating other colonies into the Empire. The British Empire was a capitalist free trade area, not a pure empire, even though it was much of that as well.

For Arrighi, alongside this institutional Concert of Europe, which protected Britain politically and militarily, was the newly built mythical principles of political economy and the God-like concepts of the free market and the wealth of nations. Arrighi indicates that these principles and concepts were generated and instituted as a witting and unwitting means of protecting private property and promoting free trade imperialism that comparative advantage had implied would be forthcoming if this ideology was put into practice. Political economy protected the *bourgeois-landlord alliance* for a time, while *Pax Britannica* saw the establishment of global systems of settler capitalism and colonial systems ensuring the availability of surplus resources for property rights and colonial control and exploitation through the 1800s.

Arrighi lists the contradictions contributing to the demise of British hegemony as the rising power of the rentier economy, competition for colonies via the scramble for Africa, Asia, and Latin America in the late 1800s and early 1900s, and the rising power of the US and Germany, which collectively eclipsed Britain economically and militarily. London still held some degree of financial power long into the 1900s and even in relative terms when New York established primacy. The colonial system continued into the 1900s while settler colonies developed at the expense of indigenous cultures.[10] (My analysis pays more attention to economic factors and climate change; otherwise, it is quite similar.)

---

[10] Some scholars compare or examine just two hegemonies. For instance, North and Thomas (1973) investigate Britain and US global leadership, but their inquiry is dominated by the concept of transaction costs, which is somewhat distant from this current work, although they do also discuss more "practical issues" to some degree (on this see Mokyr 2008).

6.7 The "Great Depression of 1773–1796?" and Price Waves

An analysis of British growth, technological change, long waves, hegemony, and climate change would be remiss without some (extended) discussion of the so-called Great Depression of 1873–1896, and the related issue of price waves. Long-wave theory and empirics (the "standard model") has historically been hypothesized and often plainly stated that the world or at least major parts of it have undergone long-wave periods when performance has been majorly subdued, and that they tend to recur every fifty years or so. Hence, the existence in the standard model of the so-called long-wave upswings of the 1780s–1810s, 1850s–1870s, 1890s–1910s, 1950s–1970s, and for some of the 1990s; and long-wave downswings of the 1820s–1840s, 1870s–1890s, 1920s–1940s, and 1980s–2020s (regarding the 1980s–2020s, some argue for an upswing in, say, the 1990s and a downswing since the GFC). I found that Britain had no long-wave upswing during the 1780s/1790s–1810s, nor did they have a *long*-wave downswing in the 1820s–1840s, and that they had a long-wave borderline performance during the 1870s–1890s. But is that the end of the story, and what of long waves of prices?

We scrutinize briefly long waves of prices. It is true that some long-wave scholars emphasize growth, others concentrate on prices, and some both. Mostly since the 1970s, they have stressed real growth due to the rise and fall of productive output (and US hegemony) since the Second World War. I emphasize growth per capita, but some reference or understanding of price waves may assist in comprehending the era. In this chap. I did argue above that there were long-wave upswings in numerous prices during the wars of the 1790s–1810s, followed by long-wave price declines during the 1820s–1840s (and later as well for some commodities), then rises during the 1850s–early 1870s, and declines in the early 1870s to the 1890s for several commodities. This periodicity is consistent with the standard model as far as prices are concerned.

Relatively recently, an econometric analysis undertaken by Marco Gallegati et al. (2017), has provided a comprehensive investigation of long waves of prices for Britain, France, and the USA from the late 1700s to the 2010s. Through wavelet analysis, and several changes in structural conditions over time, they found distinct waves of wholesale prices that accord well with the empirical results obtained by Kondratieff (early data) and several other scholars (early and later data) over time, which mirror the standard model, not necessarily of growth but certainly prices. The authors conclude that for the post-1945 data, there is little or no correspondence between prices and production (e.g., GDP), but they don't say anything (that I could find) about the pre-1945 link between production and prices. Nevertheless, it is useful to investigate their main results, for the price data, shown in Table 6.3.

Let us delve into the British case in more detail, by plotting the data, see Fig. 6.7, to examine more easily the pattern of waves for the price series:

Price waves correspond *moderately well* to the standard model (of growth), except for the post-1930s price wave, which, as with Rostow's (price) system discussed in Chap. 3, is a major anomaly (and the British and French price wave during

Table 6.3 Long waves of wholesale prices: UK, USA, France: Late 1700s to Early 2000s

Long-wave phase	UK	USA	France
1st upswing	17??➔1811	17??➔1813	17??➔1811
1st downswing	1811–1837	1813–1846	1811–1837
2nd upswing	1837–1870	1846–1869	1837–1870
2nd downswing	1870–1897	1869–1895	1870–1897
3rd upswing	1897–1919	1895–1918	1897–1919
3rd downswing	1919–1937	1918–1937	1919–1937
4th upswing	1937–1953	1837–1953	1937–1953
4th downswing	1953–1969	1953–1969	1953–1969
5th upswing	1969–1989	1969–1985	1969–1988
5th downswing	1989➔[2022?]	1985➔[2022?]	1988➔[2022?]

Source: Adapted from Gallegati (2015, 18)

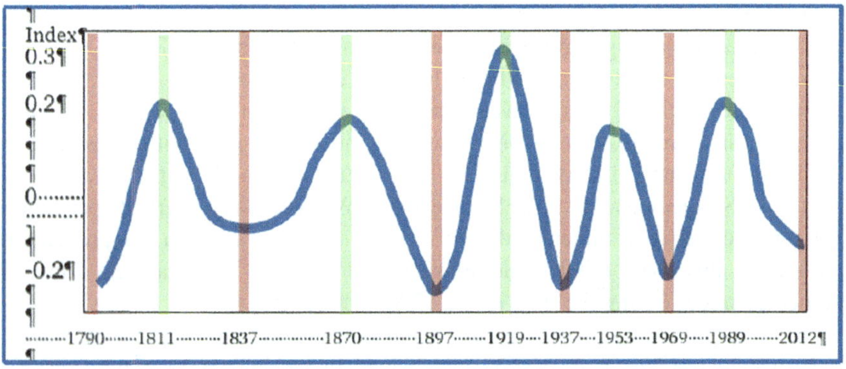

Fig. 6.7 "Wavelet" long waves of prices, UK, 1790 to 2012. (Source: Adapted from Gallegati et al. (2015, 18). *NOTE:* Based on Christiano-Fitzgerald filtered long-wave components of the wholesale price index.)

1837–1845). In most other respects (circa) before 1945, we have a price upswing when we expect a long-wave upswing, and a price downswing when we expect a long-wave downswing, for GDP per capita growth patterns. Perhaps the postwar 1945 price wave is a major anomaly or a general problem with price waves.

Regarding Britain during the so-called Industrial Revolution, we know that there was no long-wave growth per capita upswing during the first stage (1790–1820), mainly due to the Revolutionary and Napoleonic Wars. Yet there was a price upswing from the late 1700s to 1811. And we know there was a growth long upswing during the 1820s–1860s, which overlapped with the price wave downswing of 1811–1837 and the price upswing of 1837–1870.

More significant in some respects is the price-long wave downswing of 1870–1897, which was synchronous with the so-called Great Depression of 1873–1896. The question arises as to whether there is a causal link between the two. It should be noted that this ("first") Great Depression (the "second" being the so-called Great Depression of the 1930s) was cited by numerous authors as potentially or otherwise applying to numerous regions/countries of the world, including (among others) Britain (see Beales 1934–1935, Musson 1959, Coppock 1961), Central Europe (Rosenberg 1943), the USA (Veblen 1923; Fels 1949), comparative accounts (Gourevitch 1977), numerous other areas, and a critique of the hypothesis of this 1873–1896 Great Depression itself (Saul 1985).

The main issue that interests us is whether there was, in fact, a depression of prices that resulted in a much lower rate of average profit for business, due to overproduction, or some variant, leading to a depression of growth. One hypothesis is that a price drop resulted in more output, at lower prices, and thus less profit per unit output. But we do not yet know whether the greater output (in physical terms) translates into a GDP upswing or downswing, once output is given a (lower) price, and when services have been included. This outcome may manifest itself in GDP expansion or decline because real output is much higher even though (or rather because) prices are lower. (This is a classic conundrum of GDP assessment that statisticians deal with in national income accounting.[11])

Reading the literature on the first Great Depression, including the excellent paper by Beales, the profit decline was said to be due to overproduction, insufficient demand, and too much competition, but indeterminant GDP results. It was serious enough to warrant a *Royal Commission on the Depression of Trade and Industry* in Britain during the 1880s, including representations and papers by business interests, especially during the 1880s–1890s. One is left in no doubt about the extreme level of uncertainty of the era, and Beales does cite many more years of "slump" (1872–1879, 1882–1886, and 1890–1896) than "recovery" (1879–1882 and 1886–1890). It is unfortunate that we do not have more substantive data for the 1800s and into the 1900s, which hampers long-wave investigations.

We do have data on the profit share of Net National Income (NNI), and growth data as well. The share of profits (including profits from overseas) in NNY for the UK shows a definitive wave-like pattern, as shown in Fig. 6.8.

The wave-like character of the profit share indicates low*er* profits during the so-called Great Depression (the so-called Second Kondratiev downswing) and high*er* profits during the so-called Third Kondratiev upswing. Growth data is similar, except for the cyclical re-adjustment during the 1880s and the mid-1890s. "Net accumulation" (net investment) overall follows a similar trajectory, but with more of a cyclical character, with major declines during the 1870s, rise and decline in the 1880s, and rise and decline in the late 1880s and early 1890s (Phelps Brown and Weber 1962, 290). Using data from Fig. 6.2, above, I calculate the AAGR GDP pc for 1850–1873 as 1.31%, and for 1873–1993 (rather than 1896 since 1894–1896 was an upswing) the AAGR is 0.92%. In relative terms, 1850–1875 was a

[11] Technically, in theory, in GDP analysis, if we have higher physical output with, say, equal quality compared with earlier data with higher prices, then physical output should perhaps be multiplied by the earlier price series, or somehow we need to have a standard measurement of value for all years.

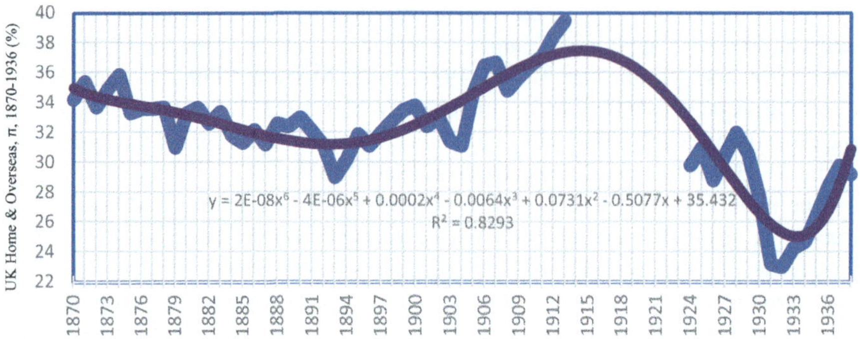

Fig. 6.8 UK, 1870–1936, Home & Overseas Profits (π), Percent of Net National Income. (Source: Adapted from raw data of Phelps Brown 1962, 299–300). Break in the data 1914–1923. NOTE: We use a polynomial trend not to differentiate the trend from cycle but mainly to provide an estimate of profit for the missing years and to provide a gauge of the trend of data (polynomial degree 6) (hence the high correlation). KEY: Raw Data (blue bar); Polynomial Trend (deg. 6) (Purple bar)

long-wave upswing, and 1873–1893,[12] taken *as a whole,* was borderline performance (based on Fig. 6.2 categories). The period 1870s–1890s underwent at least one depressive phase in every decade. It seems more likely that this period should be classed as "borderline," in between upswing and downswing. Not quite consistent with the standard model. The long-wave upswing before the 1870s–1890s lasted from the 1820s–1860s, counter to the standard model (where the downswing is during the 1820s–1840s, and the upswing lasts from the 1850s to the early 1870s).[13]

We thus interpret the so-called "depression" of the 1870s–1890s (1873–1893) in Britain as a borderline period (in general), but more significantly it represents a period of declining hegemony with structural polycrises of low growth, declining expectations, and faltering profits. Also, the standard model's results of long-wave upswing during 1896–1913 period (or 1896–1919) are not supported by the evidence, at least for Britain, because growth per capita was insufficient during 1896–1913.

In general terms, the "first Great Depression" was a period of considerable economic difficulties and uncertainties and therefore not too far removed from the standard model. The period from 1873 to 1945, taken as a whole, was one of polycrises

[12] For these calculations of per capita real annual average compound growth rate (CAAGR) for Britain I used the following formula, using annual real GDP levels: Compound AAGR = (((EndValue/StartValue)^(1/T))-1)x100 also shown as $((GDPL_{t+1}/GDPL_t)$^(1/T)-1)x100, where L = levels, $_{t+1}$ = end year, t = start year, T = number of years.

[13] Even the book that discusses the "myth of the Great Depression of 1873–1896" (Saul 1972) *seems* to be doubtful that the Great Depression did *not* exist. As he said: "The events of the 1870s and 1880s, whatever the factors underlying them, caused a serious decline in business confidence" (p. 53); and "This is not to ignore the fact that at some time during the last quarter of the nineteenth century Britain and several other countries overseas went through unusual and worrying economic experiences which sometimes they characterised at the time as a 'great depression'" (p. 54).

for Britain (at least) of world wars, volatility, depression, and financial crises until the next hegemon emerged to unite large parts of the world through the Marshall Plan, BWS, the UN and a whole series of public (global and national) goods regimes (e.g., oil, money, and trade for the world economy) to protect the system from systemic failure (for a time).

6.8 Conclusion

First, we found in this chapter that Britain underwent the most durable long-wave upswings during (circa) two bouts of hegemony, one was during the period of British hegemony, 1820s–1860s, and another during US hegemony (1950s–1980s). A third period was one modest *short-wave* upswing during the 1660s. Otherwise, in between periods of Dutch and British hegemony, there was erratic and subdued growth per capita. This provides prima facie evidence for the hegemonic stability hypothesis, that in the past, hegemons have directly or indirectly helped to sustain growth waves and stability for certain nations and areas, especially those closely linked to the hegemon.

Second, this conclusion also provides preliminary prima facie evidence for a new, second hypothesis, called the "just after hegemony" thesis, where at the time of the dissolution of absolute hegemony and in the early phases of *relative* hegemony the power most likely to be the next hegemon has experienced a brief or more extended period of rapid growth. The British experience of the 1660s is a much weaker version of this thesis. Chapter 7 examines this hypothesis in the light of the late 1800s when British absolute hegemony was transitioning to relative hegemony, in relation to the performance of the United States; while Chap. 8 studies the situation when US absolute hegemony was transitioning to *relative* hegemony, starting in the 1980s and 1990s and continuing into the 2000s in relation to Chinese performance.

Third, a major conclusion of this chapter is that Britain did not undergo major growth waves and absolute hegemony during what has been called the first Industrial Revolution of the late 1700s and early 1800s. In fact, in agreement with numerous studies, it appears that the onset of Industrial Revolution was a more gradual process, not a spurt as such and that the growth and hegemony benefits for Britain (and likely other nations) of industrial development had to await the outcome of the Revolutionary and Napoleonic Wars before structural stability and confidence (within the CSD) could contribute to durable performance into the 1820s onwards for five decades.

Fourthly, British hegemony and growth waves were very durable for five decades, but contradictions led to a deterioration of British performance that was to continue, with minor interludes, from the 1870s through to the mid-1900s. Meanwhile, especially German and US capitalism developed through the late 1800s and early-to-mid-1900s, and as the quest for German hegemony failed US power ultimately led to the most robust period of capitalist development ever during the mid-late 1900s.

Fifthly, evidence is emerging that during the period of British hegemony, there were two trends relating to climate change that impinged on Britain and much of the world. The first was the cooling period during the first half of hegemony (1820s–1852), when, on balance, the generation of greenhouse gasses did not result in warming (mostly it cooled). The second was the last half of hegemony (1850s–1880s) when rising temperatures were the net result of industrializing, trading, financing, and military activities. Whereas for Dutch hegemony there was the Little Ice Age that the United Provinces managed to adapt to much more than others in the Northern Hemisphere, the British experience was a mixed one of stability and cooling (a later phase of the LIA during the next solar cycle minima) and then heating, the latter what one would normally expect during periods of rising growth and industry around the world.

Sixthly, the principles of political economy (PoPE) contingency paradigm and the new long wave statistical method were very useful for analyzing British long waves, hegemony, and climate change (LWHegCC). In general, PoPE hypothesized that LWHegCC is contingent upon an array of factors, including historical processes and events, changes in political-economic power, heterogeneous agents and groups, CCC processes, contradictions, degrees of risk and uncertainty, the inception and demise of innovations, policy and governance, and (most importantly) the workings or otherwise of the circuits of socioeconomic dynamics. Each of these played a key role in the British experience, which led to our conclusions regarding the evidence of long waves, hegemony, and climate change.

Some brief examples of how PoPE applied to the British experience are in order. First, the whole chapter has shown how history is important to an understanding of waves of growth, hegemony, and climate change. Changes in political-economic power are crucial for the successful emergence of a durable long-wave upswing. LWHegCC depended upon an array of amplified and magnified processes that impinged upon upswings and downswings throughout, for instance, the 1800s (CCC). A multitude of innovations were essential to the emergence of Britain as a world power, including geo-eco-spatial, technical, mechanical, social, and political changes in ways of doing things. Britain depended much on the heterogeneous groups and agents alliance between bourgeoisie and landed interests and the exploitation of the working classes, as well as colonial peripheries, for the provision of economic surplus and thereby the successful development of trade, finance, and the factory system. Risk and uncertainty rose and fell over the wave, hegemony, and climate change, which fundamentally conditioned rates of rise and fall. Politics and policy were of profound significance to the whole process, especially relating to free trade imperialism, free markets, double movements, and parliament, monarchy, and workers' movements. Overall, the circuits of socioeconomic dynamics enabled British capitalism to be successful for a time through successive rounds of geo-eco-spatial production, distribution, exchange, polity, and household relations. Contradictions were embedded in the whole trajectory of the durable dynamic circuit, especially relating to the emergence of competition, declining rates of innovation, the relative exhaustion of potential, and the eventual dominance of finance, rentier income, and less productive activities.

References

Abram, Nerilie J, Helen V. McGregor, Jessica E. Tierney, Michael N. Evans, Nicholas P. McKay, Darrell S. Kaufman, and 2K Consortium of Co-Authors. 2016. Early onset of industrial-era warming across the oceans and continents. *Nature* 536 (26 August): 411–434.

ACAPS. 2023. *El Nino overview: Anticipated humanitarian impact in 2023*. Oslo: ACAPS.

Arrighi, Giovanni. 1993. The three hegemonies of historical capitalism. In *Gramsci, historical materialism and international relations, 148–185*, ed. Stephen Gill. Cambridge: Cambridge University Press.

Beales, H. L. 1934. 1. The "great depression" in industry and trade. *Economic History Review* 5 (1): 65–75.

Black, Robert A., and Claire G. Gilmore. 1990. Crowding out during Britain's industrial revolution. *Journal of Economic History* 50 (1): 109–131.

Bliss, Barbara A.; Mitch Warachka and Marc Weidenmier. Forthcoming. How the stock ticker decreased price efficiency in the early 20th Century. *Critical Finance Review.*

Bottomley, Sean. 2014. *The British patent system during the industrial revolution, 1700–1852: From privilege to property*. Cambridge: Cambridge University Press.

Broadberry, Stephen, Bruce M. S. Campbell, Alexander Klein, Mark Overton, and Bas van Leeuwen. 2015. *British economic growth, 1270–1870*. Cambridge: Cambridge University Press.

Broadberry, Stephen, Jagjit S. Chadha, Jason Lennard, and Ryland Thomas. 2023. Dating business cycles in the United Kingdom, 1700–2010. *Economic History Review* 76:1141–1162. https://doi.org/10.1111/ehr.13238.

Brooke, John L. 2014. *Climate change and the course of global history: A rough journey*. Cambridge: Cambridge University Press.

Chase Dunn, Christopher. 1998. *Global formation: Structures of the world-economy*. Boulder, CO: Rowman & Littlefield Publishers Inc.

Clark, Gregory. 1953. *The great escape: The industrial revolution in theory and history.* Mimeo. 76pp. University of California, Davis.

Coleman, David, and John Salt. 1992. *The British population: Patterns, trends and processes*. Oxford: Oxford University Press.

Conroy, Stephen J., and Tisha L. N. Emerson. 2007. Ethical cycles and trends: Evidence and implications. *Journal of Business Ethics* 8 (4): 905–911.

Coppock, D. J. 1961. The causes of the great depression 1873-1896. *The Manchester School* 29 (3): 205–232.

de Vries, J. 2008. *The industrious revolution: Consumer behavior and the household economy, 1650 to the present*. New York: Cambridge University Press.

Denoon, Donald. 1983. *Settler capitalism: The dynamics of dependent development in the southern hemisphere*. Oxford: Oxford University Press.

Derry, Thomas Kingston. 1965. *Britain since 1750: Part 2 of a short economic history of Britain*. Oxford: Oxford University Press.

Fels, Rendigs. 1949. The long-wave depression, 1873–97. *Review of Economics and Statistics* 31 (1): 69–73.

Flamant, Maurice, and Jeanne Singer-Kerel. 1968. *Modern economic crises*. London: Barrie & Jenkins.

Freeman, Chris, and Francisco Louçã. 2001. *As time goes by: From the industrial revolution to the information revolution*. Oxford: Oxford University Press.

Gallegati, Marco; Mauro Gallegati, James B. Ramsey and Willi Semmler. 2015. Long waves in prices: New evidence from wavelet analysis. *Cliometrica.*

Gallegati, Marco, Mauro Gallegati, James B. Ramsey, and Willi Semmler. 2017. Long waves in prices: New evidence from wavelet analysis. *Cliometrica* 11 (2): 127–151. Long waves in prices: new evidence from wavelet analysis | Cliometrica (springer.com).

Gelber, Harry G. 2004. *Opium, soldiers and evangelicals Britain's 1840–42 war with China, and its aftermath*. New York: Macmillan.

Geraghty, Thomas M. 2007. The factory system in the British industrial revolution: A complementarity thesis. *European Economic Review* 51:1329–1350.
Gilpin, Robert. 2001. *Global political economy: Understanding the international economic order*. Princeton, New Jersey: Princeton University Press.
Gourevitch, Paul Alexis. 1977. International trade, domestic coalitions and liberty: Comparative responses to the crisis 1873-1896. *Journal of Interdisciplinary History* 8 (2): 281–313.
Harley, C. Knick. 1999. Reassessing the industrial revolution: A macro view. In *The British industrial revolution: An economic perspective. Second edition, 160–205*, ed. Joel Mokyr. Boulder, Colorado: Westview Press.
Heim, Carol E., and Philip Mirowski. 1987. Interest rates and crowding-out during Britain's industrial revolution. *Journal of Economic History* 47 (1): 117–139.
Heim, Carol E., and Philip Mirowski. 1991. Crowding out: A response to Black and Gilmore. *Journal of Economic History* 51 (3):
Hobsbawm, Eric. 1962. *The age of revolution 1789–1848*. London: Abacus.
Hobsbawm, Eric. 1968. *Industry and empire: An economic history of Britain since 1750*. London: Weidenfeld and Nicolson.
Holmes, Richard. 2001. Crimean war. In *The oxford companion to military history*, ed. Richard Holmes, 235–240. Oxford: Oxford University Press.
Izumikawa, Yasuhero. 2001. Free trade imperialism. In *Routledge encyclopedia of international political economy*, ed. R. J. Barry Jones, 576–577. London & New York: Routledge.
Keohane, Robert O. 1984. *After hegemony: Cooperation and discord in the world political economy*. Princeton: Princeton University Press. 2005. New Preface by Author.
Kindleberger, Charles Poor. 1974. The formation of financial Centres. *Princeton Studies in International Finance* 36 (1): 1–78.
Kindleberger, Charles Poor. 1975. The Rise of Free Trade in Western Europe, 1820 to 1875. *Journal of Economic History* 35 (1): 20–55. Reprinted in C.P. Kindleberger (1978) Economic response: Comparative studies in trade, finance, and growth. Cambridge: Harvard University Press, 39–65.
Kinealy, Christine. 2002. *The great Irish famine: Impact, ideology and rebellion*. New York: Macmillan.
Koyama M (2009). The Price of time and labour supply: From the Black death to the industrious revolution. Oxford Economic and Social History Working Papers, No. 78.
Kwon, Roy. 2011. Hegemonies in the world-system: An empirical assessment of hegemonic sequences from the 16th to 20th century. *Sociological Perspectives* 54 (4): 593–617.
Lambert, Thomas E. 2020. Paul Baran's economic surplus concept, the Baran ratio, and the decline of feudalism. *Monthly Review* 72 (7):
Lambert, Thomas E. 2023. The Baran ratio, investment, and British economic growth and development. *Journal of Post Keynesian Economics* 46 (1): 142–172.
Lambert, Thomas E. 2024. British public investment, government spending, housing, and the industrial revolution: A study of governmental and social surplus absorption. *Journal of Economic Issues* 58 (4): 1378–1401. https://doi.org/10.1080/00213624.2024.2418651
Landes, David S. 1969. *The unbound Prometheus: Technological changes and industrial development in Western Europe from 1750 to the present*. Cambridge: Cambridge University Press.
Leonard, E.M. 1962. The [E]nclosure of common fields in the seventeenth century. In *Essays in economic history: Volume two,* ed. E.M. Carus-Wilson, 227-256.
Maddison, Angus. 1991. *Dynamic forces in capitalist development: A long-run comparative view*. Oxford: Oxford University Press.
Maddison, Angus. 1982. *Phases of capitalist development*. Oxford: Oxford University Press.
Maddison Project. 2024. *Maddison historical statistics database*. Maddison Historical Statistics | Historical Development | Groningen Growth and Development Centre | University of Groningen (rug.nl)

Marx, Karl. 1853. *"The East India company: Its history and results" (1853), "The British rule in India"*. (1853), and "The future results of British rule in India" (1853), *New York daily tribune*. Republished in Karl Marx and Friedrich Engels. *On colonialism*. Moscow: Progress Publishers, 1968.

McMichael, Philip. 1985. British hegemony in the nineteenth-century world economy. In *States versus markets in the world system*, ed. Peter Evans, Dietrich Rueschemeyer, and Evelyn Huber Stephens, 117–148. Beverly Hills, California: Sage Publications.

Merriment, John, and Jay Winter, eds. 2006. *Europe 1789–1914: Encyclopedia of the age of industry and empire. 6 vols*. San Diego: Thomson Gale.

Mokyr, Joel. 2008. The institutional origins of the industrial revolution. In *Institutions and economic performance, 64–119*, ed. Elhanan Helpman, 64–119. Boston: Harvard University Press.

Mokyr, Joel. 2017. *A culture of growth: The origins of the modern economy*. Princeton, New Jersey: Princeton University Press.

Musson, A. E. 1959. The great depression in Britain, 1873–1896: A reappraisal. *Journal of Economic History* 19 (2): 199–228.

Naoriji, Dadabhari. 1901. *Poverty and un-British rule in India*. London: Swan Sonnenschein & Co., Ltd.

Nierode, Dale Irwin. 2022. The cyclical sine model for climate change. *International Journal of Plant, Animal and Environmental Sciences* 12 (4): 175–191. https://www.fortunejournals.com/articles/the-cyclical-sine-model-explanation-for-climate.pdf.

Nogues-Marco, Pilar. 2021. Measuring colonial extraction: The East India company's rule and the drain of wealth (1757–1858). *Capitalism: A Journal of History and Economics* 2 (1): 154–195. https://doi.org/10.1353/cap.2021.0004.

Nye, John Vincent. 1991. The myth of free-trade Britain and fortress France: Tariffs and trade in the nineteenth century. *Journal of Economic History* 51 (1): 23–46.

Nye, John Vincent. 2010. Political economy of Anglo-French trade, 1689-1899: Agricultural trade policies, alcohol taxes, and war. In *Political economy of distortions to agricultural incentives*, ed. K. Anderson, 25–42. Washington DC: World Bank.

O'Brien, Patrick Karl. 1992. The French wars (1793-1815) and capital formation during the industrial revolution. In *New directions in economic and social history, Volume 2*, ed. Anne Digby Charles Feinstein and David Jenkins, 37–50. London: Macmillan.

O'Brien, Patrick Karl. 2011. The contributions of warfare with revolutionary and Napoleonic France to the consolidation and Progress of the British industrial revolution. In *Working paper no 150/11*. Department of Economic History, London School of Economics.

Phelps Brown, Henry, and Bernard Weber. 1962. Accumulation, productivity and distribution in the British economy, 1870-1938. In *Essays in economic history 280–301. In essays in economic history*, ed. E. M. Carus-Wilson. London: Edward Arnold.

Polanyi, Karl. 1944. *The great transformation*. Boston: 1968.

Preda, Alex. 2006. Socio-technical agency in financial markets: The case of the stock ticker. *Social Studies of Science* 36 (5): 753–782.

Rosenberg, Hans. 1943. Political and social consequences of the great depression of 1873–1896 in Central Europe. *Economic History Review* 13 (1/2): 58–73.

Rostow, Walt Whitman. 1978. *The world economy: History and prospect*. London: Macmillan.

Ryan, Lyndall. 2024. *New evidence reveals aboriginal massacres committed on an extensive scale*. https://www.newcastle.edu.au/newsroom/featured/new-evidence-reveals-aboriginal-massacres-committed-on-extensive-scale.

Saul, S. B. 1985. *The myth of the great depression, 1873–1896*. London: Macmillan.

Semmel, Bernard. 1970. *The rise of free trade imperialism: Classical political economy and the empire of free trade and imperialism, 1750–1850*. Cambridge: Cambridge University Press.

Stearns, Peter N. 2013. *The industrial revolution in world history*. 4th ed. Boulder, Colorado: Westview Press.

Taylor, Peter J. 1996. *The way the modern world works: World hegemony to world impasse*. New York: Wiley.

Temin, Peter, and Hans-Joachim Voth. 2005. Credit rationing and crowding out during the industrial revolution: Evidence from Hoares Bank, 1702–1862. *Explorations in Economic History* 42:325–348.

Tylecote, Andrew. 1992. *The long wave in the world economy: The present crisis in historical perspective*. London and New York: Routledge.

Van Neuss, Leif. 2015. *Why did the industrial revolution start in Britain?* Belgium: Working Paper, Economics Department, HEC–University of Liege.

Zanden, Van, Jan Luiten, and Jutta Bolt. 2021. Two concerns about the interpretation of the estimates of historical national accounts before 1850. *Journal of Global History* 16 (2): 294–300.

Zanden, Van, Jan Luiten, and Bas Van Leeuwen. 2012. Persistent but not consistent: The growth of national income in Holland 1347-1807. *Explorations in Economic History* 49:119–130.

Veblen, Thorstein Bunde. 1919. *The vested interests and the common man ("the modern point of view and the new order")*, 1964. New York: Augustus M. Kelley.

Veblen, Thorstein Bunde. 1923. *Absentee ownership and business enterprise in recent times: The case of America*, 1964. New York: Augustus M. Kelley.

Wallerstein, Immanuel. 1993. The three instances of hegemony of the capitalist world-economy. *International Journal of Comparative Sociology* 1 (1–2): 100–108.

Williamson, Jeffrey G. 1984. Why was British growth so slow during the industrial revolution? *Journal of Economic History* 44 (3): 687–712.

Williamson, Jeffrey G. 1991. Did English factor markets fail during the industrial revolution. In *Quantitative economic history, 45–82*, ed. N. F. R. Crafts, N. H. Dimsdale, and S. Engerman. Oxford: Oxford University Press.

WMO (World Meteorological Organisation). 2024. *WMO Confirms that 2023 Smashes global temperature record*. Media Release: WMO. https://wmo.int/news/media-releases.

Chapter 7
US Hegemony, Long Waves, and Climate Change

Abstract Using the Principles of Political Economy (PoPE) Contingency Paradigm and New Long Wave Method (NLWM), this chapter begins with an outline of the key features of US long waves, hegemony rise and fall, and climate change, from the year 1800 (when yearly Maddison Project data starts for the USA) to the 2020s. Then we detail the dynamic structural evolution, transformation, and relative decline of the US pathways and circuits of socioeconomic dynamics (CSD), from the 1930s–1940s through to the 1990s. Special reference is given to the ecological-geospatial-international structures of the post-war corporate system, Fordist accumulation and distribution, Keynesian welfare state, regulated financial system, and households-community that structured the relations of reproduction. Throughout we outline the contradictions within the circuit, and within and between all the components of the circuit, that led to long wave downswing, the transition from absolute to relative hegemony, and the climate change crisis. We extend the analysis of long waves, hegemony, and climate change into the 2020s while keeping the extended discussion of structural polycrises (during the 1980s–2020s) for chap. 9. A conclusion follows.

Keywords PoPE Contingency Paradigm · United States Hegemony · Long waves · Climate change · US Pathways and Circuits of Socioeconomic Dynamics · Postwar corporate system · Institutions and technologies · Rise and fall

7.1 Introduction

Using the PoPE contingency paradigm and the new long wave method, in this chapter, I analyze the relationship between United States long waves, hegemonic evolution, and climate change during the 1800s–2020s. Special attention is given to the era of US hegemony and its relative demise (1940s–2000s). The forces of hegemony, long waves, and climate change are interrelated. The techno-institutional-ecological

P. A. O'Hara, *Long Waves of Growth, Hegemonic Power, and Climate Change in the World Economy*, https://doi.org/10.1007/978-981-96-4132-1_7

factors and structures that provided the basis of long-wave upswing and downswing and climate change were also structural conditions underlying US hegemony and its demise.

The chapter starts by examining the pattern of growth per capita, geopolitical power, and climate change of the US and global economies during this period, what has been called "The Age of Growth" (Robinson 1978). In successive sections, we then, first, outline the technological, institutional, and geospatial-ecological circuit of reproduction of US capital during the "Golden Age" of the 1940s–1970s (Marglin and Schor 1990). Secondly, we examine the contradictions within the eco-spatial-techno-institutions that generated increasingly anomalous socioeconomic performance during the 1970s–2000s. We extend the analysis of long waves, hegemony, and climate change into the 2020s while keeping the extended analysis of structural polycrises (1980s–2020s) for Chap. 9.

7.2 United States Growth-Hegemony Wave Pattern 1800s–2020s

Firstly, we provide an outline of some of the performance measures underlying US power and long waves. We start with a summary of US decadal gross domestic product (GDP) per capita growth patterns for the 1800s–2020s, outlining the differences between trend and waves. As with Dutch and British cases (chaps. 5–6), we arrange GDP per capita annual growth in decadal averages, to moderate short cycle and chance factors in performance indicators. Then we arrange a linear trend line (using the least squares method) and transform that into a bar (20-point thickness) to highlight growth above and below the trend bar. Within the trend bar is "borderline" performance, above the trend, is the upswing, and below trend is downswing. Two or more decades above the trend bar is a long-wave upswing, two or more decades below the trend is long-wave downswing and two or more decades within the trend bar is long-wave borderline performance. One decade up, down, or borderline is short-wave upswing, downswing, or borderline, respectively. We are especially interested in durable performance which results in three or more decades of long-wave upswing, and usually numerous decades of hegemonic power. Climate change also varied through the decades, and they are predictably *hypothesized* to be worse during long-wave upswings, although as already noted in previous chapters this is usually not the case due to counteracting influences.

The pattern of short and long waves of upswing, borderline, and downswing for the US 1800s–2020s is shown in Fig. 7.1.

Table 7.1 summarizes the results of Fig. 7.1.

Analytically, Table 7.1 illustrates that the results accord with all the major long waves cum hegemony hypotheses. First, the best US long wave upswings are during periods of absolute hegemony for the US, i.e., 1940s–1960s, and much weaker

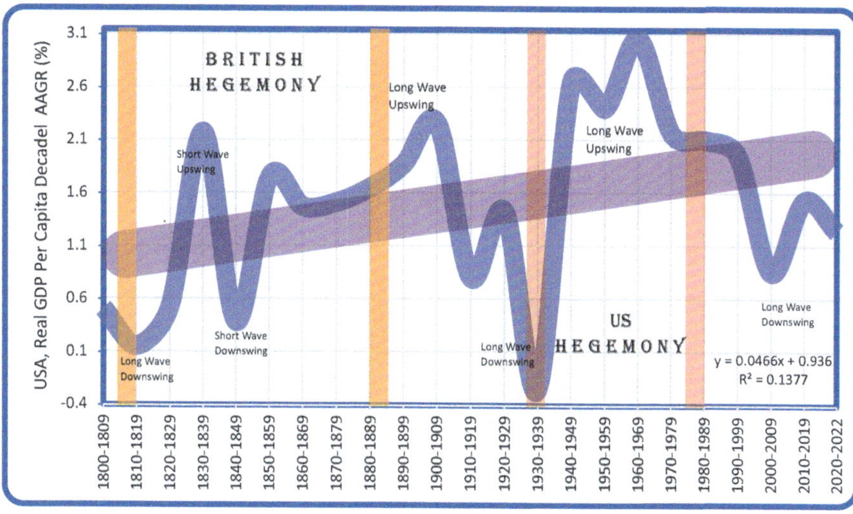

Fig. 7.1 USA real GDP per capita decadal AAGR, 1800–2023 (Blue bar). Linear trend bar (Purple). (Source: Adapted from the raw figures of the Maddison Project 2024.) ($y = 0.0466x + 0.936$; $R^2 = 0.1377$ = trend *line*)

LWUs during the 1970s–1980s. Second, during the latter phase of British absolute hegemony (1880s) and during British relative hegemony (1890s–1900s), the US underwent moderately good LWUs. As we indicated, this is a tendency, for the likely next hegemon (US) to undergo relatively good performance during the latter phase of (British) hegemon's absolute and early relative hegemony. Third, periods of no absolute hegemony were the worst for US performance (1910s–1930s and 1990s–2020s) as polycrises emerged (world wars, financial crises, Great Depression, etc.). Fourth, when the US underwent absolute hegemony, not only it but also its best allies and economic partners (e.g., Britain, Europe, including the Netherlands) underwent impressive economic performance (during the 1990s–2020s, we would expect China, the most likely next hegemon, to undergo robust long-wave upswings, as indeed it did, see chap. 8).

Now we present the Gallegati et al. (2017) results of the (filtered) USA wholesale price index for 1790–2012 in Fig. 7.2, and compare it with (a) the standard model and (b) the GDP per capita growth data from Fig. 7.1.

In terms of periodicity, for the 1790–1950 period, the US wholesale price index wavelet is broadly comparable to the standard model of long waves outlined in chapter one, with usually some modest variations, while the period since 1950 is disjointed relative to the standard model, as was Rostow's analysis of long waves. Since 1950, the real problem here is the declining price wave during 1956–1972, and the rise from 1972 to 1984; this is broadly counter-cyclical vis-à-vis growth of

Table 7.1 USA, long waves "Map," ratio of upswing to borderline and downswing performance, 1800–2022 (222 years)

1800–1819 (20 yrs)	1820–1889(70 yrs)	1890–1909 (20 yrs)	1910–1939 (30 yrs)	1940–1989 (50 yrs)	1990–2022 (33 yrs)
No Hegemony Era	British Absolute Hegemony	Relative British Hegemony	No Hegemony (Absolute or Relative)	US Absolute Hegemony	US Relative Hegemony
LWD (1800–1819) = [20 yrs]	$\frac{1}{3}$ LWU (1880s) = [10 yrs]	$\frac{2}{3}$LWU (1890s–1900s) = 20 yrs	SWBD (1920s) = [10 yrs]	50LWU (1940s–1980s) = [50 yrs]	SWB (1990s) = [10 yrs]
	SWU (1830s) (1850s) =20 yrs		SWD (1910s) (1930s) = [20 yrs]		LWD (2000–2022) = [23 yrs]
	LWB (1860s–1870s) = 20 yrs				
	SWD (1820s) (1840s) = 20 yrs				
0 U/20D	**30 U/40UB = 0.75**	**20 U/0DB = ∞**	**0 U/30DB**	**50 U/0D = ∞**	**0 U/33DB**

Note: *U* upswing, *D* downswing, *B* borderline, *LWU* long wave upswing, *LWD* long wave downswing, *SWU* short-wave upswing, *SWD* short-wave downswing, *DB* on border of D and B

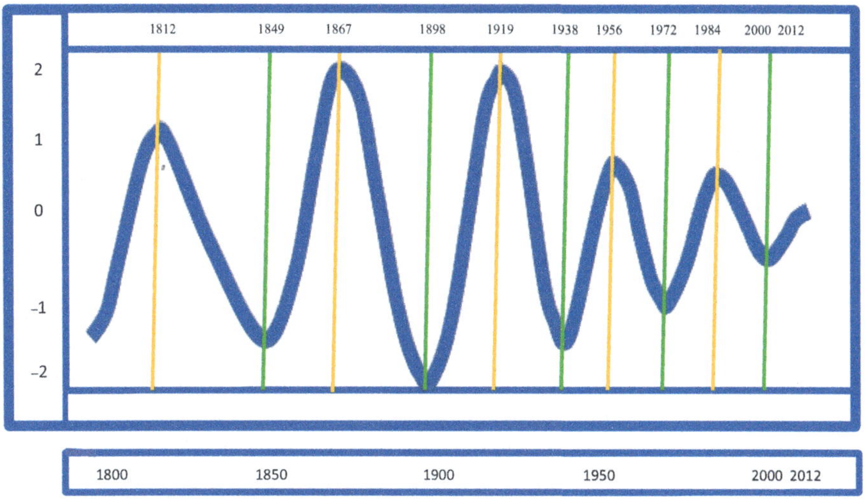

Fig. 7.2 USA, 1790–2012, MODWT LA(8) wavelet filter long-wave components of the wholesale price index. (Source: Adapted from Gallegati et al. 2017, 21)

GDP per capita, reinforced by the stagflationary spiral ("high inflation, lower growth") from 1972 to 1984. After that things become more confusing.

Compared with our PoPE model of long waves, applied to the US, the price wavelet is far more deviant. During 1800–1939, the PoPE growth wave postdates the price wave by 20 years (the price wave is counter-cyclical); during the 1840s, the PoPE growth wave coincides with the price wave, up to the 1860s, the price wave was ahead of the PoPE growth wave by a decade, during the late 1800s, prices descended while growth is robust, and, during the 1919–1956 period, the two move in the same directions (down and up). After 1956, the only similarity is a decline in both measures from the 1980s to 2000s.

Brian Berry's (1991) comparison of US wholesale price indices and US GDP AAGR (*not* per capita) for the period 1800–1990, finds mostly counter-cyclical variations of prices during 1800–1930 and 1970–1990, and one short procyclical variation during 1935–1950. Like the PoPE model, unsurprisingly, Berry's growth waves are different from the standard model, since he shows good rates of growth of GDP (again, *not* per capita) during the so-called first Kondratieff downswing (1820–1850) and during the so-called third Kondratieff downswing (1870s–1890s).

The rest of this chapter comprises detailing the nature of these evolving structures of technology, institutions, and geo-climate change affecting US performance, especially underlying the pattern of US history during the 1940s–1990s (and then briefly to the 2020s). In short, we provide a salient outline of the techno-institutional-ecological foundations of the postwar corporate system, including its positive impact on performance, and the inherent contradictions that undermined socioeconomic activity. Thereafter, we scrutinize linkages between growth, hegemony, and climate change.

7.3 US Pathways and Circuits of Socioeconomic Dynamics 1940s–1990s[1]

There were two periods in post-1800 US political economy history when evidence supports the hypothesis that there were structural conditions in the techno-geo-institutional regimes promoting the 'pathways and circuits of capitalism' (CSD) into long-wave upswing. The first was cut short by the civil war and long-wave upswing did not emerge until the 1880s–1890s–1900s. Without civil war, the short-wave upswing of the 1850s may have continued into long-wave upswing during the 1850s–1870s and possibly later as well. Although the civil war may have enabled the upswing to emerge more fully. To my knowledge, no one has developed this hypothesis in more detail from a long-wave perspective, although others have looked at this vis-à-vis the standard model (Mager 1987) or studied certain structural relations, such as capital–labor relations (Gordon et al. 1990). Mager's analysis centered on prices, but he does provide some material on the geo-techno-institutions, although not enough to help with our investigations (especially because of his standard (price) wave periodicities).

This section is not the place to *detail* these eco-techno-institutional structures, underlying the 1880s–1900s long wave upswing since our main concern is the second period of long wave upswing, during the 1940s–1960s, followed by smaller long wave (almost borderline) upswing conditions during the 1970s–1980s, and much lower growth per capita thereafter. We are concerned with long waves, hegemony, and climate change linkages, which were more pertinent during the postwar (1945→) period. Nonetheless, a *brief* preliminary mention of some *possible* eco-techno-institutional conditions of the late-1800s–early 1900s *hypothetical* CSD could assist with future research.

We merely mention some of the most iconic structures emerging from the late-1800s onward, culminating in the new era of business (Veblen 1923) of the late 1890s and early 1900s, including (1) The Reconstruction process after the civil war (including the "north-south binary"), (2) the extensive regime of production (see Sect. 7.3.3, below), the technology style of electricity, chemicals, combustion engines, turbines, railways (Mager 1987, ch. 7), and canals, (3) the evolution from initial proletarianization to labor homogenization in the workplace (Gordon 1982), (4) metals-mining and farming (esp. sugar and cotton), (5) the first wave of European migration, householding (and building), (6) the banking, debt, and investment regime, and (7) GHG emissions and temperature rises; plus associated (8) agents, classes, and other groups involved in these dynamics.

[1] The topic of US long waves and the techno-institutional circuit, 1940s–1990s, is the subject of my PhD (O'Hara 1992), which was published after rewriting as (O'Hara 2000), which won the *Myrdal Prize* for *Book of the Year* from EAEPE. This chapter utilizes some of these arguments and passages from these works.

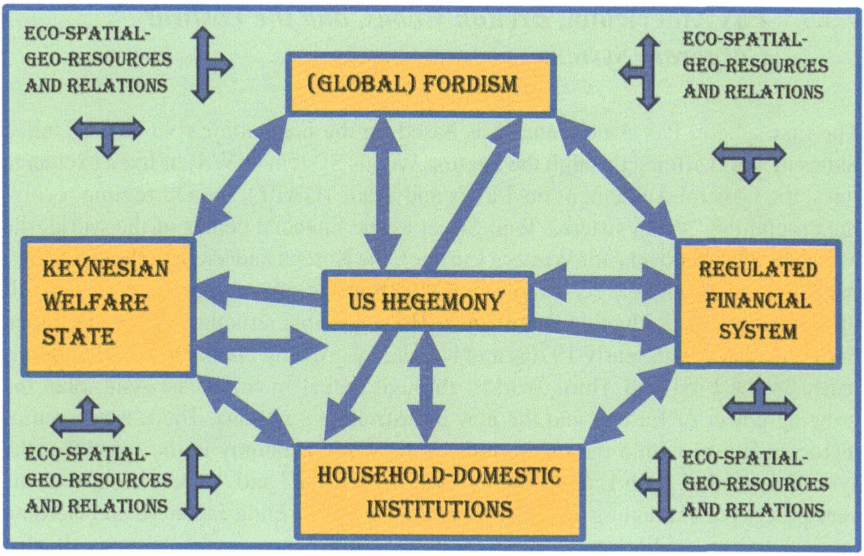

Fig. 7.3 United States pathways and circuits of socioeconomic dynamics (CSD) (*Shortform* version)

We now analyze the 'postwar corporate system' CSD in the US during the 1940s–1990s (followed by the Chinese CSD in chap. 8; and the 1980s–2020s general polycrises in ch. 9). Six *interdependent* core techno-institutional-ecological structures of postwar U.S. capitalism within the circuit of the CSD include (1) Pax Americana-US hegemony, (2) geo-eco-spatial systems (3) (Global) Fordism and the capital–labor accord, (4) the Keynesian-Welfare state, (5) the regulated financial system, and (6) the structures of family and community. Each of these are illustrated in Fig. 7.3 and outlined in the six sections that follow:

Key: 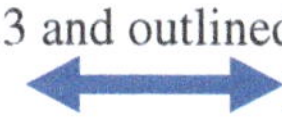Inter-sphere interdependencies: flows, stocks, agents, and groups.

These six interdependent CSD dynamic structures cumulatively provided the reproductive foundations for relative stability, profitability, and investment for three decades during the long boom of the late 1940s, 1950s, 1960s, and early 1970s. As the contradictions within (and between) the structures cumulatively merged to form a ruptured disunity, instability led to lower expectations of profitable investment, and hence the recessions in the 1970s, 1980s, 1990s, and 2000s (and afterward).[2]

[2] See O'Hara (2000). For a detailed policy and governance analysis of the new institutions-technologies and ecologies required for a new CSD, see O'Hara (2014b). For an outline of "reproduction," see O'Hara (2001).

7.3.1 Pax Americana, *Bretton Woods, and the Postwar Corporate System*

The first sphere, Pax Americana, was based on the hegemonic role of the United States in world affairs, through the Bretton Woods System (BWS) of fixed exchange rates, the General Agreement on Tariffs and Trade (GATT), the Oil regime revolving around the "seven sisters," Wall Street as the financial center of the world, the Marshall Plan (recovery for Western Europe), the Korean and Vietnam Wars to combat communism, and the central place of U.S. transnational corporations in technology transfer and production dominance. However, this structure was undermined during the late 1960s, early 1970s, and beyond by growing challenges to U.S. dominance in the First and Third Worlds, through defeat in Southeast Asia, plus the growing power of Europe and the new industrializing nations. There were contradictory relations within the institutions of the world economy in the sense that the system depended upon U.S. hegemony for "leadership" and "supervision," but the very process of expanding Western capitalism and reforming Japanese and German fascism led to challenges to U.S. capitalism and hence to the system. (It also included core elements of the other spheres of the CSD, both for upswing and downswing.)

There are four major perspectives on the question of hegemony and the postwar era:[1] (1) the rise and fall thesis, (2) the cultural hegemony thesis, (3) the institutional rise and fall thesis, and (4) the rise and still strong thesis. The first three of these are, in some respects, complementary because each seeks to emphasize a particular aspect of domination, leadership, and/or cooperation in the world economy. The "rise and fall" thesis states that the USA contributed to Western accumulation and growth in the 1945–1970 period by the provision of hegemonic stability, leadership, and/or domination, but that instability and deep recessions emerged in the 1970s, 1980s, and 1990s (in part) because hegemony declined.

This "rise and fall" thesis is by far the dominant one in terms of the number of authors subscribing to it, including, among numerous others, Wallerstein, Kindleberger, Bowles, Gordon, Weisskopf, and MacEwan (among many others). Wallerstein says that "Hegemony refers to the ongoing rivalry between the so-called great powers that is unbalanced so that one power can impose its rule and its wishes (at the very least by effective veto power) in the economic, political, military, diplomatic, and even cultural arenas" (Wallerstein 1983, 101).

The "material basis of this power" is said to have depended on "home enterprises" being dominant in the areas of agro-industrial production, commerce, and finance. "Agro-industrial" activities include agricultural, manufacturing, and high-technology industries. Commerce represents the buying and selling of goods and services in the national and world economies. Finance is defined to include the system of rules for international (and domestic) exchange of currencies (plus the activities of banks, general finance companies, and stock markets). Wallerstein (1983) postulates that hegemony "refers to the process of having an edge in each sphere simultaneously," but that dominance is achieved initially in agroindustry,

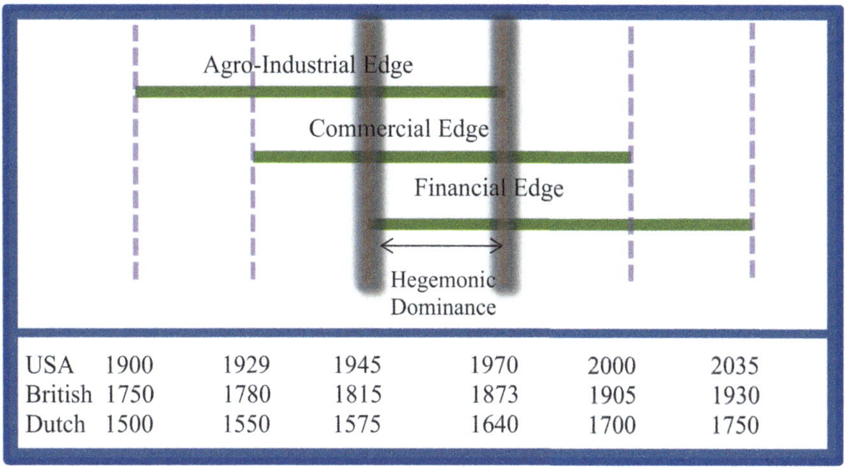

Fig. 7.4 Three dimensions of Dutch, British and United States hegemonic evolution. (Source: Adapted from Wallerstein (1983), O'Hara (2000, 2025)

then in commerce, and lastly in finance. Dominance is so significant that "allied major powers are *de facto* client states and opposed major powers feel defensive *vis-a-vis* the hegemonic power" (p.101). Figure 7.4, above, illustrates the core elements of this definition of hegemony:

This diagram illustrates the pattern of capitalist hegemony (circa) for the Dutch (1575–1640), British (1815–1873), and US (1945–1970) (see Knutsen 1999 for details on other, non-capitalist "Empire" systems). The dates are only approximate because hegemonic trends are qualitative changes linked to processes that cannot always be specified precisely. Wallerstein's theory of hegemony is said to be, not comparative-static, but dynamic-processual in orientation. Hegemonic trends are not random, but the result of specific historical processes which have a major influence on the evolution of the capitalist system.[3]

There are said to be internal contradictions within these processes that led to the demise of dominance, and which have implications for the stability and overall performance of capitalism.[2] The central contradiction of hegemony, according to Wallerstein, is associated with the rise of the ideology and practice of "global liberalism." Hegemony promotes the material conditions of the hegemonic nation, encouraging parliamentary institutions, "free trade," and a distaste for revolutionary "political" change. Despite this, domestic repression could be high within the

[3]The major journals of political economy that have explored the question of hegemony in the world economy include, for instance, *International Organization*, *Review of International Political Economy*, *Review*, *Review of International Studies, Capital and Class,* and the *Journal of World-Systems Research,* including authors such as Robert Keohane, Robert Cox, Immanuel Wallerstein, Arthur MacEwan, Stephen Krasner, Susan Strange, Stephen Gill, Robert Gilpin, Giovanni Arrighi, Christopher Chase-Dunn and Henry Nau. This debate has close links with the social structures of accumulation (SSA) and regulation approaches to political economy.

hegemonic nation, promoting "the national consensus." Externally, liberalism led to the spread of technological knowledge, which eventually reduced the "edge" that (Dutch, Britain, and later) USA experienced in production. Internally, liberalism led to rising real wages and declining productivity, which eventually reduced the edge on this front.

The other theories of hegemony are variants of, or modifications to, the hegemonic stability thesis. The second theory is the "cultural hegemony thesis,[3] which holds (in one variant of the argument) that the nature of USA hegemony has changed from a large degree of formal power to shape the rules and structures of the world economy during 1945–1970, to substantive power to shape the trends and cultural fabric on a world scale during the 1970s–2000s (and beyond). Increasing instability during the 1970s and 1980s (and thereafter) is thus said to be due to changes in the institutions of hegemony (Arrighi 1982). This is a different but, in the case of Arrighi, largely complementary view of hegemony to the "rise and fall" thesis. Arrighi's version of the "rise and still strong" thesis emphasizes cultural hegemony: Dominance of the "American way of life," especially consumerism, a belief in "laissez faire," free trade, deregulation, business principles, transnational corporate society, individualism, and (neo)liberalism.

Arrighi agrees with most of the "rise and decline" thesis (see also Rupert and Rapkin 1985), that the system of USA imperial rule declined with defeat in Vietnam, the "collapse" of Bretton Woods, and Organization of Petroleum Exporting Countries (OPEC) oil price rises—what he calls the "formal" (enforced) aspects of hegemony. However, the informal structures of USA hegemony, "the unity of the world market and the transnational expansion of capital" are said to have become stronger since the 1970s. The change from *state-orientated hegemony* to *market-orientated hegemony* represents, for Arrighi (1982, 66), the increasing dominance of USA cultural imperialism, with the USA economy being the center of a more integrated world system. Increasing instability in the 1970s, 1980s, and 1990s (and later), in this line of argument, is thus seen as the product of a changing system of hegemony: the crisis and decline of formal, state-inspired hegemony; the crisis of the rising substantive hegemony in the form of market dysfunctions; and the conflict between the two systems of hegemony. The contradictions of formal hegemony led to the abandonment of some aspects of the Bretton Woods System (e.g., fixed exchange rates and the gold standard linked to the US dollar), the rising power of OPEC members, and defeat in Vietnam. Declining formal hegemony and the rise of informal hegemony led "from 1973 up through the present, [to] the destruction of previous institutional arrangements[,] … anomalous behaviour of the world economy … and … generalised institutional instability." (Arrighi 1982, 53; see also Arrighi 1993) (In our terminology, "structural polycrises," see chap. 9.)

The contradictions within informal, market-inspired, hegemony are said to be manifesting in the form of (a) a lack of leadership and cooperation in the third world, especially in the form of wars in the Middle East and other areas; the (b) increasing dominance of supranational speculative ventures over industrial production; (c) the relative and absolute expansion of some semi-peripheral economies, such as South Korea, Taiwan, and Hong Kong (and later other nations including

China); and, in general, the (d) the unpredictability, uncertainty, and instability characteristic of certain aspects of the disembedded, market-dominated [neoliberal] institutional structures (manifesting, for instance, in the Asian crisis of 1997–98, the Internet crash, and the global financial crisis [GFC]).[4] The important point for Arrighi (1982, 72) is that "the current crisis is not simply a crisis in U.S. hegemony but, more fundamentally, a crisis of world capitalism." The onset and continuation of socioeconomic instability are the product of fragile institutional structures, and changing hegemonic regimes are linked closely to this, though they are not the only (or central) processes.

This emphasis on institutions is also the central message of the third hypothesis, the "*institutional rise and fall thesis*," which states that, in relation to the world economy, the causes of socioeconomic upswing and relative demise must be sought in the structures, functions, and contradictions within the institutions, rather than hegemony forces per se. Keohane (1984) defines international hegemony as a situation in which one nation has sufficient socioeconomic power that it may provide considerable direct and persistent leadership to promote cooperation between the nations linked closely to the hegemonic power for their common good. He criticizes the simple hegemonic stability hypothesis (HSH) for assuming capitalism or other systems necessarily need to rely on a dominant power to provide enough leadership and coercion to unite the Alliance toward common goals, and that such stability and cooperation are necessary for sustained socioeconomic growth and development. Historical evidence may often support the HSH, but this does not necessarily mean it is a general theory that will apply in the immediate or distant future. This explanation is often presented as a critique of hegemony theory and empirics.

Important to Keohane's criticism of the HSH is the notion of "regime" in particular "international regime," which he and other conference participants defined collectively as "sets of implicit or explicit principles, norms, rules, and decision-making procedures around which actors' expectations converge in a given area of international relations. Principles are beliefs of fact, causation, and rectitude. Norms are standards of behaviour defined in terms of rights and obligations. Rules are specific prescriptions or proscriptions for action. Decision-making procedures are prevailing practices for making and implementing collective choice" (Krasner 1983, 2).

During the postwar period, the USA provided leadership, cooperation, and control between the nations of Europe, North America, Australia, Japan, et al., to create

---

[4] According to Strange (1987), the decline is due to factors which are largely independent of the question of hegemony. She believes that the USA was still hegemonic (at the time she wrote), but that its institutions and agents have decided not to "lead the world" in a suitable fashion. As she says: "The use of hegemonic structural power in ways that are destructive of international order and cooperation has been a major cause of world economic instability and continuing crisis…. A necessary condition, therefore, for greater stability and cooperation lie within the United States, rather than in the institutions and mechanisms of international cooperation" (1987, 554). Clearly in this context, it is crucial to distinguish between absolute and relative hegemony. Revisiting this question of America's decline, Winecoff (2020) argues that US structural power (especially relating to strategic networks) is still very strong, and the relative rise of China (especially vis-à-vis the US) has been exaggerated. On this, see chap 8 below.

unifying international regimes (institutional structures). Despite protectionist measures by the European Economic Community (a forerunner of the European Union) and elsewhere (including the USA), and early difficulty including Japan in the regimes, as the 1950s progressed certain nations were united in the pursuit of stable and predictable regimes which are important for stability and certainty. Keohane suggests three such regimes, or what we could collectively call a *global (aspects of the) circuits* of socioeconomic dynamics (CSD): the *international monetary regime* (loosely called the Bretton Woods System), the *trade regime* (associated with the principles of GATT, transnationals, etc.), and the *oil regime* (an ad hoc selection of less stable institutions) (see Koehane 1984; Gill and Law 1988).[5]

The postwar (informal) oil regime saw the dominance of the "seven sisters": the major oil companies, backed by Western governments at the apex of which was the United States. Increasingly the US treated "oil" seriously as it was warned of the "net importer" position it might face. The postwar boom led to an enormous expansion in the demand for oil, and, eventually, in the early 1970s, OPEC members challenged the hegemony of the Western oil alliance by nationalizing many of the oil facilities. They also contributed to oil prices rising more than tenfold between 1973 and the 1980s (Nasr 1984). Varying cycles of oil price rises (and declines) emerged between the 1970s and the 1990s (and beyond), which contributed substantially to unemployment and inflation in Western nations (and elsewhere) (Rivera-Batiz and Rivera-Batiz 1989). Despite recent declines and various cycles in the oil price, no stable post-hegemonic oil or energy regime emerged into the 1990s (onward) to provide a foundation for cheap energy into the twenty-first century. (Nor yet for renewables.)

The postwar international monetary regime was based on the Bretton Woods System of fixed exchange rates, limited International Monetary Fund (IMF) credit in the case of balance of payments difficulties, the establishment of the World Bank, US financial dominance, and some capital controls to protect national development programs and international currency imbalances. With the decline in US dominance, and its military role in Vietnam, fixed exchange rates were eventually discarded by Richard Nixon in the early 1970s. Block (1977) in his remarkable analysis of this regime summarizes his conclusions about the conditions underlying its relative demise:

> In the previous two chapters, I have argued that the breakdown of the postwar monetary order was rooted in the inability of the United States both to pursue its global aims and to live within the rules of international monetary behavior it had earlier devised. [Block 1977, 215]

Block goes on to say that a new system would likely have to rely on what he terms "joint management" of the regime with other advanced nations, but that it is

[5] Keohane's thesis is similar to aspects of Veblenian institutionalism in relation to the collective foundations of socioeconomic wealth. Ultimately it is the nature of the cooperative organizational relations (and regimes) which predicates potential development. The exploitation and waste of hegemony is merely one (unacceptable and limited) means of uniting certain nations to common goals.

likely the US would ignore these rules periodically in pursuit of its own narrow objectives, which would likely cause retrenchment (anti-inflationary actions). The decline in the monetary regime was only partial, however, for while a new system of flexible exchange rates was instituted, many of the other aspects of the regime (e.g., the IMF, World Bank, and US financial dominance) continued, though often with changing functions (for instance, in practice the IMF typically 'supports' peripheral and semi-peripheral nations).

A postwar trade regime was established through GATT, including the principle of non-discrimination between nations. Ruggie (1994) argues that GATT was implemented within a system of "embedded liberalism": with an eye to national priorities of domestic intervention, improving the standard of living of workers, and promoting the welfare state. In the 1970s–1990s, during the Tokyo and Uruguay Rounds of discussions, the principles of free trade have been promoted (unevenly), devoid of concern for domestic embeddedness. Relative free trade was expanded at the expense of national socioeconomic policies, especially with the development of the World Trade Organization (WTO). GATT and related agreements have not declined in spirit, however, despite the absolute decline in US hegemony, and into the twenty-first century, we may have a multipolar system of trade. However, recently, the US, China, and others have instituted a system of protectionism and industry policy, a likely new institutional system to replace much of the old free trade system.

The HSH or "rise and fall theory" postulates that hegemony promotes cooperation through regimes and that declining hegemony leads to the decline of such regimes. This simple thesis, however, Keohane found to be only partially "true," since, during the period of declining hegemony in the late 1960s–early 1970s, the oil regime declined considerably, but only certain aspects of the Bretton Woods System were disbanded, while GATT arrangements have only partially dissolved (they have evolved). In the 1970s, 1980s, and 1990s, there was more cooperation in international regimes (within the possible global CSD) than the HSH predicts. If this is true, what factors promoted this "surplus cooperation," providing the basis for some *limited degree* of stability, profitability, and resolution of conflict? The solution to the problem—according to Keohane—was found to be institutional. The immediate postwar period was one of simultaneous institutional innovation and hegemony—the two were intertwined; and declining hegemony did not lead to a *complete* collapse of regimes (global aspects of the CSD) in the 1970s onward, as some argued,[6] (nor did it result in the complete collapse of hegemony, since *relative hegemony* is still operational).

To some extent hegemony promoted institutional structures which led to greater stability and development, but, ultimately, the major variable determining

[6] An important criticism of hegemony theories could be postulated, that, at least in their primary works on hegemony, they underplay the importance of the institutions of the state, the family, and finance operating at the national level (in addition to the other "regimes"). The "surplus cooperation, stability, and accumulation" could be due (at least in some measure) to stability in these (and the other) regimes. Hence, analysis of the CSD eco-techno-institutions in this chapter.

development and growth is a set of suitable geo-spatial and techno-institutional structures and rules within the CSD. To the extent that hegemony promoted such structures, it can be the critical variable; but it is by no means essential in principle, even if it was crucial historically (in the past, partially in the present, and potentially in the future). Hegemony is thus neither a necessary nor a sufficient condition for stability and growth. This relates to the collective foundations of wealth: Ultimately it is the nature of the cooperative organizational relations (within the CSD) that predicate potential development. The exploitation and waste of hegemony (especially as practiced internationally through Dutch, British, and later US dominance) is merely one limited means of uniting certain nations to common goals. Although, it may turn out to be the most important of them all, historically (although possibly not in the future).

Absolute hegemony of the US (in Wallerstein's sense) has declined, yet a major collapse did not occur until 2008–2009 (and 2009–2015 via the Eurodebt crisis) because of the certain degree of stability contributed by certain international *and* domestic institutional structures (regimes). In 1950, in both aggregate and relative terms, the USA was the ultra-dominant nation of the world, enabling it to have a major say in the building of postwar international institutions. However, within 25 years, this *absolute dominance* (in Wallerstein's sense) vanished as other nations developed through the postwar boom and thereby collectively challenged but did not replace U.S. supremacy. Multilateral institutions are also playing a considerable role, although often leading to stalemate as Russia, China, or the USA (and others) refuse to take (some of) them seriously.

The fourth (4th), *rise and still strong thesis,* states either that (1) US hegemony did not decline and indeed rose again during the 1990s and 2000s, and/or that (2) US hegemony should have been regenerated into the 1990s and 2000s by a unilateralist thrust, which was missing during the 1980s (Nau 1990) and 1990s. The unilateralists waited until 9/11 when George W. Bush gave them *carte blanche* to put into practice their theory with the invasions of Iraq and Afghanistan along with supportive allies, which were a failure not only vis-à-vis their rationale but also their long-term impact on the region.

Kwon (2011) provides empirical evidence, concerning GDP per capita, military power, and percent of world GDP, to support the trend to a re-emergence of US power from the 1990s to 2005. In this context, it has been argued by various authors that U.S. power was enhanced through the decline of the former Soviet Bloc during the late 1980s and 1990s; the defeat of Iraq in the war over Kuwait in the early 1990s; and the spread of U.S. unilateralism in international relations (plus cultural hegemony).

We believe this line of argument and the so-called evidence to be wrong. Against Kwon's evidence are several others. For instance, Ray Dalio (2021) presents a multi-factorial approach to US hegemony. His approach includes eight core variables, including (1) education, (2) competitiveness, (3) innovation and technology, (4) economic output, (5) share of world trade, (6) military strength, (7) financial center strength, and (8) reserve currency status. His work on hegemony comprises various phases of evolution, including the emergence of the new order, the rise, the height of hegemonic power, and the decline, followed by eventually a new order (hegemonic power). He applies this approach to the rise and fall of the Dutch, British, US, and the potential hegemony of the Chinese; see Fig. 7.5 for an outline of his conclusions, especially in relation to the US:

This shows rising US hegemony relative to Britain during the 1800s and especially the 1900s, leading to absolute hegemony by the 1940s, with declining levels from the 1960s, and only relative hegemony in more recent decades. It also shows the rapidly rising Chinese power since the 1980s.[7] One source of power it ignores is the non-state power of terrorists, which rose especially during the 1990s–2020s (giving a misleading indication of US power during this time).

Over the past fifty years, several trends that may have renewed US power have failed to do so. This is due to six main contradictions (see Wallerstein 2006 for an outline). The first contradiction is that the Washington Consensus contributed to the rise in neoliberalism, with a mandate to improve economic performance and contribute to US power through association. Neoliberalism led to an escalation in the number of financial crises and declining economic conditions, including the GFC, the Eurocrisis, several recessions/financial crises, and a deterioration of the social fabric of health, education, and infrastructure capitals in several nations. Ultimately it also led to the *relative* decline in neoliberalism during the post-GFC period, including the period of the coronacrisis. (See chap. 9, below.)

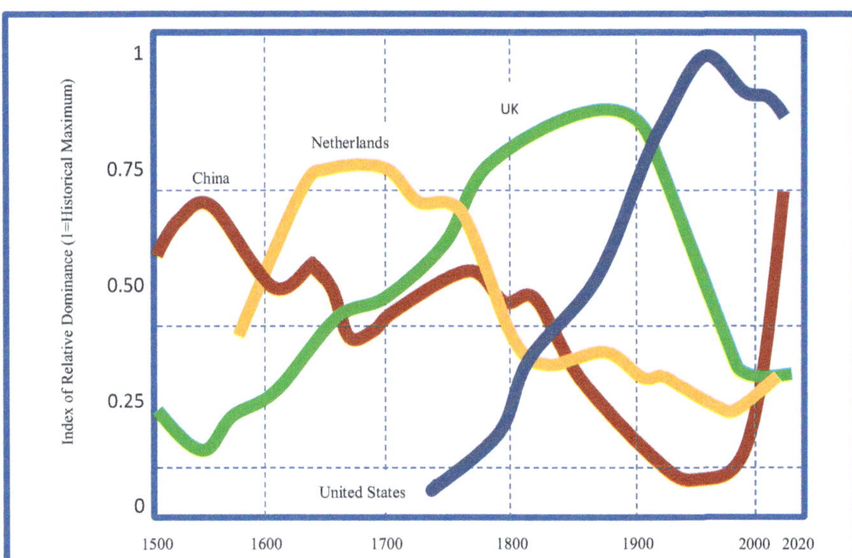

Fig. 7.5 US, China, UK, Dutch: Index of Relative Dominance, 1500–2015, Three Hegemonies + Rise of China, 1500–2020. (Source: Adapted from Dalio 2023)

[7] One specific aspect of this figure that is likely problematic is the high ranking of China especially during the 1500s and early 1600s.

The second contradiction is the demise of the Soviet Bloc, noted by Dalio but not explored relative to other rising forces. This decline reduced the main *reason d'etat* for supporting the US: anti-communism and the need to negate Soviet-style power. As Kotz (1994) recognize, while "the Cold War promoted unity among the major capitalist powers, under US leadership," the dissolution of the Soviet Union "[made] … it more difficult for the … US … to create the kind of unity behind its leadership that prevailed in the immediate postwar decades. [O]ver the long run it … reduce[d] the ability of the U.S. to exercise power in the world" (1994, 310).

The third contradiction, especially ignored in the work of Kwon and Dalio, emanates from the second, namely, that the decline in Soviet power generated an alternative power against US (relative) hegemony (in the Middle East and elsewhere): the rise of *Islamic radicalism and terrorism,* including 9/11 and the wars in Iraq (II), Afghanistan, Syria, Lebanon, Israel, and elsewhere. This links to the rise of the neoconservative trend in the US during the late 1990s and early–mid-2000s in order to challenge US decline. The invasions of Iraq and Afghanistan, etc., were complete failures, and several factors led other powers to lose trust and faith in the US (including its own agents) to act according to international law and scientific evidence, and in the military and logistics abilities of the US. (See O'Hara 2023, chap. 10; chap.10 below.)

The fourth contradiction (noted by Dalio) is associated with the rise in China which has and continues to challenge existing US economic, political, and military power, and the evolutionary change from US relative hegemony to merely multipolar power structures. (See chap. 8, below.)

The fifth contradiction is this: That the Trump era sees the dissolution of aspects of US multilateral engagement as it sought to "make America great again" at the expense of the rest of the world. Globally there are two dichotomies, the first is that between the increasing significance of autocratic-authoritarian powers such as China, Russia, Iran, and North Korea, against the democratic-liberal allies such as the EU, North America, Japan, and Australia (trade, military, and diplomatic conflict). The second is increasing national (internal) dichotomies of a similar nature (autocratic vs. liberal) *within* various nations/areas, especially the US, Hungary, India, Brazil, and EU.

Some authors subscribe to the view that a "post hegemony" (multipolar) system of international organization is emerging and that it may (or may not) be a viable system which aids stability, accumulation, and growth. Some think, for instance, that a tripolar system of "blocs" may provide the required stability to promote international relations, especially the EU, Asian, and North American organizations-arrangements. These blocs may be able to organize internal free trade, expand economic relations, and include more peripheral nations in the system of relations. Some degree of healthy competition and economic balance of power it is said may emerge between the three blocs which enhances global accumulation. (Kupchan 1998.) This is still very speculative.

Still others (e.g., Robinson 1996) believe that hegemons are a thing of the past and that the twenty-first century will see the consolidation of a polyarchic world system dominated by a transnational corporate elite. This large concentration of economic power is said to abrogate democracy and justice while it leads to a (double movement) struggle to democratize global society which will be ongoing. This (poly) centric world system, in propelling the power of transnational capital elites, may enhance accumulation and growth, or it may not. However, the countervailing influence of those who seek justice and participation may be a continual source of contradictory tension. (See several papers in the *Journal of World-Systems Research* for themes along these lines.)

Further empirics support declining US absolute hegemony. The first dimension, based on Fig. 7.1, above, shows the declining performance of the US in parallel with the movement from long wave upswing to long wave borderline and downswing. This is the principal thesis of this book. Second, Fig. 7.6 outlines the trend of *levels* of GDP per capita from the 1900s to 2022, comparing US with British, Dutch, Norwegian, Chinese, and Saudi Arabian levels:

This time series shows US levels of real GDP per capita overtaking British levels by 1900, dipping by the 1930s, and then taking a clear lead during the 1940s. The lead increased until the 1970s when other nations edged ahead. Small oil nations such as Qatar (not shown) had doubled US GDP per capita levels by 1970, and despite a large dip in the 1980s, by 2022, Qatar had tripled the level of the USA, while Norway had edged ahead of the US by the late 1990s and was 50% ahead of the USA by 2022. Saudi Arabia, another oil magnate, had equaled the US by the 2010s. Switzerland (not shown) also went ahead of the USA by the 2010s. China had by 2022 significantly reduced China–US relative differentials of real GDP per capita but was still a long way behind, the US being more than three times ahead of China. Previous hegemons such as the Netherlands are currently very close behind the USA, while Britain is not too far behind them (but the distance is getting greater). Also, as is typically the case, real GDP *levels* continue to be very high long after long wave upswings (real GDP decadal AAGR), as was the case earlier for the

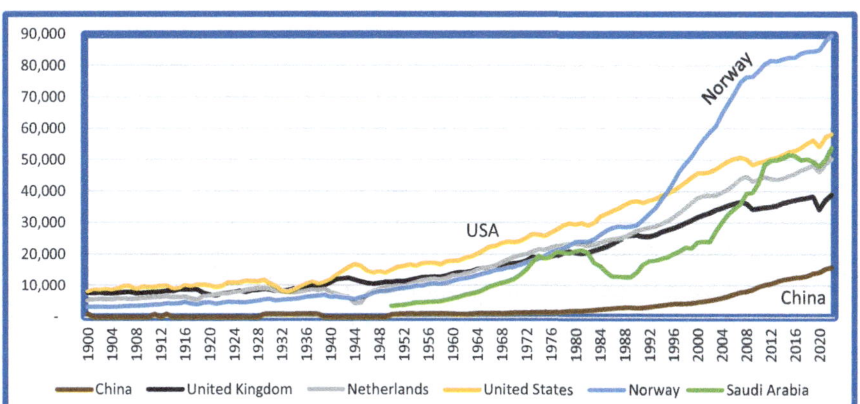

Fig. 7.6 Real GDP per capita *levels*, 1900–2022, US, UK, Netherlands, China, Norway, and Saudi Arabia. (Source: Adapted from the raw data of the Maddison Project (2024))

Dutch and the British, and also for the US during its era of *relative* hegemonic power (but with short-crisis brief declines).

According to Figs. 7.1 and 7.6, the US has long ago lost the edge in terms of real GDP growth per capita and real GDP per capita levels. Now we outline the nature of potential US dominance in production, commerce, and finance. Regarding United States productivity relative to other nations, Fig. 7.7 provides a comparison over the 1950–2023 period:

This illustrates the United States had the highest productivity in the world during the 1950s–1960s, which deteriorated during the 1970s, and was surpassed in the 1980s–1990s by some EU nations. Thereafter, US-EU productivity converged and stabilized somewhat. Meanwhile, other nations, such as China, have gained majorly since the 1990s but the level of catchup has not been major relatively speaking, even though China has advanced especially in high-technology sectors more recently (see ch. 8, below). In the meantime, other core nations continue their climb relative to the US (e.g., South Korea, with short-crisis "blips").

Regarding commercial dominance, Table 7.2 provides an indication of the US relative position regarding the *Global* 500 *Fortune* Corporations:

During the 1950s–1970s, the US dominated global production and trade through their home-based transnational corporations and an array of subsidiaries embedded in other nations to take advantage of local conditions (e.g., behind tariffs). This started to change during the 1980s and 1990s as European and Asian companies made inroads, and, by 1994–1998, there was a clear multipolar balance between corporations from the USA, Europe, and Asia, with the US no longer having

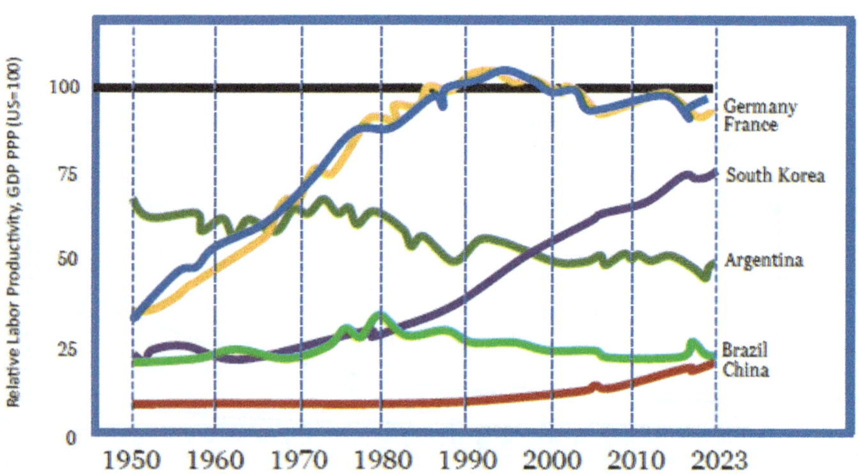

Fig. 7.7 Relative labor productivity, 1950–2023. GDP (PPP) per hour, US, China, France, Germany, South Korea, Brazil, and Argentina. (2023 = forecast.) (Source: Adapted from Fernald 2023)

Table 7.2 (A) Multipolar, (B) specific nations, *Global 500,* 1994–1998, 2000–2023 (Head Office), percentage/number of corporations

A: Multipolar powers		B: Specific nations' power				
	1994–1998 Mean	Year➔	2000	2010	2020	2023
USA	33%	USA	178	140	123	131
Europe	34%	China	12	40	125	138
Asia	29%	Japan	105	71	52	44
Other	4%	Germany	36	34	30	28
	100%	France	33	36	30	31
		UK	42	27	20	15

(**a**) Multipolar regional percent of total Global 500 Corporations, Head Office; (**b**) Number of *Global500FortuneCorporations,* HeadOffice,USA,China,Japan,France,Germany,andUK.(Source: (a) Bergesen and Sonnett (2001)); (b) Adapted from raw data provided by Global 500, Fortune Magazine 2024

dominance. In terms of specific nations rather than areas, by the new millennium, the US had long ago lost dominance of *Fortune* 500 companies.

Chinese firms grew and, by the 2020s, Chinese companies edged ahead of US ones in absolute terms. Large Chinese companies, defined by the location of Head Office, have begun to slightly dominate in terms of revenue (Fortune 2024). This relative numerical balance is moderated by two factors. The first is that almost three-quarters of Chinese firms are currently state owned, and privately owned ones are often heavily indebted to the state. The second factor is that US giant firms are far ahead of Chinese ones in profitability by the 2020s. The 15 UK companies in the *Fortune* Global 500 list had an average profit rate of 10.8%; 11 Swiss ones had 9.1%; followed by 136 US ones with 8.4%; and much further down the list were 143 Chinese (mostly state-inspired) firms with an average of 3.9% profit rate (Morrison and Stewart Black 2024). In these contexts, neither US nor Chinese corporations come close to dominating the dynamic corporate circuits of capital at the global level.

What of financial power? We argued above that hegemons tend to gain financial power in several ways, such as having a core financial center such as Amsterdam, London, or New York; having the most powerful banks; and having the de facto or official ruling currency. In the case of the US, all three of these applied. Hegemons achieve production and commercial dominance, and through financial power, they have the ruling global currency (and key financial center), which enhances their development. Since their currency is used like gold as a global safe asset ("safe haven") it is in persistent demand and can be used to finance balance of payments deficits. Buying cheap overseas goods, selling dearer domestic goods, and having a group of global subsidiaries to produce under local conditions globally, hegemons generate impressive long-wave upswings and a good means to finance public, military, and social services (where necessary) including having more groups in class alliances.

Hence, while absolute US hegemony declined into the 1970s, 1980s, 1990s, and afterward, it could be said that the US held relative (rather than absolute) hegemony during the 1980s–2020s,[8] while Chinese power is increasing (and more distantly, also Indian and Indonesian power).

The principal hypothesis of this study has been that the most buoyant long wave upswings tend to coincide (relatively closely) with global power apogees (and that these periods are characterized by specific, often idiosyncratic, forms of climate change). Similarly, periods devoid of hegemony are eras of more short-wave upswings, borderline periods, and especially long-wave downswings and financial crises (greater volatility/uncertainty) and other crises (e.g., climate; polycrises). At least one caveat hypothesis should be added here: namely, that the area that is most likely to be the next hegemon tends to have a relatively buoyant performance *just after* the start of the decline of the previous hegemon, for a certain time (e.g., 1–3 decades): for instance, Britain during the 1660s (a weak example); the US for a few decades after the 1870s (a good example); chap. 8 below examines this vis-à-vis China (a good example).

Another core hypothesis of this study is that the foundations of hegemonic eras and the most dynamic long-wave upswings are the dynamic structures of technology, institutions, and potential ways of managing geo-climate change. Hegemonies and waves are thus conditioned by the durable structures of socioeconomic capital that provide a foundation for aggregate effective demand, economic surplus, and productive investment of various types. In short, the PoPE, including the CSD, are the guiding structures that explain the success or otherwise of long waves, hegemony, and climate change. The next section scrutinizes the second aspect of the postwar US CSD relating to geospatial ecologies.[9]

7.3.2 US Eco-Spatial-Geo Systems

The United States is situated within the North American continent, and during the period of absolute US hegemony (circa 1940s–1970s), it had a population of between 133 and 236 million people. It comprises 48 mainland state clusters plus Alaska and Hawaii and control over several inhabited and uninhabited islands in the Pacific and Atlantic Caribbean. It is a constitutional liberal democracy, with two main chambers of parliament, the Senate, and the House of Representatives, with the third largest land mass of any country in the world. The mainland was typically

---

[8] Silvia and Stanaitis (2013) study the literature of the hegemonic stability thesis (HST), especially the work of Charles Kindleberger, Robert Keohane, Robert Gilpin, Susan Strange and David Lake. Their main emphasis is the question of trade, and specifically openness to trade, using inferential statistics to test certain hegemony hypotheses. They conclude that neither single hegemonies nor collective hegemonies necessarily promote openness of trade, but that diffusion of power promotes trade openness. They also conclude that both ability *and* willingness to lead the world economy are important in the analysis (rather than just ability).

[9] Recent references we found useful for understanding US hegemony and its demise, include those by Evgeny Balatsky (2024), Payne and Silver (2023), Fernández (2021), Grinin and Korotayev (2021), and Cha (2020).

violently expropriated from numerous so-called Indian tribes, and much of (especially) the west USA was expropriated from Mexico (either through wars or unequal treaties/deals). US administrations have applied their own Monroe Doctrine in Latin America, giving them unilateral action in whatever way they chose south of the Border, including organizing invasions, coups, and other aggressive actions (see Robinson 1996 for examples). The USA became the largest economy in the world around 1900 but did not assume the position of absolute hegemon (due to disengagement with foreigners and neutrality in world wars) until the 1940s. While the US aided Western Europe with military assistance during the Second World War, until the Japanese attacked Pearl Harbour, it subscribed to neutrality, then it participated majorly and was the factor that tipped the balance in favor of the allies by the end of the Second World War.

The large landmass, population, and performance of the US have given it a large domestic market, which contributes to economies of scale and scope, agglomeration; vertical, horizontal, and conglomerate association; and high levels and periodically high rates of growth of GDP per capita. Having access to large areas of both the Pacific and Atlantic seaboard contributes majorly to production, trade, finance, and military prowess. Having the best universities and networks of scholars, teachers, administrators, and businesspeople historically has contributed to high levels of human and social capital. Generating well-developed private and lesser-developed public transportation systems contributed to high rates of intra-migration and turnover of goods and services. Having a well-functioning economy has given it access historically to up to 100 million migrants (including their offspring) joining the workforce and contributing to socioeconomic performance over three centuries.

The postwar boom was a time of unprecedented GHG emissions, and as has been explained often throughout this book, one would normally expect more GHG emissions, temperature increases, and more extreme climate events during these times. However, this has often not been the case, due to cyclical and long-term changes in various other counteracting factors, which have impacted on climate, especially before more recent decades. Figure 7.8 illustrates the record for the index of heatwaves for the USA during the period 1895–2021.

The data in Fig. 7.8a display some very clear results. The first main one is that the greatest heatwaves occurred during the early–mid-1930s in the USA, which is a counter-intuitive stylized fact since this was during the Great Depression when economic activity was at its weakest, and one would have expected, prima facie, lower GHG stocks, and lower temperatures. The second is that the least number of heatwaves occurred from the mid-1950s through to the 1970s, again a counter-intuitive result since this was the greatest long wave (growth per capita) upswing in the whole history of capitalism, when one would have expected a higher levels of GHG stocks, and hence higher temperatures, and therefore a greater sequence of heat waves. Third, the heatwaves during the 2000s–2020s were not especially major compared with some other periods of US history, such as the 1910s and 1950s (and especially the 1930s), yet this (2000s–2020s) is the period when we are supposed to have seen the greatest increase in both GHG stocks and temperature rises (and more heat waves globally). Why the apparently strange results?

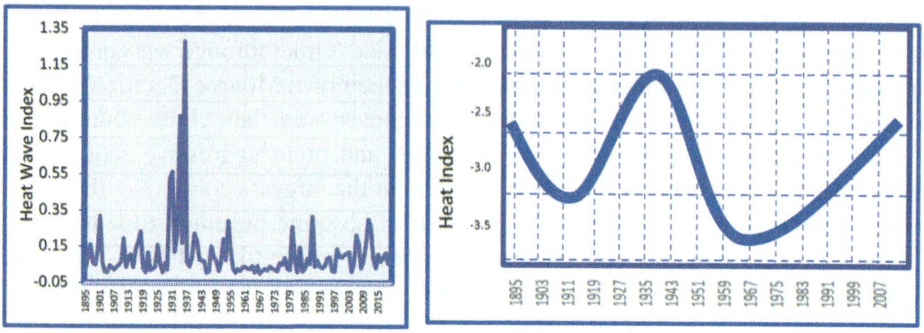

Fig. 7.8 (**a**) Heat-Wave Index (NOAA), USA, 1885–2021. Contiguous 48 States. (Source: Adapted from raw data of EPA 2024.) ** (**b**) Heat Index Natural Log. Fitted Trend. USA, 1895–2005. Contiguous 48 States. (8°Freedom, Fitted ∑ Series.). (Source: Adapted from CCSP 2008, 130) ** "This index defines a heat wave as a period lasting at least four days with an average temperature that would only be expected to occur once every 10 years, based on the historical record. The index value for a given year depends on how often heat waves occur and how widespread they are" (EPA 2024)

Figure 7.8b was published by the US Climate Change Science Program (CCSP 2008,), for a report that was subject to public review and by the National Science and Technology Council. The results produce a long wave of climate change (LWCC), for the heat index, between 1915 and 1965, including upswing (U) 1915–1936 and downswing (D) 1936–1965, surrounding the Dust Bowl crisis of the early–mid-1930s, and a LWCC upswing in the heat index for the period 1965–2008 (ongoing into the 2020s). It also shows that the LWCCU during 1915–1936 had greater amplitude per unit time than the LWCCU during 1965–2008. Special note that it does highlight the LWCCD in the heat index during 1936–1965, which we discussed in Chap. 4, and further almost immediately below.

Some authors treat the 1930s extreme heatwaves as an outlier, caused by a specific series of processes, that are perhaps unlikely to recur in the same fashion again. The 1930s experience of the so-called dust bowls of the Great Plains of the US, during the Great Depression, was investigated by a Great Plains Committee (1936), which outlined three main reasons for the great heat waves that caused many deaths, destruction, and loss of farm income. The first was soil erosion, caused by certain practices such as over-cultivation, expansion into marginal areas, lack of planning, and insufficient farm improvement. The second was a lack of forage cover for grazing due to factors such as expansion to marginal lands. The third was inefficient use of water due to lack of soil moisture and low levels of irrigation. An extensive set of policy proposals was set in motion both by government and local farmers, including practices such as creating erosion control districts, expansion of agricultural research, water retention, and irrigation schemes, conservation of groundwater, and expansion of farm sizes. McLeman (2014) argue that these and later policies instituted by the state plus adaptation measures activated by farmers were effective in reducing soil erosion and dust storms while increasing the viability of the farming sector in the upcoming postwar corporate system, with many of the measures being useful in adjusting to later climate change.

Others have scrutinized more climatological factors underlying this largest heat-wave record in recent history during the 1930s. Cowan et al. (2017) analyzed the climate record during 1920–2012 and found that of the 13 summers with the most severe heat waves on the Great Plains, 8 of them occurred during the 1930s. They linked the Dust Bowl syndrome to "anomalous circulation patterns arising over the continent, leading to strong subsidence-induced warming during heat wave onset, followed by warm advection from the north increasing the event severity." They also recognize that land degradation practices and dust forcing also played a role, and that "exceptional heat wave summers occur more often following an El Niño (15 events) than a La Niña (10 events)" (p. 2459). It also mentioned that more research is needed to see if a possible early 1900s GHG-forcing process might have contributed to the Dust Bowl phenomenon.

As we know from Chap. 4, the greatest long-wave growth upswing in the history of world capitalism (or most parts of it), during the 1940s–1970s, based on the "US hegemony" postwar corporate system, saw the opposite trend from the early–mid-1930s Dust Bowl heat waves: namely, a *Small Cooler Era*. This era was just as counter-intuitive as the Dust Bowl heat waves (as with the *Little Ice Age* during the period of the Dutch Golden Age of the late 1500s and early 1600s, as well as for the British experience), relative to growth since one would have expected a rising heat-wave during the 1940s–1970s long wave upswing. Data specifically shows the cooling being greater during the Second World War (1939–1945) and the 5 years thereafter (1945–1950), followed by a cyclical pattern of low-level cooling and heating (1950–1975) (IPCC 2007, chap. 1, 101; IPCC, 2022, chap. 2, 322). Thus, during the war and the largest and greatest worldwide long wave upswing ever recorded, along with US hegemony, there was a period of climate cooling in the US. Why?

Most analysts now believe that this global cooling was due to rising anthropogenic aerosols from pollution which dimmed the sun's rays through smog and cloud-type cover preventing a proportion of solar energy from reaching the oceans and lands. It is also recognized that to some degree volcanic ash played a role; for instance, the eruption of Mount Agung in 1963 which cooled the lower atmosphere by perhaps half a degree (Brahic 2007). Regarding the aerosols, there are two processes at play. As Flynn (2023, 15,122) states, "Aerosols may affect the radiation balance through aerosol-radiation interactions (ARIs), or the scattering and absorption of radiation directly by aerosols, and through indirect aerosol-cloud interactions (ACIs).

The ACIs include the "aerosol-cloud albedo effect," also known as the first indirect or Twomey effect …, and the "aerosol-cloud lifetime effect,", or the second indirect effect …; these interactions exist for all cloud phases." However, these aerosol impacts do not seem to totally explain the cooling period circa 1940–1970, and there is a high degree of uncertainty and complexity associated with them, which may in time lead to a better explanation of the total effect, especially relating to aerosol interactions with other aspects of the climate system (Flynn 2023,

15,130). Flynn et al. outline a few possibilities as to what other factors may be involved in the Small Cooler Era, including "among other possibilities, the *complexity* of the aerosol scheme in models and *differences* in how aerosol cloud and aerosol radiation *interactions* are *represented*" (italics added). They still think aerosols are involved, but in a more complicated fashion, especially relating to *uncertainty* and aerosol *interactions* with other aspects of the climate system (in a cascading fashion).

Relating climate change again to US hegemony and long waves, it remains to link these questions with the history of climate change since the 1970s, since during the period of the 1980s–2020s the climate crisis became part of the core polycrises of the postwar long wave downswing of this era. This strictly comes within the purview of chapters 8 and 9, so I will leave this question until then to provide more detail. (It is also covered to some degree in Chap. 4, above.)

7.3.3 Fordism, Capital–Labor Accord, Postwar Corporate System

The third dominant eco-techno-institutional sphere of CSD comprises the capital-labor truce, Fordism, and the postwar corporate system from the 1950s through to the 1970s. Fordism is very broadly situated within the framework of a system of production, the capital-labor truce, a system of working-class consumption, a corporate system of hegemony, and a technological and institutional system of suburban expansion. We start with a brief analysis of the evolution of the pre-Fordist system to the Fordist systems of production and consumption. It is argued that, overall, this CSD sphere contributed to stability, the resolution of class conflict, and profitability during the 1950s and 1960s boom (especially in the USA).

Within the developing "Regulation" conceptual paradigm, it is hypothesized that there are two main "regimes of accumulation" that have evolved under capitalism—extensive and intensive. De Vroey (1984, 45) points out that these regimes can be studied at varying levels of analysis, such as the technical, the sectoral, and the socioeconomic. Here we emphasize primarily the socioeconomic realm, but there are interdependencies between these levels of analysis. The extensive regime is said to have been dominant between 1850 and 1919, followed by a transitional period (1919–1945), then an intensive regime (1945–1966), and a similar transitional period (1966 to, perhaps, the 1980s) (see Davis 1978, 258, De Vroey 1984, 47). The transitional periods are times when the system undergoes a crisis of transformation and readjustment (and possibly depression); for instance, many scholars examined the evolution of "post-Fordist" relations (or the "flexible system of production") (e.g., Mathews 1989; Roobeek 1987; Petit 1999; Marshall 1999) during the 1980s and afterward.

The *extensive regime* (1850s–1910s) is said to have been based on potential productivity via changes to the organization of labor. In the latter stages of this regime,

Taylorism was an important mode of subordinating labor in the interests of profitability. Under Taylorism, productivity was more advanced in the capital goods rather than the consumer-goods sector. An important reason for this is that the commodity "conditions of existence" of working-class reproduction were narrowly formulated. The union movement was not institutionally fused very substantively with capital in a way that enabled substantial increases in real wages, and demand, and hence realized profits and investment.

According to De Vroey, within the extensive regime, the wage relation is partial, the mode of working-class consumption is dominated by non-commodity relations, household labor is based to a high degree on goods-production, men are dominant in the (partial) wage relation, the unemployed are largely cared for by the (extended) family, and unions are embryonic, British hegemony is starting to decline, lender of last resort facilities are limited, and the balance of power favor relatively competitive specific capitals. In this regime, the development of capitalism is fundamentally limited by low rates of institutional innovation for working-class consumption norms and wage levels. Extensive accumulation was dominant as capitalism evolved from "initial proletarianization" (1840s–1890s), to the early-middle phases of "homogenization" of the working class (1890s–1910s) (Edwards 1979), as the machine process and later "scientific management" reduced the breadth of worker skill in favor of specialization of tasks and the smooth flow of the labor process. This regime started to break down as certain industries became more concentrated, the centripetal development of power progressed, there was more divergence of ownership from control (*a la* (in the style or manner of) Berle and Means) and an increasing dominance of "absentee owners," especially financial interests (*a la* Veblen 1923).

In this context, the regulation school of political economy sees the period from the end of the First World War to the end of the Second World War as a transitional phase. During this phase, the developing regime of intensive accumulation suffered major limits, which manifested primarily as underconsumption. Expansion of the means of production and large-scale production were limited by a mode of distribution that inhibited demand within the circuit, culminating in the realization crisis of the Depression of the 1930s, which saw low profits, high unemployment, and low confidence in the future.

However, the *intensive regime* gradually evolved, characterized through the postwar corporate system by increasing oligopolization, economies of large-scale production, and the rising power of US capitalism. After the Second World War, institutional innovations emerged promoting a more balanced reproduction of new production-distribution-exchange systems. This postwar form of regulation, Fordism, is said to be "the principle of an articulation between a process of production and a mode of consumption" (Aglietta 1976, 117). The *central innovation* of Fordism was a more fully developed wage relation, the capital-labor "truce" between big capitals and big unions, and, more generally, the institutionalization of a working-class consumption pattern that is commodity-based. (See Mazier et al. 1999 on the European situation with Fordism.)

In a wider sense, Fordism includes the increasing institutionalization of segmented labor markets, expansion of household labor into consumption and services, the rapid growth of the "welfare state," the gradual re-emergence of women into the workforce, collective bargaining, parallel growth of capital and consumer-goods sectors, administered oligopoly pricing, lender of last resort, open market operations, American hegemony, and "Bastard" Keynesian policies, (De Vroey 1984, 48–9). It is important to recognize this interdependency, even though the emphasis here will be placed on production, distribution, and exchange, and the linkages to production, distribution, and consumption expenditures and norms.

Aglietta (1976, chap. 2) argues that Taylorism became a dominant aspect of the relations of production during the 1890s–1920s, but that this was superseded by a wider set of structures under Fordism by the post-Second World War period. Taylorism is said not to have disappeared, but to have been transformed or deepened through the application of complementary principles. The broad view of Taylorism includes the principles of the (a) maximum fragmentation of work into the simplest elements, (b) separation of planning from laboring, (c) eliminating independent worker preparation and organization of work, (d) minimum skill requirements, (e) minimum material handling, (f) division of management under the control of a central department, (g) time study methods-monitoring, and (h) minimal interaction of workers to atomize the workforce (Littler 1982, chap. 5).

The central point of Taylorism is the emphasis on bureaucratic control within the workplace, the transfer of power from the shopfloor to the planning department, and a balance between production, distribution, and consumption. Fordism deepened Taylorism (viewed in this wide sense) through changes to the technical system of production, expansion of the sphere of consumption through changing norms of working-class reproduction, modification of bureaucratic power, and the institutionalization of internal (and more segmented) labor markets.

The *production process of Fordism* is characterized by "semi-automatic assembly-line production … especially for mass consumer goods produced in long production runs," the further evolution of mechanization and real subordination of labor, and the increasing intensity of work (Aglietta 1976, 116–8). As Fordism developed, Taylorism (the "scientific management" of labor) became deeper through what Aglietta calls the "application of two principles." The first principle relates to the operation of the semi-automatic assembly-line processes, which promotes the "integration of different segments of the labor process by a system of conveyors and handling devices ensuring the movement of the materials to be transformed and their arrival at the appropriate machine tools" (p.118). This saves time and labor in the transfer and manipulation of cumbersome and heavy objects, promotes the normalization of the production process, and necessitates generalized large-scale production and use of electrical power. The second principle is complimentary to the first, representing the "fixing of workers to jobs whose positions [are] rigorously determined by the configuration of the machine system" (p.118). Work autonomy is abolished in this continuous linear flow system of production, and many factory-floor jobs have been simplified to a few repetitive motions.

Fordism was also based on a symbiotic relationship between production, distribution, and consumption to promote the circuit of capital. A major internal factor promoting the postwar boom was that this mode of consumption evolved and represented, along with the system of distribution, an *institutional innovation* from the point of view of capital-in-general. Aglietta sees this as promoting a balance between industry A (means of production) and industry B (means of consumption), but in a wider context it can be seen as an innovation that promotes the reproduction of the wider CSD.

Aglietta's analysis of the postwar production process needs to be supplemented by the recognition of the institutional relations of control, which were central to the process of converting labor power to active human labor. Institutional innovations associated with capital-labor relations were by no means limited to technical relations of production but included changing modes of organizational control, expansion of internal labor markets, labor market segmentation, and increasing oligopolization within the centrally planned large corporations. The analysis of the social relations of production has been influenced greatly by Harry Braverman (1976), but constructive criticism of his work has led to a less functionalist investigation of these relations (see Edwards 1979; Littler 1982). This relates to the buying of labor power in the market and the extraction of labor from workers in the production process.

Edwards argues that capitalist power in the production process evolved from a type of "simple control" in the nineteenth century, to "technical control" from the late 1800s to the early middle 1900s, to "bureaucratic control" after 1945. The existence of problems in extracting labor through the technical subordination of labor by capital, the onset of economic problems in the period up to and including the Great Depression of the 1930s, and increasing segmentation of labor led to the gradual dominance, in the oligopolistic sector, of bureaucratic control in the 1930s and 1940s. The essence of such control is "the institutionalization of hierarchical power," where company policy, formalized job descriptions, prescribed rules, procedures, and expectations, and layered superior-subordinate accountability transformed the social relations of large capitalist firms. Bureaucratic control does not extinguish simple and technical control but often uses these for added flexibility in the production process.

Edwards notes four main changes in the social relations inherent in so-called bureaucratic control. First, power relations became increasingly invisible and embedded in the institutional organization of the firm. Second, the evolution of hierarchy promotes job differentiation with specific status, responsibilities, and power. Third, supervisors engage in the roles of monitoring and evaluating performance, rather than being active overseers, and their own performance is monitored more closely. And fourth, bureaucratic control created more career ladders and institutional rewards for work: internal labor markets. Workers tended to comply with the interests of capital through institutionalized work rules, "habits of predictability and dependability," and the growth of incentives whereby workers tend to "internalis[e] … the enterprize's goals and values" (Edwards 1975, 93). The growth of "bureaucratic power" led to the expansion of supervisory personnel to instill such work rules, goals, and values into practice on the shop floor (Bowles et al. 1983, 74).

This is linked to the evolution in the postwar period of what Bowles and Gintis (1982a, b) and Bowles, Gordon, and Weisskopf (1989; 1990, 53–57, 66–72) call the "capital-labor accord" (or "truce") an institutional innovation in the age of bureaucratic control. With the accord, the labor movement in the United States relinquished major claims of control of the production process, in return for major distributive gains in the form of wages, overtime, and the social wage.[10] The "truce" led to the relative stability of direct production, and an expanded sphere of consumption which increased the realization of commodities, profit, and investment during the 1950s and 1960s. Naples (1986) describes how the truce worked through the inclusion of no-strike clauses, health/welfare benefits, productivity factors in wage clauses, supplemental unemployment benefits/pensions, acceptance of unionism, the automatic deduction of union dues from pay, the seniority principle for layoffs/promotions, grievance mechanisms, and close union links with the Democratic Party. Workers gained real wage rises and capitalists benefited through productivity increases during the 1950s and 1960s. For instance, the average labor productivity growth rate for industry rose from 1.5% (1913–1950) to 2.2% (1950–1973) (Maddison 1991:150), and the index of real wages per hour rose from 56 (1949–1954) to 71 (1958–1961) and 83 (1961–1970) (1977 = 100) (Sherman 1990, 109).

An important part of these relations was the increasing nature of corporate hegemony, greater collusion between capitals, transnational capital, and the evolution of the two-sector system of (1) private sector central planning and (2) entrepreneurial-style smaller firms. In 1929, the top 1% of wealthholders in the United States owned 62% of all corporate stock, while by 1953 this had increased to 76%. And by 1967, the largest 200 manufacturing corporations had control of 42% of the value added in manufacturing in the US (Peterson 1974, 495–6). Dugger explains the evolution from the "unitary form" ("U-form") to the "multiple division form" ("M-form") of corporate organization in the postwar period, comprising greater financial responsibility for managers in production and marketing of the various product lines, and the rising power of the Chief Financial Officer. Under this system "[o]verall coordination and long-term planning at the central corporate level are now more important than ever" (Dugger 1988, 85), and the revolution in computing, communications, and organizational design has generally led to a symbiotic expansion of such central planning.

The logic of the "centrally planned company" is the process of internationalization, internalization, transfer pricing, and worldwide sourcing of labor. Dugger indicates that the expansion of the corporate form contributed to deindustrialization of important parts of "America"; greater financial control led to the rise of long-term planning based in many cases on shorter-term market returns; and the development of corporate culture initiated the decline of traditional family and community values (Dugger 1988, 90–98). The emulation of hegemonic corporate culture promoted the

[10] But for a different interpretation, see Fairris (1994, 1997).

consumer mentality, competition for status, and the rise in "bureaucratic occupations" from 17% to 25% of the total economically active population from 1940 to 1970 (Dugger 1989, 138).

Dugger's analysis of this M-form shows that not only were workers under the control of the production plan and supervisory workers but also managers were increasingly under corporate control from above (hence the "bureaucratic" form of control). The postwar corporate managerial culture was "homosexual" (based around men; patriarchal) and "homosocial" (based on social similarities) (Dugger 1980, 403). Munkirs' analysis of the dual economy, involving the private centrally planned corporations and the entrepreneurial sector ("Adam Smith" style smaller firms), is in continuity with Dugger's thesis through the recognition of the nature of the centripetal development of power in the US economy. By use of interlocking directorships, mergers, family ties, market concentration, and cultural norms, the Centralized Private Sector Planning (CPSP) system, centered in the Central Planning Core of 12 financial institutions and 126 nonfinancial corporations, has evolved through the postwar era as the central power structure of U.S. capitalism (Munkirs and Knoedler 1987). It represents the dominance of collusion over competition, plan over market, and, in Veblenian terms, the dominance of the vested interests to exploit the social wealth, rather than the promotion of competition which may run the risk of overproduction in the sense of too many producers via the competitive process. The private planning apparatus continued to evolve and gain in strength in the 1980s (Munkirs 1985).

The above has sought to delineate the dominant relations within the postwar Fordist SSA and the capital–labor accord: The semi-automatic assembly-line process; the system of consumption and distribution; labor market segmentation; and the bureaucratic workplace/financial control within the centrally planned oligopolistic corporations. The point to emphasize now is that this set of relations had *internal contradictions*, which led to institutional instability and contributed to lower growth, and deep recessions during the 1970s (1974–1975) and 1980s (1982–1983) (and beyond). The contradictions and limits within the system of production and distribution promoting crisis and instability were numerous. They relate primarily to the contradictions of capitalism which emanate from the power relations between capital and labor, and the bureaucratic structure of corporate organization. This corresponds to the use of institutional structures for the promotion of vested interests and the medium-term interests of capital (not its general interests). The institutional *innovations* initiated in production and distribution were narrow in their structure and failed to solve some of the anomalies in the structure and linkage of institutional forms.

Firstly, an important contradiction relates to the distributive successes of labor. The accord gave primary segment and upper secondary segment labor monetary rewards, especially in the oligopolistic planning sector, while leaving nominal control of production in the hands of supervisors and thereby corporate managers. Oligopoly industry and big unions formalized a system of institutionalized distributive cooperation/conflict, through collective bargaining, which resulted in wage increases broadly in line with productivity gains from the 1950s to the 1960s in the

United States. Profits were historically higher than average during this period due to a considerable degree of capacity utilization, labor productivity, and less than excessive wage increases. The ratio of gross operating surplus/gross capital stock for the industry was historically high around 19%–20% in the 1950s and around 22%–24% during the 1960s (Downe 1986, 106).

Of relevance here is the reserve army of labor (RAL) analysis of cycles (see Sherman 1990). National income equals wages and property income (especially profit). The labor share of income equals the real hourly wage rate multiplied by productivity. The rate of unemployment increases (changes) by the degree that the rate of increase of income is less than required to employ those entering the labor force. Sustained low rates of unemployment (as in the late 1960s and early 1970s), in an environment of declining workmanship, increase the power of workers to gain real wage increases. The wage share of income is positively related to the extent and period when the unemployment rate is lower than the "critical rate" of unemployment, required for worker power to increase.

In the 1950s–1990s there were, according to Sherman and Kolk (1996), eight cycles in economic activity in the United States: the "peaks" occurring during 1953 (quarter 3), 1957 (3), 1960 (2), 1969 (4), 1973 (4), 1980 (1), 1981 (3), and 1990 (2); and the "final troughs" occurring during 1949 (4), 1954 (2), 1958 (2), 1961 (1), 1970 (4), 1975 (1), 1980 (3), 1982 (4), and 1991 (2). Sherman and Kolk argue that the cycles of 1949–1970 were structurally distinct from those of 1970–1991. One important difference is that there was much more volatility in investment, profit, and national income during the latter period, especially in relation to the major recessions of 1975, 1982, and 1991. The earlier period was characterized by moderate recessions and major booms, especially in the late 1960s, including the "missed recession" of 1967–8.

There were low rates of unemployment in the late 1940s–early 1950s, but they occurred in an environment of postwar conciliation, and little organizational worker power. Workers thus did not challenge capital sufficiently to result in lower levels of investment and workmanship. Net property income was relatively high in this period, despite the low rates of unemployment. The reserve army of labor was re-established at a relatively high rate during the 1950s, due to the high rate of increase in the adult population joining the labor force (especially women through their "latent reserve" facility, and migration). During the 1950s, as the accord was fully intact, labor did not question the power of capital significantly, strikes over wages/hours/job security/plant organization were low (Wallace 1989, 19), the injury frequency rate in manufacturing was historically modest (Naples 1986, 117), and labor productivity was exceptionally high (Wolff 1986, 96).

However, this period of relative historical tranquility was upset as capacity utilization increased, unemployment dropped, and the capital-labor truce started to break down. The problem emanates from the long length of expansions and the shortness of contractions over the 1948–1970 period, and the fact that the reserve army effect (of restoring profitability) seemed to work well during long upswing (1948–1970) but not during the subsequent period of relative instability (1970s–1990s) (Sherman 1990; Sherman and Kolk 1996). For instance, in the cycles of the postwar boom, the expansions lasted 16 quarters (1949–1953), 14 qrs (1954–1957), 9 qrs (1958–1960), and a sizable 36 qrs (1961–1969), while the contractions were short and shallow at 3qrs (each for 1953–1954, 1957–1958, and 1960–1961) and 4qrs (1969–1970) (Miller 1990, 90). The 36-quarter expansion between 1961 and 1969 is especially important in reducing the rate of unemployment to historically low levels, resulting in a higher wage share of national income (Sherman 1990), through increases in real hourly wages (and decreases in productivity). Institutional instability was inherent in the postwar boom which led workers to question their servility to capital.

Naples (1986) and Wallace (1989) studied the rise in labor militancy in some detail. The accord or truce, they argue, had inherent anomalies. It failed to institutionalize the nature of wage arrangements in cases where productivity growth faltered; it was based on a narrow economistic framework, especially distributive gains, which ignored workers' alienation in a bureaucratic workplace; and it assumed continued United States supremacy in the world economy, which began to falter. The economistic framework of worker interests came to the fore as their wage share of GNP rose substantially in light of low rates of unemployment and a heightened aspiration for consumption gains. While the 1948–1965 profit share experienced an average annual decline of −0.71%, for the 1965–1972 period the decline increased to −3.87% (and during 1972–1985, the share increased by an average of only 0.18%).

Second, there were numerous barriers, limits, or contradictions largely internal to the labor process. A major one was the cost of corporate control. Workers in the oligopoly sector of industry in the postwar period were situated in a contradictory position of wanting both greater material benefits and workplace power simultaneously. However, the institutionalized structure of the capital-labor truce, which brought together big capitals and big unions, led to the unions abrogating power within production in return for the benefits of distributive rewards. In this case, the industrial relations environment was ceremonially dominated by pecuniary and emulative values plus corporate hegemony. This dominance of "economism" over "industrial power" created greater worker alienation, and subordination, and eventually led to costs that promoted declining labor productivity, while capital sped up production to counteract the declining profit rate. Aglietta (1976, 120) discusses these costs vis-à-vis the rise in fatigue, nervous exhaustion, absenteeism, accidents, and defective products.

The uniform pace of the production process within the Fordist aspect of the CSD sphere is consistent with the subordination of labor by capital, but not with ideal conditions of production. Performance can be increased by variable pace, worker control over machine motion, and resting time, as argued by, for instance, Booth (1985) and Hodgson (1982-83). However, the tendency for uniformity and increasing production pace promoted fatigue, nervous exhaustion, absenteeism, accidents, and defective products, which increased as Fordism evolved. The extension of bureaucratic control became harder to implement as workers' alienated conditions led them to rebel against a system of production over which they had little control, and which increasingly led to health risks and lack of interest (Gordon 1982, 220).

With the declining reserve army, a speed-up of the production process occurred to counteract the already declining rate of profit, and labor productivity fell during the late 1960s/early 1970s. The power of capital to exploit social wealth declined somewhat, which propelled considerable instability and uncertainty.

Weisskopf (1983) argued that a major factor contributing to the decline in productivity in the mid-1960s was a drop in "work intensity," especially with the exhaustion in the supply of the reserve army, which reduced the cost of job loss for workers, and contributed to the lowering of the degree of effective subordination of labor by capital at the point of production. The low rate of unemployment reduced the degree of work intensity (the "Marx effect"), and it is the "factors affecting work intensity [which] account for far the largest share of the first period of slowdown (1966–1972), more than 98% of the predicted decline" (Weisskopf 1983, 421–2). Michl argues that, whereas the declining rate of profit during 1965–1972 (the first period of profit decline) was due largely to an increase in labor share, during 1972–1985 (the second period) it was largely due to a decline in the rate of growth of capital productivity (based on the output/capital ratio), some of which may be related to a decline in "work intensity" (Mitchl 1988, 15–20). Maddison (1991, 150) illustrates the decline in labor productivity (gross value added per person employed) from an average annual growth for "industry" of 5.2% (1950–1973) to 2.5% (1973–1987) in the United States (a similar decline to other Western economies).

A major problem with Fordism and thereby the truce was the bureaucratic structure of production in large oligopoly firms, incorporating detailed job-task descriptions, close monitoring of performance, and reward within internal labor markets. There are sharp limits to the successful reproduction of a system that transfers decision-making, information, and knowledge from the shop floor to managers. Booth (1985) emphasizes the problems of worker motivation and innovation in such a bureaucratic system.

Evidence points to rising worker antagonism to bureaucratic control in the 1960s and 1970s. One manifestation of this conflict lies in strike behavior. Wallace illustrates that strike behavior was strong in the late 1940s-to-early 1950s, that it declined considerably during the capital-labor truce from the early–mid-1950s to the late 1960s, and then it rose strongly during the late 1960s through to the mid-1970s when challenges were being mounted to the truce. The rise in strikes relating to "wages and hours" represents, in part, the success of labor in the sphere of distribution during a period of sustained decline in the reserve army. The issue that especially concerns us here is the rise in strikes over "plant administration" issues. Wallace (1989) argues that "plant administration strikes" (and "wage and hours strikes") challenged the truce (plus Fordism in general), and part of the reason for this relates to challenging capitalist control per se.

Naples (1986, 118; 1996, 118–123) shows that, during the late 1960s, pressures on profitability led capitalists "to delay maintenance of their machinery and to rely more heavily on speed-up [techniques] to retrieve profit margins," which led to major health and safety problems. For instance, she cites an instance in 1968 when 1.33% of all full-time equivalent miners were killed on the job. Workers were understandably against treating this case as a "productivity bargaining tool." She also cites examples in the manufacturing sector where shop stewards dropped to a low one per thousand employees, which undermined the accord because of the expansion of unresolved grievances (Fairris 1997). Rank and file workers more willingly engaged in "wildcat" strikes, defined as all strikes happening during the life of a contract, usually of a short duration, such as a few days, to speed-up such unresolved disputes.

Workers rebelled against capitalist control (and their unions) due to (1) greater consciousness and perception of being able to challenge, their alienated conditions per se; (2) "resistance against union policies that continued to sacrifice control-related job issues to higher wages and fringe benefits" (Wallace 1989, 27); and (3) deteriorating work conditions, due to speed-up techniques and delaying the maintenance of machinery as profitability declined, which severely compromised worker health and safety (Naples 1986). All three factors had an impact, but it is more likely that health, safety, and speed-ups were the principal factors, linked to resistance against union policies of distribution, and that challenges to capitalist control were of a more derivative source.

Labor did thus rebel against the internal conditions of production which affected productivity and hence the ability of capital to be reproduced within bureaucratic firms. As Naples (1986, 163–164) wrote, the "deterioration in industrial relations [was] … an endogenous outcome of the low levels of unemployment in the postwar era and the contradictions embodied in the postwar pattern of labor-management relations". She therefore concludes that the truce (as part of the Fordist element within the CSD),

> embodied *contradictions*, since it constituted relations … which were inherently conflict-ridden. During the extended expansion of the sixties those conflicts surfaced. As unemployment fell, the number of strikes rose. As profits were squeezed and working conditions deteriorated, the truce became less tenable and strikes over working conditions and wildcat strikes accelerated…. Obviously this shift in the terrain of union-capital conflict from wage determination to production itself, interfered directly with corporate control of the labor process. As a result, productivity growth suffered: the greater the constraints on capitalist freedom of enterprise, the greater the weight given to other considerations besides increasing output, the slower the growth of productivity. (Naples 1986, 110-11, 118; emphasis added)

Third, we turn to the contradictions of Fordism directly linked to the institutions of technology and consumption. One aspect of Fordism is the linkage between mass production and mass consumption. The mass production system of the postwar period included "large batch production; infrequent changes of model or die; cost minimisation through standardisation; … time and motion studies; [increasing] returns to scale"; and "break[ing] down [the labor process from] complex tasks into simpler (ones) for which less skilled labor could be employed." The costs of supervision and planning needed to be offset by economies of scale through large production runs (Mathews 1989, 130).

But the success of Fordism through the postwar boom goes well beyond the simple technical concerns of mass production, depending on, among other things, "the creation and maintenance of mass markets where mass produced goods may be bought, and the maintenance of mass purchasing power through high wages and social welfare systems" (Wallace 1989, 131). Central to this process was the growth of the motor vehicle industry, "white goods," televisions, infrastructure, housing, petroleum, petrochemicals, engineering, the military-industrial complex (which provided the technological basis for many consumer and engineering innovations), and the spatial-organizational context of production-consumption, including especially suburbanization, the network of highways, and the vehicle, steel, rubber, glass, electrical, pharmaceutical and electronics industries (Roobeek 1987).

Roobeek (1987, 134) adds that "technological determinism does not exist, but … the impact of technology is shaped by the power relations in a specific country in any particular period in history." An important process leading to the disruption of the power of capital-in-general was the life-cycle of the Fordist system, particularly the commencement of the maturity phase which many durable consumer-goods and process technologies entered by the late-1960s (Roobeek 1987, 137). During the maturity phase, the rate of increase in sales, productivity, and innovation slowed down, while the emergence of new industries was not fast enough to compensate. This thesis is developed especially by Schumpeterians such as Mensch; also Forrester; and those who argue that the transition between Fordism and Post-Fordism styles may be a very time-consuming process, and by no means inevitable (Tylecote 1992). Cars and durable consumer goods, which the U.S. specialized in, became saturated in international markets; while chemicals, steel, and metal industries evolved to a point of over-capacity (see Pfaller 1991, 51).

We have argued in this section that the Fordist system contributed to stability, certainty, and cooperation between capital and labor for a time, and thereby promoted an environment for real profit and real wage increases during the 1950s and 1960s. However, there were limits inherent in this CSD sphere, and the potential to stabilize industrial relations became exhausted as workers gained some measure of effective power over distributive processes and the ability to control their labor in the late 1960s and 1970s. There were also challenges from abroad. In the postwar era the relations between capital and were modified due to "institutional change," but this led eventually to the under-exploitation of the social wealth by the capitalist classes, and hence to a degree of circular and cumulative slide into a period of fragility and instability into the 1970s–1990s as uncertainty heightened.

The Fordist-truce CSD sphere evolved into crisis through the late 1960s and especially the 1970s as growth declined, recessions became deeper, and financial instability and crises recurrent, and these growth anomalies, deep recessions, and financial crises continued into the 1980s, 1990s, and thereafter. The question arises as to whether there was a transitional era during the 1970s–2000s (similar in some degree to 1919–1945) when the Fordist system was evolving into a new mode which may have helped solve some of the problems of capitalism. Questions have arisen, for instance, as to whether a new CSD sphere of production-distribution-exchange emerged and whether such a structure is related to the system variously called the "flexible system of production," "Toyotism," or "Post-Fordism"; or whether a more "neo-Taylorist" system is evolving either separately or in a type of dual system with the flexible system in the US (and elsewhere) (Mansfield 1992; for details see O'Hara 2000, chap. 14).

7.3.4 Keynesian-Welfare State

The third sphere of the CSD, the state-citizen accord and the Keynesian-welfare state (KWS), was based on rising welfare payments, a higher dole, and greater influence of the state in economic life, especially during the 1950s, 1960s, and early 1970s. Rising state expenditure propelled growth and thereby contributed to the reverse reserve army effect and rising working-class power. By acting on citizen rights to environmental controls, occupational health and safety, and consumer protection legislation, the state upset the profit needs of the business through regulations and taxes (Gordon et al. 1990, 166–7). The KWS had immanent contradictions in the sense that, while expansionary policies promoted growth, the growth eventually became inflationary; and the degree of "welfare," regulation, and protection reduced the incentive to invest and work thus reducing growth. Despite the Thatcher and Reagan conservative reactions against labor, and the development of neoliberalism, a new set of state institutions have not been constituted as a new sphere of the CSD to propel stable reproduction and *growth*, reduce climate change, or attenuate adequately some of the other polycrises (see chap. 9 below).

This section outlines the nature of the KWS, including the capital-state truce, especially in the US, paying special attention to the degree to which the KWS influenced growth and accumulation through promoting socioeconomic stability, resolution of class conflict, and profitability during the 1940s–1980s. We find that the KWS did tend to promote growth and accumulation during the 1940s–1960s through an array of methods, including welfare provision, stabilization policies, military expenditure, and moderating the conflict between capital and labor. However, the KWS had no unified dynamics and thereby failed to sustain growth and accumulation through the 1970s–1980s onward as its contradictions began to manifest. From the late 1960s onward, it contributed to declining profit through supporting worker and citizen rights vis-à-vis capital; expanding worker power in distribution and working conditions; and generating instability through questioning established truths and institutions. The decline in the KWS then led to attempts to re-establish stability, profit, and the power of capital through the Reagan revolution and other measures of the 1980s and 1990s (through neoliberalism; see Chap. 9 on polycrises).

During the late 1920s, problems of reproduction became manifest throughout dominant areas of the capitalist system. The financial system became increasingly speculative, the state-supported laissez-faire, the international economy became unstable, and industrial capital less innovative. This contributed to a serious drop in confidence during the 1930s, and the depression itself led to further institutional disorganization and disarray. The depression, the Second World War, and its aftermath, however, led also to a massive devaluation of capital and, eventually, some degree of institutional reorganization emerged. The institutional structures were put into place by which US hegemony emerged, the KWS gradually flourished, Fordism evolved as a predominant system of production, distribution, and consumption, the financial system was reorganized and regulated, and household labor began a period of "baby boom" and consumerism that promoted reproduction for a time.

The state was involved in all these developments. The BWS was organized and developed primarily by representatives of the state apparatus (Phillips 1985). The KWS saw the gradual development of policy centered on preventing depression, providing for full employment, and indirectly expanding the sphere of the capitalist enterprise (Bleaney 1985). The continual war effort (e.g., 1939–45, Korea, and later Vietnam) contributed to the development of many commercial innovations, expanded demand, and established closer links between the state and industry, through the "military-industrial complex" (Reich and Finklehor 1970). The state played an important organizational role in the creation of the capital-labor truce (Bowles and Gintis 1982a, b), and spending policies of the state promoted consumption patterns necessary for expansion (Bowles and Edwards 1993).

The state improved the functions of the Central Bank, especially lender of last facilities, and instigated laws to promote a regulated regional and national banking system for retail and commercial purposes (Wolfson 1993). The state ensured that women who had worked in industry during the Second World War were coaxed back home to perform their maternal duties, which provided a basis for reproduction and the latent reserve army of labor (Power 1983). Gold (1977) has shown linkages between Keynesian strategy and aggregate demand, state centralization, the labor movement, the world economy, "military Keynesianism," and the "Keynesian coalition."

Both the New Deal policies of the 1930s and the "Great Society" programs of the 1960s laid the foundations of the welfare aspects of the state in the US (Pfaller 1991, 85; Stanfield and McClintock 1999, 1246). The Social Security Act of 1935 established an insurance system for old age, unemployment compensation, and various assistance packages on a means-tested basis. The 1935 Revenue Act increased tax rates on the wealthy, and, in 1936, there was a new tax on undistributed profits. The watered-down Employment Act of 1946 specified the need for "maximum employment," a Presidential annual Economic Report, a Joint Committee of Congress, and a Council of Economic Advisers (Bleaney 1985, 46, 87–89) The record of Depression and war contributed to a sense of national emergency and unity of purpose in which "the pursuit of private profit seemed strangely antiquated and immoral, [and, over time,] … Keynesian techniques … conquered the academic world[,] … became familiar in government circles, and seemed ideal for the new requirements of economic management. With the help of wartime experience, Keynesianism ceased to be depression economics and became a central tool of stabilisation policy" (Bleaney 1985, 82, 90).

Developments after the Second World War very gradually took root in the United States in which the formerly dominant laissez-faire ideology declined in favor of a liberal democratic viewpoint. Bastard-Keynesian economic policy taught that an equilibrium position could be established at less than full employment and that government spending/lower taxes and monetary policy may help push demand to full employment levels. Keynes himself emphasized the need to design institutions to help solve the pressing problems of economic policy. Important in this context is what James Cypher analyzed as the "corporate state," or "Cold War Keynesianism," namely, the enormous financial and strategic commitment to the war machine during the so-called Cold War against Soviet-style states. During 1951–1955, 22% of net United States investment was subsidized by the military, while during 1945–1970 over 50% of R&D was associated with the military. Much of this is said to have been modified for non-military developments, such as computers, airplanes, satellites, artificial intelligence, microcircuitry, and steel/aluminum fabrication plants (Cypher 1979, 519).

During the 1960s, a new wave of welfare measures was enacted, including medical insurance, Medicare, Medicaid, food stamps, Aid to Families with Dependent Children, job training, and other public assistance programs (Peterson 1985, 603). Real social welfare expenditures under public programs grew in real terms from \$10b (1950) to \$29b (1960), \$86b (1970), \$351b (1980), and \$938b (1992) (Walker and Vatter 1997, 188). However erratic, tentative, and late in coming, some of these employment, welfare, and military programs represented a qualitative source of change in capitalism and a major escalation in the role of the state. Despite neoliberal efforts to curb these developments in the 1980s and 1990s, the state continues to this day to provide important welfare, warfare, and counter-cyclical functions in the United States and elsewhere. The KWS techno-institutional system penetrated the whole system and conditioned the reproduction of capitalism in the US and elsewhere.

The KWS promoted both reproductive and nonreproductive institutional relations, from the point of view of the general interests of capitalism. But, as the postwar structure evolved in the 1970s, the nonreproductive relations began to dominate, and the contradictions of the KWS began to manifest as greater instability and uncertainty, lower rates of economic growth-profit, and gradually a reduction in the degree of legitimacy of the KWS.

To provide some degree of embeddedness of economy within society, however, the KWS techno-institutions always ran the risk of promoting disembedded modes of human reproduction. There are two reasons for this. First, many of the KWS programs were "developments from above," which did not necessarily promote integrity and community. And secondly, the KWS developed some programs which adversely affected capital accumulation and, to that extent, promoted the fragmentation of capitalism, without reproducing viable and effective alternatives to capital's mode of reproduction. These are the contradictions that Ian Gough (1979) recognized as fundamental limits to the KWS and to the development of "liberal (social democratic) capitalism."

Offe (1984, 147) identifies the welfare state as corresponding to a "peace formula" involving, first, state assistance to fulfill certain basic needs which are not satisfied by the dominant market system, and secondly, the institutionalization of labor unions in the wage and general policy process. To transform this into the KWS within the CSD, it is important to add anticyclical economic policy and the expansion of public works and military programs. Under the KWS, there was an expansion of minimum wages, social security, job security, education, medical services, subsidized housing, compulsory insurance schemes, automatic stabilizers, discretionary policy, and regulation.

But the contradictions were not that long in manifesting themselves, especially during the late 1960s and 1970s. A major contradiction of the KWS is that it "exemplified bewildering contradictions between systemic capitalist needs, individual capitalist interests, and working-class needs" (O'Connor 1984, 200). The KWS was unable to develop the warranted knowledge and alternative institutions to capital, which might have provided the foundations for a more "progressive" instrumentalist or socialist system. In addition, it had trouble developing systematic and well-defined policies over the long-term horizon, due to (1) the election needs of parties, (2) conflicting objectives, (3) changing priorities, (4) changing personnel in the state apparatus, (5) pressure groups, (6) the "disjointed and incrementalist" tendency of policy, (7) lack of information (and the availability of wrong information), (8) incompetence, and many other factors. Electoral pressure, immediacy, and the uncoordinated nature of the KWS, plus class conflicts and compromises inherent in modern capitalism, led to greater policy confusion as the postwar system evolved. There was no systematically patterned logic to the workings of the KWS which might have propelled, in a different socioeconomic environment, a more unified (socialist) reproductive framework.

Offe (1984) recognizes that the KWS was initiated, in some measure, to counter the contradictions inherent in the struggle between capital and labor, to institutionalize and moderate the distributive conflict that plagued capitalism since early times. It succeeded to some degree in this objective, but, in place of the old contradictions, new ones emerged which promoted accumulation crisis, although the crisis was not as extreme as in previous periods of structural and processual dislocation (e.g., the 1930s) (at least not until the late 2000s and early 2010s in parts of the Eurozone). He further argues that "the welfare state apparatus imposed a burden of taxation and regulation upon capital which amounts to a disincentive to invest"; and secondly, "grants claims, entitlements, and collective power positions to workers and unions which amount to a disincentive to work, or at least to work as hard and productively as they would be forced to under the reign of unfettered market forces" (Offe 1984, 149). He believes these arguments have some validity, but that one need not accept policy prescriptions that were often instituted in the light of them (e.g., neoliberalism).

He points to the contradiction between citizen/worker rights and the accumulation process, and how the welfare state reinforced this division, and thereby destabilized both processes. The KWS promoted citizen/worker rights without an autonomous and completely embedded institutional structure to reproduce them in a thorough fashion. Thus, "welfare payments to the poor [were] everywhere made conditional upon their conformity to standards of behaviour which the better-to-do strata of the population are perfectly free to violate," while "Bureaucracies absorb more resources and provide less services than typically democratic and decentralized structures of social policy" (Offe 1984, 155–156).

The fundamental contradiction, Offe believes, is between, on the one hand, the historically developed reproductive needs of humans to cope with rapid change, social stress, the "secularization of the moral order," alienating work conditions, and the life process of the community, and, on the other hand, the (modified) logic of capital which exacerbated such sources of instability. Or, as another author puts it: "The state's role of securing the reproduction of capitalist social relations exists in fundamental tension with its effort to facilitate collective action to improve the adjustment of instituted power and status to the fuller unfolding means and purposes of generic humanity" (Stanfield 1991, 778). Historically, however, "while capitalism cannot coexist with, neither can it exist without, the welfare state. This is exactly the condition to which we refer when using the *concept of 'contradiction'*" (Offe 1984, 153) (emphasis added).

As interest groups increased their effective power over distribution, the KWS drifted further from the interests of capital-in-general. The policy tendency was for demand-induced transfers and spending patterns, which, while important for the realization of commodities, essentially failed to promote competition, innovation, and institutional reorganizations which might have stimulated capital accumulation. The development of a bureaucratic state apparatus expanded the system of regulations, rules, and limitations on the activities of capitalist enterprise. Gradually, the KWS encroached on the effective power and hegemony of business, and, during the 1960s, the protest movements campaigning for the environment, worker safety, and consumer protection effectively influenced the legislative state process. This led to the development of the National Highway Safety Commission (1970), the Occupational Safety and Health Administration (1970), the Environmental Protection Agency (1970), the Consumer Safety Administration (1972), the Mine Enforcement and Safety Administration (1973) and other measures. Government regulation of business rose from an index of 1 (1948) to 2 (1965) to 8 (1975), which contributed to declining profitability by reducing U.S. international competitiveness and expanding national resistance to capital (Bowles et al. 1990).

The KWS contributed to the declining hegemony of "traditional values and norms of social integration such as patriarchy and respect for formal authority" plus "carrot-stick economic incentives and labor mobility" (O'Connor 1984, 220, 222). The very success of the KWS in providing welfare, education, and reducing the intensity of recessions (in association with Fordism as a whole) led to the search for higher values, and the questioning of established truths. This is consistent with Maslow's hierarchy of needs, in which, once the basic needs of food, clothing, shelter, and partner contentment are satisfied, human beings, in general, are more capable than normal of seeking higher truths such as moral values, quality of life issues, and "idle curiosity."

As discussed in the Fordism section, above, higher levels of demand reduced the size of the reserve army of labor (see O'Hara 1999, 989–991), which contributed in its own way to the distributive successes of labor, a lower level of worker subordination, the formation of counter cultures, and a decline in the work ethic. Rising levels of unemployment benefits and welfare reduced the cost of job loss. All this inhibited the intensity of labor and hence labor productivity, and eventually promoted the wage share of the national product. Under these contradictory conditions, "[e]xploitative production relations coexist[ed] with expanded possibilities to resist, escape, and mitigate exploitation" (Offe 1984, 152).

The KWS regime slowly gained legitimacy during the 1940s and 1950s in the United States and much elsewhere, especially in the core, and during the 1960s, it became a dominant aspect of American political economy (and most other advanced capitalist economies). There was a massive increase in welfare payments during the 1960s, particularly during President Johnson's "war on poverty" and the building of the "great society" programs (Brown-Collier 1999). The KWS gained hegemonic dominance as the democratic party had "huge majorities in both houses" and a "reform-minded Supreme Court" to help it along (Murray 1989, 71). A plethora of reforms emerged, such as training strategies, housing programs, educational subsidies, and medical insurance. Murray (1989) shows that, during 1960–1975, Federal expenditure (in real terms) on welfare for those of "working age" increased more than five-fold; this contributed to a reduction in the "cost of job loss" from an index of 15.0 (1965) to 11.4 (1975), and 10.3 (1979) (Bowles et al. 1990, 71). During this period, births to single women more than doubled, the participation rate of 18–19-year-old blacks dropped from 72% to 55%, and the work ethic declined (Murray 1989, 75, 76).

These changes have been shown to have contributed to a reduction in the ability of capital to extract work from labor in the production process, through a drop in the degree of competition between workers. During the "first phase of decline" (1966–1973), 84% of the decline in productivity from 2.96% (1948–1966 yearly average) to 2.07% (1966–1973 average) has been attributable to a reduction in "work intensity." During the "second phase of decline," 1973–1979, real output per production worker rose by only 0.83% (yearly average), a major decline compared with 1948–1966, 30% of which was attributed to a decline in work intensity. The changes instigated by the KWS which reduced the cost of job loss contributed to the decline in work intensity (Bowles et al. 1990). This is linked to what Bowles and Gintis (1982a, b, 1986) term the contradiction between the principles of private capital, which require rights in property, and the principles of liberal (social) democracy, which vests rights in persons or citizens independent of property.

Overall, in the postwar period, some semblance of balance was ensured in the early- to mid-phases of the long boom, but as the KWS structures gained in strength the contradictions manifested themselves more openly, thus questioning the basis of accumulation without establishing the conditions suitable for a new social order. The deep recessions of the 1970s–1990s were in part contributed to by the activities of the KWS. In response, a right-wing backlash was instigated, leading to the development of many important think tanks, university departments, and, of course, the Reagan Administration of the late 1970s and 1980s (Thatcherism in Britain). Monetarism, supply-side economics and later new classical economics evolved to support business and conservative governments. A neoliberal state apparatus was developed in the US and many other nations, which we examine in Chap. 9.

7.3.5 Regulated Financial System and its Demise

The fifth sphere of the CSD, the regulated financial system, was a critical part of the postwar corporate system of institutions into the 1940s–1970s. During the mid-late 1930s, 1940s, and onward, the U.S. financial system evolved into a regulated form as fixed interest rates, deposit insurance, lender of last resort, controls on interstate banking, and financial segmentation provided enough certainty to propel stability and certainty through the socioeconomic circuit. No major financial crises were ensured as growth and accumulation were relatively strong from the 1950s to the late 1960s. From the late 1960s, uncertainty started to rise, escalating into the 1970s–1990s and beyond as financial crises became periodically institutionalized into the system. The move from a financially robust system with hedge finance to a more fragile system with speculative finance led to the emergence of more Ponzi financial positions as cash flow and profitability declined while debt servicing increased. In this climate, pressures built during the mid-late 1970s, 1980s, and 1990s to deregulate the financial system for interest rates, exchange rates, and flows of capital to be more flexible. Currently, as we move into the early decades of the twenty-first century, the failures of neoliberalism have seen some changes but not a robust new CSD for growth, accumulation, and climate change mitigation and adaptation (see chap. 9 for more on this).

The purpose of this section is to comprehend the role of the U.S. financial system during the postwar era of the 1940s–1990s. Special attention is placed on the role of finance in the forces promoting growth and accumulation during the 1950s and 1960s and the contradictions which manifested themselves in financial fragility and instability during the 1970s–1990s. In developing this theme, political economy work in finance will be scrutinized, especially the financial instability hypothesis and writers who broadly link to this framework.

Fundamental to the financial instability hypothesis (FIH) is the notion that "[c]apitalist market mechanisms cannot lead to a sustained, stable-price, full employment equilibrium" (Minsky 1985, 173). Capitalism is ever in the process of change, and "whatever happens changes as institutions evolve, so that even though business cycles and financial crises are unchanging attributes of capitalism, the actual path an economy traverses depends upon institutions, usages, and policies" (p.174). This ever-changing system, linked to *circular and cumulative causation*, produces a non-equilibrium tendency that generates cumulative upswing and downswing, with the existence of stabilizing institutions such as the lender of last resort and big government.

Capitalism is seen by Hyman Minsky to include privately owned means of production, monetary returns to the owners of capital, the determination of asset prices in markets, and large-scale production with a sizable investment goods sector. It is said to undergo "periods of relative tranquility" (such as the postwar boom), not equilibrium, in which disruptive influences are not great. But during these periods forces internal to the operation of the economy evolve which predicate financial instability in the long term.

Minsky, Martin Wolfson, and others ask, first, why were there no major financial crises during the 1940s–1960s, but severe crises into the 1970s–1990s (and beyond)? Secondly, why were the moderately severe crises during the 1970s–1990s not as severe as the Great Depression of the 1930s? Drawing on Minsky's model, Aliber and Kindleberger (2015) ask the same questions and reply that the financial system during the 1980s–2010s, especially in the US, experienced the most intense long-period of financial instability and crises in the history of Western capitalism.

As to the reasons for this, answers link to long-wave theory (Minsky 1964; Wolfson 1994, 232) and the qualitative differences between the 1900s–1940s and the 1940s–1990s (Minsky 1982, xi-xxiv; Wolfson 1994). Minsky believes that there are forces that develop systematically during the boom of the wave which subsequently lead to fragility and crises. Major recessions and financial crises were absent during the postwar boom (1950s–1960s), while mostly decadal major recessions and numerous financial crises emerged during the long "contraction" of the 1970s onward.

The message of Minsky is that the long boom of the 1950s and 1960s provided the *institutional and environmental conditions for the evolution of fragility*, which transformed into periodic deep financial instabilities during the long wave downswing of the 1970s–1990s circa. Wolfson complements this by demonstrating that short business cycles during the long contraction led to recessions which endogenously precipitated major financial crises shortly after the upper-turning point in the cycle. These processes are endogenous in an environmental rather than deterministic sense. But the role of the state, primarily, in providing lender of last resort functions, discretionary policy, deposit insurance, and Chinese Walls between retail and wholesale banking, historically usually prevent(ed) major depression under capitalism (until these conditions change).

Recovery after the Second World War was aided by a regulated financial sphere within the CSD in an environment of debt reduction, greater government spending, plus the gradual emergence of stability and confidence. Wolfson explains some of the robustness of the 1945–1965 period as being due to a degree of financial conservativeness, and a reduction in the stock of debt as corporations, individuals, and families emerged from the depression. The postwar boom seemed to suppress anomalies due to the creation of circular and cumulative bouts of optimism. The postwar system of corporate and banking finance, emerged from changes instigated in the 1930s (especially the Banking Act of 1933), 1940s, and later. It is said to be qualitatively different from previous times due to a combination of big government, deposit insurance, the separation of commercial and investment banking, the Federal Home Loan Bank Board, the emergence of the discount window, the prohibition of interest on cheque accounts, and a further series of regulations and "innovations" (plus changes linked to the world economy such as fixed exchange rates) (Wolfson 1993). Most of these changes increased the viability of financial organizations and the stability of the system. No major depressions emerged in the postwar long upswing, Minsky and Wolfson agree, due to these institutionalized support networks (Minsky 1982, 117–155; Wolfson 1994) that stabilized a financial system that otherwise periodically tends toward substantial incoherence and instability.

The postwar economy, especially during the 1950s and 1960s, was relatively embedded (in Polanyi's 1944 sense) in the political and social fabric of U.S. capitalism ("embedded liberalism"), with a considerable degree of financial robustness. Pfister and Suter (1987) and Suter (1992) differentiate between competitive, cooperative, and centralized financial systems. The pre-war era (1900–1939) was said to be based on a more competitive model, in which system stability was lacking, culminating in the Great Depression of the 1930s. The postwar period, however, saw a transformation toward system stability through primarily cooperative self-organization within many of its subsystems, including at the international level, which is said to have reduced the potential for systemic instability. At the national level, there was a larger element of centralized organization as the financial system became heavily regulated. Consistent with Polanyi's analysis, increasing institutionalization of financial relations in the postwar period reduced crisis-potential through cooperative and embedded financial institutions such as lender of last resort, deposit insurance, and interest rate controls.

Political economists have historically been somewhat critical of the role of finance in the economy, especially in relation to "fictitious capitals," speculative bubbles, and the conflict between industrial and money capitals. While these dimensions of capital are important, such scholars have more recently recognized the critical role money plays in providing endogenous finance, stimulating production (money is not a "veil"), and enhancing the circuit of money capital, especially in an embedded financial system such as the postwar circuit. For instance, as David Harvey emphasizes, a financial system is essential to capital, for individual agents, groups, and the system-as-a-whole. This is true since "the circulation of interest-bearing capital performs certain vital functions and the accumulation of capital requires that money capitalists achieve and actively assert themselves as a power external to and independent of actual production processes" (1982, 261).

Included in the functions of the credit system under capital are the mobilization of money as capital; a reduction in the cost and time of circulation; the role of fixed capital circulation and consumption fund formation; the formation of fictitious capital as bills of exchange and other marketable assets; the rate of interest acting as a "barometer and thermometer" for the movement of money into different assets/investment areas; and the promotion of large-scale production and economies of scale (Harvey 1982, 262–272).

These functions of credit are central to the reproductive relations of capital since they variously promote the creation and realization of surplus value and protect the property relations of the system. Even "markets for fictitious capital," as Harvey states, "are vital to the survival of capitalism since it is only through them that the continuity/flow of interest-bearing capital can be assured. This flow … performs some vital coordinating functions … in capitalist society" (Harvey 1982, 278), including the buying and selling of securities to "preserve flexibility and liquidity"; abstracting wealth holders from the barriers of specific use-values, which promotes added flexibility; and representing a claim upon the future production of surplus value (p. 266–272). Also, in relation to the credit system in general, the potential functions of "the sphere of circulation" are considerable (see Harvey 1982, 284).

The postwar financial SSA contributed to growth and accumulation through core essential functions. The financial aspects of the circuits and pathways were, on balance, a source of stability, relatively high profitability, and a moderation of intracapitalist conflict between industry and finance. The stability was provided by the system of regulation and the national–subnational orientation of finance. Profitability was enhanced by the system of credit expansion and relatively safe markets. The moderation of intra-class conflict, vis-à-vis *heterogeneous groups and agents*, was due to finance being directed to expanding the industrial base of Fordism. As Wolfson said:

> Stability was assured by the renewed confidence in financial institutions made possible by the system of government support and protection, and by the environment of low and stable interest rates made possible by the low levels of debt and inflation. The profitability of financial institutions was enhanced by the monopoly rents provided by "compartmentalization," by the subsidy implicit in federal deposit insurance, and by the assured profits made possible by the positive spread between long-term and short-term interest rates. … Conflict between financial and industrial capitalists was moderated by high absolute levels of profitability, which eased pressures over the relative division between the two groups. … The increased stability, profitability and moderation of class conflict all helped to provide an environment conducive to rapid economic growth [Wolfson 1994, 137]

However, as the 1960s and early 1970s progressed, the postwar financial SSA started to break down. The system of fixed exchange rates gave way to more flexible rates as the contradictions of the international monetary system (BWS) started to impact quite sharply (Fred Block 1977). The regulated system of national banking started to crumble as divisions between institutions declined. The process of globalization was enhanced through Euromarkets and foreign banking, which increased competition in the US and threatened the profitability of established financial interests. Technological change brought new pressures to bear on the institutions and opened up new avenues and threats to the old players. The old order was in decline while the new order disrupted the balance of class forces, reduced profit, and increased instability. All this at a time, during the 1970s–1990s (onward), when global instability was high, deep recessions prevalent, and financial crises common (Brenner 1998).

The period since the 1970s has thus been one of generalized and cyclical financial fragility. The technical basis for this instability is said to be "the changing relations between debts and incomes, the variable margins of safety in financing contracts, and the evolution of financial practices over time" (Minsky 1984, 25). Minsky (1985, 1995) differentiates between the "era of tranquility" from 1945 to 1970 and the time of "contained turbulence" during the 1970s–1990s (onward). He believes that, during the postwar period, the endogenous workings of the system, with its long lags and circular and cumulative motion, eventually produced incoherence (financial instability). Incoherence is defined as a state where initial fragility sets off further fragility due to the amplifying nature of the instabilities. Incoherence tended to manifest itself during the long wave downswing of the 1970s–1990s onward. However:

> The result of the processes need not be a great depression. Policy interventions of the lender of last resort nature and the impact of big government and the deficits it generates when income falls have succeeded in containing the thrust towards deep depressions. However, the medicine that succeeded—like most powerful medicine—has side effects. The inflation, stagflation, and turbulence since 1966 are prices paid, in our times, for not having deep depressions. [Minsky 1984, 22-23]

It is in light of the creation of financial fragility from a long boom to a long wave downswing that financial crises emerged, especially during the 1970s onward. The long boom brought pressure to bear on money markets, labor markets, and commodity markets which raised input costs to capitalists, and endogenous money supply exacerbated this pressure along with the expansion of debt created out of cumulative optimism and overexpansion. The institutions of private financial-corporate relations are geared to expansion but have no universal counter-cyclical processes to stabilize the boom nor to promote stability in an environment of fragility. The lender of last resort function, big government, and deposit insurance elements can, if used wisely, prevent the emergence of depression, but it cannot stop the fragility that is endogenously generated through the institutions of capitalism. Financial-corporate relations were not well structured to cope with heightened uncertainty, disorganization, and socioeconomic instability, which contributed markedly to the periodic emergence of deep recession and financial crises as the postwar circuits and pathways declined.

We need to explain in more detail the rise of financial fragility (Minsky) and financial crises (Wolfson) from the late 1960s or early 1970s onward. How did financial fragility emerge as the CSD declined, leading to instability and crises? Minsky (1974) has presented a formal explanation of the trend from financial robustness, during the 1950s and 1960s, toward fragility, during the 1970s, 1980s, and 1990s. Central to this explanation is the relationship between the (expected and actual) flows of current income (Y) and (expected and actual) current contractual cash commitments (C); which provide an estimate of cash flow. The other measures that are important are balance sheet-related items: The capitalized (K) value (stock) of expected income (in period t) over many years (K(Y)) and (expected) contractual payment commitments (in period t) over many years (K(C)). We thus have a measure of net cash flow:

$$Y_t - C_t \tag{1}$$

and a stock of accumulated or capitalized income minus payments (expected) over many years:

$$K(Y)_t - K(C)_t \tag{2}$$

The cash flows provide an indication of the current operating potential of the firm, sector, or economy, while the stocks indicate the long-term viability of the firm, sector, or economy reflected in the state of the balance sheet.

Minsky then introduces a long recovery, such as the postwar boom, resulting, through many years, in a net cash flow that is rising, an expected income (Ye_t) that is less than actual (Ya_t) and rising (i.e., $Ye_t < Ya_t$) as *uncertainty*, a core factor, declines (see Runde 2001), with an expansion of net worth, $K(Y)_t > K(C)_t$, and hence rising investment during the late 1940s and 1950s. After a lag, businesses revised upwards their estimates of profitability and, as actual profit continued to rise on average during the 1960s, expected profit rose in a gradual (although lopsided) fashion. (A series of lags could be introduced here, corresponding to Forrester's (1977) "bootstraps process.")

In the earlier years of the long boom, Minsky implies, corporate finance is in a very sound state. Potential investment sources (Is) include current internal income (W), previously acquired cash/other financial assets (Pcf), and external funds (the issue of equities (E) or borrowing (B)):

$$Is = W + Pcf + E + B \tag{3}$$

In an environment of tranquility, during the 1950s, when firms were constrained for funds by depression, war, and postwar renewal, the internal sources and past acquisition of liquid assets were generally low, compared with expectations of profit in the future, and the value of capital assets. Consumers had a relatively low level of savings to draw on to buy equity and other assets. Therefore, firms depended more heavily on borrowing. Gradually, expected income increased in line with an increasing level of actual income, although at this stage net expected income is still smaller than actual. As time goes on, both expected and actual cash flows rise. Since existing banking institutions are more conservative than producer corporations in their assessment of the level of contractual debt commitments that are prudentially feasible for the firms to hold, "the profit situation is conducive to financial innovation and a growth of 'fringe' banking relations" (Minsky 1974, 270). Firms expand their debt commitments, often through non-traditional sources, on the assumption that the growth of the previous decade will continue, as happened during the 1960s.

During all phases of the long boom, except the period sometime before the upper-turning point, the financial position of most firms, Minsky believes, are such that $Y_i > C_i$ (expected and actual cash flows are high) and $K(Y) > K(C)$ (the stock of net worth is high). This is the situation that he calls a generalized situation of "hedge finance": current income is greater than payment commitments at least by a "margin of safety"; and the balance sheet is sound in that capitalized expected income is greater than capitalized contractual payment commitments. Expected cash flows cover the payments of interest charges plus some of the principal sum of debt. This financial soundness is typical of periods when a suitable financial CSD sphere is in place.

However, most firms do not recognize limits to growth inherent in the full employment level of resources. They tend to extrapolate good (or bad) results into the future if high levels of uncertainty and instability are long-since-past (see Courvisanos 1996), and the general trend of demand has been on the increase for two decades or so, as was the situation in the late 1940s through to the late-1960s.

Their expansionary plans tend upward based on past behavior, with less weight given to more distant events, such as the Great Depression, and with no indication of any deep recessions or depressions on the horizon. More fundamentally: "Whereas the utilisation of existing capacity is determined by price, cost, and therefore by profit expectations over a relatively short period (6 months, 1 or 2 years), the decision to expand capacity is determined by profit expectations over a much longer time horizon: 10, 20 or even 40 years" (Minsky 1985, 34–35). With optimism high, firms continue to finance both the existing contractual commitments and expansionary plans. If there are limits that lead to the demise of the long boom, there is an endogenous force leading firms to engage in debt financing to an extent that is inconsistent with the (realistic) prices of capital assets.

Financial fragility increases when units move cumulatively from hedge to speculative, and, especially, from speculative into Ponzi positions. Speculative finance is where $Y_i < C_i$ but $K(Y) > K(C)$; Minsky approximates this to the situation where many units in the economy borrow to repay interest charges. As the financial position of firms gets worse, Ponzi finance, which is an extreme form of speculative finance, arises when many units operate with $Yi < Ci$ as well as $K(Y) < K(C)$; and are technically insolvent. They not only need to borrow to repay interest charges but also possibly extra fees for late payments, and this situation is not expected to change significantly in the foreseeable future. The dominance of Ponzi finance is typical of situations when the financial sphere of the CSD is in disarray.

Minsky argues that there is an endogenous process that leads to the movement of hedge into speculative and speculative into Ponzi finance, resulting in fragility and the potential for deep recession (Schroeder 2009). This is linked to the decline in the financial aspects of the CSD as the stabilizing institutions give way to more speculative relations. A high level of dependency on financial markets, when speculative finance is strong, implies the creation of an environment in which apparently accidental events, which in normal times fail to promote uncertainty, may trigger a financial crisis. This movement can result from a multifarious set of factors, which are highly likely as the long boom moves into the contractionary phase of the long wave. Ultimately a financial crisis occurs when there is an intense demand for money and usually a run on a bank and financial market (a "Minsky moment?").

As the financial CSD sphere declines there is a deterioration in the state of long-term confidence, which adversely affects investment in this and other CSD spheres. There is a drop in expected capital asset prices, due to a reversal of the circular and cumulative causative (CCC) upward motion. As the euphoria of the boom eventually leads to pessimism, high levels of uncertainty reduce the prospective yield of projects. Linked to this is a series of related processes. For instance, there is usually an increase in short-term interest rates, especially if the sudden drop in long-term profit expectations leads to financial uncertainty and a sudden increase in demand for money; and when the monetary authorities raise interest rates to moderate demand pressures. There is also usually an increase in the ratio of input prices to output prices, particularly due to the high prices for interest, oil (energy), labor, and general commodities. There is also typically an increase in the ratio of external to internal funding of projects and short- to long-term debt. The is typically an increase in the gestation period of investment, due to supply bottlenecks inherent in the height of the long boom, and an increase in the gap between expected completion of projects and the sale of capital goods.

The boom in the long wave in the late 1960s and early 1970s, the endogenous supply of finance which expanded the boom, and inflation, all created an institutional environment for these instabilities to arise. Thus, "Once the price of capital assets reflects inflationary expectations, an end to those expectations will lead to a sharp fall in investment. The upward instability of capitalism is a necessary condition for the possibility of a deep recession" (Minsky 1980, 512). Capitalism does not have sufficient investment in *embedded institutional relations* to stabilize the level of uncertainty inherent in its functioning when the financial sphere of CSD declines.

When firms need external funds beyond traditional sources they finance contractual commitments from non-traditional sources. This led to a rise in endogenous credit money to satisfy corporate demand for funds. As Minsky says of the postwar era:

> The portfolio adventuring that led to the current [1970s and 1980s] fragile structure was taking place in the 1950s ... in the innovations in financial markets that were taking place.... The Federal Funds Market [FFM] ... enable[d] a given volume of reserves to carry a larger volume of bank liabilities and thus earning assets, and ... it change[d] the way banks ma[d]e position ... [from] Treasury debt to ... a set of devices such as federal funds, commercial paper, Eurodollar borrowings, and varieties of repurchase agreements.... The growth of the [FFM] ... was a response to profit-making opportunities [which] ... increased the volume of financing that was available with a given reserve base.... With an endogenous supply of finances, stable expansion destabilizes the economy: stable expansion is impossible. [Minsky 1984, 26-27]

These (structural) endogenous sources of funds enabled a multiple expansion of deposits in the financial system by expanding loans in areas where reserve requirements were lower than average or missing altogether. Financial innovation, according to Minsky, is in large measure a way of "reinvent[ing] new" forms of money, substitutes for money in portfolios, and financing techniques for various types of activity" (Minsky 1985, 178; see also Wray 1990 and Pollin 1991). Thus, a series of such endogenous credit processes over 10 or 20 years, even without the emergence of long wave downswing, results in substantial debt accumulation. The real problem arises, according to Minsky, when interest rates suddenly rise, or, according to Wolfson (and Pollin 1986), when the rate of profit declines during long wave downswing, which reduces the ability of firms to finance the repayment of debt; and when the search for short-term finance exacerbates the problem. In the light of reduced profit and/or higher interest rates, an expansion of (especially short-term) debt from non-traditional sources raises the debt/equity ratio and reduces the quality of existing debt. Financial relations contributed in their own way to these contradictory relations via the endogenous credit process. As Minsky says:

> The model sketched here makes a debt-deflation process [see Fisher 1933] up to the triggering event an endogenous phenomena [sic] *not in any deterministic sense* but in the sense of

> creating an *environment* in which the likelihood of such an event taking place increases. [Minsky 1982, 226, emphases added]

In this environment, then, how did the financial crises of 1970, 1974, 1980, 1982, 1984, 1990, and so on emerge in the US? Wolfson's model of the financial crises depends to some degree on the financial instability framework of analysis developed by Minsky (except he and Pollin (1991) think that factors adversely affecting profitability are more important than mere interest rate rises in precipitating fragility). He starts with the process of expansion during the upward phase of the short business cycle (Juglar cycle) during the long wave decline. Recovery and expansion led to higher levels of confidence, an expansion of production, and renewed profitability. During periods of rising confidence, the net value of capitalized future earnings minus capitalized payment commitments (K(Y)-K(C)) increased, as did the net level of cash flow (Y-C), and the desired capital stock is greater than actual. Net investment expands. As the upswing continued, typically wages increased, oil/material prices rose, and central bank reductions in credit led to credit crunches and higher interest rates.

Firms producing final commodities suffered cash flow problems, but not yet major reductions in (expected) net worth, which led to endogenous finance (usually financial innovations) creating new sources of finance to circumvent central bank contractionary policies. As Wolfson says:

> To meet these loan commitments, the banks use liability management ... Near the expansion peak they rely increasingly on purchased funds, particularly certificates of deposit. Other purchased funds include Eurodollar borrowings, federal funds and repurchase agreements, and commercial paper issues by holding companies. In addition to being expensive, purchased funds are quite volatile.... Th[e] lack of insurance adds to their volatility. [Wolfson 1994, 127-128]

These endogenous and more volatile sources of funds expanded as the regulated financial SSA declined and a more global and open system gradually emerged in the 1970s onward. Endogenous credit expanded debt, especially short-term debt, and, after profits declined for 6–12 months, firms believed that the drop in the rate of profit was longer-term in nature. Cash flow and net worth were adversely affected, which reduced net investment in Fordist and other sectors, and the upper-turning point was reached in the short cycle. At this point, the economy, which has already commenced a downward part of the long wave, experiences, in addition, a recession in the short cycle. Hence, the multiple forces of reduced optimism, as happened in the recessions of 1970, 1974, 1980, 1982, and 1990–1991 onward.

During the long downswing, financial fragility became deep-seated, and, in this fragile environment, all that was necessary was "an unexpected negative event" to push the economy into financial crises, which Wolfson (1993) defines as a period in which there is an "sudden, increase demand for money." The process is called a "Minsky moment" (see Whalen 2007). This sudden intense demand for money can result from firms (including banks) needing cash to meet payment commitments because their normal financing sources have been disrupted. Or it can come from "financial investors" who fear that their funds may be unobtainable from banks

(Wolfson 1994). This leads to panic, a sudden intense demand for money, and the *potential* for major debt deflation and depression. The crisis ensures and often lasts a considerable time.

The lender of last resort facility of the reserve bank typically upsets the potentially devastating effects of financial crises, and hence depression is potentially averted and after some time the recession usually subsides.

Wolfson applied his model to financial panics in the United States during the credit crunch of 1966 (a "near-panic"), when the savings and loan associations were squeezed; the panic of 1970, when Penn Central went bankrupt; the November 1974 failure of Franklin National Bank, which had international ramifications affecting the Eurodollar market; the silver crisis of 1980; the 1982 crisis associated with the anomalous operations of Drysdale Government Securities Inc., Penn Square Bank, and Third World multinational bank lending; and the 1990 crisis of confidence (Wolfson 1994:chap. 10). He showed that as a rule, the profit rate declined 6–18 months before the peak in the short cycle, firms then maintained investment through borrowing, and the upper-turning point in the cycle arose with reductions in the rate of increase in investment, and then a surprise negative event (a Minsky moment) occurred 2–13 months after the recession commenced, which led to the financial crisis. This was followed by lender of last resort functions which reduced the intensity of the crisis. Overall, then, as Wolfson says:

> A system of financial regulation was crafted out of the financial turmoil of the 1930s.... This institutional structure was created in conformity with the concrete conditions at the time (low debt, high liquidity, low inflation, and low interest rates). ... The high profit rates in the early postwar period also helped to create a situation in which no financial crises occurred. Eventually, however, these conditions changed: debt increased, liquidity declined, profits fell, and inflation and interest rates increased. The worsening financial conditions in the latter postwar period contributed directly to the re-emergence of financial crises. The old institutional structure ... resulted in instability and financial difficulties in the context of these new conditions. ... Financial crises increased, as did failures of thrifts and commercial banks. Eventually the banks and thrifts searched for riskier, potentially more profitable, but ultimately more speculative areas of lending. The analysis points to the need for a new system of financial regulation. [Wolfson 1994, 232]

The evolution from financial robustness in the 1950s and 1960s to financial instability and crises of the 1970s–1990s onward is thus very complex (see Wolfson 1993). The system of regulatory and business finance instituted in the 1930s and 1940s played a critical role in the postwar boom and thereby performed crucial CSD functions. The international financial institutions established at the Bretton Woods System were also an important part of the structure. However, the postwar financial structure had internal contradictions that manifested themselves in financial crises and deep recessions; and the contradictions emanating from the financial system accommodating the needs of industry and overextending finance, along with the periodic onset of recessions from the general economy. The periodic onset of financial instability and crises, however, did not emanate purely from the financial system, although the endogenous credit and sudden increases in interest rates helped to produce Ponzi financial positions. As financial crises recurred during the 1970s–1990s, the domestic and global financial systems became more deregulated.

However, the deregulated structure did not constitute a *suitable* institutional sphere (even though it was instituted), because, in its neoliberal form, it also contributed to instabilities and contradictions of the system (see chap. 9 below).[11]

7.3.6 Household Labor and the Nuclear Family

The sixth system of the CSD, household labor and the nuclear family, was critical for the reproduction of labor power and domestic relations into the 1940s–1960s (O'Hara 1995, 2004, 2014a). Household labor contributed to the reproduction of potential labor power and economic agents, the expansion of the sphere of consumption, the double day, and patriarchal relations during the 1950s and 1960s. This provided an underlying institutional foundation for growth and accumulation. However, there were inherent contradictions in the postwar system of household–family relations, which eventually contributed to the anomalous reproduction of the system. The family became riddled with instabilities as the 1960s transformed into the 1970s onward, which led to an escalation of divorce, a deterioration in familial capital, and a decline in the bonds of community, which are essential for stable reproduction. As a result, it is hypothesized, uncertainty rose, productivity declined, and wages rose, which adversely affected the growth and accumulation process of capitalism into the 1970s, 1980s, 1990s, and the early years of the twenty-first century.

This section studies the historical functions of household labor and its contribution to macroeconomic stability in the US during the 1940s–1970s and beyond.[12] Stable institutional arrangements are essential for long-term development and growth. One aspect of this necessary stability is household relations within the family, which has the potential to promote human communication, nutrition, emotional development, preparation for work, population growth, consumption, a latent reserve army of labor, total labor time, and work transfer in supermarkets. The labor of houseworkers and the organization of the family is historically crucial for the provision of underlying organization and reproduction upon which macroeconomic performance in part depends. It is argued that such activities, on balance, positively conditioned postwar growth in the United States during the 1950s and 1960s.

Household labor is the exertion of human endeavor on specific tasks such as cooking, cleaning, child counseling, shopping, reproducing babies, repairing,

---

[11] See also the chapter on the political economy of money, credit, and finance, including modern monetary theory (MMT), and linkages to instability and crises, with updated references (O'Hara 2023, chap. 9).

[12] This section is based on a paper (O'Hara 1995, 2014b) that won the *Research Article of the Year Award* from CBS. It is a summarized version of the argument, updated somewhat according to further evidence. This theme is also examined in a further paper on the topic (O'Hara 2009: chap. 9), and much further work was done to redirect the analysis to issues of the nurturance gap (O'Hara 2023: chap. 12).

gardening, and bringing up children, whereas the family/house-community environment is the usual institutional base from which such labor is activated. A family may be defined as "a group in which people typically live together in a household and function as a cooperative unit, particularly through the sharing of economic resources, in the pursuit of domestic activities … [and] consisting of at least one adult and one dependent person" (Popenoe 1993, 529).[3] Household labor may be provided by members of families, or it may be provided in part by the state or private corporations. Daycare centers undertake some of the functions of the family, as do schools, some workplaces, foster homes, and community relationships between people. Household labor may be provided by men, women, transsexuals, and/or children and others, but in the postwar United States economy it was provided primarily by women and must be linked to the role of women as wage labor, and the gender division of labor.

The early years of the postwar era saw the emergence of a qualitatively new social structure of the family. The qualitative aspects that collectively define family life in this era include the stable nuclear family, the baby boom/child-centered ideology, the importance of the sphere of consumption, and the emergence of the double day for women. A new era of optimism emerged.

The contribution of "effective" household labor to the reproduction of the postwar family aspect of the CSD in the postwar United States economy was considerable.[4] First, the household labor aspect of the CSD contributed to the reproduction of potential labor power or children who in their teenage or later years contributed to gross domestic product and economic surplus (over-and-above consumption costs).[13] At the higher realms of organization, household labor is potentially linked to the formation of cooperative and loving family relationships, and the bonding that emanates between partners and their children. From the view of reproducing babies and children, household labor is associated with the "moments" of menstruation, ovulation, copulation, alienation, conception, gestation, labor, pregnancy, birth, appropriation, and nurture" (O'Brien 1981, 47–64). The population of the United States increased, due to immigration and internal fertility from around 140 million people in 1945 to 213 million in 1974 and then to 249 million in 1990 (Maddison 1991, 234, 238; Hoffman 1991, 385). Household labor and the organization of the family is an institutional sphere that has historically specialized in the complex tasks of population reproduction, nurturance, clothing, feeding, nourishing, transporting, and loving.

Household labor contributed in some measure to the socialization of children in the arts of communication and education, as well as to their nutritional requirements, which are necessary for proper growth and development. Such labor may enhance the formation of personality, social integration, and stability through the provision of love, care, and psychological counseling (O'Hara 2014b). Given this, a positive role of household labor is central to the long-term requirements of

[13] On the economic surplus see Paul Baran (1957). He defines the actual economic surplus as "the difference between society's actual current output and its actual current consumption" (Baran 1957, 132).

production, distribution, and exchange—especially in the baby boom years of the postwar period.

Secondly, the household labor system also contributed to the reproduction of economic agents—actual labor power, workers, capitalists, rentiers, financiers, government workers, other household laborers, members of the reserve army of the unemployed, and the like. The postwar period was of central importance for feeding, clothing, caring, and generally enabling classes to be mentally, physically, and organizationally prepared for work (and for interviews) to (potentially) contribute to the production, utilization, or redistribution of economic surplus. Without such functions, socioeconomic agents may be undernourished, uncommunicative, late for work and interviews, and the like. The workforce in the U.S. increased from around 65 million in 1950 to 92 million in 1973, and then to 129 million in 1992 (Maddison 1991, 267; ILO 1993, LIII). This is a sizable increase that necessitates constant attention to adequate nutrition, sleep, and education/training for a nation to have an adequate supply of healthy, diligent, and/or skilled people to contribute to the reproduction of the political economy.

Thirdly, the household labor sphere contributed to the expansion of the sphere of consumption through the promotion of emulation, mass consumption, and coordination of household functions. In the postwar years in the U.S., Fordism was the dominant mode of regulation of production, distribution, and exchange, in which the benefits of high productivity were distributed between labor and capital, which led to the expansion of the sphere of consumption, and a higher level of viability for global capitals during the 1950s and 1960s. In general, working-class organizations lost interest in the question of control of the production process, in return for distributive rewards for their members in the capital-labor truce (as argued earlier in this chapter). This led to greater responsibility for household labor in "the labor process of consumption." Game and Pringle (1983, 120) examine what they call "a major shift from housework as production to housework as consumption activity," in which "shopping and managerial tasks" increased from an average 2 h per week in 1935 to over 10 h in 1966 in the US (Vanek 1974).

The greater emphasis on shopping, convenient foods, fashion, and buying rather than making/mending clothes and producing material use-values changed the nature of much household labor. "Consumption-propelling" aspects of household labor promote effective demand and profitability, which was especially important in the postwar Keynesian age when the sphere of consumption enhanced the sphere of production, the state, the world market, and hence the CSD (at least for a time). Much of this consumption improved the living standards of the population and potentially made the drudgery of housework less pervasive, but much of it was also enculturated by emulation and conspicuous consumption in which invidious comparisons are made with other members of the community. As Veblen (1899, 79–80) recognized, consumption may be useful in the sense of being directly instrumental in promoting life, or it may be wasteful in being purely invidious or emulative, or it may be a combination of the useful and wasteful to varying degrees.

These activities include what Glazer calls "work transfer," which is a major tendency of modern capitalism to transfer personal shopping services from wage labor to non-wage household labor. It includes, for instance, the work of searching, reaching, transferring, and transporting groceries within "supermarkets" from the shelf to the checkout. There has been a transfer of this work from paid employees in small shops to customers in supermarkets. The evolution from the dominance of independent stores and food chains to supermarkets during the 1930s–1950s corresponds to the increasing dominance of self-service methods of shopping. Although advertising and rents may be more costly under this system, the great advantages of combining high advertising costs and low service costs to customers are the significance of "impulse buying" and the "lower labor costs [of] eliminating workers and making the customers do the clerks' work" (Glazer 1984, 71). The expansion of unwaged consumption work contributed to the cheapening of the value of labor power through the lower price of the product, and hence to an increase in the ability of capital to potential lower real wages (ceteris paribus). (Gimenez 1990, 28).

This is related to the fourth role of household labor: linking household and paid work through the "double day." The double day is a phenomenon of growing importance during the postwar era, in which women participated in paid employment but also performed most of the domestic chores. Many women emerged from the home and undertook industrial and other forms of labor during the Second World War. Immediately after the war, they were encouraged to concentrate more on domestic duties and contribute to the baby boom years of reproduction and nurturance. The forces of the postwar boom, shortages in various sectors, the transition from home to school (and eventually to work) for many children, and changing norms and mores, enabled many women to move into the full- and part-time labor force on a more permanent basis, especially during the 1950s–1970s (and later).

However, regardless of how much women undertake wage labor, household duties will still need to be done. There are many household tasks that private capital could produce for profit, and many that they would find difficult. The family in total could not be emulated for profitable intentions (Zaretsky 1976, 49). The total household labor process is difficult to copy commercially because of (a) large gaps between production time and labor time, (b) the sporadic nature of the work, (c) an absence of a specialized and layered division of labor, and (d) the importance of emotional attachments which cannot so easily be created through commodity production (Blumenfeld and Mann 1980, 301).

Nevertheless, an increasing number of household products have been subsumed by private capital and sold on the market. Power (1983) stresses the gradualism of the transition from household to capitalist domination of production in relation to fruit and vegetables, poultry, clothing, and baking. She suggests that the main reason for the gradual decline of household production in some areas is the increasing relative efficiency of the capitalist inner circuit of reproduction. By the 1920s, the era of the "mass market" had begun in its infancy, providing the material preconditions for the large-scale entry of women into the labor market. Production work ("growing food, preserving, weaving cloth, sewing clothes," and the like) is said to have been gradually replaced by maintenance or service work ("caring for the ill, house cleaning, laundry, shopping" and the like), without reducing the total requirements of household labor. The growth of maintenance work during the postwar era increased the ties of the family to the market and the need for wage labor to buy such goods and services, without reducing the time spent in the laundry (Gershuny 1983), providing general family care and performing shopping and managerial tasks (Vanek 1974, 119). Hence, the rise of the norm of the double day.

During the 1940s, 1950s, and 1960s, many women were drawn into the "latent reserve army of labor," which potentially existed for them to join the labor force much more so than in the 1920s and 1930s. This occurs "when capitalism, in the course of its expansion, invades and takes over sectors of pre-capitalist production" (Power 1983, 74). Household workers are potentially and actually engaged in waged work for capital during periods of rapid accumulation, especially in the post-war period.

The double day is important because many women were expected to perform adequately both in the home and paid employment, without the normative expectation that men would adequately share household labor. It is argued that this double day represents a central contradiction of postwar capitalism, which helped to promote domestic and macroeconomic uncertainty and instability. In like measure, women usually had the power to decide about the reproduction of children, even when "the relationship" ended, which contributed its own contradictory forces to the whole process.[14]

This links to the fifth function of the household: the maintenance of patriarchal relations in the home, and within the dominant institutions of the state, production, finance, and the world economy. The postwar era of capitalist development was based on central patriarchal structures of reproduction; "the institutional structure of male domination," especially in the wider society (Kramarae and Treichler 1985, 323). Household labor, and the gender division of labor, backed up by the media, the state, and business, contributed in varying degrees to the reproduction of values and behaviors that perpetuated respect for male authority, developing/building male egos, maintaining household peace, and promoting emotional stability, without fundamentally questioning the institutions of male domination. By failing to challenge such structures during the 1950s and most of the 1960s, many women actively encouraged the reproduction of unequal power relations between men and women. Marx and Engels argued that patriarchy would decline with the entry of women into the workforce in the relatively early phases of industrialization. Clearly, the latter was not the case for Western capitalism, although aspects of patriarchy declined in the postwar era through women entering the labor force in large numbers, having

[14] Shelton (1990) presents U.S. data for 1980–1981, which implies that full-time female homemakers worked on average 42.6 hours on household duties while their spouses worked 13.7 hours on these duties. When the women worked full time, their household duty hours dropped from 42.6 to 21, while spouses' hours dropped from 13.7 to 13.1. Working women prepared most of the meals, did most of the shopping, and spent more time with the children than men, while men spent more time on certain tasks of cleaning up after meals, repairs, and acquiring services. Some studies (such as Blair and Lichter 1991) do not include childcare hours in their study on the basis of the assumption that childcare includes "work" and "leisure" and they only want to measure "work." (This is problematic. A possible analogy is to exclude the time worked by men in the paid workplace, which they find enjoyable as distinct from burdensome.)

more options available, greater sexual freedom, access to better-paying jobs, and some improvement in the gender wage differential. Seccombe (1980a, 64) recognizes that Marx and Engels ignored forces that, until the (later) postwar era, reinforced women's role in the home.

Through these five functions, the household part of the CSD became critical to postwar stability and economic performance during the 1950s and 1960s. But we must not be blinded by the functions into believing in the "final cause of social integration or pattern maintenance," and thereby implicitly "reject any tendency toward long-run social disintegration" (Frank 1969, 98–101). Marital instability, conflict, and stress were prevalent in the family during the 1940s–1960s, but they intensified during the late 1960s and 1970s and stayed at a high level into the 1980s and 1990s (and thereafter). This magnification of household contradictions, it is hypothesized, adversely affected macroeconomic instability after the 1960s, which in turn affected the domestic sphere, and so on ad infinitum in a circular and cumulative fashion.

The question arises as to what *contradictions* emerged within the household CSD sphere, and between the household and other institutions, to contribute toward instability and uncertainty within the U.S. CSD. Frederick Engels (1884) emphasized a major contradiction of capitalism which has special relevance here, and which links to feminist, Polanyian, and CSD concerns. This is that labor power is a very special commodity in that private capitals are unable to secure the collective and social wealth necessary for its reproduction, as a general rule, and have no direct control over household labor to ensure a steady supply of the right type of labor power at the right price, place and time. A commodity that contributes an important human element to production is thus not directly under the control of private capital. This led to supply problems, which, particularly in the postwar period, were only partially resolved by the state and household labor. Seccombe (1980b, 247) similarly hypothesizes that "private capital is structurally indifferent to labor power's production, and tends, without external regulation, to jeopardize and destabilize its long-term reproduction." This is inextricably linked with the more general problem of the tendency of private capital to underinvest in the social capital of durable human relationships, skills, organization, information, and institutions.[17]

Household labor and the family became more dysfunctional as the postwar "growth and development process" evolved. This important social structure underlying the reproduction of the circuit became ridden with instabilities that reciprocally influenced and in turn were affected by the wider CSD. Carlson (1980) explains some of the factors involved in this circular and cumulative process of destabilization. From the late 1960s and 1970s, the baby boom generation sought to innovate and began to dominate the social and political landscape through rebellion against parental and conservative political ideologies and practices. The sexual and social revolution contributed to innovation by challenging the values of monogamy, female virginity at marriage, and male domination of the household. The innovation of abandoning the norm of the nuclear family was accelerated by the Marxist and feminist critique of the bourgeois family, the rise of ethical relativism, plus alternative lifestyles/norms.

Popenoe (1993) exposes the myth that "the family [has not] declined, it is just changing." While the 1950s and early 1960s saw an unusual era of stability in the family, the period since then is said to have been characterized by

> an unprecedented decline of the [traditional nuclear] family as a social institution. Families have lost functions, social power, and authority over their members. They have grown smaller in size, less stable, and shorter in life span. People have become less willing to invest time, money, and energy in family life, turning instead to investments in themselves.... Familism as a cultural value has diminished.... [M]arriage is becoming deinstitutionalized. [Popenoe 1993, 528, 533]

The family "lost functions to such institutions as organized religion, education, work, and government," while "pro-familial normative pressures have [been] eroded in all areas of ... life" (Popenoe 1993, 538). The family is said to have been reduced to two main functions, child-rearing and affection/companionship, and while it is not always good at undertaking even these limited functions, it is better at doing them than the other institutions. The problem is that, from the late 1960s onward, there have been stresses and strains that inhibited the performance of these limited functions, which exerted a negative influence on the CSD as *uncertainty* accelerated.[18]

In a circular and cumulative fashion, it is argued that the postwar boom endogenously set in motion forces that led to family instability; that this helped (along with other factors) to propel long-term macroeconomic uncertainty and disarray; and that these macroeconomic problems reciprocally affected family stability in a negative fashion. The major contradictions emanate from the inability of capitalism to sustain the social fabric (including the supply of labor power) underlying accumulation due to its disembedded tendencies.

Nuclear family instability began to rise in the late 1960s, accelerated in the 1970s, and remained at a high level through the 1980s, 1990s, and beyond. Many more people now live alone or with a nonrelated person; people are marrying later; there are many more single parents; the probability of divorce has risen considerably; more parents choose not to have children; and kinship patterns in the family are far weaker than in the mid-1960s. A landmark occurred in 1974 when more marriages ended in divorce than in death (Popenoe 1993). The hegemony of the nuclear family is thus considerably weaker in the 1970s–1990s and thereafter compared with the 1950s and 1960s.

Divorce itself has the potential to promote stability or instability, depending on the balance of resources and stresses (Amato 1993).[19] While rising family instability is the principal phenomenon we are concerned with, divorce itself on balance contributes its own momentum to the fragmentation process. While all married people initiate divorce, women started to initiate it more than men from the late 1960s onward. Women in general were more financially capable of leaving problematic marriages than before, and men often found it difficult to adjust to rising women's achievement in the workforce as well as to share the housework more evenly. Sanders (1985, 522) notes that "the divorce rate is positively related to the earning ability of women in market work." Houseknecht (1985) recognizes that it is not so much the achievement of women in the workplace that promoted family instability, but inflexible norms and mores, which acted as a fundamental limit on the ability of a two-wage family to adjust to an era of greater female participation in paid work.

Greenstein studied the relationship between women's employment/income and divorce through the postwar period in the U.S. and concluded that the "independence effect" of women working (which increased divorce) was often outweighed by the "income effect" (which stabilizes marriages). However, he found that "women with the greatest threat of marriage disruption are low-income wives who average 35–40 h at work" per week (Greenstein 1990, 675). One factor promoting family instability and separation is that these full-time working-class women, had the least support of their husbands in household labor, hence the women's double day and dissatisfaction in marriage. Another factor is that these women often worked in enterprises and work environments that were subordinating, uncreative, physically demanding, and not conducive to human interaction and the resolution of conflict. Thus, women who are more likely to experience domestic disharmony "have little work commitment or … are dissatisfied with the type of work they are doing" (Greenstein 1990, 675).

The other side of this contradiction is that women mostly had control over reproduction and child-rearing, and many men felt alienated from these processes, and thereby put more effort into work, sports, and other activities such as drinking. Being culturally unable or unwilling to share familial duties with women as other activities crowded them out, contributed majorly to instability within the family and the rising rate of divorce.

Nazzari (1980) shows that during the 1960s, the rate of divorce in the US increased by over 50%, while the population increased by 13%.[20] Greenstein (1990) shows that during this time the divorce rate and the labor-force participation rate increased more or less in synchrony. Between 1960 and 1976, the percentage of married women in the workforce increased from 23% to 52%, while divorce increased from 2.2 per 1000 population to 4.85 (rising to a high of 5.2 in 1980, and then dropping slightly to 4.6 in 1991). A more extreme perspective is gained when examining divorced persons per 1000 married persons with a spouse present: Rising from 47 (1970) to 100 (1980) to 142 (1990) and 148 (1991).[21] Divorce was found to be higher among working-class, black, and urban families (as well as among families where the wife has five or more years of college) (Houseknecht 1985, 125).

During the early 1970s, 61% of separated/divorced women did not receive any alimony, and despite state support, children in such families "lack[ed] access to basic essentials," while, in black female-headed families, "five out of every six children [were] deprived of essentials" (Nazzari 1980, 70). Such families had less access to proper nutrition, physical space, and play areas. Demo and Acock (1988) argue that, without well-defined institutionalized alternatives to the traditional nuclear family, many in such broken homes have lower levels of "well-being" than other children. Particularly anomalous is the negative impact on "personal adjustment," including gender-role identification, self-control, responsibility, leadership, and the development of independence. Male children were most disadvantaged as they often had no stable sex-role model to learn from. For this reason, "boys in divorced families manifested significantly more maladaptive symptoms and behaviour problems than boys in intact families" (Demo and Acock 1988, 622–26). Amato (1993) evaluated 180 studies of the influence of divorce on children. His most important conclusions are that long-term personality and developmental problems often emerge due to parental conflict (before and after divorce); the custodial parent lacking resources; children having the stress of moving, changing schools, and losing friends; the custodial parent adjusting to post-divorce life, and boys losing contact with their fathers. In many cases, divorce retains/creates more problems than it resolves, especially for children.

It is hypothesized that these three problems linked with the declining household aspect of the CSD—decline in the latent IRA, lower work effort, and social fragmentation—contributed to the uncertainty and instability associated with lower expected productivity, profit, and growth. The degree of fragility of the family environment influences the state of long-term expectation upon which long-term economic performance rests. Circular and cumulative linkages between different spheres of the macroeconomy periodically result in marked turning points: of an upward nature when optimism is growing, and of a downward nature when optimism is falling. Sustained fragmentation of the household inhibits the degree of predictability of events and thereby lowers confidence in the long term. This manifested periodically in the deeper recessions of 1974–1975, 1981–1982, 1990–1992, and thereafter, which indicates the presence of a lower level of underlying socioeconomic robustness and the ease with which systemic confidence can be eroded within the CSD.

There were thus important contradictions of modern capitalism related to household labor and the sexual division of labor. At the general level, capital underinvests in the social capital necessary for long-term institutional stability, leading to the demise of institutions and macroeconomic problems. Related to this problem is the inability of capital to directly control the reproduction of labor power, especially after the late 1960s, which led to difficulties in the supply and quality of human skills. Systemic family fragmentation and disarray influence the macroeconomic environment through a decline in the underlying level of confidence and trust. Overall, the increasing commodification, individuation, suburbanization, deregulation, and mobility of labor since the 1960s led to a greater degree of uncertainty and discontinuity within the circuit of reproduction. These contradictions are linked to the tendency of market processes to operate in abstraction from the necessary bonds of community, stability, and trust which underly long-term economic performance.[15]

[15] In terms of policy and alternatives: The "communist alternative" for the household appears to be the most democratic and egalitarian. Fraad, Resnick and Wolff (1989, 57–58) describe this alternative as being 'now widely regarded as components of the definition of successful modern family life [including …] equal sharing of the performance, management, and fruits of domestic labor and all household decision-making. The broad goal is to share wealth, work, power, and emotional intimacy [;] all adult members … do necessary and surplus labor collectively … All decide together as a collective household how (to whom) to distribute this surplus …'. This alternative is a far-cry from the household-family structures that emerged into the 1990s–2020s (see O'Hara 2023: chap. 12).

7.4 Conclusion

This chapter started with an overview of the differences between trends and waves in the US economy since the 1800s. These differences revealed relatively poor and erratic performance during much of the 1800s, a long wave upswing during the 1880s–1900s, followed by a long wave downswing during the 1910s–1930s (close to borderline in the 1920s). Then there was the greatest long wave upswing in the history of (US) capitalism during the 1940s–1960s, followed by much weaker long wave upswing during the 1970s–1980s, borderline performance in the 1990s, and long wave downswing during the 2000s–2020s. We found that the biggest US long wave upswings operated during the period of absolute US hegemony (1940s–1970s) when climate change underwent a cooling due to pollution and volcanic aerosols preventing dangerous rays of heat from penetrating the Earth's atmosphere. The subsequent weak upswing, borderline performance, and long wave downswing performance (1970s–2020s) operated during a period of major climate crises (global warming, major heatwaves and bushfires, massive floods and coastal erosion, etc., which also increased the prevalence of social, political and economic crises).

We hypothesize that the major long-wave upswing and absolute US hegemony during the 1940s–1960s were associated with the effective establishment of a productive circuit of socioeconomic dynamics, and that declining hegemony and gradually declining performance were associated with a declining CSD during the 1970s–2020s.

The chapter then outlined the shape, contours, rise, evolution, and contradictory demise of the postwar CSD in the US during the corporate system of the 1940s–1990s. The study of the CSD spheres started with the system of US hegemony rise and fall, particularly the factors involved in generating hegemony and the contradictions that led to its demise.

Second, the geo-spatial-climate system was scrutinized. I summarized the geophysical order of the US system and provided some details of the climate system's evolution from the "dust bowl" heatwaves of the 1930s, to the Small Cooler Era of the 1940s–1970s, and an introduction to the climate crises of the 1970s–1990s and into the twenty-first century.

Third, Fordism, the capital-labor accord, and the postwar corporate system were analyzed, including its major constituents, evolution, contradictions, and demise. The fourth part of the CSD, the Keynesian welfare state, was then outlined, especially how it contributed to the postwar system and played a core role in its demise. The fifth sub-system examined was the regulated financial system, which played a significant role in the long-wave upswing and hegemonic dominance of the US, but also exhibited major contradictions that led to its demise through greater financial crises and slumps, especially during the 1980s, 1990s, and beyond.

Lastly, details were provided for the role of the household and the family in the postwar corporate system, especially in generating substantial stocks-flows of labor power and familial capital which underlay the postwar system. It too, however, contributed to the demise of the system through generating substantial instability and fragmentation during the 1970s–1990s (and beyond).

Overall, the six subsystems exhibited a relatively unified organic whole in which they played core circular and cumulative (interdependent) roles in contributing to hegemonic power, long waves, and climate change. However, the contradictions within and between the CSD spheres promoted the demise of these systems of power, performance, and climate. Substantial polycrisis system failures emerged during the 1980s–2020s with the rising power of neoliberalism when there was no hegemon, which are analyzed in Chap. 9 below, including decadal instabilities, climate crises, GFC, corona crisis; and geopolitical crises (see Chap. 10). China emerged as a dominant player through long-wave upswing to challenge the US for hegemonic power, especially during the 2000s–2020s, which is discussed in Chap. 8 immediately below.

References

Aglietta, Michel. 1976. *A theory of capitalist regulation,* English Edition, London, New Left Books, 1979. Translated from the French by David Fernbach.

Aliber, Robert Z., and Charles P. Kindleberger. 2015. *Manias, Panics and Crashes: A History of Financial Crises*. 7th ed. New York: Palgrave Macmillan.

Amato, Paul R. 1993. Children's adjustment to divorce: Theories, hypotheses, and empirical support. *Journal of Marriage and the Family* 55:23–38.

Arrighi, Giovanni. 1982. A crisis of hegemony. In *Dynamics of global crisis*, ed. S. Amin, G. Arrighi, A. G. Frank, and I. Wallerstein. London: Macmillan.

Arrighi, Giovanni. 1993. The three hegemonies of historical capitalism. In *Gramsci, historical materialism and international relations*, ed. S. Cox. New York: Cambridge University Press.

Balatsky, Evgeny. 2024. The American model of global dominance. *Terra Economicus* 22 (2): 96–113. https://doi.org/10.18522/2073-6606-2024-22-2-96-113.

Baran, Paul. 1957. *The political economy of growth*, 1973. Harmondsworth: Penguin.

Bergesen, Albert J., and John Sonnett. 2001. The global 500: Mapping the world economy at century's end. *American Behavioral Scientist* 44 (10): 1602–1615.

Berry, Brian J. L. 1991. *Long-Wave Rhythms in Economic Development and Political Behavior*. Baltimore: John Hopkins University Press.

Blair, Simpson Lee, and Daniel T. Lichter. 1991. Measuring the division of household labor: Gender segregation of housework among American couples. *Journal of Family Issues* 12: 91–113.

Bleaney, Michael. 1985. *The rise and fall of keynesian economics: An investigation of its contribution to capitalist development*. London: Macmillan.

Block, L. Fred. 1977. *The origins of international economic disorder: A study of United States international monetary policy from World War II to the present*. Berkeley: University of California Press.

Blumenfeld, Emily and Susan Mann. 1980. Domestic labour and the reproduction of labour power: Towards an analysis of women, the family and class,. in Bonnie Fox 1980.

Booth, Douglas E. 1985. The problems of corporate bureaucracy and the producer cooperative as an alternative. *Review of Social Economy* 43:298.

Bowles, Samuel. 1975. Unequal education and the reproduction of the social division of labor, *Review of Radical Political Economics* 3(4). Reprinted in Martin Carnoy ed., *Schooling in a Corporate Society: The Political Economy of Education in America*. New York: David McKay Company, 38–66.

Bowles, Samuel, and Herbert Gintis. 1986. *Democracy and capitalism: Property, community, and the contradictions of modern social thought*. London: RKP.

Bowles, Samuel, and Herbert Gintis. 1982a. The crisis of liberal democratic capitalism: The case of the United States. *Politics and Society* 11 (1): 51–93.

Bowles, Samuel, and Herbert Gintis. 1982b. The crisis of liberal democratic capitalism: The case of the United States. *Politics and Society* 11 (1): 1982.

Bowles, Samuel, and Richard Edwards. 1985. *Understanding capitalism: Competition, command, and change in the U.S. economy*. New York: Harper and Row Publishers.

Bowles, Samuel, and Richard Edwards. 1993. *Understanding capitalism: Competition, command, and change in the U.S. economy*. 2nd ed. New York: Harper and Row Publishers.

Bowles, Samuel, David Gordon, and Thomas Weisskopf. 1983. *Beyond the Wasteland: A democratic alternative to economic decline*. New York: Doubleday.

Bowles, Samuel, David M. Gordon, and Thomas E. Weisskopf. 1989. Business ascendancy and economic impasse: A structural retrospective on conservative economics, 1979-87. *Journal of Economic Perspectives* 3 (1): 107–134.

Bowles, Samuel, David Gordon, and Thomas Weisskopf. 1990. *After the Wasteland: A democratic economics for the year 2000*. Armonk, New York: M E Sharpe Inc.

Brahic, Catherine. 2007. Climate myths: The cooling after 1940 shows CO_2 does not cause warming. *New Scientist* 194:34.

Braverman, Harry. 1976. *Labor and monopoly capital: The degradation of work in the twentieth century*. New York: Monthly Review Press.

Brenner, Robert. 1998. The economics of global turbulence. *New Left Review* 229 (May/June): 1–265.

Brown-Collier, Elba. 1999. Johnson's great society: Its legacy in the 1990s. *Review of Social Economy* 56 (3): 259–276.

Carlson, Allan C. 1980. Families, sex, and the liberal agenda. *The Public Interest* 58:62–79.

CCSP. 2008. *Weather and climate extremes in a changing climate. Regions of focus: North America, Hawaii, Caribbean, and U.S. Pacific Islands.* A Report by the U.S. Climate Change Science Program and the Subcommittee on Global Change Research. [Thomas R. Karl, Gerald A. Meehl, Christopher D. Miller, Susan J. Hassol, Anne M. Waple, and William L. Murray (eds.)]. Department of Commerce, NOAA's National Climatic Data Center, Washington, D.C., USA.

Cha, T. 2020. Is anybody still a globalist? Rereading the trajectory of US grand strategy and the end of the transnational moment. *Globalizations* 17 (1): 60–76. https://doi.org/10.1080/14747731.2019.1611011.

Courvisanos, Jerry. 1996. *Investment cycles in capitalist economies: A Kaleckian behavioural contribution*. Cheltenham, UK and Brookfield, US: Edward Elgar.

Cowan, Tim, Gabrielle C. Hegerl, Ioana Colfescu, and Massimo Bollasina. 2017. Factors contributing to record-breaking heat waves over the great plains during the 1930s Dust Bowl. *Journal of Climate* 30:2437–2361.

Cypher, James. 1979. The transnational challenge to the corporate state. *Journal of Economic Issues* 13 (2): 513–542.

Dalio, Ray. 2023. *Principles for dealing with the changing world order: Why nations succeed and fail*. New York: Simon and Schuster.

Davis, M. 1978. Fordism in crisis: A review of Michel Aglietta's *Regulation et Crises du Capitalisme*. *Review* 2.

De Vroey, Michel. 1984. A regulation approach interpretation of contemporary crisis. *Capital and Class* 23:45.

Demo, David H., and Alan C. Acock. 1988. The impact of divorce on children. *Journal of Marriage and the Family* 50:619–648.

Downe. 1986. The behavior of postwar rates of return in capitalist countries. *Review of Radical Political Economics* 18:101–110.

Dugger, William M. 1980. Corporate bureaucracy: The incidence of the bureaucratic process. *Journal of Economic Issues* 14 (2): 399–410.

Dugger, William M. 1988. An institutional analysis of corporate power. *Journal of Economic Issues* 22 (1): 79–112.
Dugger, William M. 1989. *Corporate hegemony*. New York: Greenwood Press.
Edwards, Richard C. 1975. The social relations of production in the firm and labor market structure. *Politics and Society* 5:83.
Edwards, Richard. 1979. *Contested Terrain: The transformation of the workplace in the twentieth century*. New York: Basic Books.
EPA (USA Environmental Protection Authority). 2024. *Heatwave Index for the United States, 48 Contiguous States,* 1895–2021. https://www.epa.gov/climate-indicators/climate-change-indicators-heat-waves
Fairris, David H. 1994. Shopfloor relations in the postwar capital-labor accord. In *Social structures of accumulation: The political economy of growth and crisis*, ed. David M. Kotz, Terrence McDonough, and Michael Reich. Cambridge, UK and New York: Cambridge University Press.
Fairris, David H. 1997. *Shopfloor matters: Labor-management relations in 20th century American manufacturing*. London and New York: Routledge.
Fernald, John Huiyu Li. 2023. Productivity in the world economy during and after the pandemic. Federal Reserve Bank of San Francisco. *Working Paper 2023-29.*
Fernández, D. 2021. The hegemony crisis, the neoliberal model, and the United States power structure. *Critical Sociology* 47 (7–8): 1283–1293.
Fisher, Irving. 1933. The debt-deflation theory of great depressions. *Econometrica* 1 (4): 337–357.
Flynn, Claire Marie, Linnea Huusko, Angshuman Modak, and Thorsten Mauritsen. 2023. Strong aerosol cooling alone does not explain cold-based mid-century temperatures in CMIP6 models. *Atmospheric Chemistry Physics* 23:15121–15133.
Fortune Magazine. 2024. The fortune global 500 companies. *https://fortune.com/ranking/global500/.*
Fraad, Harriet, Stephen Resnick, and Richard Wolff. 1989. For every knight in shining Armor, there's a castle waiting to be cleaned: A Marxist-Feminist analysis of the household. *Rethinking Marxism* 2:10–69.
Frank, Andre Gunder. 1969. *Latin America: underdevelopment and revolution*. New York: Monthly Review.
Gallegati, Marco, Mauro Gallegati, James B. Ramsey, and Willi Semmler. 2017. Long waves in prices: New evidence from wavelet analysis. *Cliometrica* 11 (2): 127–151.
Game, A., and R. Pringle. 1983. *Gender at work*. Sydney: Allen and Unwin.
Gershuny, Jonathon. 1983. *Social innovation and the division of labour*. Oxford: Oxford University Press.
Gill, Stephen, and David Law. 1988. *The global political economy: Perspectives, problems and policies*. Baltimore: John Hopkins University Press.
Gimenez, Martha E. 1990. The dialectics of wages and unwages work: Wages work, domestic labor and household survival in the United States. In *Work without wages: comparative studies of domestic labor and self-employment*, ed. Jane L. Collins and Martha Gimenez. Albany, New York: State University of New York Press.
Glazer, Nona Y. 1984. Servants to capital: Unpaid domestic labor and paid work. *Review of Radical Political Economics* 16:61–88.
Gold, David A. 1977. The rise and decline of the Keynesian Coalition, *Kapitalistate*, no 6, Fall 1977.
Gordon, David, Richard C. Edwards, and Michael Reich. 1982. *Segmented work, divided workers: The historical transformation of labor in the United States*. Cambridge: CUP.
Gordon, David, Thomas Weisskopf, and Samuel Bowles. 1990. Power, accumulation and crisis: The rise and demise of the postwar social structure of accumulation. In *Radical political economy, Vol 2*, ed. Samuel Bowles and Richard Edwards. Aldershot, UK: Edward Elgar.
Gough, Ian. 1979. *The political economy of the welfare state*. London: Macmillan.
Great Plains Committee. 1936. *The future of the great plains*. Washington DC: Government Printer.

Greenstein, Theodore N. 1990. *Marital disruption and the employment of married women*, 657–676. August: Journal of Marriage and the Family.

Grinin, L., and A. Korotayev. 2021. Seven weaknesses of the U.S., Donald Trump, and the future of American hegemony. *World Futures* 77 (1): 23–54. https://doi.org/10.1080/02604027.2020.1801309.

Harvey, David. 1982. *The limits to capital*. Oxford: Blackwell.

Hodgson, Geoffrey M. 1982-83. Worker Participation and Macroeconomic Efficiency. *Journal of Post Keynesian Economics* 5 (2):

Hoffman, Mark S. 1991. *The World Almanac and book of facts 1993*. New York Pharos Press.

Houseknecht, Sharon K. 1985. Achievement of women outside the home as the phantom factor in marital breakdown. In *Current controversies in marriage and family*, ed. Harold Feldman and Margaret Feldman. Beverly Hills: Sage Publications.

Keohane, Robert O. 1984. *After hegemony: Cooperation and discord in the world political economy*. Princeton: Princeton University Press. 2005. New Preface by Author.

Knutsen, Torbjorn L. 1999. *The rise and fall of world orders*. Manchester and New York: Manchester University Press.

Koehane, Robert. 1984. *After hegemony: Cooperation and discord in the world political economy*. Princeton, N.J: Princeton University Press.

Kotz, David M. 1994. The regulation theory and the social structures of accumulation approach. *Kotz, McDonough and Reich* 1994:85–98.

Kramarae, Cheris, and Paula A. Treichler. 1985. *A feminist dictionary*. London: Pandorapress. With the assistance of Ann Russo.

Krasner, Stephen D. 1983. Structural causes and regime consequences: Regimes as intervening variables. In *International regimes*, ed. Stephen Krasner, vol. 36, 185. Ithaca: Cornell University Press.

Kupchan, Charles. 1998. After Pax Americana: Benign power, regional integration, and the sources of a stable multipolarity. *International Security* 23 (2): 40–79.

Kwon, Roy. 2011. Hegemonies in the world system: An empirical assessment of hegemonic sequences from the 16th to the 20th Century. *Sociological Perspectives* 54 (4): 593–617.

Littler, Craig. 1982. *The development of the labour process in capitalist societies*. London: Gower. Second Edition.

Maddison Project. 2024. *Global historical statistics*. University of Groningen. https://www.rug.nl/ggdc/historicaldevelopment/maddison/releases/maddison-project-database-2020?lang=en

Maddison, Angus. 1991. *Dynamic forces in capitalist development*. Oxford: OUP.

Mager, Nathan H. 1987. *The Kondratieff Waves*. New York: Praeger Publishers.

Mansfield, Edwin. 1992. Flexible manufacturing systems: Economic effects in Japan, United States, and Western Europe. *Japan and the World Economy* 4:1–16.

Marglin, Stephen A., and Juliet B. Schor. 1990. *The golden age of capitalism*. Oxford: Clarendon Press.

Marshall, M. G. 1999. Flexible specialization, supply-side institutionalism, and the nature of work systems. *Review of Social Economy* 57 (2): 199–219.

Mathews, John A. 1989. New production concepts. *Prometheus* 7.

Mazier, Jacques, Maurice Basle, and Jean-Francois Vidal. 1999. *When economic crises endure*. Armonk, New York and London: M.E. Sharpe.

McLeman, Robert A., Juliette Dupre, Lea Berrang Ford, James Ford, Konrad Gajewski, and Gregory Marchildon. 2014. What we learned from the dust bowl: Lessons in science, policy, and adaptation. *Population and Environment* 35:417–440.

Miller, John A. 1990. *Women's unemployment patterns in postwar business cycles: Class difference, the gender segregation of work and deindustrialization, review of radical political economics* 22, 22.

Minsky, Hyman P. 1964. Longer waves in financial relations: Financial factors in the more severe depressions. *American Economic Review: Papers and Proceedings* 54 (May): 324–332.

Minsky, Hyman P. 1974. The modelling of financial instability: An introduction. *Modelling and Simulation* 5:267–272.

Minsky, Hyman P. 1980. Capitalist financial processes and the instability of capitalism. *Journal of Economic Issues* 14 (2): 505–522.

Minsky, Hyman P. 1982. *Can it happen again? Essays on instability and finance*. Vol. 25, 5. Armonk, New York: M. E. Sharpe Inc.

Minsky, Hyman P. 1984. Financial innovations and financial instability: Observations and theory. In *Financial innovations: Their impact on monetary policy and financial markets*, ed. Federal Reserve Bank of St Louis. Boston: Kluwer-Nijhoff Publishing.

Minsky, Hyman P. 1985. *Money and the lender of last resort*, 12–19. March–April: Challenge.

Minsky, Hyman P. 1995. Larger waves in financial relations: Financial factors in the more severe depressions II. *Journal of Economic Issues* 29 (1): 83–86.

Mitchl, Thomas R. 1988. The two-stage decline in U.S. Nonfinancial corporate profitability, 1948–1986. *Review of Radical Political Economics* 20 (4): 1–20.

Morrison, Allen J. and J. Stewart Black. 2024. *Is chinese economic dominance at an inflection point?* Harvard Business Review. Published Online. https://hbr.org/2024/02/is-chinas-economic-dominance-at-an-inflection-point.

Munkirs, John R. 1985. *The transformation of American capitalism*. Armonk, New York: M.E. Sharpe.

Munkirs, John R., and Jenet Knoedler. 1987. The existence and exercise of corporate power: An opaque fact. *Journal of Economic Issues* 21 (4): 1679–1706.

Murray, Charles. 1989. The American experience with the welfare state. In *The welfare state: Foundations and alternatives*, ed. Michael James. Sydney: the Centre for Independent Studies.

Naples, Michele I. 1986. The unraveling of the union-capital truce and the U.S. industrial productivity crisis. *Review of Radical Political Economics* 18 (21 & 2): 110–131.

Naples, Michele I. 1996. Labor relations and the social structure of accumulation: The case of U.S. coal mining. In *Beyond survival: Wage labor in the late twentieth century*, ed. Cyrus Bina, Laurie Clements, and Chuck Davis. M.E. Sharpe: Armonk, US and London, UK.

Nasr, F. 1984. Implications of the recent OPEC crisis. *Journal of Economic Issues* 29 (2): 483–491.

Nau, Henry R. 1990. *The Myth of America's decline: Leading the world economy into the 1990s*. Oxford: Oxford University Press.

Nazzari, Muriel. 1980. The significance of present-day changes in the institution of marriage. *Review of Radical Political Economics* 12:63–75.

O'Connor, James. 1984. *Accumulation crisis*. New York: Basil Blackwell.

O'Hara, Phillip Anthony. 1992. *A critical analysis of the reproduction of institutions within capitalism: Integrating macroinstitutional themes from marxist and institutionalist political economy*. PhD Thesis, University of Newcastle, Australia, Department of Economics.

O'Hara, Phillip Anthony. 1995. Household labor, the family, and macroeconomic instability in the United States: 1940s–1990s, *Review of Social Economy,* vol 52, 89–120. See O'Hara (2014a).

O'Hara, Phillip Anthony. 1999. *Encyclopedia of political economy*. Vol. 2. London and New York: Routledge.

O'Hara, Phillip Anthony. 2000. *Marx, Veblen and contemporary institutional political economy: Principles and unstable dynamics of capitalism*. Cheltenham: Edward Elgar.

O'Hara, Phillip Anthony, ed. 2004. *Global political economy and the wealth of nations: Performance, institutions, problems and policies*. London & NY: Routledge.

O'Hara, Phillip Anthony. 2014a. Household labor, the family, and macroeconomic instability in the United States: 1940s-1990s, *Review of Social Economy,* vol 52, 89–120. In *Social structure of accumulation theory Volume II*, 514-545. Eds. Terrence McDonough, David M. Kotz and Michael Reich. Cheltenham, Edward Elgar, 53,

O'Hara, Phillip Anthony. 2014b. Political economy of love: Nurturance gap, disembedded economy and freedom constraints within neoliberal capitalism. *Panoeconomicus* 612:161–192.

O'Hara, Phillip Anthony. 2023. *Principles of institutional and evolutionary political economy: Applied to current world problems*. Revised Edition. Singapore: Springer Nature.

O'Hara, Phillip Anthony. 2025. *Long waves of growth, hegemonic power, and climate change in the world economy: Dutch, British, US and chinese capitalism and structural polycrises*. Singapore: Springer.jvv.

Offe, Claus. 1984. In *Contradictions of the welfare state*, ed. John Keane. London: Hitchinson.

Payne, C., and B. Silver. 2023. Domination without hegemony and the limits of US world power. *Political Power and Social Theory* 39:159–177. https://doi.org/10.1108/S0198-871920220000039009.

Peterson, Wallace C. 1974. The corporate state, economic performance, and social policy. *Journal of Economic Issues* 8:483.

Peterson, Wallace C. 1985. The U.S. welfare state and the conservative counterrevolution. *Journal of Economic Issues* 193:601–642.

Petit, Pascal. 1999. Structural forms and growth regimes of the post-fordist era. *Review of Social Economy* 57 (2): 220–243.

Pfaller, Alfred. 1991. The United States. In *Can the welfare state compete? A comparative study of five advanced capitalist countries*, ed. Alfred Pfaller, Ian Gough, and Goran Therborn. London: Macmillan.

Pfister, Ulrich, and Christian Suter. 1987. International financial relations as part of the world-system. *International Studies Quarterly* 31:239–272.

Phillips, Ron. 1985. The failure of keynesianism and the collapse of bretton woods. *Research in Political Economy* 8:1985.

Polanyi, Karl. 1944. *The great transformation: The political and economic origins of our time*, 1944. Boston: Beacon Press.

Pollin, Robert. 1991. Two theories of money supply endogeneity. *Journal of Post Keynesian Economics* 13 (3): 366–399.

Popenoe, David. 1993. American family decline, 1960-1990: A review and appraisal. *Journal of Marriage and the Family* 55:527–541.

Power, Marilyn. 1983. From home production to wage labor: Women as a reserve army of labor. *Review of Radical Political Economics* 15, no 1, Spring:71–91.

Reich, Michael and Finklehor, David. 1970. Capitalism and the military-industrial complex: The obstacles to conversion, in David Mermelstein ed. *Economics: Mainstream readings and radical critiques,* New York, Random House, 1976. 3rd Edition. Reprinted and Abridged from *Review of Radical Political Economics*, vol 2, no 4, Winter 1970.

Rivera-Batiz, F. L., and L. Rivera-Batiz. 1989. *International finance and open economy macroeconomics*. New York: Macmillan Publishing Company.

Robinson, Joan. 1978. The Age of Growth. In *What are the questions? And other essays: Further contributions to modern economics*, ed. In J. Robinson, 33–42. Armonk, New York.

Robinson, William I. 1996. *Promoting polarchy: Globalization, US intervention, and hegemony*. Cambridge, UK and New York: Cambridge University Press.

Roobeek, Annemieke J. M. 1987. *The crisis of fordism and the rise of a new technological paradigm, futures*, 19, 129.

Ruggie, J. G. 1994. Trade, protectionism and the future of welfare capitalism. *Journal of International Affairs* 48:1–11.

Rupert, Mark E., and David P. Rapkin. 1985. The erosion of U.S. leadership capabilities. In *Rhythms in politics and economics*, ed. Paul M. Johnson and William R. Thompson. New York and Toronto: Praeger.

Sanders, William. 1985. Women, work, and divorce. *American Economic Review* 75:519–523.

Schroeder, Susan. 2009. Defining and detecting financial fragility: New Zealand's experience. *International Journal of Social Economics* 36 (3): 287–307.

Seccombe, Wally. 1980a. Domestic labour and the working-class household. In *Hidden in the household: Women's domestic labour under capitalism*, ed. Bonnie Fox. Toronto: The Women's Press.

Seccombe, Wally. 1980b. *The expanded reproduction cycle of labour power in twentieth century capitalism, in Bonnie Fox 1980*. 217–266.

Stanfield, James Ronald. 1991. The dichotomised state. *Journal of Economic Issues* 25 (3): 765–780.

Stanfield, James Ronald, and Brent McClintock. 1999. Welfare State. In *Encyclopedia of political economy*, ed. Phillip Anthony O'Hara, 1245–1248. London and New York: Routledge.

Shelton, Beth Anne. 1990. The distribution of household tasks: Does wife's employment status make a difference? *Journal of Family Issues* 11:115–135.

Sherman, Howard J. 1990. Cyclical behaviour of the labor share. *Review of Radical Political Economics* 22 (2-3): 92–112.

Sherman, Howard J., and David X. Kolk. 1996. *Business cycles and forecasting*. New York: HarperCollins.

Silvia, Stephen J., and Michael Stanaitis. 2013. *Is economic hegemony necessary for maintaining open trade? An empirical challenge to the hegemonic stability theory*. Washington DC: Working Paper. School of International Service, American University.

Strange, Susan. 1987. The persistent myth of lost hegemony. *International Organization* 41 (4): 551–574.

Suter, Christian. 1992. *Debt cycles in the world economy: Foreign loans, financial crises, and debt settlements, 1820–1990*. Boulder and San Francisco US: Westview Press.

Tylecote, Andrew. 1992. *The long wave in the world economy: The current crisis in historical perspective*. New York: Routledge.

Vanek, Joann. 1974. Time spent in housework. *Scientific American* 231:116–120.

Veblen, Thorstein Bunde. 1899. *The theory of the leisure class: An economic study of institutions*, 1970. London: Unwin Books.

Veblen, Thorstein Bunde. 1923. *Absentee ownership and business enterprise in recent times: The case of America*, 1964. New York: Augustus M. Kelley.

Walker, John F., and Harold G. Vatter. 1997. *The rise of big government in the United States*. Armonk, US and London: M.E. Sharpe.

Wallace, Michael. 1989. Aggressive economism, defensive control: Contours of American labour militancy, 1947-81. *Economic and Industrial Democracy* 10:7.

Wallerstein, Immanuel. 1983. The three instances of hegemony in the history of the capitalist world-economy, *International Journal of Comparative Sociology*, vol 14, 1983. Also published in G.T. Crane and A. Amawi eds., *The theoretical evolution of international political economy: A reader*, New York: Oxford University Press, 1991.

Wallerstein, Immanuel. 2006. The curve of American power. *New Left Review* 40:1–20.

Weisskopf, Thomas, Samuel Bowles, and David M. Gordon. 1983. Hearts and minds: A social model of U.S. productivity growth. *Brookings Papers on Economic Activity* no 2.

Whalen, Charles. 2007. *The U.S. credit crunch of 2007: A minsky moment. Public policy brief 92*. Annandale-on-Hudson, NY: Levy Economics Institute of Bard College.

Winecoff, William Windred. 2020. "The persistent myth of lost hegemony" Revisited: Structural power as a complex network phenomenon. *European Journal of International Relations* 26 (1): 209–252.

Wolff, Edward N. 1986. The productivity slowdown and the fall in the U.S. rate of profit, 1947–1976. *Review of Radical Political Economics* 18 (1 & 2): 87–109.

Wolfson, Martin H. 1993. The evolution of the financial system and the possibilities for reform. In *Transforming the U.S. financial system: Equity and efficiency for the 21st century*, ed. Gary A. Dymski, Gerard Epstein, and Robert Pollin, 133–156. Armonk, New York and London: M.E. Sharpe.

Wolfson, Martin H. 1994. *Financial crises: Understanding the postwar U.S. experience*. Armonk, New York: M. E. Sharpe Inc. Second Edition.

World Bank. 2024. *World development indicators (WDI)*. World Development Indicators | DataBank (worldbank.org).

Wray, L. Randall. 1990. *Money and credit in capitalist economies: The endogenous money approach*. Cheltenham, UK and Brookfield, US: Edward Elgar.

Zaretsky, Eli. 1976. *Capitalism, the family and everyday life*. London: Pluto Press.

Chapter 8
Chinese Long Waves, Potential Hegemony, and Climate Change

Abstract This chapter provides an outline of Chinese growth waves of real GDP per capita (decadal AAGR), and real GDP per capita levels, during the 1780–2020s, and surveys Chinese techno-institutional, ecological, and potential hegemonic performance during the 1970s–2020s. Section 8.2 summarizes the data for the 1780–2020s, and presents hypotheses for investigation. Section 8.3 details the pathways and circuits of socioeconomic dynamics (CSD) associated with the seven spheres vis-à-vis their contribution to long waves, potential hegemony, and climate change. This section compares and contrasts China with the USA since potential Chinese hegemony depends crucially on such comparisons. Section 8.4 scrutinizes the contradictions associated with Chinese performance and its significance for future long waves, hegemony, and climate change. Section 8.5 analyzes hegemony from a comparative perspective for China, USA, Britain, and the Dutch. A conclusion follows.

Keywords Chinese potential hegemony · Long waves · Climate change · Empirics · Historical specificity · Principles of political economy (PoPE) · Pathways and Circuits of socioeconomic dynamics (CSD) · Rules and stylized facts

8.1 Introduction

In a previous paper (O'Hara 2006), I examined whether China had at the time a viable macro-social structure of accumulation (SSA) for capitalist long-wave upswing into the early decades of the twenty-first century. The paper commenced with the SSA Index of Proficiency and Potentiality (IPP) through which phases of capitalist development can be scrutinized. The rest of the paper detailed the components of the IPP, first the more technical institutional factors and then broader indicators of development. The paper concluded that China in the 2000s was an emerging *state capitalist economy* and that it is likely to continue through a

P. A. O'Hara, *Long Waves of Growth, Hegemonic Power, and Climate Change in the World Economy*, https://doi.org/10.1007/978-981-96-4132-1_8

long-wave upswing with core industrialization during the 2006–2020 period, though at a lower level. I concluded by stating that: "There are critical limits to capitalist development in China—including problems associated with capital productivity, innovation, pollution, and rural-urban dynamics—and these are likely to restrict long-term performance [significantly] by about 2020" (p. 397).

The purpose of this current chapter is to reevaluate the performance of China in the light of further developments and a broader periodicity (1780–2020s, especially 1950s–2030s), and with a somewhat different approach. Here we utilize the principles of the political economy (PoPE) paradigm, paying special attention to the contribution of the dynamic circuit of techno-institutional-ecological (socioeconomic) reproduction (CSD) to long waves, hegemony, and climate change up to the 2030s–2040s. Such a paradigm is an innovative new approach to applying a technological, institutional, ecological, and world capitalist system view of long waves and hegemony. I also utilize the new long-wave method as used in earlier chapters to examine the statistics of decadal GDP per capita average annual growth rates (AAGR).

In this context, China has been integrating into the capitalist-world economy, especially over the past 45 years, notably by joining various global organizations and agreements, encouraging foreign direct investment (FDI), enhancing market relations, and promoting capital accumulation and profit. Chinese-Asian growth and development has been one of the few success stories in a world where most continental engines of growth have faded since most of Europe, North America, South America, sub-Saharan Africa, Eastern Europe, and the Middle East have been in relative economic malaise since the 1980s and 1990s, although short upswings were conspicuous at times in most places (see details in Chap. 11, below), and some subareas have performance better than others. Could China and the region be the main engine of growth for the world economy to inspire growth and accumulation into the future? While most areas of the world suffer from poor performance, could China be undergoing a capitalist long-wave upswing, hegemonic ascendency, and climate change mitigation/adaptation, or has it turned the corner into long-wave downswing, potential hegemonic demise, and climate anomalies? This is the subject matter of the current chapter.

8.2 Long Waves and Hegemony in China

Figure 8.1 scrutinizes China's rate of real GDP per capita decadal average annual growth rates (AAGR) from 1780 to 2022 (blue bar), the linear trend bar (purple), with aeas British and US hegemony outlined.

Table 8.1 summarizes the results of Fig. 8.1.

This Figure shows four clear trends. The first trend in the data is that between 1780 and 1950, China's growth was usually close to zero or in some cases majorly negative (1938–1950) (LWD for 170 years). However, the growth rate would rise noticeably, but not majorly, for a decade or more. For instance, one such period was

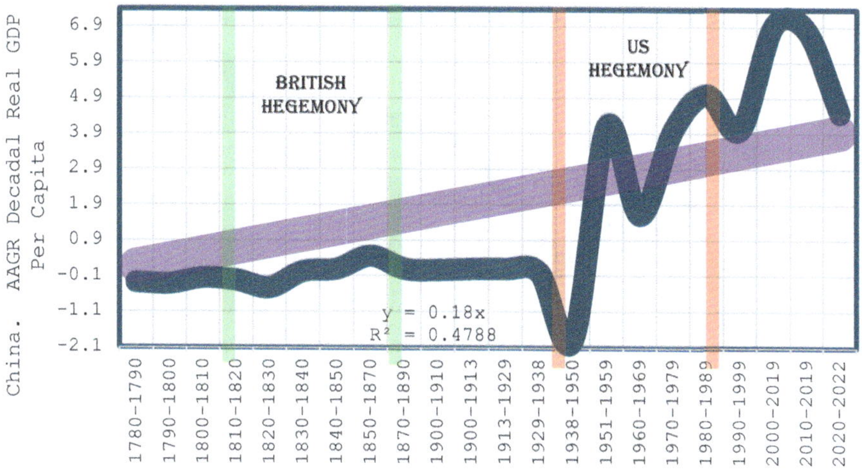

Fig. 8.1 Chinese Real GDP per capita decadal AAGR, 1780–2022 (blue line). (Source: Adapted from the raw figures of the Maddison Project (2024). Linear Trend Bar (purple) (y = 0.18x; R^2 = 0.6258 for trend line)

Table 8.1 China, long waves "Map," ratio of upswing to borderline and downswing performance, 1780–2022 (242 years)

1780–1950 (171 yrs)	1951–1969 (19 yrs)	1970–2022 (53 yrs)
Varying power dynamics	US absolute hegemony	Relative US hegemony
170 year LWD	SWU (1950s)	LWU 1970–2019)
	SWD (1960s)	SB (2020–2022)
0 U/171D	**9 U/10D) = 0.9**	**50/3 = 16.7**

Note: *U* upswing, *D* downswing, *B* borderline, *LWU* long wave upswing, *LWD* long wave downswing, *SWU* short-wave upswing, *SWD* short-wave downswing, *SB short borderline* B

during the two decades of 1850–1870, when China was engaged in the second Opium War against Britain (1854–1860), being forced to open various ports for trade with Britain and others, hand over territory, and legalize opium. But the worst long-wave downswing was during the 1930s–1940s when China underwent a civil war (revolution) and the second Sino-Japanese war.

The second trend in the data is that over 1780–2022 only one period illustrates a clear long wave *high* upswing and possible downswing (high ceiling and high floor), namely, the years from the 1970s–2010s (long wave upswing), and the start of a possible long wave downswing, *moving toward* short-wave borderline during 2020–2022. Growth has fallen from an average (AAGR) of 6.88% for the 2000s–2010s to 4.49% (2020–2022), a drop of 35% as several contradictory forces have begun to impact (see sect. 8.4 and chap.11 below for details). More importantly, as we analyze later in this chapter, many think this drop will continue into the future rather than being *purely* cyclical.

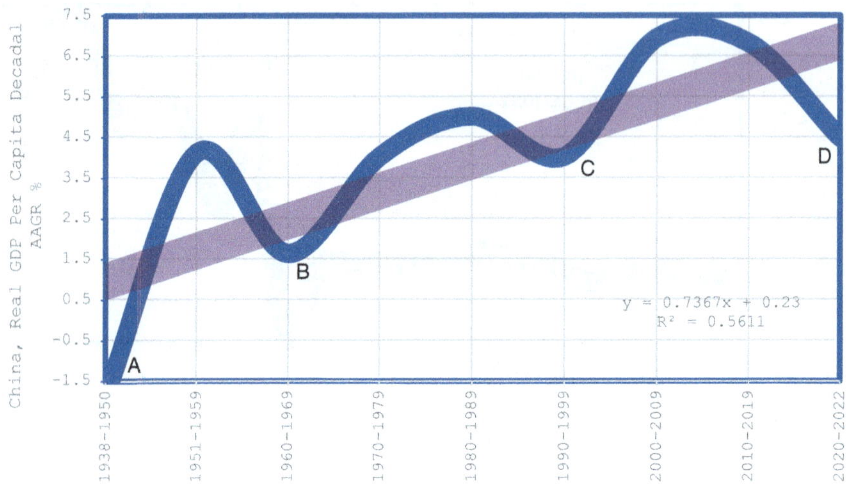

Fig. 8.2 Chinese small waves or swings (1938 to 2022) (Blue bar is decadal GDP per capita AAGR; purple bar shows trend borderline performance)

The third trend can be observed in Fig. 8.2, where China has undergone three shorter waves or swings since the 1950s.

When measured from downswing to downswing, China can be seen to have undergone its first (1st) medium wave/swing between point "A" and "B," followed by another (2nd) between "B" and "C," and the third short wave or swing between "C" and "D" (3rd). The first emerged from the Second World War and revolution through to the first five-year plan, the Great Leap Backward and the Cultural Revolution of 1966–1976 (Robinson 1974). The second developed from the Cultural Revolution to the recovery of the late 1970s, and the initial establishment of the market economy in the 1980s, to the slight decline of the 1990s (Wilson and Morris 1997). The third emerged from the slight decline of the 1990s to the large boom of the 2000s and 2010s during the property escalation and the subsequent property crash and corona crisis of the early 2000s (Cordesman 2023). These medium-scale 25–30-year waves or swings were undergone during the institutional workings of state capitalism and the movement of around 300 m people from the rural areas to the towns and cities.

This cyclical pattern in the data shows clear patterns of short-wave upswing and downswing, corresponding to upswings during the 1950s, 1970s–1980s, and 2000s–2010s and downswings during the 1960s, 1990s, and 2020s (so far).[1] The trend recently in the literature (say past 5 years) is to consider the "infrastructure

[1] GDP per capita growth figures especially for the period before the 1970s are replete with high levels of uncertainty and margins of error (see details analyzed by Deng and O'Brien 2016). They are still subject to uncertainties and margins of error during and after the 1970s, but these are somewhat lower levels of error compared with the earlier periods, but nevertheless significant, often as much as 2% or 200 basis points (Wei Chen et al. 2019).

bust—Covid-19 downswing" as being potentially more durable than a few years because it also included several other contradictions. The most notable anomalies are the debt and property crash in China in recent years, which has generated a modest trend to deflation, and prompted the President to call for more productive investment in the future ("from quantity to quality"). There is also the likely exhaustion of the movement from rural to urban areas, which was a core element of China's industrialization process. The trend to a more elderly population, as their domestic reproduction rate declined with the first drop in the aggregate population level since 1961, will reduce levels of GDP per worker and likely erode safety nets for the elderly and others. Having the highest greenhouse gas (GHG) flows in the world will require a more robust movement to renewables and adaptation than is currently the case. A rising level of centralization of decision-making has already reduced the scope for political-economic and cultural creativity and innovation. There is also the continuing conflict with the US and, to a lesser extent, the EU (and various Asia-Pacific nations) over protectionism, tariffs, subsidies, and Taiwan, which may generate continual anomalies for China and others.

Fourth, this declining growth has implications for hegemony and climate change dynamics. This is due to several factors. Hegemonic nations need to have, among other things, the highest real GDP per capita in the World for several decades, long-wave upswings (usually) in the middle of (or just before) absolute hegemony, and possible low growth in the future will severely inhibit this trajectory. Hegemonic nations also tend to move onto absolute hegemony through a major war of ascendency, and low levels of growth will inhibit China's ability to win such a war (and possibly make the strain of high rates of military expenditure unsustainable). Low growth may also lead China to renegotiate its climate change responsibilities because doing so may lessen the costs of adaptation and mitigation.

Fifth, one could hypothesize from this date two interrelated types of waves occurring at once. The first being the long wave upswing representing the vibrant long-term growth during the 50 years of 1970s–2020s (with possibly a downswing on both sides of these dates). And the second being three Kuznets swings from 1938–1950 to 2020–2022: The first one from 1938/1950 to 1960–1969, the second from 1960–1969 to 1990–1999, and the third from 1990–1999 to 1920–2022. These three possible Kuznets swings are clearly isolable from visual inspection. Ascertaining whether they could reasonably be considered Kuznets swings is a hypothesis in need of further inquiry into the future, in terms of theory, causality, factors, and so on. Here, our main concern is with the long wave upswing over the period of the 1970s to the 2020s, and especially the CSD that underpins it.

In this context, the major task of this chapter is to analyze the seven main dimensions of the Chinese pathways and circuits of socioeconomic dynamics (CSD), comprising its main institutional, technological, and geo-ecological structures, dynamics, and flows over recent decades onto the present and immediate future. An analysis of the CSD provides a structural-dynamic view of the Chinese political economy underlying long-term performance during the long waves from the 1970s to the present and into the future. The CSD conditions long waves, hegemony, and climate change dynamics.

8.3 Chinese Pathways and Circuits of Socioeconomic Dynamics

In this section, we review the structure and dynamics of seven major techno-institutional-geospatial aspects of the Chinese circuits of socioeconomic dynamics (CSD), which are illustrated in Fig. 8.3. These include the role and power of China vis-à-vis (1) global political economy, (2) state capitalism, (3) techno-innovation, (4) households–rural–urban dynamics, (5) market-finance capital, (6) corporate performance, and (7) geoecological dynamics. There are core interdependencies and relative autonomies within and between the seven major dynamic structures of the CSD that generate cascading tipping points (CTP) that propel the political economy into a long upswing, followed by the buildup of contradictions and uncertainties, and onto long-wave downswing.

Key: ⟷ Inter-sphere interdependencies: Flows, stocks, agents, groups.

We start with the nature of the Chinese CSD system within the global political economy in the first of these sections.

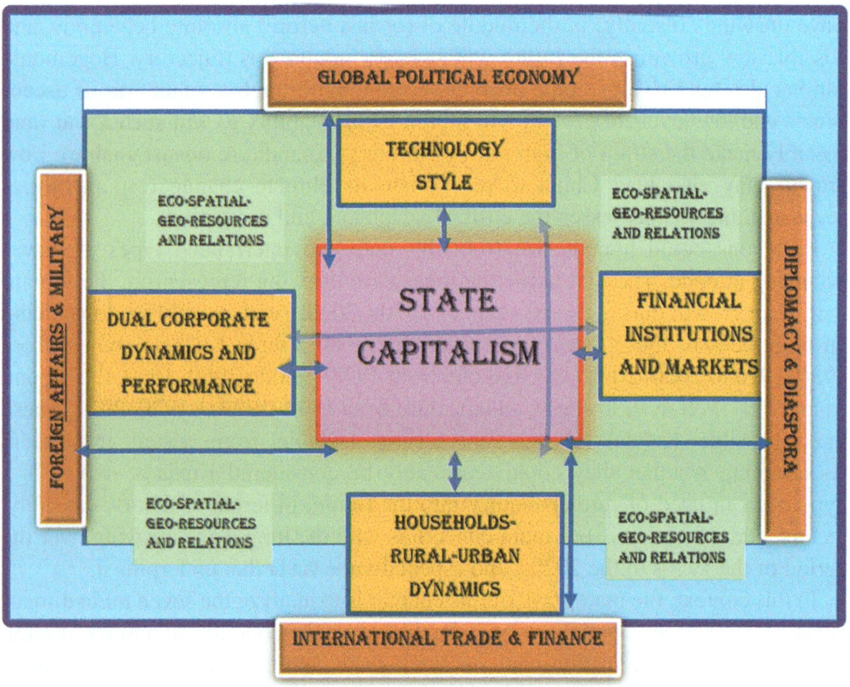

Fig. 8.3 Chinese pathways and circuits of socioeconomic dynamics (CSD) (*Shortform* version)

8.3.1 *China's Power in the Global Political Economy*

China has undergone a number of socioeconomic developments since the revolution of the 1940s (see Elsner 2020). This started with industrial rehabilitation (1949–1952), then the foundations of industrial development during the first five-year plan (1953–1957), followed by the backward movement of the Great Leap Forward and Cultural Revolution (1958–1976), the market-oriented reform period (1978–present), and more recently the period when President Xi Jinping has lead China (since 2012), reinforcing his position in 2022 by securing his third term as Chinese Communist Party (CCP) General Secretary and in 2023 being elected State President for the third time.

Before the 1978 reforms, China's political economy centered on communal systems of production and state firms, along with centrally planned and controlled structures. Since 1978 major reforms have been made to promote strategic alliances between state and private companies, open up the country to foreign trade and capital flows, and encourage competition, investment, and private property relations, all while keeping state power over the system as a whole, and expanding it into the Asia-Pacific region and beyond where possible.

The People's Republic of China has been building and then consolidating institutions to succeed in the power stakes of the global political economy. Soon after official recognition by many nations in the early 1970s, and gaining a seat at the UN, China began its reform agenda. In the 1980s, the People's Republic joined the International Monetary Fund (IMF) and World Bank, as it tried to cast Taiwan into the diplomatic wilderness (attempting to incorporate it formally into the mainland), and has been active in the Asian Development Bank. It went on to join the World Trade Organization (WTO) in 2001 and ratify the Kyoto Protocol in 2002. By the new Millennium, it had joined all the major international institutions and agreements, as well as the informal G-20, where it often mediates between developing and developed nations (Yu 2005). It has also increased its global power through the "Belt-and-Road Initiative" (BRI), which assists nations in the provision of infrastructure and related structures, plus enhancing its diplomatic and military power through numerous agreements around the world.

Gaining a power base in the global political economy is a way of enhancing its world standing, potentially promoting a good reputation, and having a say in what happens in all areas of finance, trade, diplomacy, and even global culture (the diaspora is especially useful here). In addition, it helps boost China's position in the global division of labor, stimulates networks and strategic alliances, as well as value chains and production networks (Athukorala and Ravenhill 2016). If China is to be the next hegemonic power, past hegemonic trends may be instructive here, since one stylized fact is that hegemons tend to be liberal democracies. If this is true, movements in this direction are likely to enhance its prestige and position, but nowhere seems to be in process.

The Chinese state has also been undermining its "good reputation" through various threats and actions, often associated with "naked power" (Russell 1938). For instance, it massacred many during the 1989 Tiananmen Square demonstrations, which itself was, in part, a reaction to the death of the pro-reform CCP General Secretary, Hu Yaobang (1915–1989). In 2012, it elected an authoritarian leader, Xi Jinping, as General Secretary, and for a third time in 2022 (for "Life"). It has been sending millions of (especially Uyghur) Muslims (and other religious and ethnic groups) into re-education camps in north-east China, especially since the 2010s. It has effectively absorbed Hong Kong into the mainland's polity and emasculated democracy in the region. In recent years it has been enhancing its sea power in the region through the building of artificial islands and military harbors, threatening neighbors, and accelerated efforts to control Taiwan. It has also supported Russia in its invasion of Ukraine. With the re-election of Xi Jinping as General Secretary of the CCP in 2022 (for a third term), Chinese authoritarian power has become normalized. These actions are important because there are two main parts of hegemonic dominance, one being effective threats, and the second moral leadership. China has often shown a lack of moral leadership.

The US has seen China as the main threat to its (relative-declining) hegemony for a decade now, in military-diplomatic terms, trade and production, and finance.[2] In response, and ironically in a similar fashion to China itself, it has instituted several industrial policies such as subsidies and tax incentives for productive investment in domestic manufacturing, instituted several forms of protection, especially against Chinese competitors, encouraged ongoing nationalist sentiment against foreigners, migrants, and global competitors such as China, and reinforced its diplomatic-military attachments notably in the Asia-Pacific region. These similar policies undertaken by both China and the US have seen a shift in ideology from variously neoliberal (US) and pro-market (China) sentiments to promoting more self-reliance and domestic sources of investment and innovation and to some degree addressing the issue of inequality and national uneven development. Globally, nations are tending toward more protectionism, nationalism, and self-sufficiency. The trend toward inward development, protectionism, and industry policy is a common historical trait of world economies for several decades after the demise of a major hegemon (Dutch, British, US).

In the Chinese context, several indices have been developed to measure global power, including soft power, military power, and related dimensions. For instance, the *Rand Global Power Index* (GPI) (Heim and Miller 2020) estimates GPI using a composite of military, economic, technological, political, and human capacities for

[2] This is similar, to some degree, to the changing power relations between the Dutch and English in the 1600s, which eventually led to diminishing Dutch hegemony especially after the 1650s (the English Navigation Acts), the first of 1661, and the second Anglo-Dutch War of the 1660s, even while Britain took another 155 years to gain full power. This is notably quite different from the relationship between British and US power into the late 1800s and through the 1900s, during which British and US relations were relatively friendly; indeed, US power was achieved through similar cultural and ethnic lines.

various nations.[3] It estimates that by 2017, the US was still ahead of China in GPI, but by 2022 China was likely to have made major inroads vis-à-vis the US. They then study several future scenarios for 2040. This includes, for instance, the scenario of a lost decade for China, where several key indicators of power are well below historical trends, resulting in China not potentially overtaking the US totally until the mid-2030s. Other scenarios link to climate change policies and population changes, with China overtaking the US by the mid-2020s. However, none of the different scenarios for 2040 show China having even near the relative power *differential* over the US (or any other nation) that the US had over, for instance, the USSR in 1960.

Current trends involving multilateral differentials between global powers are unlikely to move China to absolute hegemonic dominance by the 2040s, although a movement toward relative hegemony is possible if India (or Indonesia) does not escalate its power base majorly in future decades. This indicates that no major single power will be able to coordinate an array of nations toward major long-wave upswings of socioeconomic performance. However, since evidence suggests absolute hegemony is not a strict requirement for long-wave upward motion, and that the hegemonic stability theory is subject to serious objection, at least in theory, other arrangements of the techno-institutional fabric of nations and regions may well establish structures underlying successful performance for the world economy (or key members) into the foreseeable future (at least for a time, through multipolar developments).[4] We examine hegemony issues further throughout this chapter.

8.3.2 Chinese State Capitalism

The question of what style of socioeconomic and political system developed in China during different phases of its transformation is a complex one, as anyone who reads Richard Westra's (2023) introduction to a special issue on the subject for the *Journal of Contemporary Asia* will realize.

Officially, China's system is said to be called "socialism with Chinese characteristics" (SCC). The basics of this system have been examined by numerous scholars, Chinese politicians, and policymakers. I briefly scrutinize this concept and practice, discussed by two Chinese scholars of "Marxist political economy." Xia Lu and

[3] Some of the other global power indexes, *available in the public area*, include, for instance, Brand Finance's Global Soft Power Index, ISSF's World Soft Power Index, Monocle's Soft Power Survey, and Portland's Soft Power 30 Report (see Wikipedia 2023).

[4] China may well edge ahead of other areas and nations in technological leadership and even military leadership without being hegemonic in the absolute sense. However, if the world moves closer to the dual bloc process, China-Russia-North Korea, etc. vs. US-EU-Japan-Australia, etc. (including dichotomous blocs within nations and areas), a World War may lead to one bloc winning and imposing their wishes on others (but if this is to happen, historical processes indicate that liberal-democracies tend to win, for both moral and innovation reasons).

Xiaoqin Ding (2022) undertook a survey of the concept by a number of scholars associated with the *New Marxian Economics Synthesis School*, which discussed it conference during 2021.

It is clear from this document that SCC derives from the basic framework that is said to have started with Marx and Engels, through to Lenin and Stalin, onto Mao and Deng Xiaoping, and onto Xi Jinping. Little or no mention is made of other socialists, or Western Marxism, or any possible divergence between Marxian economics and socialist economics. In fact, the synthesis school mainly examines SCC through the lens of "political economy" (In general terms), rather than through the prism of experts of socialist economics.

Principle number one of their view of SCC is linked to contributing to solving some core *contradictions* within the Chinese economy. The main one is between "people's growing demand for a better life and inadequate and unbalanced development" (p. 478). Much emphasis is given to solving this problem through more emphasis being given to public commodities rather than private commodities, by which they mean public enterprises. Domestic demand is given priority, along with self-reliance ("*dual circulation*").

Principle number two is to expand and enrich the *productive forces* through new innovations in science and technology, AI, and qualitative dimensions of commodities, through the "socialist market economy," with "diverse forms of ownership but with public ownership as its main component," and with "distribution according to work" being fundamental (p. 480–481). Industrial policies are crucial along with "modernization of industrial supply chains," through the triad of *party, state, and market* to generate such advances.

Principle number three of SCC is for the development of "*socialist capital*," with the "*external compulsion of capital over labor still appl[ying]*," and with other forms of capital also being used, such as private capital and collective capital (p. 482). *Common prosperity* is to be developed through various means of distribution to reduce inequality and promote poverty alleviation, better coordination, and more inclusiveness. A progressive tax system is said to be important, along with taxes on capital gains and inheritance, and preventing asset transfers overseas through offshore trusts (p. 485; emphasis added). What would Marx say?: "External compulsion of capital over labor?" "I don't think so!" This is a characteristic of capitalism.

Principle number four of SCC enunciated at the conference was that China should follow the lead of previous great powers such as the US, Britain, and the Soviet Union to develop *hegemonic power*. This can be done via the "maritime silk road," a "shared community" in the South China Sea, "world class enterprise groups," and "leading-edge technology." Currently, there is a "struggle for world dominance between hegemonic empires and new rising powers," also involving "a [Sino-US] trade war, a technology war, and an information war." In this context, a "complete, multidimensional strategic plan" is said to be necessary through the leadership of the CPP (p. 492–493). What about the hegemony-stylized facts mentioned in this current book? Liberal democracies? Hegemony emerging from a major war? Free trade?

Participants at the conference recognized that "the Communist Party of China does not engage in abstract disputes over whether China's system is peculiar to "capitalism" or to "socialism" (Xia Lu and Xiaoqin Ding 2022, 482). Indeed, apparently, no discussion was held at the conference as to whether China's "socialism with Chinese characteristics" (also called market socialism) may perhaps be considered "state capitalism" (as many think it is, e.g., Birley 2023), "party-state capitalism" as one group of authors call it (Pearson et al. 2020) or even simply "capitalism" as Minqi Li (2020) argues it should be termed.

In this context, Minqi Li (2020) briefly examines the historical transformation of China over the past hundred years, and cites the conflict between Mao Zedong and Deng Xiaoping plus other members of the Party elite as a pivotal movement, leading to the Cultural Revolution (1967–1976); after which, when Mao died, an impetus was generated for "China's transition to capitalism." Li then examines the sudden transition to market relations, the rise of private property, the sale of state firms, capitalist sweatshops, and "capitalist relations of production" (p. 76). He summarizes the Chinese class structure as comprising (in 2017) 3% capitalists; 2% party and state bureaucrats, the top layer which "should be considered part of the capitalist class" (p. 82); 9% urban middle class, who are said to be paid a "loyalty rent," including highly skilled workers such as "managers, engineers, technicians, scientific researchers, doctors, lawyers, and professors"; 24% urban proletariat; 15% semi-proletariat, including the urban self-employed, unemployed, and unclassified; and 46% rural semi-proletariat.

"*The Chinese System*" (TCS) can thus be seen from many angles in terms of classification: socialism, market socialism, state capitalism, party-state capitalism, and capitalism. Maybe we should just call it "TCS." However, due to obvious linkages between the state and capital inherent in its structure and dynamics, I will call it a system of "state capitalism." The Chinese authorities have, probably knowingly, set in motion a style of "state capitalism," where it has encouraged competition, globalization, capital accumulation, and profitable enterprises, along with several classes of bourgeoisie and workers. The bourgeoisie includes financial capitalists, industrial capitalists, entrepreneurs, state-business elements, compradors, merchants, and venture capitalists. The workers include an array of unskilled, skilled, aristocratic, bureaucratic, and clerical personnel. The CCP has been utilizing the capitalist mode of production and reproduction to stimulate industrialization, through a high degree of competition on the world market. Expanding capital accumulation and thus raising the share of investment in GDP to over 40% has increased labor productivity to successively high levels.

This is an ingenious plan by the Chinese authorities in which they use capitalist processes and systems as a means of industrializing their nation as well as improving the standard of living of its citizens. Schweinberger (2012) defines state capitalism as "a political, social and economic system which combines state power with some policy tools and institutions of liberal capitalism to promote a sustained and rapid growth of … GDP and economic development" (p. 172). He argues the Chinese have been developing state capitalism by instituting several policy measures over several decades.

The first such tool is *industry policy*, which encourages innovative investment in several key sectors, such as high-tech manufacturers, electronics and electric vehicles. Relying mostly on small-flexible firms to develop innovations and large state firms to expand improvements through access to finance and public goods enables total factor productivity to grow.

The second is the *building of trust between networks* of heterogeneous agents and groups in several sectors of the economy (alliances). Especially important is trust between party and citizens, which depends upon continual long-term performance. Also crucial is that between business and government, where the government is said to lay down certain rules and business reaps rewards while enhancing the so-called common good. Good relations between small private companies and large enterprises also play a core role, as the synergy between them enables a more coordinated process of expansion.

The third is *relational interaction* between Chinese people and others operating in several areas and nations of the world since access to ethnic, language, and cultural networks (roles, mores, and diaspora) help build business organizations and productivity. Especially important is the expansion of knowledge (tacit and specific) within and between business agents, state officials, and others. Schweinberger argues that these networks may enable China to eschew the potential "middle income trap" on the East Coast by spreading innovations and development to the hinterland and thereby potentially enabling sustainable growth.

State capitalism is said to have advantages over the more specifically (neo)liberal policies of the West (especially in the 1980s–2010s), such as enabling China to protect itself from some of the instabilities of the global financial crisis (GFC). The more collectivist model enhances communication and relationships between groups and agents, expands the flow of information and knowledge, and thereby reduces risk and uncertainty between lenders and borrowers, underwriters and investors, officials and entrepreneurs, and potentially between citizens and "the Party" (O'Hara 2009). The more financialized model of the West (especially the US) has (historically) more risk embedded in its institutional edifice, which subjects it to greater uncertainty and thereby less long-term investment.

Despite these advantages, the state capitalist model (SCC) exhibits several ongoing contradictions, which may hinder long-term progress more severely than the growth decline of the 2020s (shown above). As mentioned above, the Chinese state has, more recently, explicitly encouraged (1) "quality over quantity," (2) "national development" (domestic demand), (3) socialist capital, and (4) rising Chinese hegemonic power. On the first of these, Chinese competitive advantage for several decades was in producing cheap products with global sales in mind, and often unsustainable spending in unproductive areas such as property and equity. The move to more value-added industries and less unstable ones is one that will likely reduce levels of (unstable) growth further as quality is given priority. The second, placing more emphasis on the domestic market may reduce growth, especially as the population ages and the movement from rural to city life exhausts its momentum. The third objective is subject to several contradictions. If indeed, as Xi Jinping apparently believes, "We commemorate Marx in order to pay tribute to the greatest thinker in the history of mankind" (quoted by Cheek and Ownby 2018), we will come up against numerous anomalies, as Marx would likely have had major objections to authoritarian modes, inadequate civil society, and war mongering especially in the Asia-Pacific (and in supporting Russia against Ukraine).

Xi Jinping's pretense of socialism likely would not have convinced Marx, who was known to have said that he was "not a Marxist" (O'Hara 2016). Xi Jinping realized that Chinese development up until the 2010s was too much state capitalism and not enough "socialism," but his responses hardly do justice to Marx's vision of such a system, or suitably adjust the vision to account for Marx's anomalous perspectives on the matter. Why, I ask, treat Marx as a God, rather than as a brilliant (but contradictory) human being? (see O'Hara 2016).

Then there is the serious question of the (in)adequacy of state socialist governance. In general terms, the state has done very well in improving the material conditions of life for the domestic population over the past several decades, even though inequality has increased, hence their new policies relating to this. For the rest of the world, something usually ignored, it has provided a mass of products at usually cheap prices for consumers, businesses, and governments, thus aiding their material quality of life. But what about more technical issues of governance, such as China's relative and absolute position in the global governance index (GGI, World Bank) and performance vis-à-vis the coronavirus crisis, as proxies of how state socialism may cope with challenges in the future? Table 8.2 shows the GGI for the USA and China from 1995 to 2022, decomposed into its six components, including a mean for the components as a whole:

The GGI is a composite index comprising six sub-dimensions, including (1) Voice and Accountability, (2) Political Stability and No Violence/Terrorism, (3) General Government Effectiveness, (4) Regulatory Quality, (5) Rule of Law, and (6) Control of Corruption. First, the overall results (7) show that there has been some degree of convergence between the USA and China over the 26 years, with the USA having dropped quite significantly from 90 to 78, with China improving marginally from 38 to 41. In terms of governance power between the two nations, reflecting leadership in this realm, the US is so far ahead of China that there is almost no comparison. Given the recent trends in the USA, one might think this could easily change, but since China has what could be called similar trends, this process of (major) convergence is unlikely in the foreseeable future, even though the US is likely to decline further while China may rise.

Regarding individual components of the index, areas where both nations are moderately close include (2) Political Violence and No Violence/Terrorism, where both have declined in value recently, plus (3) Government Effectiveness, an area where China has improved a lot recently. At broader levels, though, with both nations being in the "pre-war stage" (World-War 3?) over Taiwan and Ukraine, and with authoritarian trends rising in both the US and China, one might think this is "good" for China since hegemony theory shows major wars are generally necessary for hegemony to emerge. Counter this, though, is another general rule of hegemony theory and empirics: since all hegemonic nations, including the Dutch, British, and US, were all liberal democracies, at least domestically, whereas China is not, this

Table 8.2 Global governance index, 1996–2022, USA and China

	1. Voice and accountability		2. Political stability and no violence/terrorism		3. Government effectiveness		4. Regulatory quality		5. Rule of law		6. Control of corruption		7. Global governance index mean	
	USA	China	USA	China	USA	China	USA	China	USA	China	USA	China	USA	China
1996	91	13	80	45	90	42	94	45	93	38	93	48	90	38
2022	73	6	45	28	87	68	91	37	89	53	83	55	78	41

Source: Adapted from raw data of World Bank 2024

could be a major limit to China's rise to hegemony. While China may generate major levels of comparative military and technological power, this may not transfer into effective leadership in a moral sense, since all the global powers that lost hegemonic (or Empire) wars were all autocratic-world empires (potentially or actually), such as the Spanish (80-year war), France (Revolutionary and Napoleonic Wars), and Germany (two world wars). Stylized facts are not on their side.

8.3.3 Chinese Technology Style

In this section, we undertake three tasks. First, we outline the dynamic structure of China's innovation system. Second, we scrutinize the ongoing success of this dynamic structure. Third, we critically evaluate the system's operational anomalies associated with likely declining growth in the long term.

Li (2020) argues that the Chinese innovation system comprises four key elements. The first involves an evolutionary economics approach. Such an approach centers on the nature and relationship between institutions, social technologies, and physical technologies. Nelson (2008) defines an institution broadly as the ways of doing things that are dominant in society, and which include norms, customs, routines, laws, basic rules of the game, regularized actions, organizations, and behavioral patterns. Social technologies include the structured environments within which institutions and technologies are actioned, especially vis-à-vis patterns of knowledge, science, and organization of factories, banks, corporations, households, states, and trading systems. Physical technologies are the innovations that generate new products, processes, infrastructures, minerals-mining resources, agricultural goods, and so on. Successful innovation systems thus require a productive and efficient set of coordinating processes, setting in motion the institutions, social technologies, and physical technologies by several heterogeneous groups and agents.

We study the changing innovative potential of China compared with the US via the Global Innovation Index (GII). This is done by investigating the evidence for 2007–2008, 2015, and 2022–2023 in Table 8.3.

Progress with the index reveals important results over 2008–2023. First, it illustrates that China has enhanced its global innovation from 37th (2008–2009) to 29th (2015) to 12th (2022–2023) while the USA has moved down and up from 1st (2008–2009) to 5th (2015) to 3rd (2022–2023). Of all areas of innovation, China is the best in the world with 0 (2008–2009) to 7 (2015) to 9 (2022–2023) of the areas, while the USA is the best in 10 (2008–2009) to 8 (2015) to 13 (2022–2023) areas. During 2022–2023, China was judged the global leader for (a) PISA scales for reading, math, and science (in Beijing, Shanghai, Jiangsu, and Zhejiang); (b) utility model applications for patents with a short life span and less stringent requirements; (c) labor productivity growth rates; and (d) certain intangible assets (trademarks and creative goods exports) (WIPO 2022–2023). Overall, China has major improvements to make to become technologically dominant, especially since it is currently eighth in the world for innovative outputs, but only 25th in the world for innovative

Table 8.3 Global innovation index, China, USA, 2008–2009, 2015, 2022–2023

	China	China	China	USA	USA	USA
	2008–2009	2015	2022–2023	2008–2009	2015	2022–2023
GII rank [score] (general)	37 [3.6]	29 [47.5]	12 [55.3]	1 [5.3]	5 [60.1]	3 [63.5]
Number of best rank global score areas	0	7	9	10	8	13
1. Institutions rank	56	91	43	17	16	16
2. Human Capital & Research Rank	38	31	22	1	14	12
3. Infrastructure rank	48	32	27	10	14	25
4. Market sophistication rank	46	59	13	3	1	1
5. Business sophistication rank	49	31	20	1	9	2
6. Knowledge & Tech. Outputs rank	28	3	6	6	4	12
7. Creative outputs rank	n.a.	54	14	n.a.	23	14
Innovation input index rank [score]	47 [3.85]	41 [48.4]	25	2 [5.72]	5 [67.3]	2
Innovat. Output index rank [score]	29 [3.33]	21 [46.6]	9	1 [4.81]	9 [52.9]	4
Rising ranks 1–7 ∑		+25 Rks	+152 Rks		−18	−6

Source: Adapted from various parts of WIPO (2023), Cornell University et al. (2015), INSEAD (2009)

inputs. For instance, problematically, it is 118th in the world for environmental performance, 89th for quality of the regulatory environment, 88th for certain measures of schooling and tertiary education (all inputs), and 123rd for online creativity. Despite the anomalies, China's performance in innovation and knowledge has been exemplary, especially in the development of electronic vehicles, solar panels, lithium batteries, scientific research, and high-technology innovation. However, these developments are nowhere sufficient to generate absolute or even relative hegemony overall.

The US during 2008–2023, on the other hand, while declining from the overall top position of first to fifth in innovation and knowledge areas, has recently increased its ranking from fifth to third, as it improved its top ranking from 8 to 13 sub-areas. It now has the top spot in areas of (a) redundancy dismissal costs, (b) top 3 R&D investors, (c) top three university rankings, (d) venture capital values, (d) scale of domestic market, (e) cluster development (all inputs); plus (f) citable documents, (g) unicorn valuations, (h) software spending, (i) intellectual property (IP) receipts, (j) intangible asset intensity, (k) entertainment-media market penetration, and (l) generic top-level online domains (outputs). But currently, it has anomalies in pupil–teacher ratios in schools, graduates in S&E at university, FDI net inflows (inputs), quality-management-system outputs for consumers, and aspects of creative outputs. Overall, like most other mature economies, the US has settled into long-wave downswing conditions for some decades now; and while it long ago lost absolute hegemony, it still holds aspects of relative hegemony. China is at its heels, but it too has possibly settled into a lower trajectory of long waves than previously, but at a higher rate of growth than the US.

8.3.4 Households, Demography, and Rural–Urban Dynamics

A crucial part of the Chinese techno-institutional-geo-spatial CSD is the process of people being included in the production-distribution dynamics of state capitalism. One primary aspect is the movement of people from areas of underemployment to areas of active formation of employment, accumulation, and profitability. The movement of people from households in rural areas to those in town, urban, and city areas is crucial to this. China's population has risen from 550 m (1950) to over 1.4 b (2024) people. During the 1950s, they mostly lived in the countryside and towns. When the economy was transformed into a market economy with core elements of private property in the late 1970s, 1980s, and beyond, manufacturing enterprises were expanded in areas where they could develop economies of scale and scope, agglomeration, and networks of strategic alliances.[5]

During the 1980s to the 2010s, when long-wave upswing occurred, more than 300 m people moved from the countryside to towns, and from rural and township areas to cities and urban areas. Some were glad to move, others were forced off their land, and others still were cajoled into moving. In many cases, young adults moved households while leaving their parents behind, and often their children as well. Those who moved usually had fewer rights to resources such as childcare, housing, medicine, education, and pensions. Most of those who left areas of underemployment as surplus labor joined the productive sectors, especially of manufacturing, trade, and finance.

The process of creating markets has led to a reallocation of resources from rural to urban and town/city households and areas, which has stimulated productive industries at the expense of rural agriculture. This transformation of peasants into potential and then actual workers, according to Michael Francis et al. (2005), contributed substantially to the expansion of total factor productivity in the post-reform period. To free up resources, the communes were disbanded, state enterprises increasingly privatized (or with dual state-private ownership), workers' remuneration decisions gradually shifted to managers, property rights strengthened, urban infrastructure and education greatly improved, and migration rules very gradually modified. In addition, the government encouraged new economic zones, special tax incentives, joint ventures with foreign companies, and foreign direct investment.

[5]An analysis of the intellectual foundations of the rural to urban dynamics is provided by the Lewis-Fei-Ranis Model of development. However, as Fan Gao (2022) points out, this model has various assumptions which may not apply to this example of China. For instance, the notions of equilibrium and assumptions about the capital-labor ratio and the perfect nature of markets.

Sun (2019) proposes four stages in the Chinese migration of farmers from rural to urban households: "prohibition (1949–1983), permissiveness (1984–1991), liberalization (1992–2001), and facilitation (2002 onwards)." Along with the rising sophistication of the labor market and the slow easing of restrictions on the flow of people, there has been a tumultuous process of surplus labor moving to built-up areas with fewer household members. The process of Chinese capitalism creating a large class of waged workers and capitalists depends largely on this regional movement of people.

Currently, China seems to be in an advanced stage of development from stage II to stage III of Zelinsky's theory: "During Phase II, the early transitional society, a sharp rise of rural–urban migration took place due to the development of urbanization, which absorbed most of the rural labor force. This phase constitutes the peak of the countryside-to-town/city movement. A crucial source of growth has largely been exhausted as the process of rural–urban-city migration and settlement has long passed its zenith.

Phase IV, the later transition, is a stage of "declining fertility and decelerating rural–urban migration" (Sun 2019, 15). Table 8.4 provides a good indication of the crucial indicators of the rural–urban and peasant-worker changes, comparing China with the US.

The rate of growth of urban and city households in China during 2022 is the lowest over the past 60 years, gradually declining from 5.16% growth in 1980 to 1.65% in 2022. The scope for more growth in urban populations is limited, mainly due to the exhaustion of natural growth forces and partly due to the policy of improving conditions of rural populations, which has had limited success to date. This process of rural–urban transformation has been a crucial factor associated with productivity growth in China, including both capital and labor productivity, and since both labor productivity and total factor productivity (TFP) have been in decline especially over the past decade, while volatility has expanded (see Prasad 2023, 27), this shows the limits to Chinese growth into the future from this important source.

In comparison, US rural-to-urban transformation has also long since lost its growth potential, while the rate of growth of urban households in 2022 is the lowest over the past 40 years. The US growth and productivity performance have been anomalous for many decades. No change is likely to the rural-to-urban growth

Table 8.4 Rural to urban households-regions, China and USA, 1950–2022

	1960	1970	1980	1990	2000	2010	2020	2022
China population	667 m	818 m	981 m	1.14 b	1.26 b	1.34 b	1.41 b	1.41 b
China urban population (%$\sum$)	16.20	17.4	19.36	26.44	35.88	49.23	61.43	63.56
China urban growth population (%)	n.a.	2.03	5.16	4.31	3.69	3.26	2.08	1.65
US population	180 m	205 m	227 m	250 m	282 m	309 m	332 m	333 m
US urban population (%$\sum$)	70.00	73.60	73.74	75.30	79.06	80.77	82.66	83.08
US urban population growth (%)	n.a.	1.53	1.02	1.41	1.51	1.04	1.21	0.63

Source: Adapted from World Bank WDI (2024)

potential in the future, as with China. In conclusion, both Chinese and US rural-to-urban dynamics have seemingly lost their potential to generate growth in the future from this source. From a Chinese perspective, this is likely to inhibit long-wave and hegemonic rise into the future, although factors associated with other dimensions of the CSD may counter this to some degree.

8.3.5 Financial Institutions and Markets

A core part of China's growth model, especially in recent decades, has been its domestic market, which is (potentially) the largest in the world. As China's middle class expands and urbanization spreads, the growth of the domestic market creates enormous potential for growth and accumulation. The development of market capitalism in China has seen the process of promoting exchange relations in many areas of socioeconomic life. Some of the legal and constitutional changes include the creation of Special Economic Zones in the early 1980s, the incorporation of Hong Kong into China in 1993, and the 1999 amendment to the Constitution elevating the private sector to parity with the state. Commodity markets, for instance, have expanded tremendously over the past several decades.

A further indication of the degree to which market capitalism has been instituted in China, and how much capacity there is left to move in this direction, is given by the *Economic Freedom Index*, undertaken annually by the Heritage Institute. The Economic Freedom Index (EFI) has been drawn up annually for 127 nations according to the theoretical foundations inspired by Adam Smith, Milton Friedman, and Friedrich Hayek, associated with personal choice, voluntary exchange, open markets, and protection of private property. The index itself examines the size of government, the legal structure and security of property rights, access to sound money, freedom of exchange with foreigners, and regulation of credit, labor, and business. While this current book is not based on Friedman-Hayekian principles, this indicator is important for this specific aspect of CSD, since we are indeed dealing with core elements of capitalism (albeit state capitalism).

Table 8.5 provides a summary of key indicators of the EFI for China and the USA over recent decades.

The EFI illustrates five things relevant to the financial and market performance of China and the USA over the 1990s–2020s, from a Hayekian, Friedman, and neoliberal perspective. First, it shows that the USA is far ahead of China in economic freedom, from a financial/market capitalist point of view, especially for US property rights, plus investment, business, and financial freedom. The US historically has believed in market capitalism since its inauguration, whereas China has historically abhorred the excesses of market relations, and more recently has begun controlling business somewhat (again).

The second factor is that government integrity from a financial capitalist view is much more advanced in the US since US financial capitalists trust governments much more than capitalists do in China. This is understandable since the US

Table 8.5 Economic freedom index (EFI), 1995–2023, China and USA

Nation	Index year	∑EFI	Property rights	Govt integrity	Tax burden	Business freedom	Labor freedom	Monetary freedom	Trade freedom	Investment freedom	Financial freedom
China	2023	48.3	45.3	42	69.5	68.3	55.2	72.5	73.6	20	20
China	2020	59.5	60.9	46	70.4	76.8	64.4	71.1	72.4	20	20
China	2010	51	20	36	70.2	49.7	53.2	70.6	72.2	20	30
China	2000	56.4	30	35	70.4	55	n.a.	84	42.6	50	50
China	1995	52	30	30	70.6	55	n.a.	68.4	20	50	50
US	2023	70.6	94.7	73.4	75.4	83.8	76.3	78	75.4	85	80
US	2020	76.6	81.8	77.2	74.6	83.3	87.9	75.5	79.8	85	80
US	2010	78.0	85	73	67.5	91.3	94.8	78.1	86.9	75	70
US	2000	76.4	90	75	63.8	85	n.a.	86.3	78.4	70	70
US	1995	76.7	90	90	64.8	85	n.a.	83.8	78.4	70	70

Source: Adapted from Heritage Foundation (2023)

government, whatever its persuasion, believes in capitalism, whereas the Chinese government is nominally a communist government, although one advancing the cause of state capitalism (in practice).

The third point is that labor freedom is more advanced in the US than in China since the freedom to hire and sack workers (and dealing with wages and conditions in market-friendly terms) is more developed in the US. However, gaining employment in both nations utilizes social connections (social capital [USA] and *Guanxi* [China]) more than merit, despite the rhetoric (see DiTomaso and Bian 2018).

Fourth, some dimensions of freedom are similar in magnitude in both nations, especially relating to tax burden, monetary freedom, and trade freedom. This is so since both China and the US are relatively light in their tax take compared with Scandinavia, Britain, and other West European nations. Also, the US and China are much more concerned with money and trade independence than many nations in Europe, Asia, and Latin America. The trade freedom data for 2023 and 2020 (relative to 2010) show that the US has slipped majorly (about 11 points), whereas China has improved a little. The slight improvement for China is perhaps surprising since, especially in the past decade, both nations have been undergoing a massive trade war. Indeed, neoliberalism is, according to many, such as the *Economist,* out of fashion, and the new fashion is that of nationalism, protection, and industry policy, especially (re-)establishing hegemonic power in the case of China and the US (and regional hegemony in the case of Russia, India, NATO, and some other areas). Indeed, free marketeers and even (some) US/(many) UK liberals are skeptical of such inward-looking policies, in the belief that they will inhibit growth and development into the future for all nations that have joined the new club of "national-builders." It is an area where both countries are converging somewhat.

In like fashion, fifth, some of the figures have been regressing in recent years in the US and China, notably the general EFI index, as well as business freedom, and "labor freedom" (which has more to do with the freedom of capital). Probably these declines are part of the general movement against neoliberalism just discussed since both China and the US have been trying to tackle abuses of market power by addressing issues like inequality, monopoly power, and the need for more self-sufficiency (more recently).

China and the US have experienced greater financial risks in recent decades, especially in the Chinese property market, which has been in freefall, and in the US Congress, which is having problems with budgetary measures. While the US currently nominally has global financial dominance, although it has lost production and commercial dominance, it has been under heightened pressure at the financial level as well. Outside the Americas, the US dollar no longer has the financial clout it has historically experienced, as more global exchanges are made in other currencies (e.g., the Euro and Chinese Renminbi/Yuan). Its financial dominance is also deteriorating in the light of the Congressional conflicts over US Budgetary measures and the probability of defaults rising (declining integrity). Globally, the US/West's former control of global finance is moving toward a segmented system as new financial centers challenge US financial hegemony and enemies such as Russia and Iran develop new levers of financial flows (Economist 2024). China, on the other hand, is currently reevaluating its commitment to market relations, in the light of the increasing (contradictory) importance of "Xi Jinping thought" and greater emphasis on state enterprises (declining investment and financial freedom).

From a more general viewpoint, the US is a classic case, especially up to the time of the GFC, of finance-dominating industry, where relatively unproductive financial activities have been crowding out industrial accumulation, as finance has been structurally transferring from industrial to financial activities. The incentive to build productive stocks of investment has deteriorated in recent decades, while shareholder value and short-term valuation methods have increased financial risk and instability. Some lessons have been learned from the GFC and other crises, but the structural polycrises of US capitalism still operate. (See Chap. 9 below.)

Chinese finance has historically been under some degree of state control since its "coming out" during the late 1970s, but to some degree, China has allowed the financial system to "infect" industry and contribute to instability in more recent decades, ironically likely having been influenced by US financial capitalism. As Eswar Prasad (2023) rightly said of these anomalies:

> [Recently,] the [Chinese] government has … deal[t] with episodes of housing market and stock market volatility. The government has … [been] caught in a schizophrenic effort to strike a balance between maintaining confidence in the market and allowing the market to discipline itself, which has … heighten[ed] market turbulence. This on-off approach to intervention has sometimes injected a strong dose of uncertainty on[to] [an] already fragile investor sentiment and added to market volatility. … Another lesson to be taken from these episodes of volatility is … that market-oriented reforms can … add to volatility and generate more risks if they are not accompanied by broader reforms. China needs a better institutional framework—[such as] more transparency in policy-making, better corporate governance and accounting standards, and more operational independence for the central bank and regulatory authorities—to supplement its financial and other market-oriented reforms. … The government has … done little to improve corporate governance … or their accounting and auditing standards. The resulting opacity has contributed to large fluctuations in stock and bond markets, as investors have little information about the companies they are investing in, leading them to follow and exacerbate market swings.

8.3.6 Corporate Performance in the CSD: Accumulation and Profit

Here we analyze the political economy processes underlying China's corporate growth and development. We investigate the rate of profit, rate of surplus value, organic composition of capital, and unproductive activities. What strategy is in place to generate potential movement over the next 15 years? Figure 8.4a, b, below, summarizes these variables in the context of China's past few decades since reform started in 1978, compared with its rival, the USA.

We, first, compare the macro rate of profit (surplus divided by business assets) of corporations in China vis-à-vis the USA. The key trend for the Chinese macro rate of profit since the 1980s has been for rising rates from 1983 until the mid-1990s,

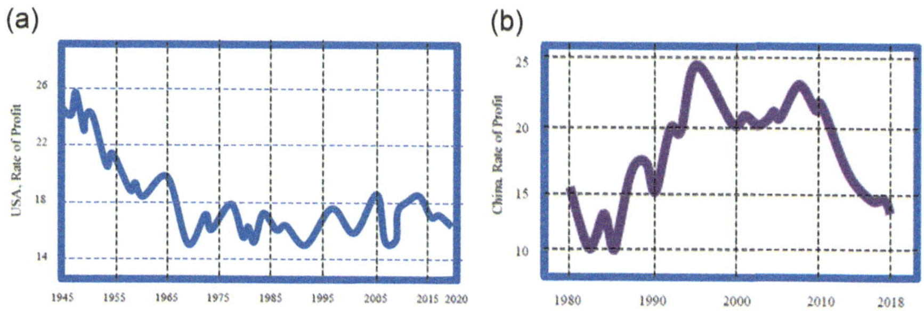

Fig. 8.4 (**a**) USA, macro rate of profit (ROP), 1946–2020, (Source: Adapted from Michael Roberts 2021.) (Note: RoP (π) is defined here as: $\pi = [s/(C + v)]$ as a percent, where s = surplus value, C = constant K, v = variable K. C = historical cost of fixed assets (FA). Similar trend to market cost of FA.) (**b**) China, rate of profit, 1980–2018. (Source: Adapted from Minqi Li, 2018, 84) (Note: Profit rate (π) is defined as the ratio of total domestic profit divided by business sector net stock of fixed capital (as percent)

with 1995 being the highest rate experienced of around 25%. Thereafter, diminishing profit rates were the norm, from 25% in 1995 to 20% in 2003, staying around those lower rates until 2011. Then another slide occurred with the ROP declining to 12.5% in 2018, and since then evidence shows a continuing decline. Hence, overall, a rise from 1983 to 1995, a decline from 1995 to 2003, and then another slide from 2010 to 2018 (likely continuing into later years). Rates in the 2010s are about what they were in the 1990s. This trend shows a clear long-wave pattern for profit rates. Longer movements of "up and down" motion are more noticeable than shorter cycles, notably in 1995–2018.[6]

The USA ROP pattern overall is quite similar, with a high but rapidly declining rate from the 1940s to the early 1960s, then a steep decline in the late-1960s, and since then low rates of profit until 2020. Since the late 1960s the dominant trend has been low but cyclical rates of profit, and a slight increase from the mid-1980s to 2006, followed by the GFC and again cyclically low rates. Overall, this illustrates rates of between 18 and 26% during 1945–1968 followed by rates of between 15% and18% between 1969 and 2020. The slightly higher rate from the 1980s–1990s to 2006 is due to a rising share of the surplus being redistributed to the financial system, and thereby away from productive investment in capital.

A similarity between profit rates in China and the USA is thus for relatively lower rates during the most recent decade (China) and many decades (USA). For China, these lower rates are during the 2010s (and likely especially so for the 2020s) and for the USA lower rates were prevalent during the 1970s–2010s. Both nations are currently undergoing profit anomalies with their respective corporations. These results are comparable to those cited by Marquetti et al. (2021, 124) who note a definite convergence of profit rates in China and the USA.

[6] See also the work on the US rate of profit by Tsoulfidis and Papageorgiou (2019, 437), which is very similar to that of Roberts (2021).

There are of course major differences in the rate of profit between and within sectors. Marquetti et al. (2021) compare Chinese and US sectoral rates of profit (net income) over 2007–2014. The main sector from both nations with the highest *long-term rate* of profit (high profit and low standard deviation) is manufacturing, typically including pharmaceuticals, medical, and chemical areas; with computing, electronic, and optical areas faring well in China, and transport equipment and food-beverages-tobacco in the USA; with information and communication areas performing well in both nations. The areas with the most volatility (and often high profits) include mining and quarrying (MaQ) plus to some degree agriculture, forestry, and fishing (in the US), and MaQ in China. The lowest rates of profit for both nations were typically in finance and insurance, and for the US, additionally, real estate and professional, scientific, and technical areas in the years examined.

These Chinese mean ROP trends do not sit well for Chinese potential hegemonic power relative to the USA in the future. We provide more details about this anomaly in the next section, where we scrutinize the contradictions inhibiting long-wave upswing and rising hegemonic dominance for the Chinese political economy.

As to what factors caused lower rates of profit in both nations, there are specific factors at play, including rising unproductive activities (especially services), increasing real wages in China, and expanding global and local competition. The rising level of services especially relates to greater funds being allocated to financial sectors (rather than real investment) and state activities. Rising real wages in China are counterposed to the declining real wages in the US (until recently). The heightened global (especially for US and China) and local (especially for China) competition corresponds to firms adopting new technology earlier, thus raising depreciation and associated costs.

Much of the literature documents a greater trend toward monopoly in the US in recent decades. This is well illustrated vis-à-vis the major technology and media companies, such as the "Big 6" high-technology companies, Alphabet, Meta, Alpha, Amazon, Microsoft, Nvidia, and the "Big 6" media companies, Viacom, Disney, Time-Warner, CBS, NBC, and Newscorp. However, this way of looking at the problem ignores the many small-to-medium businesses, including numerous start-ups, and more seriously also global competition in relation to China, India, the EU, South Korea, the West, and so on. Within specific nations such as China, there is also a major level of competition, not only in general but also in high-technology sectors such as electric vehicles and solar panels, for instance.

To my knowledge, no one has adequately analyzed competition within this wider context (global, regional), even though it is discussed incessantly in the media. Briefly, it can be explained as follows. The rising organic composition of capital (OCC) is an important part of any explanation of declining profit rates in both China and the USA, a factor long ago emphasized by Holz (2005) for China and Gilman (1958) for the US (plus of course Mandel). In light of the crises of capitalism in the 1970s, where wage pressures played a key role, the organic composition of capital tended to lay low (papers concentrated on the rate of surplus value, and rising real wages). But more recently this trend has changed, as shown by the work of Jones (2021) and Herrera and Long (2017). Herrera and Long (2017, 79) demonstrated a distinct rising trend in the Chinese OCC from 1952 to 2014, and cyclical changes in OCC over this time. Jones (2017) studies the rate of profit in the US and tentatively cites the rising OCC as a core explanation for this trend.

When explaining the declining rate of profit for China during 1978–2002, Holz (2005) cited the importance of the declining rate of exploitation and the rising organic composition.[7] Knight and Li (2005) point out that during the period of central planning in China, state-owned enterprises were "highly profitable" since they employed a price-scissors policy of "keeping industrial prices high and agricultural prices low to finance industrialization" (p. 206). But during the period of reform, 1978 onward, greater competition reduced margins and cut profit rates for both state and private firms. The profit rate was reduced through the incessant expansion of capitalist production, especially the continual investment and replacement of labor by capital in the ongoing process of global competition. The higher capital/labor ratio translated into a higher organic composition of capital, which reduced the rate of profit (Robinson 1978).

As competition continues and Chinese products penetrate the global market, the ever-replacement of old technology with newer methods and processes, in an environment of greater competition (a greater number of private and overseas firms), results in an expansion of the organic composition of capital as the cost of capital has not declined. This led to a relative escalation in depreciation costs in GDP. The rate of exploitation has also declined as real wages (variable capitals) have expanded. These two main changes led to a decline in the rate of profit, although they also changed in a short-cycle fashion. The expansion of depreciation costs is an underplayed trend in the Chinese and US economies and brings home the importance of the General Law of Capitalist Production associated with capital-using technology (Marx 1867; the "Marx effect").

The reason firms introduce new technology when the rate of profit declines (eventually) is that otherwise they would go out of business, and at least in the short term, there is a transfer of surplus from the inefficient firms and sectors to the more efficient, which justifies their innovative actions. As Emma Xiaoqin Fan and Jesus Felipe (2005, 27) argue:

> As individual entrepreneurs race to adopt more profitable technologies there is a general increase in labor productivity, which eventually will lead to increases in real wages. If the wage increases proportionally to labor productivity, so that the labor share remains approximately constant, and technical change is Marx-biased, the profit rate will fall. To understand how this happens, it is important to understand the difference between how each individual entrepreneur behaves and what happens at the level of the whole economy. …

They go on to explain the paradox:

---

[7] There are several ways of examining the composition of capital, including the organic composition, the technical composition, and the value composition of capital. For a discussion of these various versions, see Saad-Filho (1993) and Paul Zarembka (2020, ch 8). See also Robert Pauls (2022, 286) on the value composition of capital vis-à-vis the rate of profit for China during 1995–2015.

> Indeed, once a new, lower cost method becomes feasible, the investment picture changes. The first few firms to adopt the new method are in a position to lower their selling prices, undersell their competitors and expand their own shares of the market[.] … The average rate of profit declines due to a fallacy of composition, that is, actions that appear advantageous to individual firms … are not always advantageous when all firms try and pursue them. …

This complex scenario does pose critical potential limits and contradictions for Chinese industrialization, albeit one which has already befallen the advanced capitalist nations. China's industrialization is based on capital-using changes in production leading to higher productivity and rising real wages. But the other side of the coin is that the high rate of accumulation results in an escalation in the depreciation rate. The higher rate of depreciation is due to competition necessitating continual changes in technique and product (Carchedi 2015).

8.3.7 Climate Change, Long Waves, and Hegemony

Currently, China has the highest *aggregate* annual contributions to global greenhouse gas emissions, at 14.5 $GtCO_2e$, which have been escalating, with minor cyclical changes, for many decades. The gap between China's emissions and the emissions of the nearest major economy, Brazil, has been getting wider since 2004. China's per capita emissions have also been escalating, while most other major nations' per capita emissions have been declining or moderating; China's emissions per capita are the third highest in the world, after the USA and Russia. In both cases, China's emissions are a grave problem and need to be moderated majorly for any successful global decline in GHG emissions to below 1.5 °C temperatures (compared with preindustrial levels) (UNEP 2023, 7). Many analysts have now concluded that "1.5°C" is now not practicable as an upper limit given the lack of concerted action around the world; we are already at a global average increase of 1.5°C (i.e., 1.45°C) during 2023.

China's climate change dynamics are crucial not only for future global sustainability, mitigation, and adaptation but also for China's long waves and hegemonic power into the future. Regarding long waves of growth, the move from the Chinese upswing into the 1980s–2010s to a relative downswing in the 2020s would normally be expected to have reduced GHGs majorly (due to reduced GDP growth per capita), yet (as just mentioned) their emissions have continued to grow. And for China's hegemonic power to grow, they will not only need to reduce their emissions majorly to solve, to some degree, this ecological problem at the national level, but also to provide (moral) leadership at the global governance level. At both levels, on balance, there are disappointing results for China.

But there is another level of consideration vis-à-vis long waves, which relates to climate change long waves, considered at the global level in Chap. 4, above, and in relation to the Dutch (Chap. 5), Britain (Chap. 6), and the USA (Chap. 7). Put simply, it has to do with China moving from upswing of GHG emissions to downswing

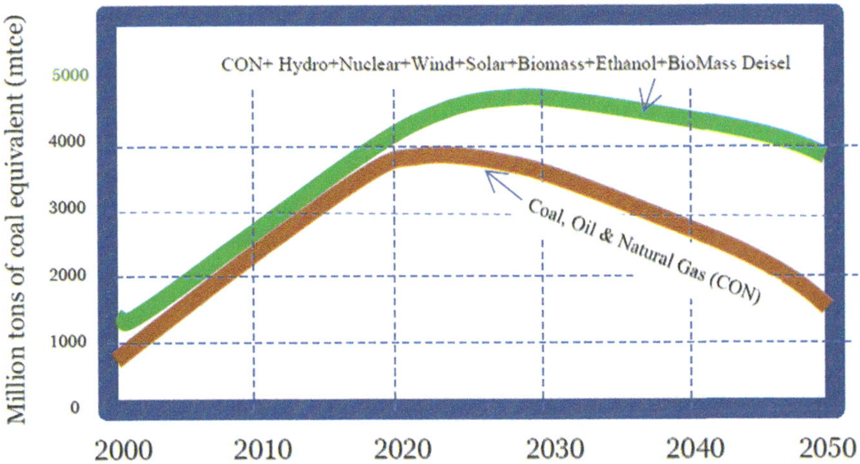

Fig. 8.5 Past and future (optimistic) long wave in coal-oil-gas-renewables, etc.: Core energy demand transition scenarios, China, 2000–2050. Millions of tons of coal equivalent (mtce) (Source: Adapted from UNCTAD 2023, 29)

of GHG emissions, which collectively would represent a potentially full GHG long wave (of upswing and downswing), as shown in Fig. 8.5.

This shows a possible optimistic policy mitigation and adaptation strategy whereby past energy dominance by coal, oil, and natural gas (CON, red line), compared with CON plus renewables (green line), during 2000–2020, may undergo a radical transformation from 2020 to 2050, resulting in a cumulative (combined) rapid escalation in solar, wind, biomass, ethanol, bio-diesel, hydro and nuclear energy use (green line) consistent with major reductions in GHGs. If China can generate a real long-wave downswing in the use of coal, oil, and natural gas by 2050 whereby these GHG emitters constitute less than 2000 million tons of coal equivalent (mtce), while CON plus renewables constitute slightly less than 4000 mtce, this would be a major achievement for the national and global ecologies, economies and polities.

It is well known and researched that climate change is causing escalating conflicts throughout the world in terms of more intense famines, droughts, floods, heatwaves, rising waterways, cyclones, and hurricanes (Schaar 2018). This ecological crisis tends to generate greater conflict over resources, leading to more regular civil wars, tribal uprisings, competition for land, faltering confidence in institutions, and geo-political unrest domestically and globally (analogous somewhat to the Little Ice Age during the 1600s; see chaps. 4–5). It also leads to great species extinction and declining bioavailability through more intense habitat destruction, unavailability of food stocks, and competition within and between species. In a circular and cumulative change (CCC) process, these multiple interactive impacts of climate change correspond to cascading tipping points of path dependence, multiplier, and accelerator-magnified consequences.

And in like fashion, the greater conflicts, competition, deaths, declining trust, and the like have a reciprocal magnified impact on climate change. Wars and conflicts tend to increase GHGs, reduce flora and fauna, dislocate global agreements and regional accords on climate change, and reduce resources for sustainability projects (Mayoral 2012, SIDA 2018, Scheffran et al. 2023). This raises the question of the empirical research on hegemonies indicating the stylized fact that hegemonies arise out of important wars and conflicts, which have potential links to the current war in Ukraine, escalating global spending on armaments and military in obvious preparation for global conflict, and the question of rising conflict in the Asia-Pacific and increasing likelihood of war over Taiwan (see Ruiz Estrada 2023). We scrutinize this question in the next two chapters (chaps. 9 and especially 10).

Regarding China's push toward possible hegemony, their responses to the climate crisis are important for several reasons. First, as the major emitter, they have a responsibility to reduce the impacts of CC on climate and conflicts. Second, as a potential hegemon, they have leadership qualities to consider, as one component of the package required for dominance. In this context, we again consider China vis-à-vis the USA on this score, relative to the Climate Change Performance Index (CCPI). Figure 8.6 compares both nations on the CCPI, first relating to GHG emissions and the Paris Commitment relative to 1.5 °C.

This Figure shows both China and the USA having per capita GHG emissions (blue lines) which are consistently deviating above (after 2006 for China) their Paris Commitments (black/dashed line). The orange area above the dashed line is their level of emissions above the Paris Commitments. Regarding the CCPI, no country, including either China or the USA, is regarded as making enough progress to prevent dangerous climate change, and indeed, as shown elsewhere, the world is currently on track to reach more than 2.5°C from current commitments by 2100 (compared with preindustrial levels). China and the USA are far worse than average.

For the CCPI, of the notionally 67 nations, China in 2024 came 51st (score of 45.56) for the second year in a row, which is defined as "very low" in terms of their commitment to GHG emission reductions. It has one of the largest oil and gas reserves in the world and few plans to scale back exploitation of them anytime soon. On the other hand, it has a good track record on renewables, is the largest supplier of electric vehicles and solar heaters, and has some good policies for sustainability. The USA is worse, with a CCPI of 42.79, being notionally the 57th ("worst") nation (down five pegs since 2023) for climate performance. It has a very bad score (very

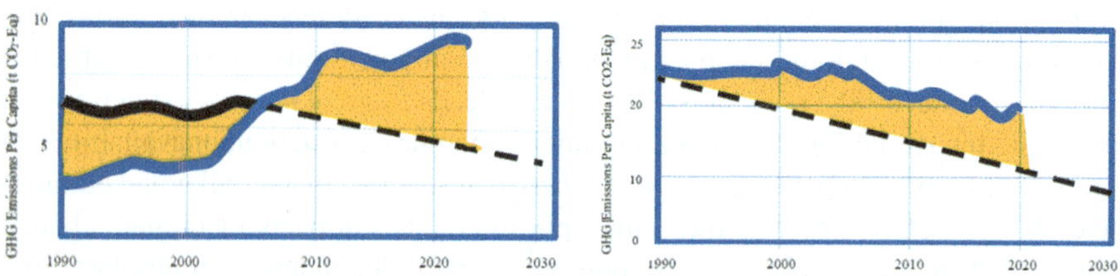

Fig. 8.6 Greenhouse Gas (GHG) emissions and Paris Commitment, China (LHS) and USA (RHS), 1990–2030. (Source: Adapted from Germanwatch 2024)

high) on GHG emissions, renewables, and energy use. However, due to the Inflation Reduction Act, the US is seen as improving on policy. Overall, neither is serious about their climate change commitments. Ironically, one reason for this is that US economic performance has been dismal over several decades and declining over the past decade and a half (China, recently), which puts added pressure on resource exploitation and includes an extra policy objective that is not being met, even though lower GDP per capita growth typically reduces emissions.

8.4 Chinese Contradictions: Long Waves, Hegemony and Climate Change Prospects

Thus far, this chapter has outlined the key elements of the Chinese socioeconomic circuits and pathways (CSD) underlying long-term performance and potential hegemony. We showed how China underwent long-wave upswing during the 1980s–2010s, and how long-wave relative downswing has possibly started to become ingrained in the circuit into the 2020s. (We also tentatively illustrated Kuznets swings, subject to further research in the future.) This implies the Chinese established a successful CSD during the 1980s–2010s, which was based on general Asian dynamics and specific Chinese characteristics of state capitalism, as a prelude to potential Chinese (and Asian?) hegemony into the future. We value the current Chinese global power as an "ascendant power."

Six techno-institutional elements of the Chinese CSD were outlined as contributing to long-wave upswing and potential hegemony, the current long-wave downswing (relatively speaking), and ascendant hegemony. They all have potential and actual positive and negative elements, i.e., contradictions, which, on balance, cumulatively amount to a considerable barrier to further long-wave upswing and hegemonic power. In this section, we scrutinize these contradictions and how they may well inhibit the wave upswing, absolute hegemony, and climate change resolution into the future.

The first contradiction concerns the Chinese place in the global political economy. While Chinese structural dynamics generate rising power, such power is contentious and conflictual. Siding with Russia in the invasion of Ukraine, threatening to invade Taiwan, taking over Hong Kong, harassing neighbors in the Asia-Pacific region, building artificial bases on human-made (artificial) islands in the Pacific, engaging in trade wars with the US and other parties, refusing to offer debt relief for southern regions, and a host of other actions have led others to fear Chinese power and perceive it as an untrustworthy partner in the world political economy. On balance, this generates uncertainty, transaction costs, and deteriorating relations with numerous parties in the world economy. In the future, these social, political, and economic costs may well heighten.

The second contradiction applies to state capitalism. Especially since 2012, when Xi Jinping's tenure was confirmed as General Secretary of the CCP, and especially since 2022, when his tenure became secure for "life," state capitalism has lost much of its vitality, adaptability, and evolvability toward regional and global norms. Like many other autocratic rulers, Xi has inculcated into state capitalism an extreme nationalist bent, being more concerned with internal stability, external protectionism, controlling business interests, and reducing the scope of civil society. Some previous leaders of the CCP promoted a more liberal-democratic *potential* in state-civil institutions, which some felt would evolve into a truly participatory series of institutions into the 2010s and 2020s. On balance, current trends have emasculated these potential changes, leading to lower socioeconomic performance, greater social control of its people, and reducing the potential legitimacy of Chinese state capitalism. In this context, it must be remembered that, historically, a core philosophy and policy of hegemonic nations has been liberalism in general and specifically free trade at least notionally. Could this rule exclude China as a potential hegemon, or should we change such rules and include an oligarchy as a caveat?

The third contradiction concerns the Chinese innovation system (technology style). China has made major strides, especially in developing innovative *output* systems, yet its innovative *input* systems are lagging. At present, China is 12th while the US is third in the Global Innovation Index, but China's output index at 9th (US is 4th), is well ahead of its input index at 25th (US is 2nd). China is especially anomalous in the input areas of institutions, infrastructure, human capital, and business sophistication. The US has been engaging in advanced capitalist development for over two hundred years, while China has been involved in capitalist development for less than 50 years. In short, the Chinese government is less committed to business interests, infrastructure is heavily indebted and of dubious business acumen, human capital is subject to control and direction, while companies and contract laws have irregularities. Many of these anomalies are likely to continue or get worse in the future.

The fourth contradiction concerns rural–urban relations. Over the past 4–5 decades, around 300 m people have moved their households (or parts of them) from the countryside to the towns, cities, and urban areas of China. This was one of the key dynamics propelling growth and accumulation through rising labor productivity, agglomeration, and reduced underemployment of resources. It generated a major endogenous social movement and a source of social dislocation as these migrants were subject to discrimination and separation from family and community, with transliteration of the urban landscape. It was, however, a core geo-economic fulcrum around which Chinese growth was based since the 1980s. But its rate of growth has come to a standstill at a level not seen since the 1970s. Hence, this dynamic motion has ceased to contribute majorly to socioeconomic performance, and a critical element of the growth model has effectively been nullified (despite recent efforts to revive it).

The fifth contradiction concerns finance, property, and markets. A major part of the growth strategy of the CCP historically was to establish private property laws and protections, sell off, and modernize many state enterprises, develop joint ventures between state and private companies, institute effective banks and stock markets, and generally support businesses nationally and overseas. However, this movement has reversed somewhat as the state seeks more control over the business, market relations have stalled, and the CCP seeks quality over quantity, which is anomalous vis-à-vis the trend to speculative bubbles and property crashes. The Chinese debt deflation and highest levels of uncertainty since the Cultural Revolution (SLFed 2024), in light of the property crash, poses the greatest threat to performance in several decades. In consequence, the state seeks to moderate business power as a way of generating more control over economic affairs with a turn to quality over quantity. This is potentially a good trend but is likely to exacerbate contradictory movements between state and business, at least in the transition period.

The sixth contradiction involves declining corporate dynamism as the rate of profit has declined over recent decades. A coevolutionary path has been created of lower profit generating lower growth per capita (supply side) and lower consumption creating low profit (demand side). A core part of this process is competition necessitating general adoption of newer technology, or otherwise being beaten by competitors, and meanwhile, the new technology increases the organic composition of capital (e.g., greater depreciation), and reduces the rate of profit in general. The lower profit rate leads to low growth per capita while the deteriorating consumption share reduces the rate of profit through bidirectional causality.

The seventh contradiction concerns ecology, resources, and climate change. We saw above how the high rate of GHG emissions and few effective means of remission negatively impact both future CSD effectiveness and hegemonic moral leadership on mitigation and adaptation. Being the highest emitter of GHGs in absolute terms and the third highest emitter per capita, and rising, places major responsibilities on their shoulders if they are to solve these two anomalies. China cannot move forward without an effective growth-sustainability accord and a forward-looking plan for the world if it hopes to ascend to the top position in the hegemony stakes.

There are several other core contradictions, including an aging population, greater inequality, unemployment, especially for graduates, but also others, and limited social welfare safety nets. In a sense, these contradictions are closely related as being all imbued with social security implications. Being able to solve these problems will help immensely in inculcating the population of China to support the regime despite the recent trend toward greater autocracy and lower consumption. Dealing effectively with issues of pensions, social equity, youth employment, general social safety nets, and population issues in the demand equation will undoubtedly assist their movement to long-wave upswings, hegemonic power, and climate change resolution, and an inability to solve these problems will inhibit these developments.

We now summarize the potential for Chinese long-wave and hegemonic performance over successive future decades in the light of discussions in this chapter so far, and likely developments into the future. Table 8.6 looks at past growth and likely future growth (not per capita), following explanations of the reasons behind the analysis.

Based on the tendency to converge with the US, it is likely that the Chinese pattern of growth will continue in the current trajectory of declining performance, due to the contradictions within and between the techno-institutional-climate fabric

Table 8.6 Past and projected future Chinese growth and its contributions

Years	Actual/Projected GDP growth %	K contribution	L contribution	HC contribution	TFP contribution
2001–2005	9.8	5.2	0.9	0.3	3.9
2006–2010	11.3	5.6	0.3	0.1	4.3
2011–2015	7.9	4.8	−0.1	0.6	2.9
2016–2020	6.6	5.1	−0.1	0.5	1.3
2021–2025	5.3	3.4	−0.2	0.5	1.7
2026–2030	3.5	2.1	−0.5	0.4	1.5
2031–2035	2.7	1.5	−0.5	0.6	1.1
2036–2040	2.0	1.2	−0.4	0.2	1.0

Source: Adapted from parts of Peschel and Liu (2022, 45)

within the socioeconomic circuit (in a cyclical or long swing fashion). To date, this has manifested itself in a major cut to growth from the highs of the 2000s–2010s to much lower rates during the 2020s. This will likely follow through to a relatively long-wave downswing during the 2020s–2030s and possibly beyond. The contribution of growth to rising hegemony will likely decline as the contributions of capital (C), labor (L), human capital (HC), and total factor productivity (TFP) fall toward single digits (K, HC, TFP) and for some (L) negative rates of growth into the 2020s–2030s (possibly with deflation). Chinese long waves during the 1920s–2030s will likely thus exhibit major parallels to the US and Europe as shown during the 1980s–2020s. There is little doubt that China has a productive technology style, especially in high-technology areas, AI, robotics, electric vehicles, solar systems, and science and engineering research and development. Indeed, much of the West earlier evolved a highly efficient technological apparatus (ICT), especially since the 1990s, and more recently with AI. But the failure of these innovations to raise productivity, and to develop an effective and matching set of economic, social, and political institutions, seems to be afflicting all areas as we move into the second quarter of the twenty-first century.

8.5 Comparative Hegemony Issues: China, Dutch, British, and USA

In this light, we comparatively examine the record of hegemony for Dutch, British, US, and potentially Chinese cases. Table 8.7 provides a summarized and qualitative measure of the phases of hegemonic power, based on this chapter (for China) and chapters 5 (Dutch case), 6 (British), and 7 (USA).

This Table illustrates that "rising influence" was hypothesized to be characteristic of Dutch power during 1500–1540, British power 1650–1770, US power 1820–1880, and China 1970–2010. Ascending power was held by the Dutch in 1540–1580, British 1770–1820, US 1890–1945, and China 2010 onward. Absolute

Table 8.7 Hypothesized phases of (Potential) hegemonic power, 1500–2020s, Netherlands, Britain, US, and China

	Rising influence (3–4)	Ascending power (5–6)	Absolute hegemonic power (7–10)	Relative hegemonic power (5–6) (Decline)	Major decline in hegemonic power (4–5)	Little or no hegemonic power (3–4)
Dutch	1500–1540	1540–1580	1580–1650	1650–1700	1700–1760	1760 onward
British	1650–1770	1770–1820	1820–1890	1890–1920	1920–1940	1990 onward
US	1820–1880	1890–1945	1945–1975	1975–2035	2035–2055?	2055 Onward?
China	1970–2010	2010–Onward	?	?	?	?

Table 8.8 Hypothesized US hegemonic power index (HPI): (Out of 10)

	1850	1900	1930	1945	1960	1975	2005	2024
1. Production	3	5	6	9	9	8	7	6
2. Commercial	2	4	5	8	10	8	7	6
3. Financial	2	3	5	7	9	10	8	7
4. Military	2	4	6	9	8	6	5	5
5. Cultural	2	4	6	8	10	9	8	7
6. General	2–3	4–5	5–6	8–9	9–10	7–8	6–7	5–6

hegemony was hypothesized to be held by the Dutch during 1580–1650, British 1820–1890, US 1945–1975, and China not yet (or ever?). Relative (declining) hegemonic power was held by the Dutch during the 1650–1700, British 1890–1920, and US 1975–2035. A major decline in hegemonic power was characterized by the Dutch during the 1700–1760, British 1920–1940, and US 2035–2055? Little or no hegemonic power was held by the Dutch 1760 onward, and the British 1990 onward.

Detailing the six dimensions of hegemonic power is only possible from more recent times, mainly during the era of US rising hegemony and its decline, when most of the works about hegemony were written. Hence, China can be included to some degree in these metrics. See Table 8.8 (US) and Table 8.9 (China) for the hypothesized results.

The most important hypothetical comparative results from these two Tables are fourfold. The first is that in 1960 while the US had absolute hegemonic power, which it acquired especially during the 1940s, China in 1960 had virtually no international power. Chinese power during 2024 was quite comparable to US power in 1900. The second result is that during 2024 the degree of comparative general *relative* hegemonic power in the US is still significantly higher than in China, especially in areas of culture and finance. China is currently slightly behind the US in production dominance. Third, the US is currently a relatively hegemonic power, while China is the main ascendant hegemonic power, and both are significantly distant from absolute hegemony. And fourth, China by 2040 could be either achieving

Table 8.9 Chinese hegemonic power index (HPI): 6 Aspects (Out of 10)

	1960	1980	2000	2024	(a) 2040?	*or* (b) 2040?
1. Production	1	2	3	5	8?	7?
2. Commercial	0	1	3	5	8?	6?
3. Financial	0	0	2	3	7?	5?
4. Military	1	2	3	5	9?	7?
5. Cultural	1	2	3	4	6?	6?
6. General	1	2	4	4–5	7.5–8.0?	6?

absolute hegemonic power ("a") or having declined in relative hegemonic power since 2025 ("b").

A *crucial conclusion* is that the British and US experienced *hegemonic power* while also undergoing a crucial period of *very long wave upswing*. British and US hegemony and long-wave upswings also stimulated long-wave upswings in numerous other nations and areas. Also, the Dutch achieved significant (but not *very*) long-wave upswings just before their development of hegemonic power (or about the same time).

Another conclusion is that the Chinese long wave upswing, during the 1980s–2010s was not achieved concurrently with Chinese absolute or relative hegemonic dominance and was not achieved on the back of hegemonic power or long wave upswing of any other power(s) (except for East and South Asia in general?). Long wave upswing was achieved in many, especially Asian economies during the 1980s–2020s (circa), which was part of the general process of rising Asian power and challenges to previous Western dominance. This is the crucial stylized fact associated with rising Chinese (and Asian) power and long-wave upswings.

It is not so unusual, however, for nations and areas to experience major long-wave upswings without hegemonic dominance. For instance, many nations underwent long-wave upswings during the period of British hegemony, and during US hegemony (see chap. 11, below), followed thereafter by downswings. This is under the general umbrella of hegemonic powers stimulating other nations to undergo long-wave upswings.

Crucially, soon after one hegemonic power declines, it is usual for another, rising power to undergo long-wave upswing (or at least good short-term performance), usually a power that will eventually become the new hegemon. This was the (weak) case for British performance soon after Dutch hegemony (during the 1660s), US performance immediately after cessation of British hegemony (during the 1880s–1910s), and Chinese performance immediately after US hegemony (1980s–2010s). But this could be theorized as being part of the associated process of Western (and other) nations drawing on combined *Western hegemonic processes* during these times, plus the *longue duree* of rising Asian power upon declining Western power currently.

The above qualitative results for Dutch, British, and US hegemony ascendency and decline are broadly comparable to the empirical results obtained by Kwon (2011), who analyzed three main nations, including the Dutch, the British, and the Americans. Kwon (see chaps. 5, 6, and 7) promotes interactive scholarly

Table 8.10 Periods of hegemony, long waves, and wars: Dutch, British, and US, possibly China 1570–2030[a]

	1. Dutch	2. British	3. US	4. Possibly China
Absolute hegemony	1580–1650	1820–1880	1945–1975	2030s–2040s?[b]
Relative hegemony	1650–1700	1880–1914	1975–2030s?	2050s–2070s?
1st long wave(s)	1570–1589	1820–1870	1940–1975	1980s–2020s?
2nd long wave	1600–1619			2030s–2040s??
War(s) of ascendency	1570–1590	1790–1815	[1914–1918] 1939–1945	2020s? Over Taiwan (& Ukraine)?
War(s) of descending Hegemony	End of 30-years war (1648) (& 80-years war)	Scramble for Africa (1880s➔)	Vietnam War End (1975)	??

[a]In this context, papers that enhanced our understanding of Chinese power vis-à-vis the US include those by Rojo (2022) and Santibañes (2009)
[b]Seymour Itzkoff (2003) predicts that the Chinese will attain hegemonic power by the middle of the twenty-first century (2045–2055). As he says: "China, considering its geopolitical situation, its massive control over … water resources, and relatively high intelligence and educability of its population will emerge as the dominant world power by the middle of the twenty-first Century." He goes on to say that "The author suggests that its power will create a new Asian hegemonic association of states. … Only internal instability can prevent it from attaining world dominance of the late twenty-first century" (p. 487)

convergence between world-systems analysis (e.g., Wallerstein and Chase-Dunn) and political science work (e.g., Modelski) on the relationship between hegemony (global "leadership"), long waves, and wars. But our results are somewhat closer still to that of Ray Dalio (2023), see chap. 7, who used a multiple-factor approach to estimating the leadership index for Dutch, British, US, and Chinese capitalisms during their eras of actual or potential hegemony (but Dalio ignored rising non-state terrorist power, and over-reached Dutch hegemony and Chinese power [in the past and currently]). Our overall results are summarized in Table 8.10.

We could now state several rules of hegemony, long waves, and climate change (HegLWCC) based on established stylized facts. They may or may not apply to the future (e.g., to China).

First HegLWCC Rule or Stylized Fact: Hegemons have war(s) of ascendency prior to hegemony. (I doubt the general existence of wars of consolidation during hegemony) This could apply to the Dutch Revolt (1570s–1580s), British success in the Napoleonic Wars (1815), and US success in the Second World War (1939–1945). Applied to China, they would need to win a war of ascendency over Taiwan (and/or Ukraine?). (Otherwise, we may have to reformulate this rule.)

Second HegLWCC Rule or Stylized Fact: Hegemons tend to have wars of descending hegemony. These may include the end of the 80-years war in 1648 (for the Dutch, the Treaty of Westphalia), the Scramble for Africa (for the British), and the Vietnam War (for the US). This is still a tentative hypothesis to be confirmed or otherwise by further research, and applied, where relevant to China.

Third HegLWCC Rule or Stylized Fact: Hegemons often have one very long wave upswing during periods of hegemony, e.g., British 1820–1860; US 1940s–1960s and long upswing near borderline (US 1970s–1980s); and sometimes they have multiple reasonable or modest long waves before hegemony and partially during hegemony, e.g., the Dutch during 1570s–1589. 1600–1619). Linked to China, sometime in the (near) future, China would need to have another long wave upswing broadly linked to their hegemonic status (were they to be hegemonic).

Fourth HegLWCC Rule or Stylized Fact: Hegemons tend to be liberal democracies advocating (a) free trade [imperialism], (b) parliamentary electoral institutions, and (c) a good degree of civil society. This applied to the Dutch, British, and US situations. China currently has none of these characteristics.

Fifth HegLWCC Rule or Stylized Fact: Immediately following a period of *absolute* hegemony, the power most likely to be the next hegemon tends to have modestly or good waves (upswings) during periods of *relative* hegemony for the "original" power. This applies to the British after Dutch hegemony (1660s); the Americans after British hegemony (1880s–1910s); and the Chinese after US hegemony (1980s–2010s).

Sixth HegLWCC Rule or Stylized Fact: Before and during hegemonic periods with long wave (upswings) and climate change dynamics, the socioeconomic circuit (CSD) is required to be operating effectively through durable structures of eco-spatial, institutional, and technological capabilities. Were China to be the next hegemon it would need to have a renovated CSD in the future, especially to bring its technology style into line with the economic, political, and social institutions (EPS).

Seventh HegLWCC Rule or Stylized Fact: In between periods of hegemony there tend to be long periods characterized by (many more) structural polycrises, such as various depressions, major financial crises, major wars, unstable short-wave ups and downs, rebellions and revolutions, very poor performance, climate crises, for the previous hegemonic power and many others. This applies potentially to the 1700s after Dutch hegemony; and also applies to the period from 1914 to 1945 after British hegemony; and especially the 1980s–2020s after US hegemony. (We investigate briefly whether it applied to the post-Dutch and post-British situation in the early stages of chap. 9, below; most of chap. 9 studies the polycrises of the 1980s–2020s.) (It obviously does not yet apply to China.)

Eighth HegLWCC Rule or Stylized Fact: Prior to and during periods of hegemony and long-wave upswings, alliances between various groups of heterogeneous agents and classes tend to emerge that lead to relatively successful periods of coordination, cooperation, agreements, interactions, and strategic processes that promote the relatively stable development of the CSD for a time. This applied to the Dutch vis-à-vis alliances between merchants, local and federal state bureaucrats, and capitalist entrepreneurs; the British in relation to business classes and landlords; and the US for large businesses, state-political elements, and unionized workers. (This does not yet apply to China.)

Ninth HegLWCC Rule or Stylized Fact: During hegemonic periods, there are structural contradictions within the eco-spatial, technological, and institutional CSD of the hegemonic power, which tend to manifest themselves and which lead to the dissolution of hegemony (and long wave upswings) through time. All the major dynamic-structural spheres of CSD tend to undergo these contradictions, vis-à-vis households, businesses, states, the world economy, and eco-geo-spatial relations.[8] (This does not yet relate to China in total.)

Tenth HegLWCC Rule or Stylized Fact: Normally, one would expect rising global temperatures during the height of long wave upswings and hegemonic powers, but the empirical material seems to mostly fit the opposite trend due to certain counter-tendencies to this trend. Also, normally one would expect major global and regional climate crises (polycrises) during global long-wave upswings, but these have mostly been activated during global long-wave downswings (1930s; 2000s–2020s).

Eleventh HegLWCC Rule or Stylized Fact: The world at present is dichotomizing between two forces: autocracy and liberal democracy. The main autocratic forces include Russia, Iran, China, Venezuela, North Korea, and several others, and the main liberal-democratic forces include the EU, Britain, USA, Japan, Taiwan, Australia, New Zealand, and several others. In the light of the Ukrainian war, in particular, the two camps are increasingly trading internally rather than with the other camp. Within nations, there are also the dual forces of autocracy versus liberal forces (e.g., *within* USA, Poland, Hungary, Italy, and so forth).

Tensions are building from the Ukrainian war, and further tensions are developing from conflicts over Taiwan and other actions by China and the USA, especially. Nations are increasing their military spending majorly from these two conflicts. It is widely believed that a major conflict will arise from the Taiwan situation; in fact, it is virtually inevitable since China says it will eventually incorporate this area into the mainland (*de jure*), while America says it will defend Taiwan.

A core question is whether a world war is likely. If hegemonies require major wars as a prelude to their absolute power, as research suggests, then China will need a win a war over, say, Taiwan to become the next hegemon. But if hegemonic powers as a rule *need* to be liberal democracies, then this counters this thesis. Since Spain (an autocratic power) lost the conflict over the Netherlands in the 1560s–1570s, France (an autocratic power under Napoleon) lost the Napoleonic Wars to Britain in 1815, and Germany (an autocratic power during the First and Second World Wars)

[8]This may have relevance for China: of the three cases of hegemony, Dutch, British, and US, the Dutch case is the weakest, for four reasons. First, most of the data is for Holland, not for the Dutch Republic as a whole. Hence, maybe the whole case needs to be revamped to relate to Holland only. Second, that being the case, the Dutch Hegemony Index calculated by Kwon may not be higher than the British or Spanish HI with hypothetical data for the Netherlands included rather than simply that of Holland. Third, almost all analysts conclude that the Dutch experienced hegemony during at least the 1610s–1630s (often 1600–1650 or 1620–1700), but this is unlikely to include the 1620s as this was a decade of depression for the Dutch, due to partly financial crisis and mostly war with the Spanish (even though they came out of it quite well). Hence, my conclusion of hegemony during the 1610s and 1630s–1640s, and two long upswings, 1570–1590 and 1600–1619.

lost to Europe and the USA, it may follow that China (an autocratic power under Xi Jinping) will lose to the EU and USA, etc.

In the current scenario, no major global long waves or hegemonies have emerged to propel sustained recovery for the world economy. It has been 40–50-odd years since the postwar long wave upswing (and hegemony) declined, and no major innovations in technologies, or in economic, social, political, or climatic processes have contributed majorly to long-term performance. This does raise the issue of whether the current capitalist-world system is moving into long-term sclerotic demise through several polycrises and no upswings (outside of China/Asia, etc.). Upswings are exogenous and nothing has propelled such motion in recent decades. Several counter-movements may be successful in generating progressive change, or perhaps regressive movements. This issue is raised again in the conclusion.

8.6 Conclusion

This chapter has examined Chinese performance in light of its record of long waves, hegemony prospects, and climate change. We investigated the performance of Chinese capitalism through the pathways and circuits of socioeconomic dynamics, including the various spheres of the pathways and circuits. We found that the Chinese role in the global political economy has historically been one of productive engagement but that more recently this has moved into areas of increasing conflict and disharmonious engagement. The sphere of state capitalism was evaluated as one of the positive developments and anomalous governance measures that have been deleterious to democracy and participatory engagement. The Chinese technology system has been advancing majorly in recent decades, but still faces challenges concerning the shape of institutions and the nature of productive inputs. The system of households, demography, and rural–urban transition has been of major benefit to Chinese growth, but has dissipated, and potential growth will decline in the future on these fronts. The financial system has played a major role in establishing market relations in China, but the lack of proper institutions and risky elements will likely continue to impact socioeconomic performance. The declining rate of profit has placed China in a similar position to that of the US and Europe as maturity and relative decline settle into habitual modes. China is the top GHG emitter and has not advanced its moral or economic power to demonstrate leadership on this front, although it is the leading producer of electric cars, batteries, and solar panels (and advancing strongly in AI).

Several contradictions are affecting Chinese performance that may inhibit to some degree long-wave upswings, hegemony, and climate change mitigation and adaptation into the future. The first involves China's intrusion into conflict with other nations over Taiwan, democratic deficits, and control of atolls in the (so-called) South China Sea. The second relates to state capitalism's anomalous involvement in industry policy, nationalism, and inward development. The third comprises several areas of innovation underperformance. The fourth pertains to the demise of the rural–urban dynamic whereby the underemployed become employed in productive activities. The fifth refers to the property collapse, potential debt deflation, and associated macro instability. The sixth applies to the declining rate of profit and the associated demise of corporate power. The seventh alludes to climate change and the difficulty in gaining the moral high ground when China is the greatest single GHG emitter. The eighth has relevance to weaknesses in China's social security system in the light of several population trends.

The chapter ends with an elucidation of several stylized facts and rules that impact China's waves, hegemony potential, and climate change. They relate to wars of ascendency and decendency, the relationship between long-wave upswings and hegemony, hegemons tending to be liberal democracies, the effective workings of the socioeconomic circuits and pathways, structural polycrises, agents and class alliances, structural contradictions, long-wave climate change correlations, and the rising conflict between autocracies and liberal democracies.

The Chinese experience of long-wave upswing was long-ranging and now will likely be similarly expansive through long-wave moderation (though perhaps with a high ceiling) as it matures and settles into mediocrity. China's hegemonic evolution will likely thus dissipate relative to production, commerce, and finance, even if militarily it continues to expand at the expense of other areas such as consumption and productive investment. It is unlikely that a nation seeking empire without liberal democracy and sufficient civil society can take the mantle of hegemony unless it radically changes the rules of command. China needs, at a minimum, a suitable set of economic, political, and social institutions to fit with its technology style to propel further long-wave upswings, hegemonic power, and mitigation/adaptation to climate change.

References

Athukorala, Prema-Chandra, and John Ravenhill. 2016. China's evolving role in global production networks: The decoupling debate revisited. In *Working paper no 2016/12*. Canberra: Crawford School of Public Policy, Australian National University.

Birley, Lewis Michael. 2023. Cycles and transformation: China's state-capitalism as adaptive strategy in the arc of capitalist governance. *Journal of World-Systems Research* 29 (2): 505–523.

Carchedi, Guglieleo. 2015. Profitability and modern capitalism. In *The future of capitalism after the financial crisis: The varieties of capitalism debate in the age of austerity, 205–227*, ed. Richard Westra, Dennis Badeen, and Robert Albritton. London and New York: Routledge.

Cheek, Timothy, and David Ownby. 2018. Make China Marxist Again. *Dissent* 65 (4): 71–77.

Chen, Wei, Xilu Chen, Chang-Tai Hsieh, and Song Zheng. 2019. A forensic examination of China's national accounts. In *NBER working paper*. Boston: National Bureau of Economic Research. http://www.nber.org/papers/w25754.

Cordesman, Anthony H. 2023. *China's emergence as a superpower*. Washington DC: CSIS.

Cornell University, INSEAD and WIPO. 2015. *The global innovation index 2015: Effective innovation policies for development*, Fontainebleau, Ithaca, and Geneva.

Dalio, Ray. 2023. *Principles for dealing with the changing world order: Why nations succeed and fail*. New York: Simon and Schuster.

Deng, Kent, and Patrick Karl O'Brien. 2016. *China's GDP per capita from the Han dynasty to communist times. Economic history working paper 229/2016*. London: London Schools of Economics.

DiTomaso, Nancy, and Yanjie Bian. 2018. The structure of labor markets in the US and China: Social capital and Guanxi. *Management and Organization Review* 14 (1): 5–36.

Economist. 2024. Special report: Deglobalisation of finance. *Economist*. 11–17 May. 12pp.

Elsner, Wolfram. 2020. *Das chinesische Jahr Hundert: Die neue Nummer eins ist Anders*. Frankfurt/Main: Westend.

Fan, E. X., and J. Felipe. 2005. The diverging patterns of profitability, investment and growth of China and India, 1980-2003. In *CAMA working paper 22/2005*. Canberra: Centre for Applied Macroeconomic Analysis, Australian National University.

Gao, Fan. 2022. *Political economy in the evolution of China's urban-rural economic relations*. London New York: Routledge.

Germanwatch. 2024. *CCPI: Climate change performance index*. Bonn: Germanwatch. https://ccpi.org/country/chn/; https://ccpi.org/country/usa/.

Heim, Jacob L., and Benjamin M. Miller. 2020. *Measuring power, power cycles, and the risk of great power war in the 21st century*. Santa Monica: California: Rand Corporation. https://www.rand.org/content/dam/rand/pubs/research_reports/RR2900/RR2989/RAND_RR2989.pdf.

Herrera, Rémy, and Zhiming Long. 2017. Capital accumulation, profit rates and cycles in China from 1952 to 2014: Lessons from the evolution of Chinese industry. *Journal of Innovation Economics & Management* 23 (2): 59–82.

Heritage Foundation. 2023. *Economic freedom index, 1995-2023*. https://www.heritage.org/index/.

Holz, C. A. 2005. China's economic growth 1978-2025: What we know about China's economic growth tomorrow. *World Development* 36 (10): 1665–1691.

INSEAD. 2009. *Global innovation index 2008–2009*. Singapore: INSEAD Business School.

Itzkoff, Seymour. 2003. China- emerging hegemony: A speculative essay *journal of social. Political and Economic Studies* 28 (4): 487–496.

Jones, Peter. 2021. *The falling rate of profit and the great recession of 2007–2009*. Leiden: Brill.

Jones, Peter. 2017. Turnover time and the organic composition of capital. *Cambridge Journal of Economics* 41 (1): 81–103.

Knight, J., and S. Li. 2005. Wages, firm profitability and labor market segmentation in urban China. *China Economic Review* 16:205–208.

Kwon, Roy. 2011. Hegemonies in the world-system: An empirical assessment of hegemonic sequences from the 16th to 20th century. *Sociological Perspectives* 54 (4): 595–626.

Li, Minqi. 2020. *Profit, accumulation, and crisis in capitalism: Long-term trends in the UK, US, Japan, and China, 1855–2018*. London & New York: Routledge.

Lu, Xia, and Xiaoqin Ding. 2022. Socialist political economy with Chinese characteristics and research on the Chinese and foreign economies. *World Review of Political Economy* 13 (4): 476–501.

Maddison Project. 2024. *Maddison historical statistics*. Groningen, Netherlands: University of Groningen. Maddison Project Database 2023 | Releases | Groningen Growth and Development Centre | University of Groningen (rug.nl).

Marquetti, Adalmir Antonio, Catari Vilela Chaves, Leonardo Costa Ribeiro, and Eduardo da Motta e Albuquerque, Rate of Profit in the United States and in China. 2021. A look at two trajectories and strategic sectors. *Review of Radical Political Economics* 53 (1): 116–142.

Marx, Karl. 1867. *Capital: The process of capitalist production as a whole*, 1981. Harmondsworth: Penguin.

Mayoral, Amanda. 2012. *Climate change as a conflict multiplier*. Washington DC: US Institute of Peace. https://www.usip.org/sites/default/files/PB%20120_0.pdf.

Nelson, Richard R. 2008. What enables rapid economic progress: What are the needed institutions? *Research Policy* 37 (1): 1–11. https://doi.org/10.1016/j.respol.2007.10.008.

O'Hara, Phillip Anthony. 2006. A Chinese social structure of accumulation for capitalist long-wave upswing? *Review of Radical Political Economics* 38 (3): 397–404. https://doi.org/10.1177/0486613406290905.

O'Hara, Phillip Anthony. 2009. The global securitized subprime market crisis. *Review of Radical Political Economists* 41 (3): 318–334.

O'Hara, Phillip Anthony. 2016. The contemporary relevance of Karl Marx's heterodox political economy. In *Marx, Veblen and the foundations of heterodox economics, 50–78*, ed. Tae-Hee Jo and Frederic S. Lee. London: Routledge.

Pauls, Robert. 2022. Capitalist accumulation, contradictions and crisis in China, 1995–2015. *Journal of Contemporary Asia* 52 (2): 267–295. https://doi.org/10.1080/00472336.2020.1861640.

Pearson, Margaret, Meg Rithmire, and Kellee S. Tsai. 2020. *Party-state capitalism in China*. Working Paper 21-065. Harvard Business School.

Peschel, Dominik, and Wenyu Liu. 2022. The Long-term growth prospects of the People's Republic of China. In *ADB East Asia working paper series*. Manila: Asian Development Bank.

Prasad, Eswar. 2023. Has China's growth gone from miracle to malady? *Brookings papers in economic activity: BEA conference drafts 30-31st march 2023*. 33pp.

Roberts, Michael. 2021. The US rate of profit in [1945-]2020. *Left Horizons*. 12(6). https://www.left-horizons.com/2021/12/06/the-us-rate-of-profit-in-2020/

Robinson, Joan. 1974. *The cultural revolution in China*. Pelican: Harmondsworth.

Robinson, Joan. 1978. The organic composition of capital. *Kyklos* 31 (1): 3–18.

Rojo, J. 2022. United States, China and the dispute for global hegemony: A comparative analysis. *Human Review* 11:2–13. https://doi.org/10.37467/revhuman.v11.4302.

Ruiz Estrada, Mario Arturo. 2023. Exploring world war III scenarios with Wolfram Mathematica. *Econographication Virtual Laboratory (EVL)*. https://doi.org/10.13140/RG.2.2.24945.86882.

Russell, Bertrand. 1938. *Power: A new social analysis*, 1975. London: Allen & Unwin.

Saad-Filho, Alfredo. 1993. A note on Marx's analysis of the composition of capital. *Capital and Class*. 50 (1): 127–146.

Santibañes, F. 2009. An end to U.S. hegemony? The strategic implications of China's growing presence in Latin America. *Comparative Strategy* 28 (1): 17–36. https://doi.org/10.1080/01495930802679728.

Schaar, Johan. 2018. The relationship between climate change and violent conflict. In *Working paper 2017*. Stockholm: SIDA(Swedish International Development Cooperation Agency).

Scheffran, Jürgen, Weisi Guo, Florian Krampe, and Uche Okpara. 2023. Tipping cascaded between conflict and cooperation in climate change. *EGOsphere Preprint Repository*. https://doi.org/10.5194/egusphere-2023-1766.

Schweinberger, Albert. 2012. State capitalism, entrepreneurship, and networks: China's rise to a superpower. *Journal of Economic Issues* 48 (1): 169–180.

SLFed. 2024. *World Uncertainty Index for China, 1953–2024*. St Louis Federal Reserve Bank. World Uncertainty Index for China (WUICHN) | FRED | St. Louis Fed (stlouisfed.org)

Sun, Li. 2019. *Rural urban migration and policy intervention in China: Migrant workers' coping strategies*. Singapore: Springer Nature (Palgrave Macmillan).

Tsoulfidis, Lefteris, and Aris Papageorgiou. 2019. The recurrence of Long cycles: Theories, stylized facts and figures. *World Review of Political Economy* 10 (4): 415–438.

UNCTAD (United Nations Conference on Trade and Development). 2023. *China's policy strategies for green low-carbon development: Perspective from south-south cooperation*. Geneva: UNCTAD. https://unctad.org/publication/chinas-policy-strategies-green-low-carbon-development-perspective-south-south.

UNEP (United Nations Environmental Program). 2023. *Emissions gap report 2023. Broken record: Temperatures hit new highs, yet world fails to cut emissions (again)*. Nairobi: UNEP.

Westra, Richard. 2023. The question of socialism in China: An introduction. *Journal of Contemporary Asia* 53 (5): 749–766.

Wilson, Ron, and Kevin Morris. 1997. *Changing China: Opening windows to the west*. Wheaton, ILL: Harold Shaw Publishers.

World Bank WDI. 2024. *World development indicators*. https://databank.worldbank.org/reports.aspx?source=World-Development-Indicators

Wikipedia. 2023. *Soft power*. https://en.wikipedia.org/wiki/Soft_power

WIPO. 2023. *Global innovation index 2023*. Geneva: World Intellectual Property Organisation.

Yu, Y. 2005. G-20 and China: A Chinese perspective. *China & World Economy* 13 (1): 3–14.

Zarembka, Paul. 2020. *Key elements of social theory revolutionized by Marx*. Leiden: Brill Publishers.

Chapter 9
Structural Polycrises of the 1970s–2020s: Decadal Crises, Debt Crises, GFC, Eurocrisis, Coronacrisis, and Climate Crisis

Abstract This chapter outlines the ongoing and successive polycrises that have emerged from the demise of US (and Western) hegemony and long wave upswing vis-à-vis the deteriorating pathways and circuits of socioeconomic dynamics (CSD). As the hegemony, long wave upswing, and climate moderation underwent contradictory movements, and neoliberalism rose during the 1970s, 1980s, 1990s, and 2000s, polycrises got worse, and as neoliberalism went into relative decline during the 2010s, its vestiges helped to precipitate the health crises of the early 2020s. These ongoing polycrises include, for instance, the decadal financial crises and recessions, the global financial crisis (GFC), four waves of debt crises (including the Eurocrisis), the coronacrisis, and the climate crisis. These are the subjects of this chapter (the ongoing crisis associated with the Ukraine/Taiwan anomalies is investigated in Chap. 10). A conclusion follows.

Keywords Neoliberalism · Structural polycrises · Pathways and circuits of socioeconomic dynamics (CSD) · Global Financial Crisis (GFC) · Eurodebt crisis · Coronacrisis · Institutions · Technologies and ecologies · Contradictions & crises · Principles · Long waves · Hegemony · Climate change · 1970s–2020s

9.1 Past Structural Polycrises

The purpose of this chapter is to *outline* the key techno-institutional-climate developments and polycrises of global and regional capitalism during the 1970s–2020s and to subject these dynamic structures to a critique based on their complex operational and contradictory motion. The reason it is an *outline* is that I have written several books and dozens of papers relating to this subject, and therefore I will merely outline the basic contours of the subject (see O'Hara 2000, a, b, 2013, 2023 for details). We aim to outline the structural and evolutionary nature of neoliberalism, its dominant contradictions, and its *relative* fall, paying special attention to the

P. A. O'Hara, *Long Waves of Growth, Hegemonic Power, and Climate Change in the World Economy*, https://doi.org/10.1007/978-981-96-4132-1_9

anomalies of the decadal crises, the GFC, the Eurocrisis, the coronacrisis, and the climate crisis.

One of the basic stylized facts of hegemony studies, not a rule but a recurring tendency, is that in-between times when hegemonies decline and others subsequently rise to dominance, there tends to be instability, subdued performance, and polycrises. For instance, during the period when Dutch hegemony had declined, yet British hegemony had not yet emerged (especially the 1700s), and when British hegemony had declined yet US dominance had not yet developed (1880s/1890s to the 1930s), and since the relative demise of absolute US hegemony (the 1980s to the present), we tend to have major polycrises and instabilities. This usually includes lower levels of socioeconomic performance, especially in the core economies. We know in theory this need not be the case, but it has been a recurring trend.

Kindleberger (1996, 7, 4), who relies "to a great extent on Fernand Braudel," argues that Dutch "leadership, or economic hegemony as some call it," in the first half of the 1600s was based on (some) other nations following the lead of the Dutch Republic. As he said: "The United Provinces of the Netherlands in the seventeenth, century, though small in comparison with the great powers, led by example, not by military or political power" (p. 13). He adds, "This is … true [also] of Britain in the last half of the nineteenth century, and of the United States in the third quarter of the twentieth" (p. 13). In relation to the Dutch, "Particularly admired were the Dutch industry; frugality; the patent system; government support of trade, including standardization of output and control of its quality; the low rate of interest coming from thrift; and the aggressive fishing in specially built busses" (p. 43). In the periphery, though, they were not so admired as the Dutch external mercantile war-mongering, monopolization, colonializations, massacres of whole peoples on some islands, slave trading, and related activities rendered them aggressive agents.

In Chap. 5, we illustrated that the Dutch experienced two long-wave upswings (during the late 1500s and early 1600s) which coincided with or were followed by hegemony as the circuits of socioeconomic dynamics (CSD), per capita real GDP, and successful military strategy were buoyed during the Dutch Golden Age. I have dated Dutch hegemony during 1580–1620 and possibly 1630–1650, but others have used the 1600s as the hegemonic period for the Dutch. Domestic and external factors were important to the decline in hegemony and in the subsequent subdued economic activity. The Dutch underwent domestic life cycle changes through 30–60 years of buoyant activity to declining performance, along with external threats to livelihood from mercantile powers such as Britain (and France). The CSD matured, and as Kindleberger (1996, chap. 6) argued, they experienced lower levels of invention after 1640, declining trade (commerce) from the 1680s, and financial disarray by 1763, while mercantile aggression against them rose, especially from the 1650s onward.

Bear in mind also, as noted in chap. 5, that many have posited a global (or European) series of polycrises during the 1600s, mainly or partly due to the Little Ice Age (LIA) (one of the cycles of the Ice Age). So polycrises are not to be seen only due to inadequate hegemonic direction. Wallerstein (1980) and others have also posited the 1600s and 1700s as a structural downswing in the world economy.

Prominent long-wave upswings and hegemonic dominance are causally related. The Dutch (and some others in the North Sea area) displayed resilience and innovation in the face of the Little Ice Age 1600s circa (many other economies did not), which helped long-wave upswings and hegemony. When long waves and hegemony declined, mediocre performance emerged in the Netherlands. The next 150 years and more after the end of Dutch hegemony saw Dutch performance decline with volatility, numerous wars, aggression, and mercantile battles that prevented standards of living from rising (per capita real GDP levels were fairly constant).

We noted earlier a stylized fact applicable to Britain (later the US and potentially China): that when Dutch hegemony declined from the mid–late 1600s, British short-wave upswings became more pronounced for a short time, even though volatility was extreme (short waves were the norm). But no long waves emerged for the British until they achieved hegemony.

To my knowledge, no one has applied the notion of the hegemonic stability hypothesis (HSH) *explicitly* to the Netherlands during this period (critically or otherwise). HSH states that hegemonies provide the basis for public goods, which the hegemon and its allies (and possibly others) can benefit from. These public goods include relative peace, international lender of last resort, common trade, international monetary rules, and international systems of patents and copyrights. The most important public good provided by the Dutch during their era of hegemony was emulation. They were looked up to, jealously, envied, hated, but forever copied and mimicked. Amsterdam also provided financial and commercial services for the region and beyond.

Although the so-called Peace of Westphalia (1648) did generate some stability along the lines of the balance of power principle, especially between European powers, this was exaggerated by some authors and short-lived. For many areas, there was a deterioration in economic performance and especially erratic performance, certainly for the Dutch and the UK, and many nations of Europe and beyond. The Little Ice Age (LIA) was still in play throughout the 1700s, including the coldest winter for half a millennium in 1709 affecting many areas and the apogee of the LIA around mid-century. During the whole of the 1700s, Britain and France plus their allies and enemies engaged in numerous wars and struggles for supremacy. For instance, the (original) "First World War" (as it is known) (1756–1763) was a critical one, involving several powers, especially in Europe and the Americas (Pocock 1998). The outcome was a success for Britain and Prussia, especially over Austria and France. The last third of the 1700s saw four wars between Britain and the Mysore Kingdom (in south India). There were also the American Revolutionary Wars, French Revolutionary Wars; and the Napoleonic Wars, the last of these saw the Congress of Vienna (1815) and related agreements, which contributed to *relative* stability, especially among European powers for (as many argue) 100 years (Polanyi 1944).

The ending of (British) hegemony from the 1880s and its relative hegemony until the First World War also established an unstable/conflictual set of conditions. These included the unofficial "great depression" of the 1870s–(*early*)1890s, which did affect many countries (although may not have been quite a "great" depression for most). The scramble for Africa and the era of imperialism in general is typically seen by some political economists as one of many responses to the general crisis of the 1870s–1890s, usually called a "Great Depression" but in our own terminology from Chap. 6 called "a period of great instability, turmoil, and change" (borderline performance). It also included the "scramble for Africa (and other areas)" during the 1880s–1930s (the "age of imperialism"). From a series of conferences, e.g., the Berlin Conference of 1884–85, Europeans formally sought to eliminate "slavery," but de facto still exploited and killed Africans through "forced labor" (i.e., slavery by any other name). Through bilateral negotiations and unilateral actions, the "informal imperialism" of the early–mid-1800s transformed into full-blown imperialism, especially from the 1880s to notably the First World War (and onto the Second World War).

Responding to the crises of the late 1800s, the European powers saw Africa and related conflicts as a rational response to the overproduction and limited markets of Europe. It was a way of gaining cheap resources (such as labor, copper, gold, and diamonds), exporting home products (such as textiles, engines, and electricity), absorbing the surplus from the home country, and gaining surplus labor, product, and value from the colonies (Rodney 1972). Solving balance of payments problems was, however, secondary to the core objectives of expanding the Empire-building power of European nation-states and white Europeans. In all of Africa, only two countries initially failed to be colonized (Ethiopia and Liberia), but much later Ethiopia was colonized by the Italians with their population decimated (275,000 killed) under Mussolini's orders during the mid–late 1930s. All in all, during the Scramble for Africa and its extension through other wars, possibly up to 100 million Africans were killed, while many African nations were devoid of populations through slavery, many of whom were also killed or died of malnutrition and mistreatment.

In one country alone, the so-called Congo Free State, during 1885–1908, where the hands of locals who failed to fulfill production quotas were often cut off on orders of Belgian authorities, up to ten million locals possibly died from forced labor. The second most significant impact of the Scramble for Africa was the drawing of artificial borders, which dislocated indigenous networks right up to the present, precipitating numerous wars and crises. As mentioned, the main purpose of the imperial pursuits of the 1880s–1910s-circa was to enhance Empire building, with Britain, for instance, increasing its colonies to around one-third of the globe (Hobsbawm 1987, 74).

When Britain lost both absolute and related hegemony, the two "official" world wars (1914–1918 and 1939–1945), and the official Great Depression of the 1930s generated disarray for most nations. It was in relation to this period of "no-hegemony" that the HSH was unofficially espoused by Kindleberger, who developed these ideas in relation to the two world wars and the Great Depression of the 1930s. As he said, "The world economic system was unstable unless some country stabilized it, as Britain had done in the nineteenth century and up to 1913. In 1929, the British couldn't and the United States wouldn't provide the required leadership. When every country turned to protect its national interest global or multiregional public interest was emasculated (Kindleberger 1973, 292). As he said in relation to the causes of the Great Depression:

> The explanation of this book is that the 1929 Depression was so wide, so deep and so long because the international economic system was rendered unstable by British inability and United States unwillingness to assume responsibility for stabilizing it in three particulars: (a) maintaining a relatively open market for distress goods; (b) providing counter-cyclical long-term lending; and (c) discounting in crisis. [Kindleberger 1973, 292]

Perhaps viewing them as coevolving factors, the overproduction of primary products, the halting of lending to Germany, and the stock market crash of 1929, he concentrates on one core central process (general leadership). No one was willing to provide such leadership in the context of the 1927 and 1933 World Economic Conferences, and "It was not until 1942 that Harry D. White began preparing a world plan for discussion at Bretton Woods – together with the plan of Lord Keynes—a world plan for limited discounting" (p. 298).[1]

The imperial phase of capitalist development was an early manifestation of the wars between the so-called great powers that engulfed the world during 1914–1918 and 1939–1945, and which coevolved with the so-called 'Great Depression' of the 1930s. Between the ending of British hegemony, their one major long-wave upswing (1820s–1860s), and the start of US hegemony, thus was clearly established a whole list of instabilities and conflicts. The decline in US hegemony also established a period of relative instability and poor economic performance (1970s–2020s). This chapter examines these post-hegemony instabilities and mediocre performances. They include a whole series of financial crises and deep recessions on a decadal basis, including four successive and major debt crises, the GFC of the late 2000s, the Eurocrisis of the late 2000s and early 2010s(ff), the coronacrisis of the early 2020s, climate change crises of the 1990s onward, and a possible World War III (the current "pre-war era" is analyzed vis-à-vis Ukraine (and Taiwan) examined in Chap. 10).

As neoliberalism has been in relative decline, especially since the GFC, we have seen the emergence of another tendency in governance. This involves the more recent relative rise of nationalist-autocratic blocks (e.g., Russia, China, Iran, etc.) versus the liberal and social democratic blocks (e.g., North America, Europe, parts of Oceania, and East Asia), that have established rivalry, especially during the past decade. There are, of course, still lingering vestiges of neoliberalism, and some would argue large swabs of it, still operating in the crevices and in more conspicuous places (Mavroudeas and Papadatos 2011). But the stylized fact of autocratic vs.

[1] Kindleberger discusses the issue of global power in terms of leadership rather than hegemony per se, and he tends not to distinguish absolute from relative leadership (or hegemony). This results in him discussing Dutch global power (leadership) from the 1600s to the early 1700s (in our terminology through both absolute and relative hegemony) and British leadership from the 1800s to the First World War (through both absolute and relative hegemony). Ironically, he discusses US leadership between 1945 and 1975 (through absolute hegemony), and adds that the US could have chosen to "lead the world" during the 1920s or 1930s; which may have affected the nature of and possible outcome of any world war 2 that may have transpired.

liberal democratic trends, along with the associated rise in protectionism, industry policy, and the trend toward possible World War III, have become more recently emergent stylized facts of the world in recent years. The autocratic vs. liberal powers' contradiction some think is moving planet Earth into a pre-(world) war situation.[2] A related autocratic vs. liberal dichotomy has also been pervading many national economies, such as, especially, the US, Hungary, India, Brazil, etc.

Section 9.2 summarizes the emergence and development of neoliberalism, while Sect. 9.3 dissects the conditions and unstable contradictions emerging under neoliberalism. Section 9.3 outlines the key polycrises that have emerged since the 1970s, and Section 9.4 summarizes key features of the subprime and global financial crises. Section 9.5 examines the four waves of debt crises (including the Eurocrisis), while Section 9.6 discusses the anomalous forms of governance that led to the global outbreak of the coronacrisis and future policies to prevent a recurrence of health crises. Section 9.7 discusses the climate crisis, one of the core themes of this book. The chapter ends with a conclusion.

9.2 Emergence of Neoliberalism and Beyond

According to the theory of long waves of growth, hegemony, and climate change espoused in this book, sustainable long-term growth and accumulation require a set of suitable dynamic structures for promoting public goods or system functions. The structures that have been the main subject of this book have been summarized as the pathways and circuits of socioeconomic dynamics (CSD), which comprises a set of eco-geo-spatial, technological, and institutional capitals upon which long-term economic performance depends. These dynamic structures essentially comprise a set of CSD eco-geo-dynamics, technological elements, corporate relations, state apparatuses, financial structures and flows, and household-community bonds of association. These relations are set within the context of subnational, national, regional, and global dynamics, circuits, networks, pathways, and peoples.

In this context, Western nations (in particular) are said to have experienced a long-wave upswing in the 1940s (for some), 1950s, and 1960s (and for some, the 1970s and 1980s). Deep recessions and major financial crises were largely absent,

[2] The current trajectory of the world historical system of capitalism, likely including its events, conjunctures, and *longue duree*, does include other trends and stylized facts besides neoliberalism per se. For instance, there is also a trend of various forms of extreme nationalistic and militaristic forces at play in various nations and areas, which could be seen as (*attempting* to develop) a form of protection against free market processes, but also which may be considered an extension of neoliberalism toward the inclusion of force to promote the interests of the vested interests and the military-industrial complex. Briefly, such forces, which may be termed autocratic (and some "proto-fascist"), include the current (2025) regimes in the US, Russia, China, the Philippines, Hungary, Brazil, and many others. (There are also other tendencies in motion, such as the much-discussed "populist" trend, which includes many right-wing, but also some left-wing, groups and parties around the world.) See chap. 10.

and growth was quite strong for the two or three decades after World War II. These results were thought to be the result of numerous geo-techno-institutional dynamic structures. However, these geo-techno-institutional arrangements faltered from the 1970s to the 1990s (and beyond) as contradictions within and between these structures led to greater uncertainty, conflict, and instability. A long-wave downswing emerged, with periodic deep recessions, lower productivity, financial crises, and slower economic growth. Along with this, US hegemony declined, and climate change took a very severe escalation. An in-depth analysis of the periodicities, amplitudes, and regularities of these long waves is provided in Chap. 11 for around 100 nations of the core, periphery, and semi-periphery. Because of uneven development, China and numerous Asian nations (plus some others) underwent robust long-wave upswings during the downswings experienced by most elsewhere. But the world as a whole mostly continued to be in a downswing.

As mentioned throughout this book (and as Kindleberger and Louçã, among others, also critically note), some analysts confuse the short 1990s boom (in some nations) with the start of a long-wave upswing, whereas I see it as being comparable to the 1920s in some nations (a speculative bubble rise followed by a crash). During the 1970s–2020s, core nations especially underwent a Juglar boom and slump through successive decades, while the peripheral and semi-peripheral areas had varying experiences depending upon their specific eco-techno-institutional dynamics, the worst involving successive debt crises, the periodic slumps in oil prices (for OPEC members and others), plus the decline in Soviet-style economies in the 1990s, including the civil war in the Balkans, and innumerable troubles elsewhere.

In Chap. 7, we delimited the scope of the analysis to several spheres of CSD activity in the US and similar economies. The state impacted all these spheres. US hegemony was inextricably linked to military spending and the role of the state in facilitating sustainable growth and accumulation both during and after World War II. The state contributed to the capital-labor accord by facilitating legal and industrial relations outcomes that enhanced agreement. The state was implicated in other CSD spheres through systems of corporate law, financial regulation, and family assistance packages. Main state functions were the Keynesian welfare policies that dominated the 1950s, 1960s, and early–mid-1970s in most advanced capitalist economies. These included automatic and discretionary stabilizers; welfare benefits such as unemployment insurance, pensions, and sickness benefits; and an array of military, legal, and regulatory arrangements (Bleaney 1995). Indeed, during the postwar era, the state became the dominant institutional player in unison with the transnational corporate system. Nonetheless, the contribution of companies, unions, and families to governance processes was quite strong, as Chap. 7 specifies.

According to many long-wave arguments, the Keynesian welfare state contributed to this long-wave upswing by enhancing stability, conflict resolution, and profitability. Stability was promoted by government spending, raising the floor of the business cycle, and thereby reducing uncertainty. Conflict resolution was provided by reducing antagonism between capital and labor, finance and industry, and national and global economies. And profitability was stimulated by the provision of government contracts with the private sector in areas such as military, infrastructure, and communications.[3]

During the late 1960s and early 1970s, the state was said to inhibit long-term accumulation through greater regulations, higher taxes, red tape, long policy lags, and incompetence. The Vietnam War contributed to stagflation and declining US hegemony; welfare policies led to a drop in the cost of job loss; the search for higher values questioned the work ethic; and long-term industrial profit was inhibited by higher taxes, regulations, and wages. Many non-state institutions contributed to the long-wave downswing, including the maturation of technology associated with product cycles of consumer and producer durables, a reform movement that questioned many of the values of capitalism, and developments in Europe, the Middle East, and Asia that challenged US power, as worker power expanded for a time also (Bowles et al. 1990).

When long-wave downswings start after prolonged periods of buoyancy agents often reassess long-term growth and accumulation strategies. While some are conscious and reasoned responses, many are "groping in the dark" (e.g., disjoined incrementalism), since proxies for structural dynamics are often not obvious, and not all policymakers recognize long-wave processes (structural conditions). There are many ideologies of policy and by no means a monolithic set of themes. Central to the struggle for renewed stability and profitability since the 1970s has been an attack on the Keynesian welfare state and the rise of free market ideology (*at least* until the GFC and the coronacrisis but likely longer than this as well in many cases). Since the mid–late 1970s, this economic philosophy has had a strong influence on policy in most nations of the world.

The Thatcher and Reagan revolutions during the 1980s questioned welfare state regulation and stabilization practices. These coevolved with supply-side economics, monetarism, and new classical economics, which constituted the more theoretical sides of the movement. These policy coevolutions saw the rise of neoliberalism, a conservative form of economic policy and governance that relies on the free market and individual initiative. Neoliberal analysts advocate(d) the sale of state enterprises, less government spending, capital ruling over labor, reduced taxes, and moderate regulations on business. We also saw the relative decline in Fordism and the rise in aspects of the flexible system of production, including just-in-time stock adjustments and more flexible relations within and between supply chains. During

[3] Samuel Rosenberg (2003) pays particular attention to the role of the state in the postwar US experience. As he says about Keynesian policies: "During the 1940s and 1950s, Keynesian demand management policies were not systematically applied toward economic stimulation. Nevertheless, growing federal expenditures on goods and services helped to maintain aggregate demand and economic growth. Military expenditures were an important part of such spending, reflecting changes in overseas military activity, which did destabilize the economy at times" (Rosenberg 2003: 63). He goes on to say that "A conservative form of Keynesianism dominated macroeconomic policymaking in the 1960s. Government policymakers believed that if aggregative macroeconomic policy tools were suitably utilized the economy would be able to grow steadily with low rates of inflation and low rates of unemployment. However, by the early 1970s, this view was demonstrated to be overly optimistic" (p. 122).

the 1990s, and continuing into the new millennium, the ideology and practices of neoliberalism became dominant worldwide.[4] (Some also use the term the "Washington consensus," although others believe this was somewhat different from neoliberalism.)

However, especially through the decadal series of financial/corporate crises and recessions, plus the GFC (2007–2009), four waves of debt crises (including the Eurocrisis 2009–15ff) and the coronacrisis (2020–2023), neoliberalism was found wanting, and a host of policies and practices were utilized that went far beyond neoliberalism. These include functional finance (including extensive use of discretionary fiscal and monetary policies), some (short-term?) nationalization of companies, monetization of the debt, and so on.

There are cascading factors merging that generated polycrises, not simply neoliberalism, which led especially to limits on required health, education, and infrastructure spending, but also the destabilizing impacts associated with inadequate hegemons, including lack of leadership, insufficient global lender of last resort facilities, major wars, and numerous public goods failing to be generated to protect the system from crises; and the linked movement from long-wave upswings to downswings. The causes of the polycrises are multiple, but they all coevolved with typical neoliberal anomalies. In this context, we outline the major contradictions of neoliberalism in the next section.[5]

9.3 Structure, Dynamics, and Contradictions of Neoliberalism

In this section we utilize interrelated principles to (1) explain the horizontal (8 eco-techno-institutional spheres) emergence of neoliberal capitalism; (2) as it underwent vertical contradictory systemic and periodic emergence of instability and crises; (3) through conjunctural but also core event and long-term processual temporal emergence.

In this context, Gordon (1991) noted that Nicholas Kaldor's use of the *principle of circular and cumulative causation* (CCC) embodied too much cumulation and not enough contradiction. But 1974 Nobel Laureate Gunnar Myrdal (e.g., 1968), from whom Kaldor got the CCC term, was more specific about how CCC links to contradictory processes. Indeed, the dominant contradictions of neoliberal capitalism can

---

[4]As I argue in O'Hara (2009a, 2009b, 2009c) and O'Hara (2013), neoliberal globalization was a key set of institutional, technological, and eco-geo-spatial structures and relationships that were also embedded within ideological and psychological traits of the systems, which included global-regional-national-sub/national arrangements, governance systems, corporate organization, financial institutions, and familial groupings.

[5]I have written a whole book on this (O'Hara 2009a, which won an award for *Scholarly Book of the Year* from CBS), so this is an outline-summary of the core problems that also goes beyond the book and includes much more recent material.

be understood by linking the three principles of (1) the (dis)embedded economy, (2) contradiction, and (3) circular and cumulative causation. The (dis)embedded economy and the double movement are the core *general* contradictions of capitalism, associated with the major *specific* contradictions of *neoliberal* capitalism, while CCC enables one to scrutinize the upward and downward movements *generated by these contradictions.* The circular aspect of CCC emphasizes the interaction between the eco-techno-institutional relations, and especially the linkages between the contradictions that are embedded in the relationships. The cumulative aspect of CCC helps to comprehend the waves and phases of metamorphosis of institutions and the multifarious (variously positive and negative) feedback processes that produce magnified impacts, resulting in novel crises. Figure 9.1 illustrates certain horizontally emergent relationships associated with eco-techno-institutional CSD spheres through the workings of these three related principles.

Neoliberal CSD processes are emergent in a complexity sense since, first, the *interaction* within and between institutional spheres is critical to the *whole system*;

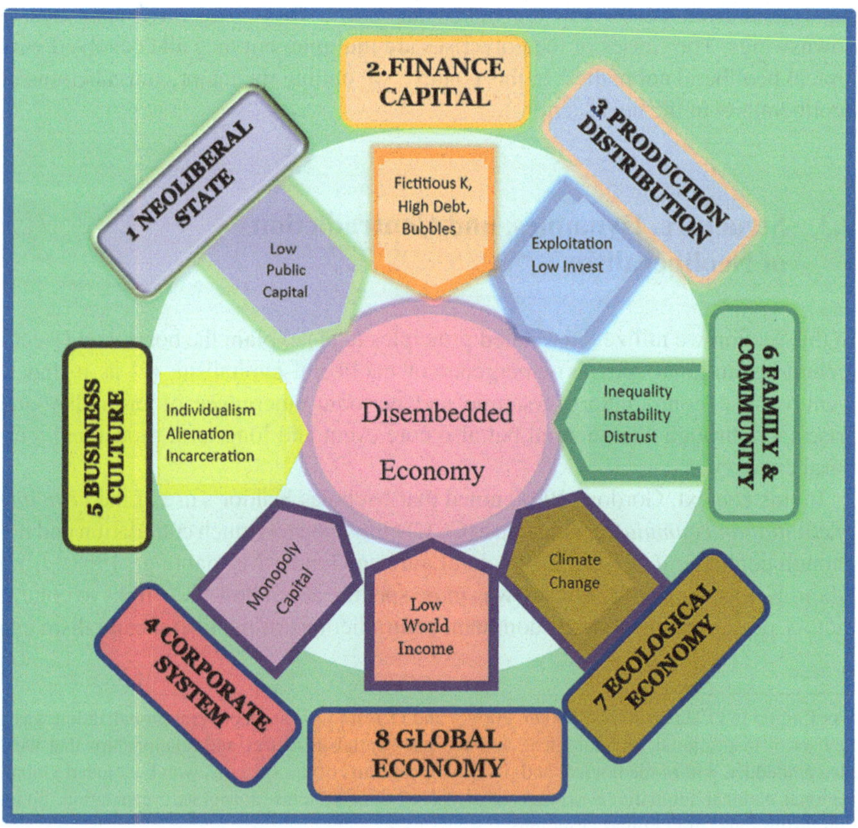

Fig. 9.1 Anomalous neoliberal CSD: ecological-techno-institutional spheres and CCC contradictions. (Short form; Adapted from arguments of O'Hara 2009a, b, c, 2023)

and second, this interaction can generate contradictory "coherence" at the meso-level, negatively affecting the performance outcomes of the whole system. Thus, situating this horizontally emergent level vertically (eschewing voluntarism and structuralism), neoliberal capitalism generates elements of "freedom" at the individual level (especially for rich and powerful individuals and groups), while, at the novel meso-level of the institutional clusters, core elements of *contradictory coherence* emerge, and at the macro/regional/global system levels, the contradictions multiply negative outcomes, generating emergent systemic and periodic instability, crises, and potentially terminal struggles and outcomes.

Following Ron Stanfield (1986), Stanfield (2011), Brennan and Kalsi (2015), O'Hara (2023), plus numerous other scholars, the dominant contradiction of capitalism is said to be that of the (dis)embedded economy and the double movement. As we saw above, the disembedded economy thesis reveals that neoliberal capitalism attempts to expand markets by destroying nonmarket transactions of reciprocity, redistribution, householding, plus informal markets, and replacing them with formal exchange transactions (Polanyi 1944). This process of destructive creation is necessary for commodity production to *potentially* enhance accumulation, profit, and growth. Mostly this is done by attempting to more deeply commodify "fictitious commodities," such as labor power, money-credit, ecological resources, and knowledge, thereby largely replacing reciprocity, redistribution, householding, and informal markets within and between corporations, families, world economies, financial systems, state systems, ecological structures, and industries. This represents the commodification of previously non-commodified goods and services and the more intense commodification of goods and services that were partially commodified in the past.

Neoliberal commodification has been widespread and generated instability, uncertainty, and anomalous interactions within and between ecological, technological, and institutional relations involving individuals and groups. Because these destructions (outcomes of contradictions) are interactive, they generate CCC destabilizing forces throughout the system.[6] Here the analysis of neoliberalism will con-

[6]While these destructions are ongoing, Polanyi posited the generation of ongoing protective responses to these destructions so that a double movement of destruction and protection becomes institutionalized into the system. For instance, there are ongoing protective responses to neoliberalism. While they may not question neoliberalism at the systemic level, at lower vertical levels alternatives have historically been generated. These include an array of movements, such as the recreation of worker cooperatives to promote alternatives to orthodox capital dynamics, the generation of ecological niches to enhance species diversity, and the promotion of indigenous rights through extension of property to first nation ethnic groups (Gibson-Graham 2003). These double movements also include efforts by unions to protect worker rights on the job and enhance especially minimum wages; innovative fishing practices to enhance species diversity and reduce ecological footprints; as well as promoting embedded households and institutions to challenge the dominance of capital space (Roelvink et al. 2015). Ways of stimulating embeddedness are ongoing through various ethical practices to challenge quid pro quo, formal exchange, and alienation on the job (Gibson-Graham and Roelvink 2009). There are ongoing proposals and realized policies to protect against neoliberal-inspired deep recessions, financial instabilities, and debt crises (O'Hara 2013). Many of these double movements, including anti-hegemonic movements, black-lives

centrate on the horizontally emergent eco-techno-institutional spheres, from which linkages are made to the vertical forms of emergence through periodic structural crises. We also illustrate the need to concentrate on *conjunctural* processes while including some critical *long-term* tendencies (e.g., the rise of Asia, especially China, and the growing ecological disaster of GHG emissions) plus *Great Episodic Events* (e.g., the GFC of 2008ff and the coronacrisis of 2020–2023ff).

In this system of global neoliberalism, most national, regional, and international structures of the "*1. Neoliberal State*" have historically, since the 1980s, been enforcing austerity, low inflation, and deregulation of the economy as the power of finance, capital, and the rich has been increasing (Dugger 2022). There are different varieties of neoliberalism, such as the "traditional neoliberal" economies (UK, USA) and the "newly deconstructed neoliberal" economies of Central Europe (Poland, Hungary) as well as the "partly coordinated" neoliberal states (Germany, Japan). Typically, neoliberal economies have negatively impacted public capital as the use of resources for transport infrastructure, education, and public health has been well below community requirements over several decades (O'Hara 2013). Public capital has declined while (relative) spending on transfer payments has increased as un(der)employment and community deterioration have expanded (periodically) in the neoliberal era.

Being dominated by "*2. Finance Capital*" led to periodic and secular excess fictitious capitals in the form of nonindustrial and unproductive spending on speculative real estate, equity, and liability management practices (including securitization). These unproductive uses of resources led to shareholder, real estate, and financial derivative values undergoing periodic bubbles and busts, which during 2008–2016 had especially major international ramifications as neoliberalism entered its worst systemic crises since its inception (Elsner 2016); and capitalism its worst depression since the 1930s with the "global financial crisis" (a major series of events *in the core*) since 2008, the Eurodebt crisis, as well as the greatest period of uncertainty since the Great Depression of the 1930s with the coronacrisis (globally).

Low growth rates of investment and wages in industry, as resources are redirected toward finance, led to the crowding out of productive industry by finance. Corporations no longer prioritized industrial expansion but sought financial growth as a core road to profits. Lower real wages and public capital negatively impacted profit, investment, and growth in the industry, especially in the core, as workers and companies increased debt (periodically and structurally) within "*3. Production-Distribution*" relations (Beitel 2009; Elsner 2016; UNCTAD 2024). Financial wheeling and dealing took over industry so that the (periodic and structural) "sabotage" (Veblen 1921) of production and services shaped the reigning norms and routines of business. Louçã (2021) and Perez (2016) believe these anomalies are due to the system not having an appropriate set of eco-geo-institutional relations to realize potential surpluses in markets, while Gordon (2017, 2018) has repeatedly stressed

movements, LGBQTIA movements, and so on, are analyzed in the *Journal of World System Research.*

that the technological styles of the post-1970s, especially US capitalism, have not contributed to productivity improvements (and GDP growth) like previous waves of innovation.[7]

Through the *"4. Corporate System,"* declining levels of reciprocity, redistribution, householding, and informal markets in corporations led to excess competition, especially global competition as Asia (e.g., China) has reemerged as a major player (linked to the *longue duree*), which reduced the profits of industry, especially in the declining yet still "core" nations, while it enhanced the profits of finance (within both finance and industry) (Walker 1999). Much has been written about merger movements and the power of the Big Five (Alphabet [Google], Microsoft, Apple, Amazon, and Facebook [Meta]) and other high-tech companies. But overriding this is the global competition between the US and China and (more generally) between the liberal-democratic allies vs. autocratic powers and their respective corporate systems.

Expanding contractual relationships with other firms and workers through international supply chains, commodity chains, and subcontracting reduces agglomeration benefits, economies of scale, and scope for private returns. These rising transaction costs of attempting to mimic pure market relations in corporate systems put more pressure on workers and middle managers while enhancing the power of CEOs and CFOs. They especially pose problems when crises erupt and dislodge the inner connectedness of the chains, and when the relative power of leading firms within the chains (especially powerful retailers) squeezes necessary profits from less powerful members of the chain and sends them bankrupt or into yet another merger and acquisition "opportunity," to try and counter the global competitive forces through efforts to reduce competition wherever possible.

It is for this reason that the earlier "flexible manufacturing" trend of (a) just-in-time stock adjustment (and customized supply), (b) total quality management, (c) participatory inclusion, and (d) total quality management has been majorly adjusted. In its place have been (i) enhanced cost considerations in a demand-constrained system, (ii) the eschewing of participatory inclusion in favor of rule by capital (neo—Taylorism) and robotics, and (iii) heightened debt ratios in wage and

---

[7] As Gordon (2017, 635) shows, productivity (average growth rate of output per hour [worked]) in the US economy for 1948–1970 was 2.71%; while during 1970–1994-1994 and 2004-2015, combined, it was 1.38% (1.08% with educational adjustment); while the forecast growth of productivity for 2015–2040 is 1.20% (with educational adjustment). Productivity has basically halved from long-wave upswing to long-wave downswing, with likely downswing continuing into the foreseeable future. The educational adjustment figure relates to educated persons working in low-education jobs. The reason for the lower productivity is said to be that the technology style does not generally raise GDP (or productivity) since, for instance, robots have not penetrated consumer markets, 3D printers are not being mass produced, and the smartphone enhances consumer surplus but not growth. Gordon recognizes a modest short-term increase in productivity during 1994–2004, but not one relevant to waves of long-term growth. He also recognizes a problem when the top 1% of the population benefits most from the low productivity rises while the bottom 99% do not. (annual Growth rate of income in the US for the top 1% of income earners has been 4.05% compared with the bottom 99% of income earners of 1.28% [post tax] during 1979–2011; Gordon 2017, 611.) Growth rates were all about equal during 1948–1972.

profit-constrained systems. The idea of reducing costs by having "complete" contracts and pure markets rather than organizations per se never worked due to the real needs for profitability, power, and long-term continuity within the circuit of capital in the light of major crises.

The relative power of capital was enhanced within *"5. Business Culture,"* which generated greater levels of alienation, exploitation, and incarceration as individualism was given priority over norms of fairness, equity, and participation. Since the 1980s, most workplaces have been generating greater power for upper-level management while workers and lower (and middle) management were squeezed (Kristal 2013). Minorities and "lumpens" were controlled through expanded resources for incarceration as law and order were prioritized. Individualism raised the prospects of a few while reducing opportunities for the many and increasing the power of conspicuous consumption through "keeping up with the Joneses," as inequality expanded, as much recent research has highlighted (see, e.g., Stilwell 2019, Piketty 2024).

Within the systems of *"6. Families and Communities,"* families have been losing resources as divorce rates remain high, fewer people are marrying, and the institution of the family is being deinstitutionalized. Family functions have increasingly been commodified as cooking, making clothes, repairs, and potential labor-power-enhancing activities, and others have shifted to the market, and more time is spent away from home at work, markets, educational institutions, and traveling. The community lost bridging networks within and between especially lower classes and civil society; political space has been crowded out by efforts to make money; and voluntary associations are increasingly needed but less capable of providing resources for the needy (and in decline). The increase in inequality, declining trust, and rising institutional instability have negatively affected the quality of life and public resources for the family and community (O'Hara 2004, 2023, chap. 12; Ciscel and Heath 2001). In like manner, deindustrialization and declining cities and towns in many areas, as well as the reduced ability and desire to procreate given these anomalies, in much of the world, result in population growth that is often lower than reproductive levels, even often after migration. This poses threats to GDP per capita and GDP per worker and risks further bankruptcy of pension funds and backlogs in hospitals as the average age of the population rises majorly (GBD 2024).

In the *"7. Ecological Economy,"* the disembedded economy has especially taken a toll on the environment as nations have increased their ecological footprint well beyond biospheric capacity. Declining profits and wages have placed even greater pressure on ecological resources, leading to a higher rate of greenhouse gas emissions, declining natural habitats, and species extinction, especially emanating from the *longue duree*, but also impacting the conjunctures and events. Climate change is now seen as the greatest challenge (crisis) of the global system, which requires a new "environmental" performance-based geo-techno-institutional dynamic underlying accumulation to resolve the issue before it becomes irreversible (many think it is by now, which leaves adaptation as our main hope and a hoped-for major innovation in the future to reduce the sun's rays on Earth). Core nations have been attempting to partly resolve their ecological/resource crisis by transferring the problem to the periphery, where public controls over (legal and illegal) logging, mining, and pollution are generally weak (O'Hara 2023; Foster 2014). Meanwhile, international agreements to solve this problem are below par, have not been ratified by the most powerful nations, and do not stabilize global and regional temperatures enough to prevent catastrophic outcomes for the planet (IPCC 2023).

In the *"8. Global Economy,"* historically low rates of real investment and wages, higher debt, transfers from real investment to spending on fictitious capitals, cost-cutting measures, and declining public investment have inhibited productivity and placed a severe limit on the growth of world income (World Bank 2021). Most nations give priority to expanding exports (and "microeconomic reform") rather than coordinating expansionary measures for global performance. With a restricted global market, greater competition inhibits demand (profit rates, productive investment, and wages) and prevents sustained growth per capita.

Eschewing voluntarism and structuralism, we see that these eight major systemic contradictions emanating from within the eco-techno-institutions (at the meso-level), linking to habits and norms (at the micro-level), cultural hegemony, and the vested interests (at a "higher" level) are inextricably intertwined. The circular causation between the contradictions generates multiple cumulative motions, building on each other through multiplier impacts that amplify the process of dampened and unstable socioeconomic performance. The institutional changes of the neoliberal institutional conjunctural system, including some core events and *longue duree* processes, exert negative impacts on real output (including services), productivity, growth, inequality, and the quality of life for especially the lower and middle classes. These multiple and interdependent anomalies of neoliberalism put more pressure on institutional systems, thus exacerbating periodic and structural crises of uncertainty and instability. As Bob Jessop (2013, 17) says, the neoliberal "finance-dominated model continues to destabilise [potential] growth regimes in many areas."

At the horizontal emergence levels, the multiple contradictions of neoliberalism within and between the eco-techno institutions magnify the negative impacts through contradictory circular and cumulative causation as it runs through several iterations of anomalous reproduction. Here the meso-systemic contradictions do indeed become a novel reality magnified from the parts, especially generating novel outcomes of the system and impacts (through downward causation) cascading majorly on individual persons, lower and middle groups, families, communities, and corporations. The paradoxes and contradictions through conjunctures, phases of evolution, events, and long-term processes reveal a vast gulf emerging between the social needs of capitalism (and alternative historical systems) and the emphases on individual motivation, deregulation, and competition that encapsulate neoliberalism.

9.4 Decadal Crises and Other Polycrises

In the next three sections, we situate the (a) GFC, (b) Eurodebt Crisis, and (c) coronacrisis within major postwar (post-1970s) economic crises of capitalism. There were no major economic crises during the period of absolute US hegemony and long-wave upswing between 1945 and 1970 (Sherman and Kolk 1996). There were short-run Juglar cycles, some minor recessions, numerous wars (especially Korean and Vietnam), plus geopolitical crises such as the Cuban Missile Crisis. The major economic crises emerged during the long-wave downswing and *relative* (not absolute) US hegemony during the 1974–75–2020s.

The first *general* principle of political economy is the *principle of historical specificity*, that an understanding of society should be embedded in history. What is the historical environment in which the GFC emerged? How does history help to comprehend the problem? This is closely related to the principle of path dependence, where processes that emerge historically often become locked in and difficult to change. This also relates to business cycles, long waves, and eco-techno-institutional change. Cycles and waves are embedded in the dynamics of the history of the US and other economies. For instance, the historical operation of cycles and long waves impacts financial/housing crises. Since the mid-1970s, the US economy (Wolfson 1994) and the global economy (O'Hara 2004, 2023) have been undergoing long-wave downswing and serious periodic financial crises. Financial crises tend to occur variously before or during recessions, but they are closely linked to wave and cycle downswings as cause and/or effect.

Since the 1970s, the following crises, financial and economic, have been especially notable in the US and many global economies, as shown in Table 9.1.

Our analysis of long waves and hegemony during the postwar period of the 1940s–2020s demonstrated that there were, especially in the core, no major depressions, deep recessions, or major financial crises during the 1950s–early 1970s, but increasingly severe recessions and financial crises during the 1970s–2020s. The core tended to experience long-wave upswings during the 1950s–early 1970s, under conditions of US hegemony, and major crises and subsequent long-wave downswings during the 1970s–2020s under relative US hegemony.

Suter (1992) showed that debt crises have tended to emerge during long-wave downswings, especially in the periphery. The number of countries in default and the share of defaulted debt were highest during the 1820s–1830s, the 1870s, and the 1930s, and during the more institutionalized workings of default, rescheduling numbers and percentages were very high during the 1980s (p. 63, Appendix). Perhaps the most general way to describe the 1970s–2020s polycrises globally is that there were four major waves of debt accumulation throughout the world, which tended to result in major financial crises (World Bank 2021).

The first wave of debt (crisis) was during the 1980s–1990s, especially in the periphery (some in the semi-periphery) of Latin America and the Caribbean and Africa. The second wave of debt crises occurred during 1990–2001, comprising nations in East Asia and the Pacific and Eastern Europe and Central Asia, culminating in the Asian and Russian financial crises. The third wave was associated with

Table 9.1 Major postwar economic crises of capitalism

Crises	Periodicity	Geographies, institutions, ecologies, and markets involved	Crisis example?
1st major recession of postwar capitalism	Mid-1970s	Multiple institutional demise (oil regime, exchange rate regime)	Franklin National Bank
2nd major recessions of postwar capitalism	1980s, 1980–1983	Debt crises in third world, monetarist, neoliberal, new classical demand anomalies	Commercial banking crisis
3rd major postwar crisis of capitalism	Late 1980s & early 1990s	1987 stock market crash, market crashes, and recession (1990–92)	Stock market crash, (global) recession
4th major postwar crisis of capitalism	Late 1990s & early 2000s	Asian financial crises, Russian crisis, corporate crisis, internet bubble, 9/11, recession	Enron, WorldCom, & Tyco corporate crisis, stock market crash, terrorism, wars
5th major postwar crisis of GFC & Eurodebt crises	Late 2000s & early–mid-2010s	GFC and Eurodebt crisis	Credit crunch & financial panic; depressions (EU)
6th major postwar crisis: Coronacrisis	Early 2020s	Debt, insufficient health capital, uncertainty	Chinese Wuhan virus
7th major postwar crisis: Climate crises	1990s–2020s➔	Ecologies, planet earth	Heat waves, droughts, wildfires, floods, hurricanes, species extinction, rising waterways

Source: Adapted from O'Hara (2000, 2009a, b, 2023), Wolfson (1994), Kindleberger (2000)

rising private borrowing from US and European banks, which cascaded into the GFC of 2007–2009 and the Eurodebt crisis thereafter. The fourth wave during 2010–present represents the largest rise in debt and the greatest number of nations of all four waves, especially among emerging and developing nations, the impacts of which are ongoing.

The similarities between these debt waves were that they occurred in an environment of low or falling interest rates, financial deregulation and innovation, and an upswing in the short cycle. Prudential regulation was generally lacking while there were clear incentives for private businesses to lend and borrow freely. There were differences between the four waves, with the first wave involving private firms in the core lending to public institutions in the periphery, and inflation being higher than during the other three waves. Moving from the first to the fourth wave represented increasing institutionalization of multilateral renegotiation and rescheduling of debt. (World Bank 2021) The fourth wave is still in motion and has more safety nets in place to protect the system from collapse, but we still do not know whether its trajectory will end in major multinational financial crises like the others (although the experience of China has been tumultuous).

For the core, the long-wave downswings commenced during the period of US relative hegemony, the 1970s to the 2020s, and it is during these Juglar highpoints, especially of the mid-1970s and early 1980s, late 1980s and early 1990s, late 1990s, early 2000s, late 2000s, early–mid-2010s, and the early 2020s that prominent crises occurred, linking to recessions. Partly these instabilities were influenced by long-wave downswing, lack of absolute hegemony, and short-cycle expansion excesses, and instabilities deepened long-wave downswings, cycle excesses, and absolute hegemony absences. Much of the evidence for these tendencies is provided by Marty Wolfson, O'Hara, Minsky, and Kindleberger, who attribute the system-upsetting financial crises to the lack of LLR and possibly the absence of hegemony, while Minsky himself said no Great Depression had occurred for the global economy (or the core) since the 1930s (until the GFC and Eurodebt crisis), due to big government and LLR.

Kindleberger's successive editions (with various co-authors) of his *Manias, Panics and Crashes: A History of Financial Crises* (up to the 2015 edition *only*, e.g., Aliber and Kindleberger 2015) utilize Minsky's model of financial crises to help explain the major instabilities of the mid-1970s, early 1980s, late 1980s/early 1990s, late 1990s/early 2000s, and late 2000s/early 2010s. They conclude that these successive crises were collectively the most volatile and extreme in the whole history of capitalism.[8] Kindleberger is less interested in the cycles and more concerned with financial crises. He uses a qualitative historical method, devoid of technical tools, to comprehend these crises.

To capture the broad contours of the financial crises and recessions, below we present the World Uncertainty Index (WUI) for the years 1990–2024 in Fig. 9.2, which only commenced inception in the 1990s[9]:

Apart from the crises of the early 1990s, there was the Internet rise and crash of the late 1990s and early 2000s, which included the corporate crisis, clashes with terrorists, wars in the Middle East, and a recession in many areas. This was followed by the GFC of 2007–09, which *affected mostly the highly developed deregulated capitalist economies*, along with (especially) the Eurodebt crisis of 2010–2015. The greatest upsurge in uncertainty throughout the *whole world* was the coronacrisis of 2020–2022 (continuing into 2023 in China), hence the major spike. Thereafter, we saw another hike in the face of the invasion of Ukraine (2022 onward), which also impacted supply chains and inflation, along with interest rates, for a time. Currently, we are in another crisis, what many describe as a "pre-war" era, which could mean

---

[8] However, the most recent edition (2023), without the supervision of Kindleberger or the previous coauthor, is completely different, without the use of Minsky or mention of the greatest crises ever in the history of capitalism. Because it is so different from previous editions, we do not think it deserves to be placed in the Kindleberger camp, and hence do not recognize its authenticity in this respect. It will not be mentioned specifically.

[9] "The WUI is computed by counting the percentage usage of the word 'uncertainty' (or its variant) in the Economist Intelligence Unit country reports. The WUI is then rescaled by multiplying by 1,000,000. A higher number means higher uncertainty and vice versa. For example, an index of 200 corresponds to the word uncertainty accounting for 0.02% of all words, which—given the EIU reports are on average about 10,000 words long—means about 2 words per report." (WUI 2024).

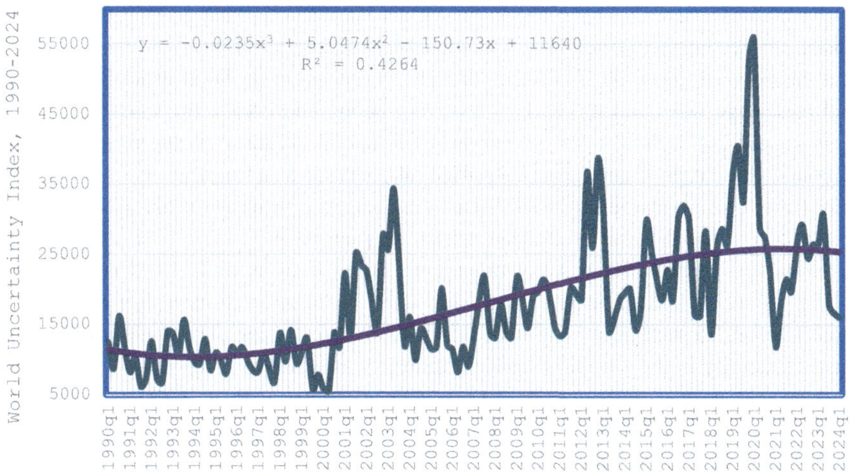

Fig. 9.2 World uncertainty index, 1990–2024. (Source: Adapted from the raw data provided by Ahir et al. 2024) Note: The purple line is the polynomial trend line (Order No. 3)

"pre-WW3" (see Chap. 10 for details), including another major spike in uncertainty during the 'Trumpian 2025' (possibly being ongoing; not shown).

Neoliberalism in practice promoted the interests of capital at the expense of labor, financial innovation rather than productive industry, the power of capital rather than the state, global rather than national, and urban rather than rural interests. In this context, the period of especially the late 1970s through to notably the GFC, Eurocrisis, and to some degree the coronacrisis, especially in the core, was notable for the use of extensive financial innovations, rising debt through financial deregulation, declining real wages, and higher, especially financial, profits, greater global mobility of finance, and in more recent decades greater oligopoly rather than competition (domestically), but globally more competition (especially between China and the US). The past decade and a half have seen a tendency away from neoliberalism and globalization, but they still impact to some degree.

We need to comprehend the events of the 2000s leading to the subprime mortgage market crisis in the US, then the international spread leading to the GFC, Eurodebt crisis, and further to Depression in nations such as initially Iceland and Ireland and extensively later Italy, Portugal, Greece, etc. into the 2010s.

The subprime (USA) and global financial crisis (GFC) were not simply financial crises, but also economic crises, and more generally, socioeconomic crises of legitimacy for deregulated capitalism. They were socioeconomic crises because they structurally affected finance, economics, and society. Their onset is linked to historical trends of corporate power, dampening real wages, and rising debt, and they are part of the trajectory of successive financial crises and recessions over the past several decades (see Wolff 2009). But they are also financial and economic crises in the narrower sense. The usual pattern is recession followed by financial/corporate crises, which occurred during 1974, 1980, 1982, 1990–1991, and 2001–03 (especially in the US). However, sometimes booms in the short cycle have generated financial crises before the recession. This was the case with the stock market crash of 1987 and the GFC of 2007–09. After the mid-1970s recession in the aftermath of the oil and real wage rises and the early 1980s recessions and crises, the mid–late 1980s upswing set the scene for a whole series of financial escalations, such as leveraged buyouts, share repurchases, and corporate takeovers, often financed by credit. Low-debt firms often became high-debt firms very quickly, which stimulated a speculative bubble (globally and in the US), which crashed in 1987.

However, a recession did not emerge in many nations until 1990 (often until 1992), as a real estate boom manifested itself in many nations (after the equity crash) before expectations declined, bringing on a recession. The 1990s boom and bust, especially in the core and semi-periphery, was a classic long-wave downswing Juglar cycle as the subsequent boom was more than negated by the ICT crash, corporate crisis, and 9/11 (2001) trend to recession (especially in the US) (much like the 1920s). Recession emerged in the US during 2001, while the corporate crisis continued through 2002 and 2003 (affecting also the equity market), followed by major wars in Iraq and Afghanistan, and recovery did not eventuate until 2004 onward. The associated corporate crisis, linked to Enron, WorldCom, Global Crossing, Arthur Anderson, and a host of other companies, continued to be played out in the courts even until well into the 2010s. As recovery and boom established itself, various financial innovations and institutional changes led to the emergence of a subprime mortgage market expansion in the US. This was stimulated by the so-called low-risk environment established by the boom of the mid-2000s.

The key difference between 1987 and 2007/09 is that the stock market crash in 1987 was generally followed by a boom in another market (e.g., property), and the recession did not emerge until subsequent market decline around 1990–92 (especially in the core). The recovery of the early–mid-2000s, especially in the US, was slow, but again the emergence of exuberance into the mid-to-late 2000s led to the biggest crash of core economies since the Great Depression of the 1930s (to that time). The subprime crisis, GFC, and subsequent Eurodebt crisis were different since a credit crunch occurred first in the US (late 2007), then financial panic mainly in the US (late 2008) and recession (late 2008 and 2009), followed by Eurodebt crisis (2010–2015ff). A decline in several markets had been ongoing, including equities, housing, subprime/collateralized debt, and resources. The economic crisis become interregional in nature, leading to the EU crisis, especially in places such as Greece that went into the Depression.

9.5 Subprime Crisis, GFC, and CCC

Figure 9.3 shows linkages between the subprime crisis, GFC, and CCC processes:

To start with, we need to be cognizant of the fact that, as Kindleberger (2000, 3), alluding to Minsky, says: "Financial crises are associated with the peaks of business Cycles." Kindleberger himself was not especially interested in business cycles, only

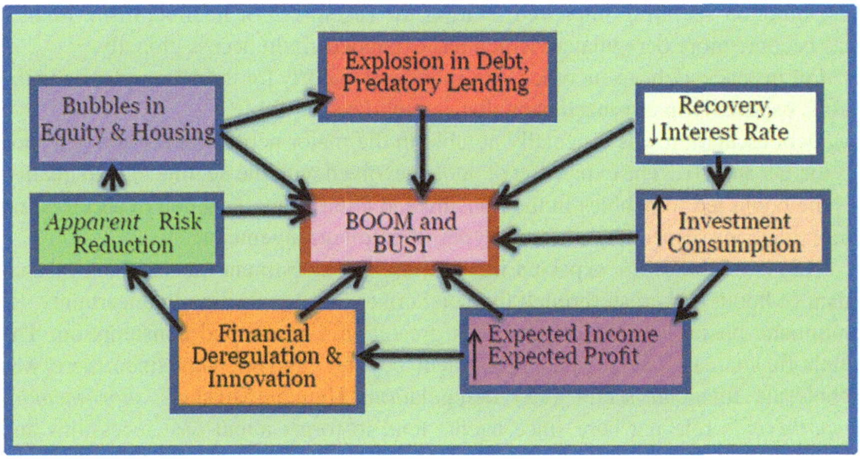

Fig. 9.3 Subprime circular and cumulative upswing and downswing. (Source: Adapted from O'Hara (2009b) Note: Green *background* area = eco-geo-spatial environment)

the crises, but we must provide some basis for the cycles. The US recession resulting from the dot.com upswing and crash, corporate crises, and terrorist attacks of 9/11 lasted for 8 months, from March to November 2001. It had been 10 years since the previous recession. The stock market crashed from an index of 1550 (Jan 2001) to 750 (Jan 2003) over 2 years. Interest rates declined from 7 to 1% between 2000 and 2003.

Several interacting factors were at work, and the subprime crisis cannot be reduced to a single factor (as Mian and Sufi 2008 attempt). Many authors recognize this interaction between many variables in a multicausal model (see Wray 2007). Gunnar Myrdal and Nicholas Kaldor call this multifactor approach a model of CCC since the variables are multiple and the magnified multiplier of all factors combined is very sharp and cascading.

In the US, the initial recovery of aggregate demand from the early 2000s recession, lower official interest rates, and less uncertainty eventually stimulated investment and consumption spending. This led to a period of optimism, lower unemployment, eventually an expanded share market, and expected income and profits over 2004–2006.

During post-US-hegemony cycle upswings, credit typically overexpands dangerously relative to income, because euphoric conditions enhance *expected* corporate income and profitability much greater than the growth of *long-term* actual corporate income, due to speculative bubbles. Real wages are also dampened due to rising prices, while consumption is financed often by debt (since real wages have been declining since the 1970s). Greater debt ratios, including the so-called democratization of debt and predatory lending/debt, contributed to boom-fragility. In an environment of uncertainty, when prospective yields reflect long-term conditions, the prevailing business climate is often a proxy for future profit. Hence, *apparently* "good times" and low *apparent* risk lead to expanded credit as investment and consumption spending improved. During the recent era of neoliberalism, finance has become more deregulated, which has expanded credit access globally.

For instance, debt-to-income ratios increased majorly for the 10 years prior to the GFC, especially in advanced capitalist economies; see Table 9.2.

Debt escalation was especially notable in the major neoliberal economies, such as the US and UK. The expansion of debt coevolved with the decline in loan quality, as the boom led to bubbles in the housing and equities markets due to accelerating debt financing, especially different types of credit arrangements.

This is linked to the expected income—credit—investment transmission mechanism of boom and crash through financial crises. First, a decline in uncertainty via optimistic business climates generates greater investment and consumption. The euphoria increased credit and investment beyond fundamentals since there was wholesale financial sector (FS) deregulation. Hyman Minsky's *short-memory hypothesis* is relevant here since agents tend to forget about past recessions and financial crises and set up expectations based on the *prevailing business climate*, especially as *new generations* of financial and speculative agents are active in the markets. Much of the so-called investment is misallocated during eras of wholesale financial deregulation as the public good of stability declines. It is especially misallocated to the relatively cyclical and speculative sectors, such as the secondary equity markets, property markets, and foreign exchange markets.

Financial innovation and deregulation, including much greater levels of disintermediation and securitization of mortgage market securities, enhanced the boom and fragility. The "financial innovation" of securitizing subprime mortgages (used more and in different ways than in the past) led to problems of lack of available market information about who had the mortgages, what was the quality of the collateral, and what would happen if the boom in housing and equity markets faltered. The complexity of the securitized mortgage bond was an especially critical problem leading to informational anomalies in the bond system.

Rating agencies and institutional mispricing of risk played a role. There was a conflict of interest between rating agencies, such as Moody's and Standard and Poor's, providing ratings for companies and providing financial advice as well. The lack of suitable information exchange between borrower and broker, broker and originator, issuer and originator, trustee and issuer, asset fund and trustee, plus investors and asset managers, followed through to credit rating agencies. Appropriate ratings depended mainly on the quality and quantity of information, and rating

Table 9.2 Liabilities as a percent of disposable income, advanced capitalist nations, 1996, 2001, 2006

	1996	2001	2006	% ↑1996–01	% ↑ 2001–06
USA	92	106	140	15.22	32.08
UK	105	118	168	12.38	42.37
Canada	107	114	128	6.54	12.28
EU	n.a.	73	81	n.a.	10.95

Source: Adapted from Mizen (2008, 535)

agencies and others failed to incorporate appropriate risk (or rather, higher levels of *uncertainty*) into their calculative models. However, these rating agencies also provided financial advice on how the buyer of the risk assessment might organize its bond offerings, which depends in part on the risk assessment provided. They were thus unlikely to criticize their own risk assessment in advising how to offer the bonds. The "risk" models also were highly contingent on rising housing prices, for instance, so that if alternative risk assessment scenarios (and other aspects of "stress testing") had been the *norm,* this would have likely moderated instability somewhat. Certain various quasi, semi, or total government institutions, such as Freddie Mac, Fannie Mae, and Ginny Mae, also played a key role in the rise and fall process, as they ultimately lost control of their portfolios through the securitization process.

These multiple factors generated housing, securitized bonds, and equity booms, which in turn enhanced aggregate demand while circular and cumulative causation ran through several runs over the business cycle. All major factors contributed to the bubble and hence fragility and subprime crisis. Debt overexpanded based on euphoric expectations and bubbles in the housing and equity markets. Governments played a critical role in reducing interest rates to historic lows and then increasing them relatively rapidly. All this happened while agents assumed risk was relatively low, while systemic risk (*uncertainty*) was rising, especially since midway through the boom (after the inflection point).

During 2007–09, housing prices declined, demand for securitized bonds evaporated, and equity markets went into freefall in the US, as the credit crunch and financial panic took hold. Eventually, agents realized their calculative models of risk were wrong, and they reformulated risk assessments *suddenly* to reflect high levels of uncertainty as confidence in markets evaporated. Increases in liquidity preference led to greater demand for money, flight to quality, decreasing aggregate demand, and negative GDP growth.

US liquidity problems affected especially *core* nations in proportion to the extent that financial institutions and agents were buying US securitized bonds (high levels of uncertainty were not shown in the *global* uncertainty index for these earlier years). Close global linkages between financial institutions in the circuit of money capital led to chains of bankruptcy for financial institutions, especially in Iceland, the UK, Europe, and Japan; but there were also linkages to Chinese institutions and eventually a flow-on effect to oil-based economies, many other developing nations, and regional growth and investment.

The economic crisis became international (but not global) in nature, and it has been the biggest crisis and recession for many nations up to then since the Great Depression of the 1930s (the coronacrisis was worse *globally*). The Icelandic economy was "temporarily destroyed," since it was based mainly on financial institutions (since deregulation), with its equity market crashing 92% and real GDP declining by 10% in 2009, indicating a depression. Most of the *major* stock exchanges around the world crashed in the order of 40–60% over the 12 months to late October 2008. New York, London, Tokyo, Hong Kong, and Sydney exchanges were severely impacted by the securitized subprime dislocation. Subprime and related financial linkages were increasingly affecting the real economy of production, employment, and income, as the figures for 2009 imply. Sharp recessions occurred in the US, UK, and Japan (as indicated above), plus the world economy (−0.5% real GDP), Europe (−2.5%), and Canada (−1.5 to −2.0), with much of the rest of the world experiencing positive but much lower growth (RGE Monitor 2009). In this light, governments around the world were variously responding with rescue packages associated with lender of last resort facilities, nationalization of financial enterprises, fiscal and monetary incentives, and even some bailing out of manufacturing firms (some being temporary) (see O'Hara 2013).

9.5.1 Principle of Contradiction, Financial Crises, and the GFC

The *principle of contradiction* surfaces again. Contradictions are opposing tendencies associated with institutional processes, which are a source of movement, periodic instability, and crises (see O'Hara 2001, 2008a, b, 2023 Glossary). Contradiction is crucial for comprehending various opportunity costs between forces that have varying levels of power through time. There are many contradictions relevant to the subprime crisis, GFC, and EU crisis, including those between capital and labor, finance and industry, and monopoly and competition (just to mention three).

In this specific section, we are especially interested in the contradiction between financial stability and financial freedom, or an associated one between finance and industry (plus to some degree other contradictions, such as that between capital and labor). In political economy, Karl Marx (1894), Thorstein Veblen (1923), Schumpeter (1911), and Keynes (1936) wrote about these contradictions, which have been added to by various neo-Marxian, post-Keynesian, and institutional political economists. Deep periodic financial crises tend to occur *historically* when there is (a) a long-wave downswing and (b) a large degree of financial deregulation. These two conditions help to generate deep financial crises. Long-wave downswings often occur when there is, over often 30 years, a combination of (i) product cycle maturation, (ii) general low industrial profit and investment, (iii) low real growth per capita, culminating in (iv) eco-techno-institutional systems that are not working well (i.e., CSDs).

Historically, major financial crises have occurred when the financial system was excessively deregulated (in principle, it should also occur when finance is *excessively* regulated, under capitalism). Most advanced capitalist economies deregulated their economies in the 1970s–1980s, generating instabilities into the 1980s, 1990s, and 2000s and beyond. Most Asian economies deregulated finance during the 1980s–early 1990s, leading to the Asian crisis of the late 1990s (their CSDs were much stronger). The state tended to respond to these crises by reregulating to some degree, through the intervention of a proper reserve bank, prudential controls, and lender of last resort (especially in Asia). In the US, the corporate crisis of the early 2000s led to the Sarbanes-Oxley Act (2002) to improve governance in corporations (to *hopefully* prevent fraudulent reporting of financial information). However, especially in economies controlled by finance (e.g., the US, UK), the subsequent boom led to a *distant memory* of these earlier problems and further financial innovations that had been untested in history (e.g., expanding use of securitized subprime mortgages). This led to major instabilities a few years later.

When finance dominates industry through deregulation, historically a misallocation of resources from industry to finance evolves, which reduces productive investment and emphasizes short-term market rates of return in equity markets, the payment of fees on innovative financial instruments, and the rate of turnover rather than the quality of debtors. To some degree, this is merely a declining metamorphosis of previously dominant economies as the rate of return from industry declines and activities turn to finance as an alternative (one of the rules/stylized facts of declining hegemony, see chaps. 5 to 8). The rise in finance (and other services) is thus both a cause and an effect of declining profit for highly productive sectors. As the industrial-capitalist sector of industry becomes depleted, the "household" sector takes on a life of its own through higher credit rates and consumption demand, partly because real wages have been falling and partly because deregulated finance enables it.

Developments in the USA are typical of developments in other advanced neoliberal economies, such as the UK and France (see Stockhammer 2004; Binswanger 2004). For the US, financial sector (FS) debt as a proportion of total debt increased by over 200% from the mid-1970s to the mid-2000s. Mortgage debt for households increased relative to GDP by over 100% during this period. And financial assets as a proportion of tangible assets for nonfinancial corporations rose by 200%. One technical reason finance was able to grow faster than the industry in mature capitalist economies, especially, is that speculative bubbles (and fees) enhance the growth of finance if bubbles crash/decline back to near "fundamental values," rather than *below* fundamentals. Likely this is what happened in the mid-1970s, early 1980s, late 1980s, and early 1990s, and again in the early 2000s. However, when they crash below fundamentals, as likely happened during the GFC, this upsets the dynamics of financial dominance and propels reregulation of the financial system. Reregulation and post-neoliberal practices are expanding around the world.

Financial deregulation and innovation thus expand the rate of credit, during business cycle upswings, toward often dangerous levels, which result in crises. More latterly in the US, much of this credit came through the capital account surpluses (to balance current account deficits). But it came not just as potentially productive FDI, but more importantly also as European and Asian debt money buying securitized mortgage-backed securities (MBSs), i.e., bonds. In this way, US debt escalated while Europeans and Asians came to hold many of these problem bonds. The crisis was thus typically a period of dangerous overexpansion of lending and credit to risky customers. The bubble was especially important for the housing and stock markets, which crashed in the US, and through regional and global linkages affected other areas.

There was much variability throughout the US, with housing prices declining (Aug 2007—Aug 2008) by 18.0% in the "West," 9.3% in the "South," 3.9% in the

"Northeast," and 2.3% in the "Midwest" (Integrated Asset Services 2008). An international study showed that for the first time in the past 100 years, the housing bubble has become closely synchronized, at least vis-à-vis the four nations studied. The housing bubble was shown to be (as of March 2006) in the order of 20% above fundamentals in the US, 56% in the UK, 67% in the Netherlands, and 35% in Norway. The multiple bubble crashes of 2007–2009 have moved prices closer to fundamentals, probably eventually below fundamentals. This has instigated major uncertainty around the globe, generating, as noted, the biggest financial and economic crisis since the Great Depression of the 1930s (prior to the coronacrisis).

9.5.2 Principles of Financial Innovation, Heterogeneous Groups/Agents, and the GFC

The *principle of financial innovation* is especially important. Where innovations generate more power to finance major crises often emerge, usually during short-cycle upswings. Consider disintermediation and securitization of subprime mortgage markets. These revamped innovations enhanced the power of finance. Initially, however, these "innovations" exacerbate instabilities since they were new (and/or existing securities that experienced rapid overuse) and no one was sure about their impact on the economy because of lack of experience in their use and lack of knowledge about the changes wrought by their power and motion.

The *principle of heterogeneous groups and agents* in political economy argues that operators in the economy are not homogenous but act through different social roles. The major roles include different class and nonclass processes associated with workers and capitalists, industrialists and financiers, buyers and sellers, men and women, and different ethnic groups. Also important are some micro-roles in the securitized subprime circuit (as part of the wider circuit of money capital), shown in Fig. 9.4.

Stage one in the circuit is when mortgage loan arrangers (brokers) bring a multitude of borrowers and lenders together for contractual commitments relating to mortgages. The second stage is when many mortgage lenders sell loan arrangements to issuers of securitized bonds, while borrowers make monthly repayments to servicers. The third stage is when issuers of securitized bonds, made up of a multitude of hundreds or thousands of different mortgages, sell securitized mortgage bonds to "investors" (underwriters may assist and rating agencies [RAs] rate the bonds). The fourth stage is when servicers remit monthly repayments to the issuers of the bond (and service bad debts with the trustee), who in turn pass a percentage of the funds onto investors. The fifth stage of the circuit is when degrees of confidence held by "investors" generate varying degrees of action by the arranger to continue such practices on an ongoing basis. This circuit undergoes successive rounds of action, usually of a cumulative nature, due to the dynamics and contradictions embedded in the institutional relationships between heterogeneous agents.

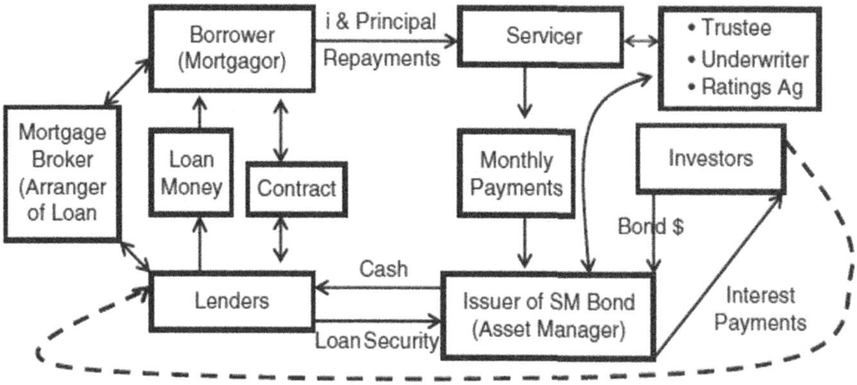

Fig. 9.4 Heterogeneous agents-groups, securitized circuit of finance. (Source: O'Hara 2009b)

Securitized mortgage debt includes different classes of mortgages bundled together and sold as a package by a chain of agents and institutions, resulting in the formation of a mortgage bond. In this package are prime and subprime mortgages. Originally these bonds were sold as investment-grade securities, thanks to the rating agencies, even though by the mid–late 2000s, subprime components represented an increasing proportion of the total. Securitized mortgages as a percentage of total mortgages rose from 0% (1965) to 5.3% (1975) to 22.5% (1985) to 50.0% (1995) to 56.5% (2005) (Schnure 2005, 23).

There are four classes of mortgage loans: Agency, Jumbo, Alt-A, and Subprime. Agency loans relate to prime borrowers conforming to government underwriting standards. Jumbo loans include prime borrowers with a principal balance larger than government standards. Alt-A loans relate to borrowers not conforming to government limits due to high leverage or lack of documentation of income. Subprime loans link to borrowers with a lower-than-prime credit rating. The recent subprime crisis has been linked to both subprime and Alt-A loans, which collectively rose from 7.42% (2001) to 42.02% (2006) of total issued mortgage loans (Ashcraft and Schuermann 2007, 7).

The main debtors in the subprime market were minority ethnic groups. During 2005 in Washington, DC, African American borrowers represented 70% of subprime home borrowers, followed by Latino borrowers at 9%; while in New York during 2006, 41% were African American, 29% Hispanic, and 14% Asian. In New York, the ten worst-hit neighborhoods were from "poor" (mostly "ethnic") communities (Sassen 2008). Generating financial innovations that depend on rising (often relatively unsecured) debt among the poorest sections of the community is a recipe for disaster, especially when the "honeymoon interest rates" typically disappear after a couple of years, during which interest payments tend to double. The best way to stimulate house ownership among the poor is to encourage the building of durable skills and jobs that stimulate sustainable income flows (Fernandez et al. 2008).

The development of these new financial relationships between economic agents created difficulties in an informational and social capital variety. During the 1950s to 1970s, housing finance linkages were based on trust, direct interaction, and the copious gathering of information. Finance was instituted to look after the collective action problems of providing finance for businesses and households. Deregulation stimulated anonymity between parties, market pricing rather than historical costing, and the pricing of risk based on dubious calculative norms. For instance, deregulation stimulated a marked shift in the relationship between borrowers and lenders. The previous borrower-lender style was broken in favor of more distant relationships between agents.

During long-wave upswing (1940s–early 1970s), the old style generated substantial home ownership among working people, since growth and income expanded majorly. The new style (e.g., 1980s–2000s) was based on increasing the velocity of lending to subprime mortgagees, along with rapidly growing securitization of MBS, while at the same time unwittingly generating a system crisis of uncertainty, which led to foreclosures for more than 3 million poor mortgagees in the US alone. This was associated with a decline in both bonding (within groups) and bridging (between groups) social capital. As Raymond Brescia (2008) found, the new financial instruments seemed to be based on encouraging low-income households to acquire property while also doing exactly the opposite (a classic contradiction). Poor mortgagees were encouraged to take on mortgages while paying excessive interest rates (after a couple of years), having difficulty renegotiating terms when foreclosure was likely, being worse off than if they never purchased a home (in losing whatever deposit—and dignity—they might have had), and having little information about alternative arrangements that could have been made with other institutions.

This decline in social capital led to worse communication between lenders and borrowers, inadequate information flows, lack of contract flexibility, higher risk-taking, dubious ethical standards of financial intermediation, and, as a result, high levels of *systemic uncertainty*. The complexity of the relationship between agents and institutions involved in mortgage-backed securities, collateralized debt obligations (CDOs), and credit default swaps (CDSs) led to a whole range of other factors enhancing risk and uncertainty.

9.5.3 Risk, Uncertainty, and the GFC

Issues of risk and uncertainty are critical to the subprime crisis and the GFC. The work of Frank Knight (1921), J.M. Keynes (1936), and G.L.S. Shackle (1955) has laid the ground rules of this analysis, and other political economists have taken this further. Risk is when financial aspects are said to be calculable and relatively determinate, such as the throwing of a die or the chance of being in an automobile accident. Uncertainty is when there is relative ignorance, such as having projects that are financed with the debt lasting into the future when knowledge is lacking or ambiguous. One can place risk and uncertainty on a continuum, as shown in Fig. 9.5, with risk at one end and uncertainty at the other, with elements of both in the middle.

The Basal Accord (Mark II) incorporated specific risk assessment models into the equation, due to persuasive corporate risk assessors who had "learnt the lesson" of the Savings and Loan crisis of the 1980s and the limits of Basel I. While Basel II applied primarily to international banks and had only recently come into play, some of the techniques have become widely used. Calculative, risk-based pricing models are one of these techniques that came into general normative practice, especially in the 1990s and 2000s, specifically linking to the presumed ability of clients to repay their debt. The idea behind these calculative models is that if interest rates paid are closely linked to the specific risk of clients, then expansion could proceed logically and rationally. The normative convention or "enabling myth" (Dugger 1996, 29–33) of the so-called scientific assessment of risk thus emerged so that economic action could be justified from a technical analysis of the factors involved. It thus *appeared* that, for instance, people with a poor credit history could be included in the market if their risks were adequately priced and lenders compensated accordingly. Scores based on these models, such as FICO scores, tend to adopt this philosophy of compensating institutions for greater risk by charging higher rates.

It is well known that these calculative models tend to assume risk moves in an anti-cyclical fashion (with a lag) because the risk weightings are based on expectations about the future determined by the *prevailing business climate*. Hence, "recognised risk" (rather than actual risk) will tend to rise some months before the cycle reaches its upper turning point and (especially) into recession and decline just before the lower turning point and into recovery through to high boom. The models do not consider the desirability of high-risk individuals with unsecured debt not being extended loans due to a threshold expansion of risk in the face of unlikely but possible scenarios. They also assumed erroneously that bundling higher-risk subprime together with lower-risk mortgages into a bond would cancel out much of the risk of the subprime element, even as the proportion of subprime in the bond increased (Mizen 2008: 554). Stress testing by use of alternative assessments based on changes in various markets and environments was not standard practice.

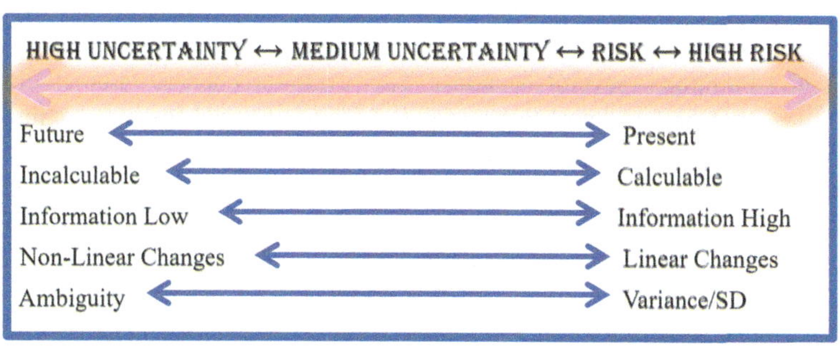

Fig. 9.5 Uncertainty↔Risk Continuum (*Source:* Adapted from O'Hara 2009b)

In general, risk assessments made by financial institutions, including Moody's, Standard & Poor's, and Fitch, did not incorporate *systemic uncertainty* into the equation. In attempting to calculate the risk of individual borrowers, broader questions of interdependencies, the complexity of the securities, and systemic linkages were abstracted. Business cycle upswing was *assumed* to generate low risk (for most of the upswing), with risk likely rising during the recession. This core problem is compounded by the fact that many individual risk assessments were done with speedy acceptance and with little regard for rigorous information gathering and analysis.

The calculative risk assessment models did not adequately consider uncertainty that may (suddenly) rise in the future, even in broad terms of including different scenarios in the assessments. In being deterministic, the calculative models exaggerated the degree of certainty about their assessments and ignored *systemic sources of uncertainty* at the macro or global level that emerge due to interdependencies between agents, markets, instruments, and institutions. There was no attempt to use what Martin Hellwig (2008:21) calls a "holistic approach" to risk and uncertainty, combining specific data with a broader understanding of cycles and tendencies of the macro and global economies.

These problems could have been alleviated by building on the work of Michal Kalecki, Hyman Minsky, and Martin Wolfson (see O'Hara 2001). This tradition recognizes that risk and uncertainty tend to be procyclical (with some lags), with cycle upswings (especially during long-wave downswings) eventually leading to much higher and sudden increases in uncertainty when instability reaches a tipping point (threshold effect). This *principle of increasing risk,* considered broadly, is important for recognizing the endogenous systemic risks and uncertainties that tend to rise during a boom. The Kalecki–Minsky–Wolfson tradition helps comprehend the subprime experience of massive credit downgrades, bankruptcy, liquidity crisis, and recession during 2007–09 (but is ignored in the calculative models of risk). This tradition especially helps to comprehend the following problems in the subprime crisis and the GFC:

(a) Evolution from Conservative to Market Accounting. There has been a switch from *historical cost* (conservative) to *fair market value* accounting and shareholder value over recent decades. This generates a "discrepancy" between the "financial investment" horizons of agents (daily or weekly) and the long life of real estate houses and buildings (several decades). This eventually led to bubbles crashing below fundamentals, as "market pricing" led many financial institutions into both illiquidity (a common problem in a credit crunch) *and* insolvency (common during recession), since in the face of a liquidity crunch *and* panic, they *immediately* had their assets devalued according to "market prices" (Hellwig 2008, 7). However, during the credit crunch and especially financial panic, it became difficult to ascertain what "fair values" were due to information problems and uncertainty.

(B) Increasing Distance between Underlying Assets and Instruments: Financial dependence and dominance led to innovations based on profit-making schemes that *expanded the distance* between underlying assets (mortgages) and financial instruments (securitized mortgages). This "originate-and-distribute model" generated a

major contradiction with securitization, namely that "outsourcing the funding side of an originator's balance sheet undermines its incentives to monitor the quality of the loans it originates" and results in "troubled loans becom[ing] the property and problems of someone further down the transaction chain" (Caprio Jr. et al. 2008, 12). There were informational frictions between borrower and mortgage broker; originator and arranger; arranger and third parties; servicer and borrower; servicer and third parties; asset manager and investor; and investor and credit rating agencies (see Ashcraft and Schuermann 2007, 2–3).

(c) The Emphasis on Velocity rather than Quality. There was a disproportionate emphasis on the *velocity of growth* of securitized subprime mortgages (assuming property prices would keep growing), rather than on the *quality of the mortgages* in the securities (bonds). The importance of velocity became a normative standard of judgment embedded in the collective consciousness of the players in the markets (quality was assumed to be reflected in mechanical calculative risk assessment models). (Sassen 2008:204.) Eventually "recognized risk" rose during 2008 to (broadly) equate with "actual risk" after a long lag.

(d) Credit Default Swaps (CDSs). One factor increasing systemic uncertainty was the use and abuse of CDSs. A buyer purchases a CDS from a seller for use as hedging against a loss in their (mortgage-backed) securities, or as speculation that other companies will experience a loss, or for arbitrage purposes. During late 2007, the private market in CDS had reached US$45 trillion, with 45% for speculative purposes. Illiquidity and insolvency problems for AIG and Lehman Brothers, in particular, generated panic in the CDS market (and the wider national and global economies) during late 2008, as these companies had a large stake in CDSs. Trillions of dollars of CDSs became worthless as Lehman Brothers became insolvent. Systemic *uncertainty* suddenly increased as thousands of firms were exposed to losses. (A "Minsky moment.")

(e) Calculative Risk Models ignored Systemic Risk and Uncertainty. The mechanical calculative models of risk were unable to include "systemic uncertainty" in the analysis. The risk-based pricing models were legitimized through "rigorous" credit scores and letter-rated risk for MBS, along with the use of credit default swaps, which led many borrowers to be indifferent to (or to encourage) default on the part of debtors. There was, to this point, only a limited history of mortgage securitization, which made it difficult to ascertain the future impact of their rapid expansion. Moody's, S&P, and Fitch concentrated on the rising market rather than potential future decline in real estate prices, rising interest rates, rising default rates, and recession (or different scenarios). (Langley 2008, 477–85).

(f) Use of Structured Investment Vehicles (SIVs). SIVs issue short-term commercial paper (liabilities) to fund longer-term assets such as CDOs. To evade Basel guidelines, many banks organized SIVs to deal with these assets and liabilities to prevent them from being shown on their balance sheets, which reduced the (low risk) capital requirements of banks. The assumption was that SIVs could engage in these activities without affecting the viability of the banks themselves. When problems emerged in these vehicles, many banks, such as Northern Rock and Bank of America, saw the need to include SIV positions on their balance sheets, which

affected bank profits and net worth positions, often leading to liquidity problems and insolvency.

(g) Securitized Mortgage Bonds Infected Global Circuits of Finance. Through national, regional, and global networks, the procyclical innovations such as subprime mortgage bonds, collateralized debt obligations, and credit default swaps with high system risks infected not only national but also international markets (especially in advanced nations). As they entered the financial circuits, their growing velocity gradually built up a massive "system-risk" (uncertainty) that mechanical calculative models failed to recognize. System problems became obvious in late 2007 (Sassen 2008, 208) and much worse in late 2008. The inability of calculative models of risk and deterministic worldviews to quickly "solve" the contradiction between individual risk and systemic uncertainty helped to initiate a breakdown of the financial and economic system (credit crunch, financial panic, and recession) in economies directly and indirectly linked to the circuit of securitized subprime financing (mostly in the core).

Such was the record of the subprime and global financial crises of 2007–09, which then contributed causal processes to the Eurodebt crisis 2009–2014–2017 circa.

9.6 Eurodebt Crisis

These especially core nations (notably in Europe) were also adversely affected by intersectoral linkages between defaulting securitized bond markets, credit default swap markets, structured investment vehicles, anomalous credit rating agencies, asset-instrument distance, velocity throughput, and bank-NBFI anomalies. In short, the American-style financial system was so riddled with vulnerabilities and uncertainties that it failed to function effectively and upset the whole global financial system and eventually the world capitalist system. Areas were affected in proportion to the extent that they incorporated neoliberal-style governance systems and American-style finance into their institutional edifice. However, even the European systems that depend more upon banks than nonbanks were not immune from the crisis since these uncertainties easily dominated banking-style systems. It also opened up cracks in the edifice of financial systems with large amounts of debt, corruption, and incompetence (see O'Hara 2011, 2013).

Advanced capitalist economies, especially in Europe, held masses of mortgage-backed securities as packaged bonds often financed through debt from overseas. When US markets imploded, the value of securitized mortgage-backed bonds dived, and many, especially European nations, were unable to recoup their massive borrowings, leading to balance of payments crises, market crashes, and deep recession. Iceland was the worst country affected initially since its economy comprised mainly financial assets and liabilities, due to deregulation, leading to market failure and Depression over multiple years.

Deregulation and financial system dominance held sway as crises and recessions were potentially catastrophic, as they were also in Ireland and much of continental

Europe (especially Greece, Portugal, and Spain), and to a *much lesser extent* in other continents outside of the core. Neoliberalism and deregulation were coming home to roost, and had governance systems not responded, the result would have likely been as catastrophic as the Great Depression of the 1930s for more than just these few (especially Greece). Governance systems and memories of previous policies (that could be used) saved most nations from Depression. Lower interest rates, bailing out financial institutions, takeovers of anomalous institutions, a series of nationalizations, incorporating concepts such as financial system instability, recognizing the problems of high debt in deregulated systems, assistance with mortgage payments, deepening deposit insurance, and major fiscal expansions (among a host of measures) prevented the third Great Depression from taking hold of the world economy (but not specific nations such as Greece, Spain, Portugal, Ireland, and Iceland). (See O'Hara 2011 on such policies.)

In this context, major attempts to avert depression led to even worse problems with further crises. For instance, in Ireland, unlimited deposit insurance and other spending led to massive government debt, and these high debt anomalies also existed in other European nations. Fraudulent accounting techniques spread to government fiscal accounts, as the Greek government admitted its sovereign debt was much higher than treaties allowed. Attempts to reduce the GFC led to other nations, such as Germany, even admitting to having debt levels higher than allowed. Soon, bond markets were factoring in systemic anomalies for the whole area, especially for the European periphery, such as Greece, Ireland, Portugal, and Spain, which had much higher debt levels than average and needed bailouts from multiple organizations to survive (IMF, EU, ECB, etc.). In return, they promised to institute structural reforms and austerity to reduce debt and deficits and satisfy international creditors.

This was the worst polycrisis ever to hit the Eurozone: financial crisis, sovereign debt crisis, austerity crisis, political crisis (and climate crisis). Greece was hit much worse than others because of systemic fraud including (among others) the underreporting of government debt, tax evasion, uncompetitive industries, and current account deficits. During the late 2000s to 2017 and beyond, Greece experienced major depression, high unemployment, and default on its debt. Greece also experienced the negative impacts of certain structural problems that all members of the EU were subject to and are still impacted by to some degree.

These structural problems were a combination of characteristics of the EU architecture, neoliberal aspects of policy, and plain corruption/incompetence. The structural problems involve, first, the fact that nations using the common currency (the Euro) are absent a core policy tool: devaluation or revaluation of their (no longer present) *national* currency to alleviate certain socioeconomic anomalies such as unemployment or inflation. Second, they also were unable to officially utilize effective fiscal policy to alleviate domestic problems because of treaty obligations to restrict government debt in accordance with provisions (which many ignored or hid). And third, with the increasing power of the ECB and the need for the independence of central banks, there are restrictions on the use of monetary policy. Historically also, the Euro bloc has been subject to the anomalies of neoliberalism, including the repeated use of austerity measures not only in daily policymaking but also when accepting bailouts and other measures of assistance to enhance financial capabilities. They have been subject to structural adjustment policies to eschew core aspects of the national policy-political environment.

Greece was thus subject to the full force of these structural anomalies, in addition to having its own socioeconomic and policy anomalies associated with low productivity, inadequate competitiveness, taxation-budget fraud, and excessive debt. The Greek people voted against the "austerity referendum" of 2015 (which proposed financial support with austerity and structural adjustment), but the eventual package accepted by the government was even worse austerity, resulting in a string of policies that further upset the fabric of the social economy. Overall, the Depression in Greece has been far worse in magnitude and timing than the typical experience of the 1930s Great Depression, as, for instance, GDP per capita is not anticipated to return to its 2007 level until possibly 2034. The IMF did, however, agree that the austerity and structural adjustments and policies enacted during the Greek crisis did unjustly fall on the shoulders of workers (Thomsen 2019).

But soon the whole world (rather than just the highly developed capitalist economies) would be subject to an even greater crisis, namely, the coronacrisis of the early 2020s, which is discussed below.

9.7 Coronacrisis, Early 2020s, and Future Pandemics

Around 20 million "excess deaths" were purported to have been experienced worldwide from the coronavirus during the early 2020s, according to the *Economist*'s research portal (compared with 35–40 m having died from AIDS and 20–100 m having died from the so-called Spanish Flu during World War 1 and thereafter) (see O'Hara 2023 for details). This generated a crisis worldwide for many years. Given the socioeconomic and policy background within which the global coronacrisis emerged, it was not difficult for policymakers to utilize policies that were *not* neoliberal in their conceptual edifice to tackle the problems (see O'Hara 2023, chap. 3 for details), since neoliberal policies were implicated in its genesis (insufficient public health infrastructure). Very early on many nations of the world, especially those with financial and technical resources to do so, started instituting measures to discover suitable vaccines to fight the viruses, as well as having lockdowns, lowering official interest rates, and eventually using fiscal policies to support individuals and businesses, and in many cases mandating masks and work from home arrangements.

Numerous commenters and analysts came to believe that the coronacrisis was a type of practical-empirical test for modern monetary theory (MMT), since functional finance, printing money to finance fiscal incentives, and using the bond market to adjust interest rates were core parts of anti-corona policy in many areas. The GFC was seen by many as a direct result of the use of anomalous neoliberal policies and practices, which was fought with a package of predominantly anti-neoliberal policies, especially in the USA. So it was not seen as strange to use MMT-type policies to fight the coronacrisis uncertainties that otherwise may have caused a Depression in many nations. In addition, during this time, and generally since the GFC, various governments have been attacking free market policies in other ways, by, for instance, promoting protectionism, industry policy, and self-sufficiency in domestic economies. This is the case, especially for the two core economies of the world, the USA and China, but also for a multitude of others on all continents.

Some analysts believe that despite these multiple attacks on neoliberal-style policies, neoliberalism itself keeps coming back and reasserting its ugly head; indeed, neoliberalism has become embedded enough to evade complete destruction of most economies (e.g., see Cahill et al. 2018). While one can still see neoliberal traditions at work in the economy, even in the light of these supposedly anti-neoliberal trends, it is true that, as many other analysts have noticed, neoliberalism is currently "out of fashion" in economics and policy circles (see e.g., *The* Economist 2022). This trend is likely to increase, as right- and left-wing autocracies and governments, center-right and center-left administrations, Islamic states, and others eschew neoliberal and internationalist ideology. Amazingly, to some, the Boris Johnson Conservative Government (2019–2022) seemed to emerge as a big government communitarian institution committed to reducing the rural–urban/north–south divide in Britain, while *The* Economist (2023) has argued persuasively that the Republican Party in the US is beginning to *regain* its earlier dominant traditions of protectionism, nationalism, and isolationism against globalization and free markets. China likewise, as noted earlier, is moving further away from its more liberal-market form of state capitalism to a more protectionist and nationalist variety of state capitalism under President Xi Jinping (2013 to present).

Something more substantial needs to be added to the coronacrisis predicament from the view of socioeconomic policy. The GFC was the biggest crisis of capitalism, at the core, since the Great Depression. But the coronacrisis era exhibited greater levels of uncertainty for the world as a whole than the GFC, and the coronavirus downswing in many places was more intense but short-lived. The corona era taught us more than anything that pandemics can and will continue to cause havoc throughout the world at various stages unless we are suitably prepared for them. In this context, it is very necessary to propose policies to help in this regard in the future.

Thus, here we look at the principles of uncertainty, innovation, and policy/governance linked to lack of preparedness for the pandemic and policies that can be instituted to reduce uncertainty by preparing adequately for the next socioeconomic health crisis (O'Hara 2023, chap. 4). Prior to the coronacrisis, there were several specific policies and institutions used by authorities throughout the world to prepare for biological pandemics/attacks to reduce uncertainty and crises. These preestablished preparedness structures were critically scrutinized by the 3 years (2017–19) global research initiative associated with the Global Health Security Index (GHSI), undertaken jointly by the *Economist* Intelligence Unit, the John Hopkins University Bloomberg School of Public Health, and the Nuclear Threat Initiative (EIU, JHU, NTI 2019). The GHSI was finalized in late 2019 and sought to assess the potential of the world and its areas and nations to tackle *biological risks* that are likely to impinge on areas in the future, especially pandemics, epidemics, terrorist attacks, and accidental (e.g., laboratory) leaks. The timing and nature of this GHSI exercise were perfect for assessing preparedness for the SARS-CoV-2/COVID-19 anomaly, given that it was done with an emphasis on the ability of areas to respond to a biological crisis and was published a month or two before the first COVID-19 case was officially detected in China. The six areas studied include [1] prevention of the release of a pathogen, [2] detection and reporting, [3] rapid response, [4] robust health system, [5] compliance with international norms, and [6] overall risk environment (EIU, JHU, NTI 2019, 65).

Table 9.3 summarizes the GHS Index for major areas of the world:

A core result of the GHSI exercise was that the whole world was unprepared for a global catastrophic biological risk, since "at least 75% of countries received a low score in biosecurity, oversight for dual-use research, emergency response operations, linking of public health and security operations, and medical countermeasure dispensing" (EIU, JHU, NTI 2019, 42). The average for all six indicators was 40.2 out of 100 for the 195 countries in aggregate (population weighted). The GHSI group concluded that "national health security is fundamentally weak around the world. No country is fully prepared for epidemics or pandemics, and every country has important gaps to fill" (EIU, JHU, NTI 2019, 12).

More specifically, as Table 9.3 indicates, the advanced capitalist economies of North America (NA), Europe (EU), and Oceania (Australia and New Zealand) were mostly "somewhat prepared," though many were "not very prepared." The countries of Asia were mostly "not very prepared," although some were "somewhat prepared" and "unprepared." Those from the Middle East and North Africa (MENA) were mostly "not very prepared," though others were "somewhat," "badly," and "unprepared." Latin American nations were usually "unprepared," though a lot were "not very prepared" and a few "somewhat" and "badly" prepared. With some exceptions (such as South Africa), nations of Sub-Saharan Africa were mostly "unprepared" and "badly prepared," while small island states in the Pacific, Oceania, were almost entirely "badly prepared" for the pandemic.

Even for the advanced capitalist economies of North America and Europe, which were "somewhat prepared," major gaps existed, which led to much uncertainty. For instance, in the USA, which was at the top of the list (1/195) for preparedness, there

Table 9.3 195 Nations in Regions: GHS Index, Pandemic Preparedness, 2019

GHS Index	Degree prepared	EU & NA	ASIA	MENA	Latin America	Sub-Saharan Africa	Oceania
0–50	Somewhat Prepared	28	8	4	6	1	2
51–100	Not very prepared	15	11	10	11	7	0
101–150	Unprepared	4	9	4	14	17	2
151–195	Badly unprepared	1	3	6	6	17	11

Source: Based on the data in EIU, JHU, NTI (2019, pp. 20–29)
NA North America; *EU* Europe; *MENA* Middle East and North Africa.

was no exercise of rapid response plans, major defects in the emergency response operation, serious deficiencies in access to medical care for many citizens, and a low level of responsible science culture for many people (EIU, JHU, NTI 2019, 303). The UK (2/195) was documented as having problems with biosafety prevention, detection and reporting, emergency response operations, and access to health care for numerous citizens.

China, where the virus first manifested itself, overall came 51st out of 195 nations for the GHS Index, with a score of 48.2/100. This is higher than the average score of 40.2, but not epidemiologically optimistic for the future of COVID-19 once it becomes active in the human population. China got abysmal results, especially for dual-use research and culture of responsible science; data integration between human, animal, and environmental health sectors; exercising rapid response plans; linking public health and security authorities; communication between healthcare workers during an emergency; aspects of compliance with international norms; and emergency rapid response operations (EIU, JHU, NTI 2019, 152). It is thus not surprising that China failed to share epidemiological data on the very first cases of COVID-19 and to prevent the disease from ultimately becoming national and transnational in scope and transfer.

Although the Index has been criticized, it does appear to have calculated quite well the capabilities of certain nations to respond to an emergency. As mentioned, it documented several limitations, even for top-scoring nations, such as the US and UK; and what is a capability may not transfer to action if the politicians and administrators do not adequately activate and communicate properly with health care workers and citizens. Indeed, critics of the index often centered on these differences between technical preparedness and the broader political and social determinants of pandemic response, especially for the leading nations (e.g., see Manjari Mahajan 2021).

Critics have also attacked the GHSI (as well as the Economic Preparedness Index and the National Health Security Preparedness Index) for failing to predict *specific national rates* of COVID-19 mortality (Keim and Lovallo 2021; Baum et al. 2021). These critiques argue that now and into the future, we need broader social and political indicators of how policies and institutions adequately deal with pandemics. For instance, Baum et al. (2021) put forward eight such factors necessary to consider for adequate pandemic preparation and prevention dynamics, which should assist policymakers in dealing with present and potential future crises. *The first is the need to consider globalization, geography, and global governance.* For instance, larger island states, such as Australia and New Zealand, were able to isolate from global forces for a long time, instituting lockdowns, social distancing, contact tracing, limits on overseas (and domestic) arrivals, face masks, and the like, and reduce deaths to a minimum, even before vaccines became widespread.

The second is participatory rather than just authoritarian governance: they argue it is necessary to include civil society groups and decentralized factors to ensure community participation in governance. This helps explain some individuals and groups attacking government mandates and rules where communities required integrating into policy.

The third is the need for universal, public, well-funded health systems that are not privately outsourced, which they say help to explain some of the *initial* success of policy in Thailand and Vietnam, plus Australia and New Zealand more generally.

The fourth factor is political leadership and ideology, which helps explain why populist forces underlying nations, such as the US, Brazilian, Indian, and UK responses, led to high rates of mortality in these nations.

Fifthly, the importance of context, including the unevenness of subnational structures, helps explain some regional differences in federations, such as the US, India, South Africa, Belgium, and Australia.

The sixth factor critiques the indices' obsession with GDP levels being (indirectly) a major determinant of pandemic preparation and performance. They point to, for instance, the effectiveness of the Rwandan and (initially) Vietnamese solid pandemic response despite being poor nations.

The seventh factor relates to heterogeneous agents and groups, as marginalized groups within nations have tended to suffer most from the pandemic, yet this inequality was not analyzed in the indices (at least not directly).

The *eighth factor* required for pandemic preparedness and low levels of uncertainty in the present and future is the *use of government support for households and businesses* in the form of furlough schemes, unemployment benefits, income support schemes, interest rate decreases, ad hoc handouts to people, business lockdown payments, accelerated investment depreciation schemes, extended sick leave allowances, and the like. These schemes have been accelerated majorly, especially in the advanced nations of the EU, USA, UK, Australia, Japan, Canada, and New Zealand, primarily because they have sophisticated financial and budget systems. Neoliberalism is also declining majorly in these nations, at least *relatively*, especially in the light of the GFC and the pandemic, which helps explain the quick implementation of functional finance, handouts, and monetary easing. The least developed nations are generally unable to utilize these schemes effectively due to their underdeveloped technological, financial, and budget systems. Finally, it is also important for policies not to revert to neoliberal priorities (as has often happened in the past), which typically will inhibit proper preparation for the next major crisis.

One core additional factor for reducing uncertainty now and into the future, vis-à-vis the principle of innovation, is the ongoing role of vaccinations in the defense of the population from COVID-19 and other infections. Many advanced nations, while not *consistently* emphasizing lockdowns, social distancing, facemasks, and so on, have managed to institute an effective global system of science and manufacturing for the production and distribution of effective vaccines. They are pinning their hopes on opening the economy while having a large proportion of their population with sufficient antibodies through vaccinations and previous infections to achieve herd immunity. The US, UK, EU, and others eventually had such immunity but at the cost of large numbers of infections and enormous numbers of deaths in many such areas.

As mentioned, most less developed economies have difficulty getting access to vaccines to reach 80–90% immunity and activating sophisticated functional finance and discretionary fiscal and monetary policies to prevent major dislocation. One other anomaly may generate renewed uncertainty and dislocate global and national political economies in the light of the Coronacrisis. This includes *major inflationary/stagflationary forces* precipitating higher interest rates that dislocate the circuits of capital in the light of high levels of international debt, supply-side anomalies, and demand forces. Currently, for instance, much of the EU is in recession (in terms of per capita growth), which may get worse, especially in the light of the war in Ukraine, which is increasing uncertainty.

In relation to the principles of innovation and policy/governance, the pandemic has had some crucial political and health impacts, which will affect the world majorly into the future. For instance, it led to the creation in a short period of several effective vaccines, sharpened the scientific edifice of virology and immunology, and laid the policy foundations of potential pandemic reactions that will likely put certain areas of the world (the core) in good stead for future such crises. Second, it led directly or indirectly to Donald Trump's defeat in the US presidential election and majorly reduced the popularity of several other populist-nationalist politicians, especially in Brazil, Poland, and other nations. Third, it taught and is still teaching the world about the limitations of austerity and neoliberalism, the need to speed up reactions to potential pandemics, and assistance to the poorest nations to make available sufficient vaccines and other supports through global governance.

One cannot ignore climate change in the context of the coronacrisis and future policies and practices (Dieter Helm 2020; Sarkodie and Owusu 2021). The pandemic crisis led to moderated carbon emissions during the 2020 recession phase, while the 2021 recovery increased emissions. The pandemic crisis also crowded out climate change endeavors to some degree as the world concentrated on the "immediate pandemic tasks," even while extreme events such as wildfires, floods, tornadoes, heatwaves, and droughts became ever more evident in reality. All this as the IPCC (2021) documented the greater speed and intensity of climate events now and into the future. Multiple simultaneous crises can lead to some of them, such as climate change, being underplayed, which happened during both the GFC and the coronacrisis. It was found that coronacrisis demand policies that focused on labor-intensive green projects were good for the environment, employment, and recovery, while those green policies that were capital-intensive and large-scale helped climate change but not so much employment and recovery (Engstrom 2020). Should another biological or other threat emerge, climate change policies should be kept in full view and deepened now and into the future.

9.8 Climate Crises

Much detail has already been provided on climate change in this book (especially chapters 1 and 4–8) and the previous volume in this series (O'Hara 2023, chap. 5). Here, I will specifically delineate the various climate crises and their impact. In this context, the climate emergency includes various climate crises, such as the much more intense heat waves, hurricanes, droughts, wildfires, floods, coastal erosion, and species extinction. These examples of crises that generate existential emergencies have become more extreme, especially because of the onset of numerous interconnected climate events that manifest themselves in a circular and cumulative fashion through cascading tipping points of climate change.

Climate change uncertainties relate to the lack of knowledge about key ecological, behavioral, and modular relationships as they change through historical times. The extreme weather events and catastrophes linked to threshold impacts ("tipping points") are the greatest source of uncertainty. At these crucial tipping points, rapid escalations occur in critical environmental processes that radically upset the climate, producing a whole series of catastrophes (IPCC 2007, chaps. 6, 19; Keller et al. 2008, Lenton et al. 2008, Lenton 2021). The key idea underlying threshold effects is that a small change can generate major impacts in a circular and cumulative fashion. Some of the tipping points are already happening, such as coral bleaching, West Antarctic and Arctic ice sheet disintegration, and Greenland ice sheet melting, among others.

These threshold effects have some element of nonlinearity, hysteresis, and irreversibility as feedback processes change parameters, thereby producing cumulative effects. The uncertainty relates to the timing or states (multiple) when the changes and effects manifest *suddenly*. The complexities involve a multifarious linking of numerous variables that are difficult to predict. Threshold effects are important because they challenge the idea that climate change will bring linearly related impacts on the system. Threshold effects are likely to happen sooner than linear models predict, and Keller et al. (2008, 5) argue that "only subtle warning signs" are likely in many cases "before climate thresholds have been crossed" due to "multiple parameter" interaction.

Cascading tipping points are the most important CCC processes likely to lead to a severe breakdown of the Earth's climate system, systemic nonlinear changes in climate, and even more severe climate events such as major droughts, floods, hurricanes, heat waves, cold snaps, and sea level rise. These cascading tipping points are caused by multiple interacting tipping point breakdowns involving some of the dozen or more regional climate systems that constitute the basis of the Earth's ability to resist major temperature rises. These multiple structural interacting crises are of significant probability at 1.2 °C and a high chance of happening at 1.4 °C, more so at 1.8 °C temperature rises, relative to 1850–1900 mean levels. 2023 was the first year that average global surface temperatures reached almost 1.5 °C above preindustrial times (1.45 °C) (ECMWF 2024).

The individual tipping points that are potentially culminating in cascading interacting tipping points involve an array of core Earth systems. A new report authored by more than 200 scholars associated with 25 institutions (Lenton et al. 2023a) decided to change the name of the CTP to *global tipping points* (GTP), since they do impact the whole of planet Earth. They identify "more than 25 Earth System tipping points" from observations, models, and past records: 6 in the cryosphere, 16 in the biosphere, and 4 in ocean/atmosphere systems (p. 20).

Some of the major ones include collapse of the West Antarctic ice sheet; disintegration of the Greenland ice sheet; transformation of the Atlantic meridional overturning circulation; dieback of the Amazon rainforest; thawing of the northeast permafrost; death of the tropical coral reefs, mangroves and seagrass; major shifts of the northern boreal forests; thawing of the northern permafrost; collapse of the Arctic summer sea ice; destruction of the alpine glaciers; a major shift in the West African monsoonal system; chaotic instability of the Indian monsoonal system; collapse of the eastern Antarctic ice sheet; more persistent El-Nino regime; and major instability of the Arctic winter ice sheet. *Individual* tipping points for these ecological systems are a function of linear *or* nonlinear increases in mean global temperatures, extreme northern hemisphere mean temperatures rising well above most other areas, and land mean temperatures rising more than ocean temperatures (Cai et al. 2016).

When temperatures and extreme events impact simultaneously several of these individual tipping elements, the process transforms into an interacting series of nonlinear global tipping points for the whole Earth and regional systems. The reason for this is that the different tipping point elements experience interacting influences that heighten, magnify, and accelerate the individual elements into an emergent novel major system crisis of symbiotic processes (in an emergent and complex fashion). For instance, we know that there has been a major melting of sea ice and ice sheets in the Arctic, Antarctic, and Greenland regions, and that Greenland ice (GIS) tipping contributes to changing patterns in the Atlantic meridional (AMOC) by increasing the flow of freshwater into the region. A tipping of El Nino increases the likelihood of Amazon rainforest dieback by increasing temperatures and reducing rainfall. The melting of ice sheets and sea ice tipping points due to rising temperatures increases the likelihood of permafrost thawing and boreal forest dieback. Through time, the growing number of tipping elements and the increasingly interconnected nature of their transformations amplify the process of temperature rises, extreme events, and evidential global crises in a CCC fashion (Cai et al. 2016).

Chapter 4 provided some empirical data relating to the teleconnections between the various cascading global and regional tipping points. Already numerous individual elements have begun tipping, or more specifically are on the *cumulative gradation* upward trajectory, including parts of the (1) west Antarctic, (2) Greenland, (3) Arctic summer, (4) Alpine glaciers/ice sheets, and (5) coral reef systems (Schellnhuber et al. 2016: 650; McKay et al. 2022). With at least five systems in varying degrees of interactive synchrony, 1.5 °C relative to the 1850–1900 mean temperature looks decidedly too high for two main reasons. The first is that we are currently seriously involved in teleconnections with several CGTP at above the 1.5 °C temperature rise. And second, the slower-moving impacts of GHG stocks on climate will be ongoing in their impact (even without further rises in GHGs).

It is the stocks of GHGs that impact tipping points, rather than simply the flows of GHGs, and it takes many years for stocks to decline if flows even start to decline, and currently, even the flows are increasing. The more tipping points that interrelate, the more such interdependencies generate even greater numbers of cascading global processes into the future, and hence the worse the climate crises and emergencies will be.

As Lenton et al. (2023a) said of "existing" temperature rises[10]:

> Our estimate that global warming since 1960–1990 has put more than 600 million people outside the temperature niche is consistent with attributable impacts of climate change affecting 85% of the world's population. Above the present level of … global warming, exposure to unprecedented [mean annual] temperatures (MAT ≥29 °C) [are] predicted to increase markedly, increasing exposure to temperature extremes. … This is consistent with *extreme humid heat* having more than doubled in frequency since 1979, associated with labour loss of 148 million full-time equivalent jobs, with exposure in urban areas increasing for 23% of the world's population from 1983 to 2016 (due also to growing urban heat islands) and the total urban population exposed tripling (due also to demographic change). [Lenton et al. 2023b, 1242; emphasis added.]

As the multiple climate crises escalate, the social, political, economic, and ecological crises become more intense, since more intense heatwaves, floods, droughts, wildfires, rising waterways, hurricanes, and cyclones also generate greater competition between humans for resources and between humans and other species for scarce habitats and their provisions. Concurrently, they also generate more severe financial crises, recessions, depressions, social revolts, revolutions, wars, and other forms of anxiety-generating dynamics. The climate and society are inextricably interrelated as they coevolve through long historical times.

9.9 Conclusion

This chapter started with a review of global polycrises emerging from situations lacking in hegemonic power. We provided a summary of situations during the 1700s, 1880s/early 1900s, and late 1900s–early 2020s. Then we had numerous sections dealing with aspects of the current period of no absolute hegemony. This included the emergence of neoliberalism, its structural contradictions, and the various decadal crises arising from the disembedded economy. Thereafter, we scrutinized specific instances such as the GFC, the Eurocrisis, the coronacrisis, and climate crises. These examples were not examined to *completely* support the hegemonic stability hypothesis, but at least to put weight to the view that hegemonies can be useful if they do provide useful public goods, club goods, or system functions upon which many economies benefit.

Relying on hegemonies for club goods that only benefit some nations and regions (mainly in the core) and which eventually dissipate with the hegemonic fall is perhaps a good argument for trying to develop multipolar systems with cooperative relationships embedded in their operational dynamics. Currently, we are experiencing a rising China and a falling USA, but at a wider level also potential major

---

[10] 2023 was the hottest year on record for average global temperatures (14.98 °C) and the greatest increase (1.48 °C [i.e., 1.5 °C]), relative to the average for preindustrial times (1850–1900), according to Copernicus data (ECMWF 2024). Slightly less rises have been suggested by other authorities (e.g., increase of 1.45 degrees C; see chap. 4).

conflicts between liberal-democratic allies versus several autocratic powers, the outcome of which is uncertain. We turn to analyze this issue in Chap. 10.

Acknowledgments I wish to thank without implication the anonymous referees, Svetlana Kirdina-Chandler, Asimina Christoforou, Torsten Heinrich, and participants of the special AFEE-EAEPE session when I was an invited speaker at the EAEPE Conference for their comments and encouragement on some of the issues examined in this chapter. Thanks also go to Helen Gunn, Ian Kerr, and Kosta Josifidis for comments and suggestions.

References

Ahir, Hites; Nicholas Bloom, and Davide Furceri (2024). *World uncertainty index, 1990–2024*. About us–World Uncertainty Index (Accessed 1 May 2024.)

Aliber, Robert Z., and Charles P. Kindleberger. 2015. *Manias, panics and crashes: A history of financial crises*. London: Palgrave Macmillan.

Ashcraft, A. B., and T. Schuermann. 2007. *Understanding the securitization of subprime mortgage credit*. Federal Reserve Bank of New York.

Baum, Fran, Toby Freeman, Connie Musolino, Mimi Abramovitz, Wim De Ceukelaire, Joanne Flavel, Sharon Friel, Camila Giugliani, Philippa Howden-Chapman, Nguyen Thanh Huong, Leslie London, Martin McKee, Jennie Popay, Hani Serag, and Eugenio Villar. 2021. Explaining Covid-19 performance: What factors might predict National Responses? *BMJ* 372:N91.

Beitel, K. 2009. The rate of profit and the problem of stagnant investment: A structural analysis of barriers to accumulation and the spectre of protracted crisis. *Historical Materialism* 17:66–100.

Binswanger, M. 2004. Stock returns and real activity in the G-7 countries: Did the relationship change in the early 1980s? *Quarterly Review of Economics and Finance* 44:237–252.

Bleaney, Michael. 1995. *The rise and fall of Keynesian economics: An investigation of its contribution to capitalist development*. London: Red Globe Press. https://doi.org/10.1007/978-1-349-16666-4.

Bowles, Samuel, David M. Gordon, and Thomas E. Weisskopf. 1990. *After the waste land: A democratic economics for the year 2000*. Armonk, NY: M.E. Sharpe, Inc.

Brennan, Andrew John, and Jaslin Kalsi. 2015. Elephant poaching and ivory trafficking problems in sub-Saharan Africa: An application of O'Hara's principles of political economy. *Ecological Economics* 120:312–337.

Brescia, Raymond H. 2008. Capital in Chaos: The subprime mortgage crisis and the social capital response. *Cleveland State Law Review* 56:271–318.

Cahill, Damien, Melinder Cooper, Martijn Konings, and David Primrose, eds. 2018. *Sage handbook of neoliberalism*. London: Sage.

Cai, Yongyang, Timothy M. Lenton, and Thomas S. Lontzek. 2016. Risk of multiple interacting tipping points should encourage rapid CO2 emission reduction. *Nature Climate Change*. Advance Online Publication.

Caprio, G., Jr., A. Demirguc-Kunt, and E. J. Kane. 2008. *The 2007 meltdown in structured securitization: Searching for lessons, not scapegoats*. Washington, DC: World Bank. October. Policy Research Working Paper No. 4756.

Ciscel, David H., and J. A. Heath. 2001. To market, to market: Imperial capitalism's destruction of social capital and the family. *Review Of Radical Political Economics* 33:401–414.

Dugger, William M. 1996. Four modes of inequality. In *Inequality: Radical institutionalist views on race, gender, class and nation*, ed. William M. Dugger. Westport, CT: Greenwood Press.

Dugger, William M. 2022. The doleful dynamics of competition: Inequality and fakery in modernity. *Forum for Social Economics* 51 (1): 43–64. https://doi.org/10.1080/07360932.2017.1374196.

ECMWF. 2024. *2023 was the hottest year on record Copernicus data show*. ECMWF. 2023 was the hottest year on record, Copernicus data show | ECMWF.

Economist. (2022) *Covid-19 data: The pandemic's true death toll: Our daily estimate of excess deaths around the world*, 21 March 2022. https://Www.Economist.Com/Graphic-Detail/Coronavirus-Excess-Deaths-Estimates

Economist. 2023. American isolationism: Losing their religion: How the Republicans went from isolationism to internationalism and back again. *The Economist* 449 (9369): 33–35. (28 October 2023).

EIU, JHU, NTI. (2019) *GSI index: Global health security index: Building collective action and accountability*. October 2019. Economist intelligence unit, John Hopkins University, Nuclear Threat Initiative. Https://Www.Ghsindex.Org.

Elsner, Wolfram. 2016. Speculative financial capitalism Wacking out over an "impossible" profit rate: The infeasibility of a "usual" real average profit rate, considering fictitious capital, and its implications. In *Marx, Veblen, and the foundations of heterodox economics: Essays in honor of John F. Henry*, ed. Tae-Hee Jo and Frederic S. Lee, 199–227. London: Routledge.

Engstrom, Gustav, Johan Gars, Niko Jaakkola, Therese Lindahl, Daniel Spiro, and Arthur A. Van Benthem. 2020. What policies address both the coronavirus crisis and the climate crisis? *Environmental and Resource Economics* 76:789–810. https://doi.org/10.1007/S10640-020-00451-Y.

Fernandez, L., F. Kaboub, and Z. Todarova. 2008. *On democratising financial turmoil: A Minskian analysis of the subprime crisis*. Working Paper 548. Levy Economics Institute of Bard College.

Foster, J. B. 2014. The theory of unequal economic exchange: A Marx-Odum dialectic. *Journal of Peasant Studies* 41:199–233.

GBD. 2024. Global fertility in 204 countries and territories, 1950–2021, with forecasts to 2100: a comprehensive demographic analysis for the global burden of disease study 2021. *The Lancet*. Published online March 20. https://doi.org/10.1016/S0140-6736(24)00550-61.

Gibson-Graham, J. K. 2003. Enabling ethical economies: Cooperation and class. *Critical Sociology* 29:123–161.

Gibson-Graham, J. K., and G. Roelvink. 2009. An economic ethics for the Anthropocene. *Antipode* 41:320–346.

Gordon, D. M. 1991. Kaldor's macro system: Too much Cumulation, too few contradictions. In *Nicholas Kaldor and mainstream economics: Confrontation or convergence?* ed. Edward J. Nell and Willi Semmler, 355–383. London: Macmillan.

Gordon, Robert J. 2017. *The rise and fall of American growth: The US standard of living since the civil war*. Princeton: Princeton University Press.

Gordon, Robert J. 2018. Slowing economic growth despite ongoing innovation. *Explorations in Economic History* 69 (2): 1–12.

Hellwig, M. 2008. *Systemic risk in the financial sector: An analysis of the subprime-mortgage financial crisis*. https://doi.org/10.1017/S1049023x20001521.

Helm, Dieter. 2020. The Environmental Impacts of the Coronavirus. *Environmental and Resource Economics* 76:21–38.

Hobsbawm, Eric. 1987. *The age of empire 1875–1914*. London: Phoenix Press.

Integrated Asset Services. 2008. *IAS360 house price index*. Denver, CO: IAS.

IPCC. 2007. *Climate change 2007: The physical science basis. Contribution of working group 1 to the fourth assessment report*. Cambridge: Cambridge University Press.

IPCC. 2021. In *Climate change 2021: The physical science basis. Contribution of Working Group I to the sixth assessment report of the intergovernmental panel on climate change*, ed. V. Masson-Delmotte, P. Zhai, A. Pirani, S. L. Connors, C. Péan, S. Berger, N. Caud, Y. Chen, L. Goldfarb, M. I. Gomis, M. Huang, K. Leitzell, E. Lonnoy, J. B. R. Matthews, T. K. Maycock, T. Waterfield, O. Yelekçi, R. Yu, and B. Zhou, 2391. Cambridge, United Kingdom and New York, NY, USA: Cambridge University Press. https://doi.org/10.1017/9781009157896.

IPCC, 2023: *Climate change 2023: Synthesis report. Contribution of working groups I, II and III to the sixth assessment report of the intergovernmental panel on climate change* [Core writing team, H. Lee and J. Romero (eds.)]. IPCC, Geneva, Switzerland, 184 pp., https://doi.org/10.59327/IPCC/AR6-9789291691647.

Jessop, B. 2013. Revisiting the regulation approach. *Capital And Class* 37:5–24.

Keim, Mark, and Alex Lovallo. 2021. Validity of the national health security preparedness index as a predictor of excess Covid-19 mortality. *Prehospital and Disaster Medicine* 36 (2): 141–144.

Keller, K., G. Yoke, and M. Schlesinger. 2008. Managing the risks of climate thresholds: Uncertainties and informational needs. *Climatic Change* 91:5–10.

Keynes, John Maynard. 1936. *The general theory of employment, interest and money*, 1973. London: Macmillan.

Kindleberger, Charles P. 1973. *The world in depression 1929–1939*. Berkeley and Los Angeles: University of California Press.

Kindleberger, Charles P. 2000. *Manias, panics, crashes: A history of financial crises*. 3rd ed. London: Macmillan.

Kindleberger, Charles P. 1996. *World economic primacy: 1500–1990*. Oxford University Press.

Knight, Frank. 1921. *Risk, uncertainty and profit*, 2005. New York: Cosimo Classics.

Kristal, T. 2013. The capitalist machine: Computerization, workers' power, and the decline in labor's share within U.S. Industries. *American Sociological Review* 78:361–389.

Langley, P. 2008. Sub-prime mortgage lending: A cultural economy. *Economy and Society* 37:469–494.

Lenton, Timothy M., Hermann Held, Elmar Kriegler, Wolfgang Lucht, Stephan Rahmstorf, and Hans Joachim Schellnhuber. 2008. Tipping elements in the earth's climate system. *Proceedings of the National Academy of Sciences* 105:1786–1793.

Lenton, Timothy. 2021. Tipping points in the climate system. *Weather* 76 (10): 325–326.

Lenton, Timothy M., D. I. Armstrong Mckay, S. Loriani, J. F. Abrams, S. J. Lade, J. F. Donges, M. Milkoreit, T. Powell, S. R. Smith, C. Zimm, J. E. Buxton, E. Bailey, L. Laybourn, A. Ghadiali, and J. G. Dyke, eds. 2023a. *The global tipping points report 2023*. Exeter, UK: University Of Exeter.

Lenton, Timothy M., Chi Xu, Jesse F. Abrams, Ashish Ghadiali, Sina Loriani, Boris Sakschewski, Caroline Zimm, Kristie L. Ebi, Robert R. Dunn, Jens-Christian Svenning, And Marten Scheffer. 2023b. Quantifying the human costs of global warming. Nature Sustainability 6(October): 1237–1247.

Louçã, Fransisco. 2021. As time went by–why is the long wave so long? *Journal of Evolutionary Economics* 31:749–771. https://doi.org/10.1007/s00191-021-00724-9.

Mahajan, Manjari. 2021. Casualties of preparedness: The global health security index and Covid-19. *International Journal Of Law In Context* 17 (2): 204–214. https://doi.org/10.1017/S1744552321000288.

Marx, Karl. 1894. *Capital, volume 3: The process of capitalist production as a whole*. Harmondsworth: Penguin.

Mavroudeas, S., and D. Papadatos. 2011. Neoliberalism and Washington consensus. In *International encyclopedia of public policy: Volume 3: Public policy and political economy*, ed. Phillip Anthony O'Hara. Perth: GPERU. 408-420. http://Pohara.Homestead.Com/Encyclopedia/Volume-3.Pdf.

McKay, David I. Armstong, Arie Staal, Jesse F. Abrams, Ricarda Winkelmann, Boris Sakschewski, Sina Loriani, Ingo Fetzer, Sarah E. Cornell, Johan Rockström, and Timothy M. Lenton. 2022. Exceeding 1.5°C global warming could trigger multiple climate tipping points. *Science* 377 (6611). https://doi.org/10.1126/science.abn7950

Mian, A., and A. Sufi. 2008. *The consequences of mortgage credit expansion: Evidence from the 2007 mortgage default crisis*. University Of Chicago Graduate School Of Business.

Mizen, P. 2008. The credit crunch of 2007-2008: A discussion of the background, market reaction, and policy responses. *Federal Reserve Bank of St. Louis Review* 90:531–567.

Myrdal, Gunnar. 1968. *Asian Drama: An inquiry into the poverty of nations*. Vol. 3. Harmondsworth: Allen Lane–The Penguin Press.
O'Hara, Phillip Anthony. 2000. *Marx, Veblen and contemporary institutional political economy: Principles and unstable dynamics of capitalism*. Cheltenham, UK and Northampton, US: Edward Elgar.
O'Hara, Phillip Anthony. 2001. Contradiction. In *Encyclopedia of political economy, 140–143*, ed. P. A. O'Hara. London & New York: Paper Edition.
O'Hara, Phillip Anthony. 2004. A family-community social structure of accumulation for long wave upswing in the United States? *Forum for Social Economics* 34:51–80.
O'Hara, Phillip Anthony. 2008a. Principle of circular and cumulative causation: Fusing Myrdalian and Kaldorian growth and development dynamics. *Journal of Economic Issues* 42:375–397.
O'Hara, Phillip Anthony. 2008b. Can the principles of heterodox political economy explain its own re-emergence and development? *On The Horizon* 16:260–278.
O'Hara, Phillip Anthony. 2009a. *Growth and development in the global political economy: Social structures of accumulation and modes of regulation*. Oxford and New York: Routledge. Paper Edition.
O'Hara, Phillip Anthony. 2009b. The securitized subprime market crisis. *Review of Radical Political Economics* 41 (3): 318–334.
O'Hara, Phillip Anthony. 2009c. Political economy of climate change, ecological destruction and uneven development. *Ecological Economics* 69:223–234.
O'Hara, Phillip Anthony. 2011. International subprime crisis and recession: Emerging macroprudential, monetary, fiscal and global governance. *Panoeconomicus* 58 (1): 1–17.
O'Hara, Phillip Anthony. 2013. Policies and institutions for moderating deep recessions, debt crises and financial instabilities. *Panoeconomicus* 60:19–49.
O'Hara, Phillip Anthony. 2023. *Principles of institutional and evolutionary political economy: Applied to current world problems*. Singapore: Springer Nature. Revised Edition.
Perez, Carlotta. 2016. Capitalism, technology and a green global golden age: The role of history in helping to shape the future. *The Political Quarterly* 85 (S1): 191–217.
Piketty, Thomas. 2024. *Nature, culture, and inequality*. London: Scribe Publishers.
Pocock, Tom. 1998. *Battle for empire: The very first world war 1756–63*. London: Michael O'Mara Books.
Polanyi, K. 1944. *The great transformation*. Boston: Beacon Press.
RGE Monitor. 2009. *Navigating the first global economic recession*. RGE Monitor Newsletter, 14 January.
Rodney, Walter. 1972. *How Europe underdeveloped Africa*. London: Verso, 2018. Foreword by Angela Davis.
Roelvink, G., K. St. Martin, and J. K. Gibson-Graham. 2015. *Making other worlds possible: Performing diverse economies*. Minneapolis: University Of Minnesota Press.
Rosenberg, S. 2003. *American economic development since 1945: Growth, decline and rejuvenation*. Basingstoke: Macmillan Press.
Sarkodie, Samuel, and Phebe Asantewaa Owusu. 2021. Global assessment of environmental, health, and economic impact of the novel coronavirus (COVID-19). *Environment, Development and Sustainability* 23:5005–5015. https://doi.org/10.1007/2Fs10668-020-00801-2.
Sassen, S. 2008. Mortgage capital and its particularities: A new frontier for global finance. *Journal of International Affairs* 62:187–212.
Schellnhuber, Hans Joachim, Stefan Rahmstorf, and Ricarda Winklemann. 2016. Why the right climate target was agreed in Paris. *Nature Climate Change* 6 (July): 649–653.
Schnure, C. 2005. *Boom-bust cycles in housing: The changing role of financial structure*. IMF Working Paper No. 05/200. Washington, DC: IMF.
Schumpeter, Joseph A. 1911. *The theory of economic development*, 1969. Oxford: Oxford University Press.
Shackle, G. L. S. 1955. *Uncertainty in economics and other reflections*. Cambridge: Cambridge University Press.

Sherman, Howard J., and David X. Kolk. 1996. *Business cycles and forecasting*. New York: Harper Collins.

Stanfield, James Ronald. 1986. *The economic thought of Karl Polanyi*. NY: St Martin's Press.

Stanfield, James Ronald. 2011. Some social economics concepts for future research. *Forum for Social Economics* 40 (1): 7–18.

Stilwell, Frank. 2019. *The political economy of inequality*. London: Polity.

Stockhammer, E. 2004. Financialization and the slowdown of accumulation. *Cambridge Journal of Economics* 28:719–741.

Suter, Christian. 1992. *Debt cycles in the world-economy: Foreign loans, financial crises, and debt settlement, 1820–1990*. Boulder, Colorado: Westview Press.

Thomsen, Poul M. 2019. The IMF and the Greek Crisis; Myth and Reality. https://Www.Imf.Org/En/News/Articles/2019/10/01/Sp093019-The-Imf-And-The-Greek-Crisis-Myths-And-Realities

UNCTAD (United Nations Conference on Trade and Development). 2024. *Trade and development report update 2024*. Geneva: UNCTAD, April.

Veblen, T. B. 1921. *The engineers and the price system*. London: Transaction Publishers.

Veblen, T. B. 1923. *Absentee ownership and business enterprise in recent times*, 1964. New York: Kelley.

Walker, R. A. 1999. Putting capital in its place: Globalization and the prospects for labor. *Geoforum* 30:263–284.

Wallerstein, Immanuel. 1980. *The modern world-system II: Mercantilism and the consolidation of the European world-economy, 1600–1750*. Boston: Academic Press.

Wolff, Richard. 2009. *Capitalism hits the fan: The global economic meltdown and what to do about it*. Northampton, MA: Olive Branch Press.

Wolfson, Martin H. 1994. *Financial crises: Understanding the postwar U.S. experience*. 2nd ed. Armonk, New York and London: M. E. Sharpe.

World Bank. 2021. *Global waves of debt: Causes and consequences*. Washington DC: World Bank.

Wray, L. R. 2007. *Lessons from the subprime meltdown*. Levy economics institute—Bard College of New York. Working paper no. 522, December.

WUI. 2024. World Uncertainty Index, 1990–2024.

Chapter 10
Liberal-Democratic Allies vs. Autocratic Powers: Prewar Era and World War 3?

Abstract The purpose of this chapter is to examine the nature and likely causes and the trajectory of the ongoing conflicts between several *liberal-democratic allies* [LDAs] (especially NATO) and numerous *autocratic powers* [APs] (especially Russia and China) using core general principles of war and political economy. We situate this paper within the context of the ongoing wars and conflicts involving the situation in Southeast Europe (e.g., Ukraine) and the Asia-Pacific (e.g., Taiwan), also involving agreements, military bases, competitive struggles, hegemonic battles, and geopolitical rivalries, and how they may evolve in the future. The ten dialectical (contradictory) principles of war in the information age are interrelated with the core principles of political economy (PoPE), such as historical specificity, hegemony/uneven development, contradiction, heterogeneous groups and agents, innovation, uncertainty, circular and cumulative causation (CCC), socioeconomic circuits (CSD), plus policy and governance. We make conclusions about the likely trajectory and possible outcomes of these ongoing conflicts using these principles and concurrent developments, noting their significance for long waves, hegemony, and climate change.

Keywords Hegemonic struggle · Contradictions & crises · Principles · Long waves · Ukraine · Taiwan · 2010s–2020s · Liberal-democratic allies · Autocratic powers · World War 3 · Waves · Hegemony · Climate change · Prewar era

10.1 Introduction: Historical Specificity of War

The first major principle of political economy is the principle of historical specificity (O'Hara 2023), that political economy should utilize a historical and evolutionary approach to scrutinizing major problems emerging throughout the world. Doing so enables the problem, such as geopolitical conflict, to be situated and understood,

P. A. O'Hara, *Long Waves of Growth, Hegemonic Power, and Climate Change in the World Economy*, https://doi.org/10.1007/978-981-96-4132-1_10

providing the basis for both potential solutions and analysis of the ongoing evolution of the anomaly in current and future trajectories.

In this context, understanding the nature of the current ongoing conflicts between NATO and its liberal-democratic allies (LDAs), on the one hand, and the dominant autocratic powers (APs) such as Russia, China, and their global allies, on the other hand, requires us first to understand the conflict historically. We thus need to comprehend the nature of wars and other conflicts to understand the background and political economy processes that have been affecting the situation as we move well into the twenty-first century. We start this process by analyzing the nature of the first three major global conflicts since 1900, including the First World War (WW1) during 1914–1918, the Second World War (WW2) during 1939–1945, and the so-called Cold War (CW) between 1949 and 1989, and their relationship to the ongoing conflicts between LDAs and APs ("WW3?").

The issue of the conflicts over Ukraine and Taiwan is directly linked to three aspects of the core thesis of this book. First, we know one of the core propositions of hegemony theory and empirics (a core stylized fact) is that a new hegemon requires a successful war of *hegemonic ascendancy*; in the same way that the Dutch were successful over the Spanish in their republican revolution (or revolt) of the late 1500s, the British were successful over Napoleon in 1815, and the US were successful in 1945. Hence, the conflicts in Ukraine and Taiwan are potentially very relevant to China's potential hegemony in the future, as well as the future of the world, including that of the US, NATO, and Russian power.

Second, the Ukraine and Taiwan conflicts are relevant to other issues of hegemony, long waves, and climate change. The Ukraine conflict and potentially the conflict over Taiwan may be seen as another structural crisis that occurs in between two hegemonic positions (the US and [China?]). Such crises not only link to hegemony but especially to more severe long-wave downswings as the conflicts waste resources on war and armaments when other spending commitments will likely be more productive of long-wave upswings and climate change mitigation and adaptation. A war of ascendancy is likely to be less productive of global socioeconomic performance than, for instance, multilateral agreements to stabilize conflicts.

And third, the conflicts over Ukraine and Taiwan are very likely not only to exacerbate the climate crisis directly through (a) destruction of fauna and flora and (b) greater pollution, but also through (c) reducing resources for fighting the climate crisis due to concentrating on other crises. It is well known that as the number of global or regional crises escalates, the resources spent on (some of) them per unit number decline.

The First World War (1914–1918), according to David Fromkin (2004) in *Europe's Last Summer: Who Started the Great War in 1914?*, was ultimately blamed on Germany, and their defeat temporarily prevented them from ascending to a hegemonic position in the region/world. The Second World War (1939–1945), as A.J.P Taylor emphasized in *The Origins of the Second World War* (1964), finally ended Germany's aim of world domination, as they sought to concentrate on economic rather than military-political power thereafter. C.W. Mills in *The Causes of World War Three* (1958) investigated the early stages of the world war between capitalism and so-called communism (or 'state capitalism', as some Eurocommunists or democratic socialists may prefer to call "it"), as each side sought to promote their hegemony or enhance their power, respectively. In some circles, it is commonplace to refer to the *so-called* Cold War (CW) (1947–1989) as "ww3" (this is put in small letters to prevent confusion with the current "prewar" situation that alludes to WW3 into the 2020s). For instance, the work of former CIA director James Woolsey (2003), Norman Podhoretz (2005), and so on demonstrates a whole literature on "ww3." The so-called Cold War was an earlier conflict between liberal-democratic and autocratic powers closely linked to the current one.

Despite this, most analysts of the "Cold War" underplay the extent to which this was a "hot" world war, involving dozens of nations, between capitalism and "communism," especially during 1947–1991 (from the Truman Doctrine to the dissolution of the USSR). Briefly, these include (among others) the Korean War of 1950–1953ff, involving 3m troops, 2–3m civilian deaths, half a million troop deaths/missing, and 27 countries. The Vietnam War of 1955–1975 involved 28 nations, with Vietnam being the most bombed country in history; Cambodia close behind, with 3.5m Vietnamese, Cambodians, and Laotians killed, and with US$1trillion (1955–1975 units) being spent on the war by the US alone. There were dozens of other mass killings with the complicity of major powers, e.g., the massacre of *circa* 1m leftists in Indonesia during 1965–1970, plus similar events in Guatemala (1954), Iran (1963), Brazil (late 1960s), Chile (1970s), El Salvador (1979–1992), similar ideological civil wars in Africa, etc., as well as the well-known ones in China during the Cultural Revolution, North Korea since the war, and numerous other nations. A hot (and warm) world war it certainly was.

More recently, many have touted the possibility of a new world war. For instance, former President Biden said there was a choice between "sanctions and World War 3," and since then he has mentioned "World War 3" (WW3) numerous times. He noted that he would support NATO "to the point of World War 3," and that if Taiwan was invaded, he would intervene on its behalf, which would also start (or continue) World War 3 (Wingrove 2022; Bickerton 2021). Enforcing a no-fly zone in Ukraine, which a large proportion of Americans support, would amount to, many have said, the start of WW3, since NATO/USA would have to shoot down Russian planes to enforce it. Russian state TV also stated that "World War 3 has definitely begun," with the sinking of Russia's prime battleship, Moskva (Stewart and Sharman 2022).

There are ongoing global divisions generated between autocratic regimes on the one hand (e.g., China, Russia, North Korea, etc.) and liberal-democratic regimes on the other hand (e.g., the US, UK, EU, Japan, Australia, etc.). The invasion of Ukraine has shocked the world, especially through the atrocities that have occurred, and this links to other incursions by Russia into Georgia, Crimea, Belarus, etc. For some time now, the world has been alarmed also by China's rising hegemonic potential, involving military activities in small islands in the South China Sea, incursions of warplanes into Taiwan's air defense zone, their plan to invade Taiwan, support for Russia in the Ukrainian conflict, attacks on Filipino and other ships, evolving "defense" agreements with numerous nations, including the Solomon Islands and others in the Asia-Pacific region, and a host of other such activities. The major nations/areas of the world and many others are now preparing for major ongoing geopolitical conflict and war by, among other things, increasing the percentage of GDP spent on defense and military hardware, software, and personnel to 2% and beyond (while Russia spends almost 6%).

However, there are numerous relatively recent examples of problematic events on the other side of global politics. This includes the US's support for Israel against the Palestinians, especially during 2023–2025, in the light of over 50,000 Gazans (and thousands of Lebanese, a couple of thousand Israelis) having been killed, including perhaps over 25,000 children, and over 100,000 injured. The US has historically provided Israel with hundreds of billions of dollars of weapons. If the war in Gaza/Lebanon develops into an even wider war, it may link with the war in Ukraine structurally or incidentally (e.g., through Hezbollah's link to Iran and their link to Russia). The US also engaged in an invasion of Iraq in 2003, based on fraudulent intelligence, with up to a quarter of a million dead. The Iraq War contributed to the rise of the Islamic State (ISIS), especially in Iraq and Syria, which temporarily held power in some areas and is a (somewhat) more radical organization compared with *Al Qaida.* The Islamic terrorist networks provided a complementary counter-US and western movement that replaced the Soviets, including also in Afghanistan, while now Russia is taking the lead in challenging NATO as well, along with their allies such as China, Iran, North Korea, and others.

This chapter examines the ongoing growing geopolitical conflict between the LDA and AP through the lens of core general principles of political economy (PoPE) (O'Hara 2023) and *war*. We continue using the principles of *historical specificity and hegemony/uneven development* in the next section, tracing the recent, current, and likely future history of the conflict between LDAs and APs. We then use the principles of *circular and cumulative causation* (CCC) and *contradiction* (K) to isolate the dominant forces leading to instability and disarray through military build-up, conflict, war, and discord. After that, we scrutinize how these ongoing conflicts can be viewed through the (contradictory) principles of war in the information age. This is linked to the principle of uncertainty, as instability is studied regionally and globally from 1900 to 2024, situating current trends within a wider historical context. The paper also examines the principles of *innovation* and *policy/governance*, where moderating influences could reduce the contradictions and CCC processes, thereby reducing the potential for world war.

10.2 Historical Specificity II: The Four Wars

As mentioned, the principle of historical specificity states that scholars and others should place in historical context the problems and issues they scrutinize, since this enhances understanding of the phenomenon and assists in moderating the anomalies. In this context, all the major conflicts since the start of the twentieth century (WW1, WW2, Cold War, and recent LDA-AP conflicts [WW3?]) have similarities and these similarities expose subtle and not-so-subtle differences that make them

Table 10.1 Similarities between WW1, WW2, CW, and potential WW3

Similarities WW1→WW3	WW1	WW2	"Cold War"	Potential WW3
1. Conflict of "West" vs. Central/Eastern Powers	Allies vs. Central Powers	Allied Powers vs. Axis Powers	Capitalist vs. "Communist" Powers	Liberal-Democratic Allies vs. Autocratic Powers
2. "Hegemony" at Core of Conflicts	War for European-World Hegemony	War for European-World Hegemony	Hegemony of Capitalism vs. "Communism"	Hegemony of Liberal Democratic vs. Autocratic Powers (Russia, China, Iran, etc.)
3. "West" Won WW1, WW2, CW	Allied powers won	Allied powers won	State capitalism won	Uncertainty about the 'Winner'
4. Innovations Played Critical Roles	Submarine, aerial, poison gas, tank warfare	Short-range atom bombs; radar; jet propulsion, ballistic rocketry	AK-46, F-4 Phantom, FN-FAL Battle Rifle, Chieftain Main Battle Tank FV4201[a]	Drone warfare, cyber warfare, unmanned vehicles, hypersonic missiles, AI, nuclear threat
5. "Europe" At Core Of Each War; Asia Semi-periphery Of Wars	War in Europe, colonial linkages, Japan in Asia-Pacific	War in Europe, colonial linkages, Japan in Asia-Pacific, US role critical	Conflicts in Europe, Asia-Pacific, Latin America, and Africa	Wars in Europe, the Middle East, China–US, etc. Conflicts in Asia-Pacific
6. Micro-Regional Issues	Balkans War, Belgium War	Germany annexed Austria, occupied Czechoslovakia, and invaded Poland	Communist uprisings in Greece & Turkey led to Truman Doctrine	Ukraine War, Taiwan Conflict. Russia Lost Central & Eastern Areas. China wants Taiwan back, Middle East
7. Each War "Causally Linked" to Previous War(s)	7-Year War (1756–1763), 1871 Treaty "Causally Linked" to WW1	1919 Treaty of Versailles "Caused" WW2	Winners of WW2 "Causally Initiated" CW (Russia & USA)	Outcome of CW "Causally Linked" to WW3

Source: [a]Adapted from Kyle Mizokami (2019); Modified and Added to by O'Hara

unique. To promote specificity, Table 10.1 outlines some of these core similarities. Note that information is lacking for many aspects of LDA-AP conflicts (WW3?), so we raise questions in the context of these potential similarities.

The first similarity of the major conflicts-wars involves groups of nations forming alliances, including the protagonists and other groups fighting the protagonists, while sometimes nations change sides. For instance, WW1 involved the triple alliance of Germany, Austria, and Italy, but after Italy joined the allies, this became the *Central Powers*, including Turkey and Bulgaria. The other side was called the *(Triple) Entente* of Britain, France, and Russia, and later simply called the Entente or the *Allied Powers*, with also Japan, Italy, Portugal, Romania, Greece, and the USA.

WW2 comprised the *Allied Powers*, Britain, France, and Russia, versus the *Axis Powers* led by Germany with Italy. Japan started the war in Asia by invading China in 1937 and officially joined the *Axis Powers* in 1940 when they signed the Tripartite Pact. Japan's attack on Pearl Harbor (followed by campaigns in east and southeast Asia) led to direct US involvement in the war on the side of the *Allied Powers.*

The so-called Cold War (1947–1989), between "communism" and capitalism, also included alliances, with the US leading other western nations such as Britain, France, West Germany, Australia, Japan, Spain, Portugal, and New Zealand in the capitalist camp, while the USSR, China (initially allied with Russia), Cuba, Central and Eastern Europe, and several other nations were in the communist camp. There was also a so-called non-aligned movement, involving several nations in south(-east) Asia, Latin America, Africa, and the Middle East.

The currently emerging series of conflicts also involves a series of alliances. On the one side are the *autocratic powers*, including China, Russia, North Korea, Iran, Belarus, and potentially also Venezuela, Myanmar, and some African nations. The other side is called the *liberal-democratic allies* (or *Allied Powers)*, including (among others) the US, EU, Britain, Canada, Australia, New Zealand, Japan, Taiwan, Ukraine, and (potentially) several other nations from Asia, Africa, the Middle East, and Latin America.

This system of alliances is especially important for two reasons. First, as discussed below, it often causes a *bandwagon effect* of circular and cumulative causation (CCC) that accelerates the course of the conflicts and potentially makes the end of the conflicts different to engineer. And second, there are always opposite sides involved in an alliance. On the latter, the current system of conflicts is (not unlike the other major wars) rather more complicated since the nations of the Allied Powers also include autocratic *forces* (e.g., Trumpians, far right in Europe, "One Nation" elements, Hungarian government, etc.,), while the nations of the autocratic powers have citizens who are liberal democratic in tendency (though many of them are "gagged"). These dichotomies are global, regional, national, and subnational.

The second similarity is that the issue of hegemonic power/uneven development is at the core of all the conflicts-wars. The first two world wars were associated with ongoing major conflict within and between the major European powers, with linkages to regional and global powers. The 7-year war (1756–1763, which some call the "*real* first world war") and the mostly European wars ending in treaties in 1871 left especially France bereft of territory, while Germany established an empire. By the first decade of the twentieth century, alliances had been established with massive military build-up by most European states, leading many to surmise that war was "inevitable." David Fromkin (2004) argues that Germany strategically planned the war(s) to begin with while it was still in an apparently powerful position. Similarly, in the late 1930s, Germany was keen to take back territory lost in WW1 and possibly extend far into Western and Eastern Europe and possibly further if successful (with links to Japan in the Asia-Pacific). In the shadows of both world wars, Britain had long lost global hegemony while the USA was the most powerful nation and the global absolute hegemon by 1945 or earlier (until the 1970s, when it declined to *relative hegemony*).

The USSR and USA engaged in their global infighting for supremacy during the Cold War (1947–1991) while both underwent long-wave upswing during the 1950s–1970s (1940s also for the US). Major conflicts over communism versus capitalism emerged between numerous nations over Korea and Vietnam, while more localized struggles were happening in China, Iran, Greece, Malaya, Chile, Indonesia, the Philippines, Argentina, Brazil, numerous areas of Africa, the Middle East, and a host of other regions. When the US deployed nuclear missiles in Turkey and Italy in 1961 and supported an invasion of Cuba, the Russians and Cubans responded with nuclear missiles in Cuba, and the ensuing crisis nearly started a nuclear war, known as the Cuban missile crisis of 16–28 October 1962. Into the 1970s onward, a mostly global (excepting much of Asia) long-wave downswing started (undergoing lower long-wave dynamics or borderline performance until the 1980s or 1990s, then a severe downswing) that affected both camps. Economic performance malaise more severely affected the Soviets and their satellites, due to their less proficient circuit of eco-techno-institutional reproduction, with military over-expansion exacerbating downswing. Hence, the resultant victory of one version of "state capitalism" (US, NATO) over another form of state capitalism (USSR) (Resnick and Wolff 2002).

The demise of the Soviet Union adversely affected the territory controlled by Russia, which for a decade resulted in serious negative growth and the embezzlement of millions of its citizens' bank deposits during the 1990s. Many former Russian areas gained independence. The resulting power struggles eventually led to the emergence of crony capitalism and ultimately an autocratic regime in Russia by the 2010s bent on reestablishing some of their old Russian Empire and Soviet client states. These forces led to the likely origins of the current "prewar" situation (and possibly WW3) as Russia, China, and several other autocratic regimes flex their muscles reestablishing territory, while liberal democratic regimes, most notably in the UK, EU, and USA (NATO), have been reluctantly adapting to this changing geopolitical environment.

In recent years, Russia occupied parts of Moldova, Georgia, and Crimea, while China continued to be aggressive in the Indo-Pacific region and the South China Sea, while North Korea has upgraded its nuclear arsenal majorly in recent years. Iran has also upgraded its nuclear capability and networks of armies and allies in the region. Things came to a head during 2022–2025 as Russia invaded Ukraine, China established a security pact with the Solomon Islands and engaged assertively with South Pacific island nations while continuing the Belt and Road Initiative (with a lesser trajectory). President Putin several times threatened to use nuclear strikes if the West got in his way, and China has supported Russia's invasion as a "logical response" to NATO's encroachment in central, southern, eastern, and northern Europe.[1]

The third similarity is that the Allied Powers (e.g., UK, Western Europe, US, etc.) have won the first three wars (WW1, WW2, and CW), but it is perhaps an open question of who will win the possible fourth war (WW3?). The first three wars were fought in the context of US and Western European hegemony, at least relative (rather than absolute) hegemony in the case of WW1, WW2, and the later phase of the CW. But WW3 potentially emerged in the context of potential Chinese hegemony, which appears much more substantial (economically) than any degree of *actual* long-term German power during the 1900s. China has a population of 1.4b, strong links throughout Asia, the Americas, Africa, the Middle East, the Pacific, and Europe, and an increasing degree of production, commercial, financial, and military power. An autocratic alliance between China, Russia, North Korea, Venezuela, Belarus (and potentially Hungary de facto), and several other nations with little or no domestic constraints could prove disastrous for the liberal-democratic allies.

The fourth similarity is that technical innovations were crucial during all these conflicts-wars. Such innovations during WW1 include submarines, tank warfare, airplanes, and poison gas. WW2 innovations include short-range atom bombs, radar, jet propulsion, and ballistic rocketry. CW innovations include AK-47 rifles, F4 Phantom jets, the FN-FAL battle rifle, and the Chieftain main battle tank. The innovations in use during current conflicts (WW3?) include drone strikes, cyber warfare, unmanned vehicles, hypersonic missiles, AI, and nuclear threats.

The fifth similarity is that all four conflicts initially involved local wars, but because of alliances between nations and regions, they became more general wars (pending WW3). WW1 started in the Balkans but quickly became European-wide due to the networks associated with the Allied and Central Powers, respectively, and later much wider in scope. WW2 initially spread from Germany to Austria and then especially Czechoslovakia and Poland, with alliances and agreements between the allies and central powers quickly involving Europe as a whole and later spreading, including independence struggles in Asia against European powers (which the Japanese encouraged). The Cold War heavily involved the USSR and the USA, but the conflict eventually included wars in Korea and Vietnam, almost a nuclear war during the Cuban missile crisis, and later also Indonesia, China, Argentina, Brazil, and Chile, plus several areas of Africa and the Middle East. In many ways, the Cold War was much more global than the first two world wars (or three, including the 1756–1763 war). The emergent phases of potential WW3 have involved around 30 nations providing arms and artillery to Ukraine, which has been invaded by Russia, which is supported by Iran, China, and several other nations, to some degree, such as India, Turkey, Myanmar, and Belarus (e.g., through supply chains). China has been expanding its power in the Asia-Pacific region through the creation of new military islands, military bases in Djibouti, and (security) agreements with Solomon

[1] See Wolfram Elsner (2020) for an investigation of the Chinese situation.

Islands, Vanuatu, Namibia, Cambodia, and elsewhere, while China has said it will eventually incorporate Taiwan "formally" into the PRC.

The sixth similarity is that all four conflicts-wars have been causally linked in part to the previous conflicts-wars. WW1 was a continuation of the outcomes of the 7 year's war of 1756–1763 (the "real first world war"), the 1871 Treaty, and the generalized military and alliance build-up to 1914. WW2 was causally associated with the asymmetric 1919 Treaty of Versailles, which led Germany to seek vengeance, especially after the catastrophe of the Depression. The Cold War was contributed to by the power gained by the USSR, US, and Europe in the context of WW2 and the relative expansion of China while Japan/Germany was defeated and demilitarized after the war. The Cold War was never really "finished" as China is now seeking hegemonic dominance (and seeing itself as a "communist" power) while Russia is trying to reestablish peripheral-buffer power bases lost during the end of the CW (1990s, and potentially expanding further). The core issues of all these wars have been sovereign general, national, and ethnic property rights in Europe, European/Asia-Pacific/global hegemony, and the settlement of boundaries and buffers within and between powers.

A seventh similarity is that all these wars *ceteris paribus* majorly increase(d) greenhouse gasses and certainly global temperatures, pending certain countertendencies such as albedo, while also destroying stocks of biologically active species and generating major deforestation. The current tension and localized wars and conflicts between the allies and the Axis powers will have a more cascading impact on GHGs and global temperatures if it does escalate into a world war. It especially has the potential to push planet Earth even more into the realm of interacting, cascading global (and some regional) tipping points involving the whole world, which would produce substantial circular and cumulative forces of destruction. Many more heatwaves, droughts, floods, hurricanes, coastal erosion, and other forms of extreme climate events will engulf the world, with some areas warming more than twice as strongly as other regions (e.g., the Arctic region). It would also likely result in (tens of) millions of human deaths, injuries, and future births that are prevented due to the conflicts.

These similarities between the "four wars/conflicts" have also revealed differences. World War I involved mostly conventional warfare: a militaristic orientation; trench warfare; kinetic capital; troops on the ground, air, and sea; mainly actioned within a few hundred miles of Western Europe; and the use of official uniforms and rank insignia. The Second World War was characterized by fewer trench tactics as mobility was more important; it was more worldwide in scope; it actioned more advanced weaponry, including nuclear; and it was more racially motivated through the killing of 6 million Jewish civilians (WW1 included the killing of up to 1m Armenians by the Ottoman Turks and tens of thousands of North Africans). The so-called Cold War included much guerrilla warfare, a series of regional wars and killings, the greater use of intelligence services, a heightened political-ideological battle, and a more extensive temporal dimension. The current potential WW3 involves an array of wars, conflicts, diplomatic fissures, and trade/commercial battles; more extensive use of nuclear weapons as a threat and potential defense/attack; sophisticated cyber warfare, drones, AI, short-medium and long-range missiles; hypersonic missiles, greater use of disinformation, and agents to distort information.

10.3 Contradictory Principles of War/Action in the Information Age

Any science must make use of its core principles to understand critical problems and issues of the world. The science of war, for instance, makes use of its core principles of war, which have been debated and analyzed for centuries now (Algar 1982). Ancient principles were developed by Sun Tzu (500 BC), Chanakya (350 BC), and more recently by Henry Duke of Rohan (1644), Marquis de Silva (1778), and Henry Lloyd (1781). The most famous historical principles of war emanate from Carl von Clausewitz (1812) in his major work, simply entitled *Principles of War*. These include general principles of war, strategic principles (offensive and defensive), plus tactical principles associated with defense, offense, troops, and terrain, as well as notes on how to apply these principles to temporal/spatial/contextual dimensions of war.

As time went by, national governments also developed principles of war. The UK and its commonwealth of nations typically made use of those developed by J.F.C. Fuller (1926). Other nations such as the USSR, Russia, the USA, China, France, Canada, Israel, and so on have their own principles. Comparing, for instance, the principles developed by autocratic systems vis-à-vis western principles, the former tends to place more emphasis on *central control* and preparedness, while the latter places more emphasis on *decentralized initiatives*, whereas Chinese principles also give scope to *regional issues.*

It is perhaps surprising how durable these various national principles have become and how similar they are, despite regional differences. For instance, the US principles of war have been perennially concerned with the famous nine principles (Fuller had nine principles as well). These one to nine principles are shown below (Leonhard ch. 2). More latterly, they have included three additional principles, making it 12 (USDOA 2019):

(1) Have clearly defined objectives.
(2) Seize and maintain the offensive.
(3) Synchronize and mass forces in one decisive element of combat power.
(4) Economy of force (only employ forces that have a strategic or tactical purpose).
(5) Maneuver (distribute forces relative to the enemy with a positional advantage).
(6) Seek unity of command and effort.
(7) Security: protect your forces from enemy attack.
(8) Strike the enemy when they are surprised.
(9) Utilize simple plans and concise orders.

(10) Restraint (judicious use of force).
(11) Perseverance (prepare for potential long-term engagement with military, diplomatic, economic, and informational resources).
(12) Legitimacy (moral, humanitarian, and public support).

The three additional principles (10–12) are certainly an innovation, but even in this revised form, they (principles 1–12) have been critically evaluated especially among military academics over recent decades. The main areas of criticism and necessary innovation concern three issues. First, they have been revised on the basis that they are contradictory: processually, conceptually, and logically (this is a statement of fact more than criticism). Second, the revisions have been undertaken based on institutional, technological, and strategic changes that have occurred. And third, they have been especially attacked for largely ignoring (or underplaying) the recent principles and practices of Russian and Chinese military and political-economic strategies.

In this light, there have been many newer publications, especially books, that have sought to revise these principles based on such changes. Most of even these documents have unfortunately concentrated on war as battles or tactics on the battlefront (e.g., McIvor 2005). Some attention has been given to broader issues of long-term strategy, even in these publications (but not enough), for instance, principles of human rights (Mary Kaldor 2005; an extension of, e.g., principle 12). But a full-blown rethink of the principles of war as a long-term strategy linking tactics, economy, diplomacy, politics, legitimacy, information warfare, and human rights has not been the focus.

Some effort, however, to develop general principles of war encompassing these broader issues has been made. For instance, Robert R. Leonhard (1999, 2015) and, to some limited degree, Marvin Pokrant (2021) follow this course. After examining the history of war principles and those of different countries, Pokrant rewrote the principles to accord with contemporary principles of complexity (rather than simplicity), knowledge of the environment, self, and enemy; deception and surprise; prioritized objectives and relative advantage (rather than objective and mass); plus sustained initiative and unity of effort. These are certainly better principles of war, but what we really need are principles of long-term sustained military–political–economic–diplomatic–humanistic principles of policy and governance to sustain prolonged geo-strategic action in the global political economy. The current principles of war should accord with principles of action in a complex global environment.

Leonhart intuitively knows this and goes part of the way toward fashioning the "principles of the information age" (including war). Like Pokrant, he recognizes the anomalous nature of the enduring extant principles and modifies them to keep in tune with current developments and complex modes of thinking and strategizing. He sees the core task at hand of providing tools of thinking for all concerned with great power battles at global, macro, meso, and micro levels. He also sets out to provide an explicitly dialectical mode of analysis for all parties to use as a means of assessing their situation. Rather than positing principles of war per se, he posits

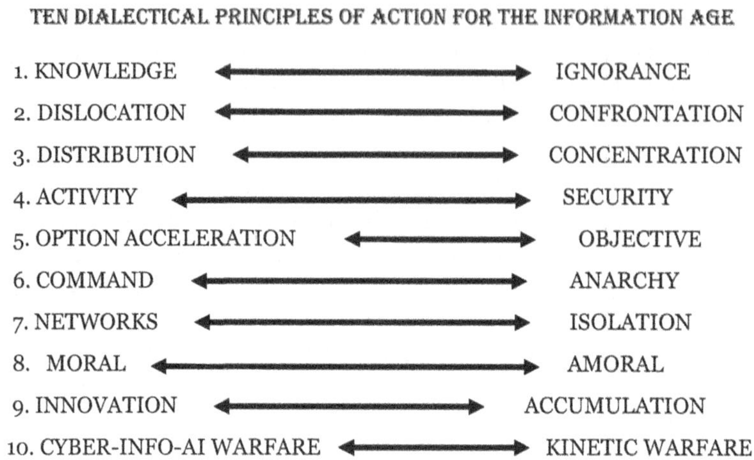

Fig. 10.1 Ten dialectical principles of action for the Information Age. (*Source:* Principles 1–6 Adapted from Leonhard (1999); 7–10 Added by O'Hara)

principles of action for virtually any occasion or problem. This is the true emergent innovation.

Figure 10.1 outlines his principles of action in a complex environment (1–6) plus four (7–10) I have added to make these additional issues more explicit, collectively called the *Ten Dialectical Principles of Action for the Information Age*:

War 3 (Global) Postulate 1 What this figure indicates is that the forces, whether *liberal-democratic allies* or *autocratic powers*, will be able to "win" WW3 (and any action concerning this *or other matters*) if they are able to utilize this complex array of dialectical contradictory principles to their strategic, operational, and tactical advantage.

At the core of Leonhard's analysis is the *First Contradictory Principle of Knowledge↔Ignorance (K↔I).* He posits the thesis that all levels of military-diplomatic strategic (S), operational (O), and tactical (T) action (SOT) need to solve the dialectical contradiction between knowledge and ignorance by assessing how it relates to the issues under consideration. Some instances will require much more knowledge than others, while under pressure action will have to be taken under conditions of extreme ignorance. It depends upon the context, the specificity of the environment, and the abilities of the various groups and agents. This K–I contradiction applies to all the other contradictions illustrated and is thus the prime one. For instance, applying this to the threat of war, several weeks prior to Russia invading Ukraine in 2022, the Ukrainian government would have taken various forms of action in an environment of relative ignorance when risk and uncertainty were at high levels.

The *Second Contradictory Principle is that between Dislocation (D) and Confrontation (C),* where the SOT needs of the situation require various levels of

D↔C along a continuum depending on the situation. The action required will also depend upon the levels of knowledge and ignorance at various levels. For instance, especially for a nation such as Ukraine, fighting a much bigger Russian force with more sophisticated software/hardware, a greater degree of dislocation is likely required relative to confrontation. This includes actions such as temporal dislocation, where Ukrainian forces attack Russian forces when they are unprepared (which obviously requires knowledge of their habits and patterns, plus local knowledge). It can also involve moral dislocation, such as the Ukrainian forces having more legitimacy than the Russians who are invading a sovereign nation and engaging in terrorist actions (targeting civilians to some degree) against international law. Functional dislocation has also been helpful by, for instance, Ukrainians utilizing anti-tank missiles and thereby upsetting troop movements in their attempts to confront Russian forces. Positional dislocation is also helpful as Ukrainian forces may have superior knowledge of when the Russian military is in very difficult terrain or moving in the wrong direction.

The *Third Contradictory Principle states that* various *forces will need to use an array of different dynamics of Distribution↔Concentration (D↔C)* to get advantageous positions and results. Different balances of D↔C are required to be enacted through time and space depending upon the situation and environment. Nations with smaller forces (e.g., Ukraine, Taiwan), for instance, are likely required to have distributions scattered around the region at different times, *engaging in guerrilla tactics*, while states with large-scale battalions will likely often achieve better results through more concentrated engagements. However, likely a degree of variation is required to increase the degree of uncertainty on the part of the enemy. It has become an almost established fact that Russia over-distributed its forces during the early phase of its 2022 invasion of Ukraine and got better results in the east and southeast of Ukraine when it concentrated its forces, especially in the light of Russia's major losses in the meantime.

The *Fourth Contradictory Principle shows that different arrays of Activity↔Security (A↔S) are required,* depending on knowledge and circumstances. Forces that perpetually secure their forces against attack will never win a war unless enemies make repeated errors of judgment due to incompetence or ignorance. Leonhard notes the significance of the *law of economy* for this contradiction, as the more knowledge available, the fewer the resources needed for security. Forces will never prevail, however, unless successive efforts at forward thrusting are instigated. For instance, Taiwan will be more likely to prevail as an independent nation (*de facto* at least) if the US has given a definitive assurance that it will come to its aid in the case of an attack from China. President Biden gave this assurance in, e.g., May 2022 (despite caveats by his officials and considering potential changes in the future). Another example is that Ukraine was able to engage in some successful attacks on Russian forces when supplied with many different types of modern military hardware and software by outside forces. Ukraine could, therefore, reduce the emphasis on security per se and strike out more against the Russians, even on

Russian soil (as it did in the northeast during May 2022 and several times during 2023 and 2024; especially in the Kursk Oblast region during August 2024, etc.).

The *Fifth Contradictory Principle concerning Objectives Layering and Acceleration↔Objective Centring (OL↔OC)* also requires trade-offs between the various alternatives. OL↔OC shows that it is important to have specific objectives in mind when undertaking strategic, operational, and tactical moves. The more knowledge liberal-democratic allies or autocratic powers have, the faster objectives can be actuated, and the greater the ignorance, the slower objectives can be achieved, if at all. Relevant here is Pokrant's (2021, ch. 5) use of the principle of complexity, for instance, when he introduced *the new principle of prioritized objectives*, a layer of key objectives that have differential priority. Liberal-democratic allies and autocratic powers need to develop prioritized objectives, including lower and higher objectives, where the lower ones should help attain the high-order objectives (which may change over time). Some of these objectives may be contradictory in themselves, and there may be differential objectives for different nations within the respective alliance. An example of prioritized objectives is where, more recently, the US has made Asia-Pacific power and stability a higher-level objective over Eurasian power and stability (enabling their European allies to do the opposite and thereby provide a potentially useful balance between objectives), although this depends entirely upon geopolitical circumstances.

The *Sixth Contradictory Principle in need of resolution is that of Command↔Anarchy (C↔A),* where varying levels of balance are required in different contexts. An example crucial for the ongoing evolution of WW3 is where the autocratic powers (e.g., Russia, China, and North Korea) historically have privileged command at the expense of anarchy at most levels of strategic, operational, and tactical planning and action, whereas the liberal allies have tended historically to provide more of a balance between command and anarchy. In the world wars to date, the more balanced provision between C↔A has tended to be more successful in warfare because of the ability to innovate at higher, medium, and lower levels of command, depending on the knowledge at hand and specific circumstances. This posits two postulates associated with these ongoing conflicts-wars:

War 3 (Meso) Postulate 2 The *liberal-democratic allies* are more likely to prevail over the *autocratic powers* due to their better (historical) balance of command and anarchy, enabling more innovative decisions and actions to be successful.

War 3 (Global) Postulate 3 The autocratic axis is more likely to engage in nuclear strategic first strikes (not simply tactical) and have already made several such threats, relative to the *liberal-democratic allies* because of their command tendencies, which, ironically, can lead to apparently anarchistic actions (ad hoc command actions), such as this, which will likely lead to retaliation, followed by re-retaliation, and potentially major regional or global destruction where likely no one succeeds and we all lose tens or hundreds of millions of lives and numerous cities and countries. (cf. the interrelated eight contradictory principles.) (*Economist* 2022a).

As mentioned, I have added four principles to Leonhard's list, since these four are required, as most are listed as various principles by some authors and/or nations or buried in the details of some of Leonhard's arguments. They do, however, require to be included as principles, in their own right, due to their significance:

The *Seventh Contradictory Principle, between Networks (N) and Isolation (I),* N↔I, is that between the networks nations and blocs can establish, on the one hand, relative isolation in terms of alliances and bases, on the other. There is choice through the establishment of various trade-offs. More often, though, these networks are established historically due to various trends and power arrangements that nations and blocks have with others. For instance, historically, the US has established a whole series of alliances, military agreements, and trade relations that became intermeshed with its role as an absolute global hegemonic nation during the 1940s–1970s and relative global hegemonic nation during the 1980s–2020s. These include, for instance, NATO, ANZUS, and AUKUS, plus a whole series of military bases in over 30 nations, including Australia, several areas of the EU, South Korea, Japan, Germany, Kuwait, Israel, Italy, Iraq, Cameroon, Bulgaria, Belgium, Bosnia & Herzegovina, Niger, Estonia, Diego Garcia, Saudi Arabia, Honduras, the UK, Spain, Turkey, and Cyprus, to mention some of the more obvious ones.

Russia lost many of its bases and military linkages with the breakup of the USSR, but it has been trying to reestablish territory, alliances, and soft-strong force in Belarus, Georgia, Moldova, Syria, Ukraine, Tajikistan, Kyrgyzstan, Kazakhstan, and Georgia, plus several in parts of Africa. It thus has limited networks, with hardly a global dimension, and many of these are subject to strong force. China has (limited) bases in places such as Djibouti, Myanmar, Tajikistan, and Equatorial Guinea and has planned to expand the list majorly into the future, perhaps as an extension of its Belt and Road Initiative. But China too has limited military alliances and bases in a global context, although this will expand in the future.

War 3 Postulate 4 Currently, the liberal-democratic allies have a far greater network of allegiances and bases than the autocratic powers, and this should put them in good stead for any expansion of WW3 tendencies. However, as China expands its global influence, its alliances and bases will grow in the future. But with the cluster of major alliances and bases that the West has, and the greater the number that the autocracies will engender in the future, this inevitably expands the CCC tendencies of WW3 as allies adhere to principles and support their members. The "chain of alliances," or "chain ganging" thesis, often spoken of in relation to wars, highlights the CCC potential of tight alliances, which will likely heighten the intensity of conflicts-wars in the current multipolar world (see Tierney 2011, 302).

The *Eighth Contradictory Principle, between Moral (M) and Amoral (A),* (M)↔(A), is between those nations and areas with positive moral attitudes versus those with an amoral tendency. Having a clear and moral path to their military-industrial tendencies allows nations and areas to gain a high moral ground and potentially heighten their morale, as they try to stay clear of terrorist activities against civilians, engage in drunken brawls at night, and destroy the cultural capital of nations whose geographical territories they operate within. This is, for instance, very clear in the case of Ukrainian forces fighting for their homeland versus Russian forces trying to decimate cities, peoples, and icons throughout Ukraine. It is also clear in the case of liberal-democratic allies versus the autocratic powers that through time autocratic powers may lose much support of their citizens when they act irresponsibly and against human rights locally and within outside conflicts-wars (ditto for the allies when they do this).

War 3 Postulate 5 This moral-ethical principle gives liberal-democratic allies a strong force supporting their strength and success in the various conflicts in Europe, Asia, and elsewhere against the autocratic axis (since they support the underdog in both cases, Ukraine and Taiwan, who are being invaded [potentially or actually]).

Likewise, the West loses moral authority when it engages recklessly in various areas of the world. This especially applies to the US and its allies in Iraq during the early 2000s onward, when it propelled a war that led to hundreds of thousands of deaths on false pretensions (no weapons of mass destruction and "no" (direct) links to terrorists). Similarly, the US and others support Israel in Gaza despite the 50,000-plus Gazan deaths (plus Lebanon); in the face of the ICC and UN efforts to balance the equation, they lose moral support for the West.

The *Ninth Contradictory Principle*, *Innovation↔Accumulation*, states that there are trade-offs between major innovations and general accumulation, which will impact the successes and failures associated with WW3. Too many resources being given to major innovations may be at the expense of the general accumulation of military capital and military and intelligent human capital. It may also be at the expense of other social resources. Some emphasis on innovation may generate solutions that lead to an early end to the war, but it may also lead to major escalation. A good balance between innovation and backwardness may be ideal in terms of some innovation and some capital accumulation. While the autocratic axis can engage in major innovation at their whim, without any likely backlash from the electorate or parliament, this is not the case for the liberal-democratic allies. In general:

War 3 Postulate 6 It is perhaps more likely that the *liberal-democratic allies* (LDAs) will engage in more successful military and intelligence innovation due to (a) having the moral high ground and more successful creativity and freedom of innovation in society/MIC; (b) more converts and migrants flowing to the LDAs due to citizens, scientists, and academics preferring or being forced into LDA areas due to lack of academic freedom and other liberties within the *autocratic powers* (APs). (This is likely to counter to some degree the tendency in recent years for democratic governments to have been reduced in number significantly around the world, while autocratic governments have been increasing majorly, and in principle have more carte blanche power to innovate (Smeltzer and Buyan 2022.)

The *Tenth Contradictory Principle*, *Cyber-Info-Warfare↔Kinetic Warfare*, is that between Cyber-Info-Warfare and Kinetic Warfare. This states that there is a productive balance between traditional kinetic warfare that involves large and smaller-scale military equipment and personnel with the skills and knowledge to utilize it, on the one hand, and the use of information and cyber-capabilities in conjunction with the Internet, computers, and AI along with skilled strategic-tactical knowledge workers, on the other. Kinetic warfare involves artillery, fighter jets, nuclear weapons, tanks, conventional rifles, and (some) drone warfare. Cyber-Info-Warfare involves utilizing information to confuse the enemy, disinformation campaigns to seek an advantage, planning to minimize/"optimize" the use of kinetic offenses and destruction, plus the use of cyber warfare to distort and disable information streams that lead to kinetic impacts.

For instance, as Leonhard (2015) argues, Russia used a sophisticated array of plans and strategies concerning the manipulation of information to intervene in Lithuania (1991), Transnistria (1990–1992), Chechnya (1994–1996), Dagestan and Chechnya (1991–2000), Georgia (2008), plus Crimea and (Eastern) Ukraine (2013–2014). Similar programs, including further innovations, have been in motion in Ukraine from 2022 to 2024. All these actions are said to be in response to Mr. Putin's belief that greater encroachment of NATO into Eastern, Southern, and Northern Europe constitutes a major threat to Russia. The "stimulation of reactionary movements among Russian conservatives" saw Putin situate himself as a defender of Russian nationalism and orthodoxy, creating and sustaining pro-Russian "political parties, unions and paramilitary groups"; using Russian agents to engender local protests and paramilitary operations; importing numerous "volunteer" forces; denial of Russian operations; using hacktivists, bloggers, actors, and "journalists" to portray themselves as Ukrainian nationalists; "relief columns importing military supplies to pro-Russian forces; invasion operations used by tactical groups; and the so-called defensive actions to protect pro-Russian populations (pp. 2–3).

These tools of psychological deception and manipulation are said to be part of a sophisticated strategic-operational-tactical six-phase and four-threat plan of Russia to take over more peripheral territory, as illustrated in Fig. 10.2.

The first phase (t) involves covert origins and differences of interest through potential military threats. The second phase (t+1) involves the escalation of conflict from differences to actual conflict (but not yet official military action). The third

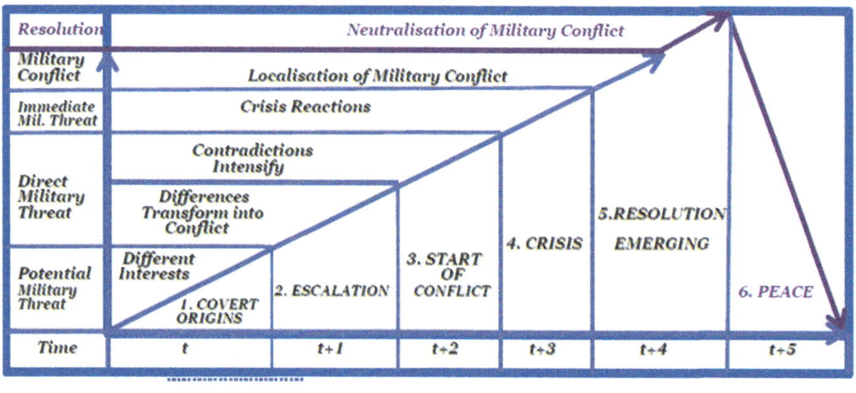

Fig. 10.2 Russia's six-phase plan of extending peripheral territory. (Source: Adapted from Leonhard 2015, 50)

phase (t+2) includes the intensification of *contradictions*, including military *threats*. The fourth phase (t+3) involves crisis, including reactions such as military conflict. The fifth part of the plan (t+4) is for the localization of military conflict and methods of resolving the conflict. Last, the plan (t+5) seeks a post-conflict resolution to promote peace as Russia succeeds in gaining more territory. The six-point plan thus commences with Russia promoting political opposition plus various coalitions against those seeking stronger links to the EU and NATO, leading to economic sanctions, breaking of diplomatic relations, opposition forces, embargoes, and strategic deployment; then having the economy on a war footing plus a changing military leadership; and finishing with seeking ways of promoting peace through peacekeeping operations. All through the plan, the use is made of information warfare.

Part of the contradiction requiring resolution is the use of cyber warfare ↔ kinetic warfare by combatants. Much has been written about cyber warfare alongside conventional and potentially nuclear warfare. This involves the use of electronic and electromagnetic means of gaining kinetic advantage (land, air, space, sea) in war through information and communications technology and associated infrastructure. Several principles of cyber warfare are crucial to the process (Parks and Duggan 2015).

The first principle of cyber warfare is that they must have real-world impacts that enhance the war effort. The second principle is to disable, confuse, misdirect, misinform, destroy, delay, attack, and promote uncertainty within minds by the anomalous workings of the physical and financial capitals of the enemy. The third *principle is uncertainty*, that one can never be sure of the exact impact of cyber warfare, and therefore they need to be carefully preplanned and pre-executed. The fourth principle is that cyber warfare operates in the virtual–artificial domain that is constantly changing, literally every hour, and therefore continual, ongoing, daily modification and innovation are required to keep ahead of the enemy. For instance, Russia is said to have used cyber warfare in many effective campaigns, such as to promote Mr. Trump in the 2016 US elections; Mr. Putin is said to have seen Trump as a fellow traveler (and vice versa) and certainly preferable to Hillary Clinton or (President) Biden. The use of cyber warfare was also apparently used to negatively target Mrs. Clinton in that election, which may have cost her the presidency as US authorities mentioned in the final week of the elections her "anomalous" use of emails in official duties. Russian authorities believed Mr. Trump to better enhance the probability of Russia gaining peripheral territory compared with Democratic rivals. The same is true in the context of President Trump.

China is well aware of its military inadequacies relative to the US and NATO (and Russian) capabilities and is utilizing a "holistic" form of warfare in its objective of global hegemony. This holistic view, which is also used by the West, seeks to defeat the "West" not simply by military means but also through diplomatic, economic, and financial means plus the distribution of AID (and, e.g., BRI) to less developed nations. An important part of this strategy is the use of cyber warfare to engage in espionage, propaganda, sabotage, economic dislocation, and cyberattack. In the long term, China will engage in more economic–political–diplomatic cyber warfare to gain hegemony and also control of Taiwan, but in the short-to-medium term, if it turns to military action, this will engender a much different sort of war with the *liberal-democratic allies*, a potentially more violent one, more in tune with the current happenings in Ukraine but with likely more US intervention.

War 3 Postulate 7 Modern warfare thus leads to fewer or less potential for major large-scale world wars such as WW1 and WW2, and more the type of concentrations of numerous nations in combat formations in smaller wars, such as the Cold War, with the likely ongoing potential of WW3 including the actual and likely wars associated with Ukraine and Taiwan, as well as enhancing the array of bases around the world, economic domination, and cyber warfare on a large scale. As Wallerstein (2001) recognized, military hegemony is largely derivative from economic, financial, and commercial dominance. Hence, all components of the war conflict must be kept in view, including multipolar segments, when determining even one of them, such as cyber and kinetic warfare. (A "complete" world war cannot be ruled out, however, over Ukraine and Taiwan, and more broadly, even linking to the Middle East.)

War 3 Postulate 8 As numerous commentators have stated, as a general (meso) *principle* relevant for Ukraine and especially notable (potentially) for the Taiwan situation (e.g., *The Economist* 2022b: 8): "*War Tends to Favour the Defender.*" The reasons for this are numerous, such as the advantages of having local knowledge; greater morale for those attacked to save their homeland; supply-side anomalies for the invaders; international actions against the invaders; strategic-operational-tactical errors made by the attacker; and so on. Of course, this can be countered in some cases by greater resources, knowledge, personnel, weapons, and information warfare *potentially* held by the attacker. The "3:1 Rule" states that attackers will generally need three times the resources (capital, human power) of those attacked, given these asymmetries; subject, of course, to numerous caveats (such as our ten principles of war). (See "3:1 Rule" in Mearsheimer 1989.) (But note, the application of this principle needs modification in the light of the large Russian population in eastern Ukraine and other factors such as the success or failure of sanctions and the ability to enforce them. For instance, due to alternative supply chains and new systems of finance, Russia has successfully surmounted sanctions. This is crucial.)

Thus, the informational principles of contradiction and trade-off between the dialectical opposites with potential resolution are fundamental for assessing the current and future success or otherwise of the *liberal-democratic allies* versus the *autocratic axis* in their quest for world-regional domination. The likely trajectory of potential WW3 is heavily dependent upon the resolution of these oppositional but interdependent factors as they interplay through historical time. Associated with these contradictory opposites and interdependencies are numerous factors that lead to a magnified and amplified impact of the wars through cascading circular and cumulative causation, which are scrutinized more explicitly in Sect. 10.4.

10.4 Contradictions and CCC: Principles, Alliances, and Nuclear Strikes

The *principle of contradiction* in political economy states that there are numerous structural conflicts and forces of opposition ingrained in the institutions of society that tend to manifest themselves in varying degrees of instability, crises, and uncertainty depending on the balance of forces (see O'Hara 2001, 2023). The ten opposing forces mentioned above were introduced as methodological devices to assess where along the continuum the heterogeneous groups and agents of strategists, tacticians, operators, applicators, and workers can be situated to improve their position in struggles and conflicts by viewing the contradictions as a Hegelian mechanism of thesis, antithesis, and synthesis.

Normally in political economy, contradictions are used as a means of strategy but more especially also as a means of critical analysis. Several of these contradictions link with CCC forces of magnification (O'Hara 2001), the threat of major wars, and conflicts between liberal-democratic allies and autocratic powers, leading to global insecurity and uncertainty in the present and the future. The contradictions spread beyond this realm to the CSD and everyday situations as well.

A primary political economy contradiction is associated with beliefs and actions held/made by *liberal-democratic allies* and *Authoritarian* protagonists. On one side of this contradiction is the argument of the *LDAs*, that Russia, China, and others such as North Korea and Iran have been threatening and starting wars (e.g., in Ukraine) for their own personal interests. In the case of Russia, it is in the personal interests of Mr. Putin and his group to try to protect and increase Russia's zone of protection against NATO encroachment (and/or to enhance Putin's *political* longevity and personal security). The allies say Putin has been attempting to expand his territory in line with the old Soviet and before that Russian Empire boundaries and spheres of interest. But, they add, this has no validity in either international law or international norms since he has continually invaded various democratic regimes, especially in Ukraine against the wishes of the Ukrainian people. His wars are thus incendiary and likely to lead to nuclear catastrophe if unchecked, as he has threatened nuclear action numerous times, for instance, if the West does not back down, and especially if they intervene *directly* on Ukraine's behalf.

The other side of this contradiction, an argument of rebuttal, is made by Russia, China, and North Korea, and their allies, the group of authoritarian-undemocratic regimes. It is also made, in some form, by some scholars who otherwise would be unlikely to support these regimes (e.g., Thomas Palley 2022). This argument is that NATO, with the US as its head, has been encroaching on Russian geopolitical space at least since the dissolution of the USSR, around 1990. These incursions include the expansion of NATO through the inclusion of Poland, Czech Republic, and Hungary in 1999; Bulgaria, Estonia, Latvia, Lithuania, Rumania, Slovakia, and Slovenia in 2004; Albania and Croatia in 2009; plus Montenegro (2017) and North Macedonia (2020) thereafter (WPR 2022). Others such as Ukraine, Moldova, and Georgia have also been encouraged to join NATO, but Russia has "rightly" stymied this through support for Russian populations in these nations. This increasing incursion of NATO into Russia's geopolitical space is said to be a clear violation of historical norms and against the interests of global peace and normality.

What are we to make of these two contradictory arguments that are obviously counter to each other? First, they are both quite logical in their own way. The authoritarian-undemocratic argument that NATO has violated Russian historical geopolitical space is correct. But equally, the right of Ukraine, Moldova, and Georgia to seek NATO membership for their own protection is equally valid. This is what we call a *classic contradiction.* The arguments are two sides of the same coin, both valid, but equally both in contradiction with each other. In short, the contradictory but valid logic of both these arguments is a core reason for the ongoing LDA-AP (W3) conflicts and wars. The current situation in Europe is arguably as volatile as it was during the lead-up to WW1, WW2, and the Cold War, and the 7-year war during 1756–1763 (the first real world war, being fought in Europe, India, and the Americas).

A second core contradiction involves a CCC process to which all the major wars of WW1, WW2, Cold War, and WW3 were linked. This involves the process of developing alliances, generating multiple players in each of the wars, all supporting their own team, sometimes changing sides, and leading to accelerated military build-up, war preparation, and action on the field. WW1 was generated by the assassination in Serbia, invasion by Austria, Germany's support for Austria as it moved through Belgium into France, which led to Britain joining the war, while Russia engaged in complete mobilization as it supported Serbia in its defense against Austria. WW2 involved Germany moving into Austria, then Czechoslovakia and Poland, with Britain supporting Poland, leading to World War; while Japan invaded Manchuria, then expanded further into Southeast Asia, eventually bringing the US into the war by bombing Pearl Harbor in Hawaii, and the US also therefore supported the allies in Europe against Germany, Italy, and other axis territories. The Cold War involved hegemonic competition between the US and USSR, violation of the Monroe Doctrine in Cuba, the alliance between China, North Korea, and the USSR (early on), McCarthyism in the US, colonial wars in Vietnam, Cambodia, and Burma, and political conflict all over the world between capitalist and communist ideology.

The buildup to WW3 involves NATO expansion into Central and Eastern Europe and more latterly into Northern Europe; Chinese expansion in the Asia-Pacific and elsewhere; the Russian invasion of Ukraine with 30 nations militarily supporting Ukraine; and further Russian threats to Finland as well as established presence in Moldova and Georgia. Without the "chain ganging" support Russia is getting from a stream of countries for both Russia's "special operation in Ukraine" (supposedly "*not* a war or invasion") by China and support for Russian export/import of oil and/or gas/other items/supply chains, especially by China, Hungary, India, and a host of others (also negating sanctions), the Russian invasion of Ukraine would likely have been less proactive/"successful."

The third major political economy contradiction with the CCC-type motion involves Russia threatening the use of nuclear weapons several times against any direct NATO presence in Ukraine or expansion elsewhere. (Likewise, autocratic elements in the West have also engaged in such threats, e.g., Mr. Trump vis-à-vis "rocket man," the President of North Korea). Robert Litwak (2022) explains that Putin's risk-taking and miscalculation on the nuclear threat increase the chance of full-scale war in Europe and elsewhere, as any use of tactical or strategic nuclear weapons would lead to NATO replying and lead to accelerated conflict in a wider environment. As mentioned, *The Economist* (2022a) agrees that Russia's threat of using nuclear weapons, but especially the cavalier discussions in Russian media about nuking Ukraine and NATO allies (especially Britain), moves the nuclear issue into the realm of normal *social* mores. It normalizes and thereby escalates the nuclear threat to the world, rather than simply leaving it in the arena of needing to eschew mutually assured destruction (MAD).

The security agreement made in May 2022 between the UK, Finland, and Sweden represents another such CCC process likely to accelerate the military situation of WW3. The agreement stated that if Finland, Sweden, or the UK were attacked, the other parties to the agreement would come to their military (and/or other) aid if requested. During 2023 and 2024, all impediments to Finland and Sweden joining NATO have been negated (they are now members). Putin has said that such nations seeking to join NATO, or similar actions, would incur a "military-technical response" (BBC 2022). The current situation looks even more severe than what happened in the early phases of WW1 and WW2. In WW1, when Germany invaded Belgium en route to France in 1914, Britain declared war against Germany due to an agreement held between the UK and Belgium. And in WW2, when Britain gave "assurances" to Poland to defend their independence, and Germany invaded, Britain declared war against Germany. Other CCC processes followed in due course in both WW1 and WW2 due to the other military alliances between nations. It seems that Finland and Sweden are members of NATO, and the retaliatory threats made by Russia may lead to an extension of the fighting from Eastern Europe to Scandinavia (and likely to Central Europe) sometime in the future.

With the agreement that "an attack on one is an attack on all," the problem is that expanding NATO leads to a potential heightening of Putin's aggression, which in turn generates an expanding NATO, which leads Putin to aggress further, and so on and so forth in a typical CCC fashion. The fact that Putin is an autocrat, with no real limitations to his military incursions (by parliament or custom), potentially enhances the CCC process further.

The political economy *principles of innovation and policy governance* (O'Hara 2023) state that effective agreements established by conciliation and moderation could moderate these contradictory CCC processes/wars. One such global or regional agreement may center on trying to gain accord to eliminate attacks on civilians. A second agreement may try to reinforce existing nuclear treaties while developing new ones where necessary and moderating public nuclear threats. A third agreement may center on Ukraine/allies acceding to Russian control over eastern Ukraine in return for NATO non-membership of Ukraine with circa 20% less territory. And a fourth agreement may be to cede Taiwan to China as an *independent* territory of China while enhancing security for the rest of the Asia-Pacific region.

For some, these options are nonnegotiable, which enhances potential CCC multiplier-accelerator processes (I make no statement about whether they are good plans).

War 3 Postulate 9 With both sides of the LDA-AP conflict keeping to their principled beliefs, gang-busting alliances, and nuclear threats, these innovations are unlikely to gain traction. For Ukraine-NATO, the principles are the right of nations to self-determination and the right of NATO to protect such nations from invasion. For Russia, the principles are comparable to the US's Monroe Doctrine, that Russia has the right to protect itself from threats that endanger its historical space and buffers. Likewise for China, which argues that they have the right to gain from their increasing (relative) hegemonic power in economic, diplomatic, and defensive ways in the same way that the US, and before them, Britain and the Dutch, developed powerful modes of accumulation and regulation (especially given the historical position of Taiwan). With both sides sticking to their fundamentalist "principles" (and guns), there is no end in sight, and escalating aggression is much more likely.

10.5 Global and Regional Geopolitical Uncertainty 1900–2026

A critical element of political economy dynamics is associated with the *principle of uncertainty and risk*, which states that we need to scrutinize the nature, degree, and distribution of uncertainty (vis-à-vis risk) to assess the current and especially the potential performance of national, regional, and world economies (O'Hara 2023). Uncertainty can also provide us with an indication of the degree to which the current geopolitical uncertainties associated with the conflict between liberal democratic allies and the autocratic axis (WW3?) have developed to the level of the first three wars (WW1, WW2, and Cold War). It therefore potentially provides us with an indication of the phase of the evolution of WW3 (or prewar situation) and the degree to which we can call it a major integrated series of conflicts in the immediate future.

There is a negative relationship between geopolitical uncertainty and socioeconomic activity (within the CSD), since as uncertainty rises, expectations of future (and therefore current) levels of profit and growth tend to decline. It also dampens trade, stock-market returns, supply of resources, supply chain dynamics, demand, and usually increases costs. In constructing the index of geopolitical risk (GPR), Caldava and Iacoveillo (2022) state that:

> We define geopolitical risk as the threat, realization, and escalation of adverse events associated with wars, terrorism, and any tensions among states and political actors that affect the peaceful course of international relations. In the measurement step, we ... construct the GPR index with an algorithm that computes the share of articles mentioning adverse geopolitical events in leading newspapers published in the United States, the United Kingdom, and Canada. These newspapers cover geopolitical events of global interest, often implying an involvement of the United States. (Caldava and Iacoveillo 2022, 1195)

While it is called the GPR, geopolitical *risk*, it is really an index of GPU, geopolitical *uncertainty*, since it is not using deterministic measurement tools associated with statistics on the weather or insurance claims ("risk"), but rather is attempting to elicit a measure of something very general and systemic, i.e., geopolitical instability and disarray ("uncertainty"). Examining newspaper articles discussing such adverse geopolitical events is one way of evaluating this.

In this context, first, we investigate national and regional uncertainty linked to the opposing trends of liberal democracies versus the autocratic axis, especially in the light of Russian-NATO-East European and Chinese-US-Asia-Pacific geopolitical uncertainties. Figure 10.3a, b illustrates the index of geopolitical risk (GPR) for Ukraine and Russia during 1900–2024 and 1985–2024 (to 1 April 2024).

This shows that for Russia and Ukraine, the current levels of uncertainty are extremely high. For Ukraine, they are the highest they have ever been, even surpassing those by a massive factor vis-à-vis WW1 and WW2, and certainly astronomically higher than for any period over the past 40 years. Ending the war in Ukraine does not resolve all the contradictions as new ones emerge dealing with reconstruction, people returning, and what to do in the East of the country.[2]

For Russia, current uncertainty is massively higher than for any period over the past 40 years, while current levels also surpass uncertainty levels during WW2, although those for WW1 are slightly higher (GPR of 5.65) than those in 2022 (GPR of 5.58). These are even higher now than during the Cuban missile crisis of 1962

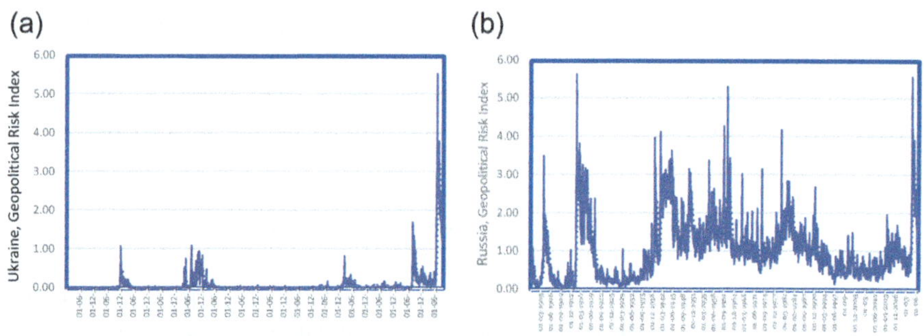

Fig. 10.3 (**a**) Ukraine GPR Index 1900–2024. (**b**) Russia GPR Index 1900–2024. *Source:* Adapted from raw data of Caldava and Iacoveillo (2024) (10-month moving average); see also Caldava and Iacoveillo (2022)

[2]These other contradictions are affected by "Ukraine's estimated reconstruction and recovery needs amount[ing] to around EUR 453 billion, on top of the colossal human suffering inflicted on the country, as recorded by the World Bank. This is roughly 2.8 times Ukraine's estimated nominal GDP in 2023. But these estimates don't include the further damage done since the beginning of 2024 and of course, the longer the war continues, the more war damage there will be. It's noteworthy that the direct damage to buildings and infrastructure within the first 2 years of the war amounts to around EUR 138 billion. But the needs for recovery are more than three times higher than the direct damage itself, as reconstruction needs also include the costs for repairs, restoration, and reconstruction with a dedicated 'build back better premium' on top of the direct damage and losses incurred" (Akhvlediani 2024, ii).

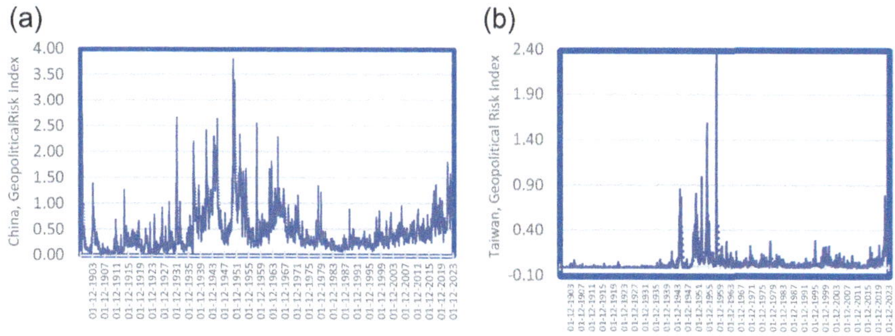

Fig. 10.4 (**a**) China, GPR 1900–2024. (10-year mov. av.). (**b**) Taiwan, GPR, 1900–2024. (10-year mov av.). *Source:* Adapted from raw data of Caldava and Iacoveillo (2024); see also Caldava and Iacoveillo (2022)

(GPR of 5.33). Whatever conclusions one makes, it must be said these uncertainty levels are consistent with major geopolitical adversity on a par with a very major war; it is hardly *simply* "early days" in the global conflict. WW3 is potentially imminent.

Turning now to Fig. 10.4 for relevant parts of the Asia-Pacific region, geopolitical uncertainty has been historically very high over the past few years in the light of the virtual takeover of Hong Kong by China, the intimidation over Taiwan by China, and the message received by Taiwan from Russia's invasion of Ukraine (in comparison with China's threat to invade Taiwan). Geopolitical uncertainty has been higher in China during 2022 than at any time since the Cultural Revolution, and in Taiwan higher than at any time since the late 1950s. Tensions are thus historically very high in China and Hong Kong, though relatively more moderated in Taiwan.

Based on these data, the Ukraine–Russia conflict has generated much more geopolitical uncertainty than the Chinese-Asia-Pacific connection. This is understandable as China has virtually taken over Hong Kong but has not directly threatened Taiwan (yet), and the message of the Ukrainian–Russian conflict for Taiwan is likely that China would be under severe pressure if it did invade Taiwan. This message is now well-established, after the continuing impact of sanctions on Russia over its invasion of Ukraine and the direct threat to China by President Biden that the US would come to Taiwan's military and other assistance in the event of such an invasion. This latter has lowered the threat to Taiwan but ironically increased the threat of escalating world war in the event of China invading Taiwan, as the US has now said it would intervene (despite the caveats).

In this context, we are very interested in the GPR for the world as a whole, in the light of the above data and issues. See Fig. 10.5.

This shows that *military-buildup uncertainty* (green line) during 2022 is even higher than it was during WW1 and about equal to those during WW2, though the degree of *escalation of war uncertainty* is nowhere near the levels of WW1 and WW2. The military build-up uncertainty during 2022 is also on par with levels during the hot cold war of 1947–1989. But, again, it is early days so far, although the military build-up uncertainty has been relatively high during 2014–2022 and rising majorly in 2022.

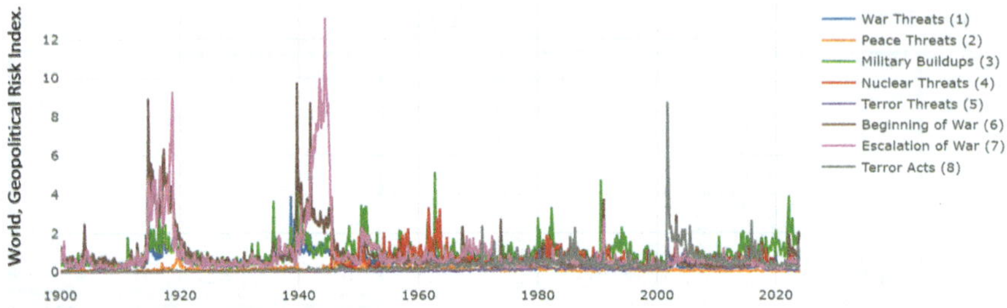

Fig. 10.5 GPR for World, 1900–2023 (to Dec 2023). *Source:* Adapted from raw data of Caldava and Iacoveillo (2024); see also Caldava and Iacoveillo (2022)

Much therefore depends upon the future degree of escalation of military buildup and especially the threat and actuality of war, as well as the future networks of military bases and defense treaties (especially for China) over the next several years. Geopolitical uncertainty thus is part of and implicates socioeconomic activity and the principles of war and political economy.

War 3 Postulate 10 Geopolitical uncertainty is at historically high levels, especially in Ukraine and Russia, but also, to a much lesser extent, in Hong Kong and Taiwan. Russia runs the risk of being demoralized and globally pushed into a corner, which may lead to a lashing out in Eastern Europe and against the Liberal-Democratic Alliance; certainly, the serious threat of a nuclear attack is higher than at any time since the Cuban missile crisis. China, for its part, is perhaps more likely to play the long waiting game regarding Taiwan, but in the meantime will escalate aggressive actions in the Asia-Pacific region, which will majorly increase uncertainty in that arena. Geopolitical instability looks likely to heighten.

10.6 Comparative Nuclear Arsenals/Assets of the Two Groups

A crucial test of capabilities for WW3 is the stockpile and potential utilization of nuclear weapons. This is so because Vladimir Putin has threatened to use them in Ukraine, and he would likely use them if the West tested his sanity too much. Susan D'Agostino (2022) of the *Bulletin of Atomic Scientists* presented the views of some 20 international experts on nuclear likelihood, and perhaps the most poignant of these was that of the current CIA director, William Burns, from 14 April 2022, and that of Scott Sagan:

> [G]iven the potential desperation of President Putin and the Russian leadership, given the setbacks that they've faced so far militarily, none of us can take lightly the threat posed by a potential resort to tactical nuclear weapons or low-yield nuclear weapons[.] (William Burns, CIA Director)
>
> Putin could order the Russian military to drop a single nuclear bomb on a Ukrainian city to try to coerce the Zelensky government into immediate surrender. This frightening

scenario is not fanciful. It is, after all, effectively what the United States did to Japan in 1945[.] (Scott Sagan, Spogli Institute for International Studies, Stanford University.)

The most likely candidate for the current ongoing global conflicts-wars to become emergent as a critical long-term process is either the dropping of a nuclear bomb on Ukraine (tactical or strategic) (or other Eastern or Central European context) or the invasion of Taiwan by China. Since the former is more emergent historically than the latter, given current uncertainty levels, this section will concentrate on the nuclear threat.

Global nuclear warhead inventories have displayed a declining long-term trend between 1986 and the present (FAS 2024). But this long-term trend underplays the fact that it has recently stopped declining, and more importantly, that the upgrading of nuclear warheads is now at a much higher level than previously. Providing more specificity for such nuclear warheads, Table 10.2 provides details of the nuclear warheads inventory total stockpile and whether they are "deployed strategic," "deployed nonstrategic," "in reserve/non-deployed," or simply "stockpiled."

This balance sheet shows that the West has a significant advantage over Russia and especially China in "strategically deployed" nuclear warheads, since they amount to 2000 nuclear warheads for the West compared with just under 1600 for Russia and none for China. However, for the total inventory, the balance is about equal (or possibly in Russia's favor). For an all-out nuclear war, after Russia potentially explodes a strategic warhead in Ukraine or another European area, the West may retaliate, while the world likely disintegrates.

But if China invades Taiwan, it has little ability to effectively fight a nuclear war with the US or the West, unless Russia and North Korea assist. Given that at present, Russia may well feel isolated and vulnerable over a war in Ukraine that has gone against them (compared with original objectives, even though they currently have an edge given US tardiness in getting major military hardware and software to Ukraine), or become very limited, Putin may well feel the need for a limited nuclear

Table 10.2 Status of global nuclear forces, number, nine countries, 2024

Country	Strategic deployed	Nonstrategic deployed	Reserve/ non-deployed	Stockpile	Inventory total
Russia	1710	0	2670	4380	5580
USA	1670	100	1938	3708	5044
France	280	n.a.	10	290	290
UK	120	n.a.	105	225	225
China	0	n.a.	500	500	500
Pakistan	0	n.a.	170	170	170
India	0	n.a.	170	170	170
Israel	0	n.a.	90	90	90
Nth. Korea	0	n.a.	50	50	50
TOTALS	~3780	~100	~5703	~9583	~12,119

Source: Adapted from FAS (2024)

strike to intimidate Ukraine, but the odds are likely against him winning even a limited nuclear war given the West's likely response. And at present, China could not likely win a war over Taiwan either.

War 3 Postulate 11 There is a possibility of a nuclear strike in Ukraine by Russia, but taking the likely retaliatory actions into account, no country or region is going to benefit from such actions, even if it is merely strategic. Regarding Taiwan, China will likely enhance its regional buffers and threats, which will increase tension in the Asia-Pacific region in the intermediate term. China is likely to try and enhance its economic, diplomatic, strategic, defensive, and hegemonic potential into the 2020s and 2030s before likely drawing Taiwan into its sphere of power until it can eventually encapsulate Taiwan without too much opposition. No nuclear threat is likely in relation to Taiwan as a more conventional war is more likely, but not before China enhances its pressure in the region and when it decides to take a gamble through the strategic initiative being in its favor.

War 3 Postulate 12 China has been losing per capita growth potential in the face of coronacrisis lockdowns, property debt-bankruptcy crises, declining productivity per worker (as the population ages), and higher unemployment (especially for graduates). There is a chance that China's hegemonic trend will deconstruct significantly and that its perceived rising dominance in the Asia-Pacific elsewhere, and potential in the long run to encapsulate Taiwan, will diminish significantly, at least in relation to its economic resources. Likewise, Russia, the US, and the EU have been suffering from deteriorating performance over the past several decades, which will limit their potential to enhance military spending per unit GDP, although more so in the liberal-democracies than for autocratic regimes (Russia's growth per capita has recently risen thanks to the success of sanctions busting and people leaving the country). To some degree, the greater control over resources in autocracies is a benefit that assists them in WW3. But this is countered by the transfer of human knowledge to the West as internal enemies of autocracies migrate to the liberal-democracy lands and assist them in many projects, including geopolitical ones.

10.7 Conclusion

We started with the principle of historical specificity and found that "World War 3" (prewar era) was a sound concept, as world wars have changed somewhat in the light of the threat of nuclear weapons and (dis)information/AI technology. They have tended to become prolonged but involve an array of smaller wars rather than one big one. The possible exception is where nuclear weapons have been activated, in which case it is likely to become a war no power can win, and the CCC processes will likely lead to disarray and dislocation rather than a clear outcome in this case.

We also used the principle of contradiction to analyze "WW3" through the characteristics of the information age. It was hypothesized that whether the liberal allies or the autocratic axis is successful (and whether *any project for anyone/group* can succeed) depends upon whether they successfully utilize the balance of forces associated with the ten contradictory trade-offs. We have little advanced knowledge of the degree to which they activate these trade-offs, but one thing did emerge: the liberal allies have an advantage in balancing more equally the command versus anarchy (centralized versus decentralized decision-making) contradiction, which can lead to more effective innovations and may engender success. The allies also likely have a military advantage over the autocratic powers in moral power, though not if all powers keep to their principles.

We also outlined the nature of the military-industrial complexes of the various powers, especially noting the spending patterns and plans, stock of military personnel, and software-hardware relating to nuclear weapons. At present the liberal allies and Russia have broadly similar stocks, and the Russians have been advancing their nuclear and other arsenals significantly, while the Chinese have and will continue to increase their arsenal majorly, especially over the next decade. The biggest threats will come from the liberal allies and autocratic axes keeping strictly to their principles of (a) Russia reestablishing a substantial buffer between them and NATO forces, (b) China pressuring Taiwan, (c) NATO protecting Central and Eastern nations from being part of the buffer, and (d) the US militarily protecting Taiwan against invasion. Unless we have people with heightened diplomatic power, the contradictions are likely to eventually lead to "WW3" of some type, through chain-ganging alliances advancing cascading escalations of military activities.

In this context, no clear success of either of the axes/powers is obvious, except that two things emerge out of the complexities of the situation. The first is that Russia is more likely to incite nuclear war, after which no power is likely to succeed, leading to disarray and destruction all around. The second is that Chinese hegemony may emerge, leading to their political-economic success at the expense of the liberal allies, including military success, which is derivative from the economic, especially in terms of increasing soft power, and thereby eventually transforming political power as well. However, third, if China invades Taiwan too soon and too destructively, it may well lead to US intervention, which will generate more global responses and possibly another regional bout of "WW3" (another regional war), the outcome of which is indeterminate. However, autocracies can generate more military resources devoid of Congressional oversight, which gives them an advantage (in terms of per capita GDP). On the other hand, successful hegemonic dominance by the autocratic powers is countered by various stylized facts of the past, including (a) all past hegemons have been liberal democracies, (b) liberal democracies have the high moral ground over autocracies both domestically and externally, and (c) greater innovation and freedom (including through migration to LD lands) will likely support the liberal democracies.

Overall, one would have to conclude, in addition, that there are numerous signs of a world war, of a similar nature to that of the hot-cold war of 1947–1989, but that it would likely have to continue through some (limited?) years of further build-up and escalation to be definitively called a major war. The nuclear option would majorly escalate conflict in that direction, were Putin to take that course, while the

Chinese nuclear option would likely have the same impact were it to invade Taiwan before it has (potentially) gained entrenched regional or global hegemony. But if it keeps playing the waiting game, it likely has more chances of succeeding. In the meantime, "World" War 3 still looms on the horizon (even if it becomes a multiregional contest). The principles analyzed in this paper should help us determine the groundwork, process-in-motion, and possibly the outcome of this likely conflict.

Regarding climate change and WW3, two core issues need emphasizing. The first is that the trend of regional and/or world wars over currently developing issues regarding potential extensions to Russia's and China's buffer areas is increasing the flows and stocks of species deaths, greenhouse gasses, and hence global mean temperatures. Ceteris paribus, this is what wars historically have done (with a caveat regarding albedo and other countervailing processes). And second, as regional and global wars require major resources of capital, knowledge, and governance, they will reduce efforts to moderate other crises in the current series of polycrises, most notably the climate crisis. There is always a trade-off in the distribution of policy attention and governance resources between wars and the environment, both with respect to the impact of one (wars) on the other (climate change) and the redirection of attention and policy from one (climate crisis) to the other (wars).

References

Akhvlediani, Tinatin. 2024. *Explaining Ukraine's Recovery and Reconstruction: What, How and When?* Brussels: CEPS.

Algar, John I. 1982. *History of the Principles of War*. Westport, CT: Greenwood Press.

BBC. 2022. UK Agrees [to] Mutual Security Deals with Finland and Sweden. *BBC News*, May 12. https://www.bbc.com/news/uk-61408700

Bickerton, James. 2021. Jo Biden Could Trigger Major War with China: Pentagon Insider Breaks Cover. *Express*, June 25. https://www.express.co.uk/news/world/1454630/Weorld-War-3-news-Joe-Biden-China-Taiwan-conflict-Franz-Gayl-South-China-Sea

Caldava, Dario & Matteo Iocoveillo. 2024. *Geopolitical Risk Index*. https://www.matteoiacoviello.com/gpr_country_files/gprc_sweu.htm

Caldava, Dario, and Matteo Iocoveillo. 2022. Measuring Geopolitical Risk. *American Economic Review* 112 (4): 1194–1225.

D'Agostino, Susan. 2022. Will Putin Go Nuclear? A Timeline of Expert Comments. *Bulletin of the Atomic Scientists*, 22 April.

Economist. 2022a. A New Era: Why the War in Ukraine Makes Nuclear Conflict More Likely. *Economist*, June 4–10, pp. 9, 15–17.

Economist. 2022b. Ukraine: The Relief of Kharkiv. *Economist*, May 21–27, p. 48.

Elsner, Wolfram. 2020. *Das chinesische Jahrhundert: Die neue Nummer eins ist anders*. Frankfurt: Westend Publishing.

FAS (Federation of American Scientists). 2024. *Status of Nuclear Forces: Who Owns the World's Nukes?* https://fas.org/issues/nuclear-weapons/status-world-nuclear-forces/

Freedom House. Freedom in the World 2025. The Uphill Battle to Safeguard Rights. *Washington D.C., USA*, 2025. https://freedomhouse.org/report/freedom-world (2025).

Fromkin, David. 2004. *Europe's Last Summer: Who Started the Great War in 1914?* New York: Vintage Books.

Fuller, Col. John Frederick Charles. 1926. *The Foundations of the Science of War*. London: Hutchinson & Co.

Kaldor, Mary. 2005. Principles for the Use of the Military for Human Security Operations, in Anthony D. Mc Ivor (Ed.), *Rethinking the Principles of War* Annopolis, MD: Naval Institute Press, pp. 388-400.

Leonhard, Robert R. 1999. *The Principles of War for the Information Age*. New York: Ballantine Publishing Group.

Leonhard, Robert R. 2015. *"Little Green Men": A Primer on Modern Russian Unconventional Warfare, Ukraine 2013-2014*. Fort Bragg, NC: United States Army Special Operations Command. ('Unclassified' version of original document.)

Litwak, Robert S. 2022. Russia's Nuclear Threats Recast Cold War Dangers: The "Delicate Balance of Terror" Revisited. *Hindsight Up Front: Ukraine*. https://www.wilsoncenter.org/article/russias-nuclear-threats-recast-cold-war-dangers-delicate-balance-terror-revisited

McIvor, Anthony D., ed. 2005. *Rethinking the Principles of War*. Annapolis, Maryland: Naval Institute Press.

Mearsheimer, John T. 1989. Assessing the Conventional Balance: The 3:1 Rule and its Critics. *International Security* 13 (4): 54–89.

Mills, C. Wright. 1958. *The Causes of World War Three*. New York: Simon & Schuster.

Misokami, Kyle. 2019. The Cold War Led To Amazing Military Innovations, But These Five Are The Best. *The National Interest*, November 4. https://nationalinterest.org/blog/buzz/cold-war-led-amazing-military-innovations-these-five-are-best-92856

O'Hara, Phillip Anthony. 2001. Contradiction. In *Encyclopedia of political economy*, ed. Phillip Anthony O'Hara, 140–143. London: Routledge. Paper edition.

O'Hara, Phillip Anthony. 2023. *Principles of Institutional and Evolutionary Political Economy: Applied to Current World Problems*. Springer Nature. Revised Edition. https://link.springer.com/book/9789811941573.

Palley, Thomas. 2022. *Ukraine: What Will Be Done and What Should be Done?*. https://braveneweurope.com/thomas-palley-ukraine-what-will-be-done-and-what-should-be-done

Parks, Raymond C., and David P. Duggan. 2015. Principles of Cyberwarfare. *ISEEE Security and Privacy*. September/October: 30–35.

Podhoretz, Norman. 2005. World War IV: How It Started, What It Means, and Why We Have to Win. In *The Right War: The Conservative Debate on Iraq*, ed. Gary Rosen, 102–169. Cambridge: Cambridge University Press.

Pokrant, Marvin. 2021. *New Principles of War*. Lincoln, NE: Potomac Books (University of Nebraska).

Resnick, Stephen A., and Richard D. Wolff. 2002. *Class Theory and History: Capitalism and Communism in the U.S.S.R.* New York & London: Routledge.

Smeltzer, Mike, and Noah Buyon. 2022. *Nations in Transit 2022: From Democratic Decline to Authoritarian Aggression*. Washington DC: Freedom House, 25pp. https://freedomhouse.org/report/nations-transit/2022/from-democratic-decline-to-authoritarian-aggression.

Stewart, Will, & Laura Sharman. 2022. Full-Scale World War Three Has Now Begun, Russian State TV Declares. *The Mirror*, April 15. https://www.mirror.co.uk/news/world-news/full-scale-world-war-three-26719035

Taylor, A. J. P. 1964. *The Origins of the Second World War*. Harmondsworth: Penguin, 1991.

Tierney, Dominic. 2011. Does Chain-Ganging Cause the Outbreak of War? *International Studies Quarterly* 55:285–304.

USDOA (United States Department of the Army). 2019. *ADP-3 Operations. Army Doctrine Publication*. Washington DC: Department of the Army.

von Clausewitz, Carl. 1812. *Principles of War*. Online: www.Abika.com

Wallerstein, Immanuel. 2001. *The essential wallerstein*. New York, New Press. (Trans. Chinese 2002, Portuguese 2002, Spanish 2003.)

Wingrove, Josh. 2022. Biden Says He'd Fight World War Three for NATO, But Not for Ukraine. *Bloomberg Asian Edition*, March 12. https://www.bloomberg.com/news/articles/2022-03-11/biden-says-he-d-fight-world-war-iii-for-nato-but-not-for-ukraine

Woolsey, James. 2003. *This is World War IV.* A speech given at UCLA, 2 April 2003.

Chapter 11
Long Waves of Global, Regional, and National Economies, 1940–2020

Abstract This chapter examines the complex evolution and metamorphosis of decadal real GDP per capita AAGR for the global, continental, and national political economies over the period from 1940 to 2020. This is during the period of US hegemonic rise and fall, China's eventual rise (and relative fall), and climate change's fall and rise. The data used is Maddison's mostly for 1940–1960 and the World Bank online WDI database mainly for 1961–2020. Emphasis is given to changes in the rate of per capita economic growth over time, arranged by decades, including the periodicity, amplitude, and phases of short, long, and secular waves. The chapter starts by summarizing the stylized long wave pattern for 1940–2020, which is then compared with the World, seven continents/regions, and 105 nations. Stylized facts about short, long, and secular wave patterns are scrutinized in relation to amplitude, periodicity, deviations from the stylized model, and the World wave, plus multiple and erratic waves and patterns.

Keywords Short, long, & secular waves · Periodicity, amplitude, & phases · Empirics · Principles · Historical specificity · US hegemony · China rising · Climate crisis

11.1 Introduction

Consistent with the *principle of historical specificity and evolution*, we scrutinize historical patterns of growth per capita for various regions, nations, and World economies to understand the anomalous growth waves associated with high-amplitude financial instability, recessions, depressions, and other crises. We study in detail the unstable movement of growth of the system and its constituents through a long-wave perspective. Undertaking this task enables one to gain knowledge about these long-term changes in the political economy. While we briefly outline some aspects of the theory of long waves, the primary concern of this study is to try out some new

P. A. O'Hara, *Long Waves of Growth, Hegemonic Power, and Climate Change in the World Economy*, https://doi.org/10.1007/978-981-96-4132-1_11

empirical methods and flexible perspectives of long-term growth. We study the rate of growth of GDP per capita over time in the context of changing hegemonic power and climate change crises.

As the empirical material of this study indicates, the core nations or regions of the world have been in a long-wave downswing (LWD) phase (and to some degree borderline performance) for several decades now, especially North America (NA) and Europe, plus several other areas and nations. These core areas have very low levels of decadal average annual growth during the long-wave downswing of the 1980s or 1990s to the 2020s. During downswings, growth tends to be lower, recessions deeper, and financial crises and instabilities more intense. Recognizing these growth anomalies in the core and others is part of understanding the polycrises of the decadal crises, GFC, Eurocrisis, coronacrisis, climate change, and the prewar era affecting numerous areas of the world.

Concurrently, several Asian nations (notably China) have been, over numerous decades, undergoing a secular long-wave upswing (SLWU) as their regime of accumulation has been vibrant and sustainable, although contradictions are emerging, especially more recently. The situation in the periphery and semi-periphery of Africa, the Middle East, Latin America, and South Asia is generally more erratic and subject to more (extreme) long-wave downswings, a series of short waves, far fewer long-wave upswings (LWUs), and hardly ever very long (secular) wave upswings (but with some notable exceptions).[1]

The first section of the chapter compares the long wave stylized model with the world pattern of long wave for the period 1940–2020, plus the wave for various continents, including Asia (south and east), the Middle East and North Africa (MENA), Latin America and the Caribbean (LACA), sub-Saharan Africa (*SSA*), Western Europe (WE), Central and Eastern Europe (CEE), plus North America (NA). We examine the details of the regions vis-à-vis how *nations* are variously similar and different from the general trend or pattern for the specific continent/area, plus the world and stylized model. Sometimes the continental averages give a good indication of the trends for the nations, and sometimes the average hides major differentials for individual nations. We also isolate specific patterns of growth at the national level, including those nations that variously outperform or underperform relative to the region as a whole, while several nations exhibit highly interesting and complex patterns in themselves that are of considerable interest to political economists, macroeconomists, and historians.

We follow the analysis of O'Hara (2001, 677) who concluded his survey of long-wave theory/empirics by suggesting that future studies should be more *flexible, creative, and complex* in dealing with the historical data, rather than making rigid preconceptions of wave periodicity, amplitude, and metamorphosis. We also follow Wesley Mitchell (1951) and Howard Sherman (1991), who both studied *short cycles*, in bringing to *long-wave* research issues of periodicity, amplitude, and phases in short, long, and secular waves.

[1] Some authors study waves of a longer duration than we have in this book (see, e.g., Frank and Gill 1993). These are well beyond the scope of this current study.

11.2 Phases, Full Waves, Stylized Model, and Hypotheses

We center on long waves in a broad tradition that includes approaches such as those of Sam de Wolff (1924), Nikolai Kondratiev (1928), Joseph Schumpeter (1939), Ernest Mandel (1975, 1995), Michel Aglietta (1976), David Gordon (1980, 1994), Andrew Tylecote (1992), and Freeman and Louçã (2001). We have been following a hybrid theory throughout this book, comprising the PoPE contingency paradigm and model, paying attention to the pathways and circuits of socioeconomic dynamics (CSD) and its various eco-geo-spatial, institutional, and technological spheres in interdependent motion through historical time. This book has scrutinized the record of the historical transformation of the Dutch, British, US, and Chinese CSD. Here we provide a foundation for extending this framework to other nations and regions. However, the chapter does not delve deeply into these circuits and spheres, which would be impossible in a broad survey chapter such as this. This is left to further analysis beyond this volume.

Following the *principle of uneven development*, we are less interested in the process of convergence per se than the complex differences, similarities, and asymmetric wave trends and processes operating at the global, regional, and national levels. Asian nations, for instance, have a somewhat different style of long waves, with China undergoing a secular wave upswing (SECWU) over 1980–2020, embedded in key institutional spheres, but with a declining trajectory during the 2020s. Despite several contradictions playing out in areas of the environment, technology, party norms, and regional–urban dynamics, the growth performance has become remarkably directive, although subdued performance may continue into the foreseeable future (see Chaps. 8 and 9).

The established wave model, in terms of one single long wave, upon which this empirical chapter will be compared, includes five main theses, which will be critically scrutinized and modified accordingly. Figure 11.1 illustrates the primary thesis of the *hypothetical* stylized full long-wave model, from the late 1940s through to the 2020s:

The *first hypothesis* is that there are 40- to 80-year waves, divided roughly between 20 and 40 years of upswing followed by 20–40 years of downswing (with various patterns of borderline performance). Specifically for this study, we will be testing the usual hypothesis behind most long-wave scholars concerning the key phases of capitalism for the core: the movement from the Fordist-Keynesian movement of the 1940s–1970s to neoliberal capitalism and (partially) beyond into the 1980s–2020s. Only the periodicity relating to this specific long wave will be tested, not the whole circuit of socioeconomic reproduction. This phase of the evolution of the core will also be linked to the periphery and semi-periphery in terms of periodicity.

We will be testing a specific form of this periodicity and amplitude through the use of the Stylized Full Long Wave Model, shown above (roughly following O'Hara 2010, 2012a, 2023; Freeman and Louçã 2001, Louçã 2019). Figure 11.1 illustrates idealized decadal per capita GDP growth rates of 2.25% [(1940s) borderline-up],

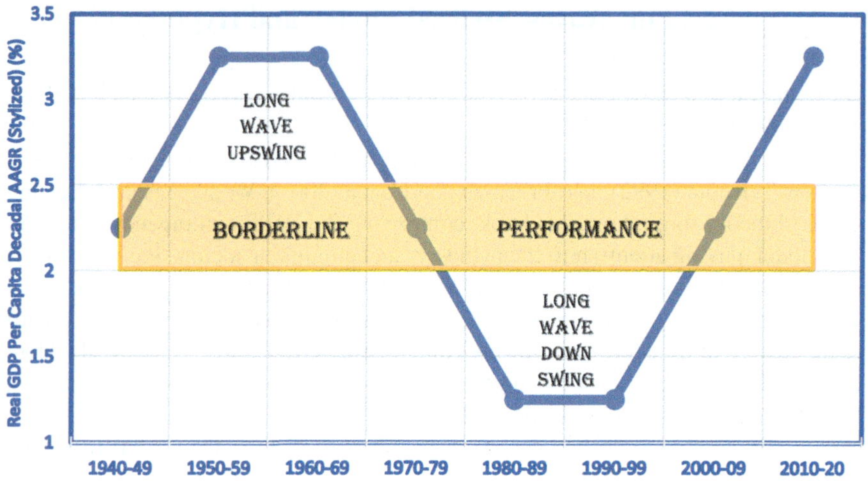

Fig. 11.1 Stylized (Standard Model) full long-wave model, 1940–2020: GDP per capita AAGR (decadal averages). Note: The orange bar represents "borderline" performance in between upswing and downswing

3.25% (1950s), 3.25% (1960s) [long-wave upswing 1950s–1960s], 2.25% [(1970s) borderline-down] 1.25% (1980s), 1.25% (1990s) [long-wave downswing 1980s–1990s], 2.25% [(2000s) borderline-up]. We have added an extra decade to the Stylized Wave Model (1940–2009) to represent the start (first decade) of another (stylized) wave (2011–2020); from "borderline" performance to upswing. The orange bar represents borderline positions in between downswing and upswing; usually borderline performance is needed (or moving through borderline) before variously undergoing upswing as well as downswing and possible upswing again.

This stylized model is empirically scrutinized to ascertain the stylized facts of the waves, from which modifications to established theory can be made. For instance, the evidence in this chapter does not support recovery and upswing in the long wave for the vast majority of nations and regions during the 2010s–2020s, nor usually borderline performance during the 2000–2009 period.

The *second hypothesis*, following Jacob van Duijn (1983), is that the established long-wave pattern tends to emerge for the whole global economy, but not necessarily for the individual nations or regions. The world capitalist system is subject to uneven developments due to the complex way in which knowledge, institutions, and production-distribution networks are shaped and formed (see Marshall 1987). Nevertheless, some nations and regions will tend to be closely associated with global trends, and these are likely to be the core economies of North America, Western Europe, and some nations elsewhere (such as Japan, Australia, and New Zealand), given their trajectory since the 1940s.

Other areas are likely to have greater volatility than average, being from the periphery and semi-periphery, because they tend to be impacted by problematic issues associated with authoritarian regimes, wars, low/unstable primary product prices, dependence on the "West," debt crises, revolutions and civil wars, more intense climate crises, low levels of geopolitical power, and so on. The study seeks to establish the validity of this idea, especially for *SSA*, MENA, and LACA (and some nations of south and west Asia).

Other regions may establish wave patterns impacted by high or low ceilings or floors in the wave. Crucial Asian nations such as China may have a dynamic that is influenced partly by the core but with dynamics peculiar to itself, especially regarding the CSD, which may now (2020s) be maturing, with lower levels of growth per capita. Broadly speaking, we hypothesize that China (and the Asian region) started to undergo long-wave upswings when the West and the East (Soviet Bloc) began lower performance through borderline and downwave declines during the 1980s, 1990s, and possibly earlier.

The *third hypothesis* is that the long wave may be usefully defined, in this chapter, relative to the mid-point of recovery (borderline) to the next mid-point of recovery (borderline) (Schumpeter 1939, 213). The "mid-points in recovery"—*borderline-up* to *borderline-up*—method of long wave periodicity potentially includes all the phases of long wave motion. It includes, in this context, for the "West" and dependent economies: the postwar reestablishment of the regime of accumulation during the 1930s through to the 1950s (when the institutions were mostly set in place); the boom of the 1950s through to the early 1970s; the onset of periodic deep recession and financial crises during the mid-1970s–1990s, followed by recovery and upswing into the 2000–2020 period. (To anticipate the typical results, such a recovery and upswing have almost always failed to materialize; the results for the 1970s–1980s are better than anticipated; and the 1990s–2020 represent a long-wave downswing.)

The *fourth hypothesis* is introduced to engender more complexity and realism into the analysis (beyond the stylized model), namely, that it is useful to include three types of *wave phases* and three types of *full waves*, both defined in terms of periodicity and amplitude. There may be *short-wave phases* of about one decade (upswing *or* downswing *or* borderline), *long-wave phases* of two or three decades (upswing *or* downswing *or* borderline), and *secular wave phases* of four or more decades (upswing *or* downswing *or* borderline). These *phases* of the wave combine to generate *full waves*, which always include an upswing and a downswing, and possibly also various borderline decades. (Although we also hypothesize adjusting this to account for lower or higher floors and ceilings for specific areas or nations, such as sub-Saharan Africa and Asia.)

The evidence supports this fourth hypothesis, especially regarding the full waves. The hypothesized *full secular waves* include, in addition, 90–100 long waves years in duration from borderline-up to borderline-up, including at least two decades each of long upswing and long downswing phases. Ideally for the short, long, and secular full waves, there would be a borderline-up, followed by an upswing; then a borderline-down, followed by a downswing; and lastly a borderline-up, which represents a recovery. However, sometimes the downswings *pass through* borderline to upswings, and similarly, upswings pass through borderline to downswings. The core thing about these full waves is that there is a movement from lower to higher growth (usually into "upswing"), then from higher to lower growth (usually into "downswing"), and then into higher growth again (usually into "borderline"). The empirics also support, to some limited extent, some *abnormal variants* of long waves.

The analysis also supports short waves. *Full short waves* are usually two decades in length, including upswing and downswing; possibly also one to two decades of other phases (such as borderline), making it a total of possibly three to four decades maximum for many nations and areas. Since we study over 100 nations and areas, the results obtained in this chapter are necessarily subject to further analysis, such as may be provided in future work. Mostly, this chapter provides hints of more extensive work required concerning the CSD of the various areas and nations and more detailed historical inquiry.

11.3 World, Stylized Model, and Continents/Regions: Periodicity, Amplitude, and Phases

We estimate the periodicity and amplitude of phases of the short, long, and secular waves, especially for the world and its continents/regions and nations, based on the Table 11.1 taxonomy (we hypothesize varying this taxonomy under certain circumstances, such as for China and Africa; details later).

The mostly Maddison and World Bank WDI, AAGR data, arranged by decades, are shown in Table 11.2 for the period 1940–2020.

Table 11.2 examines decadal AAGR per capita for the stylized model, the world, and various continents/regions—MENA, LACA, *SSA*, Asia, WE, CEE, and NA—during 1940–2020. There is inadequate data for MENA and *SSA* during the 1940s. Now we transform this annual average decadal growth data into Fig. 11.2, showing the evolutionary movements of growth from decade to decade, below, starting with the record for the world, compared with the stylized model:

Table 11.1 Decadal AAGR, growth wave taxonomy: periodicity and amplitude, for 1940–2020

Amplitude	Decadal AAGR GDP per capita	Short wave (SW) phase	Long wave (LW) phase	Secular WU, B, or WD (SECW) phase
Very high upswing	4.51% & >	10 years	20–30 years	40 years or >
High upswing	3.51–4.50%			
Upswing	2.51–3.50%			
Borderline (B)	2.01–2.50%	10 years	20–30 years	40 years or >
Downswing	1.01–2.00%	10 years	20–30 years	40 years or >
Deep downswing	0.01–1.00%			
Very deep downswing	<0.01%			

Source: Adapted from O'Hara (2012b, 2023, ch. 8)

Table 11.2 Real GDP growth per capita (decadal AAGR, percent), stylized model, world, continents/regions: 1940–2020, eight areas

	Stylized model	World	MENA	LACA	*SSA*	Asia	WE	CEE	NA
1940–49	2.25	1.96	n.a.	2.06	n.a.	−3.33	−0.65	1.24	3.55
1950–59	3.25	2.68	3.49	2.03	1.82	3.82	4.03	3.68	2.09
1961–69	3.25	3.09	3.91	2.59	2.09	3.77	4.03	3.68	3.21
1970–79	2.25	2.01	5.77	3.19	1.32	3.39	2.94	3.26	2.62
1980–89	1.25	1.36	−1.63	0.19	−0.68	2.96	2.00	0.22	2.06
1990–99	1.25	1.22	2.07	1.18	−0.60	2.87	1.88	−3.71	1.91
2000–10	2.25	1.49	2.42	2.35	2.34	4.32	1.18	4.46[a]	1.08
2011–20	3.25	1.22	0.21	−0.08	0.23	3.65	0.36[b]	0.65[c]	1.01

Source: Adapted from raw data from the World Bank (2024) and Maddison (2024)

Note: *NA* North America, *WE* Western Europe, *CEE* Central & Eastern Europe, *LACA* Latin America & Caribbean, *MENA* Middle East & North Africa, *SSA* Sub-Saharan Africa, *n.a.* not available

[a]Based on growth for CEE5 (Russia, Hungary, Poland, Bulgaria, Czech Rep., pop. weighted); [b]Euro Area; [c]Europe & Central Asia

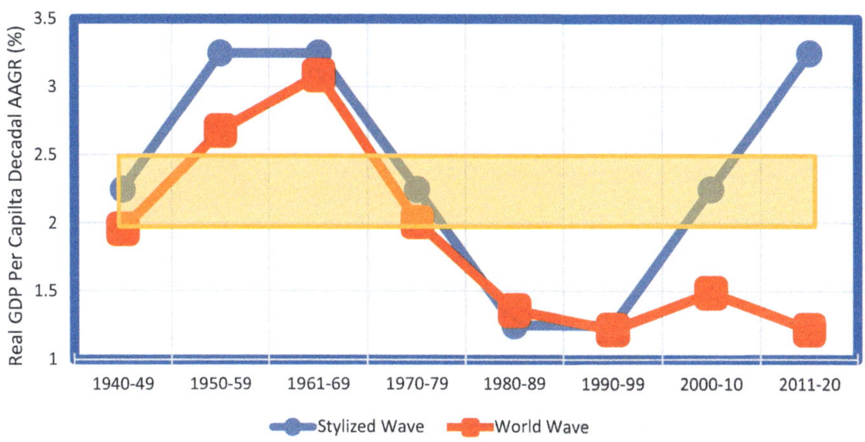

Fig. 11.2 World and stylized model, real GDP per capita decadal AAGR, 1940–2020. (Source: World data based on Table 11.2)

This world wave is easy to interpret, comprising (a) one decade of "barely" borderline results for the 1940s, (b) two decades of long-wave upswing (1950s–1960s), (c) one decade of borderline conditions (1970s), and (d) four decades of downswing (1980–2020). This 80-year-long wave for the world economy during the 1940–2020 period comprises less than one full long wave. What is missing, if we periodize it from borderline-up to borderline-up, is the borderline of the next possible upswing (2020s or 2030s?). Hence, the world wave for 1940–2020 is very similar to the stylized wave, except that the world has failed to undergo borderline recovery into the 2000–2020 period; and indeed, recently much of the world has been embroiled in the worst recessions, crises, and polycrises since the Great Depression of the 1930s, including the GFC, Eurocrisis, coronacrisis, climate crisis, and the "prewar era" (as shown in Chaps. 9 and 10).

This implies a good fit between the world and the stylized model, but it also indicates that recoveries in the wave are not necessarily endogenous to the system and may require special conditions, institutions, governance, sectors, effective demand, and technologies to restart the growth spurt, or modifying the objectives and dynamics toward a more communitarian system (e.g., center more on "quality of life" indices rather than GDP AAGR per capita). This thesis, the endogenous nature of downswing and exogenous upswing, is one held by many wave scholars, including notably Ernest Mandel (1995). This thesis may well be correct in general, or simply in certain waves. In the current temporal environment, the downswing in the wave appears to emerge endogenously through eco-geo-spatial, institutional, and technological (CSD) contradictions impacting majorly on the "system"/nation/area, the corresponding potential long-wave upswing requiring effective/innovative CSD structures and dynamics (see Chaps. 5–8).

Now we compare the stylized facts for the continents/regions, shown descriptively in Fig. 11.3 and interpreted analytically in Table 11.3.[2]

This data shows that growth per capita for most areas was generally slightly below borderline in the 1940s; at or around borderline but mostly upswing during the 1950s and 1960s; in between (mostly) upswing and borderline in the 1970s; mostly below borderline in the 1980s and 1990s; variable (downswing, borderline, upswing) in the 2000s; and almost entirely in downswing during 2010–2020. Table 11.3 presents an evolutionary view of the wave phase patterns through time

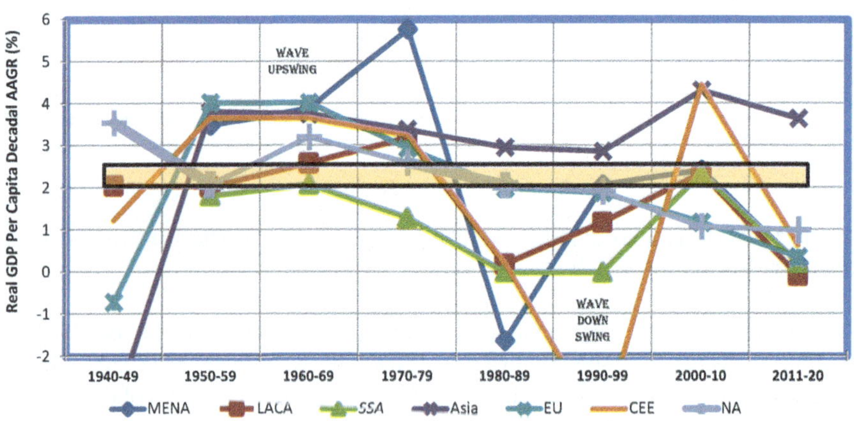

Fig. 11.3 Decadal AAGR GDP per capita, 1940–2020, continents/regions. (Source: Adapted from Table 11.2)

[2]The decadal averages are based on the second method (see footnote 4) of summing individual annual average growth rates for each year and then dividing by the decadal number of years (AAGR; mostly 10 years; sometimes 11 years, e.g., 2000–2010; sometimes other groups of years).

Table 11.3 Evolutionary pattern of wave upswing, borderline, downswing: world and continents/regions, 1950–2020, six, eight areas

	1940–1949		1950–1969		1960–1969		1970–1979		1980–1989		1990–1999		2000–2010		2011–2020	
SECWU	0	1U	0	5U	0	7U	1	6U	1	1U	1	1U	1	2U	1	1U
LWU	0		0		5		5		0		0		0		0	
SWU	1		5		2		0		0		0		1		0	
B	2	2B	2	2B	1	1B	1	1B	1	1B	1	1B	3	3B	0	0B
SWD	3	3D	1	1D	0	0D	1	1D	5	6D	1	6D	0	3D	4	7D
LWD	0		0		0		0		1		5		3		2	
SECWD	0		0		0		0		0		0		0		1	
Number	6	6	8	8	8	8	8	8	8	8	8	8	8	8	8	8

Source: Adapted from Table 11.2

Note: *SECWU* secular wave upswing, *LWU* long-wave upswing, *SWU* short-wave upswing, *B* borderline, *SWD* short-wave downswing, *LWD* long-wave downswing, *SECWD* secular wave downswing, *U* upwave, *D* downwave

over the 80-year period, including eight regions and the world, with short (SWU, SWD), long (LWU, LWD), and secular (SECWU, SECWD) upswing (U) and downswing (D) (as well as borderline (B) phases) included:

This shows, first, that the 1940s World War and its immediate aftermath was mostly an era of downswing, continuing the bad results from the Great Depression. It was especially troublesome for Europe and Asia, the two main areas involved in the war (likely also for MENA, not shown). Borderline results did not emerge since the normally good results for the late 1940s did not adequately negate the contractionary effects of World War 2 (1939–1945). For the main core area whose civilian population was not directly involved in the war, notably the North American mainland, the 1940s was a short-wave upswing (SWU) from the Depression, but war spending was not ongoing, while the 1950s was a borderline result until a robust long-wave upswing emerged into the 1960s and 1970s. This reinforces the van Duijn (1983) thesis that world wars *tend* to have a depressing effect on growth, at least in the short run, especially in territories directly involved (but perhaps not for those stimulated by war investment whose mainland civilians are not seriously attacked) and may require substantial institutional readjustment for progress to reemerge.

Except for low growth in *SSA*, all areas underwent wave upswing—the world, MENA, LACA, Asia, WE, EE, and NA—for at least 20 and usually 30 years, during the 1950s–1970s. This was the greatest long boom in the history of capitalism. The capitalist core led the way through Fordism, the Keynesian welfare state, along with US hegemony, regulated finance, and the stable family environment (see Chap. 7). These institutional spheres provided the basis for two to three decades of high profit, investment, and growth per capita. A similar growth process occurred in Central and Eastern Europe, as the system of production, distribution, and governance (state capitalism for most, state socialism for a few (?), the Soviet-style system for a few) led to a successful period of accumulation and growth. MENA, Asia, and Latin America benefited from the postwar corporate system's institutional dynamics and growth. While *SSA* did undergo borderline results in the 1950s, it was the only area to completely evade a long-wave upswing for the whole period of 1940–2020.

All areas underwent a wave downswing into the 1980s and/or 1990s, except Asia. The decades of the 1980s–2000s/1990s–2020 were mostly characterized by *long-wave downswing* for the world as well as WE, NA, and CEE, the "core" nations of the world. Fordism, the KWS, US hegemony, regulated finance, and the stable family all became subject to contradictions and institutional instability, inhibiting investment and growth through the neoliberalism era and beyond. During the 1980–2000 period, while the core was undergoing regime deterioration, LACA and *SSA* followed them, but with worse results: debt crises and very severe economic deterioration, while CEE underwent a downswing. Robust, suitable CSD conditions were lacking throughout the world system as the environment was not conducive to stable accumulation and growth (nor the quality of life considerations). As Suter (1992) showed, (semi-)peripheral areas tend to undergo debt crises during long-wave downswings (a core stylized fact, following, especially the standard model).

During 2000–2010, some degree of optimism emerged as *SSA* and LACA recovered a little to undergo borderline performance, CEE underwent a short-wave upswing, while MENA experienced borderline performance in the 1990s and 2000s. Asia continued its upward trajectory from a very long-wave upswing in the 1960s–1980s into a *secular long-wave upswing* into the 1990s and 2000s as China and later India became established players in the world economy.

This 2000s optimism waned majorly into the 2011–2020 period, with or without the coronacrisis of the early 2020s. All continents/regions of the world, except Asia, have been undergoing a downswing during 2011–2020. Global downswing got far worse during 2011–2020 (and 2021–2023, not shown) period(s), compared with all other decades. During this time, there was only one area undergoing a secular wave upswing (Asia), no areas undergoing borderline performance (2.00–2.50 decadal growth), and seven areas (out of eight) undergoing downswing during 2011–2020 (and 2021–2022 not shown). The only potentially optimistic result is that four out of eight global regions were undergoing a *short*-wave downswing (SWD) of only a decade. But the early years (2020–2022) of the next decade of 2021–2030 indicate that this decade may well be worse than any others in recent history. The fact that Chinese growth has waned, along with some other areas of Asia, indicates that the only area of good results (Asia as a whole) is likely to decline somewhat.

While the world and most areas underwent varied conditions during the 1940s, a long-wave upswing during the 1950s–1970s, and a long-wave downswing in the 1980s–1990s; and while this downswing continued for the world and the core into the 2000s, culminating in the greatest crises and recessions since the 1930s (the GFC), optimistic developments emerged during the 2000s in several continents. Critical areas of *SSA* (P), LACA (P, SP), MENA (SP), and CEE (C, SP) achieved borderline or short-wave upswing in the 2000s, but this improvement did not continue (or heighten) in the 2011–2020 period, since they underwent downswing during this decade.

Next, we *map* the wave phases and full waves in broad terms for the world and its continents or major areas, including potentially B, SWU, SWD, LWU, LWD, SECWU, and SECWD, in Table 11.4.

Table 11.4 reveals that during the 1940s–2000s, (a) *SSA*, CEE, and LACA all exhibited "full" long wave dynamics; whereas (b) the world, WE, and NA require a borderline performance—or higher—into the 2020s–2030s for full long wave motion; while (c) the availability of some good statistics for MENA in the 1940s would possibly give the region a full wave over 1940–1999. The Asian wave pattern is complex but possibly explicable as explained below. These results are quite good for Wave Empirics because they show it is possible to scrutinize short, long, and secular waves with a broad, longer-term wave pattern. Three of the areas/continents of the world have demonstrated a fully patterned short, long, and/or secular wave motion of one complete up-down-up longer-term movement with robust results, while another three areas/continents may complete the long-term wave motion into the next decade or two. One continent (Asia) underwent secular long-wave upswing motion, which may be explicable in terms of a *fully formed wave*; see below. All continents and areas appear to be historically and conceptually explained in the long

Table 11.4 "Map," wave phases, full waves: eight regions, stylized model; 1940–2020

	Stylized	LACA	CEE	SSA	World	WE	NA	MENA	Asia
Decade	Perfect full long wave (1940–2010)	"Full" long wave (1950–2010)	"Full" long wave (1940–2010)	"Full" long wave (1960–2010)	B-up needed (2021–30) for full long wave	B-up needed (2021–30) for full long wave	B-up needed (2021–30?) for full long wave	Missing 1940s data for full long wave (1940–2020?)	Secular wave upswing (1950–2020)
1940–49	B	B	SWD	n.a.	B#	SWD	SWU	n.a.	SWD
1950–59	LWU		LWU	SWD	LWU	LWU	B	LWU	SECWU
1961–69		LWU		B			LWU		
1970–79	B			LWD	B				
1980–89	LWD	LWD	LWD		SECWD	SECWD*	B	SWD	
1990–99							LWD*	BLW	
2000–10	B	B	SWU	B					
2011–20	SWU	SWD	SWD	SWD				SWD	

Source: Based on Tables 11.1 and 11.2; B#=Barely Borderline

Table 11.5 Long wave amplitude: world, continents/areas, 1940–2020

	Amplitude (BP) 1940–2020 [order from highest (1) to lowest (9)]	Amplitude intensity 1940–2020 (BP) Very high 751–1000 High 501–750 Medium 251–500 Low 0–250	Amplitude (BP) (1950–2020) [from highest (1) to lowest (9)]	Amplitude intensity 1950–2020 Very high 751–1000 High 501–750 Medium 251–500 Low 0–250
CEE	817(1)	Very high	817(1)	Very high
ASIA	765(2)	Very high	145(9)	Lowest
MENA	n.a.	n.a.	740(2)	Very high
EU/WE	468(3)	Medium	367(5)	Medium
SSA	n.a.	n.a.	302(3)	Medium
LACA	327(4)	Medium	327(4)	Medium
NA	254(5)	Low	220(6)	Low
STYLIZED	200(6)	Low	200(7)	Low
WORLD	187(7)	Low	187(8)	Low

Source: Adapted from Table 11.2

or secular wave context as having impressive wave motion. However, the downbeat results for 2011–2020, plus continuing problems during 2021–2024 (not shown), indicate for most areas that a durable upswing is not forthcoming and that eco-geo-spatial, institutional, and technological innovations are required to spur exogenous changes for a possible upswing into the mid-to-late 2020s and 2030s.

We now examine the nature of wave motion by scrutinizing the periodicity and amplitude of the *full wave* and various *wave phases*. Wave amplitude is the difference between the highest and lowest decadal growth rates during the 80-year period, measured in basis points (BP).[3] Periodicity relates to the extent that the 80-year period includes one full wave or the length of the wave so far examined empirically. Table 11.5 outlines the key findings for *amplitude*:

This illustrates that during the 1950–2020 wave amplitude was higher for those formerly "state capitalist" (i.e., "communist") economies that underwent cold turkey reform to autocratic capitalism, or "state capitalism" (in Central and Eastern Europe and Western Asia), as well as those semi-peripheral states dependent upon oil and other volatile resources (e.g., MENA). Amplitude was lowest for the newly industrialized nations of Asia (especially China) and the core nations of North America that formerly/now set the benchmark for socioeconomic performance. Amplitude was very low for the world, as this averaged out the results for the seven main areas of the globe.

Table 11.6 illustrates the actual or potential *periodicity* of the waves during the 1940s–2030s period, assessing the actual or possible chronology and degree of full wave over the period:

[3] Note: 100 BP = 1.0 full percentage change = the difference between the lowest and highest decadal growth in BP over the 1940–2010 period = growth change from, e.g., 1.0% to 2.0%.

Table 11.6 Periodicity of long and secular full waves: world, stylized model, continents/regions; length, chronology, 1940–2040

		Full wave periodicity (B to B years)	Full wave chronology (B to B decades)
SSA	Full shortish long wave (50–60 years)	50 years	1960–2010
MENA		60 years	Possibly [1940?]–1999
LACA		60 years	1950–2010
STYLIZED	Full medium-long wave (70–80 years)	70 years	1940–2010
CEE		70 years	1940–2010
NA		80 years?	Possibly 1950–2030/40
WE	Full secular wave? (90–100 years)	80–90 years?	Possibly 1940–2030/40
WORLD		80–90 years?	Possibly 1940–2030/40
ASIA		100 years?	Possibly 1940–2040

Table 11.7 Periodicity, amplitude, and full wave for the world, stylized model, and continents/regions; variously 1940–2040

	Periodicity	Amplitude 1950–2010 [1940–2010]	Full wave [variously during 1940s–2030s]
SSA	Short	Medium [n.a.]	Yes
MENA	Short	High [n.a.]	Almost (1940s data needed)
LACA	Short	Medium [low-medium]	Yes
STYLIZED	Medium	Low [low]	Yes
CEE	Medium	Very high [very high]	Yes
ASIA	Medium	Low [very high]	Complex [1940s–2030s?]
NA	Medium	Low [low]	Not Yet [1950s–2030s?]
EU	Secular	Medium [medium]	Not Yet [1940s–2030s?]
WORLD	Secular	Low [low]	Not Yet [1940s–2030s?]

Combining Tables 11.5 and 11.6, we obtain Table 11.7, which summarizes the amplitude, periodicity, and regularity or completeness of the wave.

What we can say from the evidence is that, at least in terms of periodicity, and *pending a full eco-techno-institutional inquiry* (CSD), three of the continents/areas seem to have experienced full long waves: *SSA*, LACA, and CEE. MENA requires data for the 1940s to be sure. For Asia, we cannot say for certain; this is discussed in some detail (two sections below). Of the areas that have experienced full long waves, the vast majority had shortish long waves of about 50–60 years, or in the case of CEE, medium-length waves of 70 years. Also, the areas having (shorter) full long waves are in the periphery and semi-periphery (Note: CEE is *partly* in the SP during the period), characterized by medium-to-high amplitude.

The areas with a likely longish long wave but low amplitude, including NA, WE, and world, all have yet to experience borderline growth of recovery—or higher—into 2020. Low amplitude thus seems to be linked to longer periodicities and less than one full wave to date. This indicates that the longer the long wave, the lower the amplitude of the wave, and the smaller the likelihood of recovery to date. Many parts of the core thus tended to have the greatest periodicities and the lowest amplitudes, along with no recovery yet on the horizon, plus the greatest crises and recessions since the Great Depression recently being experienced (e.g., the GFC, Eurocrisis, coronacrisis, climate crises, and "prewar era") (along with other areas).

We conclude that the periphery and semi-periphery have a tendency, in the period examined, to have shortish long waves and comparatively high amplitude, while the situation in the core is the direct opposite, with NA, WE, and the world having potentially longish long waves and lower amplitude. The combination of higher and lower amplitudes for the areas averaged out for "the World," resulting in low amplitude, but an inability of the world to exhibit full wave motion at this point in history. The relevance of this for van Duijn's thesis of fully formed long waves for the world as a system is that the world results (in both periodicity and amplitude) are comparable to the stylized model. The world as a whole, however, failed to achieve a recovery to the "borderline-up" position by 2020, mainly because the main areas of the core—EU and NA—have not yet achieved even a tentative new CSD for sustainable long-term growth.

None of the continents followed the world pattern exactly, comprising borderline 1940s, long-wave upswing 1950s–1960s, borderline 1970s, and long-wave downswing 1980–2020. However, the pattern for the "core" (defined during this period as including Western Europe, North America, Eastern Europe, Japan, and some other nations) mostly followed the global pattern. WE and EE were the closest to the global pattern since they both experienced 30 years of long-wave upswing (1950s–1970s) followed by 40 years of long-wave downswing (1980–2020), having *not* undergone borderline performance during the 1970s. The North American experience was similar, though a little different from global performance. North America experienced borderline performance during the 1950s, a long-wave upswing during the 1960s and 1970s, followed by borderline during the 1980s, and then 30 years of long-wave downswing during the 1990–2020 period.[4]

LACA was *slightly* deviant from the global pattern, having undergone borderline performance during the 1940s and 1950s, followed by 20 years of long-wave upswing during the 1960s and 1970s; then a long-wave downswing in the 1980s and 1990s, followed by a decade of borderline performance into the 2000s, and downswing into 2011–2020. This borderline result for the 2000s is majorly different from the global pattern, although on track with the stylized model. It shared this borderline result for the 2000s with MENA (and *SSA*), which had a long-wave upswing during the three decades of the 1950s–1970s; a very deep *short* downswing during the 1980s, followed by 20 years of borderline during the 1990s and 2000s. Having a deep but short-wave downswing into the 1980s and a long wave (20 years) borderline into the 1990s and 2000s situates MENA as an unusual case in the global economy, although with impressive wave dynamics comparable to the stylized model, until the SWD of the 2011–2020 period.

[4] These *results* for NA, particularly the USA, are slightly different from the results from Chap. 7, due to slightly different methodology used for Chap. 7 (compared with this current chapter).

The most unusual pattern is that undergone by *SSA* and Asia. *SSA* started in the 1950s with a short-wave downswing, followed by borderline conditions (1960s) suggesting a possible upswing emerging, but then experienced 30 years of long-wave *downswing*, including the major debt crisis of the 1980s with ramifications continuing into the 1990s, followed by borderline conditions into the 2000s (hence a possible full wave of low floor and ceiling; see section on *SSA*), then downswing into 2011–2020.

Asia experienced a short downswing in the 1940s but then a secular wave upswing for seven decades during 1950–2020, the most remarkable performance of all regions (then lower rates into the 2020–2022 period, not shown). Asia is the only area of the world not to experience a short or long-wave downswing during the 2011–2020 period. Or to put it another way, the current socioeconomic performance of the world is deplorable, as every region except Asia experienced short- or long-wave downswing over the 2011–2020 decade, and generally worse than the previous decade, and generally worse still during 2021–2023 (not shown).

These short waves, borderlines, and secular waves are major developments in wave research since they were previously external to "long wave" empirics. The empirical evidence supports a complex, evolutionary, and pragmatic analysis of waves. Examining the world, it seems to follow from the evidence that wave motion in the modern political economy is an interesting and powerful tool of economic analysis (at least during this postwar wave era, with rising and declining US hegemony and declining and rising heatwaves). Now we turn to the details of the continents/regions, including numerous nations, to scrutinize further the complex patterns of waves through the past eight decades (including future potential).

11.4 *Sub-Saharan African* (SSA) Wave Patterns

While the quality of *SSA* data may be questioned, the quantity of the data is very good, except for the complete absence of good data for the 1940s. We have 34 nations with full data for the whole 1950–2020 period. First, we scrutinize the specifically sub-Saharan long wave periodicity and amplitude, compared to the world and stylized model, in Fig. 11.4.

The *SSA* long wave shows a distinct wave pattern, even though there has been no long-wave upswing throughout the continent, at least vis-à-vis the structure of periodicity and amplitude shown in Table 11.1. This wave pattern is conditioned by a *very low floor* and *low ceiling* in the wave due likely to problematic CSD. A very clear full wave form is displayed of *relatively* upward growth during the 1950s and 1960s, deteriorating growth during the 1970s, continued negative performance during the 1980s and 1990s, followed by recovery into borderline during the 2000s (and a fall in growth during 2010–2020). Adjusting the borderline area to the low floor and low ceiling (1.00–1.50% GDP per capita; Green B), the sub-Saharan long wave was a subdued *full wave of impressive dynamics* (at a low level) through classic wave motion, experiencing borderline (1950s), upswing (1960s), downswing

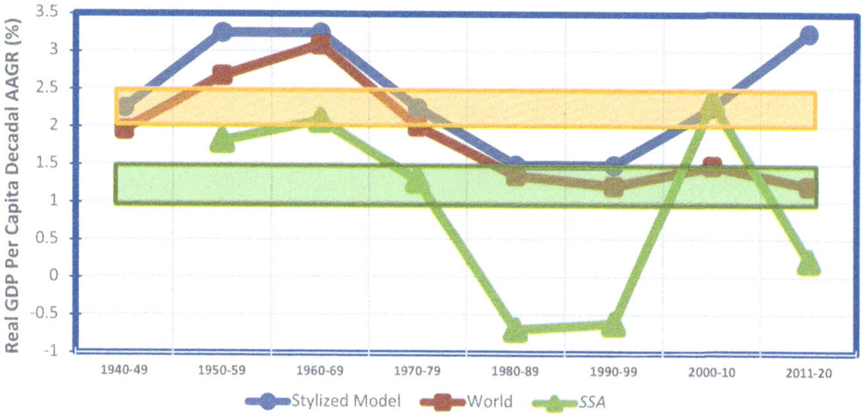

Fig. 11.4 *SSA* wave compared to the world & stylized model, 1940–2020. (Source: Adapted from Table 11.2)

(1970s and 1980s), and going through borderline to upswing (2000–2010). Periodicity was in the order of 50 years from 1960 to 2010 (B to B), while amplitude was 302BP. However, this "long wave" is so low in growth per capita as to question its validity (as applying to a growth regime and a viable CSD). This is thus an area of further inquiry beyond this book and chapter.

Decomposing the data for the 34 *SSA* nations into *evolutionary wave phase patterns* over 1950–2020, see Table 11.8.

Using the stylized long-wave pattern, the 1950s short-wave downswing dominated the area, but this moved quickly into borderline conditions during the 1960s. Then into the 1970s, 1980s, and 1990s, short and then long-wave downswings dominated, including a few secular waves as well into the 1980s and 1990s. During the 2000s, a dynamic balance existed yet again as average borderline conditions reemerged in the area. However, a major decline in the wave during 2011–2020 reversed the optimistic results of the previous decade.

We turn now to the details of a sample of *SSA* nations; see Table 11.9.

Using the classic long wave stylized model periodicities and amplitudes of Table 11.1, only two nations of *SSA* have experienced full long waves. Perhaps more importantly, only one nation has experienced a secular long-wave upswing preceded/followed by a downswing and borderline performance, indicating very strong CSD dynamics. The continent tended to undergo very modest performance in the 1950s (7/34 nations in upswing), optimistic borderline results in the 1960s (15/34 in upswing), crisis results during the debt crises and its aftermath during the 1970s–1990s (6–10/34 in upswing), optimistic borderline results for 2000–2010 (14/34 in upswing), and somber results for 2010–2020 (7/34 in upswing). The main overall result for the continent is a proliferation of secular long-wave downswings in numerous countries.

Using the stylized long-wave pattern, the main other results for these 12 nations are only three long-wave upswings and two fully formed long waves. The fully

Table 11.8 Sub-Saharan Africa 34, evolutionary wave pattern, 1950–2020

	1950–1959		1960–1969		1970–1979		1980–1989		1990–1999		2000–2010		2011–2020	
SECWU	0	7	0	15	0	10	0	6	2	6	2	14	0	7
LWU	0		2		5		3		1		3		4	
SWU	7		13		5		3		3		9		3	
BL	6		2		1		0		0		3		4	
SWD	21	21	8	17	12	23	7	28	3	28	1	17	12	23
LWD	0		9		11		17		15		5		5	
SECWD	0		0		0		4		10		11		6	
No Nations	34		34		34		34		34		34		34	

Source: Adapted from the raw data in Maddison (2024); World Bank (2024)

Table 11.9 Decadal AAGR GDP per capita, 1951–2020, 12 *SSA* nations

	Benin	Botswana	Central African Republic	Chad	Congo (DRC)	Ivory Coast	Mozambique	Nigeria	Senegal	South Africa	Togo	Zimbabwe
1951–59	–1.17	1.59	2.33	2.23	3.12	1.60	1.86	0.84	1.67	2.02	1.59	3.55
1960–69	1.51	4.80	–0.04	–1.16	1.14	4.50	2.80	1.10	–1.66	3.56	6.12	1.31
1970–79	0.04	11.65	–0.12	–3.20	–2.34c	2.90	–2.80	4.40	0.12	1.00	0.65	0.71
1980–89	0.34	7.79	–1.65	2.59	–0.85	–4.12	–0.57	–3.50	–0.50	–0.26	–0.61	1.41
1990–99	1.32	3.20	–1.07	–0.91	–8.30	–0.35	2.61	–0.22	–0.08	–0.80	–0.06	0.60
2000–10	7.09	2.90	–0.64	4.61	0.48	–1.06	4.65	4.96%	1.23	2.15	–0.07	–4.30
2010–20	2.10	1.48	–1.54	–1.28	2.29	3.30	1.85	0.01	1.75	–0.69	2.64	1.87
Amplitude	826BP	1017BP	398BP	781BP	1142BP	862BP	745BP	846BP	341BP	436BP	673BP	785BP
Long wave?	No.	LWU 50 years.	No.	No. Recurring up-down	No.	Yes. 1 LW 70 years	Yes. 1 LW. 60 Years	No. Some wave dynamic	No.	No.	No.	No.
Missing	Much missing	Missing B-up & LWD	Missing LWU & B-down	Erratic	Missing LWU	1951–2020	1960–2020	Missing LWU	Missing LWU & B-down	Missing LWU	Missing LWU	Missing LWU

Source: Adapted from the raw data of Maddison (2024) and World Bank (2024)
Note: *AAGR* Average annual growth rates (Decadal), *SLWD* secular LW downswing

formed long waves are for the Ivory Coast (1951–2020) and Mozambique (1960–2020). Nigeria experienced some wave dynamics. What this shows is that while the continent can be characterized as a very subdued wave (Green B), numerous nations in *SSA* are able to fit into more standard, mostly short but very seldom long-wave patterns (using orange B).

In terms of the relative growth rates of nations within *SSA*, only one nation stands out as a high performer through a secular wave upswing over the 1960–2010 period: Botswana. Botswana was the only *SSA* nation to clearly perform outstandingly in GDP growth per capita for 50 of the 70 years. Botswana represents an outstanding case of how to achieve economic and social progress in the region (CSD development) through good governance, workable institutions, and political democracy for others to perhaps emulate, although the cultural history of Botswana established some unique characteristics that advantaged the nation (Hope 1997). However, Botswanan growth has steadily declined over the decades, and during 2010–2020 it dropped to below borderline as it entered a short-wave downswing.[9] Nonetheless, this is a very strong case for a *major case study* of CSD generation, maturation, and relative decline along with a very long-wave upswing with no long-wave downswings for Botswana.

The worst performer in *SSA* is the Central African Republic (CAR), which has undergone a *very deep* secular wave downswing over the past 60 years. This is a serious situation, and much more assistance and advancement are needed for the CAR. Other countries in *SSA* that have been going through a *secular* wave downswing over past decades include Gambia, Ghana, Liberia, Madagascar, Mauritania, Niger, Senegal, Togo, and Zimbabwe—with Cameroon, Côte d'Ivoire (Ivory Coast), Gabon, Kenya, and Swaziland undergoing *long*-wave downswing—although most of these nations have improved performance during the 2000s while still operating in (more moderate) downswing. A major decline emerged in 2011–2020, but some areas bucked the trend with a short-wave upswing emerging in the Ivory Coast and Togo.

11.5 Asian Wave Patterns

First, we examine the specific amplitude and periodicity of the 1940–2020 Asian Wave, compared with the world and the stylized model, shown in Fig. 11.5, but modified slightly to abstract from the early–mid-1940s negatives to illustrate the wave form more clearly:

The Asian wave tends to follow the pattern of the world and with a higher amplitude and with a higher ceiling and floor. The Asian region was severely impacted by the Second World War (also the struggles for independence), as was Europe; and since the 1950s has been undergoing a secular wave upswing (SECWU), with low amplitude. This adds considerable complexity to long-wave analysis to suggest a 70-year wave upswing with no downswing forthcoming (yet). Asian evolutionary wave elements include growth being negative in the 1940s, high in the 1950s–1970s,

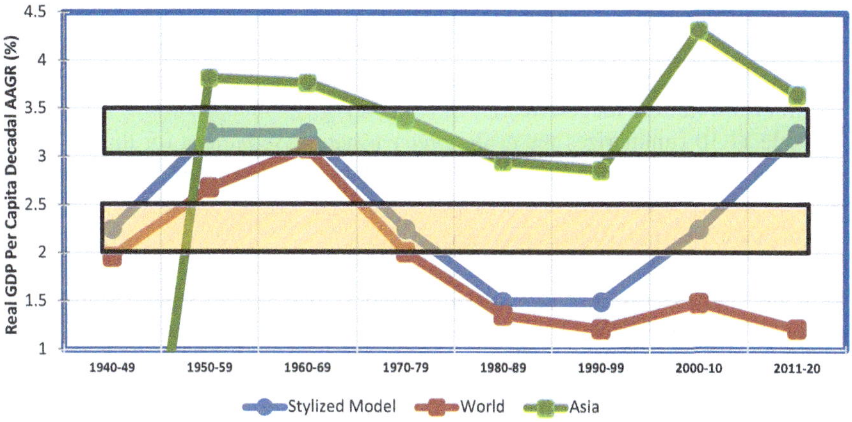

Fig. 11.5 Asian wave compared to world & stylized model, 1940s–2020, GDP growth per capita, decadal AAGR. (Source: Adapted from Table 11.2)

and declining somewhat over the course of the 1980s–1990s as some economies underwent diminishing growth. There was, for instance, declining growth in Myanmar and the Philippines during the 1980s, and during the 1990s and 2000s in Japan and Mongolia, as well as the Asian financial crisis of the late 1990s.

Asian growth grew in the 2000s partly due to the large expansion in India and continuing higher growth in numerous other nations, such as China.[5] But it dropped back to 1950s–1960s rates during 2011–2020 in the face of the Eurocrisis and trade conflict especially between China and the USA. During the coronacrisis and property crash in the 2020s, China's results dropped further (not shown).

There are at least two interpretations of the Asian data. The standard, first, interpretation, following the stylized model, reveals a wave downswing in the 1940s followed by a secular wave upswing into 1950–2020. This can be delineated further by showing a very deep wave downswing in the 1940s, a high upswing in the 1950s–1960s, an upswing in the 1970s–1990s, and back to a high upswing during 2000–2020. Here Asia has not yet experienced a full wave but could if growth dropped to 2.00–2.50% (or less) in the 2020s or 2030s. There is no reason why there should not be waves of 90–100 years in duration, as well as other waves of 50 or 60 years, and so on.

The second interpretation is that the first 70 years of the period represent *a whole wave*, with generally a high ceiling and (ignoring the *depth* of the 1940s) a high floor of the wave. This interpretation posits a (green) borderline at 3.00–3.50% (rather than an orange one at 2.00–2.50%) AAGR (averaged over decades), with the 1940s being a downswing, the 1950s–1960s an upswing, the 1970s borderline, the 1980s–1990s a downswing, and 2000–2010 passing through borderline (to

[5] For a critical analysis of Chinese GDP figures, see Takahashi (2006), who claims China is slowly adapting their statistics to international standards, but that those prior to 1987 are somewhat dubious.

upswing). This is quite a valid interpretation for Asia, with the crucial "thing" being the pattern of wave motion rather than specific rates. (This second interpretation of Asian high-floor/high-ceiling long waves is similar to but opposite the *SSA* case of low-floor/low-ceiling long waves.)

Table 11.10 summarizes the *evolutionary wave phase pattern* for the 6/24 East and South Asia nations over the 1940–2020 period, including short, long, and secular phases (and borderline).

This table illustrates the importance of differentiating between short, long, and secular wave phases (upswings, downswings, and "borderlines"). Downswings were the norm during the dislocation of World War in the 1940s, while short upswings *and* downswings were the most common form of dynamics in the 1950s and 1960s because nations were gradually gaining the eco-geo-spatial, institutional, and technological resources in a post-independent and postwar environment to stimulate economic performance. During the 1970s–1980s, the most common dynamics were long-wave upswings followed by long downswings as numerous nations achieved sustained growth (especially in East Asia) while fewer durably moved into long-wave downswings (especially in South Asia). It was during the 1980s that the first secular wave upswings emerged, with four nations experiencing such dynamics, while eight nations were in a long-wave upswing. Socioeconomic activity increased in the 1990s with 5 nations in SECWU and 8 in LWU, and further, in the 2000s as 7 countries had SECWU conditions and 11 LWU. By the 2000s, 18 of the 20 nations were undergoing short (5 nations), long (7 nations), or secular (6 nations) wave upswings, with none in borderline and only 2 in a downswing, either short or long (not secular), as the regime of accumulation developed further. However, a sudden drop in performance occurred during 2010–2020 (and likely more so during 2021–2023).

While the world economy has been undergoing a long-wave downswing over the past three decades, several positive developments are in motion, such as the seven decades of SECWU in Asia. Examining Asia in more detail reveals some complex issues. This section deals with the 14 East Asian nations of Cambodia, China, Hong Kong, Indonesia, Japan, Korea, Laos, Malaysia, Mongolia, Myanmar, Philippines, Singapore, Thailand, and Vietnam, as well as 6 nations in South(-West) Asia, including Afghanistan, Bangladesh, India, Nepal, Pakistan, and Sri Lanka. The pattern of growth for a subgroup of these Asian nations is shown in Table 11.11 (using 2.00–2.50% as borderline):

Several key trends and patterns emerge. First, the main results are that most well-developed or developing nations of Asia did not undergo a full long wave, and mostly they underwent many decades of secular long-wave upswing (SLWU). The secular wave upswing tendency, especially in recent years, while eschewing typical long-wave patterns due to an absence of downswing and subsequent borderline results, nevertheless is a very positive outcome for Asia. Apart from India, these SECWU results have also been experienced by especially China (1980s–2020), Indonesia (1970–2020), South Korea (1950–2010), and Malaysia (1960–2020) (plus Japan many decades ago and India more recently). This indicates CSD

Table 11.10 Asian evolutionary wave phase pattern, 1940–2020; 6/20 nations

	1940–1949		1950–1959		1960–1969		1970–1979		1980–1989		1990–1999		2000–2010		2011–2020	
SECWU	0	0	0	8	0	9	0	10	4	12	4	13	6	18	5	14
LWU	0		0		4		7		5		4		7		7	
SWU	0		8		5		3		3		5		5		2	
BL	0		4		1		1		1		2		0		1	
SWD	6	6	8	8	7	10	2	9	1	7	3	5	1	2	5	5
LWD	0		0		3		7		3		1		1			
SECWD	0		0		0		0		3		1		0			
No. Nations	6		20		20		20		20		20		20		20	

Table 11.11 Asia 11 nations, 1940–2020, real GDP per capita decadal AAGR

	China	India	Indonesia	Japan	South Korea	Malaysia	Myanmar	Pakistan	Philippines	Thailand	Vietnam
1940–49	n.a.	–7.74	–3.18	–3.61	–4.31	–0.48	n.a.	n.a.	–3.62	n.a.	n.a.
1950–59	6.53	1.74	2.05	9.40	5.05	–0.66	4.46	–0.17	4.45	2.38	2.26
1960–69	0.89	4.24	1.15	9.11	5.64	3.45	0.79	4.09	1.83	4.61	–0.67
1970–79	5.34	0.61	5.21	3.44	6.32	5.19	2.00	1.76	2.83	4.75	0.76
1980–89	8.19	3.45	4.20	3.74	6.39	3.05	0.09	3.36	–0.73	5.57	2.14
1990–99	8.75	3.72	3.26	1.18	5.24	4.54	4.64	1.28	0.41	4.20	5.63
2000–10	9.63	5.90	3.95	0.98	4.10	2.96	12.24	2.68	2.77	3.44	5.99
2011–20	6.27	3.31	3.46	0.52	2.21	2.62	5.83	1.60	3.12	1.88	5.11
Amplitude	874BP	1364BP	839BP	1301BP	1070BP	585BP	1215BP	426BP	807BP	369BP	666BP
Long wave?	No.	No	No.	No.	No.	No.	No.	No. Successive short waves	No. Successive short waves	No.	No.
Missing or notable trend	Missing LWD & B-up	Missing LWD & B-up	Missing LWD, B-up	Missing B-up	Missing LWD, B-up	Missing LWD, B-up	Missing LWD, B-up	DUDU; Recurring up-down pattern	DUDU; recurring up-down pattern	Missing LWD, B-up	Missing LWD, B-up

Source: Adapted from the raw data of Maddison (2006), World Bank (2024)

development in these nations through multisystem development, which should generate further research in the area.

Second, a core stylized fact is that Pakistan and the Philippines underwent successive "up-down, up-down" ("UDUD") dynamics for almost the whole period. This sort of result (see also our results for parts of Africa and Central America) is typical of nations subject to recurring instabilities of war, civil unrest, primary product specialization, and imperial domination.

Third, another notable achievement for the region is that several nations that had previously been involved in major wars and/or military governments have been undergoing a long-wave upswing for the past three decades, including Cambodia, Laos, Myanmar, and Vietnam during 1990–2020. It is a considerable achievement for these troubled areas to have reached a *very high* long-wave upswing. (However, this has ceased into the 2020s for Myanmar, given the recent coup, military crackdown, and ongoing conflicts.)

While "Asia" experienced a downswing in the 1940s and a secular wave upswing for the seven decades from 1950 to 2020, the seven-decade experience was *not* the case for *most* Asian nations in the sample. While the Asian wave was buoyant during the 1950–2020 period, the most expansive in the world, since 2011–2020 growth has deteriorated somewhat in the area. During 2011–2020, Thailand and South Korea, two high-performing nations overall, have both been experiencing a short-wave downswing. Chinese growth has declined markedly, by a third, during 2010–2020. These may be tentative signs of a further decline in the area in the immediate future as maturity sets in for these formerly dynamic nations, as perhaps their CSD underlying wave upswing is maturing, perhaps inspiring a more typical long-wave pattern over the next few decades.

11.6 American Wave Patterns

The Americas include four areas: North America, Central America, the Caribbean, and South America. Table 11.12 starts the analysis through an examination of the evolutionary wave phase pattern for 21/23 American nations collectively considered over the 1940–2020 period:

The Second World War does not seem to be part of the Full Wave, as this table illustrates a very clearly defined wave with a short-wave downswing dominating in the 1950s, especially in Central and South America, to a short-wave upswing dominating in the 1960s and a long-wave upswing in the 1960s and 1970s. Then in the 1980s, a sudden short-wave downswing emerged for the Americas, which deepened into a long-wave downswing into the 1990s. In the 2000s, conditions moderated in many nations of America, especially South America, but this reversed in 2011–2020. In short, the wave rose into the 1960s and 1970s, declined into the 1980s and 1990s, with a *very modest* recovery emerging in the 2000s, and a short-wave decline in 2011–2020. However, there were *no secular wave upswings* in the Americas for the

Table 11.12 America, 1940–2020, evolutionary wave pattern, 21–23 nations

	1940–1949		1950–1959		1960–1969		1970–1979		1980–1989		1990–1999		2000–2010		2011–2020	
SECWU	0	8	0	7	0	12	0	15	0	4	0	6	0	9		1
LWU	0		2		4		8		2		1		4		1	
SWU	8		5		8		7		2		5		5			
BL	3		2		3		1		2		1		3			
SWD	10	10	7	14	3	9	6	8	11	17	4	17	1	12	10	22
LWD	0		7		6		2		6		12		8		2	
SECWD	0		0		0		0		0		1		3		10	
No nations	21		23		23		23		23		23		23		23	

whole period, and *one secular wave downswing nation* in the 1990s, *three* in the 2000s, and *ten* in 2011–2020: a major negative wave result for the region.

We comparatively scrutinize the American waves for North America vis-à-vis Latin America (Central and South) and the Caribbean in Fig. 11.6.

The NA (USA, Canada, Mexico, and Greenland) wave seems to be upset by war spending during 1940–1945, which boosted growth from the Depression but could not be sustained into the 1950s. Therefore, the NA Full Wave started in the 1950s with borderline performance, followed by two decades of long-wave upswing in the 1960s and 1970s, then traversing into borderline during the 1980s, followed by three decades of long-wave downswing during 1990–2020. In this, it follows the world full wave, but always with a lag of one decade behind the world. During the 2000s, NA continued the decline along with the world, which picked up slightly, while the NA wave was still below the world during 2011–2020.

The North American wave of the 1950s–2020s, also like the world, thus fails to achieve a complete wave from borderline to borderline, primarily missing a borderline-up result, which may come in the 2020s or 2030s; in this sense, it may currently be one to two decades less than a complete wave. If this is the case, the complete North American wave from borderline to borderline may have a periodicity of 70–80 years (1950s–2020s) and an amplitude (so far) of 221 basis points, but this presupposes at least borderline performance soon (which may be unlikely).

From the 1950s, the LACA wave is comparable to the North American wave since it was undergoing borderline performance during the 1950s, rising into a long-wave upswing during the 1960s and 1970s, and then dropping into a long-wave downswing. LACA differs from the North since the debt crisis in LACA during the 1980s brought growth to a standstill; while the North slowly went into borderline during the 1980s, followed by a downswing in the 1990s and a deep downswing into 2000–2020. LACA went from the lower limits of a very deep downswing during the

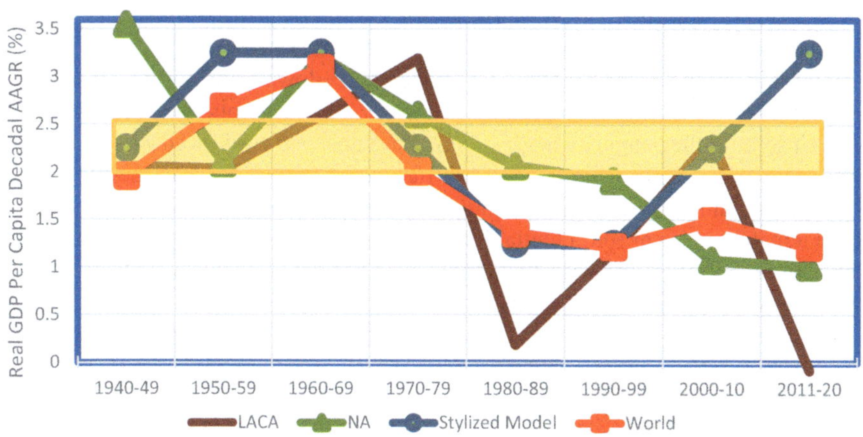

Fig. 11.6 American waves of decadal GDP growth per capita, 1940s–2000s, North America; Latin America & Caribbean. (Source: Adapted from Table 11.2)

1980s to a downswing in the 1990s and then borderline recovery into the 2000s, followed by a short-wave downswing. Hence, since LACA did move during 1960–2010 from borderline to upswing to downswing and then back to the borderline, they did undergo a full wave of 50 years (B to B).

Examining specific nations of America reveals even more differences when Latin America is broken up into Central America, the Caribbean, and South America. Selected data for North America and Central American nations are shown in Table 11.13.

All North and Central American nations had some good long-wave characteristics, but all missed core elements of the required dynamics. Table 11.14 compares waves in the Caribbean with those in South America over the standard period:

The main feature distinguishing Caribbean and South American (CASA) waves from North American waves is that in CASA there are numerous short waves, and a fairly large proportion have been dominated by downswings.

Nonetheless, some nations have moderate to good long-wave patterns, especially Brazil, Cuba, Argentina, and Peru, with three others almost emerging with full long waves, including Chile, Columbia, and Uruguay. Of course, as mentioned in the introduction to this chapter, this is purely "empirical"—formal and needs to be developed through CSD analysis for the whole period and beyond, as with all the other results in this chapter (we have done this for the USA in Chap. 7).

The Dominican Republic had a similar wave pattern to Pakistan, the Philippines, and El Salvador in having a multiplicity of *full short cycles* from 1950 to 1999. But the negative side of this equation is that these three nations experienced much erratic motion through successive UDUD (up-down, up-down) irregularities, typical of areas with some positive dynamics but generally lacking in sustainable pathways and circuits of socioeconomic dynamics.

However, the whole period, and especially more recent years, has been dominated by long-wave downswings in Haiti, Bolivia, Ecuador, Paraguay, and Venezuela. Optimistic potentials were not forthcoming as all South American nations in Table 11.14 (except the Dominican Republic) and all North American and Central American nations in Table 11.13 underwent a downswing during 2011–2020, as with most other nations of the world. North American nations were fairly uniform insofar as they engaged in good long-wave upswings, followed by major long-wave downswings, with no recovery in motion. This implies CSD development, maturation, and decline, with no significant new CSD emerging in the nations, nor even tentative renewal for potential long-wave upswings into the future. This again tends to support the hypothesis that long-wave upswings are exogenously generated while downswings are endogenous.

Table 11.13 GDP growth per capita, decadal AAGR: North America, Central America, 1940–2020

	North America			Central America				
	USA	Canada	Mexico	Costa Rica	El Salvador	Guatemala	Honduras	Nicaragua
1940–49	3.63	4.82	2.40	1.37	4.73	1.41	1.76	1.49
1950–59	1.96	2.02	2.78	3.59	1.96	1.01	0.40	2.77
1960–69	3.07	3.56	3.72	2.64	2.83	2.69	1.83	4.25
1970–79	2.60	2.62	3.42	3.72	1.53	3.16	2.69	−2.35
1980–89	2.09	1.81	0.19	−0.46	−3.29	−1.41	−0.53	−3.20
1990–99	1.95	1.34	1.58	2.91	3.67	1.70	0.24	0.82
2000–10	0.97	1.28	0.99	2.12	1.58	0.84	2.10	1.67
2011–20	0.94	0.29	0.10	1.74	0.92	1.37	0.62	1.44
Amplitude	269 BP	453 BP	362 BP	418 BP	802 BP	457 BP	322 BP	745 BP
Wave?	No.	No.	No.	No.	No.	No.	No.	No.
Missing; trend.	Missing B-up 2021–2030	Missing B-up 2021–2030	Missing B-up 2021–2030	Missing LWD in 1990s	Missing several items. Too erratic. DUDU motion.	Missing B-up during 2000–2010 onward	Missing LWU. DUDU motion, erratic	Missing B-up

Source: Adapted from the raw data of Maddison (2006) and World Bank (2024)

Table 11.14 Waves of GDP growth per capita, 1940–2020: Caribbean and South America, decadal AAGR

	Caribbean					South America									
	Cuba	Dominican Republic	Haiti	Jamaica	Trinidad & Tobago	Argentina	Bolivia	Brazil	Chile	Columbia	Ecuador	Paraguay	Peru	Uruguay	Venezuela
1940–49	3.88	n.a.	0.00	5.56	n.a.	2.17	0.78	3.14	1.70	1.06	4.30	−0.81	1.67	2.20	7.52
1950–59	−0.82	2.82	−0.42	10.16	6.26	0.57	−1.99	0.57	0.97	1.65	1.87	−0.01	2.48	0.48	3.78
1960–69	−0.54	1.60	−1.26	3.70	3.50	2.56	0.88	2.97	2.01	2.07	1.54	1.54	2.30	0.23	1.24
1970–79	4.13	5.46	3.81	−0.11	3.54	1.30	1.56	5.92	0.87	3.36	5.25	5.25	1.14	2.36	0.46
1980–89	3.35	1.54	−1.27	0.52	−2.54	−2.20	−2.58	0.82	2.72	1.21	1.09	1.09	−1.95	0.06	−2.93
1990–99	−2.53	3.10	−1.67	1.34	2.10	3.20	1.69	0.13	4.67	0.99	0.07	0.07	1.39	3.05	0.30
2000–10	5.90	3.86	−1.24	0.78	5.36	3.09	1.88	2.49	2.72	2.55	1.49	1.49	4.21	2.63	1.57
2011–20	0.66	2.97	0.14	−0.68	−1.82	−1.68	1.82	−0.52	1.00	1.36	0.07	1.76	1.28	1.16	0.41[a]
Amplitude	843BP	392BP	548BP	1084BP	880BP	540BP	440BP	644BP	380BP	237BP	518BP	606BP	616BP	299BP	1045BP
Long wave?	Yes. 50 years (1940–1999)	No.	No.	No.	No.	Yes. 60 years	No.	Yes. 60 years	Almost	Almost	No.	No.	Yes.	Almost	No.
Missing; Trend.	None.	1960–1999 SW	Missing LWU, B-up	Missing B-up & B-down	Missing B-up & LWD	LW 1960–2020	80-year SecWD	1950–2010	Missing LWD after 2000–2010 & B-up	Misses LWU	SecWD	Missing B-up & LWU	LW 1940–2010	Erratic	SecWD

Source: Adapted from raw data in Maddison (2006), World Bank (2024)
NOTE: [a]2011–2014

11.7 European Wave Patterns

European waves are based on good data for Western Europe but limited data for Central and Eastern Europe. The area includes three regions: core Western Europe (nine nations), Scandinavia (four nations), and Central/Eastern Europe (five nations). Analyzed together, these regions give a broad view of the continent of Europe, called Europe 18 (E18). We scrutinize the evolutionary wave phase pattern for E18 over 1940–2020 in Table 11.15.

The trends here are self-evident. The 1940s was a period of downswing as the war devastated numerous nations of Europe, especially Germany, France, Italy, Hungary, Austria, the Netherlands, the UK, Russia, Hungary, Poland, and Czechoslovakia. While rapid reconstruction and recovery occurred in the late 1940s in many nations, because of the earlier destruction, it took until the 1950s to become substantial (Maddison 2006, 440–41). Recovery (through borderline) occurred in the late 1940s and early 1950s, and during the 1950s, a short-wave upswing emerged, turning into a long-wave upswing in the 1960s–1970s. By the time a few secular wave upswings emerged in the 1980s, most nations had already turned to short-wave downswing while some had borderline conditions; and in 1990–2020 short and, more recently, long downswings were pronounced, while very few were in upswing. There is thus a good wave pattern but no recovery for a full wave.

Looking at the trends in Western Europe versus Central and Eastern Europe, Fig. 11.7 shows the differences in their respective wave dynamics:

This figure shows a clearly identifiable *full long wave* for CEE, starting from near-borderline in the 1940s to a long-wave upswing in the 1950s–1970s, moving to a long-wave downswing in 1980–1999, and recently recovering past borderline into a short upswing during 2000–2010 (followed by short-wave downswing during 2011–2020). This impressive CEE full long wave is in the order of 70 years periodicity and 817 basis points amplitude, with high volatility because of the crash of the 1990s and the high short-wave upswing during 2000–2010. In contrast, Western Europe has failed to undergo a borderline/upswing after 80 years, with moderate volatility of 468 BP from 1940 to 2020.

There was a similar pattern of growth within WE and CEE. They were both involved in the Second World War. In both areas, a long-wave upswing operated during the 1950s–1970s. Conditions deteriorated in both areas during the 1980s, with WE and CEE both undergoing long-wave downswing during the 1980s and 1990s; the decline was steeper and deeper in CEE, as conditions in the (state capitalist) "communist" nations deteriorated in the 1980s and then virtually collapsed in the 1990s as markets/privatization were imposed by policymakers and business interests. During the 2000s, the decline deepened in WE, while in EE, the collapse turned into a short-wave upswing. During the 2000s, the rate of growth was very much higher in EE than in the WE (for the first time since the 1970s), as CEE rebounded from the most devastating decade of short-wave downswing in living memory. While WE growth was higher than world growth during all the decades of the 1950s–1990s, it became less than the world rate in 2000–2020.

Table 11.15 Europe 18, evolutionary wave pattern, 1940–2020 (WE9, SC4, CEE5)

	1940–1949		1950–1959		1960–1969		1970–1979		1980–1989		1990–1999		2000–2010		2011–2020	
SECWU	0	1	0	16	0	17	0	14	4	5	3	5	0	4		2
LWU	0		2		16		14		1		0		1		1	
SWU	1		14		1		0		0		2		3		1	
B	1		1		1		4		5		2		2		3	
SWD	16	16	0	1	0	0	0	0	8	8	6	11	6	12	2	13
LWD	0		1		0		0		0		5		6		9	
SECWD	0		0		0		0		0		0		0		2	
Nations	18		18		18		18		18		18		18		18	

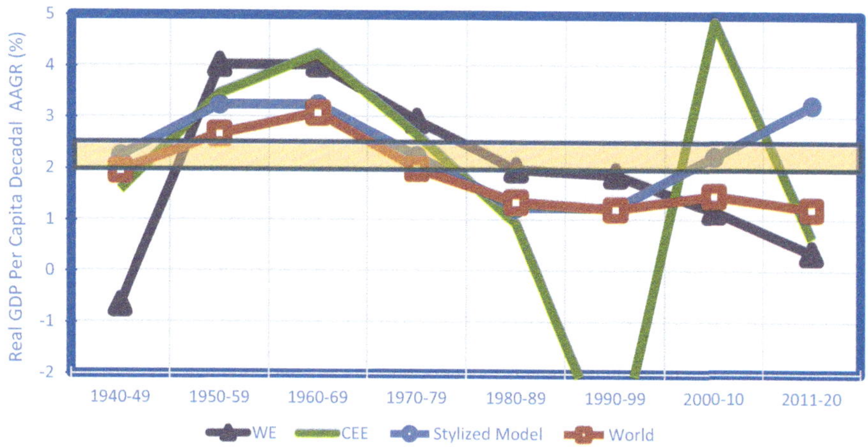

Fig. 11.7 European waves, 1940–2010, GDP growth per capita decadal AAGR. [Source: Adapted from raw data of Maddison (2006) and World Bank (2024)]

At this point in history—the 2020s—Western Europe is in a contradictory—long-wave downswing—phase of an unworkable or unsuccessful CSD; it will possibly undergo a Secular Full Wave of about 90 years, but recovery is not yet on the horizon (and is thus unlikely any time soon). This is also the pattern for North America, Japan, and the world. CEE may have joined this group of nations as it has gone through a short-wave downswing during 2011–2020, which may move to a long-wave downswing into the 2020s.

We now turn to the amplitude, periodicity, and short/long/secular wave comparison of the individual nations in a regional European context. Taking a sample of nine Western European nations, Table 11.16 shows the changing waves from the 1940s to the 2000s:

Ireland nearly experienced a full long wave, and Greece almost underwent a full long wave, while all the others have yet to recover from their long-wave downswings of the neoliberal period to the present. In this, they are similar to North America and Japan. All these areas also experienced similar CSD rises and falls, but not yet reconstruction.

Other than this, the UK underwent a secular wave borderline phase of 40 years (1950s–1980s), while Spain managed a long-wave borderline phase of 20 years (1970s–1980s). The results for Portugal and Ireland were more impressive, with a *secular wave upswing phase* of 50 years in Portugal (1950s–1990s) and 40 years for Ireland (1960s–1990s). The more peripheral economies of Greece, Portugal, Spain, and Ireland, respectively, underwent the *longest* long-wave upswings and *shortest* wave downswings for the area as a result.

The smallest amplitude was for the UK, since they underwent no long-wave upswing, while the largest amplitude was for Germany, which evolved from the highest rates of growth of all European economies (in the 1960s) to a very subdued experience in 2000–2020. Compared with the stylized long wave model, most of

Table 11.16 Amplitude, periodicity, long and short waves, "Western" European nations, 1940–2020, annual average growth rates, GDP per capita (decadal)

	UK	France	Germany	Italy	N'lands	Greece	Portugal	Spain	Ireland
1940–49	1.11	0.32	−3.93	−0.73	0.61	−2.92	1.76	1.25	1.15
1950–59	2.09	3.89	9.43	6.82	3.22	6.52	4.10	4.62	1.90
1960–69	2.25	4.47	4.55	5.01	4.06	7.00	5.84	6.67	4.02
1970–79	2.27	3.50	3.02	3.50	2.49	4.54	5.06	2.79	3.17
1980–89	2.30	1.74	1.87	2.49	1.58	2.25	3.72	2.35	2.70
1990–99	1.95	1.45	1.89	1.38	2.55	1.14	2.74	2.38	6.35
2000–10	1.12	1.18	1.14	0.03	1.14	2.46	0.55	1.03	1.59
2011–20	0.22	0.09	0.93	−0.83	0.45	−2.06	0.12	−0.21	5.74
Amplitude	208BP	438BP	1336BP	765BP	361BP	992BP	572BP	688BP	520BP
"Full" long wave?	Not yet. Subdued.	Not yet	Not yet	Not yet	Not Yet	Yes/close 1940–2010	Not yet	Not yet	Yes. 1950–2020
Missing/short wave?	Missing B-up (low ceiling)	Missing B-up	Missing B-up	Missing B-up	Missing B-up (Complex)	Missing LWD	Missing B-up	Missing B-up	SecLWU

Source: Adapted from the raw data of Maddison (2006) and World Bank (2024)

Western Europe lacked at least one phase of the long wave, mostly an upward borderline into the 2010s and/or 2020s, with a *possible* average full long wave of 80–90 years periodicity into the future (but maybe unlikely anytime soon).

Table 11.17 scrutinizes the long- and short-wave phases for specific Scandinavian and Central/Eastern nations from 1940 to 2020:

All CEE nations either achieved full long waves during the period or almost did. This is a very strong performance in long-wave terms, especially for Russia, Hungary, and the Czech Republic (Czechia). They additionally need to pass the test of CSD analyses for conclusive results. A hypothesis worth examining in the future is whether the former Soviet-style economies evolved from the postwar long-wave upswing (1950s–1970s) into the long-wave downswing during the structural dissolution (1980s and 1990s; with Polish exception) and after the cold turkey reforms reemerged for a short period but not enough for it to be sustainable. The necessary CSD reforms have thus not been developed yet.

Denmark was very close to the *prima facie* test of long wave periodicity, whereas the other three Scandinavian nations missed a borderline upward result for a full long wave. Recovery from the no-hegemony long-wave downswing has not occurred for these nations and numerous countries, especially the Western world (and Japan). While a technology style may possibly have been established, the associated eco-institutional dynamic structures (within the CSD) have not been sufficiently formed yet to provide a suitable foundation for durable performance.

11.8 Middle East and North African (MENA) Wave Patterns

Figure 11.8 compares MENA with the conditions for the world and the stylized model during 1940–2020:

The MENA wave is missing only a borderline—or downswing—result for the 1940s, giving a possible wave of 60 years for the period 1940–1999. MENA parallels the world upswing in the 1950s–1960s, but at a slightly higher level, followed by a major divergence in the 1970s as oil-producing nations expanded dramatically, while the world went into borderline conditions. Then while the world continued to deteriorate during the 1980s and 1990s, MENA collapsed in the 1980s and then jumped to borderline conditions during the 1990s, which continued into the 2000s. MENA's performance paralleled the world in the 1990s–2000s but at a borderline level rather than the downswing of the World. The new millennium has seen the world continue into a downswing while MENA fails to progress during the 2011–2020 short-wave downswing.

Table 11.18 summarizes the evolutionary wave phase pattern for the MENA12 nations over the 1950–2020 period:

This data shows that two-thirds of MENA nations were in a short-wave upswing during the 1950s, while one-third were in a downswing; then during the 1960s conditions improved as most were in an upswing (long-wave upswing), while a few were in borderline and a further few in downswing. Conditions improved further

Table 11.17 Scandinavia, Central & Eastern Europe, GDP growth per capita, decadal AAGR, 1940–2020

	Scandinavia 4 (S4)				Central & Eastern Europe 5 (CEE5)				
	Denmark	Finland	Norway	Sweden	Russia	Hungary	Poland	Czech	Bulgaria
1940–49	0.84	2.16	1.58	2.84	1.73	−1.71	1.21	1.09	0.66
1950–59	2.58	3.92	2.85	2.54	3.24	4.80	2.95	4.67	6.26
1960–69	4.02	4.04	3.60	3.72	4.26	5.07	3.70	3.29	6.93
1970–79	2.06	3.50	3.85	2.00	2.42	5.03	4.01	2.28	3.74
1980–89	1.85	3.14	2.41	2.05	0.92	1.82	−0.43	1.23	3.82
1990–99	2.05	1.25	3.03	1.35	−4.81	0.17	3.67	0.08	−1.80
2000–10	0.58	1.84	0.90	1.76	5.29	2.43	4.05	3.06	5.08
2011–20	0.95	0.34	0.36	0.65	1.07	2.48	3.07	1.46	2.14
Amplitude	344BP	370BP	349BP	307BP	1010BP	678BP	448BP	459BP	873BP
"Full" long wave?	Very close	Not yet	Not yet	No.	Yes. 1LW 1940–2010	Yes. 1LW 1940–2010	Almost	Yes. 1LW 1940–2010	Almost
Missing/short wave?	Missing B-up	Missing B-up	Missing B-up	Missing 2 B-ups	None missing	None missing	Missing LWD (1990s)	None missing	Missing LWD

Source: Adapted from the raw data of Maddison (2006) and World Bank (2024)
Note: *FLW* full long wave

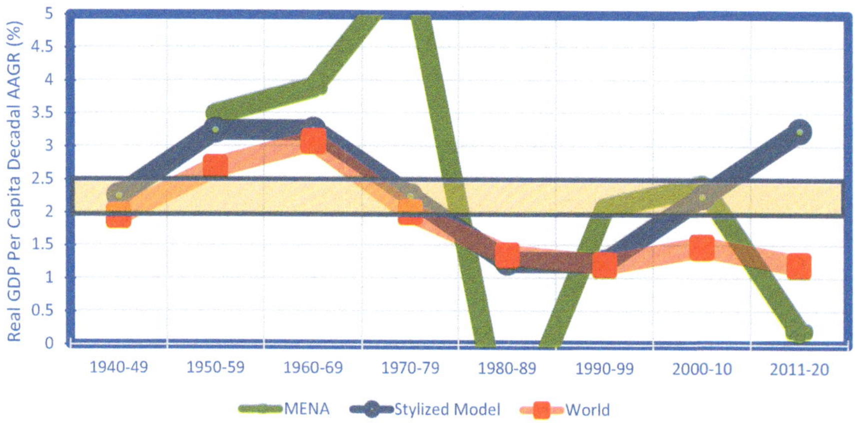

Fig. 11.8 MENA, GDP growth per capita, decadal AAGR, 1950–2020. [Source: Adapted from the raw data of Maddison (2006) and World Bank (2024)]

through OPEC during the 1970s, when all MENA nations were in an upswing phase: seven in long and five in short upswing. This was probably the most buoyant period for the Middle East and North Africa in modern times.

However, the situation reversed during the 1980s as declining oil prices and debt crises (Suter 1992) variously pushed most of the periphery and semi-periphery into a downswing for one or two decades (linked to the downswing in the core). MENA was seriously affected for the decade, with almost all MENA nations moving into a deep short-wave downswing. Things improved considerably into the 1990s and 2000s as a long-wave upswing emerged during the 2000s for a third of the area, with half going through (long or short) upswing and another third undergoing a downswing during the 1990s and 2000s. Overall, as noted, a long wave borderline performance has occurred for the area over 1990–2010, a better performance than the world and the stylized model. But, as mentioned, progress has not continued into 2011–2020.

Now we come to a specific analysis of 12 MENA nations during the 1950s–2000s, as shown in Table 11.19.

Typical MENA volatilities associated with oil prices, wars, coups, revolutions/counter-revolutions, and sanctions surprisingly led to some long waves but few perfect long-wave patterns due to erratic short upswings/downswings and insufficient borderline results. For instance, of the $MENA_{12}$ countries, Morocco almost experienced a good long wave, while Algeria, Iran, Lebanon, and Tunisia were close but missed some core elements.

These high amplitudes generated *odd short-wave downswings* for Algeria (1960s), Iran (1980s), Israel (1980s), Jordan (1980s), Lebanon (1980s), Tunisia (1980s), and the short-wave growth *crash* in the West Bank/Gaza (2000s with continued but less intense decline into 2011–2020; and much worse into 2023–2024 [not shown]). In a similar fashion, numerous nations were able to experience very long-wave upswings, including 50-year secular (Jumbo) wave upswings in Egypt

Table 11.18 Middle East and North Africa, 12 nations, 1950–2020, Evolutionary wave phase pattern

	1950–1959		1960–1969		1970–1979		1980–1989		1990–1999		2000–2010		2011–2020	
SECWU	0	8	0	7	0	12	1	2	1	6	0	6	0	0
LWU	0		5		7		1		0		4		0	
SWU	8		2		5		0		5		2		0	
BL	0		2		0		0		2		2		0	
SWD	4	4	2	3	0	0	10	10	0	4	2	4	8	12
LWD	0		1		0		0		4		2		2	
SECWD	0		0		0		0		0		0		2	
No nations	12		12		12		12		12		12		12	

Table 11.19 Average annual decadal GDP growth per capita, Middle East and North Africa (MENA12), 1950–2020

	Algeria	Egypt	Iran	Iraq	Israel	Jordan	Lebanon	Morocco	Syria	Tunisia	WB/Gaza	Yemen
1950–59	5.12	0.73	1.96	9.44	6.44	4.15	−0.16	−0.74	3.02	1.02	4.42	0.58
1960–69	1.68	2.78	8.65	4.28	5.43	2.12	1.73	2.10	3.33	2.91	4.51	0.85
1970–79	3.88	3.89	3.16	8.74	2.94	11.05	2.52	2.75	5.24	4.95	4.52	12.50
1980–89	−2.79	3.44	−3.84	−6.19	1.84	0.14	−4.38	1.41	0.50	1.03	4.51	0.05
1990–99	−0.42	2.50	2.71	−6.22	2.37	5.54	7.07	1.17	2.91	3.29	4.43	1.36
2000–10	2.03	3.24	3.75	−2.04	1.67	3.54	3.56	3.47	2.02	3.54	−5.83	0.83
2011–20	−0.19	1.47	−2.37	1.16	1.46	−1.40	−5.40	1.12	−5.92	−0.33	0.14	−7.81
Amplitude	791BP	316BP	1249BP	1566BP	498BP	1245BP	1247BP	421BP	1116BP	528BP	1034BP	2031BP
Long wave?	Nearly	No.	Nearly	No.	No.	No.	No.	Not Quite.	No.	Close.	No.	No.
Missing; Pattern.	Missing LWU	Miss. B-up, LWD	Miss. LWD	Miss. 2B-ups	Miss. 2 B-up	Miss. B-up, LWD	Missing LWD, B-up	Missing LWU	Miss. LWD; B-up	Miss. LWD; B-up	Miss. LWD; 2B-ups	SecWD

Source: Adapted from the raw data of Maddison Project (2024), World Bank (2024)

and the West Bank/Gaza, two long-wave upswings for Iran, and the very high rates of growth in alternating decades for Jordan giving it one long-wave upswing and two short-wave upswings.

MENA has the second highest degree of instability for all continents during the 1950s–2000s, with six nations having amplitudes of over 1000BP (e.g., Iran, Iraq, Jordan, Lebanon, West Bank/Gaza, and Yemen). This instability is mainly caused by the dynamics of wars, oil prices, and unrepresentative polities. Large deposits and high prices for oil in many areas led to high growth rates in the 1960s and 1970s, but this was countered by declining oil prices in the 1980s, which led to downswings in most nations. Wars also contributed to the downswing trend in several periods, including the Iran–Iraq War of 1980–1988; the civil war in Lebanon during 1975–1990; the revolutions and counter-revolutions/wars/instabilities during 2010–2023 in Tunisia, Algeria, Syria, and Yemen; and recently in Gaza. There was also problematical governance in Lebanon, sanctions on Iran, and a coup in Egypt, which affected performance. All these led the optimistic results of borderline performance during 2000–2010 to transform into a severe short-wave downswing during 2011–2020 (and 2021–2023, not shown). Things do not look promising for MENA in the future.

Very little circuit of socioeconomic dynamics (CSD) type research has been done for MENA, and their socioeconomic dynamic structures are quite different from the West and the East. Their economies are heavily dependent upon resources (especially oil and gas), and the polities are often oligarchs or semi-dictatorships, while since the US invasion of Iraq and the 2010s revolutions and 2020s conflicts between Israel and Palestinian supporters, wars have been more prominent in the area. Domestic wars are not good for long-wave upswings or CSD development.

11.9 Conclusion

Four hypotheses were present for empirical analysis at the beginning of this chapter. The first concerned the existence (and priority?) of global long waves over the 1940–2020 period. The second relates to the existence of short, long, and secular waves. The third is the borderline-to-borderline method of wave analysis. And the fourth applies to the 40- to 80-year periodicity of long waves. All four hypotheses were corroborated, though with caveats.

Regarding the first hypothesis concerning global long waves, the "World" did seem to undergo something close to a long-wave upswing and downswing over the 1940s–2020s. It was close to the borderline in the 1940s and certainly did undergo a long-wave upswing in the 1950s and 1960s, followed by borderline performance in the 1970s as it evolved into a long-wave downswing into the 1980s–2000s. Currently, as part of this downswing, we are undergoing several major crises, polycrises, especially in the core, but in several other economies as well. If the world does go into (or through) borderline conditions in the 2020s or 2030s, this will generate a full long wave of 90–100 years. A long wave periodicity of 90–100 years is longer than the stylized model, but it does have the advantage of introducing somewhat more complexity into the analysis.

Van Duijn's thesis that long waves are primarily experienced by the world (and not necessarily individual nations and continents) is not true.[6] In the first instance, the world has not yet undergone the borderline-up phase required for a full long wave. But in the second instance, numerous types of waves have been found at the continental/regional and national levels, some that fit the stylized model moderately well, some that are (multiple) full short waves, and others that have a low or high ceiling and floor. Some regions broadly followed the world record, especially the core nations of North America, Europe, and Japan. Latin America's record was close to this world pattern, except that it experienced borderline recovery into the 2000s (as with the stylized model), but the world did not. Eastern Europe fit the wave upswing of the world, but it had greater amplitude as it experienced a major slump in the 1990s and a major rebound in the 2000s.

Three areas that were moderately different from the world were sub-Saharan Africa, Asia, and, to some degree, the Middle East and North Africa. MENA experienced a stronger long-wave upswing in the 1950s–1970s than the world, while MENA had only one decade of downswing (1980s) and since then two decades of borderline performance (1990s–2000s), which the world is yet to experience, and another decade of downswing (2010s onward). *SSA* experienced a robust full long-wave pattern with a low floor and ceiling, but with no (stylized model) upswing (neither long nor short) for the whole 60 years. Asia had the most buoyant performance through 60 years of secular long-wave upswing, being the most upbeat result for the whole world over the period. It possibly experienced one full long wave with a high ceiling and floor (or simply a secular long-wave upswing since the 1950s).

The areas with the highest amplitude (during 1950–2020) were CEE and MENA; CEE due to a major slump in the 1990s and sudden reversal in the 2000s; and MENA due to a high long-wave upswing during the 1950s–1970s, subsequent negative growth as oil prices dropped during the 1980s, and severe wars, revolutions, and counter-revolutions during 2010–2022. The lowest amplitude (during the 1950s–2020s) was in Asia, as it experienced consistently high growth with no downswing, also the world; and North America, which had a modest upswing and not-too-deep downswings. Fluctuations *from successive decade to decade* were highest in the periphery, likely a result of wars, problematic governance, primary product specialization, and natural disasters.

The second hypothesis concerning short, long, and secular waves was supported. This is the first time short and secular waves have been specifically investigated in the literature, as well as the evolutionary changes from upswing through to

[6] Domestic (national) factors and long wave analysis are not contrary. Indeed, one social structure of accumulation scholar, Victor Lippit (2010), argues that long waves can *only* reasonably be explained in various *national* contexts. Some scholars would agree with him. O'Hara (2000, 2006), however, has consistently argued that long waves can be fruitfully investigated at the national, regional, and global dimensions (more work on the local level is required); his main innovation being to include global institutions and household/community relationships in the analysis.

downswing via borderline conditions. The greatest complexity emerged when nations, especially on the periphery, were analyzed, as some nations underwent great volatility, sometimes through well-formed and multiple full short waves with alternating periods of short upswing followed by downswing back to upswing and then downswing again. This volatile up-and-down tendency (with no well-formed long waves) was especially notable for Pakistan, the Philippines, El Salvador, and the Dominican Republic. In one continent, *SSA*, only one nation experienced a consistent (secular) wave upswing (Botswana, up until 2000–2010), while one nation stood out through a deep secular wave downswing (Central African Republic). Further research should study the CSD dynamics of these alternating short cycles and secular wave upswings and downswings to elicit the causes of their exceptional anomalous performance, vis-à-vis the nature of their eco-techno-institutional pathways and circuits of socioeconomic dynamics.

The third hypothesis related to the method of empirically examining long (and secular) waves from borderline (B) performance through to long-wave upswing (LWU), followed by long-wave downswing (LWD), and back to borderline (B). This "borderline-up to borderline-up" model was used to study the pattern of global, regional, and national short, long, and secular dynamics from the 1940s through to the 2020s. This was a very useful method of wave analysis, especially when used as a flexible tool to recognize movements through borderline areas (B-ups and B-downs) from lower and high areas (and higher to lower areas) as being equivalent movements for purposes of empirical analysis. The borderline bars have been used all through this book and were crucial for undertaking both theoretical and empirical inquiry. Schumpeter may well be glad of this, even though we use borderline bars for often other reasons apart from those that he proposed.

The fourth hypothesis of this chapter concerned the stylized long-wave model of 40–80 years. The study did find numerous long waves, especially the shorter long waves of 50–60 years, but none yet that had a true wave pattern for the very long periods. For the regions of the world, full shortish long waves of 50–60 years in duration were found for Latin America and the Caribbean; possibly for the Middle East and North Africa if suitable data can be found for the 1940s; and if we accept lower floors and ceilings in the wave also for sub-Saharan Africa. Full medium-long waves were also found for Central and Eastern Europe. But the potentially longer waves of 80–100 years for the world, Western Europe, and North America were missing a borderline or upswing recovery from long-wave downswing for recent decades. Perhaps this will occur in the future. Similar results were found for nations in these respective regions.

Overall, this chapter has sought to both understand recent decades of performance for the world economy, its regions, and nations and advance the state of long-wave empirics. The world economy has in recent decades been undergoing a whole series of severe ecological, financial, economic, and geopolitical crises. Recent dynamics do not indicate the emergence of (short wave) upswing or even borderline for the world or the core; rather, these areas seem to be undergoing continuing CSD decline. But a few recent optimistic results have emerged, the most notable being the continuing vibrancy of Asia (with some recent decline), only slightly more optimism in Japan, high growth in Poland, Hungary, and Ireland, plus borderline performance in the Congo (DRC, although with internal tension) and a short-wave upswing in the Ivory Coast.

The polycrises of the world have continued through anomalous GDP per capita AAGRs and numerous other crises discussed in Chaps. 9 and 10. One curious one is the climate crisis, which one might think would have been assisted by continued long-wave downswing throughout much of the world. That it has not done this on balance even though it would have possibly reduced GHGs reveals how crucial it is to work on several fronts to emasculate the climate crisis through efforts at adaptation and mitigation. And more significantly, it reveals how important it is to prioritize the ecological-climate aspects of the CSD as part of efforts to renew socioeconomic reproduction with the ecological dimensions given a central place in the edifice.

Also, efforts should be directed at renewing subnational, national, regional, and global CSDs while directing efforts toward multilateral agreements to solve world problems, instead of the problematic hegemonic efforts of the past. Greater equality in geopolitical power distributions may in the future reduce the threat of world and other wars if multilateral agreements can promote (re)conciliation, accord, and coevolutionary solutions to complex world problems. These should be the basis of efforts to moderate tension and reduce the need for great power blocks with "chain-ganging" circulatory expansions of cascading conflict in typical world-regional-national war scenarios.

Wave research helps in the pursuit of general and detailed knowledge of world, regional, and national trends and patterns of socioeconomic performance. This should stimulate wave scholars to innovate further to gain a greater understanding of the evolution and transformation of the world system through historical time. It is also necessary to complement empirical investigations with detailed investigations of the pathways and circuits of socioeconomic dynamics, which includes historical, institutional, technological, and eco-geo-spatial scrutiny. In this context, this chapter showed that most nations and regions have not experienced CSD renewal, which implies that it is exogenous and thus subject to but currently lacking sufficient concerted debate, policymaking, and proactive innovations for renewal. This should be the main area of further inquiry into long waves, hegemony, and climate change in the future.

Acknowledgments An earlier version of this chapter was presented at the ASSA meetings in Chicago. I wish to thank Pascal Petit, Maria Seccareccia, and the referees for constructive comments.

References

Aglietta, Michel. 1976. *A Theory of Capitalist Regulation*. London: NLB, 1979.

De Wolff, Sam. 1924. Phases of Prosperity and Depression. In *The Foundations of Long Wave Theory*, ed. Francisco Louçã and Jan Reijnders, vol. 1, 25–44. Cheltenham, UK and Northampton, US: Edward Elgar, 1999. Translated from the original German by J. Reijnders.

Frank, Andre Gunder, and Barry Gills. 1993. *The World System: Five Hundred Years or Five Thousand?* London & New York: Routledge.

Freeman, Chris, and Francisco Louçã. 2001. *As Time Goes By: From the Industrial Revolution to the Information Revolution*. Oxford: Oxford University Press.

Gordon, David M. 1980. Stages of Accumulation and Long Economic Cycles. In *Processes of the World-System*, ed. Terence K. Hopkins and Immanuel Wallerstein, 9–45. NY: Sage. Reprinted in D. Gordon. 1998. *Economics and Social Justice: Essays on Power, Labor and Institutional Change*, ed. Samuel Bowles and Thomas Weisskopf, 93-129. Cheltenham, UK & Northampton, US: Edward Elgar.

Gordon, David M. 1994. Putting Heterodox Macro to the Test: Comparing Post-Keynesian, Marxian and Social Structuralist Macroeconometric Models of the Post-war U.S. Economy. In *Competition, Technology and Money: Classical and Post-Keynesian Perspectives*, ed. Mark Glick, 143–185. Cheltenham: Edward Elgar.

Hope, Kempe Ronald. 1997. *African Political Economy: Contemporary Issues of Development*. Armonk, NY: M.E. Sharpe.

Kondratiev, Nikolai. 1928. The Long Wave Cycle. In *The Foundations of Long Wave Theory*, ed. Francisco Louçã and Jan Reijnders, vol. 1, 45–126. Cheltenham, UK & Northampton, US: Edward Elgar, 1999. Translated from the Russian by Guy Daniels.

Lippit, Victor. 2010. Book Review of P.A. O'Hara, *Growth and Development in the Global Political Economy*. *Review of Radical Political Economics* 42 (3): 387–389.

Maddison, Angus. 2006. *The World Economy: Vols. 1 & 2 Combined. The Millennial Perspective, Historical Statistics*. Paris: OECD, Development Centre Studies.

Maddison Project. Maddison Historical Statistics Database, *Universiy of Groningen*, 2024, https://www.rug.nl/ggdc/historicaldevelopment/maddison/?lang=en (2024).

Mandel, Ernest. 1975. *Late Capitalism*. London: Humanities Press.

Mandel, Ernest. 1995. *Long Waves of Capitalist Development: A Marxist Interpretation*. London: Verso.

Marshall, Michael. 1987. *Long Waves of Regional Development*. New York: St Martin's Press.

Mitchell, Wesley. 1951. *What Happens During Business Cycles*. New York: National Bureau for Economic Research.

O'Hara, Phillip Anthony. 2001. Long Waves of Growth and Development. In *Encyclopedia of Political Economy*, ed. P. A. O'Hara, vol. 2, 714–720. NY & London: Routledge.

O'Hara, Phillip Anthony. 2006. *Growth and Development in the Global Political Economy: Social Structures of Accumulation and Modes of Regulation*. London & NY: Routledge. (Paper edition 2009).

O'Hara, Phillip Anthony. 2010. After Neoliberalism: A Social Structure of Accumulation or Mode of Regulation for Global or Regional Performance? *Journal of Economic Issues* 44 (2): 369–383.

O'Hara, Phillip Anthony. 2012a. Institutional Regimes, Long Wave Systemic Risk and Great International Crisis of 2008-2012. *Panoeconomicus* 59:1–12.

O'Hara, Phillip Anthony. 2012b. Short-, Long-, and Secular-Wave Growth in the World Political Economy Periodicity, Amplitude, and Phases for 8 Regions, 108 Countries, 1940–2010. *International Journal of Political Economy* 41 (1): 3–46.

Schumpeter, Joseph Alois. 1939. *Business Cycles: A Theoretical, Historical and Statistical Analysis of the Capitalist Process. 2 Vols*. Philadelphia: Porcupine Press.

Sherman, Howard Jay. 1991. *The Business Cycle: Growth and Crisis Under Capitalism*. Princeton: Princeton University Press.

Suter, Christian. 1992. *Debt Cycles in the World Economy: Foreign Loans, Financial Crises and Debt Settlements, 1820-1990*. Boulder/San Francisco/Oxford: Westview Press.

Takahashi, Katsuhide. 2006. On the Credibility of GDP statistics in China: Official Historical Data Reexamined. *Kobe University Economic Review* 52:79–91.

Tylecote, Andrew. 1992. *The Long Wave in the World Economy: The Current Crisis in Historical Perspective*. London and New York: Routledge.

van Duijn, Jacob J. 1983. *The Long Wave in Economic Life*. London: George Allen & Unwin.

World Bank. 2024. *WDI: World Development Indicators, 1961–2010*. Available Online.

Chapter 12
Conclusion: Summary and Areas for Further Research

Abstract This chapter summarizes the results of the chapters of this book and outlines further research required based on the results and methods utilized. Special reference is given to the PoPE contingency paradigm, the new long wave model, and the future of the world system based on long wave, hegemony, and climate change (LWHegCC) dynamics. We then outline the stylized facts (SFs) and rules of thumb that emerge from this study, which should be the basis of future work, following the guidelines of this current book.

Keywords Long waves · Hegemony · Climate change · Stylized facts · Principles · China · Britain · United States · Netherlands · PoPE contingency paradigm · Future of the world · New long-wave method

12.1 Main Conclusions of this Book

The purpose of this book has been to reconstruct long wave theory and empirics by linking it to hegemony and climate change and embedding it in the history of capitalism back to the 1500s and through to the 2020s/2040s and vis-à-vis climate change back through the millennia and forward to 2100. For this purpose, the introduction presented the standard model of long waves and the alternative, which we called the PoPE paradigm and the new long-wave method.

Chapters 2 and 3 presented and critically evaluated long wave theories and empirics. Starting with the first long wave of long-wave scholarship (chap. 2), which included Kondratiev, Joseph Schumpeter, and others, we accepted some of the criticisms of the standard model, including the core ones of George Garvy, Simon Kuznets, and Paul Sweezy. This analysis continued in Chap. 3 vis-à-vis the second long wave of long-wave scholarship, including critically sympathetic scrutiny of the long wave schools of thought, especially generated by the work of Ernest Mandel, Walt Rostow, Alan Freeman, Francisco Louçã, Carlotta Perez, Gerhard Mensch,

P. A. O'Hara, *Long Waves of Growth, Hegemonic Power, and Climate Change in the World Economy*, https://doi.org/10.1007/978-981-96-4132-1_12

Andrew Tylecote, Michel Aglietta, David Gordon, Jay Forrester, and others. The PoPE contingency paradigm is used to conduct this reconstruction of long wave schools of thought.

Basically, we concluded that long waves, hegemony, and climate change (LWHegCC) are dependent upon several processes, which are examined through the use of the PoPE contingency paradigm. This paradigm argues that the empirical nature of LWHegCCs is dependent upon an array of factors. These include the specifics of history and evolution, the forces of hegemony and uneven development, certain heterogeneous agents and groups, contradictions, circular and cumulative changes, innovations, risks and uncertainties, policies, and the circuit of socioeconomic reproduction (CSD). These at least nine major factors (as principles) interactively determine the precise nature of LWHegCC. These processes are interrelated with and impinge on the specific ways in which the various aspects of LWHegCC manifest themselves through historical time.

In chap. 4, we develop an analysis of the historical evolution and long-wave motion of climate change. We sought to ascertain if and why the long-term history of climate change has relevance for the present climate crisis and also for climate change dynamics to be embedded in the record of hegemony and long waves of growth. We also situated climate change dynamics within the context of Dutch, British, US, and Chinese potential or actual hegemony and growth, which we incorporated in the chapters on these nations and regions. Finally, we outlined how the official documents of climate change analysts can potentially be reconciled through climate scientists studying the cycles, waves, and anthropogenetic factors impacting Earth's temperature.

Chapters 5 through 8 studied the nature of LWHegCC dynamics for the Dutch, British, US, and potentially Chinese cases. These case studies are the crux of this book. Several general and many specific stylized facts and generalizations are made in these four chapters. The 21 core stylized facts and hypotheses are the most important. These involve historical regularities about LWHegCC associated with specific tenets (see Sect. 12.2). For every such rule or stylized fact, there is a corresponding hypothesis or series of hypotheses for future research.

Chapter 9 analyzed the 1980s–2020s polycrises that emerged out of the situation where there was no absolute hegemon guiding and sometimes bullying agents, groups, nations, regions, and international institutions through various public goods of collaboration, agreement, financial bailouts, and advice. The relative US hegemony situation merged with neoliberalism to generate anomalies and crises associated with long-wave downswings, climate crises, decadal financial crises and recessions, GFC, Eurocrises, coronacrisis, and the conflict over Ukraine and Taiwan (plus the Israel–Palestine–Lebanon–Iran conflict). In especially the past decade, a *new order* of transnational contradictions has emerged to some considerable degree, which responds to these polycrises. The key ingredient of this new order comprises a new battleground between autocracy, ultra-nationalism, and liberal democracy. This is playing out so that both sides are engaging in greater levels of protectionism, industry policy, control of populations, challenges to established financial centers, and much greater geopolitical conflict.

Chapter 10 provided some details of key aspects of this geopolitical conflict vis-à-vis Ukraine and Taiwan, including the current "prewar situation" and the potential for World War 3. Some of the core principles of PoPE and war were utilized to ascertain the potential trajectory of this conflict crisis and the factors determining the specific nature of its evolution and development.

Chapter 11 analyzed the long-wave patterns and processes of the world, its major regions, and over 100 nations during the period 1940s to the 2020s. Stylized facts are ascertained and compared with the stylized model of the period and for the experience of the world, its major regions, and nations. We conclude that many regions and nations have undergone quite well-developed long waves of growth during this period. These include the changes from (a) borderline-up performance to (b) long-wave upswing, then (c) long-wave downswing, and back again to borderline (up) (as well as variations of this pattern). Some areas are yet to complete the long-wave pattern but may do so in the near future. Others still have experienced mainly long-wave upswings or long-wave downswings throughout most of the period, and others, especially those subject to systemic anomalies such as wars, despotic regions, and primary product price distortions, have been subject to numerous short waves of up and down motion.

We also added weight to the hypothesis that long waves upswings, and hence hegemonies, and therefore specific forms of climate change during such heightened activity, tend to be exogenously generated, while the movement from upswing to downswing is typically endogenous. What this means is that upwardly synchronized movements of these complex LWHegCC processes need to be systematically organized and generated through multiple events such as wars, treaties, policies, blind drifts, evolutions, and the metamorphoses of techno-institutional and environmental change. The buildup of these structures to form dynamic and innovative pathways and circuits of socioeconomic dynamics (CSD) does not develop in an upwardly cyclical fashion but is partly consciously developed and synchronized. Once they are effectively in the process, they tend to undergo phases of evolution and transformation, such as eventual maturity and demise, which happen quite naturally, as with any such complex structures that have an emergent and complex form about them. Such cycles do not exist, but long waves do, although they tend to become more effective and transformative during periods of rising hegemony, as both waves and hegemony move together at these higher reaches of performance.

12.2 Stylized Facts of Long Waves of Growth, Hegemony, and Climate Change: Hypotheses for Further Research

In this context, we now outline in summary form the major stylized facts (SFs) of LWHegCC that emerge from this book, which can also be viewed as hypotheses (H) worthy of further research in the future.

1st LWHegCC Stylized Fact and/or Hypothesis (SFH) (for Future Research): General SFH.

Combined long wave, hegemony, and climate change analytics are useful themes to merge and interrelate and can prove helpful for political economic inquiry into the future. This is a very general SFH and can apply to numerous issues, including the SFHs outlined below.

2nd LWHegCC SFH Wars of Ascendency.

Hegemons have historically experienced war(s) of ascendency prior to hegemony being successful. (I doubt the general existence of wars of consolidation during hegemony.) This applies to the Dutch Revolt/revolution (1570s–1580s), British success in the Napoleonic Wars (1815), and the outcomes of the Second World War (1945) for the US and its allies. The question arises if-and-when this stylized fact will apply to China and/or other powers in the future.

3rd LWHegCC SFH Hegemonic Stability Hypothesis and Multilateral Measures of Cooperation.

The hegemonic stability hypothesis may not be effective, and there are alternatives to it in practice. Hegemonies can operate through a continuum of forces. On the one side is a hegemon that uses its naked power to control the world in its own pure interest and possibly those of its allies, although it may use some of its power to moderate opposition from time to time (this may possibly take the form of an Empire rather than a capitalist hegemony per se). On the other hand, it is a hegemon that seeks to control the world but also balances this with efforts to promote conciliation and accord and reduce uncertainty to generate a healthy level of global reproduction of the ecological, geopolitical, technological, and institutional dynamic structures. Or we may have effective alternatives to these two options (and in-between solutions).

One alternative is collective hegemony, where certain allies band together to control much of the world's resources and potential. Another alternative is groups of opposing hegemons where none of them effectively control the world, but they may control parts of the world. A third alternative is where geopolitical organizations generate multilateral measures to promote accord on issues of climate, technology, and institutions, and where polycrises can be successfully addressed (though not necessarily completely alleviated) due to this multilateral mode of regulation.

4th LWHegCC SFH Hegemony and Long Waves.

We found historically that hegemons tend to have (a) one very long-wave upswing, or (c) two shorter long-wave upswings during (possibly one of them just before) their era of absolute hegemony. For instance, this includes two long-wave upswings for the Dutch Republic during and after the Dutch Revolt against the Spanish (1570–1620), also one very weak long-wave upswing during the time of British hegemony (1820s–1830s), and one major secular long-wave upswing within the time of US hegemony (1940s–1970s). The British experienced a secular long-wave upswing after the Napoleonic Wars (1820–1860 upswing) and during the time of US hegemony (1950s–1980s). The US had very high long-wave upswings during the era of US hegemony (1940s–1960s) and two much weaker decades of long-wave upswing (1970s–1980s; almost borderline) during the early phase of US relative hegemony. It also experienced a period of long-wave upswing during the period 1880–1910 just *after* the *Pax Britannica*.

5th LWHegCC SFH Liberal, Democratic, and Civil.

Hegemons tend to be liberal democracies advocating free trade (imperialism), parliamentary democracy, and some degree of civil society. This applied to the Dutch, British, and US situations. Does this imply that it should also apply in the future and that therefore China could not become hegemonic, or should the rules be modified in this case? Possibly it could become hegemonic in a *purely* global power sense ("Empire"), but not in a global power *and* common good sense unless it modified its governance processes.

6th LWHegCC SFH Long Wave Upswing Before Hegemony.

Immediately following a period of *absolute* hegemony (during relative hegemony), the power most likely to be the next hegemon tends to have modest or better (short or long) wave upswing(s) (during periods of *relative* hegemony for the "original" power). This applies in a very weak sense to the British experience, through a very strong short-wave upswing in the 1660s, after Dutch absolute hegemony; the Americans after British hegemony (1880s–1910); and the Chinese after US hegemony (1980–2010s➔?).

7th LWHegCC SFH Pathways and Circuits of Socioeconomic Dynamics (CSD).

Before and during hegemonic periods with long waves (upswings) the circuits of socioeconomic reproduction (CSD) are required to operate effectively through durable structures of eco-spatial, institutional, and technological capabilities. The decline in hegemony is linked to the decline in the CSD and the associated decline in LWs. Long waves and hegemonies, as well as climate change dynamics, which are part of this circuit, thus have dynamic-structural foundations underlying their motion.

8th LWHegCC SFH Structural Polycrises.

In between periods of hegemony (when there is no hegemonic power), there tend to be long periods characterized by (many more) structural polycrises, such as various depressions, wars, unstable short-wave upswings, long-wave downswings, debt crises, fiscal crises of the state, rebellions and revolutions, poor performance, and sometimes climate change crises, by the previous hegemonic powers, others, and possibly the world. This (potentially) applies to the period of the 1700s and early 1800s after Dutch hegemony and more certainly to the late 1800s and early-to-mid-1900s after British hegemony and the 1980s–2020s after US absolute hegemony.

9th LWHegCC SFH: Class Alliances.

Prior to and during periods of hegemony and long-wave upswings, alliances between various groups of heterogeneous agents and classes tend to emerge that lead to relatively successful periods of coordination, cooperation, agreements, interactions, and strategic processes that contribute to the relatively stable development of the CSD for a time. For instance, during Dutch hegemony, there was an alliance between the (con)federate governing classes and the bourgeoisie (and a small class of nobility). During British hegemony, there was an alliance between the bourgeoisie, certain landowners, and Whigs/Tories. During US hegemony, there was a capital-labor truce between the bourgeoisie and unionized workers in collaboration with a liberal-democratic class of governors.

10th LWHegCC SFH Structural Contradictions.

During periods of hegemony, there are structural contradictions within the eco-spatial, technological, and institutional CSD of the hegemonic power and its relationships to core, periphery, and semi-peripheral areas, which tend to manifest and lead to the dissolution of hegemony and long-wave upswings, and usually a new pattern of climate change through time.

11th LWHegCC SFH. Heatwaves and Rising GHGs:

During periods of hegemony (and long-wave upswings), one would, ceteris paribus, expect rising bouts of heatwaves through rising GHGs since growth per capita is expanding along with the destruction of natural capital. But other things are not equal, and the empirical record tends to often go against this expectation due to counter-tendencies. For instance, through the Little Ice Age (Maunder solar cycle minimum, 1600s, Dutch), Dalton solar cycle minimum (1800–1855, Britain), and the Small Cool Age (1940–1970, USA). Currently, the world is experiencing an ongoing climate crisis in an environment of no hegemon and mostly long-wave downswings (when one might have expected declining GHG concentrations and lower temperatures during periods of anomalous economic performance for the world).

12th LWHegCC SFH: Natural and Anthropogenic Climate Change:

The "natural" CC waves do help understand current and future CC more than the IPCC implies. Is it possible to be serious about climate change issues (especially the ongoing climate crisis) but still recognize the importance (and significance) of solar cycles, other planetary processes, and other nonhuman events on current and future climate change dynamics? Perhaps the two groups of natural scientists (natural cycle analysts; IPCC types) will work together and try to resolve this conundrum in one way or another while recognizing the anthropogenic processes underlying much (but possibly not all) of the ongoing current climate crisis.

13th LWHegCC SFH: CSD with Climate Mitigation and Adaptation:

Current trends in CC negate the potential for reasonable mitigation and rely purely on adaptation into the future, due to the cascading tipping points (or global TPs), which are likely to have catastrophic results for humans, other species, the climate, long-wave upswing potential, hegemonic potential, and CSD development. Any successful CSD in the present and future is therefore required to have adequate inclusion of climate change, both mitigation and adaptation impacts, associated with the eco-spatial, technological, and institutional dynamic structures.

14th LWHegCC SFH: Climate Change and Poor Performance.

During the era of polycrises experienced during the 1980s–2020s, climate change crises tended to be ongoing in a CCC fashion. These included more extreme events such as heatwaves, droughts, wildfires, floods, rising waterways, cyclones/hurricanes, and so on, plus the associated problems associated with these, such as more competition between groups and species, generating more crime, conflicts, civil wars, revolutions, recessions, financial crises, depressions, species extinction, and so on.

But in the short run, the climate crises along with the polycrises associated with these no hegemony periods also promote crises, during which GHGs tend to decline briefly in affected regions. This was the case with the specific multiyear crises (in numerous nations) during the early 1980s and early 1990s, the burst of the dot-com bubble/corporate crisis/9–11 (late 1990s–early 2000s), plus the GFC, the Eurodebt crisis, and the coronacrisis/property market crash. The long-term trend of course is for rising GHGs and global mean temperatures.

Furthermore, the more crises experienced, the less concentration can be given to any one of them, or more likely the current ultra-crisis (e.g., during the early 2020s, the coronacrisis) tended to crowd out other crises (climate crises) and hence to lessen climate change adaptation and especially mitigation.

15th LWHegCC SFH: Exploitation-Subordination of Ethnic Groups and Minorities.

Colonialists in all periods tended to exploit people of color and other groups potentially in their own region, as well as in the periphery and semi-periphery (where possible), in order to gain power, economic surplus, ethnic superiority, markets, and territory. This is variously done in different periods of history via the use of slavery, wars, invasion of territory, market power, the threat of lynching, and other means. The Dutch undertook multiple forms of control, especially in what is now called Indonesia and in the Caribbean and Africa (from the 1600s). The British undertook similar control measures, especially through their Empire-building activities, notably during the 1700s–1800s–early/mid-1900s, especially in the Americas, India, and Australia. European powers sought to extend their control throughout the world, especially during the stage of imperialism, the scramble for Africa, and the two world wars. The US engaged in these activities internally, in the Americas, Indochina, and much elsewhere. China engaged in internal colonialism vis-à-vis domestic citizens, Muslim minorities and Hong Kongers; threats and harassment towards Taiwan; and extension of power currently in many continents of the world.

16th LWHegCC SFH: Energy and Technology Regimes.

Every hegemon experiences peculiar or different patterns of regularity and innovation that deviate from the general pattern, and these differences mark each hegemon as being unique historically in areas of ecological, institutional, and technological structures and dynamics. A modest example relates to the energy regime. The Dutch used peat as a core form of energy during the 1600s, while the British used various forms of coal during the 1800s, and the US regime of accumulation was based on oil and gas during the 1900s.

Similarly, a core technology regime for the Dutch was the windmill (mills in general) for multiple purposes, while for the British, the factory system was a prime technology, and Fordism was the regime utilized during US hegemony. For any future hegemon (or multilateral power arrangement), AI-ICT-Biotech-Renewable energy may be the dominant technology-energy resource underlying performance.

Extending this further, every hegemon and those experiencing (especially secular) long waves have qualitatively innovative and novel CSRs, extending to the full array of eco-spatial, techno-institutions within and between the circuits.

17th LWHegCC SFH: Varieties of Capitalism.

The concern regarding Dutch, British, US, and Chinese performance in this book is with the development of several different varieties of capitalism. We have not examined purely Empire styles such as the Spanish, Portuguese, and Germans (before the 1600s) but have concentrated on the capitalist world economy. For instance, the Dutch underwent a form of proto-capitalism associated with a confederate style of governance, innovative bourgeoisie, effective merchants, and a well-developed civil society, as well as a mercantile/monopoly/discriminatory capitalist style, especially in the periphery. The British underwent both a form of industrial capitalism and Empire-building (mercantilism) simultaneously. The US underwent a form of corporate state capitalism with a dominant cultural (de facto) Empire component (linked to the military-industrial complex). The Chinese are trying to merge state capitalism with the Empire through geopolitical rivalry, domestic party control, and capitalist forms of production, distribution, and exchange.

In the current context, of course, there are various varieties of capitalism operating simultaneously: e.g., state capitalism in China, Russia, etc.; liberal market economies in Britain, the US, Australia, etc.; and coordinated market economies in Sweden, France, Germany, etc. Others have classed them differently, such as Anglo-Saxon capitalism, Nordic capitalism, East Asian capitalism, etc.

18th LWHegCC SFH: Endogenous and Exogenous Long Waves and Hegemonies.

A core rule of this book is that long waves, hegemonies, and climate changes can usefully be examined relative to the notions of (long, short wave) upswing and downswing. LWHegCC all undergo these processual changes from robust to mature to declining "performance." Rises and falls, cycles and waves, phases of evolution, and varying degrees of recurring dynamics are common to LWHegCC phenomena. However, especially for longer-term dynamics, these changes are not deterministic (i.e., inevitable, completely endogenous). They depend upon a multivariant set of conditions, according to the PoPE Contingency Paradigm. They are thus dependent upon a multifactor approach associated with history and evolution; hegemony and uneven development; various heterogeneous agents, classes, and forces; circular and cumulative processes; risk and uncertainty; contradictions and conflicts; innovations and novelties; governance and policy; and the circuit of socioeconomic reproduction.

Specifically, long waves and hegemonies are generated by forces that are thus contingent and largely exogenous at the lower turning point and largely endogenous at the upper turning point. They are largely exogenous at the lower turning point because very long-wave upswings and absolute hegemonies are subject to a large number of contingent forces that need to coalesce with sufficient force to generate long upswings/hegemony. One single factor, though, is endogenous to some limited degree at the lower turning point. That is, certain agents and classes (and forces) will be directed toward promoting these long waves and hegemonies, and they may succeed subject to the contingent and counteracting forces. Most will, however, not succeed. Success is dependent upon the coalescing of forces subject to very unique historical circumstances for specific regions and nations.

Long waves and hegemons are largely endogenous through the upper turning point because once in motion, the long waves and hegemons undergo phases of evolution and contradictions that are subject to other PoPE forces and thereby develop maturity, followed by decline. The structural dynamics within long waves and hegemons falter because the potential of the forces dissipates through a long historical time. Since few agents/classes recognize the reality of long waves, while more recognize the existence of hegemonic forces (or criticize such processes), natural/human forces of regeneration and conscious decision-making for renewal are seldom cognizant of the complexities and interdependencies involved. They are thus difficult to regenerate to enable the continuation of upswings and absolute hegemonies for hyper-long periods of time. Climate crises have more difficult trajectories because, in the current environment, for instance, right-wingers tend to be climate deniers in the US (but not necessarily in Britain), whereas left-wingers tend to be more climate change friendly (in most places).

19th LWHegCC: SFH: New Long-Wave Method.

The new long-wave method was used as an easy-to-understand tool that is ideal for book-length (and also journal article) general readers in the social sciences and business studies area.

For these purposes, we used mainly (a) the Maddison Project data (especially real GDP per capita) for numerous countries circa 1500/1800–2020s, (b) decadal annual average growth rates, (c) plotted these data, (d) used a trend line (ordinary least squares) to distinguish between wave and trend, (e) transformed this line into a thick bar, acting as a filter, within which borderline performance operates (in between upswing and downswing); higher than borderline is an upswing, and lower is a downswing, and (f) two or more decades of similar performance vis-à-vis each of the three segments equals a long wave: upswing, borderline, or downswing. This method was used for the period 1550 to 2022 (Dutch), but it was better when disaggregated to 1550–1780 (Dutch, British) and 1780/1800–2022 (Dutch, British, US, and China), including other medium periodicities. LWHegCC could all be summarized using (i) this tool (including modifications for hegemony and CC), with details triply verified (or otherwise) using also (ii) CSD and (iii) the analysis of other scholars.

20th LWHegCC: SFH: Will Secular Long-Wave Upswings Reemerge?

Since the demise of (absolute) US hegemony, the West and several other areas have been in long-wave downswings and/or borderline and/or occasional short-wave upswings (generally unimpressive long-term performance).[1] The question arises as to if and when decisive long-wave upswings may reemerge in the future. If so, will it be necessary to await a new hegemony for a new decisive long-wave upswing, and if so, will that positively impact the West (or just Asia and/or other

[1]As noted several times already in this book, others have hypothesized (alternatively) long wave upswings (for e.g., the West) already beginning and ending, for instance during the 1980s/1990s and 2007. We and some others doubt this.

areas or the whole world)? Or, alternatively, will the West (or large parts of it) and most of the world be in the cyclical/wave territory of mainly long-wave downswings into the foreseeable future (and/or generally/variably unimpressive performance/high volatility and/or low volatility/low performance/polycrises, on average)?

Or will the world, or some of its components, move to emphasize less real GDP growth per capita and more *quality of life* and *environmental quality* as constituting alternative forms of performance (or some hybrid such as standard of living indices more holistically measured)? Do GDP growth (per capita and levels) and related measures require more (supplementary) polycentric and post-material variables to compare quite different elements of reality?

21st LWHegCC: SFH: Peace Treaties and Agreements.

Wars of Ascendency tend to be associated with major peace treaties, which in the case of the *Congress of Vienna* (1815) and the *Bretton Woods Agreement/Marshall Plan/Yalta Conference* (1944–1951) led to 100 years and (to date) 80 years, respectively, with no major world war. This may be the case only when the liberal democracies (and their allies) win the war. We have no evidence to ascertain what would happen if an oligarch Empire won a possible future world war (e.g., in the current environment), except that it would probably act like an Empire and not as a capitalist economy as well.

It appears as if the *Peace of Westphalia* (1648) was not in the same order of importance as the *Congress of Vienna* (1815) and the *BWS-UN-Yalta-MP* postwar institutions (1944–1948) because it generated some *balance of power* principles around the time when Dutch absolute hegemony was (just) starting to decline into relative hegemony. Was the Dutch *Act of Abjuration* (1581), a formal declaration of independence, or the *Treaty of Antwerp* (1609), which established the 12 years' truce, adequate such peace treaties? I would hypothesize yes for the *Act of Abjuration.*

This leads me to restate a core hypothesis of this work: currently, some core political economies of the world have been undergoing a long wave downswing since their CSD are not structured adequately to generate sustainable long-term performance. Probably some elements of their CSD are well developed, since generalized depression has not emerged. Perhaps this element is the technology sphere where major progress is being made in producing cheap and effective solar panels, electric cars, AI, and electronics-biotechnology areas. But other elements are not sufficiently in motion. For instance, a suitable climate change regime has not been constructed globally, regionally, or nationally. A proper state apparatus is not currently working. A system of distribution does not favor workmanship, innovation, and relative equality. The system of households is precarious, lacking in trust, insufficiently nurturing, and too unstable. Too many resources are lost to financial wheeling and dealing, shareholder value, and mergers and acquisitions. The old system is also subject to much-disjointed incrementalism. There is also much corruption, including bribery, nepotism, fraud, embezzlement, extortion, and political funding (in public, private, and not-for-profit areas). Will the West ever regain a long-wave upswing?

22nd LWHegCC: SFH: Contradiction(s) of Autocratic vs *Liberal-Democratic Allies.* The core contradiction between autocratic and liberal-democratic allies will certainly magnify and amplify the circular and cumulative tendencies emerging in the geopolitical environment of the world. The core question is whether the world war that potentially emerges from the conflict will be a series of polywars (which collectively represent the world spatially) or a conglomerate merging of the polywars toward a generalized world war.

One core contradiction is this. The autocratic powers (Russia, China, North Korea, Iran, et al) believe that the liberal democracies (especially NATO, the US, the EU, etc.) are gaining more and more power in the vicinity of their (former) sphere of influence. For Russia, their sphere of influence used to include vast tracts of central and southern Europe and west Asia (Ukraine, Moldova, Poland, Hungary, Romania, the Baltics, etc.). Recently it has been dwindling majorly. China, for its part, sees the US and its allies invading their space in their sphere of influence in Taiwan, the South China Sea, and Southeast Asia. Chinese and Russian leaders believe that liberal democracies cannot solve their polycrises and that neoliberalism and US hegemony are now out of fashion due to their internal limitations.

The liberal-democratic allies, on the other hand, see Russia invading/seeking to influence several states that seek a Western tilt, liberal democracy, and closer links to the EU and the US. This includes the same list of countries that Russia and China are concerned about. The West (including Japan et al.) believes that nation-states have the right to self-determination, open up to global markets, and seek liberal-democratic institutions. The West believes that autocracies are undemocratic and thus need to be emasculated in the interests of the common good and the solving of complex problems of the global economy and its constituents.

This is the core contradiction that is processual and also logical. The two respective arguments are both correct in the context of their placement and significance. But they are processually in conflict, and logically they are similar but reverse sets of arguments. They lead to wars and conflicts. They also comprise several different groups of interests that propel a "chain of alliances" and the "chain-ganging" thesis. The circular and cumulative chain of causes generates cascading tipping points of differences and processes where conflicts and wars are self-propelling philosophies of action. We are in the nuclear age when tactical and strategic use of volatile missiles can be employed by the major actors but also non-state elements and lower powers such as Iran, North Korea, and Israel. Such a series of wars and potentially world wars are not only exacerbating polycrises (especially climate crises, anomalous performance, conflicts, financial crises, and wars) but also inhibiting the emergence of long-wave upswings and the resolution of climate change. Whether this becomes a war of ascendency or further CCC instability remains to be seen.

23rd LWHegCC SFH: Terminal Decline, Blind Drift, or Reemergence of the Capitalist World System?

The current period of structural polycrises seems to indicate that the capitalist world system that emerged in the 1500s and continued through three periods of hegemony, when long waves tended to be prolonged for the supreme power and some others (especially allies), and when special forms of climate change were established, may have come to the end of its life. It has been five decades since the postwar corporate system (Fordism, KWS, US hegemony, etc.) started to unravel, and when the institutions of neoliberalism and the Washington Consensus (and others) replaced it. But only a decade or less has passed since the *new order* of ultranationalism, protectionism, industry policy, and autocracy v liberal democracy started to emerge. The rise of Asia, and especially China, has been a high point, and short-term wave upswings did emerge in some nations (1990s) as they did earlier (e.g., 1920s). But a full-blown reemergence of sustained performance that impacts the world and core elements of its economies has been nowhere in sight (in terms of GDP per capita growth).

However, since hegemonies, long-wave upswings, and climate change dynamics are not endogenously generated but must be built from the existing eco-spatial, technological, and institutional fabric (CSD), and since efforts to reconstruct such performance can fail (as neoliberalism did), it is possible for some constructive developments to occur in the future. For instance, one possibility is that current geopolitical conflicts may develop into a major war or a series of polywars that may be defined as a major war, and any successors from this conflict may move to create a new world order of performance and development. In this context, it is, however, possible that the nuclear threats may lead instead to global dissolution and demise to varying degrees. Perhaps China's role in this conflict will lead to them being the next hegemonic power and leading others to a specific form of structured world organizational revolution. The liberal democracies may otherwise emerge victorious, possibly the road ahead leads to a renewed emphasis on the Green Road, quality of life, and standard of living systems. The world may alternatively move further into path-dependent blind drift with no outcome being progressive for the future of performance and development.

The capitalist world system has been in polycrises for half a century, and still no movement toward performance and development is in the wings. It thus seems that the capitalist world system itself is in a crisis of legitimacy and that socioeconomic performance is undergoing a continual turn for the worse.

12.3 Conclusion

This is the second book in the series applying political economy principles to core world problems, the first being O'Hara (2023). In this first volume, we outlined the principles from history and the current environment and applied them *explicitly* to nine core problems of the modern world. In this second volume in the series, this current volume, we do detail the principles in certain places, such as the Introduction and Chap. 5, but we sought to integrate the principles into the argument more in other chapters, rather than *highlighting* them as much as with the first volume. The reason for doing this is that, first, they had already been discussed exhaustively in volume one and in outline form in volume two. Periodically I remind readers of their importance, but I do not do it as much in this current volume. Nonetheless, the principles are just as important as in the other volume, and indeed we discuss the PoPE Contingency Paradigm in this current volume in that context.

The current volume applies some of these core principles to issues of long waves, hegemony, and climate change. In the process, it sought to innovate by recasting long waves to apply to questions of hegemony and climate change. The main empirical work in the volume involved the Netherlands, Britain, the US, and Chinese capitalism and some of their peripheral and semi-peripheral linkages. We also empirically scrutinized climate change over several millennia, structural polycrises especially in-between periods of hegemony, long waves for over 100 nations (and several regions) during the 1940s–2020s, and the rising conflict between liberal-democratic allies versus autocratic powers that may lead to wars as complex and widespread as the world wars of the past, or at least wars that have some similarity with the first two world wars (even if more regional in nature).

I encourage readers of this book to do further work on the 23 stylized facts and hypotheses developed in this volume (and others not explicitly stated), the theories and principles analyzed, and the methods utilized. I also encourage you to (re)look at the first volume in this series. And keep in mind that a third volume is in the wings (O'Hara Forthcoming). Otherwise, I hope you enjoy(ed) this book, and please do, where possible, write a review of it, use it in class, write about the issues covered in it, and communicate with me regarding what you think of the work (gperu.ohara@gmail.com). Thank you for your interest! ....Now to the Glossary, which is very important for this current volume.

References

O'Hara, Phillip Anthony. 2023. *Principles of institutional and evolutionary political economy: Applied to current world problems. Revised Edition*. Singapore: Springer Nature.

O'Hara, Phillip Anthony. Forthcoming. *Advances in political economy principles: Applied to world problems and issues.*

Glossary

This glossary is not intended to be exhaustive, simply indicative of some terms and scholars relevant to political economy, long waves, hegemonic power and climate change. For more detail on the political economy concepts, principles, terms and policies mentioned here see the *Encyclopedia of Political Economy,* edited by P.A. O'Hara (Routledge, 1999; 2 vols; paper edition 2001; pdf version 2022; Chinese Translation 2013), the *International Encyclopedia of Public Policy,* ed. P.A. O'Hara (GPERU; 4 vols; latest ed. 2022; available Online), and P.A. O'Hara, *Principles of Institutional and Evolutionary Political Economy: Applied to Current World Problems* (Springer Nature, Revised Edition, 2023). Please email me for assistance (ohara.gperu@gmail.com). See also *The Elgar Companion to Institutional and Evolutionary Economics*, edited by G.M. Hodgson, W.J. Samuels and M.R. Tool (Elgar, 1994, 2 vols), and *The Encyclopedia of Evolutionary and Institutional Economics*, edited by W. Elsner and W. Waller (Elgar, Forthcoming).

NOTE: Cross-references within this Glossary and the book are shown as (e.g.,):
"֍→ = Relevant entries, or chapter(s) to consult
REF: = A suitable reference for this topic.

British Hegemony *Pax Britannica* was a powerful world force that ruled the seas and much of the world between the 1820s and the 1880s. It emerged after the Revolutionary and Napoleonic Wars (1780–1815), especially after the Congress of Vienna (1815), when Britain (especially England; and to some degree also Scotland and Wales and, more conflictingly, Ireland) established global dominance in production, commerce, and finance (in that order), and derivatively military power. The political regime was based on liberal democracy, constitutional monarchy, free trade and crucial elements of civil society. The economic regime was based on coal (and its derivatives), the factory system, shipbuilding, trade and finance. The main class alliances were based around the bourgeoisie, landowners and Tories/Whigs. The British Empire comprised numerous dependent colonies, settler societies, trade and foreign investment outlets. During this time Britain underwent a very long and

P. A. O'Hara, *Long Waves of Growth, Hegemonic Power, and Climate Change in the World Economy*, https://doi.org/10.1007/978-981-96-4132-1

sustainable long wave upswing (with several short cycle declines) and the highest real GDP per capita in the world. Numerous contradictions contributed to the demise of *Pax Britannica*. The main ones being other nations such as the US and Germany copying and reaching beyond Britain and questioning its power. Britain itself lost its momentum due to inadequate technical education, innovation, corporate power, and scaled economies. First it lost production dominance, then commercial, and finally financial dominance. London continued to be a financial and commercial centre for quite some time into the twentieth century and beyond. As Britain's relative power continued for some time it relied more on its global empire, established institutions and culture to sustain, to some degree, its (deteriorating) wave and cyclical performance, until US hegemony arose and then declined.

֍→||Chap. 6|| ||Hegemony|| ||Dutch Hegemony|| ||US Hegemony||
֍→||Chinese Potential Hegemony||

REF: James Morris. 1992. *Pax Britannica Trilogy.* 3 vols. London: Folio Society. 1360pp.

Capitalism The four main characteristics of capitalism are (1) generalised wage labor (labor-power) exchanged for wages, and capital exchanged for profit; (2) the predominant commodity economy; and (3) capitalists owning/or controlling the means of production of buildings, machinery, equipment, commodities, and shareholdings, and (4) capitalist entrepreneurs (or their organisational equivalents) continually revolutionising products, processes, markets, resources and organisations available for capital and consumer goods markets. Capitalist economies operate through a fifth (5) sector, financial institutions, which is crucial for the flow of money and the generation of credit, shares and bonds, financial derivatives, advice, and organisational contributions. Several other spheres important for capitalism are (6) households for reproducing labor power and demand for consumer goods; (7) transportation hubs for promoting the circuit of capital; (8) states for generating public and quasi-public goods as well as club goods, military activities, and overseeing the workings of the circuit. A further component includes (9) core, periphery and semi-periphery relationships of trade, finance and production linkages and networks (including towns, cities, colonies, etc).

The circuit of social capital comprises the relational flows and stocks of money, resources, information, finance, people, and commodities between workplaces, households, financial institutions, states, and trading sectors. The spirit of capitalism is usually seen as the activity of (capitalist) innovators (or their organisational equivalents) doing something different in economic life: using money, advertising, and trade to direct these changes through markets, corporations, households, and regional/global economies. There are several varieties of capitalism, including, for instance, (a) Liberal-market forms of capitalism with advanced systems of parliamentary, public service and democratic systems of voting. (b) State capitalist systems usually have the key characteristics outlined above, but with major (often autocratic) state power for potential control of business, citizens, and linkages with the rest of the world. Social democratic forms of capitalism have most of the nine features shown above, with a state sector providing substantial social security, infrastructure, health, education along with the usual democratic institutions and increasingly the provision of climate change organisations. Other forms of capitalism also exist, such as fascist forms.

֍→||Varieties of Capitalism|| ||Circuit of Social Capital||
֍→||Circuit of Socioeconomic Dynamics|| ||Capitalism, Phases of Evolution||

REF1: Jürgen Kocka and Marcel van der Linden. Eds. 2018. *Capitalism: The Reemergence of a Historical Concept.* London: Bloomsbury Academic. Paper Ed.
REF2: Larry Neale and Geoffrey G. Williamson. Eds. 2014. *The Cambridge History of Capitalism.* 2 Vols. Cambridge: Cambridge University Press.
REF3: Joan Robinson. 1974. Capitalist Expansion. In J. Robinson, *Freedom and Necessity: An Introduction to the Study of Society*, 60–71. London: George Allen and Unwin. 3rd Impression.

Capitalism, Phases of Evolution Many political economists have hypothesized about the existence of phases of evolution of capitalism. Some of the key contributors include Karl Marx, Thorstein Veblen, Werner Sombart, John Commons, Kozo Uno, Robert Albritton, Eric Hobsbawm, Angus Maddison, Christopher Freeman and Franscisco Louçã, and many others. In many ways, a non-determinist view of long waves becomes an inquiry into the phases of evolution of capitalism, in which case many other scholars could be added to the list, such as Joseph Schumpeter and so on. All political economists need a theory and empirics of the evolution of capitalism to situate their analyses of its dynamics, problems and solutions.

Some scholars have argued that capitalism goes back thousands of years, since to them it is the networks of trade and finance that matter for capitalism, and the further these economic relations spread the more capitalist development evolves. Others believe that if not capitalism, at least various world-systems existed before capitalism, including those variously centring on China, the Middle East, and the Americas. Most political economists, however, are of the view that capitalism had its roots in the 1400s–1600s as feudalism experienced contradictory decline and mercantilism spread the motion of capitalism.

It is thus often said that the evolution of capitalism typically started with an inquiry into mercantilism, especially during the 1400s–1600s, being the first form in which its institutions develop by way of trade, merchants, sea-power, and the opening-up of the world economy to profit and accumulation. Much of the emphasis is given to the power provided by trade, especially by generating export income and the passing of imports into further exports through simple forms of quality improvement. The primary accumulation of gold and silver, slaves and workers were seen as a form of power by which national economies could develop industry, trade surplus and profits. Mercantilism has its contradictions especially in its limited development of an indigenous capitalist class of industrialists. Before such a class could sufficiently develop an agricultural revolution was required, along with agricultural capitalists, which notably evolved through the 1500s–1700s in several areas, especially in Europe and elsewhere. This revolution enabled the emergence of a larger profit, especially through machinery, fertilizer, special seeds, and greater knowhow of agricultural science. It also led to a class of landless laborers who often moved to the cities or otherwise eked out an existence on the land.

The Dutch were the first to develop a form of proto-capitalism through the agricultural revolution, innovations in windmills, shipping, fishing and land reclamation. This surplus from agriculture and an emerging proletariat population in the towns and cities led to the emergence of diverse groupings of scientists, entrepreneurs, capitalists, financiers, workers and landowners. They also specialised in colonial exploitation and the import-export of spices, herbs, tobacco, sugar, grain, and corn. For a time in the 1600s the Dutch led the first modern-world system of capitalism, during what was called the Little Ice Age which affected especially many other nations and regions.

As part of the North Sea area, Britain had learned much from the Dutch, and set out to develop their own form of capitalism. One act was to outlaw the export of processed Indian Textiles so their (British) domestic industry could develop, and secondly, use a combination of cotton, coal, mills and water-power to industrialize. This was done in an environment of laissez faire, class alliances between landowners, capitalists and their state representatives (Whigs, Tories). Industrialization spread from Britain to France, Germany, the USA and elsewhere later.

The decline in British hegemony as others copied and improved upon their methods, led to the phase of imperialism, big business and finance capital during the 1890s–1940s. The (European) imperialists agreed to divide Africa into different zones of influence, with further often implicit agreements regarding Asia and Latin America. Colonialisation was accelerated to heighten Euro-power, absorb the economic surplus, expand slave supply (often by other names), generate trade linkages, and exploit raw material and crop production. Meanwhile, through the world, big business and large financial institutions enabled economies of scale and scope to propel greater economic surplus, while workers exerted a counterveiling movement of power through unions, wage-settlements and conditions in many areas.

Declining *Pax Britannica* led to another form of counterveiling power by way of German and US expansion and consolidation. Germany underwent two bouts of accelerated warfare to promote their hegemony, as Japan joined their movement in the second world war, but failed as the world economy underwent the Great Depression and recovery, which was linked to expanding military activities and new innovations through to World War Two. Military success to the US (and their allies) led to a *Pax Americana* by the mid-1940s in concert with various White-Euro nations (and Japan) that were mostly reemerging from wartime destruction.

The new postwar corporate system established the US along with its European partners and Anglo-allies as the supreme power in the Cold War scenario of the Military Industrial Complex, with its nuclear threats, regional wars such as Korea and Vietnam, and its postwar system of Fordism, the Keynesian Welfare State, the regulated financial system, and the household-community spheres. This system enabled at least three decades of strong growth throughout much of the world, but the contradictions of Fordism and its institutions eventually led to its demise. Crises started to become quite major in the mid-1970s, became worse in the 1980s (especially in the core and periphery) and 1990s (including the Asian and Russian financial crises) and especially 2000s as the GFC emerged in 2007–2009, followed by the Eurodebt crisis and later the coronacrisis (effecting the whole world).

A concerted campaign emerged in the 1970s and 1980s to use the power of the state to reduce the power of workers and the community through free markets and the rule of capital; known as neoliberalism. The institutions of deregulated finance, free trade, individualism, corporate hegemony and multi-polar experiments failed to renew socioeconomic performance, however, as the new technology style generated only brief expansion of productivity (as R.J. Gordon showed), while the institutions of the state, economy and society also failed to live up to its promises (as argued by, e.g., Louçã, Perez and O'Hara). A series of polycrises have thus (re)emerged through decadal financial crises, debt crises, climate crisis, Pandemics, declining social capital in many areas, and a buildup in tension between the (previous) superpowers (and others). More recently Chinese potential hegemonic power has been escalating as its production dominance may lead to commercial and financial (along with military) dominance in the future. Alternatively, a multilateral system of arrangements may otherwise possibly provide production regimes for stimulating global or regional performance, although rising geopolitical conflict may render that unlikely.

֍→||Capitalism|| ||Long Waves|| ||Chaps. 3,5–11|| ||PoPE Contingency Paradigm||

REF: Robert Albritton. (With Richard Westra). 2022. *A Japanese Approach to Stages of Capitalist Development: What Comes Next?*. Second Edition. Cham, Switzerland: Palgrave Macmillan.

Cascading Tipping Points of Climate Change Climatic tipping points (TPs) are when changes occur in the climate systems that are sudden and represent a qualitative change where the future is more uncertain and subject to potential irreversibility. Cascading tipping points relate to the emergence of multiple tipping points, where they interdependently emerge through multiplier and accelerator forces leading to major increases in radiative forcing and temperature increases to the point where catastrophic climate crises emerge. There are at least 15 areas/forces of planet Earth where tipping points would coalesce resulting in points of no return. Currently we are already undergoing the early phases of tipping points relating to the destruction of (a) west Antarctic ice sheets, (b) Greenland ice sheets, (c) Arctic summer sea-ice, (d) Alpine glaciers, and (e) coral reefs. Currently, at mean temperature increases of between 1.07 °C and 1.20 °C (2020), relative to the 1850–1900 mean, and an *average global temperature rise* of just over 1.5 °C during 2024, while rises in the Arctic region (and some other areas) are approaching double the global average, we are likely already past the point of no return for many of these interdependent tipping points.

֍→||Long Waves of Climate Change|| ||Chaps. 4,9||

REF: Nico Wunderling, Anna S. von der Heydt, Yevgeny Aksenov, Stephen Barker, Robbin Bastiaansen, Victor Brovkin, Maura Brunetti, Victor Couplet, Thomas Kleinen, Caroline H. Lear, et al. 2024. Climate Tipping Point Interactions and Cascades: A Review, *Earth Systems Dynamics* 15: 41–74.

Chinese Potential Hegemony Since China began to open to the world in the late 1970s its political economic power has been increasing. Its production system has moved from specialising in mass production low-end consumer goods to medium and high-end technology goods. Now it leads the world in AI, electric vehicles and solar panels. It also has been expanding its power in commerce and finance, though these are less developed than its technology. China relies on state, private and strategic corporate alliances, though state companies dominate. It operates sophisticated financial institutions, though the state dominates and indebtedness in the property sector has been generating instability and macroeconomic malaise in recent years. Problematic medical and health institutions led to declining trust in the state during the covid crisis of the early 2020s. Increasingly autocratic trends have been increasing social conflict and/or emigration from the mainland and Hong Kong, as well as in the South China Sea. Alliances with other autocracies such as Russia, North Korea, Iran, and Myanmar have limited their moral power in the global community. Such contradictions may well inhibit the emergence of global Chinese hegemony as currently the US still out-performs it on the global stage though the latter's relative hegemony has been declining for many decades.

֍→||Chap. 8|| ||Hegemony|| ||Dutch Hegemony|| ||British Hegemony|| ||US Hegemony||

REF1: Asım Doğan. 2021. *Hegemony with Chinese Characteristics: From the Tributary System to the Belt and Road Initiative.* Oxon: Routledge.

REF2: Feng Zhang. 2015. *Chinese Hegemony: Grand Strategy and International Institutions in East Asian History*. Stanford, CA: Stanford University Press.

Circuit of Social Capital The Circuit of Social Capital (CSC) is a model developed by Karl Marx in volume two of *Capital* (the sphere of circulation), whereby the money (M) invested (exchanged) by capitalists into 'commodities' (C), such as labor power (LP) and means of production (MOP) (M↔C), is then followed by the 'hidden' abode of production (…P…), leading to the generation of output (C+c) in the form of commodities (including services) with a potential value greater (c) than that originally invested (M, C). This extra value is called surplus product (or service). Then the Keynesian problem of effective demand needs to be put into practice so potential value (surplus product, c) can be transformed into an actual surplus (s), in the form of surplus value ([C+c]↔[M+s]), which is represented as m or in this case 's'. Then, commodity value (C+c) is exchanged (↔) for M+s. The 's' may be smaller or equal to 'c' after the effective demand phase of the circuit. The 's', surplus value, can then be called profit, p, also paying bank fees (i=interest), shareholders (d=dividends) and monies to owners of property (r=rent): s = p+i+d+r. Hence: CSC = M↔C(LP,MOP) … P …[C+c] ↔[M+s] ‖ s=p+i+d+r ‖. …

Then the process of reinvestment can be activated, where some of the profits (p', retained earnings, reinvested), plus possibly bank credit (bc) and monies from issuing new shares or equity [e] is invested into the circuit of money capital, viz.: p'+bc+e→M'↔C'(LP,MOP) … P' … [C'+c] ↔[M'+s] … : Then the circular process can be set in motion to a new higher (or lower) level, through repeated circuitries/cycles. There can be interruptions to the circuit at any point which usually lead to crises if they are major. Taxes and government spending, as well as monetary policy, may be included in the circuit. In devising the CSC Marx was influenced by the physiocrats and especially the *Economic Tableau*. Essentially the CSC is a circular stock-flow diagram illustrating the major transactions/interactions of the process whereby the investments of capitalists are potentially able to eventually make a profit. In a wider schema the CSC can be transformed into the *Systemic Circuit of Social Capital* (SCSC) which includes the ecological, environmental, social and political processes linked to the CSC (O'Hara 2009, ch 8); there is also an international circuit of social capital (Palloix 1975).

→||Circuit of Socioeconomic Dynamics|| ||Economic Surplus|| →||Circular Flow Model (CFM) & Circular Stock-Flow Model (CSFM)||

REF1: Karl Marx. 1885. *Capital: Volume 2: The Process of Circulation of Capital.* Harmondsworth: Penguin, 1978. Introduced by Ernest Mandel. Translated by David Fernbach.

REF2: Christian Palloix. 1975. The Internationalization of Capital and the Circuit of Social Capital. In *International Firms and Modern Imperialism: Selected Readings,* 63–88, ed. Hugo Radice. Harmondsworth, Penguin.

REF3: Phillip Anthony O'Hara. 2009. *Growth and Development in the Global Political Economy: Social Structures of Accumulation and Modes of Regulation.* London: Routledge. Paper Edition.

Circuits of Socioeconomic Dynamics (CSD) The CSD is also known as the Pathways and Circuits of Socioeconomic Reproduction (CSR), with related terms including the Socioeconomic Circuits, and the Socioeconomic Pathways and Circuits. They represent a dynamic, systemic, evolutionary structure of institutions, technologies, ecologies, persons, classes, genders, ethnic groups, species and resources set in motion through historical time. It also involves domestic, international, global and often also interplanetary and spatial processes. Usually it takes a specific form, such as a dominant aspect of an economic and political system, for instance, some form of capitalism. It could though be applied to other types of economic systems, such as feudalism, socialism, and Islamic forms of governance. It includes structures (stocks) and flows (movements of money, people, goods, services, etc). For instance, firstly, it involves the circuit of internal and interactive relationships within and between (1) households, (2) eco-geospatial resources, (3) technology and production systems (e.g., within corporations), (4) financial institutions and roles, (5) states and governance institutions, (5) trade and international relations, and (6) the total system[s].

The degree of relational-dynamic synchrony within and between all parts of the CSD determines its overall performance in terms of its major strategic inputs and outputs. In a capitalist system, some of the major outputs/inputs include products and services; but other strategic outputs may include systemic stability and quality of life; as well as defence and offence; in addition to trade and travel. Whatever strategic inputs/outputs are given priority will hopefully be involved in the active flow of the circuit of interaction within and between the parts of the whole. The relationship within and between the inputs and outputs as well as the systems and sub-systems are not usually simple, but are typically subject to nonlinear changes, differing levels of risk and uncertainty over cycles and waves, circular (interdependent) and cumulative (magnified) causative (CCC) impacts, of an upward and downward nature. They involve *complexity.* There are also numerous potentially contradictory processes within and between the systems and subsystems in the CSD, which interact through CCC, risk/uncertainty, and historico-evolutionary processes. The whole is greater than the sum of the parts. This means that inputs and outputs are subject to magnified and often unpredictable movements through time vis-a-vis various circuitous, historical, developmental, evolutionary, cyclical and wave-like motions.

֍֍→||Holism|| ||Capitalism|| ||Circuit of Social Capital|| ||Chaps. 1,5–9|| ||New Long Wave Method (NLWM)||

֍→||Circular and Cumulative Causation|| ||Circular Flow Model (CFM) & Circular Stock-Flow Model (CSFM)||

REF: Phillip Anthony O'Hara. 2025. *Long Waves of Growth, Hegemonic Power, and Climate Change in the World Economy: Dutch, British, US and Chinese Capitalism and Structural Crises.* Singapore: Springer Nature.

Circular and Cumulative Causation (CCC) CCC is a concept in political economy, drawing especially from Gunnar Myrdal and Nicholas Kaldor, comprising two main movements. The first involves interdependency. Political economy involves processes that are intertwined. Problems tend to be caused by multiple factors that interrelate (multifactor approach). The second involves magnification. When problems and processes involve multiple factors that interrelate, they tend to produce an accelerating impact. This involves positive feedback (and at times negative feedback) between multiple variables. Gunnar Myrdal, for instance, examined the interrelated factors that cause poverty on the one hand and riches on the other. Differential skills, (un)employment, education, and remuneration, as well as discrimination, produce differential outcomes. He suggested, for instance, more extensive, accessible and free education to help moderate the differential and increase outcomes for the disadvantaged.

Nicholas Kaldor examined CCC from the point of view of regions and productivities. Aggregate demand tends to provide funds for investment and consumption (plus government and net exports), and with economies of scale and innovation these funds can generate high productivity, which in turn may expand exports, and thereby world income. But areas with low levels of aggregate demand, low economies, and modest productivity tend to be relatively worse off. These differentials can thus become exacerbated. The principle of CCC states that one needs to apply the method of CCC to comprehend socioeconomic problems and processes. CCC usually involves emergence and complexity. (One also may need to take into account backward (negative-feedback) effects.)

⑨→||Chaps. 1–12||

REF1: Sebastian Berger. Ed. 2009. *The Foundations of Non-Equilibrium Economics: The Principle of Circular and Cumulative Economics.* Oxon. Routledge.

REF2: Mats Lundahl. 2021. *The Dynamics of Poverty: Circular, Cumulative Causation, Value Judgments, Institutions and Social Engineering in the World of Gunnar Myrdal.* Charn: Switzerland: Palgrave Macmillan.

REF3: Nicholas Kaldor. 1972. The Irrelevance of Equilibrium Economics. *Economic Journal* 82(328): 1237–1255.

REF4: Gunnar Myrdal. 1968. *Asian Drama: An Inquiry into the Poverty of Nations. 3 Vols.* New York: Twentieth Century Fund.

Circular Economy The circular economy is a concept stating that we should centre on the political economy evolving from cradle to grave to cradle (C↔G↔C). This is the idea that waste can be a resource rather than simply a source of accumulated unproductive materials. All waste needs to be reinvested back into productive activities such as fertiliser, recyclable commodities and products, and reinvigorated lifestyles. Promoting the continual circuit of the economy is thus said to enhance the life process of the world and its constituents. This is a commendable objective. But there are limits to the circularity of the economy, known under the terms of circular gap, metabolic rift, and so on. For instance, there are limits to recycling, such as entropy. The more we use a resource the less of it is available for reusing, it thus becomes increasingly entropic or less usable through time. It is for this reason that some believe economics is all about turning resources into less available resources.

Economies, for instance, often use old growth forests to create tables and when they are worn out, they languish in garbage dumps. It is better to re-use them as wood chips, or better still use sustainable renewable forests to build tables and use them when worn out by re-working them again into usable resources. Better-still to reduce people's need for commodities by concentrating on quality-of-life issues for generating utility rather than promoting GDP which generates waste and entropy. Also, better to promote walking, bicycling or public transport rather than private vehicles. If private vehicles are required, better to generate electric vehicles through using electricity generated by renewable resources such as solar, wind, or hydrogen rather than coal fired power stations, petrol or gas.

The circular economy is thus virtuous, but because of entropy (which reduces the extent to which it is completely circular) it needs to be accompanied by other ways of utilising resources, such as (a) promoting quality of life rather than growth per se; (b) generating renewable resources such as the sun and wind; and (c) engaging in preventative health.

⑨→||Long Waves of Climate Change|| || Metabolic Rift|| ||Chaps. 4,9||

REF1: Aldo Alvarez-Risco, Marc A. Rosen, Shyla Del-Aguila-Arcentales. Eds, 2023. *Towards a Circular Economy: Transdisciplinary Approach for Business.* Cham, Switzerland: Springer Nature.

REF2: Julian Kirchherr, Nan-Hua Nadja Yang, Frederik Schulze-Spüntrup, Maarten J. Heerink, and Kris Hartley. 2023. Conceptualizing the Circular Economy (Revisited): An Analysis of 221 Definitions. *Resources, Conservation & Recycling* 194: 107001. https://doi.org/10.1016/j.resconrec.2023.107001

Circular Flow Model (CFM) & Circular Stock-Flow Model (CSFM) The circular flow model (CFM) is perhaps the most powerful tool in political economy, but more so when we extend the model and include stocks as well (particularly institutions, technologies, ecologies, and networks, ITEN). A major inspiration for the model was the "blood-flow" analysis of William Harvey. The CFM was developed variously by Richard Cantillon, François Quesnay, Karl Marx, J.M. Keynes, Richard Stone and others for analyzing the circular movement of financial, physical and service activities that contribute to political economic dynamics. It was formalized by Wassily Leontief in 1928. In this one can use 2–6 sector models. An expansive model uses (1) households, (2) business, (3) finance/banking, (4) state, (5) world economy, and (6) ecology/environment. The circular economy model comes to life more when using stocks and flows, and especially dynamic structures of ITEN. Thus, when we include the physico-historical institutions, of the household, business, finance, state, world economy, and ecology/environment we can analyze the evolution of institutions/organizations, along with the flow of resources, services and labor, as well as the stock of inventories, money, savings, knowledge, routines, governance measures, habits and conventions.

֍→||Circuit of Social Capital|| ||Circuits of Socioeconomic Dynamics|| ||Chap. 1||

REF1: Hans Gottfried Nutzinger. 1972. Circular Flow. In *Marxism, Communism, and Western Society; A Comparative Encyclopedia*, Vol 1, 422–435. Ed. C.D. Kernig. New York: Herder and Herder. (Part of an 8 Volume work.)

REF2: Wassily Leontief. 1991. The Economy as a Circular Flow. *Structural Change and Economic Dynamics* 2(1): 181-212. (PhD. Thesis. Originally published in German, 1928.)

REF3: Paul A. Samuelson. 1991. Leontief's 'the economy as a circular flow': An introduction. *Structural Change and Economic Dynamics* 2(1): 177–179.

REF4: Julian Kirchher. 2022. Circular economy and growth: A critical review of "post-growth" circularity and a plea for a circular economy that grows. *Resources, Conservation & Recycling* 179: 06033. https://doi.org/10.1016/j.resconrec.2021.106033

Class Class is a concept that relates to the socioeconomic position of people in society, where they stand compared with others. It is thus in part an invidious distinction, but it also does often relate to 'real' standing, while often it links to perceived standing. There are different theories of class. One theory depends upon the class position of people vis-à-vis income and/or wealth: upper, lower and middle classes. Another relates to people's position vis-à-vis their relationship to surplus value production, distribution and exchange. In this context people may be a member of the working class, the capitalist class, or the subsumed class necessary for the others to reproduce. People often undertake different class roles, such as worker, capitalist, domestic laborer, etc. Class can also be conceived as one relating to property control/ownership, vis-à-vis the means of production; or power, how much power one wields in multifarious ways. Often to solve a world problem one needs to examine classes, genders, ethnicities, species, intelligent machines and other heterogeneous roles played by people and others in the world, regional, national, subnational environments.

⊛→||Heterogeneous agents and groups|| ||Gender|| ||Ethnicity|| ||Species|| ||Age||

REF1: Massimo Modonesi, Alfonso García Vela and María Vignau Loría. Eds. 2022. *The Concept of Social Class in Contemporary Marxist Theory*. Stutgatt: Verlag.

REF2: Charles H. Anderson. 1974. *The Political Economy of Social Class*. Englewood Cliffs, New Jersey: Prentice-Hall.

Climate Change, Hegemony and Long Waves Climate change is the process of climate variability on planet Earth, that especially becomes manifested in differential temperature changes in the atmosphere, in the seas, on the surface, in the Arctic, the Antarctic, the Equator, and so on. Waves of climate change have been typical of Earth's history over the past 4.6 billion years. It variously manifests itself in cycles and waves of ice ages and ice retreats, and more specifically in cycles and waves of extreme cold periods changing to extreme hot periods. Since especially the 1970s global warming has manifested itself in rising GHGs, floods and droughts, heatwaves, extreme wildfires, glacial retreat, coastal erosion, rising waterways, declining habitats, and species extinction.

Long wave growth and hegemonic processes have been affected by climate changes. For instance, the Dutch Golden Age (hegemony and long wave upswings) occurred during the (global) Little Ice Age of the 1600s, which especially impacted (notably initially) the Northern Hemisphere. In Europe and other areas, it is said to have contributed to droughts, famines, floods, and especially cold waves, which themselves affected the intensity of riots, rebellions, and wars. The Dutch and Japanese were able to surmount these anomalies through innovations and adaptations. The Netherlands, for instance, developed well-conceived behavioural changes and innovations to sail against the wind in the open seas, using windmills to reduce the impact of floods, and technological improvements to reclaim lowlands for market gardening and settlement.

Britain experienced long wave upswing during the 1820s–1860s while hegemony continued until the 1880s. It saw declining temperatures during the 1700s, the final cycle downswing of the little ice age from 1800 until the 1840s, and rising temperatures in the second half of the wave/hegemony (1840s–1860s/1880s).

The US experienced declining or constant temperatures during their main years of hegemony and long wave upswing (1940s–1970), due to a combination of albedo and volcanic impacts, and rising rates thereafter onto the present (ironically during an era of declining growth and relative hegemony).

The Chinese recent experience with well-developed long waves of growth per capita since especially the 1980s coincided with the trend to rising global temperatures, and more latterly to global and regional climate crises such as major successive heat waves, droughts, floods, rising waterways that threaten populations, and the socioeconomic and ecological conflicts that emerge from these anomalies.

According to NASA, the year 2023 has been the hottest year ever, at 1.36 °C above the 1850–1900 average, while 2024 is expected to be even worse, ditto for future ones. The Northern Hemisphere tends to be much hotter than the Southern Hemisphere, especially around the Arctic Circle and the tropics.

֍→||Chaps. 1,4–9|| ||Hegemony|| ||Long Waves|| || Long Waves of Climate Change||

REF: Rajib Shaw. 2022. *Handbook on Climate Change and Disasters*. Cheltenham: Edward Elgar.

Community's Joint Stock of Knowledge [CJSK] The concept of the CJSK is a communitarian perspective of the origins of property, knowledge and wealth, that places emphasis on the collective generation process. In contemporary social economies wealth and property are seen as produced in unison, by various individuals within groups, institutions and organisations. But the perspective goes further than this by indicating that knowledge is a social process, residing in the general dynamic processual stock of brains, journals, books, cultures, practices, technologies, and institutions in motion throughout the community. Even in capitalist political economies it is argued that wealth and property is generated primarily by the cultural transmission of skills, techniques, appliances, knowledge, practices, designs and plans of a multitude of actors, groups, institutions, nations and world processes.

While the assets can be produced in unison, the community's joint stock of knowledge can be encapsulated by certain vested interests through numerous networks of control, institutions, patents, takeovers, legal challenges, monopoly powers, and classes. The principle of the CJSK states that one should recognise this collective social wealth and study its ongoing generation, as it can be a useful source for alleviating global problems. Since knowledge, property and wealth are collectively generated it should be relatively evenly distributed throughout the community not only as income, but also as a source of collective investment into public goods such as education, health, infrastructure, public policy initiatives, ecological sustainability and climate change mitigation and adaptation.

֍→||Chaps 1–12|| ||Innovation||

REF1: William M. Dugger. 2015. Technology and Property: Knowledge and the Commons. *Review of Radical Political Economics.* 48(1): 111–126.

REF2: Phillip Anthony O'Hara. 1999. Thorstein Veblen's Theory of Collective Social Wealth, Instincts, and Property Relations. *History of Economic Ideas* 7(3): 153–179.

Complexity The principle of complexity states that one needs to situate the problems of the world in their historical, relational, and situational context to comprehend how they emerged and how we may reduce their negative impact. The temporal (historical) emergence of problems needs to be understood. The relational networks and interdependencies associated with the horizontal emergence of the problems need to be scrutinized. And the way in which the vertical emergence of the problems as they link individuals with groups and institutions, as well as nations and the whole world, need to be comprehended. This involves concepts such as path dependence, lock-in, non-equilibrium, uncertainty, evolutionary metamorphosis and blind drift. Only by examining the contradictory circular and cumulative nature of the behaviour of heterogeneous groups and agents through an uncertain and evolutionary path of emergence can innovations potentially be enacted to tackle these complex world problems.

֍→||Chaps. 1–12|| ||Emergence|| ||Circular and Cumulative Causation ||
REF: Ping Chen, Wolfram Elsner, Andreas Pyka. Eds. 2025. *International Handbook of Complexity Economics*. Oxon: Routledge.

Concept A concept in political economy is an idea, based around a realistic process/thought, which seeks to comprehend the process/thought in more detail. For instance, the concept of historical specificity states that historical time, phases of evolution, social provisioning and transformational processes are important in the generation/resolution of world problems, while the principle of historical specificity states that one must be cognizant of these historical changes and processes in understanding as well as in ameliorating the intensity of world problems. The concept of heterogeneous agents and groups states that world problems involve different agents and groups often in different ways, both in the generation of the problem and a myriad of potential forms of resolution, while the principle of heterogeneous agents and groups states that one must be cognizant of these agents and groups in the process of both understanding and trying to ameliorate world problems (such as climate change, sustainable growth, and concentrations of power).

֍→||Chaps. 1–12|| ||Principle||
REF1: Dugger, William M. 1995. Veblenian Institutionalism: The Changing Concepts of Inquiry, *Journal of Economic Issues* 29(4): 1013–1028.
REF2: James Ronald Stanfield. 2011. Some Social Economics Concepts for Future Research. *Forum for Social Economics* 40(1): 7–17.

Contradiction and Creative Destruction The concept of contradiction is the idea that everything exists in a potential conflict, trade-off, opposition, dichotomy and so on, with other things, that operates at all levels of the political economy, including practices of groups and agents, as well as theories, concepts and principles. These contradictions are important to analyse because they usually majorly impact on the problems and processes investigated. Some of the dominant contradictions include that between (a) the vested interests versus the common good, (b) the instrumental and ceremonial functions of institutions, (c) the disembedded economy and the double movement, (d) plus the usual oppositions between capital and labor; industry and finance; monopoly and competition; state and capital; urban and regional; nation/region versus nation/region; capital/consumption and the environment; men and women (gender); ethnic group versus ethnic group; consumers versus producers; industrial capitalists versus money capitalists; innovators versus existing routine-makers; and so on. The principle of contradiction and creative destruction states one should analyse the destructive contradictions associated with a problem or a process to comprehend its complex workings, including for innovation and policy purposes to potentially ameliorate the problem (or otherwise).

֍||Chaps. 1–12|| ||Disembedded Economy|| ||Creative Destruction||

REF1: David Harvey. 2014. *Seventeen Contradictions and the End of Capitalism.* Oxford: Oxford University Press.

REF2: Paul Diesing. 1999. *Hegel's Dialectical Political Economy.* Boulder, CO: Westview Press.

REF3: Phillip Anthony O'Hara. 2006. The Contradictory Dynamics of Globalization. In *Globalization and the Third World: A Study of Negative Consequences*, 17–35, eds. B.N. Ghosh and Halil M. Guven. New York: Palgrave Macmillan. https://link.springer.com/chapter/10.1057/9780230502567_2

Coronacrisis The Coronacrisis is a global health and socioeconomic crisis involving a viral infection that started in China during late 2019 and spread throughout the whole world during 2020, thus becoming a Pandemic in the sense of having widespread infections and deaths around the globe. There have been numerous variants and subtypes of the SARS-Cov-2 virus during 2019–2023 that have been of concern which has led to Coronavirus disease 2019 (Covid-19), as it is called, undergoing various waves of several hundred million infections and more than 20 million "excess-deaths" throughout the world. Governance health principles put in place to limit the spread of the disease have been variable from region to region, including personal protective measures (e.g., masks), case and contact tracing, social distancing, isolation and management, vaccines, a degree of international collaboration, lockdowns, etc. Political economy innovation and governance measures to ameliorate the anomaly have included functional finance and private/public innovation/investment to generate and distribute vaccines, public health infrastructures, informational communication, discretionary fiscal and monetary policies, and public health principles put into action.

֍→||Chap. 9||

REF1: Phillip Anthony O'Hara. 2022. Global Coronavirus Pandemic Crisis and Future Crisis Prevention. *Panoeconomicus* 68(5): 587–623. https://doi.org/10.2298/PAN2105587O

REF2: S. Kaplan, J. Lefler, and D. Zilberman. 2022. The Political Economy of COVID-19. *Applied Economic Perspectives of Policy* 44(2): 477–488. https://doi.org/10.1002/aepp.13164

Creative Destruction Creative destruction is the global trend for capitalism to seek creative means for innovative profit, such as through product and process innovation, expansion of market relations, new means of energy provision and changes in competition. It ever-while destroys cultures, relationships, skills, businesses, ecologies, and networks in the very creative process of innovative profit generation. Creative destruction also relates to capitalism's tendency to expand on a global scale, with uneven regional consequences, as it expands markets, production, and finance throughout the world. Expansion of these relationships are especially operating through production networks and commodity chains to enhance value chains associated with profit, intangible value and financial asset value. Capitalism undergoes waves of unstable growth of creative destruction through historical time, due to uncertainty, insufficient demand, supply bottlenecks, swarms of technological change, climate change, changes in hegemonic power, and differential phases of institutional instability. The ongoing dynamic of innovation and competition for capitalism is said to provide a potential basis for its dynamic thrust, ongoing cycles and waves, and spirit of enterprise.

֍→||Neo-Schumpeterian Political Economy||

REF1: Joseph Alios Schumpeter, 1950. The Process of Creative Destruction, 81–86. In J.A. Schumpeter. *Capitalism, Socialism and Democracy.* 3rd edition. New York: Harper.

REF2: Philippe Aghion, Céline Antonin, Simon Bunel, and Jodie Cohen-Tanugi. 2021. *The Power of Creative Destruction - Economic Upheaval and the Wealth of Nations.* Boston: Harvard University Press.

Crises A crisis is a turning point for the worse for an area or sector of a political economy. During a crisis uncertainty rises, trust declines, and asset prices usually start to fall. There are several types of crises. The first is associated with a business cycle peak when boom turns to recession, speculative bubbles usually burst, and exuberance turns to panic (e.g., Juglar cycles). These are typical of the recessions in many nations during 1974–1975, 1980–1982, 1990–1992, 2000–2001, 2008–2009ff, and 2021. The second type of crisis is a financial crisis, which is usually closely linked with business cycles, but may appear before or during recessions. For instance, the stock market collapse of 1987 was not directly linked to the recession of 1990–1992 in many nations. The Asian financial crisis of 1997–1998 was somewhat autonomous from Euro-American dynamics. The Global Financial Crisis (GFC) of 2008–2009 started with the subprime crisis in the US and then spread to Europe and many other core economies. A financial crisis usually occurs once the upper turning point of the business cycle has been reached, and it has already turned into recession. In other words, it is caused by the business cycle recession and usually recedes once lender of last resort and associated policies provide liquidity to the system. There are many other types of crises, such as crises of legitimacy, crises of governance, crises of climate change, polycrises, crises of distrust, as well as those caused by wars and pandemics.

֍→||Long Waves of Growth|| ||Business Cycles|| ||Speculative Bubbles||
֍→||Chaps. 5–8,9|| ||Polycrises|| ||Juglar Cycles||Kitchin Cycles||

REF: Phillip Anthony O'Hara. 2008. Economic Crises. In *International Encyclopedia of the Social Sciences*. Vol 2, 233–236. Ed. William A. Darity. New York: Macmillan Reference.

Culture There are numerous ways of looking at culture. The one that is more embedded in the contemporary culture is that culture is associated with the arts of classical music, literature, performance and distinguished personalities. A closely related view is that culture is associated with the popular arts of music, theatre, television, the internet, politics and the media. A third one draws a distinction between high and low culture, the former being the distinguished arts and personalities, and the latter is associated with such things as football, media, television and perhaps politics.

A more authentic view of culture draws from Veblenian institutionalism, that culture is the way of life of the community in a broad sense of including the habits of groups of people, their beliefs, their ways of earning a living, their mannerisms, how they engage in consumption, their preferences, and their behaviours/habits of thought and action (as developed by e.g., Anne Mayhew). The Veblenian concept of culture seeks to develop an anthropological view of people's multifarious ways of life, their interaction with other groups, and their beliefs and lifestyles. The principle of culture states that one should utilise a cultural analysis to situate, contextualise, comprehend and help to solve anomalies that beset such cultures.

At a broader level, there are apparently several scholarly approaches to culture in political economy, such as those associated with Veblenian, 'new', and sociological political economy, but no real attempts to investigate their potential interactions, similarities and differences between, and potential associations that could result in closer analysis of these apparently autonomous views of culture. Culture is potentially very important for understanding booms and slumps, crises, long waves and especially the nexus between the eco-spatial and techno-institutional dimensions of reality, especially in relation to the role of habits, routines, norms, mores, and broad visions required to scrutinise these anomalies.

There are also theories of culture that are quite different from the "way of life of the community" perspective, being more concerned with the beliefs and values of the participants in the society, especially relating to their nature and degree of trust, ideology and skills of its members (as developed by, e.g., Joel Mokyr).

֍→||Disembedded Economy|| ||Hegemony|| ||Chaps. 5–8 ||

REF1: Anne Mayhew. 1994. Culture. In *The Elgar Companion to Institutional and Evolutionary Economics*, 119–124. Eds. Geoffrey M Hodgson, Warren J. Samuels and Marc R. Tool. Cheltenham: Edward Elgar.

REF2: Joel Mokyr. 2018. *A Culture of Growth: The Origins of the Modern Economy.* New Jersey: Princeton University Press.

REF3: Phillip Anthony O'Hara. 2004. Cultural Contradictions of Global Capitalism. *Journal of Economic Issues* 38(2): 413–420. https://doi.org/10.1080/00213624.2004.11506701

Cycles of Climate Change Nicola Scafetta from the University of Naples, Federica II. attempts to explain many of the crucial long and short cycles of climate change through a model comprising several core variables. The core thesis of the Scafetta-Bianchini model is that the periodic movement of the planets/Sun in the solar system (including Mercury, Venus, Earth, Mars, Jupiter, Saturn, Uranus, Neptune [and Pluto]) generate a series of systematic oscillations. These oscillations create periodic changes in three core processes: first in solar activity, solar luminosity, and solar wind; secondly, in the electromagnetic field (EMF) of the solar system; and thirdly, in the gravitational field (GF) of the solar system. These three impacts on the solar system in turn affect both the periodic changes in the amount of dust and cosmic radiation entering the Earth's atmosphere, which in turn influence the periodic cloudiness which induces albedo impacts; and the albedo changes have influences on the periodic oscillations in total solar radiation (TSR) reaching Earth's surface; which in turn produces wave and cycle type changes on the Earth's climate.

Scafetta and cowriters demonstrate the existence of several well-correlated cycles and waves of planetary-orbital and global temperature dynamics that signify the importance of these interactions. For instance, they show the relationship between groups of 10-year sunspot ('Schwabe') cycles, 60-year 'Milanković waves', 1200-year 'millennial (plus) waves', and global temperatures on planet Earth, including some instances when IPCC empirics *may* have under-estimated the importance of these planetary-orbital processes for climate change.

→ ||Chap. 4|| ||Long Waves of Climate Change||

REF: Nicola Scafetta and Antonio Bianchini. 2023. Overview of the Spectral Coherence between Planetary Resonances and Solar and Climate Oscillations. *Climate* 11(44): 77. https://doi.org/10.3390/cli11040077

Disembedded Economy The disembedded economy is a core conceptual contradiction of capitalism studied by Karl Polanyi and several others. It posits that market capitalism tends to develop relatively abstract (pure) commodity relations at the expense of reciprocity, redistribution, community markets and householding. This tendency leaves many groups and agents lacking in supportive resources and social networks thus inhibiting systemic reproduction in the long-term. Pure exchange leaves usually profit for business but at the expense of destruction of social, ecological and financial resources for agents and groups. The social costs of business posed by purely market relations leaves many species decimated as business moves on to exploit other commodities, and when they are similarly decimated business moves onto another species to exploit. Similar relationships hold with land and labor, as land is used and then abandoned while further land is exploited, and so on ad infinitum. Labor is often used to the extreme and replaced by more labor which is then used and abused, and so on. Money is also used in this way, as debt is generated, profits are realised, and as the overexpanded financial system leads to crisis, more money is pushed into the system, leading to greater potential fragility (and debt deflation). In this way, money, labor, and land (plus knowledge) are special resources that need protection since pure markets typically lead to abuse, which generates a series of double movements against the free market to protect the system.

This series of double movements are often generated to counter the hyper-expansion of free markets, competition, and to provide protection through redistribution, reciprocity, householding and informal markets. Families often protect labor by generating trust, support networks, and education. States often provide finance to labor for situations of unemployment, underemployment, crises and disarray; as well as for environmental, functional finance, and discretionary fiscal and monetary purposes. Corporations try and embed the economy by degrees of oligopoly, restrictive practices, economies of scale and internalisation. Civil society groups and NGOs can protect labor and the environment through handouts, support movements for environmental protection and direct action to increase reciprocity and householding.

Historically, often the economy goes through cycles of embeddedness and disembeddedness, as disembeddedness often leads to these double movements, while if the double movements evolve too far movements can push back and support pure exchange relations for business. This can lead to further actions of the double movement as social movements, states and corporations try and embed the economy more fully through social and ecological programs and financial insurance schemes. And so on, ad infinitum. The disembedded economy has generated much discourse about the trend to crisis and social instability, and the counter trend to protection and support.

֍→||Creative Destruction|| ||Culture|| ||Circuit of Socioeconomic Dynamics||
֍→||Contradictions|| ||Polycrises||

REF1: James Ronald Stanfield. 1986. *The Economic Thought of Karl Polanyi Lives and Livelihood.* New York: Palgrave Macmillan.
REF2: Karl Polanyi. (2024). *The Great Transformation: The Political and Economic Origins of Our Time.* Introduction by Gareth Dale. Penguin Books. (First published in 1944.)

Dutch Hegemony The Dutch Golden Age is a period (1600–1650) in Dutch history when their social economy represented the most vibrant, innovative and creative period in both Dutch and possibly the world's existence at the time and arguably since. Probably only the British experience during the industrial revolution (1820–1870), the US's during the postwar golden age (1940s–1970s), and the Chinese during the 1980s–2010s, are comparable waves over the centuries.

Some date Dutch hegemony from 1580 to 1620, when its rise was rapid and emergent (with two long waves), while others put it at 1600–1650, and many date it during the whole of the 1600s, including the rapid rise plus its continual evolution and transformation. It represented an apogee for the renaissance, reformation and economy when the Netherlands and especially Holland had the most innovative technologies, most buoyant society and most integrative culture in the world. While much of Europe was subject to war, religious intolerance and the Little Ice Age (including the regional or global crisis of the 1600s), the Dutch managed to surmount these anomalies, rise-up, and create a most forward-looking form of social capitalism. Within the Netherlands mercantilism was typically limited, but throughout Dutch colonies mercantile exploitation through wars, monopolies, slavery and massacres were widespread.

During Dutch hegemony protestants, Jews and others who were being ostracized, denounced or killed in other places could move to the low countries and potentially thrive. It was a land of modest religious tolerance, although it was subject to some of the most ferocious forms of protestant (especially Lutheran) internal arguments and rebellions, especially between those espousing Lutheran orthodoxy and those into more heterodox forms of Protestantism. During this time the Dutch achieved impressive long wave upswings, global hegemony and rising standards of living (the 'Dutch Golden Age').

֍→||Chap. 5|| ||Hegemony|| ||Culture|| ||Long Waves||

REF1: Helmer Helmers and Geert Janssen. Eds. 2018. *The Cambridge Companion to the Dutch Golden Age.* Cambridge: Cambridge University Press. 428pp.

REF2: Eric Wilson. 2008. *The Savage Republic: 'De Indis' of Hugo Grotius, Republicanism, and Dutch Hegemony within the Early Modern World-System (c. 1600–1619).* Leiden & Boston: Nijhoff Publishers.

East, Central and South European Long Wave Group The most important scholar in long wave history was Nicolai Kondratiev and the Moscow Conjuncture Institute undertook crucial theory, empirics and criticism into long waves during the 1920s. It is thus not surprising that 'long waves' has become a core research topic for those from Eastern, Central and Southern European areas especially in recent decades. For instance, a heterogeneous group of such scholars have been publishing on long waves in English and other languages. The work they do is quite varied, including long waves per se, also hegemony, and other long-term trends, such as Big History. They have also been publishing jointly with Western scholars. Some of the prominent members of this multifarious group include Leonid Grinin, Anton Grinin, Andrey Korotayev, and Arno Tausch. It also includes others including Eirini Ozouni, Constantinos Katrakylidis and Grigoris Zarotiadis. These works are referenced in Chaps. 1–3 especially above. There are other works on long waves and similar fluctuations by Svetlana Kirdina (2015), V. Dementyev, and so on. They seem to be the most vibrant and most innovative group of long wave scholars at present.

֍→||Chaps. 1–3||

REF1: Svetlana Kirdina. Ed. 2015. *The Evolution of Economic Theory: Economic Reproduction, Technology, Institutions.* Saint Petersburg: Aletheia. (In Russian.)

REF2: Leonid Grinin, Andrey Korotayev, and Arno Tausch. 2016. *Economic Cycles, Crises, and the Global Periphery.* Zurich: Springer.

REF3: Eirini Ozouni, Constantinos Katrakylidis and Grigoris Zarotiadis (2018) Technology Evolution and Long Waves: Investigating their Relation with Spectral and Cross Spectral Analysis. *Journal of Applied Economics* 21(1): 160–174.

REF4: Andrey E. Tyulin, Alexander A. Chursin, Julia V. Ragulina, Victoria V. Akberdina, and Alexander V. Yudin. 2023. Development of Kondratieff's Theory of Long Waves: The Place of the AI Economy Humanization in the 'Competencies-Innovations-Markets' Model. *Humanities and Social Sciences Communications* 10(54): https://doi.org/10.1057/s41599-022-01434-8

Economic Surplus The roots of the concept of the economic surplus go back to the classical economists and Marx. In modern times, it was specifically resurrected by Paul Baran as a term to analyse development and underdevelopment (potential and actual). An economic surplus is defined in numerous ways, one of which is to consider it as net income over costs (Y-C). It can be examined from the point of view of society, general capital, and/or individual capitals. It is usually a macroeconomic term, so this net income is for the whole economy, or at least a sector.

Secondly, sometimes it is defined for the whole political economy as income minus necessary social costs (Y-NSC), or actual or necessary consumption (Y-Con). The necessary consumption includes absolute subsistence plus a cultural and historical component appropriate for the country or area in question. It is a rather flexible term that can be modified according to one's concern. If one defines it as the net output/income of society minus the historically necessary costs of living (consumption) (Y_n-C_h), then the surplus can be viewed as a fund for social change, or discretionary income of society. Viewed in this way, depending on how the political economy is structured, people could vote on how to use the surplus by, respectively, investing specific proportions into health, education, technology, ecological projects, housing, pensions, national parks, and so on. There is also the notion of potential economic surplus, or what it could be under specified ideal conditions.

The economic surplus could be considered a surplus available for productive investment in durable structures such as climate capitals (e.g., electric vehicles, solar power, wind power, hydrogen power, diversity preservation), accumulation (buildings, machinery, materials, inventories), public/social capital (infrastructure, healthcare, education, democracy), and innovation (AI, robotics, ICT, etc).

The surplus usually includes profit, interest, rent, salary levels above reasonable subsistence. It may also take the form of unproductive elements such as excess advertising (beyond 'information'), military spending (beyond 'protection'), poisonous products (tobacco, alcohol, and dangerous drugs such as Fentanyl, speed, etc), and so on. The economic surplus in most nations is distributed primarily to the vested interests who control the key sectors and institutions of the system. This form of distribution, to the vested interests rather than being based on merit and opportunity, usually inhibits the productive and reproductive use of the economic surplus, and thereby inhibits GDP, quality of life and equitable/progressive change.

→||Chaps. 1,6,7|| ||Circuit of Social Capital||

REF1: John B. Davis. Ed. 1992. *The Economic Surplus in Advanced Economies.* Cheltenham: Edward Elgar.

REF2: Paul A. Baran. 1957. *The Political Economy of Growth.* New York: Monthly Review Press.

REF3: Joan Robinson. 1979. Surplus and Accumulation. In J. Robinson, *Aspects of Development and Underdevelopment.* Cambridge: Cambridge University Press.

REF4: Phillip Anthony O'Hara. 2015. Exploitation and Surplus. In *The Elgar Companion to Social Economics*, 716–734, eds. John B. Davis and Wilfred Dolfsma. Cheltenham: Edward Elgar.

Emergence Emergence is a concept that refers to features that make certain entities different or novel from others. For instance, at the very micro level human beings exist as individuals, yet when they cooperate with others; together they generate a reality quite different from the reality of the individual *per se*. In this sense we have the emergence of cooperation and group practices.

Also, individual groups have certain characteristics, but when they cooperate with other groups, they, again, can generate a reality of practices that are emergent or novel. And when these different groups within nations cooperate with other groups in other nations, they often generate practices that are more novel still than the macro-outcomes. In the future, different groups from different planets or galaxies may cooperate in such a way that they generate even newer, novel arrangements and practices.

Generally, one refers to horizontal, vertical and temporal emergence. Horizontal refers to the linking of entities at the same level; vertical to entities at different levels; and temporal processes at differing levels of time or durability. Emergence is important to political economy especially because it helps to provide a realistic ontology as to how the world and its problems emerge and operate, as well as how to ameliorate these anomalies. The process of emergence is involved in climate change, hegemony, and long wave upswings. Emergence is inextricably related to complexity and circular and cumulative causation (CCC).

֍→||Chaps. 1–12|| ||Complexity|| ||Holism|| ||Circuit of Socioeconomic Dynamics||
֍→||Circular and Cumulative Causation||

REF: Mario Bunge. 2014. *Emergence and Convergence: Qualitative Novelty and the Unity of Knowledge.* Toronto: University of Toronto Press. Paperback Edition.

Emulation and Conspicuous Consumption These concepts emanate from Thorstein Veblen (1899) who set out to constructively critique the society in which he lived. Most societies have a powerful leisure class with lots of wealth from business or inheritance, usually educated at ivy-league universities, and characteristically living or searching for a trophy wife/husband to display. They engage various forms of competition with others in society in all walks of life, such as with other companies, associates, neighbours, friends, and even members of households. The leisure class have advantages not provided to underlings of the class system, since they can engage in conspicuous consumption on large properties, famous-make cars, extravagant dinner parties, elegant garb, and sophisticated etiquette. Lower classes emulate them by buying items outside their income range, thus increasing their propensity to consume to greater than average levels. Members of society under emulative pressure often become unhappy when it fails to impress; or they fail to succeed in the conspicuous consumption and emulation game; or when people realize how destructive and wasteful the whole game can be. This can lead to alcoholism, junk food, bad sleep, depression, suicide and ailments such as heart disease and diabetes. But when they realise how wasteful the whole thing is it may lead to greater quality of life. Periodically there are movements against such social anomalies as emulation and conspicuous consumption, which attempt to promote progressive change and better lifestyles. The double movement of following the habits and institutions of the privileged and challenging it to promote better institutions continues throughout history. Institutional and evolutionary science is part of this double movement.

֍→||Chaps. 5–8||

REF1: Thorstein Veblen. 1899. *The Theory of the Leisure Class.* Harmondsworth: Penguin, 1994.

REF2: William M. Dugger. 2022. The Doleful Dynamics of Competition: Inequality and Fakery in Modernity. *Forum for Social Economics* 51(1): 43–64. https://doi.org/10.1080/07360932.2017.1374196

Ethnicity The concept of ethnicity refers to a shared set of characteristics that usually unites people as part of a culture. For instance, a tribe may operate together as a group, eating, living, hunting and cooking together. A group of people living in a nation may have elements of togetherness and feel as one group. A group of people who have similar looks may cooperate, intermarry and eat together. These cultural traits of tradition, nation, interbreeding, looks and customs are what makes (or breaks) ethnic groups. This concept is important for political economy because one's ethnicity often has ramifications for one's standard of living and quality of life. Some ethnic groups are discriminated against, others may be disadvantaged, and some may have surmounted discrimination and developed much cultural and economic capital. Others may live in specific areas which imposes climatic costs or benefits. Some ethnic groups are more subject to certain diseases than others. Ethnicity can be used to promote contradictions, such as inter-ethnic conflict, divide and rule tactics, ethnic hate groups such as the Ku-Klux Klan (KKK), Nazi Parties, and ethno-nationalist extremist governments. Religious similarities and differences can be a factor promoting cooperation and conflict. For instance, some terrorist groups are religious fundamentalists wanting to return to the practices of an earlier age when perceived norms were seen as pure, and who see contemporary Western society (especially) as corrupt, immoral and decadent (e.g., Al Qaeda, Taliban, Islamic State).

⊛→||Chaps. 1,5–8|| ||Heterogeneous Groups and Agents||

REF: John Hutchinson and Anthony D. Smith. 1996. *Ethnicity.* Oxford: Oxford University Press.

Eurodebt Crisis The Eurodebt crisis hit numerous nations of Europe during and after the Global Financial Crisis (GFC), especially Greece, Italy, Ireland, Spain, Iceland, and Portugal, part of what is (or was) often called the periphery of the EU. It hit these nations because the GFC exposed several key anomalies both in the structural workings of the EU and the differential trends between peripheral and northern/western EU states. The GFC impacted since the periphery increased debt, and when problems hit the EU they could not devalue their currency (since they used the Euro dollar). Banks and other financial institutions also suffered in the light of the GFC, and this particularly hurt the periphery which was financially rather weak. Dealing with problems of debt, unemployment, and low growth continued for many years, especially for Greece (2009–2016ff), which has only recently started to recover somewhat.

⊛→||Chap. 9|| ||Global Financial Crisis|| ||Crises|| ||Polycrises||

REF: Ali Ari. 2015. *The European Debt Crisis: Causes, Consequences, Measures and Remedies.* Newcastle-upon-Tyne: Cambridge Scholars Publishing.

Evolution The concept of evolution states that the world and its constituents, indeed probably the whole universe and its parts, is subject to change involving mutations, modifications and various adaptations that change some of its elements, and that when significant enough become qualitatively different. For instance, capitalism undergoes changes to its institutions and the habits of individuals and groups that generate various phases of evolution through time. Capitalism is said to evolve through several phases of development (not necessarily implying progress), from mercantilism to industrial capitalism, then to imperialism, the Keynesian-welfare state, neoliberalism and beyond. The principle of evolution states that political economists and others must situate world problems within specific phases of evolution in the process of understanding and ameliorating such problems. The nature of long waves, climate change and hegemony change through historical time. Mutations and emergent complexities are both endogenously ingrained in processual structures and are affected by other systems and sub-systems that impinge from without and affect their long-term trajectory.

֍→||Chaps. 1–12|| ||Institutional and Evolutionary Political Economy||
֍→||Neo-Schumpeterian Political Economy|| ||Capitalism, Phases of Evolution||
REF: William M Dugger and Howard J. Sherman. Eds. 2002. *Evolutionary Theory in the Social Sciences*. 4 Vols. London: Routledge.

Feminist Political Economy (FPE) Many FPEs are institutional and evolutionary scholars. In this they apply various theories and methods to institutional and evolutionary topics. What makes a political economist a feminist likely varies from scholar to scholar. But three things stand out. The first is they tend to place *gender issues* at the forefront of their analysis. The reason for this is that, historically and still in many cases, women have been placed lower down than men in the power stakes of society. Some may have had some limited power in the household, and in typical female jobs such as cleaning, child-rearing, secretarial, teaching and medical areas, but in the broader areas of power they have had limited authority, until more recent decades in the advanced nations.

These broader areas of power include geopolitics, national politics, CEOs, science, and criminal areas (gangs). More recently in several nations, women have increased their power in several areas, including politics, science, business, medical and computing areas. But several trends in some areas of the world have gone backwards, such as with the Taliban in Afghanistan, the military junta in Myanmar, and in the USA with declining abortion rights in several states (and more conservative Supreme Court judges). In virtually all nations women still do not have equality with men in areas of wages, salaries and superannuation.

The second thing that some women claim to be a feminist issue is their method of analysis, namely, that they tend to have a more *holistic method*, in that it often is interdisciplinary or transdisciplinary. This trend to making institutional and evolutionary issues more holistic is in keeping with the main principles of evolutionary economics, and therefore, in this context and more, feminist themes and evolutionary science are very much complementary.

The third, related thing that makes FPEs evolutionary-institutional is their emphasis on *social provisioning*. In this they are interested in the ways in which humans and other beings are provided for vis-à-vis nurturance, sustenance, food, clothing, shelter, and the cultural ways genders, classes, ethnicities, nationalities and species interact, and how identity is formed through these roles and norms.

֍→||Chaps. 5,7|| ||Heterogeneous Groups and Agents|| ||Gender|| ||Holism||
֍→||Social Provisioning||

REF1: Sara Cantillon, Odile Mackett, and Sara Stevano. 2023. *Feminist Political Economy: A Global Perspective.* Newcastle-upon-Tyne: Agenda Publishing.

REF2: Shirin Rai, Georgina Waylen. Eds. 2013. *New Frontiers in Feminist Political Economy.* Oxon: Routledge.

Fictitious Capital The concept that certain forms of 'capital' are fictitious revolves around the idea that capital proper is something real rather than merely intangible or non-fundamental. When Marx in volume 3 of *Capital* discusses "fictitious capital", he is referring to the idea of speculative bubbles, intangible capitals that do not reflect fundamentals, and shadow banking that is a sideshow to industrial capital. Hence when these fictitious capitals are growing stronger than industrial capital it is an indicator that the economy is not operating effectively. There may be excess debt, equity prices beyond real value, and real estate valuations artificially inflated by excess demand. This occurs when fictitious capitals are a sideshow to the goods and services that people depend upon for their standard of living, and whose valuation does not move linearly with productivity plus real output and services. It can also refer to various forms of new financial instruments that do not directly correlate with the valuation of real goods and services. However, declining prices for fictitious commodities can also decrease prices of real capital through declining confidence and greater uncertainty in the wider political economy.

֍→||Chaps. 7,9|| ||Financial Instability Hypothesis|| ||Crises|| ||Fictitious Commodities||

R.M. Marques and P. Nakatani. 2023. Crisis and Fictitious Capital. In *Value, Money, Profit, and Capital Today* (*Research in Political Economy*, Vol. 39), 215-229. Ed. R. Herrera. Leeds, UK: Emerald Publishing Limited. https://doi.org/10.1108/S0161-723020230000039013

Fictitious Commodities When Karl Polanyi wrote about fictitious commodities he was referring to labor (or labor-power), land and money not being commodities in the sense that they do not operate like an automobile in the motor market. One cannot get hold of labor, land or money in the same sense that, under capitalism, one can buy a vehicle. This is because labor-power is human and therefore cannot be exploited to death in the same way that an automobile can, at least not in normal circumstances. Land similarly can have the soil destroyed and minerals extracted but the land itself cannot be alienated or destroyed entirely. Money does not have a use-value in itself, since one cannot reasonably be said to be able to eat it or use it to produce some commodity. These three commodities are sui generis, public goods, that need special attention for if privatised they may lead to destruction at prices less than their social cost. Labor, land and money need to be considered from the point of view of the system. For instance, what is the state of the labouring classes in Hong Kong? How much has the soil been degraded through overuse, and how does this contribute to climate change? To what extend does the government need to provide liquidity to the system to protect markets via lender of last resort? These public goods type questions are crucial to Polanyi's vision of the common good where special attention is given to the state of labor, land and money through the various types of transactions such as reciprocity, redistribution, exchange and householding. Knowledge can also be considered a public good and hence a real commodity that cannot be fictitious unless it is debased by lies, reputational debasement, and the asymmetric distribution of material facts towards the vested interests.

⊛→||Chaps. 4,7,9|| ||Disembedded Economy|| ||Speculative Bubbles|| ||Fictitious Capital||

REF1: Maja Savevska. 2019. The Fictitious Commodification of Money and the Euro Experiment. *Culture, Practice & Europeanization* 4(1): 29–42.

REF2: Antonino Palumbo. 2020. Knowledge as a Fictitious Commodity: A Polanyian Reading of the 'Digital Economy', *International Journal of Political Theory* 4(1): 1–23.

Financial Instability Hypothesis (FIH) The FIH is a term created by Hyman Minsky (1919–1996) to describe a theory and empirical stylized facts about the cyclical and wave-like dynamics of capitalism. It appears to be influenced by the views of financial capitalism developed by Marx, Veblen, Schumpeter and Keynes, and by Minsky's extensive knowledge of finance in the macro and world economy. It concerns the dynamic movement of capitalism over cycles and waves. When recovery happens in a socioeconomic cycle or wave, confidence starts to build which leads capitalists to invest more in complex durable structures such as machinery, buildings, hardware, software, workers, robots, knowledge and land. They also tend to finance this capital investment from internal funds, shares or equity in their firm, borrowing, or other often complex financial instruments. As confidence in the prevailing business climate increases, they engage in more financial vehicles, e.g., debt instruments (shares, credit, etc). Minsky defined firms at this stage as usually being in the "Hedge Finance" position, where cash flow and net worth are positive. They tend to get exuberant as their animal instincts grow cumulatively and in a circular fashion.

However, eventually the cyclical upward dynamic starts to decline somewhat, due to a possible variety of factors often endogenous to the upswing, such as rising interest rates, wages, material costs, supply bottlenecks, conflict, strikes and so on. During these times Minsky would likely argue that many firms are moving to "Speculative Finance", where cash flow has declined majorly (possibly to negative) but still net worth is positive.

Then usually some major event happens, a "Minsky moment", such as the collapse of a famous company (e.g., Enron, Lehman Bros), or some other endogenous yet unexpected process, which reduces business confidence majorly and leads to a crash in the markets, and eventually likely to recession. Many firms then move to "Ponzi Finance", where cash flow is very low or negative and net worth is negative. If this is a major economy, such as a hegemon, these instabilities will likely affect much of the rest of the world. Debt deflation may generate a regional or global deep recession of depression.

During these crises likely reserve banks will have long intervened, or engaged in extended intervention, to attempt to stabilise matters, by actions such as lender of last resort, fiscal and monetary policy. Eventually, depending on numerous lags, the economy may eventually readjust towards at least some semblance of 'recovery', and the cycle or wave continues again, in the upwards direction and beyond.

→||Chaps. 4,7,9|| ||Speculative Bubbles||

REF1: M. Knell. 2015. Schumpeter, Minsky and the Financial Instability Hypothesis. *Journal of Evolutionary Economics* 25(2): 293–310.

REF2: Hyman Minsky. 1975. *John Maynard Keynes.* New York: McGraw-Hill, 2008.

REF3: Hyman Minsky. 1986. *Stabilizing an Unstable Economy.* New Haven: Yale University Press.

Forrester, Jay Wright Jay Forrester (1918–2016) is said to have invented system dynamics analysis and was involved in the Club of Rome research on climate change and energy consumption. He also was involved in long wave investigations, and is said to have been a coinventor of the magnetic core memory system in digital computers. His theory and empirics of long cycles are endogenously determined by the nature of expansion of the capital goods sector, and, more especially, due to the interaction between capital and consumer goods sectors. Buildup, overexpansion, and relative decline of the capital or means of production sector is the essential characteristic (and dynamic) of the long cycle. Since expansion of the capital goods sector is embodied in both capital deepening and widening, a changing technological structure is an important form of sectoral growth. Increasing consumer demand stimulates orders for more capital, which is produced in the capital goods sector by denying the consumer goods sector normal periodic supply, which increases further the demand for capital. The tendency of the capital sector to demand more from itself thus continues. Only after a long, lagged process is the initial demand satisfied, but by this time the capital sector is vastly overextended, which provides the basis for contraction. Forrester used his theory to explain the postwar long wave of economic life from the 1940s through to the 1990s.

→||Chap. 3||

REF1: Jay Forrester. 1976. Business Structure, Economic Cycles, and National Policy. *Futures* 8(3): 195–214.

REF2: Jay Forrester. 1981. Innovation and Economic Change. *Futures* 13(4): 323–331.

Freeman and Louçã Christopher Freeman (1921–2010) and Fransisco Louçã (2001) provide a comprehensive history of long waves of capitalism from 1780 to 2000. They include details on all major technological and socioeconomic spheres involving every wave during this period. In doing this they argue that successive long waves are phases of evolution of capitalism, that correspond to different techno-economic and socio-political processes and techniques that rise and fall throughout history. These waves are seen as qualitative transformations, with various quantitative elements, but ones that do not necessarily manifest in waves of majorly rising and falling real economic activity (growth). Rather, long waves tend to represent successive 'industrial' (or informational etc) revolutions, associated with socio-political changes during the upswings, followed by downswings characterized by structural crises of adjustment to new conditions, techniques, and processes. Upswings and downswings are not deterministic, but represent evolutionary processes of nonequilibrium, path dependent, emergent, and contradictory phases of capitalism.

During the upswing in each wave the 'emergence, diffusion, and clustering of innovations' (p. 338) provide the potential for 'immense profits' based on the quality of these novelties, with profits being the heart of these upswings during the 1780s–1810s, 1850s–1870s, 1890s–1910s, and 1940s–1970s in the core nations. The upper turning points of the waves tend to occur when the profit potentials decline, and during long wave downswings *crises of structural adjustment* occur as job skills, structural unemployment and mobility anomalies lead to various mismatches and declining levels of general confidence and investment. Social conflicts are hypothesized to cluster around the peaks of long waves (during high upswings) and during the structural crises of adjustment during downswings (p. 369), such as during the 1820s–1840s, 1870s–1890s, 1920s–1930s, and 1980s/1990s [to the present].

Important is the principle that the clustering of techno-economic innovations does not necessarily lead to long wave upswing in profits and performance, because there needs to be a match between the techno-economic and other sub-systems of the political economy. This has not yet occurred in any core area of capitalist development since the postwar golden age (although it has occurred in some areas such as China and much of Asia).

֍→||Chaps. 3,12|| ||Carlotta Perez|| ||Technology Style||
֍→||Neo-Schumpeterian Political Economy||

REF: Christopher Freeman and Fransisco Louçã. 2001. *As Time Goes By: From the Industrial Revolution to the Information Revolution.* Oxford: Oxford University Press.

Functional Finance This is a political economy principle of governance initiated by Abba Lerner, which states that policies to tackle socioeconomic problems should be concerned with the state of the economy and how to improve it rather than, e.g., conservative principles of balanced budgets and budgets being equal to a maximum percent of GDP. Hence if there is a lot of uncertainty throughout the political economy then policy should be pointed to reducing this over time. Under these circumstances, governments should be concerned with reducing this uncertainty through, for instance, automatic and discretionary fiscal and monetary policy. Taxes and government spending, in this context, should be seen as aggregate demand facilitators, rather than means of public accounting. Other such governance measures should be seen in this light as well. Functional finance is seen as crucial for dealing with all forms of socioeconomic crisis, recession/booms, depressions and financial crises, as well as day-to-day issues of governance, including climate change.

֍→||Chaps. 7,9|| ||Modern Monetary Theory|| ||Financial Instability Hypothesis||
Ref: Abba P. Lerner. 1943. Functional Finance and the Federal Debt. *Social Research*. 10(1): 38–51.

Gender Gender is a complex concept that relates to, partly, one's physical, genetic and/or social behaviour or structure; secondly, one's identity; and thirdly, one's relationship to sex. For some it is entirely a matter of social role, for others it links to genetics, and for others it is concerned with identity. In aggregate it concerns all these factors. One's gender could be male, or female, or transgender, or some other category. Recently there has been a tendency for gender to refer to one's identity, whether one is male, or female or transgender, and so on. Increasingly the literature differentiates between gender in terms of role, identity and behaviour; and sex, which concerns biology, sexuality and physicality. Gender role and identity have implications for all questions of political economy and is hence related to the distribution of economic power, remuneration, and role played in the social economy. It is also closely associated with class, ethnicity, nationality, age and species through the concept of heterogeneous groups and agents. More recently, especially in the advanced capitalist economies, a double movement is in process, committed to promoting rights and knowledge about LGBTQIA rather than the conservative norms of previous generation. (LGBTQIA stands for 'lesbian, gay, bisexual, transsexual, queer, intersexual, asexual' groups, tendencies, characteristics, or people.).

֍→||Chaps. 5,7|| ||Feminist Political Economy|| ||Heterogeneous Groups and Agents||
֍→||Social Provisioning||
REF: Judith Butler. 2002. *Gender Trouble: Feminism and the Subversion of Identity*. London: Routledge, eLibrary. (Orig. Pub. 1990.)

Global Financial Crisis (GFC) The GFC (2008–2010) was, at the time, the greatest economic and financial crisis since the Great Depression of the 1930s (and the subsequent second world war of 1939–1945). It started out as the subprime crisis in the United States during 2008–2009, which was caused by rising uncertainty and debt that was not sufficiently embedded in risk assessments for companies, clients and nations. Many sub-standard mortgage arrangements were bundled together with other mortgages and sold as prime assets (or at least reasonable ones) or securitized mortgage bonds. It took the market time to realise that these bonds were substandard and that they were closely linked to predatory lending, opaque information, under-pricing of risk and high debt. Once the market priced some of the risk and uncertainty into securities it affected profits of many firms and triggered declining equity prices in the US. There were many inter-sectoral linkages between the US and Europe, and the effects of US instability soon impacted other especially advanced nations, as well as many parts of Asia. Other factors also intervened which made it an international crisis, such as the move from conservative to market accounting, increasing distance between underlying assets and instruments, calculative risk models ignoring systemic risk and uncertainty, the use of structured investment vehicles, abuse of credit default swaps, and securitized mortgage bonds infecting global circuits of finance. International disarray especially impacted Iceland and soon the periphery of Europe was undergoing a Eurodebt crisis which lasted several years. Many economists and policy makers blamed the GFC on neoliberalism and it led to the latter's relative demise. This helped policy makers deal with the next crisis, the coronacrisis during 2020–2022, as functional finance was used to reduce the degree of crisis affecting the macro and global economies.

֍→||Chap. 9|| || Crisis|| ||Speculative Bubbles|| ||Fictitious Capital||

REF1: A. G. Malliaris, Leslie Shaw, and Hersh Shefrin. 2016. *The Global Financial Crisis and Its Aftermath: Hidden Factors in the Meltdown.* Oxford: Oxford University Press.

REF2: Robert J. Shiller. 2012. *The Subprime Solution: How Today's Financial Crisis Happened and What to Do about It.* Princeton, NJ: Princeton University Press.

Global Political Economy [GPE] GPE is a field of political economy involving the dynamic interplay of power, production, trade, money and conflict involving corporate, state and other actors with the concern being the functioning of the circuit of social capital throughout the world. GPE especially involves power and conflict but also cooperation and agreement through which institutions and agents seek to achieve their objectives of profit, control and power over resources. It especially links to the relative power of nations and regions and their seeking of various types of hegemonic dominance throughout the world, as they have varying capacities in areas of production, commerce, finance and military prowess. The circuit of social capital reaches the global economy as capitalism seeks to caste-aside all barriers to its growth and development through the creation of new products, processes, markets, raw materials and other means while simultaneously destroying established jobs, institutions, cultures, climate systems, and ways of life. International politics is often used as a vehicle for the expansion of capitalism, but also for other concerns such as terrorism, human rights abuses, corruption, warfare, and so on, as well as efforts to moderate these ceremonial activities. Currently the GPE is mostly concerned with the rise of China and the relative decline of the US, plus the nations and interests that are variously supporting each party, and those who are caught in the middle or playing off both parties for their greatest gain. A double power block is forming with China-Russia and other nations versus the US-EU-Australia and others dealing with issues such as trade, finance, production, military and diplomatic issues that are evolving into extreme forms of potential and actual violence, confrontation and war.

֍→||Chaps. 3,5–10||Hegemony||Long Waves of Climate Change||

REF1: *Journal of World-Systems Research (pitt.edu)*

REF2: Robert Gilpin. 2001. *Global Political Economy: Understanding the International Economic Order.* Princeton, NJ: Princeton University Press.
REF3: Theodore H. Cohn and Anil Hira. 2023. *Global Political Economy.* Oxon: Routledge.
REF4: Phillip Anthony O'Hara. 2006. *Global Political Economy and the Wealth of Nations: Performance, Institutions, Problems and Policies* Oxon: Routledge. Paper Edition.

Gordon, Robert J Robert Gordon's major thesis is that the great innovations of the 1800s and early-to-mid 1900s were revolutionary in enhancing multi-factor productivity. The first great invention was that of electricity. In 1821 Michael Faraday invented the electric motor; electrical engineering underwent major advances in the late 1800s; while Edison and Swan created the United Electric Light Company in 1883. These innovations enabled masses of people to work through the night, reducing manual labor to enhance productivity in manufacturing, and through refrigeration enabling food to last days or weeks longer.

The second great innovation was the internal combustion engine, which enabled major increases in transportation for business and consumers for many decades. In 1885 the first automobile was build, known as the Benz Motorwagen, with a four-stroke engine; and in 1897 the first functional diesel engine was built in Germany by Randolf Diesel. These and others paved the way for several new industrial sectors and consumer products such as the automobile, the aeroplane and engineering motors during the twentieth century.

The third great invention was petroleum, pharmaceuticals, and plastics, which are said to have greatly enhanced medical applications, business machines and consumer durables. For instance, aspirin was invented in the 1900s, Howard Florey and others produced the first penicillin in 1942, while Tetracycline was patented in 1953. Together these and other products have prevented several hundred million deaths from disease as well as relief from intense pain over the past 80 years and more.

The fourth great invention is said to be entertainment, communication and information via the telephone, radio, TV, music and newspapers, which greatly increased the flow of knowledge, information and enjoyment. For instance, experimental TV broadcasting started in the US in 1939, sound recording underwent multiple phases of evolution between 1877 and 1975 from acoustic to electrical, magnetic and digital, while the newspaper industry experienced dozens of innovations over successive centuries. Together they distributed information to billions of people over centuries and decades.

In contrast, Gordon argues that the first generation of information and communications technology (ICT) techniques, including VCRs, color TVs and larger screens merely represented easier ways of performing the same services as before. While the generation of ICTs was well served by the mainframe computers, later development such as the personal computer "have resulted in diminishing returns to computers operating with unparalleled force"; whereas the internet "can be viewed largely as a source of information and entertainment that substitutes for other forms of information and entertainment" (2004, 81).

Gordon then asks the question: "why was productivity growth so much faster between 1891 and 1972 than either before or after, and fastest of all between 1928 and 1964?" (p. 85). The first explanation he gives is the multitude of four great innovations that enhanced MFP more than any others. The second is the closing of migration between 1920–1960, which raised real wages and capital-labor substitution. And the third is the role of high tariffs, depression and war in reducing import competition and inhibiting convergence while heightening real wages. He concludes by saying that "diminishing returns has left the greatest benefits of the computer age in the past, not awaiting us in the future" (p. 81).

֍→||Technology style|| ||Long Waves of Growth|| ||Chaps. 3,8,9||

REF1: Robert J. Gordon. 2004. *Productivity, Growth, Inflation, and Unemployment: The Collected Essays of Robert J. Gordon.* Cambridge: Cambridge University Press.

REF2: Robert J. Gordon. 2016. *The Rise and Fall of American Growth: The U.S. Standard of Living Since the Civil War.* Princeton, New Jersey: Princeton University Press.

REF3: Robert J. Gordon and Hassan Sayed. *2024. A New Interpretation of U.S. Productivity Growth Dynamics, 1950-2023.* CEPR Discussion Paper 19569, October 2024.

Hegemony The general concept of hegemony is that a culture, region or nation tends to hold much of the power in the global economy, or in certain nations or regions. This power has varying degrees of legitimacy, due to the material benefits gained from the power relations, and/or from the enabling myths that validate the prevailing system of arrangements, and/or from the very concepts the hegemonic power develops and the agents it employs to market these concepts.

Two elements are crucial in relation to hegemony. The first is cultural leadership, emulation and patterns of behaviour, norms and mores in the dominant culture. The second has to do with power, authority, control, and the display of aggression. Hegemony can refer to a subnational, national, regional, international and global region or culture. Antonio Gramsci's main concern was with the evolution of a hegemonic culture to provide leadership and emulation for future provisioning. Charles Kindleberger's main concern was with a dominant global power that provides not only cultural leadership and emulation but also power and authority to provide public goods for stability and long-term performance.

The hegemonic stability thesis (HSH) states that the world economy needs a leader that is willing and able to provide various institutions and relationships to generate stability for the present and the foreseeable future. Such public goods include lender of last resort facilities, trading agreements to reduce conflict, production networks to ensure continuity, and (other) international institutions to deal with anomalies and crises. One needs to differentiate between Empires and Hegemons. Empires seek regional or global domination or control, such as the Spanish,

Portuguese, and Holy Roman Empire (1300s–1600s). Global Hegemons seek to provide leadership, emulation, power and authority to enable internal stability and external continuity and control.

Three such hegemons have emerged to date in the capitalist world-economy, the United Provinces of the Netherlands (much of the 1600s; 1590s–1640s?), the British Isles (much of the 1800s; 1820s–1880s?), and the USA (much of the 1900s; 1940s–1970s?). *Pax* Britannia was also a formal Empire, and the *Pax Americana* a *de facto* empire. The question arises as to whether another area or country may emerge as the next hegemon. For instance, can China provide the leadership, emulation and public goods as well as the power, authority and control to enable global stability and progress? The Dutch, British and US cases of hegemony were all liberal-democratic forms that sought domestic progress and global stability. Can another power undertake these functions into the future? If not, are we to continue through numerous ongoing polycrises with no long-term global superior performance and stability in view, as we have at present? Or could a system of multilateral arrangements (or multipolar arrangements) suitably substitute for hegemony?

֍→||Chaps. 1–12|| ||Dutch Hegemony|| ||British Hegemony|| ||United States Hegemony||
֍→||Chinese Potential Hegemony|| ||Core, Periphery and Semi-Periphery||
֍→||Uneven Development||
REF1: Immanuel Wallerstein. 1974–2011. *The Modern World System I-IV.* New York: Academic Press (I-III) and Los Angeles: University of California Press (IV).
REF2: Fernand Braudel. 1979. *Civilization and Capitalism: Volume III: The Perspective of the World.* New York: Harper & Row. Translated from the French by Sian Reynolds.

Heterogeneous Groups and Agents The concept of heterogeneous groups and agents in political economy states that the dominant roles that people play in groups are important for comprehending any major problem or process in the political economy. These roles include those based around gender, class, ethnicity, species, age, but also more technical roles that people play in institutions, and skills and attributes that they have when interacting with others in social life. People and other species always perform multiple roles in the political economy, even when one role is dominant, and they also have various traits based around gender, class, ethnicity, species, age, technical roles, that make them heterogeneous in these multiple respects. This concept is increasingly also including intelligent machines playing roles that have been attributed to human beings, and even mechanical robots and similar machines contributing AI should be included in the analysis. The principle of heterogeneous groups and agents states that one should utilise this concept to comprehend any problem or issue in the political economy, including for innovation and policy purposes to ameliorate the anomaly. Various groups and agents are crucial for generating long wave upswings, hegemonies and climate change (causation, mitigation, and adaptation).

֍→||Chaps. 1–12|| ||Class|| ||Gender|| ||Ethnicity|| ||Age|| ||Species||

REF: Phillip Anthony O'Hara. 2023. *Principles of Institutional and Evolutionary Political Economy: Applied to Current World Problems.*Revised Edition. Singapore: Springer Nature. Principles of Institutional and Evolutionary Political Economy: Applied to Current World Problems | SpringerLink

Historical Specificity The concept of historical specificity states that knowledge of the history of a problem, practice or a theory is important for comprehending the nature of it, and the way in which it can be useful for improving the performance of the political economy. The principle of historical specificity states that one should examine all problems historically to provide a better and more complex understanding of how to improve matters through innovation and policy into the future. Historical specificity and evolution are core elements affecting long waves, hegemonies and climate change.

֍→||Chaps 1–12|| ||Evolution|| ||Core, Periphery and Semi-Periphery||
֍→||PoPE Contingency Paradigm||
REF1: Mills, C.W. (1959) *The Sociological Imagination.* Harmondsworth, UK: 1970.
REF2: Hodgson, Geoffrey M. (2001) *How Economics Forgot History: The Problem of Historical Specificity in Social Science.* London & New York: Routledge.
REF3: David Christian. 2011. *Maps of Time: An Introduction to Big History.* Los Angeles: University of California Press.

Holism The concept of holism has a long history and is subject to many versions and traditions. Some of these traditions are especially relevant to institutional and evolutionary political economy. One tradition espouses that holism is the principle that people should try and develop a lifestyle that includes an array of stimulating, developmental and innovative activities. People should try always to be learning something new, being on the lookout for new experiences, while also being able to relax and absorb these experiences, so that one undergoes dynamic transformation and renewal, but never extreme instability and disarray that could lead to death or disability. This should include a balanced diet that is nutritious and developmental in its effects on the mind and body. It should also include activities that stimulate the affective domain of emotions and feelings, so that one develops emotional as well as mental intelligence; the two become intertwined when enabled.

This principle is used by political economists to advise governments, corporations and individuals to enhance the body-mind experience of all classes, genders, ethnic groups, ages, species, other groups, and individuals. The principle of holism can also be extended further into the socioeconomic and political domains, by suggesting that political economy should be interdisciplinary in the sense of including an array of social, economic, political and environmental elements together to solve complex world problems. World problems go beyond single disciplines, and therefore one necessarily scrutinises anomalies such as world poverty, inequality, insufficient trust and nurturance, Pandemics, financial crises and recessions, un(der) employment, inflation and other problems such as terrorism, corruption and artificial intelligence, by looking at these issues through a wide-scope and depth of vision. Political economists are likely to be able to do this more effectively if they have developed a holistic lifestyle that enhances the functioning of their body and mind.

More technically, holism in political economy refers to four things about the world. The first is that *the whole is greater than the parts* ('emergence'), and hence the whole is magnified, novel, different, from the parts. This may be because of interaction between the parts, communication, reproduction of a new thing, innovation, and a host of other factors. Second, quantitative change among the parts can become so great than *a qualitative change* operates within the whole (e.g., a new phase of evolution of capitalism; an innovation, a new hegemon, a long wave upswing, a downswing in climate change heating). Third, the parts interact continuously so that *the whole is forever in the process of becoming*, i.e., evolving and changing through historical time. And fourthly, some of the parts interact in processually contradictory ways that generate endogenous movement, transformation, unfolding, often through *serious crises, wars, conflict*; and often these contradictions encourage/require cooperation, coordination, *collaboration and other types of synergies*.

֍→||Chaps. 1–12|| ||Emergence|| ||Complexity|| ||Circuit of Socioeconomic Dynamics||
֍→||Feminist Political Economy|| ||Veblenian||
REF1: J.C. Smuts. 1926. *Holism and Evolution*. New York: The Macmillan Company
REF2: David Bohm. 1980, *Wholeness and the Implicate Order.* London: Routledge & Kegan Paul.
REF3: František Petrovič and František Murgaš. 2020. Holistic and Sustainable Quality of Life Conceptualization and Application. *Folia Geographica* 62(1): 77–94.

Imperialism Imperialism is a general term for when core nations and areas exploit and oppress peripheries and semi-peripheries (and perhaps peripheral areas of the core). More generally it refers to situations when powerful nations and areas exploit and oppress those with less geo-political power. The *Age of Imperialism* often refers to the period during the late 1800s to the early-mid 1900s when core nations underwent a concerted series of campaigns to exploit and oppress underdeveloped nations of Africa, Asia, the Middle East, Latin America and elsewhere. During Dutch hegemon (1580–1650) Dutch corporations and navies sought to exert power over several ethnic groups in the Americas, Asia and Africa. In doing so they reverted (externally) to typical mercantile activities such as generating monopolies, invading islands and other territories, and massacring whole tribes to prevent them from trading with competitors and to ensure monopoly power over a commodity.

During the era of British hegemony (1820–1880) the British used free trade imperialism to dominate world markets. They did this by promoting free trade for their products, and for the products of other nations and areas, so that their most efficient engines of growth could dominate world markets. Other areas with higher costs found it hard to compete with the British. In this way China was forced to allow foreign ships to trade in the country and to enable Britain to solve its balance of trade imbalance with China through the importation of large volumes of opium (during the Opium Wars). Britain was also able to drain large amounts of economic surplus from India through unequal treaties and trading arrangements that placed a premium on British rather than Indian interests. In Australia the British sought to exterminate the indigenous peoples through distributing microbes (which they had little or no immunity to), ignoring communal property rights, and engaging in recurring wars with the original inhabitants.

The core age of imperialism was in the 1880s–1930s during the scramble for Africa when European nations formally divided the continent into areas of influence and colonialisation, with no regard for the interests of the indigenous people. By the use of enslavement (often by other names such as forced labor), massacres, invasions, monopolies, and exploitation of resources and labor power, Europeans prevented the development of these areas. They created artificial borders, prevented local governance structures from developing, killed generations of inhabitants, imposed harsh penalties for unproductive labor (e.g., Belgiums cut hands off those with low quotas in the Congo), and engaged in wholesale rape and enslavement of women.

During the era of US hegemony, the US promoted various forms of imperialism, including free trade imperialism; invasions of various countries/areas such as Vietnam, parts of the Caribbean, and Iraq; US corporate control through forms of ownership, licensing rights, and profit repatriation; plus also cultural imperialism by using advertising, TV, film, and other institutions such as the press. The US also sought to control Central and South America through the Monroe Doctrine by which these areas were seen as de facto extensions of US property and influence. In the postwar period (1945–1972) the US also extended their power through having their dollar as the ruling currency of the world, with monetary policy having influences far beyond their shores. After 9/11 the invasions of Iraq (and Afghanistan) were undertaken with little or no justification or concern for the people of the region.

֍→||Chaps. 5–8|| ||Hegemony|| ||Core, periphery and semi-periphery||

REF1: John Milios and Dimitris P. Sotiropoulos. 2009. *Rethinking Imperialism: A Study of Capitalist Rule.* New York: Palgrave Macmillan.

REF2: David Harvey. 2003. *The New Imperialism.* Oxford: Oxford University Press.

REF3: John A. Hobson. 1905. *Imperialism: A Study.* New York: Casimo Classics, 2005.

REF4: Walter Rodney. 1972. *How Europe Underdeveloped Africa.* London: Verso, 2018.

Industrial Revolution The industrial revolution (IR) is a term usually meant to describe the era during the later 1700s and early-to-mid 1800s when Britain underwent a whole series of inventions, innovations and industrial transformations that qualitatively changed the economic, social and political landscape of this area. These changes included or were preceded by the agricultural revolution, which enabled the generation of economic surplus by which capitalists could enhance investment in manufacturing industry, and which itself provided the resources for developing services such as finance, education, public utilities, governments, trade, and defence. During this time but especially later other nations were able to learn from this experience and generate their own industrialisation processes. Initially these other nations include such core economies as France, Germany, USA, and eventually much of Europe, followed by other continents as time goes by.

Some scholars argue that the roots of the industrial revolution occurred much earlier, such as during the whole of the 1700s, and that other countries or areas underwent comparable qualitative phases of evolution much earlier, although they were obviously different in nature and scope. These include China in the 1400s, the Dutch in the late 1500s and 1600s, and several others throughout history. It has also been suggested that Britain underwent two industrial revolutions. The first one, based on textiles, water-power, coal and factory (mill) production occurred during the 1780s–1840s; or the 1760s–1840s, in Britain, also associated with the scientific revolution, primary accumulation, laissez faire, and a constellation of classes. The second one is said to be based on railways, steam power, mechanization, as well as processes such as shopfloor management, big business, and the continual process of British hegemony, including its gradual maturation, during the 1850s–1890s.

The fact that the Revolutionary and Napoleonic Wars prevented the first industrial revolution from developing to its full capacity and growth potential until the 1820s, indicates that perhaps the first and the second IR should be seen as merging much more than would normally have been perceived. It also led to British hegemony manifesting itself during the 1820s–1880s instead of much earlier or not at all. The industrial revolution, therefore, should perhaps be seen as multifarious in nature, subject to complex dynamics, temporally quite opaque, and spatially more expansive than normally perceived.

֍→||Chaps. 6,7|| ||British Hegemony|| ||US Hegemony|| ||Technology Style||

REF1: Peter N. Stearns. 2013. *The Industrial Revolution in World History*. 4th Edition. Boulder, CO: Westview Press.

REF2: Jeff Horn, Leonard N. Rosenband, and Merritt Roe Smith. Eds. 2010. *Reconceptualizing the Industrial Revolution*. Cambridge, MA: MIT Press.

Innovation and Novelty The concept of innovation states that there are numerous ways of contributing to solving world problems, and one can do this by innovating, which means doing something different in socioeconomic life, which contributes to the solution of these problems. Some of the methods include purely technical or material innovations, some concern changes in organisation, others relate to changes in ideas, while others concern knowledge and its application to concrete issues. Invariably they concern promoting the instrumental workings of core elements of the social, political, economic, engineering and ecological systems. Some innovations may be 'things' in the past that have been resurrected, others concern principles that are applied, while some concern quite different elements from the past. The principle of innovation and novelty states that one should promote innovations to contribute to solving anomalous world problems. Innovations have been crucial for the generation of long wave upswings, hegemonies and climate change mitigation and adaptation.

֍→||Chaps. 1,2,3,5–8||

REF1: Adedeji B. Badiru. 2020. *Innovation: A Systems Approach.* London: CRC Press (T&F).

REF2: Adedeji B. Badiru and Gary Lamont. 2024. *Innovation Fundamentals: Quantitative and Qualitative Techniques.* London: CRC Press (T&F).

Institution There are various ways of looking at the concept of an institution. One is to see an institution is a structured way of organising group behaviour, comprising various routines, roles and behavioural norms to undertake some important social practice(s). Some differentiate between behavioural, organisational and theoretical institutions, so that an institution can variously comprise, for instance, the gendered division of labor, the organisations of the state, and double entry bookkeeping. Some scholars delimit the concept to organisational institutions, such as households, corporations, financial institutions, government departments or ministries (and parliament), plus world institutions such as the United Nations, the IMF and the World Bank. In scholarly discourse, the institutions associated with neoclassical economics dominated economics for a long time, but has always been the subject of double movements, such as the social movement called institutional and evolutionary political economy. In original institutional economics, the broad contours of inquiry centre on culture, institutions, habits, routines, instincts, and systems.

֍→||Culture|| ||Circuit of Socioeconomic Dynamics|| ||Chaps. 5–8||

REF1: Ernesto Screpanti. 2001. *The Fundamental Institutions of Capitalism.* London: Routledge.

REF2: Michael Heller. 2009. *Capitalism, Institutions and Economic Development.* London: Routledge.

Institutional and Evolutionary Political Economy (IEPE) IEPE is a form of political economy that seeks to understand the dynamic and institutional nature of groups and agents as they interact and thereby form the basis of the roles that potentially enhance socioeconomic performance. Many of its adherents seek to improve performance by advocating innovations to enhance social provisioning, community, skills, learning, communication, trust, productivity, capacities and capabilities. These innovations especially seek to instrumentally promote the common good and to eschew institutional characteristics that promote ceremonial discrimination, distrust, conflict, war, and extremes of inequality. There are various traditions of IEPE, and some of them are trying to work together to generate a relatively common discourse for solving critical world problems. But the process will take some time and requires much innovation and invention to succeed. IEPE is an ideal vehicle to study the linkage of issues of long waves, hegemony and climate change.

֍→||Chaps. 1–12|| ||Veblenian|| ||Neo-Schumpeterian political economy|| ||Culture||

֍→||Technology Style|| ||LWHegCC|| ||Institution||

REF1: Phillip Anthony O'Hara. 2023. *Principles of Institutional and Evolutionary Political Economy: Applied to Current World Problems.* Singapore: Springer Nature. Revised Edition.
REF2: Geoffrey M. Hodgson, Warren J. Samuels and Marc R. Tool. Eds. 1994. *The Elgar Companion to Institutional and Evolutionary Economics.* 2 Vols. Cheltenham, UK: Edward Elgar.
REF3: Wolfram Elsner and William T. Waller. Eds. Forthcoming. *Encyclopedia of Evolutionary and Institutional Economics.* Cheltenham, UK: Edward Elgar.

Juglar Cycles Juglar cycles are typically seen as 7–11 year cycles of economic activity. Clément Juglar (1819–1905) himself saw such cycles as involving changes in interest rates, prices as well as other variables such as death and birth rates. Karl Marx and W.W. Rostow saw these cycles as comprising movements in production and investment. Joseph Schumpeter included these cycles as part of his three-cycle schema of Kitchins (2–3 years), Juglars (7–11 years) and Kondratievs (54 years). Howard Sherman's periodicity of US cycles during the 1950s–1990s revolved around one cycle approximately every decade (circa). More recent crises and recessions in the US have been occurring on a decadal basis (broadly speaking every 7–12 years: e.g., mid-1970s, early-1980s, early 1990s, early 2000s, late 2000s, early 2020s (and in several other industrial nations). Long wave scholars tend to view cycles more generally as during upswing the recessions tend to be less severe, while during long wave downswings the short-crises and recessions tend to be more extreme. This indeed tends to be the case.

→||Chaps. 2,3,5–8|| ||Kitchin cycles|| ||Kuznets swings|| ||Kondratiev waves||
REF1: Daniele Besomi. 2009. Clément Juglar and his Contemporaries on the Causes of Commercial Crises. *European Journal of Social Sciences* 143: 17–47.
REF2: Clément Juglar. 1916. *A Brief History of Panics and their Periodic Occurrence in the United States.* 3rd Edition. New York: Augustus M. Kelley, 1989.

Kitchin Cycles In 1923 Joseph Kitchin (1861–1932) published a famous paper where he examined mainly short ("minor") cycles averaging 3.5 years (2.33–4.87 years) duration (periodicity). The causes of these "Business [inventories] and price [and interest rate] cycles", in the US and Great Britain (1890–1922), were said to be "cyclical recurrences in mass psychology reacting through capitalistic production" (Kitchin 1923, 14). Several lags are involved, such as e.g., the (a) process of supply exceeding demand, (b) businesses checking information, (c) the decision to reduce production, (d) reducing supply. The factor coalescing other businesses to act in a similar fashion through CCC, if such conditions are more general, is the prevailing business climate. Kitchin argued that two or three of these minor (inventory) cycles may generate a "major" cycle (e.g., Juglar cycle), which some other economists (e.g., R.C.O. Mathews) attributed to changes in durable fixed capital (fixed investment/capital).

Schumpeter subsequently included Kitchin cycles along with Juglar cycles and Kondratiev cycles in his three-cycle schema of multiple business cycles.

→||Chaps. 2,3|| ||Juglar Cycles|| ||Kuznets Swings|| ||Long Waves of Growth||

REF1: Joseph Kitchin. 1923. Cycles and Trends in Economic Factors, *Review of Economics and Statistics*, 5(1): 10–16.

REF2: Vasilii Erokhin, Gao Tianming, Jean Vasile Andre. 2023. Economic Cycles. In: V. Erokhin, G. Tianming, and J. Vasile Andre, *Contemporary Macroeconomics*, Singapore: Springer. https://doi.org/10.1007/978-981-19-9542-2_7

Kondratiev Waves Nikolai Dmitrievich Kondratiev (1892–1938) was born in Russia 200 miles from Moscow. He enrolled at St Petersburg University where he attended lectures by M.I. Tugan-Baranovski among others. As a young teenager he joined the Socialist Revolutionary (SR) Party which promoted the idea of agrarian socialism. He became Minister for Food Supply in the Provisional Government during 1917 and was heavily involved later in the agricultural plan and the New Economic Policy. During most of the 1920s he headed the Moscow Conjuncture Institute, where most of his work on long waves was undertaken.

Much of his work involved analysing extra-economic factors and empirical dynamics associated with long waves, from which he proposed several stylized facts. The first was that during long waves of upturn and expansion, periods of prosperity are significantly more numerous than during downturn and contraction; and during long wave downturns, years of recession are significantly more numerous than during upturn and recovery. The second is that during the downturn and contraction of the long cycle a significantly larger number of important discoveries and inventions in production technique and communications are made than during other phases of the long cycle (innovations *spread* during upturns and expansions). The third is that during the upturn and expansion of the cycle the most disastrous and extensive wars and revolutions occur.

The fourth stylized fact is said to be that during the downturn and contraction of the cycle agriculture experiences an especially pronounced and long depression, e.g., especially of prices. And according to the fifth, gold production increases during the beginning of the long expansion, while the market for goods is promoted by new and especially colonial countries. Kondratiev accorded with the standard model of long waves in relation to the 1780s–1920s.

His empirical method of analyzing both prices and output data involved usually fitting trend lines (using ordinary least squares), with the deviations from the trend being filtered by a 9-year moving average (to eliminate short cycle and irregular factors). He studied especially the cases of Britain and France.

Kondratiev's endogenous theory of long cycles was that they were pure reinvestment cycles in durable fixed capital, including transport facilities, factories, warehouses, which promote the expansion, and the subsequent spreading of net investment as capital is (re)installed. The expansions of the producer and consumer sectors tend to decline, however, as investment and consumption spending adjust to the initial burst of activity, leading to a period of long cycle decline.

His opposition to Stalin's policy of collectivization of agriculture (and associated activities) led to his arrest, imprisonment, and several years of incarceration in

Siberia. While there he did much research, especially on material directly and indirectly linked to national income accounting. As Vincent Barnett (1998, 202) noted, during the earlier years of imprisonment he produced a 400-page treatise on *The Basic Problem of Economic Statics and Dynamics* (1932).

There was much criticism of Kondratiev's long wave analysis, ranging from Leon Trotsky's view that the curve of capitalist development operated but was not a cycle, to Oparin's view that his method of calculating waves was anomalous, to the typical Bolshevik view that capitalism does not undergo waves but is doomed to crisis and collapse, and the George Garvey conclusion that we should concentrate on the empirical regularities and dynamics of capitalism devoid of preconceptions about periodicity, amplitude and regularity. In terms of his statistical methods, his use of the moving average technique (and long periods) may have led to anomalous results due to the *Slutsky-Yule Effect*. Numerous modern scholars have scrutinized Kondratiev's hypotheses with mixed results. For instance, Antonio Foccacci (2023) could find no consistent cycles for prices or output per capita in his multinational empirical wavelet analyses, while others have found positive evidence, for both prices (Gallegati et al. 2017) and GDP (Korotayev and Tsirel 2007).

Had he lived a normal life cycle he may have contributed to the renascence of long wave scholarship in the 1970s–1990s, and/or innovated further into the 1940s–1960s. As Tugan-Baranovsky said of Kondratiev: "He was the best of the Russian economists".

֍→||Chaps. 1,2|| ||Long Waves of Climate Change|| ||Slutsky-Yule Effect||

REF1: Vincent Barnett. 1998. *Kondratiev and the Dynamics of Economic Development: Long Cycles and Industrial Growth in Historical Context.* New York: St Marttin's Press.

REF2: Natalia Makashiva, Warren J. Samuels, and Vincent Barnett. Eds. 1998. *The Works of Nikolai D. Kondratiev: Economic Statics, Dynamics and Conjuncture.* 4 Vols. London: Pickering and Chatto. Translated by Stephen S. Wilson. (Republished 2016 by Routledge, London in Hardback and ebook.)

REF3: Antonio Foccacci. A Wavelet Investigation of Periodic Long Swings in the Economy: The Original Data of Kondratieff and Some Important Series of GDP per Capita. 2023. *Economics* 11(231): 1–21.

REF4: Marco Gallegati, Mauro Gallegati, James B. Ramsey, and Willi Semmler. 2017. Long Waves in Prices: New Evidence from Wavelet Analysis. *Cliometrica* 11(2): 127–151. Long waves in prices: new evidence from wavelet analysis | Cliometrica (springer.com)

REF5: Andrey V. Korotayev and Sergey V. Tsirel. 2010. A Spectral Analysis of World GDP Dynamics: Kondratieff Waves, Kuznets Swings, Juglar and Kitchin Cycles in Global Economic Development, and the 2008–2009 Economic Crisis. *Structure and Dynamics* 4(1). https://doi.org/10.5070/SD941003306

Kuznets Swings A Kuznets cycle or 'swing' is typically seen as a 18–26 year recuring cycle of greater economic performance generating building and population dynamics that are associated with the opening up of areas for economic development. An example is the expansion of the West of the US during the 1800s which led to rising demand providing a magnet for the migration of people to the area who built houses, businesses, roads, transportation modes, and various vehicles and communication nodes. These expansions of demand, building and migration tend to be ongoing due to the lags and inner dynamics that generate cycles of upward and downward motion through time. During the upswings the multiplier and accelerator mechanisms enable CCC processes to heighten and overshoot through a decade or more, which lead to price and production instabilities then to downswing. The highs and lows are typically exacerbated by the complex interdependencies and behavioral dynamics involved in these real-world movements. Successive overshooting produce lags of expansion and subsequent downswing, *ad infinitum*, until the whole process exhausts itself. Some believe that the Kuznets process ran its course early in the 1900s, but subsequent opening up, migrating and building dynamics have been seen periodically since then in numerous areas. However, restrictions on the movement of people internationally, and the influence of longer-term dynamics especially in the postwar era, may have limited the workings of the Kitchin cycle swings.

Eugene Howrey (1968) argued that the Kuznets swing was an artifact of the filter used by Kuznets, which could also be generated on white noise, although Kuznets argued against this by showing global swings without the use of the filter.

֍→||Kitchin cycles|| ||Juglar cycles|| ||Long Waves of Growth||

REF1: Simon Kuznets. 1973. *Population, Capital, and Growth: Selected Essays*. London: Heinemann Books.

REF2: Moses Abramovitz. 1991. *Thinking About Growth and other Essays on Economic Growth and Welfare.* Cambridge: Cambridge University Press, pp. 243–300.

REF3: Eugene Philip Howrey 1968. A Spectrum Analysis of the Long Swing Hypothesis. *International Economic Review*. 9:228–252.

Liberal Democracy A liberal democracy is usually thought of as a socioeconomic system where capitalism is the dominant mode of production, distribution and exchange, but where the political system is subject to well-organised and respected parliamentary elections, usually where parties alternate in power, sometimes as various coalitions and often through the two dominant parties, one being centre-left and the other centre-right. The idea of liberal democracy is where elections have a high degree of legitimacy, where the rule of law is generally respected, and where people have various civil rights to freedom of expression, congregation and movement (except during pandemics and wars). A liberal democracy usually has at least a moderately strong state, where it constitutes a dominant player in providing education, health, infrastructure, plus bureaucracy, military, parliament, and legal-justice systems. Examples include the United States, the UK and Australia.

֍→||Chaps. 6,7||

REF: Nicholas Wolterstorff and Terence Cuneo. 2012. *Understanding Liberal Democracy: Essays in Political Philosophy.* Oxford: Oxford University Press.

Long Cycles There is a rather large group of scholars who work on long cycles, and those who only recognise 'Kondratievs' as long *cycles.* They thus work on or only recognise long *cycles,* in which 'Kondratiavs' have an internally generated endogenous rhythm of periodicity, amplitude and regularity through logical time (Bernard et al. 2014). Such a cycle may have varying periodicities and amplitudes but a regularity they must have as part of their endogeneity. It is much easier to have an endogenous theory of long *cycles* when only prices are considered, because there is no doubt that prices do empirically form cycles historically much more commonly throughout history than real variables such as the growth of GDP per capita. Kondratiev and Schumpeter dealt with prices much more than output in their empirical work, but that is only because they were more commonly available than macro aggregates of output and GDP (or even micro-ones). Kondratiev studied national income intensively when in the gulag in Siberia. Had he lived a normally long life he would have likely been part of the renaissance of interest in waves during the 1970s (as well as keeping it alive in the 1940s–1960s) with output at the forefront of analysis. Schumpeter likely had prices on the vertical axis of his cycle diagrams, but for him too output was a core part of his investigations.

Those who specialize in empirical critiques of long *cycles* (e.g., Solomou Solomos 1998) obviously only recognise long waves as cycles. Solomou criticised those who posited the first Kondratiev upswing in 1780–1820 (in Britain), due to low growth rates then which would have more likely rendered it a downswing. He also criticised those who used data before 1870, since he doubted the quality of it (although he may have changed his mind more recently due to increasing quality). Critics of many empirical methods call out those using moving averages to identify long cycles due to the Slutzky-Yule Effect. Solomou criticises long cycle analysts, and only thinks serious long cycle empirics involves growth rather than prices. It is paradoxical that Somolou only recognises long *cycles,* yet details the institutional complexities of especially British economic history as being a core part of understanding the pattern of growth and development. One wonders why he does not recognise the many authors who posit long waves (rather than cycles) as being conditioned by the geo-spatial, institutional and technological (including behavioral) factors involved in long-term dynamics.

֍→||Long Waves of Growth|| ||Chaps. 2–3, 5–8|| ||Slutsky-Yule Effect||

REF1: Solomou, Solomos. 1998. *Economic Cycles: Long Cycles and Business Cycles Since 1870.* Manchester: Manchester University Press.

REF2: Lucas Bernard, Aleksandr V. Gevorkyan, Tom Palley, and Willi Semmler. 2014. Long-Wave Economic Cycles: The Contributions of Kondratieff, K Kuznets, Schumpeter, Kalecki, Goodwin, Kaldor, and Minsky. In *Kondratieff Waves: Juglar – Kuznets – Kondratieff,* 120–163. Eds. Leonid E. Grinin, Tessaleno C. Devezas, and Andrey V. Korotayev. Volvograd: Ichitel Publishing House.

Long Waves of Growth The notion of long waves is a concept seeking to explain long movements of socioeconomic and political life of complex systems of institutions, technology and eco-spatial relationships. These long movements undergo phases of evolution as the institutions, technologies and geo-spatial relationships change through time. Often, they undergo sequential phases of reconstitution, expansion, maturity, and destruction of institutions, technologies, and eco-spatial structures. Industrial capitalism is one such system that tends to undergo these movements, as it has been hypothesized that such phases of growth and development have been inherent in its motion at least since the 1780s, and likely much earlier. Because of uneven development various regions, continents, nations and subnations undergo differential phases of long wave change through historical time. The principle of long waves states that analysing long phases of complex economies helps to comprehend the differential rate of growth and phases of development which assists in solving socioeconomic, political, and geo-spatial-ecological problems and anomalies.

One would normally expect differential but structurally linked wave patterns between core, periphery and semi-periphery (CPSP), and indeed within and between all nations and regions. Undertaking a global analysis of waves incorporating all the regional and CPSP complexities into the investigation would be the ideal method of approaching the subject. The principle of long waves implies that one should scrutinize long patterns of ecological, socioeconomic, and political performance to be cognizant of core dynamics of the system. Such an inquiry is useful for innovation, policy and governance purposes for solving world problems of anomalous performance, hegemonic dynamics, and climate change tendencies.

֍→||Chaps. 1–12|| ||Kondratiev Waves|| ||Long Waves of Climate Change||

REF1: Alfred Kleinknecht, Ernest Mandel and Immanuel Wallerstein. Eds. 1992. *New Findings of Long-Wave Research.* New York: St Martin's Press.

REF2: Jason Hecht. 2023. Are Long Waves 50 Years? Re-examining Economic and Financial Long Wave Periodicities in Kondratieff and Schumpeter. *Review of Political Economy*. Available Online.

REF3: Jan Reijnders. 1990. *Long Waves in Economic Development.* Cheltenham, UK: Edward Elgar.

REF4: J.J. van Duijn. 1983. *The Long Wave in Economic Life. London:* Allen & Unwin.

REF5: Nathan H. Mager. 1987. *The Kondratieff Waves.* New York: Praeger.

REF6: Franscisco Louçã and Jan Reijnders. Eds. *Foundations of Long Wave Theory.* 2 Vols. Cheltenham, UK: Edward Elgar.

REF7: Brian J. L. Berry. 1991. *Long-Wave Rhythms in Economic Development and Political Behavior.* Baltimore: John Hopkins University Press.

REF8: Chris Freeman. 1997. The Political Economy of the Long Wave. In *Environment, Technology and Economic Growth: The Challenges to Sustainable Development,* 159–183, eds. Andrew Tylecote and Jan van der Straaten. Cheltenham, UK: Edward Elgar.

REF9: Phillip Anthony O'Hara. 2003. Recent Changes to the IMF, WTO and SPD: Emerging Global Mode of Regulation or Social Structure of Accumulation for Long Wave Upswing? *Review of International Political Economy* 10(3): 481-519. https://doi.org/10.1080/09692290308426

Long Waves of Climate Change The first, *Hadeon Long Wave* (4.6b–4.0b years BP), represents the earliest stage of the formation of planet Earth, with plumes of various substances (such as H [Hydrogen], N [Nitrogen], He [Helium], H_2O [water vapor]) being ejected from volcanoes to form the atmosphere, with surface molten taking the form of super-hot lava. During the second, *Archean Long Wave* (4.0–2.5b years), life emerged, as oxygen and carbon concentrations developed, and an ozone layer began to protect life from deadly UV rays. During the third, *Proterozoic Long Wave* (2.5b–540m years) the so-called Great Oxygen Event, starting 2.4b years ago (circa), enabled the development of more complex life forms and more sophisticated climate systems. From the fourth, *Phanerozoic Long Wave* (540m years to the contemporary age, *circa* 1970s), we have clearer data of long waves of ice ages and hot periods, alternating during the era to the 1900s; with the more complex evolution of multicellular organisms that diversified into organisms currently on planet Earth; while the supercontinent *Pangaea* separated into the continents we have today.

None of these major waves or periods before the 1800s (or 1970s) were likely *anthropogenic*; i.e., caused specifically by humans (or other animals). They were caused by factors such as changes in the tilting of the Earth's axis, volcanic forcing, or solar irradiance. Current trends concerning climate are the first to be precipitated by human beings or 'non-natural' forces. The current period of expansion of greenhouse gasses commenced at a low base during the industrial revolution from the mid-1850s but did not noticeably increase until the 1970s when it started showing an upward warming trend through to the 2020s and likely beyond during the Anthropocene wave.

→||Chap. 4|| ||Cycles of Climate Change|| ||Long Waves of Growth||

REF: Phillip Anthony O'Hara. 2025. *Long Waves of Growth, Hegemonic Power, and Climate Change in the World Economy: Dutch, British, US and Chinese Capitalism and Structural Polycrises*. Singapore: Springer Nature.

Maddison, Angus Angus Maddison (1926–2010) was an economic historian specialising in national income accounting, GDP per capita, and macroeconomic development. He wrote about countries from every continent and numerous books about the world economy. His analysis of long waves revealed that the theory and empirics was impressive, but that waves were caused by accidental (exogenous) factors. His own view of long-term macrodynamics was that there were epochs and phases of evolution. His method of analysis was to concentrate on two major factors, first the institutional and socioeconomic environment, and secondly, the more technical variables. He always surveyed the socio-institutional dynamic structures while highlighting some specific statistics on various factors.

The epochs he examined included (a) Agrarianism (500–1500 AD, with average real growth per capita [gpc] of 0.00%), (b) advanced agrarianism (1500–1700, gpc 0.2%), (c) merchant capitalism (1700–1820, gpc 0.2%), and capitalism proper (1820 onwards, gpc 1.2%). Regarding capitalist development, he differentiated between the following phases: (1) 1820–1913 (subdivided into two phases), (2) 1913–1950, (3) 1950–1973, and (4) 1973 onwards. Maddison characterizes the first phase since 1820 as the movement from agriculture to industry and rural to urban lifestyles, the increasing role of government, expanding size of companies and unions, and the rise of the international monetary system. The second part of the first phase, 1870–1913, was seen as having little concern for unemployment, weak unions, the gold standard, free trade, and free factor movement. The 1913–1950 phase encompassed a beggar-thy-neighbour approach, largescale unemployment, an unstable exchange rate regime, wage declines, protectionism, and control of factor movements. The golden age of 1950–1973 saw full employment, fixed exchange rates, strong unions, freer trade and greater factor movements. The next phase, neoliberalism, saw a collapse of the international payments system, emphasis on price stability, weak unions, free trade, and free capital movements but restricted labor mobility. Maddison did not live to see the latest phase of rising conflict between Liberal Democracies and Autocratic powers, greater protectionism, and industry policy since the 2010s.

Out of his extensive experience of economic history and national account inquiry emerged the Maddison Project, which has an extensive personnel and published numerous versions of the database for most nations of the world, especially including GDP per capita, population, and the accompanying research papers, books and reports. It starts at year zero (AD) including figures where they have been estimated, with much data dating back to 1000 AD, while less developed and recent additions to the world economy often begin during 1800, or for especially the periphery 1950. The latest dataset 2024 (updated 18 Sept 2024) is available at:

Maddison Project Database 2023 | Releases | Groningen Growth and Development Centre | University of Groningen (rug.nl)

֍→||Chaps. 1, 5–8, 11||

REF1: Angus Maddison. 1991. *Dynamic Forces in Capitalist Development: A Long-Run Comparative View.* Oxford: Oxford University Press. 333pp

REF2: Angus Maddison. 2006. *The World Economy: Volume 1: A Millennial Perspective & Volume 2: Historical Statistics.* OECD. 653pp

Mandel, Ernest Ernest Ezra Mandel (1923–1995) was one of the greatest Marxist economists of the twentieth century, publishing many foundational books and articles on capitalism, socialism, long waves and dialectics. His *Marxist Economic Theory* (1963, 2 vols) produced a classic analysis of Marxian theory and empirics, being especially good on dynamics (including phases of evolution and business cycles). His magnum opus was *Late Capitalism* (1972), where he set out to comprehend the evolutionary transformation of capitalism in the latest phase of its evolution, set in historical perspective. His Cambridge lectures (Mandel 1980) were on long waves, where he developed a quite innovative approach to the dynamics of capitalism.

Mandel's analysis of long waves considers that the upper turning point of the wave is explained endogenously, while the lower turning point is largely exogenously determined. With an increase in the average rate of profit, and subsequent technological innovation (capital deepening) and general accumulation of capital (capital widening), both of which reduce average costs of production, a period of long wave expansion is set in motion at the macroeconomic level. Profit rates may be high for an extended period, partly through migration increasing the supply of labor power and potentially dampening (along with labor saving technology) the wage rate. The dominant reason for the falling rate of profit is the rising organic composition of capital through the massive level of accumulation during the upswing. Hence the drop in the average rate of profit (and the turning point from boom to recession) is due to a decline in the ratio of profits to total invested capital, resulting from a disproportionate rise in that part of capital spent on equipment and raw materials as against that spent on wages (1981, 337), while the rate of surplus value declines or is kept constant (or with the rise in the organic composition being greater than the rise in the rate of surplus value). The upper turning point (from long wave upswing to downswing) is thus largely endogenous, while the lower turning point (from long wave downswing to upswing) is primarily exogenous, since a whole series of changes are required to provide a new set of potentiality underlying growth and accumulation (1981, 338).

→||Long Waves of Economic Growth|| ||Capitalism||

REF1: Ernest Mandel. 1980. *Long Waves of Capitalist Development: The Marxist Interpretation.* Cambridge: Cambridge University Press.

REF2: Ernest Mandel. 1972. *Late Capitalism.* London: Verso, 1975. Translated from the German by Joris De Bres.

Marxian Institutional and Evolutionary PE Marxian political economy (MPE) has a tradition of including institutional and evolutionary aspects of its theoretical and empirical edifice. This does not include all Marxian traditions, but certainly it has been a major trend in some forms of Marxian analysis. It is especially noticeable in Marxian economic history (e.g., Eric Hobsbawm), Marxian archaeology (e.g., V. Gordon Childe), social structures of accumulation, the Regulation Approach, various trends in radical political economy (especially Howard Jay Sherman), and some other approaches (e.g., *Rethinking Marxism).* Often the term 'Marxian' seems redundant when writing Marxian IEPE since the important thing is the quality of the analysis rather than the category of the approach. Indeed, MIEPE has influenced so many traditions and scholars that isolating one element of the totality seems unnecessary. Marx himself was influenced by a myriad of scholars and his IE elements, including for instance, historical investigations into capitalism, its origins and evolution; the circuit of social capital, including the details on the production system, the sphere of circulation, and effective demand, and investigations into the monetary system, fictitious capitals, competition, centralisation, technological change, labor market and world economy. There is a lot in Marx to stimulate one's interest in institutional and evolutionary themes. Contemporary IEPE has used many aspects of his analysis, including innovations thereof, to investigate the dynamic motion of capitalism and its alternatives.

֍→|| ||Economic Surplus|| ||Circuit of Social Capital|| ||Chap. 7||

REF1: Eric Schutz. 2022. *Inequality, Class, and Economics.* New York: Monthly Review.

REF2: Howard J. Sherman and Paul D. Sherman. 2018. *Inequality, Boom, and Bust: from Billionaire Capitalism to Equality and Full Employment.* London: Routledge.

REF3: Stephen Maher and Scott M. Aquanno. 2024. Institutional Marxism. In *Encyclopedia of Critical Political Science*, 68–73. Ed. Clyde W. Barrow. Cheltenham, Edward Elgar.

Metabolic Rift Metabolic rift is the idea that capitalism historically sets up major rifts (contradictions) not only between capital and labor but also between capital and ecology, core and periphery, city and countryside, plus industry and agriculture. Most of the rifts of capitalism are caused by capital's need to exploit not only labor but also nature. Historically, capitalist processes and agents have tended to exploit labor as much as possible, treating workers like commodities and slaves where possible, and replacing them when they die, like a piece of earth discarded when not needed. Labor, however, may develop effective counterveiling powers to challenge this exploitation and subordination through double movements. Capital will also exploit the powers of the earth, waterways and space to gain a surplus devoid of the costs of reproduction.

Hence the norms of unadulterated capitalism will promote the dissolution of fish stocks, then turn to other (fish) stocks until they dissipate, in a circular and cumulative fashion. It will seek out rural or peripheral areas to provide resources until they disappear, then turn to other areas for exploitation until they diminish, to propagate city-urban commodification, again in a CCC fashion. Its agents and groups will annex and colonise islands and areas rich in guano (bat and bird droppings), high in nitrogen, protein, phosphorus, calcium, magnesium, as well as spices and herbs, and promote their depletion, using exploited labor to extract the resources until they collapse, when sources dry up, or promoting monocultures which threaten the viability of endogenous cultures, upsetting the ecological habitats for commercial gain. Each phase of capitalism develops new avenues for exploitation of labor and nature, to adapt and transform systems for profitable investment. Again, effective ecological counterveiling powers may seek to negate the exploitation and destruction by capital through effective double social movements.

֍→||Long Waves of Climate Change|| ||Capitalism||||

REF: John Bellamy Foster. 1999. Marx's Theory of Metabolic Rift: Classical Foundations for Environmental Sociology. *American Journal of Sociology* 105(2): 366–405.

Modern Monetary Theory [MMT] The four main principles of MMT are (a) money is a state symbol, (b) functional finance, (c) taxes drive money and (d) bonds are interest rate control mechanisms. MMT is an approach to money, production and employment that follows the Chartalist tenet that money is a mere *symbol*, established by the state, for purposes of promoting sustainable socioeconomic performance. It has historically been institutionalised by states as fiat money, and *taxes* have been imposed by states to ensure demand for state money. Functional finance is the main tool of state policy, namely, that state policy should be directed to ensuring full employment and price stability. Taxes and government spending are demand-moderating devices, while government bonds are used for moderating interest rates to regulate levels of demand. The coronacrisis period (2020–2022ff) has been described by some commentators as MMT put into practice; a scientific test of the efficacy of MMT. If so, it performed very well in preventing depression. Some scholars have presented points of conjecture about MMT, including that it has limits when interest rates rise or are high, and that it oversimplifies the complexity of the workings of governments and their monetary arms.

→||Chap. 9||Financial Instability Hypothesis||
REF: L. Randall Wray. 2024. *Modern Money Theory: A Primer on Macroeconomics for Sovereign Monetary Systems*. Palgrave Macmillan.

Multiple Capital Paradigm (MCP) The MCP is a recent approach to interdisciplinary studies, social science, and economics that seeks to open discourse to diverse ways of integrating global knowledge. It starts out by examining 'capital' as those durable structures of diverse phenomena that provide a flow of benefits over long historical time. 'Investment' is an increase in the stock of capital for new structures or replacement of old fabrics. Saving is the keeping of stocks for long-term potential benefit into the future as a type of social safety net or for 'redundancy' purposes. Consumption is the destruction of structures where use leads to demise rather than maintenance or enhancement. These terms can then be used to describe their effective demand equivalents (e.g., investment demand, etc.).

Capital is heterogeneous, lumpy, often difficult to divide, and subject to numerous types of real-world processes. One type of capital is financial capital, which represents the relatively durable and fundamental values of intangibles that depend upon goodwill, trust, institutions, and those with knowledge of subtle processes in the business of providing money, credit, advice and financial assets and liabilities. It takes various forms, of net worth, economic surplus, interest, rent, and the price of various assets. Often the market value of financial capital is greater than fundamentals which usually leads to speculative bubbles and financial instability and crises.

Another type of capital is 'durable fixed business capital', which includes things such as machinery, factories, vehicles, shipping, and perhaps inventories. There is the physicality aspect of these fixed capitals and the value aspect. Investment (demand) in durable fixed capitals tend to be subject to instabilities of the business cycle and the long wave. In the past this form of capital has been thought to be the most important.

A crucial type is knowledge capital, which includes the durable aspects of holding information, data, theories, hypotheses, concepts, and principles. There is tacit knowledge and specific knowledge, the former being subject to subtlety and learning by doing, and the latter being codified more emphatically in words, books and objects. Labor power is one form of knowledge, including the potential skills, applications, and endurance inherent in the worker. Traditionally, the value of labor may be greater than the renumeration provided by wages for labor power, in which case there is a surplus value which remains in the form of profit (or variously rent, interest and dividends).

A more recently included form of capital is that associated with trust, social networks, class and group solidarity, and relational aspects of gender and ethnic association. Here there are intra and inter-forms of social or cultural capitals. Trust is the most important form of relational capital since without it long-term processes cannot be sustained. Social class is dependent upon intra-group relations being more important than inter-group association. Yet for the political economy to continue to be a going concern key elements of inter-group trust and sociality are crucial to establish, maintain and develop. Social circles are important for establishing and maintaining community, information sharing and friendships underlying goodwill.

There are also natural capitals, which constitute various species, environmental processes, geographical resources, and spatial durability. These have to do with genetics, energy from the sun, production of chlorophyl, generation of oxygen, and layers of sediment that buildup through long historical time. A knowledge of natural capital is crucial for promoting species diversity, climate change mitigation and adaptation, and social survival on planet Earth and beyond.

The power that links to accumulating and maintaining stocks of different forms of capital provide the basis for hegemony, long wave upswing, and climate change moderation and adaptation. This takes the form not only of centripetal development of power but also sharing power with others to develop alliances, quid pro quo, treaties and export-import relationships. Production, commercial and financial power relies on complex, interactive relations of cooperation and domination, production and distribution, buying and selling, and reciprocity and redistribution.

֍→||Climate Change|| ||Hegemony|| ||Power|| ||Long waves of Growth||

REF1: Phillip Anthony O'Hara. 2001. Wealth Distribution and Global Inequality in the Multiple Capital Paradigm. *International Journal of Human Development* 1(1): 121–140. https://www.researchgate.net/publication/290991330_Wealth_Distribution_and_Global_Inequality_in_the_Multiple_Capital_Paradigm

REF2: Sean Stein Smith. 2015. Arguing for a Multiple Capital Model. *International Journal of Managerial Studies and Research* 3(5): 22–32.

REF3: Anne Elizabeth Fordham, Guy M. Robinson, Jen Cleary, Boyd Dirk Blackwell, and John Van Leeuwen. Use of a Multiple Capital Framework to Identify Improvements in the CSR Strategies of Australian Resource Companies. *Journal of Cleaner Production* 200: 704–730.

REF4: Joan Robinson. 1980. The Meaning of Capital. In *Collected Economic Papers of Joan Robinson. Vol. 5.* New York: Wiley & Sons, 59–70. (Originally published in French, *Revue d'Economie Politique*, March 1977.)
REF5: Thorstein Bunde Veblen. 1908. On the Nature of Capital, I & II. *The Quarterly Journal of Economics,* XXII(Aug-Sept). Reprinted in T.B. Veblen (1990) *The Place of Science in Modern Civilization and Other Essays.* London: Transaction Publishers, 324–386.

Neoliberalism Neoliberalism is system of thought and a socioeconomic system of governance. The system of thought is based around small government, strong and free markets, well-developed police and military (possibly privatised), state providing legality and electoral systems and a relatively small public sector. It is committed to deregulating industrial relations, the financial system, corporations, foreign capital flows, plus the health care system and education. The basic philosophy of neoliberalism is that a deregulated economy (often undertaken by a strong state) is the only form of socioeconomic organisation possible for promoting high levels of productivity, profitability and economic growth. It seeks to privatise as many public functions as possible, institute self-regulation by the business sector, and leave people free to choose commodities they prefer (vouchers for education). Historically, neoliberalism is seen as a strong global force since the late 1970s through to the 2000s. It is perhaps still strong, but has less legitimacy in the light of the Global Financial Crisis of 2007–2009, Eurodebt crises of 2008–2014, ongoing climate crises, and the coronacrisis of the early 2020s. Various contradictions of neoliberalism led to aspects of its relative demise, including e.g., that between capital and labor (lower real wages and insufficient productive demand); finance and industry (speculative bubbles and crises); ecological capital and durable fixed business capital (growing GHGs, habitat destruction); health crises (insufficient defence against Pandemics). It may well be that a new or concurrent phase of capitalism is developing with the emphasis on the schism (or merging) of liberal democratic politics on the one hand and those who believe in industry policy, tariffs, domestic development and populist economics on the other hand.

→||Policy and Governance|| ||Chaps. 7,9|| ||Global Financial Crisis||
REF1: Tibor Rutar. 2023. What is Neoliberalism Really? A Global Analysis of its Real-World Consequences for Development, Inequality, and Democracy. *Social Science Information* 62(3): 295–322.
REF2: John Komlos. 2024. *Neoliberal Economic Policy and the Rise of Right-Wing Populism: Western Civilization at the Crossroads.* Cham, Switzerland: Palgrave Macmillan.

Neo-Schumpeterian Political Economy Neo-Schumpeterian political economy is a contemporary trend in economics that draws liberally on the insights of Joseph Schumpeter but also incorporates many of the (other) advances in science that have emerged since Schumpeter's time. Especially relevant in this respect is the general (re)emergence of institutional and evolutionary themes, complexity theory, uncertainty, bounded rationality, qualitative novelty, innovation dynamics, development, change and long waves, in addition to the heterogeneity of agents, systems theory, new knowledge, industrial development, and innovative finance. An important role is given to public goods provision, especially education, knowledge, and information.

֍→||Chap. 3|| ||Freeman and Louçã|| ||Perez, Carlotta|| ||Chap. 3||
֍→||Schumpeter, Joseph Alios|| ||Innovation|| ||Creative Destruction||
REF1: Horst Hanusch and Andreas Pyka. 2007. *Elgar Companion to Neo-Schumpeterian Economics*. Cheltenham: Edward Elgar.
REF2: Christopher Freeman. 2019. History, Coevolution and Economic Growth. *Industrial and Corporate Change* 28(1): 1–44.

New Long Wave Method (NLWM) The NLWM is one of the ways in which long and short waves of growth are empirically assessed in this book. A second way is through use of the Circuit of Socioeconomic Dynamics Reproduction (CSD) and the Principles of Political Economy (POPE) Contingency Paradigm, examining the principles associated with the evolution and transformation of techno-institutional and eco-spatial factors. A third way is through use of other authors' assessments of the pattern of performance.

The statistical method of NLWM is as follows. We need a simple and straightforward method for readers of a book that seeks to be widely read. We (1) use real gross domestic product (GDP) *per capita* levels (rather than simply real GDP levels). This is because we want to emphasise the average standard of living in the economy. Then (2), and more importantly, we use real GDP per capita decadal AAGR to ascertain the wave like motion (growth rate) of the economy. Following this, (3) to ascertain the existence of upswings, borderline conditions and downswings, we transpose onto the decadal GDP per capita AAGR line a trend line (using ordinary least squares linear regression).

Afterwards (4), following Schumpeter to some degree, though for similar and different reasons, we transform the trend line into a bar (20 points width). Above the bar we have (long or short) upswing, since it is higher than average performance for the period. Below the bar we have downswing, since it is below average performance. Within the bar we have borderline conditions, since it is within the range of average performance. We utilise the wave/trend differential method as a type of simple filter, for filtering out average performance growth, and leaving us with remaining upswing (U), downswing (D) and borderline (B) performance. Multiple decades of upswing equal long wave upswing, multiple decades of downswing equal long wave downswing, and multiple decades of borderline equal long wave borderline performance. Single decades similarly equal short waves of U, D and B, respectively.

This method of wave-cycle/minus trend filter is comparable to that used by Alfred Kleinknecht (1990, 136–146) to analyse innovations deviating upwards or downwards from the trend line. Stanley Bober (1968, ch. 2) makes use of the least squares linear regression model of trend estimation and cycle comparison for his investigations of short cycles and how they depart from the trend. It is also comparable to the method used by Conroy and Emerson (2007), who examine ethical cycles moving around the trend. As they say: "attitudes may follow a cyclical pattern about a long-term trend in a similar fashion to the economy. That is, society's ethical attitudes may follow a general long-run trend with attitudes constant, increasing, or decreasing in their acceptance of ethically questionable behaviour, but that attitudes may also oscillate in a cyclical pattern around the trend" (p. 907).

The other two methods of assessing performance, apart from [1] cycle/trend comparisons, include [2] CSD-PoPE, which details the principles of political economy, including the eco-spatial, institutional and technological dynamic structures evolving over time. We use the PoPE Paradigm for assessing long waves, hegemony and climate change, by using historical inquiry for analysing the processes. And the third method is [iii] the use of other works, inquiring into whether these results are reinforced (or otherwise) by other scholarship. We use different authors and styles of science to provide a third mode of analysis into LWHegCC structures and dynamics.

֍→||Chaps. 1–3,5–8,11–12||Circuit of Socioeconomic Dynamics||
֍→||PoPE Contingency Paradigm|| ||Slutzky-Yule Effect||

REF1: Phillip Anthony O'Hara. 2024. *Long Waves of Growth, Hegemonic Power and Climate Change in the World Economy*: *Dutch, British, US and Chinese Capitalism and Structural Polycrises*. Singapore: Springer Nature.

REF2: Alfred Kleinknecht. 1990. *Innovation Patterns in Crisis and Prosperity: Schumpeter's Long Cycle Reconsidered.* London: Macmillan. Foreword by Jan Tinbergen.

REF3: Stanley Bober, *The Economics of Cycles and Growth.* New York: Wiley and Sons.

REF4: Conroy, Stephen J. and Tisha L.N. Emerson. 2007. Ethical Cycles and Trends: Evidence and Implications. *Journal of Business Ethics* 8(4): 905–911.

Path Dependence The concept of path dependence states that the future (of political economies) depends upon the path taken through time, and that these paths cannot easily be broken, although recognition of this fact can help establish a new trajectory for the future. Path dependence is closely associated with the concepts of hysteresis and lock-in. Macro and global economies do not easily tend towards equilibrium because the trajectory of evolution is complex, often involving blind drift, and subject to the impacts of multiple processes. Non-equilibrium processes, or multiple equilibria, involve complex movements and often major crises, periods of boom and crash. For instance, a major period of institutional dissonance, debt crises, depression, crisis, may generate substantial unemployment, and the longer the unemployment continues the higher the unemployment rate (hidden plus actual). The long-term unemployed take a substantial amount of time to reenter the labor force (if they re-enter it at all). Also, the establishment of a productive, investment-generating capitalist class, along with a generation of a skill-upscaled working class, and a forward-looking middle class, can help promote a long period of sustained socioeconomic performance that may last a generation, until its potential declines markedly. Similarly, an economy unable to generate substantial investment, consumption and productive government spending cannot easily eschew a downward trend as the institutional conditions underlying this underperforming economy continue into the foreseeable future. People often start relationships that are hard to break because of habits, institutions, emotions, and lock-ins. The principle of path dependence states that one needs to analyse these processes to comprehend and ameliorate world problems, including long waves of growth, hegemonic power and climate change mitigation and adaptation.

֍→||Chaps. 1–12|| ||Long Waves of Growth|| ||Long Waves of Climate Change|| ||
֍→||Hegemony||

REF: Paul A. David. 2007. Path Dependence: A Foundational Concept for Historical Social Science. *Cliometrica* 1(1): 91–114. https://doi.org/10.1007/s11698-006-0005-x

Perez, Carlotta Born in Venezuela during 1939 Carlotta Perez contributed theory and empirics to the neo-Schumpeterian task of understanding long-term change in technology, finance and socio-political-economic institutions in the performance of capitalist economies. She developed the ideas of Great Surges, the techno-economic structure, and the correspondence between different elements of business and social economy. In her framework, major changes in capitalism are initiated by successive bouts of speculative bubbles in new technology (e.g., the regime of ICT, biomedicine and AI-robots during the 1980s–2010s), which rise and fall perhaps several times (e.g., the dot.com bubble burst with a major crash in 1999–2000). These changes are required to structurally modify the organisational arrangements of the economy, including habits, mores, skills and the competitive environment. There is no certainty that techno-economic dynamics will engender a wholesale change in the system resulting in a new surge that promotes high levels of long-term growth and development. Hence the economic malaise of the past several decades in the global economy (see Chaps. 9,11 below). In short, the technology style may be well formed, but the synchronization with a suitable mode of regulation and sociopolitical institutions is weak, resulting in malaise and under-performance.

R. J. Gordon argues that the contemporary technology regime is a pale imitation of past ones (such as the Steam Engine, Railways, Telephone, Combustion engine, etc) which thus inhibits long-term growth. Perez in contrast has confidence in the financial and technological revolution but believes stumbling blocks may develop within the polity, governance, and social arrangements that may inhibit the movement from great surge to long-term growth and general performance. In her paradigm a schism has developed between the techno-economic regime and the polity-governance-social regimes. Fransisco Louçã believes this is why the Fifth Kondratiev upswing has not taken hold in the advanced nations and others since the 1980s.

Phillip O'Hara argues that contradictions within the technology style (a la R.J. Gordon) as well as wider ones within the economic-political-social regime (a la Perez and Louçã), including the absence of a new major hegemon (or a multipolar-multilateral substitute system) has prevented the emergence of major global or multinational long wave since the 1980s (although such a wave has operated in parts of

Asia, including China). In short, principles associated with the PoPE Contingency Paradigm, including the CSD, have prevented successful transformation into long wave upswing far beyond China and Asia due to the operation of major contradictions and insufficient innovations in the political economy.

֍→||Chaps. 1–12|| ||Neo-Schumpeterian|| ||Chaps. 1,6,7|| ||Freeman and Louçã||
֍→||PoPE Contingency Paradigm||.||Gordon, Robert J.|| ||Tylecote, Andrew||
REF: Wolfgang Drechsler, Rainer Kattel, and Eric S. Reinert. 2009. *Techno-Economic Paradigms: Essays in Honour of Carlota Perez*. London: Anthem Press.

Policy and Governance The principle of policy and governance states that we should seek to improve the conditions of all species of life on planet Earth (except maybe certain viruses, bacteria, etc.), since many forms of variety improve our knowledge and experience of life and thereby enhance the common good. In this context, it also involves the process of social provisioning, enhancing the quality of life, standard of living and participatory democracy while protecting the community from conflicts, wars and other forms of violence. It also includes functional finance, automatic and discretionary fiscal/monetary policy, accords and agreements, plus climate change mitigation and adaptation. In theory, governance can and should be provided by all institutions, organisations and agents, but only if they seek to enhance the common good rather than their own self-interest. Self-regulation by business is sometimes a good objective but too often undertaken out of self-interest rather than concern for the whole society. Too often also states are captured by corrupt interests, through various actions including bribery, fraud, embezzlement, nepotism, extortion, and numerous conflicts of interest. Political economy seeks to emasculate these contradictions from the edifice of the system.

֍→||Chaps. 5–10||
REF: Phillip Anthony O'Hara. Ed. 2022. *International Encyclopedia of Public Policy*. 4 Vols. Perth: GPERU. Online Edition. Second Edition. https://archive.org/details/international-encylopedia-of-public-policy-volume-1/International%20Encylopedia%20of%20Public%20Policy%20Volume%201/ https://archive.org/details/international-encylopedia-of-public-policy-volume-1/International%20Encylopedia%20of%20Public%20Policy%20Volume%202/ https://archive.org/details/international-encylopedia-of-public-policy-volume-1/International%20Encylopedia%20of%20Public%20Policy%20Volume%203/ https://archive.org/details/international-encylopedia-of-public-policy-volume-1/International%20Encylopedia%20of%20Public%20Policy%20Volume%204/ https://independent.academia.edu/PhillipOHara

PoPE Contingency Paradigm The PoPE contingency paradigm applies the major principles of (institutional and evolutionary) political economy (PoPE) to economic growth, hegemony, and climate change, showing that these applications are contingent upon integrating forces merging to potentially constitute processes of upswing and downswing. Long waves of growth, hegemony and climate change (LWHegCC) are thereby hypothesized to be contingent upon and interrelated with several factors, which are linked to the principles, that allude to several processes generating these contingencies. These principles (and contingencies) include (1) history and evolution, (2) hegemony and uneven development, (3) the principle of *the circuits of socioeconomic dynamics* (CSD), (4) heterogeneous agents and groups, (5) the amplified and magnified multifactor CCC (circular and cumulative causation) forces at work, (6) the contradictory processes in motion, (7) the degree of uncertainty in the socioeconomic environment, (8) the nature of and uneven impact of innovation and novelty, (9) the role of policies and governance. The techno-institutional and eco-spatial dynamic structures of the political economy need to be suitably arranged according to these contingencies to develop long wave upswings, hegemonic dominance, and climate change mitigation and adaptation.

֍→||Chaps. 1–12|| ||Historical Specificity|| ||Hegemony|| ||Uneven Development||
֍→||Uncertainty|| ||Circuit of Socioeconomic Dynamics|| ||Contradiction||
֍→||Heterogeneous Groups and Agents|| ||Circular & Cumulative Causation||
֍→||Innovation|| ||Policy & Governance||
REF: Phillip Anthony O'Hara. 2024. *Long Waves of Growth, Hegemonic Power and Climate Change in the World Economy: Dutch, British, US and Chinese Capitalism and Structural Polycrises.* Singapore: Springer Nature.

Political Economy Political economy has many meanings, but a core one is that it is an interdisciplinary study of the evolution, development, organisation and contradictory reproduction of the processes of social provisioning, production, distribution, and exchange of material and immaterial means of life on planet Earth and beyond. Often accompanying this is the notion that it is a study of the structured use of power by various vested interests to control the economic surplus for their own benefit, and the use of governance processes to reduce legitimacy for reproducing this asymmetric distribution of resources. One can thus use political economy to provide a theory and framework for potentially challenging this hegemonic dominance to distribute and control resources more equitably and enhancing social provisioning for the benefit of the community through a double movement.

֍→||Chaps. 1–12|| ||PoPE Contingency Paradigm|| ||Disembedded Economy||
REF1: Phillip Anthony O'Hara. 2001. *Encyclopedia of Political Economy.* 2 vols London: Routledge, paper and ebook editions.
REF2: Howard Jay Sherman. 1987. *Foundations of Radical Political Economy.* Armonk, New York: M.E. Sharpe.
REF3: Joan Robinson and John Eatwell. 1973. *An Introduction to Modern Economics.* Revised Ed. New York: McGraw Hill.

Polycrises A crisis is where there is a turning point for the worst, such as the emergence of a financial crisis and/or recession. This crisis may be affecting a nation, region or the world. A polycrisis is where multiple crises emerge when there are several turning points towards instability and dissociation within the same or similar period. Structural polycrises occur when there are several turning points towards instability and dissociation which are closely connected in time, space and causality. These structural polycrises (SP) tend to occur during eras when there is no absolute hegemony and moreso when there is no absolute or relative hegemony.

More generally, SP occur when no set of techno-institutional and eco-spatial and relationships promote socioeconomic performance in the regional or global political economy. SP are said to have emerged during the 1700s, 1890s–1940s, and 1970s/1980s–2020s. For instance, during the 1970s/1980s–2020s there emerged the variously *overlapping or sequential* structural polycrises of (a) successive decadal financial crises and recessions, (b) debt crises in the periphery (1980s in Latin America and 1980s–1990s in Africa), (c) Asian financial crisis of 1997 and Russian financial crisis of 1998, (d) GFC of 2007–2009, (e) Eurocrisis of 2009–2014ff, (f) coronacrisis of 2000–2022, (g) climate crisis of 2000s-onwards, and (h) several military crises involving terrorists, Russia-Ukraine-NATO, Palestine-Israel-Lebanon-Iran, and so on. These crises are structurally linked in different degrees during different times. When polycrises are affecting political economies their performance will generally be lacklusture. Political economy exists to moderate these polycrises and other problems in the social economy by promoting long wave upswings, climate change mitigation and adaptation, quality of life, standard of living, and social provisioning.

֍→||Crises|| ||Chaps. 5–8,9,10|| ||Global Financial Crisis|| ||Long Waves||
֍→||Freeman and Louçã||

REF1: David Henig and Daniel M. Knight. 2023. Polycrisis: Prompts for an Emerging Worldview. *Anthropology Today* 39(2): 3–6.

REF2: Mohd Shahril Abdul Rahman, Mariah Awang and Zainab Toyin Jagun. 2024. Polycrisis: Factors, Impacts, and Responses in the Housing Market. *Renewable and Sustainable Energy Reviews* 202: 114713.

REF3: Achim Szepanski. 2024.*Capitalism in the Age of Catastrophe: The Newest Developments of Financial Capital in Times of Polycrisis.* Cham, Switzerland: Palgrave Macmillan.

Post-Keynesian Institutionalism [PKI] PKI is a term to formalise the notion that Keynes and specifically many of his followers are institutionalists in the sense that the historical and institutional environment of capitalism and its alternatives (and antecedents) are core parts of their analysis. They also usually recommend institutional changes to improve the functioning of capitalism or modify it towards a more social democratic or democratic socialist direction. Some of the more well-known PKIs of recent decades include Hyman Minsky, J.K. Galbraith, Victoria Chick, Philip Arestis, L. Randall Wray, Stephanie Kelton and Charles Whalen. These PKIs have always had a strong linkage with Veblenian institutionalists, and to some degree other institutional and evolutionary scholars who share an interest in their concepts of aggregate demand, uncertainty, monetary theory of production, endogenous money and credit, financial instability hypothesis and modern monetary theory.

֍→||Modern Monetary Theory||→||Financial Instability Hypothesis||

REF1: Hiroyasu Uemura. 2023. *Japanese Institutionalist Post Keynesians Revisited: Inheritance from Marx, Keynes and Institutionalism,* Springer Nature.

REF2: Eduardo Fernández-Huerga, Ana Pardo, and Ana Salvador. 2024. Compatibility and Complementarity Between Institutional and Post-Keynesian Economics: A Literature Review with a Particular Focus on Methodology. *Economia Politica*. Available Online. https://doi.org/10.1007/s40888-023-00299-7
REF3: Charles J. Whalen. Ed. 2022. *A Modern Guide to Post-Keynesian Institutional Economics*. Cheltenham: Edward Elgar.

Power Bertrand Russel (1938) in his book *Power*, defined power as the "ability to produced intended effects" and argued that rather than sex being the motive force of human energy (as in Freud), and rather than economic self-interest being the core motive for human action (as for economists), it resides in power. People seek to increase or sustain their power, in the sense of producing intended effects to their actions. William Dugger believes that in contemporary political economies power lies in the various roles that people play, e.g., as parent, employed personnel, citizen, participant in public affairs, stakeholder, environmental activist, CEO, etc; and that business interests have most power compared with states, families and civil society groups. E.L. Wheelwright argued that corporate power was executed through the corporate domination of the world, regions and nations; market concentration; restrictive trade practices; interlocking directorates; and linkages with political-power networks. Power also resides in largescale aggregates, such as nations in the world economy, as with hegemonic power, that evolved from, e.g., Dutch (1600s) to British (1800s) to United States (1900s) to potentially Chinese (mid-2000s?) hegemony (viz. Wallerstein).

֍→||Chaps. 1–12|| ||Hegemony|| ||Heterogeneous Groups and Agents|| ||Class|| ||Gender||
֍→||Age|| ||Wars||
REF1: Bertrand Russell. 1938. *Power: A New Social Analysis*. London: Unwin Books, 1975.
REF2: Edward Lawrence Wheelwright. 1974. Concentrations of Private Economic Power, 115–126. *Radical Political Economy: Collected Essays*. Sydney: ANZ Books.
REF3: John Kenneth Galbraith. 1980. *The Anatomy of Power.* Boston: Houghton Mifflin Co.
REF4: William Waller. 2022. A Reconsideration of William Dugger's Analysis of Power. *Forum for Social Economics* 51(1): 95–111. https://doi.org/10.1080/07360932.2017.1370603

Principles of Institutional and Evolutionary Political Economy A principle in political economy is a rule of action based on a concept. For instance, the (1) principle of historical specificity and evolution states that one should examine all problems within an historically specific context to understand them more fully and how they evolve, and that this concept will assist in developing innovations and policies for moderating problems and comprehending dynamics.The other core principles include (2) hegemony and uneven development; (3) pathways and circuits of socio-conomic dynamics (CSD); (4) heterogeneous groups and agents; (5) circular and cumulative causation; (6) contradiction and creative destruction; (7) innovation and novelty; (8) uncertainty and risk; and (9) policy and governance. O'Hara (2023) developed eight of these principles, while O'Hara (2025) added a ninth principle of the circuits of socioeconomic dynamics. There are many other principles closely associated with the core general ones. Many review articles and book reviews have examined O'Hara (2023), such as (for instance) Ian Kerr (2023), Alpar Lošonc (2023), the *Journal of Economic Literature* (2023), Harry Bloch (2023), Frank Stilwell (2023), and Thomas Lambert (2025); and others have applied these principles to specific isssues and current problems, for instance, Baidyanath Ghosh (2007), Andrew John Brennan and Jaslin Kaur Kalsi (2015), and Jennifer Guerra (2022). The O'Hara (2023) book has also been subject to an online Legal-Economics-Nexus Podcast (2023).

֍→||Chaps. 1–12|| ||PoPE Contingency Paradigm|| ||Evolution|| ||Historical Specificity||
֍→||Hegemony|| ||Uneven Development|| ||Circuit of Socioeconomic Dynamics||
֍→||Heterogeneous Groups and Agents|| ||Contradictions|| ||Innovation||
֍→||Circular and Cumulative Causation|| ||Uncertainty|| ||Policy and Governance||

REF1: Phillip Anthony O'Hara, 2023. *Principles of Institutional and Evolutionary Political Economy: Applied to Current World Problems*. Singapore: Springer Nature. Revised Edition. Principles of Institutional and Evolutionary Political Economy: Applied to Current World Problems | SpringerLink

REF2: Phillip Anthony O'Hara. 2025. *Long Waves of Growth, Hegemonic Power, and Climate Change in the World Economy: Dutch, British, US and Chinese Capitalism and Structural Polycrises*. Singapore: Springer Nature.

REF3: Jennifer Guerra. 2022. *Love Capital: A Manifesto for Political and Revolutionary Eros*. Milan: Bompiani Publishers. Translated from the Italian by Alice Kilgariff.

REF4: Baidyanath Ghosh. 2007. *Gandhian Political Economy: Principles, Practice and Policy*. Aldershot, UK: Ashgate Publishers.

REF5: Andrew John Brennan and Jaslin Kaur Kalsi. 2015. Elephant Poaching and Ivory Trafficking Problems in Sub-Saharan Africa: An Application of O'Hara's Principles of Political Economy. *Ecological Economics* 120: 312–337.

REF6: Alpar Lošonc. 2023.Review Article of O'Hara (2023), *Panoeconomicus*, Vol 70, No, 2023, pp. 683-690. https://panoeconomicus.org/index.php/jorunal/article/view/2023/806.

REF7: Ian Kerr. 2023. Review Article of O'Hara (2023), *Journal of Economic Issues*, Vol 57, No 4, pp. 2023, 1375–1381. https://www.tandfonline.com/doifull/10.1080/00213624.2023.2273189

REF8: Harry Block. 2023. Book Review of O'Hara (2023), *History of Economics Review*, Vol 85, Issue 1, pp. 100-101. https://www.tandfonline.com/doi/full/10.1080/10370196.2023.2219501.

REF9: Frank Stilwell. 2022–2023. Book Notes on O'Hara (2023), *Journal of Australian Political Economy*, 2022–2023, Number 90, pp. 143–144. www.ppesydney.net/content/uploads/2022/12/10_Book-notes.pdf

REF10: JEL. 2023. Book notes on O'Hara (2023) *Journal of Economic Literature*, June, pp. 748-749. https://pubs.aeaweb.org/doi/pdfplus/10.1257/jel.61.2.745

REF11: Legal-Economics-Nexus Podcast (1923), Interview with Phil O'Hara (2023). https://podcasts.apple.com/us/podcast/an-interview-with-phil-ohara/id1569479269?i=1000610604160

REF12: Thomas Lambert (2025) Review of O'Hara (2023) (5pp), *Review of Political Economy*. https://www.tandfonline.com/doi/full/10.1080/09538259.2025.2493272

Radiative Forcing Radiative forcing is the process whereby the sun's rays on Earth has an influence on Earth's temperature; the influence can be positive, negative or in balance. If it is in balance the net incoming and outgoing radiations are equal to zero. If it is positive the net incomings are greater than zero, and Earth's climate warms. And if it is negative the net figure is less than zero, and Earth's climate cools. Much depends upon what happens when the incoming radiation is affected by natural and human activities. For instance, if trees are cut down to be replaced by concrete buildings there is more carbon dioxide relative to oxygen in the 'transaction', which usually results in warming. If wild animal habitats are destroyed and replaced by coal fired power stations, there is again more (net) carbon dioxide produced in the transaction, and temperatures rise. A reduction in glaciers and ice-sheets will likely reduce the degree of reflection of radiation to the outer atmosphere and result in warming and rising sea levels. However, a certain increase in radiative forcing, due to higher levels of GHG, may take time for the full impact to manifest itself, resulting in, e.g., gradually rising mean temperatures. *Through historical time*, a specific extant increase (or decrease) in Earth's GHG stocks and especially flows take time to fully impact crucial tipping points such as ice sheets, glaciers, monsoonal systems, coral reefs, ocean currents, and meso/macro-climate systems such as El Nino. Mean Earth atmospheric temperatures in 2023 have risen by just under 1.5 °C since 1850–1900 but the full impact of the extant increase in GHGs lies in the future. Impacts will continue to increase even if GHG stocks do not rise further; but the fact that mean atmospheric temperatures are still rising majorly equals cascading cumulative escalating back-logs of impacts to deal with. In other words, cascading tipping points of no return are happening with the current 4–5 tipping points being impacted due to magnified, amplified and CCC-type expansions of these contradictions. The change in surface temperature (Ts) caused by increases in radiative forcing (F) can be calculated using the formula: $\Delta Ts = \lambda \Delta F$, where λ is typically valued at 0.8 $K/(W/m^2)$. (The parameters may change through time.)

֍→||Chaps. 4, 9||Long Waves of Climate Change||

REF: Nicolas Bellouin, Will Davies, Keith P. Shine, Johannes Quaas, Johannes Mülmenstädt, Piers M. Forster, Chris Smith, Lindsay Lee, Leighton Regayre, Guy Brasseur, Natalia Sudarchikova, Idir Bouarar, Olivier Boucher, and Gunnar Myhre. 2020. Radiative Forcing of Climate Change from the Copernicus Reanalysis of Atmospheric Composition. *Earth System Science Data* 12(3): ESSD, 12, 1649–1677. https://doi.org/10.5194/essd-12-1649-2020

Regulation Approach The Regulation Approach (RA) to political economy emerged out of the decline of the postwar boom of Fordism, US hegemony, and the Keynesian welfare state in the 1970s. Its major adherents are Michel Aglietta, Robert Boyer, Alain Lipietz, Bob Jessop, and several others. There are also multiple schools of regulation theory and empirics. RA's primary aim was to revise and reconstruct Marxian political economy in the twentieth century institutional and technological environment, and in consequence to provide an alternative evolutionary approach to capitalist development. The core concepts of RA that emerged were (1) mode of accumulation, (2) regime of accumulation, (3) institutional forms, (4) reproduction, and (5) rupture. One 'traditional' way of explaining these is to say that the capitalist mode of accumulation (MOA) includes a regime of accumulation (ROA) and several institutional forms (F). Since the 1800s there have been two main (and a third) ROA, first the extensive ROA, typical of the period during the 1800s to the early 1900s (based on absolute surplus value); second the intensive ROA, from the early-mid 1900s to the early 2000s (Fordism); and thirdly a flexible system of production from the late 1900s to the (possibly) mid-2000s.

The Fordist system associated with the postwar (1945–1990) regime of accumulation included, firstly, the interactive tendency for unstable expansion between consumer and capital goods sectors, a technology style of internal combustion engine and semi-automatic assembly line process, and economies of scale and scope. The structural forms included the postwar corporate system, the Bretton Woods system, Keynesian welfare state, regulated finance, US hegemony, and familial organisation. These institutions and the technology style developed contradictions that eventually ruptured their reproductive forms. Productivity declined during the early 1970s and 1980s due to rising worker power and technological maturation. Finance became more unstable due to speculative bubbles and rising unproductive activities. Familial organisations underwent instability as divorce rates rose and people created alternatives to the nuclear family. Absolute US hegemony declined due to challenges to US power. The system-crises that emerged included periodic financial crises, deep recessions, social unrest and geopolitical conflicts.

However, the forms of flexible accumulation and neoliberalism that partly replaced Fordism and its associated institutions since the 1990s did not solve capitalism's problems and crises. Low levels of inventories were problematic in the light of periodic supply-chain disruptions. Total quality management was costly in the light of Chinese competition and low prices. And worker participation in management failed to widen due to greater centralisation/centripetal development of power. Neoliberalism took centre stage but did not regenerate capitalism's growth potential due to stagnant wages, insufficient productive investment and financial instability and crises.

More recently, we have seen a global (increasing) trend to a new structural form of greater protectionism, industry policy, and extreme nationalism that is in some respects reminiscent of the Begger-thy-neighbour policies of the 1910s–1930s that led to the rise of fascism and world-war II. Is history repeating itself but in some different forms? We also have developments in the regime of accumulation through information and communications technology, AI, Internet and biotechnology sectors. But according to R.J. Gordon these are promoting long-term productivity sufficiently for a new long wave upswing.

→||Chaps. 3, 7||

REF1: Michal Aglietta. 1975. *A Theory of Capitalist Regulation.* London: New Left Books.

REF2: Bob Jessop. Ed. 2001. *Regulation Theory and the Crises of Capitalism.* 5 Vols. Cheltenham, Edward Elgar.

REF3: *Revue de la regulation: Capitalisme, institutions, pouvoirs.* (*Review of Regulation. Capitalism, institutions, pouvoirs.*) Journal of the Regulation Approach. Revue de la régulation - Capitalisme, institutions, pouvoirs (openedition.org)

Rostow, Walt Whitman Walt Rostow (1916–2003) was a famous economic historian, who also provided extensive advice to multiple US Presidents, especially on foreign policy and national security (to the annoyance of some people especially during and after the Vietnam War). He also became (in)famous for his *The Stages of Economic Growth* volume (in many editions and versions), which had a very conspicuous subtitle (which also annoyed many people). His politics however tended often to out-play his economic history, even though his economic history was outstanding, He was a grand master of economic history before cliometrics emerged. Methodologically he was close to Charles Kindleberger and Eric Hobsbawm in using general themes and big issues to explain history, although he used much more extensive data and tables than they did.

His empirics and theory of long waves engage in extensive economic history for an understanding of the dynamics of especially core economies. The crucial thing about his work is that he believed in the *irreducible complexity of history,* which meant that no endogenous theory could explain core elements of motion, and that long waves should be studied from a pragmatic and thematic but not deterministic approach.

Hence, Rostow's is the least mono-causal long wave theory, since he stresses the dynamic interplay of (1) leading sectors, (2) changing profitability of the primary sector, and (3) the large international process of migration, its relationship to the size of the workforce and demand for housing. Rostow was concerned with the 'complex process of economic growth' and rejects the position that there are long waves with an endogenous mechanism propelling the cyclical movement of the economy over successive 40–60 years. Wars, extensive primary sector expansion and long gestation periods for investment are more important to Rostow in providing a dynamic framework within which the international economy exhibits periodic, regular, trend (not cyclical) and internationally synchronized movements in prices (and output). Movements in prices, especially relative primary prices divided by industrial prices, constitute the dominant empirical variable upon which he periodizes 'long-trends'. In seeing the 1950s as a long wave decline and the 1970s a rise his analysis is anomalous compared with most other accounts of these periods.

Nonetheless, his approach was refreshing and contributed much to the renewal of long wave analysis during the 1960s–1990s.

֍→||Chap. 3||

REF1: W.W. Rostow. 1980. *Why the Poor Get Rich and the Rich Slow Down: Essays on the Marshallian Period.* London: Macmillan.

REF2: W.W. Rostow. 1978. *The World Economy: History and Prospect.* London: Macmillan.

Schumpeter, Joseph Alois Schumpeter (1883–1950) was born in Austria-Hungary, was briefly a Minister of Finance in the Austrian Government of 1919 and was called by some a 'Rich Person's Karl Marx'. The reason for the link to Marx is that his economic methodology was comparable to Marx, in that he concentrated on the inner motion of capitalism, and he dedicated his book on *Capitalism, Socialism and Democracy* (1950; *CSD*) to Marx. His *magnum opus* was *The Theory of Economic Development* (1911), where he developed his theory of innovation, the role of the entrepreneur, and business cycles. He went on to write many more books, notably for long waves, *Business Cycles* (1939), which was subtitled: "*A Theoretical, Historical, and Statistical Analysis of the Capitalist Process.*

In *Business Cycles* Schumpeter starts with the circular flow of economic motion in equilibrium, with perfect competition, the existence of workers and landlords, and money functioning only as a means of simple circulation.

He then introduced the first approximation to the real world through the introduction of entrepreneurs and money capitalists that start the metamorphosis, borrowing (credit) to finance innovation, which generates a two-phase cycle of recession and recovery. Innovation is generated through product, process, market, raw material and corporate clusters of novelty.

The second approximation operated when credit is (over-)extended beyond innovation to finance general accumulation, speculation and over-indebtedness which generates a four-phase cycle of upswing, boom, recession and depression.

The third approximation introduces innovations of variable durability and periodicity/amplitude generating cycles/waves of different periodicities, volatilities and mechanisms/processes. This involved multiple fluctuations such as 'Kitchin cycles' (3–4 years), 'Juglar cycles' (7–11 years) and 'Kondratievs' (45–60 years) (He mechanized the periodicities between the three 'cycles' in Schumpeter 1939, 213.)

Schumpeter promoted the idea of 'creative destruction', in which the motivate force of capitalism generates major changes and new ways of doing things. It destroys cultures, firms, jobs, industries, ecologies and institutions, with the need to deal with the ramifications of these creations/destructions.

Three technical things are crucial with respect to Schumpeter for this current book. The first is that he utilised 'neighborhoods of equilibrium', which are areas or bars (not lines): regions that capitalism is working within, and which are somewhat indeterminate (we use these for borderline performances). The second is that during long wave upswings financial crises and recessions tend to be more moderate than during long wave downswings (and visa-versa for long wave downswings). And thirdly, credit or debt is a core potential anomaly especially during the upper turning point and the associated long wave downswing when it can generate a debt deflation, financial crises and debt crises.

His analysis of long waves has been subject to much discussion and criticism. For instance, Paul Sweezy rightly argued that he should have included capitalists in his schema not just as financiers but also as entrepreneurs and managers, and indeed as part of the largescale corporation (the latter which Schumpeter did incorporate in his *CSD*), and include surplus value in the circular flow. Kuznets heaped praise on him for asking the right questions and trying hard to incorporate them in his inquiry, but argued Schumpeter should have specifically tested his hypotheses more directly in history. Since the 1970s there has been a full-blown neo-Schumpeterian school of political economy that has used some of his methodology to study long waves, but in some respects has utilised a more historical and institutional approach than Schumpeter did.

֍→||Chaps. 1–3|| ||Neo-Schumpeterian Political Economy|| ||Perez, Carlotta||
֍→||Freeman and Louçã||

REF1: Joseph A. Schumpeter. 1970. *Treatise on Money.* Aalten, Netherlands: Wordbridge Publishing, 2014. English translation by Ruben Alvarado
REF2: Joseph A. Schumpeter. 1928. The Instability of Capitalism. *Economic Journal* 38(151): 361–386.
REF3: Christopher Freeman. 2015. Schumpeter's "Business Cycles" Revisited. *European Journal of Economic and Social Systems* 27(1–2): 47–67
REF4: Allen Oakley. 1990. *Schumpeter's Theory of Capitalist Motion: A Critical Exposition and Reassessment.* Cheltenham: Edward Elgar.
REF5: Harry Bloch. 2018. *Schumpeter's Price Theory.* Oxon: Routledge.

Shared Socioeconomic Pathways (SSP) A SSP is a concept used by ecological economists and the IPCC to describe specific types of responses to the environmental crisis of climate change. One pathway used to help solve climate change anomalies is called the Green Road to Sustainability (SSP1), where quality of life is given priority over GDP growth, GHGs are replaced by technologies such as wind and solar power to reduce emissions, and electric cars as well as bicycles and walkways assist in temperature rises to up to 1.0–1.8 °C (uncertainty differentials) by 2100, relative to 1850–1900 mean. Another SSP, the High Road of Growth (SSP5), emphasises adaptation while promoting GHG emissions, high GDP growth and rising levels of consumption, where the global mean temperature may rise by up to 3.3–5.7 °C by 2100, compared to the 1850–1900 mean,thereby not solving the climate crisis dilemmas. There are various other SSPs in between these extremes that lead to temperature increases of between 2.1–4.6 °C by 2100 compared with the 1850–1900 mean. Discussing SSPs in terms of pathways is an innovation in thinking about climate change, but usually they are not analysed in terms of the degree of structural change required, nor with respect to the likely fact that the 2024 rise in global mean temperature to just above 1.5 °C, relative to the 1850–1900 mean, is probably the highest we could go before 4–5 tipping points lead to 'points of no return'.

➔||Chaps. 4, 9|| ||Long Waves of Climate Change||

REF: Ivo Welch. 2024. *The IPCC Shared Socioeconomic Pathways (SSPs): Explained, Evaluated, Replaced.* Working Paper 32178. Cambridge, MA: NBER. 45pp. w32178.pdf (nber.org)

Slutsky-Yule Effect Eugen Slutsky (1880–1948) worked at Kondratiev's Conjuncture Research Institute in Moscow and published important works that are relevant to long waves. This summary relies especially on the work of Judy Klein (1999) and Vincent Barnett (2006). Slutsky's work was published in Russian and English. His main thesis is that summation of random factors is capable under certain conditions of producing a wave-like motion in the data. A second thesis is that the data's wave-like motion may exhibit periodic regularity over time. Together Slutsky thus posits that recurring long waves of economic motion may result from data that has no real causal basis. This may occur when random data is analysed using *moving averages* (overlapping techniques). Cycles and waves of a random nature may thus become confused with cycles and waves with specific causal processes. Much has been made of the Slutsky random causes notion of cycles and waves, often without emphasising that he hypothesised the possibility of this occurring, not that it necessarily did occur. What Slutsky did argue is that if a moving average of a random set of values is devised as trend, then a coherent wave or cycle motion *may* (or may not) result.

Slutsky's work could be interpretated as saying two things. The first is that real economic cycles could be the result of chance factors, and the second that chance factors may lead certain techniques to resemble real cycles or waves when this is spurious. The latter is the method that should be eschewed where possible. Barnett notes that many scholars have misinterpreted Slutsky's theses, especially by relating the issue to exogenous factors and equilibrium conditions. Perhaps what we can learn from Slutsky is that we should keep his main thesis in mind when doing empirical work. But we can also try to ascertain the nature of real empirical trends and waves from alternative references, not only data, but also historical inquiry, case studies and multiple sources. The Slutsky Effect is sometimes called the "Slutsky-Yule Effect" (see G.U. Yule 2026), and Ragnar Frisch was working on a parallel path.

➔||Chaps. 1–3||

REF1: Eugen Slutzky. 1937. The Summation of Random Causes as the Source of Cyclic Processes. *Econometrica* 5(2): 105–145.

REF2: G.U. Yule. 1926. Why Do we Sometimes get Nonsense Correlations between Time Series? *Journal of the Royal Statistical Society*, 89(1): 1–64.

REF3: Judy Klein. 1999. The Rise of "Non-October" Econometrics: Kondratiev and Slutsky at the Moscow Conjuncture Institute, *History of Political Economy* 31(1): 137–168.

REF4: Vincent Barnett. 2006. Chancing an Interpretation: Slutzky's Random Cycles Revisited. *European Journal of the History of Economic Thought* 13(3): 411–432.

Social democracy Especially over the past 100 years, social democracy has been seen as a sociopolitical system, or a political party, which balances the forces of socialism with the forces of capitalism, usually where most of the means of production, distribution and exchange are controlled by private or public (shareholder) corporations, but where there is a very strong state, and usually a coherent civil society. The social democratic state has a strong interest in education, health, infrastructure and social protection such as pensions, unemployment benefits, as well as often a commitment to some form of participatory democracy in business. It also has well-organised and legitimate electoral systems, police-justice systems and at least a moderately well-equipped military. Historically, the Scandinavian countries have been classed as social democracies, possibly also, at times, the Netherlands, Germany and France. In the UK the Fabian Society has been the major bearer of social democracy principles. Following the lead of these nations many others have embraced social democracy. During especially the age of the Keynesian Welfare State (KWS) (1940s–1970s) social democracy was well entrenched in many nations, and now it is strong in several states and institutions.

֍→||Chap. 7|| ||Keynesian Welfare-State||

REF1: Thomas Kastning. 2020. *Basics of Social Democracy.* Friedrich Ebert Stiftung, Ghana. https://library.fes.de/pdf-files/bueros/ghana/10519.pdf

REF2: Margaret Cole. (1961). *The Story of Fabian Socialism.* Stanford University Press.

REF3: André Liebich. 1997. *From the Other Shore: Russian Social Democracy after 1921.* Cambridge, MA: Harvard University Press, 1997. https://annas-archive.org/search?q=russian+social+democracty+after+1921

Social provisioning Institutional and evolutionary political economy is the science of provisioning in the sense that its main concern is to provide a framework where the majority of inhabitants on planet Earth can survive and develop. It seeks to provide a principled architecture for providing the material and immaterial needs and wants of all life forms on Planet Earth and beyond. In other words, it seeks to devise ways in which life forms have access to adequate habitats, ecosystems, communities, and repositories of food, clothing and shelter. It also seeks to provide a framework for promoting development of these assets for the common good. It does recognise that the system we live under, capitalism in its various forms, is subject to the dynamics of subjecting cultures to the ravages of mining, production, innovation, transportation networks and markets. In this context, it tries to moderate the excesses of creative destruction by financing the updating of skills, knowledge and tacit understandings of the changes in ecosystems that require adaptation and modification of behaviour to survive in a constantly changing environment. It also seeks to protect species and classes that are subject to the most devastating forms of destruction and decimation through safety nets and action plans. Since the forces of capitalism are rampant, and even governance measures to protect species and classes are usually modestly ameliorative at best, it is likely that we will need other planets to colonise to continue life in other places. Hopefully the governance measures implemented on other planets will learn from past mistakes and promote a more embedded system (better social provisioning) for all species and classes. Political economy should seek to provide a framework for that innovation.

֍→||Chaps. 5–8||

REF: Zdravka Todorova. 2015. Social Provisioning within a Culture-Nature Life Process, *Review of Political Economy* 27(3): 390–409.

Social Structures of Accumulation (SSAs) David Gordon developed the concept of SSAs to understand the dynamics of long waves of growth and phases of evolution of capitalism through historical time. Gordon's core hypothesis of SSAs is that durable relationships underlying institutions tend to provide a foundation for accumulation in the form of investment in durable fixed capital (including infrastructure), which fundamentally impacts on economic growth. Through these institutions capitalism also undergoes phases of evolution, such as reconstruction, expansion, maturity, and dissipation, which lead to long wave upswings and also downswings through time. Empirical work on SSAs examined various forms of institutions that impinge on the accumulation and growth (as well as phases of evolution) of capital, including (among others) the capital-labor accord, the Keynesian-welfare state, US hegemony, the financial system, corporate structure, familial relationships, and others. These are said to have provided a foundation for long wave upswing during the 1950s–1970s in various countries (especially the US), and that underwent maturation and decline (to varying degrees) during the 1970s through to the present.

As they declined, other institutions evolved, such as neoliberalism, rising Chinese power, deregulated finance, unfamilial households, and the flexible system of production. Through successive crises and instabilities, these institutions evolved as well, as neoliberalism has been challenged by especially crises such as the GFC, the Eurocrisis, and the Coronacrisis, while the flexible system has become modified through (for instance) a relative decline in the just-in-time system, increasing role of robotic production and decline in worker participation in several areas. More recently global forces have been developing institutions in a new direction, through greater protectionism, industry policy, extreme nationalism which in many ways remind us of the beggar-thy-neighbour policies of the 1920s–1930s that led to fascism and war.

֍→||Chap. 3||Regulation Approach|| ||Capitalism, Phases of Evolution|| ||Institution||
֍→||Marxian Institutional and Evolutionary PE||

REF1: David M. Gordon. 1998. *Economics and Social Justice: Essays on Power, Labor and Institutional Change.* Cheltenham, UK: Edward Elgar. Edited by Samuel Bowles and Thomas W. Weisskopf.

REF2: Phillip Anthony O'Hara. 2009. *Growth and Development in the Global Political Economy: Social Structures of Accumulation and Modes of Regulation.* Oxon: Routledge. Paper edition.

REF3: Terrence McDonough, David M Kotz and Michael Reich. Eds. 2014. *Social Structures of Accumulation Theory.* Cheltenham, UK: Edward Elgar.

REF4: Tamás T. Csontos. 2023. From Social Structures to Techno-Economic Paradigms: Comparison of Four Phases of Capitalism Theories. *World Review of Political Economy* 14(4): 511–53.

Socialism There are many models, theories and practices of socialism. They comprise arrangements such as worker controlled enterprises; state control of many leading enterprises; the socialisation of much of education, health, infrastructure development, housing, social security, child care and functional finance; involvement of the community in decisions which affect their lives in business and government; promotion of community trust, interaction, and sociality; the development of producer and consumer cooperatives; and the development of the joint stock of community knowledge and skills. Generally, political economists talk about socialism when there is a high(er) degree of community involvement, control, ownership or sharing of economic and social resources. The objectives of socialism are related to enhancing the role of the lower classes in social, political and economic life; and reducing alienation and subjugation of all classes. Socialism also links to the development of more trust, bridging social networks and voluntary association between all genders, ethnic groups, classes and ages of people plus other species involving the ecology of planet Earth.

֍→||Chaps. 2, 8||

REF1: Frederick Engels. 1880. *Socialism: Utopian and Scientific.* Moscow: Progress Publishers, 1970. (Originally published in French.)

REF2: Michael A. Lebowitz. 2010. *The Socialist Alternative: Real Human Development.* New York: Monthly Review Press.

REF3: Paul Magnette. *2025. Ecosocialism: Climate Change, Socialism and Democracy*. London: Routledge.

Species The concept of a species is one of the most complex notions in political economy, since there are so many ways of categorizing living organisms. But generally, a species is a set of 'living' organisms that share some critical traits, whether they are genetic, reproductive, evolutionary, or behavioural in nature. For instance, some define a species as those living organisms that can successfully breed together. Then there are those that undergo non-sexual reproduction. Species are important in political economy because they link to world problems, such as the coronavirus pandemic, declining biodiversity, HIV-AIDS, AI-robotics, and climate change. They are also involved in the motion of long waves of growth, hegemony and climate change. Human beings are species of *homo sapiens*, an apex predator with multiple chains of species under their control and included in their diet. Numerous microorganisms also have great power over other species, and even perform crucial functions in the human gut and elsewhere. Currently during the Anthropocene thousands of species have become extinct while numerous others are under threat of extinction.

֍→||Chaps. 4,9||Long Waves of Climate Change||

REF: Cynthia S. Parr, Nathan Wilson, Patrick Leary, Katja S. Schulz, Kristen Lans, Lisa Walley, Jennifer A. Hammock, Anthony Goddard, Jeremy Rice, Marie Studer, Jeffrey T. G. Holmes, Robert J. Corrigan, Jr. 2014. *The Encyclopedia of Life v2: Providing Global Access to Knowledge About Life on Earth (pensoft.net)*

Speculative Bubbles A speculative bubble is an overexuberant expansion of asset values (e.g., shares or equities, real estate, etc) above fundamental values (long-term dividends or long-term returns). These bubbles typically crash when they are especially high as agents believe that the bubble has run its course and will decline. Some analysts differentiate between rational and irrational bubbles. Rational bubbles may be those exacerbated by mainly professional traders, who are willing to keep trading in these assets so long as the return (R) is equal to the risk-free rate (rf), plus the normal risk rate (r) and the bubble premium (b), plus a return for unanticipated returns (u). If the bubble does not rise by an amount equal to the expected rise in the bubble next period (e), collectively expected by agents, then there is a crash.

Irrational bubbles are also hypothesised to operate, when uninformed traders push the market to unsustainable highs, under the principle of 'buy when stocks are rising and sell when stocks are declining'. The herd mentality thus pushes stock prices to very high values that may threaten the performance of the macroeconomy. Under these circumstances, a "environmental endogenous factor" such as the bankruptcy of a crucial financial institution, which has engaged in unsustainable credit overexpansion, may lead to a general crash in the market (e.g., Enron, Lehman Brothers). Another means by which asset prices may crash and/or simply return to fundamentals is when professional traders recognise the speculative bubble and start selling assets, which may lead to a crash, or otherwise a sudden but sustainable drop in prices towards fundamentals.

Bubbles are likely to have been implicated, for instance, in the stock market crash of 1929 which preceded the Great Depression of the 1930s, the stock market crash of 1987, the Internet/equity market crash and corporate crisis of 2000–2002, the subprime/equity/GFC crash of 2007–2008, the Eurozone sovereign debt crisis of 2009–2012, the Chinese property crash of 2018–2023, and numerous other examples of financial instability. Speculative bubbles tend to rise and fall especially during the onset and later in long wave downswings. According to Carlotta Perez, for instance, a Great Surge in technology stocks is necessary for the later onset of long wave upswing, and the subsequent crash (such as the Internet crash and corporate crisis of 2000–2002), may reflect short-term adjustments, as part of a long-term expansion in information and communications technology (ICT). But the technology style may have spurious fundamentals (only a short-term rise in productivity, as argued by R.J. Gordon), and may not sufficiently synchronise with the economic, political and social institutions, for systemic long wave upswing in the core during the 1990s–2020s (as argued by Perez, Louçã, O'Hara).

֍→||Financial Instability hypothesis|| ||Technology Style|| ||Long Waves of Growth||
֍→||Chaps. 5–9|| ||Crises|| ||Global Financial Crisis|| ||Eurodebt Crisis|| ||Hegemony||
REF: J. Bradford DeLong and Konstantin Majin. 2006. A Short Note on the Size of the Dot-Com Bubble. Working Paper 12011. NBER, Cambridge, Mass.

State Capitalism State capitalism is a socioeconomic system comprising two things. First, it is a system whose inner motion is driven by the continual changes in products, processes, markets, raw materials and organisations such that skills, lifestyles and ecologies are forever being modified and ravaged in the interests of productivity and growth (creative destruction). Secondly, control of such a system is directed by a group or series of agents who call themselves the government or the state. State capitalism is a hybrid of private capitalism and state, where the inner motion of capitalism is given full sway, but where the state or its representatives control much of the material and immaterial base. Currently, the Chinese system could be called state capitalism; possibly also that of Russia; numerous others as well.

֍→||Capitalism|| ||Policy and governance|| ||Chap. 8||
REF1: Albert Schweinberger. 2012. State Capitalism, Entrepreneurship, and Networks: China's Rise to a Superpower. *Journal of Economic Issues* 48(1): 169–180.
REF2: Ya-Wen Lei. 2023. *The Gilded Cage: Technology, Development, and State Capitalism in China*. Princeton: New Jersey.

Technology Style Carlotta Perez introduced the concept of the technology style to describe a new paradigm of technological dynamics with the potential to generate high levels of productivity and rising optimism for a new phase of economic development. But for this to generate high levels of GDP per capita growth the technology style must coalesce with a suitable set of socioeconomic institutions and geopolitical systems to solve complex national, regional and world problems.

Currently, for instance, throughout most of the world there is an emerging technology style of electronics, biotechnology, AI and renewable energy being developed. But it has not generated a long wave upswing throughout much of the world due to problems. According to Robert J. Gordon, in terms of its contribution to macro productivity, the new economy of ICT is a pale imitation of the great innovations of the past, such as the electric light, electric motor, automobile, aeroplane, chemicals, the telephone, radio, TV, transport networks, sanitation and indoor plumbing.

According to Francisco Louçã, the new technology style has not been adequately complemented by a suitable set of social and political institutions. In this context, Phillip O'Hara argues that a suitable replacement for the neoliberal state apparatus is nowhere in sight, the deregulated financial system has not yet entirely been replaced by a more stable system, households have become too contradictory between individual and system needs, and the international system of geo-politics is wrought with too many conflicts and instabilities. There are segments of the world economy undergoing long wave upswing, especially in China, but even here the contradictions are growing, and it is unlikely, on current trends, that long wave upswings can revitalize most areas in the global political economy.

֍→||Chaps. 1–3, 5–8|| ||Perez, Carlotta|| ||Freeman and Louçã|| ||Innovation||
֍→||Tylecote's Long Wave Analysis|| ||Gordon, Robert J.||

REF1: Andrew Tylecote. 1992. *The Long Wave in the World Economy: The Present Crisis in Historical Perspective.* London: Routledge.

REF2: Carlotta Perez. 1983. Structural Change and Assimilation of New Technologies in the Economic Social Systems. *Futures* 15(5): 357–375. Structural change and assimilation of new technologies in the economic and social systems - ScienceDirect

Terrorism Terrorism can be defined as those practices associated with the planning and executing attacks on civilians for purposes of making political, ideological, theological and/or related statements on behalf of the attacker, a group of like-minded activists or state apparatus. The purpose of such attacks is usually to bring a core issue to the mind of the public and state or other actors, and often to instil fear and intimidation into the minds of the community. Examples include the atom bombs dropped on Hiroshima and Nagasaki during the latter stages of the second world war; the strikes on many cities and towns of Britain by the Germans during the second world war, and later on Germany by the British and Russian forces; the many attacks by, for instance, Al Qaeda, Islamic State, Al-Shabaab, the Mujahadeen, and so on, against the US, its supporters, and national governments in the Middle East, Africa, and elsewhere (plus US terrorism against Arabs, etc); Israel and Palestinian attacks on civilians over the past 70 years; the IRA, Unionists and UK Police/Army in their many skirmishes; and Russia in its invasion of Ukraine, where it purposefully targets civilian suburbs, hospitals and emergency accommodation to pressure the government to adhere to its terms.

These holistic, systemic, interdependent, circular, cumulative, uncertain, contradictory, evolutionary processes associated with terrorism, are also variously subject to metamorphosis and cycle/wave motion at the micro, meso, macro, international, world and cosmological levels. Terrorism is linked directly and indirectly to issues of long waves, hegemony and climate change.

֍→||Chap. 9||Terrorist Attacks on 9/11||

Terrorist Attacks on 9/11 On 11 September 2001, four planes were hijacked in the United States, with the plan to hit hi-profile building/person-icons of US trade, finance, government and defence. Two of the planes hit the twin towers of the World Trade Centre, at the time the tallest building(s) in the world, near Wall Street, New York, and the building(s) collapsed. A third plane hit a wing of the Pentagon, US military headquarters, near Washington DC; and a fourth hit a field in the countryside after passengers intervened and stopped a likely plot to hit the White House or other icons in Washington DC. Direct casualties were about 3000 deaths, plus around 25,000 injured. Of the 19 hijackers 15 were from Saudi Arabia. The Al Qaeda terrorist network was said to be responsible for the attacks. The attacks contributed to the depth of the 2001 recession in the US and led to the invasion of Afghanistan and Iraq by US-supported allies. "9/11" is certainly one of the most significant events of the twenty-first century, due to the factors leading to it, the nature of it, and the impact on the world. It will likely lay claim to being associated with one of the most defining issues of world history.

֍→||Chaps. 7,9|| ||Terrorism|| ||Wars||

REF: Mathew J. Morgan and R.J. Woolsey. Eds. 2009. *The Impacts of 9/11 on Politics and War: The Day that Changed Everything.* London: Palgrave Macmillan.

Treadmill of Production The treadmill of production (TOP) concept uses the circuit of social capital (CSC) apparatus to explain ecological problems and climate change under capitalism. Capitalism is based on complex capital processes to reduce the input of labor as much as possible to make higher profits. Some analysts argue that this is a potential problem because reduced inputs of labor reduce the output of surplus as prices decline and competition leads to lower rates of profit. The general law of capitalist accumulation leads thus to greater accumulation of machines, robotics, buildings, packaging, and transportation as well as warehouses, shops and roadways, in addition to using iron, coal, steel, timber, oil, gas and other minerals and materials. These items of constant capital (fixed and circulating capital) may increase the organic composition of capital thus reducing the rate of profit (ceteris paribus). They also produce much pollution, waste, destruction of habitat and de-oxygenization via carbon absorbing plants and other sinks. Waterways are destroyed by constant destruction of fish species and conglomerations of waste in the form of plastics, other containers and wrappers. GDP growth generates GHGs and waste. Generating capital uses materials cheaper than their (ecological etc) reproduction costs. The treadmill of production needs replacing through structural changes to emasculate the laws of capital by promoting social provisioning, quality of life and preservation of nature.

֍→||Capitalism|| ||Climate change|| ||Chap. 4||Circuit of Social Capital||

REF: Kenneth A. Gould, David N. Pellow, and Allan Schnaiberg. 2016. *The Treadmill of Production: Injustice and Unsustainability in the Global Economy.* Boulder, CO: Paradigm Publishers.

Tylecote's Long Wave Analysis Andrew Tylecote (1992) presents an important analysis of capitalism's dynamic motion. His theory is that long wave (upswings) require (a) successive *technology styles* within an economic sub-system; (b) a specific set of social and political institutions to be suitably matched with the economic subsystem (especially technology style); (c) a regime of geopolitical institutions to moderate conflicts in the system; and (d) a set of feedback processes, comprising [1] inequality feedbacks (north, south, between north-south), [2] monetary feedbacks, and [3] population feedbacks. This theoretical architecture then is required to be related to the various hypothesised long waves throughout history. He agrees that Britain did not undergo long wave upswing during the Revolutionary and Napoleonic Wars (during the so-called upswing of the First Kondratiev (1780s–1815) since growth was insufficient). Later when Kondratiev's works became more fully available for an English audience (1998), Tylecote came to eventually believe that Kondratiev developed the endogenous rationale for long waves much more fully vis-à-vis especially 'extra-economic processes'.

→||Chaps. 3, 6|| ||Long Waves of Growth|| ||Technology Style||
→||Neo-Schumpeterian Political Economy||

REF1: Andrew Tylecote. 1992. *The Long Wave in the World Economy: The Present Crisis in Historical Perspective.* London: Routledge.

REF2: Andrew Tylecote. 1998. Politics, Technology and Economics: Kondratiev's Endogenous Theory of Long Waves. In *The Works of Nicolai D. Kondratiev:* lxxi-lllxxxii. Eds. Natalia Makashiva, Warren J. Samuels, and Vincent Barnett. Eds. 1998. *The Works of Nikolai D. Kondratiev: Economic Statics, Dynamics and Conjuncture.* 4 Vols. London: Pickering and Chatto. Translated by Stephen S. Wilson. (Republished 2016 by Routledge, London in Hardback and ebook.)

Uncertainty and Risk Institutional and evolutionary political economists tend to differentiate between risk and uncertainty. Risk is something fairly-determinate in the sense that it is moderately easy (given current knowledge and techniques) to estimate quantitatively. Examples include the weather, housing prices, stock market fluctuations, insurance costs, equestrian performance, unemployment, and inflation. The concept of uncertainty posits the notion that there are core elements of opaqueness, futurity, ignorance, complex lags, and lack of information and/or knowledge in the political economy. Risk often relates to current events and things in the not-to-distant future. Uncertainty links to the long-term future, tipping points, and very complex processes. Marx and Schumpeter, for instance, saw capitalism as having an inherently uncertain character, because it was based around seeking out new areas, new products and processes, new skills and knowledge, and new markets and corporate arrangements. In the process it generates obsolescence, unemployment, bankruptcy, poverty, decimated environments, and species extinction. For Keynes the dominant uncertainty about capitalism was the long-term generation of complex capital goods and shortish-term debt, with these different time dimensions creating potential heightened instability and crisis. Institutions are often created to moderate uncertainties in the system, such as through lender of last resort facilities, deposit insurance, unemployment benefits, certain accounting practices, climate control strategies, and poverty-reducing policies.

→||Creative Destruction|| ||Disembedded Economy||

REF: Stephen McBride, Marjorie Griffin Cohen, Laurent DobuzinskisJames Busumtwi-Sam. 2002. *Global Instability: Uncertainty and New Visions in Political Economy.* Springer, Dordrecht. https://doi.org/10.1007/978-94-010-0251-6_1

Uneven Development The concept of hegemony and uneven development states that global capitalism tends to generate uneven forces throughout the world, where some states or regions benefit majorly from the system of socioeconomic, political, and geo-ecological arrangements, but numerous others fail to achieve high rates of growth, investment, social provisioning, standard of living and climate change mitigation and adaptation. The areas that tend to benefit from the global system of arrangements include the highly advanced capitalist economies, and possibly some newly emerging states from the semi-periphery. Areas that benefit less from global arrangements are usually from the periphery, providing agricultural, market garden and raw material commodities, as well as ecological sinks for global corporations and the core; whose commodity prices tend to be low and volatile but play a positive role in promoting advanced nations' standard of living and social provisioning. Power thus tends to be unequally distributed due to agglomeration tendencies, vested interests, and centripetal processes. Colonial and post-colonial anomalies tend to perpetuate this schism through past and present surplus drain, brain drain, dubious border rules, and slavery (under many names) which generate path dependent underdevelopment, long wave downswings and extreme climate events which exacerbate socio-political problems.

֎→||Hegemony|| ||Core, Periphery, Semi-Periphery|| ||Power|| ||Chaps. 1–12||

REF1: Donald J. Harris. 2007. Uneven Development. In *The New Palgrave Dictionary of Economics*, 751–753. Eds. John Eatwell, Murray Milgate and Peter Newman. London: Macmillan.

REF2: Richard Grabowski, Sharmistha Self and Michael P. Shields. 2012. *Economic Development: A Regional, Institutional, and Historical Approach.* Armonk, New York: M.E. Sharpe.

REF3: Patrick Bond. 2024.Extreme Uneven Development, *Financial Volatility, Deep Capitalist Crisis and Super-Exploitation in South Africa and the World.* Cham, Switzerland: Palgrave Macmillan.

United States Hegemony *Pax Americana* was established as the US held absolute global power between the 1940s and the 1980s. Its power was based around firstly production dominance, followed by commercial dominance, and financial power (and derivatively military power) by 1945. Several eco-spatial and techno-institutional (sub-)systems constituted the material basis of its power. The Bretton Woods Agreement comprised fixed exchanges rates (the US dollar exchanged for a 'fixed' value of gold), the IMF providing funds for balance of payments disequilibria, and New York City being the financial centre of the world. The Keynesian welfare state contributed automatic and discretionary fiscal and monetary policy, liberal democracy, and infrastructure-education spending to sustain the social fabric. Fordism utilised semi-automatic assembly lines, the oil regime, and economies of scale and scope to ensure high productivity for 30 years. The military-industrial regime utilised innovations, a defensive-offensive system, and alliances to control much of the world. And the household system enabled the reproduction of labor power, bridging social networks and suburban housing-transport systems to sustain the social fabric.

Pax Americana had internal contradictions that eventually led to its relative demise during the 1970s–1980s onwards. These include other areas successfully competing in business networks and innovation systems (especially Europe and Japan). The US losing the Vietnam War while the working class established more relative power over capital in wages and conditions during the late 1960s and early 1970s. The KWS lost legitimacy as it led to higher inflation and greater costs for business. The financial system evolved into several decades of periodic financial instability and speculative bubble crashes into the 1970s onwards. And the household-community system became more unstable as marriage became de-institutionalised, a declining proportion of people tied the knot, social trust declined and bridging social networks went into relative demise ('bowling alone'). This led in the 1970s and 1980s onwards to several decades of periodic crises and recessions, corporate and financial crashes, the global financial crisis and the coronacrisis. The US also lost much legitimacy in geopolitics even as the Soviet system underwent demise as it acted recklessly especially in Latin America and the Middle East. China has been seriously competing globally in systems of innovation, business networks and financial arrangements for several decades now.

֍→||Hegemony|| ||Chap. 7|| ||Dutch Hegemony|| ||British Hegemony||
֍→||Chinese Potential Hegemony||

REF1: Christopher John Bartlett. 1974. *The Rise and Fall of the Pax Americana.* New York: St Martin's Press.

REF2: Immanuel Wallerstein. 2006. The Curve of American Power. *New Left Review* 40(July-August): 77–94

REF3: Joan Robinson. 1980. The Age of Growth. *Collected Economic Papers of Joan Robinson.* Vol. 5. 120–129.

Varieties of Capitalism (VOC) VOC is the notion that capitalism goes beyond its three main characteristics of (1) substantial formation of wage labor and capitalist classes (of various types), (2) generalized commodity production (buying and selling of goods and services), and (3) incessant innovation and destruction. It also states that capitalism undergoes (4) stages or phases of reproduction, in addition to (5) different varieties of capitalism historically and currently. Even in the possible stages of development of capitalism of the core through, e.g., mercantilism (1400s–1600s), manufacture (1700s), industrial capitalism (1800s), imperialism (1880s–1910s), monopoly capitalism (1920s–1950s), embedded welfare state (1950s–1970s) and globalised neoliberalism (1980s–2020s), and the current trend to *autocratic v liberal capitalism* (regionally and domestically), there are said to be different varieties of capitalism, such as, for instance, possibly the Dutch Golden Age of a coordinated market economy (CME) (1580s–1650s) (domestically) and mercantilism (globally); and also, e.g., Germany's attempt to become an Empire (rather than simply hegemon) through their *trend* to a totalitarian form of fascist-global capitalism (1930s–1940s), followed by their own tendency towards a CME.

It is also possible to analyse capitalism in the current period as being subject to different VOC globally. For instance, there is literature on the possibility of differentiating between liberal-market economies (e.g., US, UK, Australia), coordinated market economies (Germany, Japan, France), autocratic state-capitalisms (Russia, China), Nordic-style social capitalisms (Scandinavia), south-east Asian style capitalisms, Latin American styles of capitalism, and so on. Taken to its logical extreme, it should be possible not only to situate most nations within the context of their general styles/varieties, but also to dynamically analyse the evolving styles of capitalism for every relevant nation or area.

֍→||Capitalism|| ||Chaps. 5–8||

REF: Thomas Palley, Esteban Pérez Caldentey, and Matías Vernengo. 2023. *Varieties of Capitalism: Second-Generation Perspectives.* Cheltenham: Edward Elgar.

Veblenian A Veblenian is an institutional and evolutionary political economist who is influenced by or follows the method or analysis of Thorstein Veblen (1857–1929). This involves, firstly, being an interdisciplinary, multidisciplinary and/or transdisciplinary scholar, who studies world problems involving an array of economic, social, political, ecological and psychological elements. Secondly, such a scholar may adopt and utilise some of the core concepts of Veblen, such as culture, institutions, habits, and instincts; conspicuous consumption, emulation, cumulative causation, the community's stock of knowledge, and instrumental versus ceremonial functions of institutions; and the common good versus the vested interests, relative income, Veblen goods, intangible value, absentee ownership, the New Era of Business, sabotage, the Great Union of Vested Interests, blind drift, and the gendered social economy. Thirdly, Veblen also engaged in analysis of hegemonic power, the imperial state, war and peace, old and new orders, cumulative growth of waste, the economic surplus, the industrial revolution, and the master class versus the common person.

֍→||Culture|| ||Institutions|| ||Circuit of Socioeconomic Dynamics||
֍→||Institutional and Evolutionary Political Economy|| ||Hegemony||

REF1: Thorstein Veblen. 1915. *Imperial Germany and the Industrial Revolution.* New York: B.W. Huebsch Inc.

REF2: Thorstein Veblen. 1917. *An Inquiry into the Nature of Peace and the Terms of Its Perpetuation*. London: Macmillan.

REF3: Thorstein Veblen. 1923. *Absentee Ownership and Business Enterprise in Recent Times: The Case of America.* New York: B.W. Huebsch.

REF4: K.L. Anderson. 1932–33. The Unity of Veblen's Theoretical System. *Quarterly Journal of Economics* 47: 598–626.

REF5: Phillip Anthony O'Hara. 2001. The Contemporary Relevance of Thorstein Veblen's Institutional-Evolutionary Political Economy. *History of Economics Review* 35(1): 78–103.

REF6: James Ronald Stanfield. The Shape, Method and Significance of Original Institutional Economics. *Journal of Economic Issues*, 32(2): 231–255.

Wars Wars are important historically for hegemonic power, long waves and climate change. In hegemony empirics, wars of ascendency have been shown to be necessary for hegemonic power to be established. For instance, US hegemony being promoted by the success of the Allies in the second world war (1939–1945), is anexample of major wars providing an opportunity to defeat fascist regimes and provide space for renewed development of the global political economy. US hegemony, *Pax Americana*, was able to coalesce with the Marshall Plan to prevent communism in Western Europe, also the United Nations to help prevent a new world war and moderate conflict, and the Bretton Woods Agreement to institutionalise fixed exchange rates (based on gold and the US dollar) and the IMF to assist with the balance of payments.

British success in the Revolutionary and Napoleonic Wars, and the resulting Congress of Vienna (1815) enabled stability to be ensured, so that Britain could redirect resources towards more productive pursuits. *Pax Britannica* (1820–1880) enabled the circuits of socioeconomic dynamics to be put into motion to activate more fully the technology style, plus the institutions of the eco-spatial, state, finance, business and household systems to promote secular long wave upswing for 50 years. British colonialism was instituted through several wars, including the two Opium Wars which led to over 10 million Chinese being addicted to Opium, the Australian Wars in which tens of thousands of Aborigines were killed while many more lost links to their ancestral lands, and the effective imposition of Martial Law in India which resulted in regular assaults against civilians.

The Dutch case in relation to war is more complex and tentative. Many argue that the end of both the 80-years war (1568–1648), and the 30-years war (1618–1648) with the Treaty of Westphalia, enabled stability such that the Dutch golden age could be enhanced. But it was the earlier success against the Spanish, during the Dutch revolution/revolt and the resultant *Union of Utrecht* (1579) (some also mention the 21-year truce of 1609–1621) that united the seven northern United Provinces, and enabled the Dutch to emasculate their oppressors, resulting in the subsequent Golden Age, long wave upswings and hegemony during the little ice age. The Dutch managed the ongoing wars against the Spanish (and later against the English, 1650–1688) through clever innovations such as financing the wars from taxation and employing mercenaries, learning how to sail against the wind, using the waterways to dissuade incoming enemy ships, and employing intelligent principles of war. (The Dutch were much later heavily defeated in the 1780–1784 war against the English.)

Some scholars have hypothesised wars of consolidation regarding hegemony. But this is unlikely. More likely is the operation of wars of hegemonic descent, in which the Dutch, British, and US went through wars which accelerated their absolute hegemonic demise. Good examples include the Vietnam War (of the 1960s and early 1970s) which contributed to US hegemony decline, and the wars in Iraq and Afghanistan (early 2000s onwards) which reduced US relative hegemony. The three Anglo-Dutch Wars of the 1650s–1670s were good examples of struggles that reduced the resources and energy of the Dutch military machine, even though they performed at least moderately well in these wars. For Britain, one hypothesis is that the wars associated with the scramble for Africa reflected the sort of balance of power they had to share with other European powers during the demise of British hegemony.

Wars are also relevant to long waves and climate change. For instance, the Revolutionary and Napoleonic Wars prevented Britain from growing and developing more as a nation and empire while they were in process. But the wars also enabled Britain and much of Europe and the Americas to caste-aside external oppressors and develop as nation states. Hence success provided Britain with greater stability necessary for long wave upswings and hegemony. The first world war, according to J. van Duijn, upset the stability of the European economies that may otherwise have sustained further long wave upswing into the 1910s–1920s. The Chinese may require a war of ascendency to rise to become the hegemonic nation during the mid-twenty-first century. Wars typically (ceteris paribus) increase GHGs (stocks and flows) and thus contribute to global temperature rises. It also leads to greater decimation of stocks of species of both fauna and flora.

֍→||Hegemony|| ||Chaps. 1–3,5–8,10,12|| ||Dutch Hegemony|| ||British Hegemony||

֍→||United States Hegemony|| Chinese Potential Hegemony||

REF1: Joshua S. Goldstein. 1988. *Long Cycles: Prosperity and War in the Modern Age.* Yale: Yale University Press.

REF2: Paul M. Johnson and William R. Thompson. Eds. 1985. *Rhythms in Politics and Economics.* New York: Praeger.

REF3: George Modelski. Ed. 1987. *Exploring Long Cycles.* Boulder, CO: Lynne Rienner Publishers.

REF4: William R. Thompson and David R. Dreyer 2012. *Handbook of International Rivalries 1492–2010.* Washington DC: Sage Publishers.

World-Systems Analysis (WSA) WSA is an approach to social science, a classic form of political economy, that seeks to analyse the different world-systems that emerged over the centuries, and more specifically to scrutinise the capitalist world-system that started in Europe during the 1500s and which has evolved through different hegemonic movements to the present and beyond. WSA started in the 1970s under the influence of the student and workers movement of 1968ff (initially in France), and the relative decline of US hegemony into the 1980s–2020s, as various anti-hegemonic movements merged to form of an intellectual social movement and thereby a new historical social science. Some of the specific influences in its development include Immanuel Wallerstein, Andre Gunder Frank, Samir Amin, Giovanni Arrighi, and Terence Hopkins, the journal *Review* (Fernand Braudel Centre) and the *Journal of World-Systems Research.*

Firstly, it has variously been called "unidisciplinary" (Wallerstein 2010, 518) and "transdisciplinary" (Babones and Chase-Dunn 2010, 4), whereby it integrates culture, economics and politics into its edifice as an *integrative social movement.* Secondly, it is not so much concerned with the whole "world economy" as with a "world-economy" that includes many nations and areas around the globe. Thirdly, it differentiates between "world Empire", such as the former Chinese Ming Dynasty (1368–1644) or the Hapsburg Empire (1273–1700), and the "capitalist world-economy", which emerged due to the limits of feudalism, into the 1400s onwards, with the first power starting with the *Pax Netherlandia* (1600–1650s), followed by the *Pax Britannica* (1820–1880), and *Pax Americana* (1945–1975). Fourthly, Wallerstein and some others have argued that since the 1970s–1980s the attempt to establish a viable new regime of accumulation through neoliberalism and the Washington Consensus failed as successive decadal financial crises and recessions led to further structural crises such as the GFC, the Eurodebt crisis, the coronacrisis, climate crises, and currently geopolitical crises in the shape of multiple wars in Ukraine, the Middle East and elsewhere.

Fifthly, WSA seeks to develop a strong knowledge of the different elements of the world-system, especially including the core, the periphery and the semi-periphery, plus various mutations such as the periphery of the core (Wallerstein 1974). For instance, under Dutch hegemony, the core was the north-west region of Europe, the centre of which was the United Provinces of the Netherlands. The periphery included areas in Europe such as the Baltic region from which the Dutch specialised in acting as merchants for the grain that was shipped around the world, after being warehoused and stored in various places in the low countries. Colonial peripheries included the Dutch East Indies, various places in the Americas (e.g., Brazil, the Caribbean), and parts of Africa. Semi-peripheral areas of the core included England and France during Dutch hegemony (Braudel 1979).

With Dutch to British to United States hegemony passing away, many decades have passed since the core and numerous other nations have recorded several decades of strong growth of GDP per capita. Long wave upswings seem to have become emasculated, along with successive hegemonies. The capitalist world-system may well have come to the end of its potential as no viable system has led to sustained productivity, ongoing productive demand, and sustained resolution of its structural polycrises into the second quarter of the twenty-first century.

WSA examines not simply successive hegemonies, but also long waves and ecological problems of the world-system, and various social movements to improve the functioning of social economies. Some of its main contributors believe that sustainable growth of the system may well be a thing of the past and that we are currently seeing the evolution towards a new system, perhaps a different form of world-system, that may well be concerned more with quality of life, standard of living and ecological sustainability than the growth fetish of the past which is apparently well past its prime and unable to be resurrected.

֍→||Hegemony|| ||Dutch Hegemony|| ||British Hegemony|| ||United States Hegemony||

֍→||Long Waves of Growth|| ||Metabolic Rift||

REF1: Immanuel Wallerstein. 2012. World-Systems Analysis as a Knowledge Movement. In *Routledge Handbook of World-Systems Analysis*, 515–521, eds. Salvatore J. Babones and Christopher Chase-Dunn. Oxon: Routledge.

REF2: Salvatore J. Babones and Christopher Chase-Dunn. 2010. Introduction to *Routledge Handbook of World-Systems Analysis*, 1–6, eds. Salvatore J. Babones and Christopher Chase-Dunn. Oxon: Routledge.

REF3: Immanuel Wallerstein. 1974. *The Modern World-System 1: Capitalist Agriculture and the Origins of the European World-Economy in the Sixteenth Century.* San Diego: Academic Press.

REF4: Fernand Braudel. 1979. *The Perspective of the World: Civilization and Capitalism, 15th-18th Century*. Vol 3. New York: Harper & Row.

Name Index

P. A. O'Hara, *Long Waves of Growth, Hegemonic Power, and Climate Change in the World Economy*, https://doi.org/10.1007/978-981-96-4132-1

Subject Index

P. A. O'Hara, *Long Waves of Growth, Hegemonic Power, and Climate Change in the World Economy*, https://doi.org/10.1007/978-981-96-4132-1

D

H

I

J

K

Q

R

S

The manufacturer's authorised representative in the EU is Springer Nature Customer Service Centre GmbH, Europaplatz 3, 69115 Heidelberg, Germany. If you have any concerns regarding our products, please contact ProductSafety@springernature.com

Printed and bound by CPI Group (UK) Ltd, Croydon, CR0 4YY
30/09/2026
02225303-0018